The Ultimate Linux Scripting Guide

Automate, Optimize, and Empower tasks with Linux Shell Scripting

Donald A. Tevault

The Ultimate Linux Shell Scripting Guide

Senior Publishing Product Manager: Reshma Raman
Acquisition Editor – Peer Reviews: Gaurav Gavas
Project Editor: Meenakshi Vijay
Content Development Editor: Soham Amburle
Copy Editor: Safis Editing
Technical Editors: Aneri Patel and Kushal Sharma
Proofreader: Safis Editing
Indexer: Pratik Shirodkar
Presentation Designer: Rajesh Shirsath
Developer Relations Marketing Executive: Priyadarshini Sharma

First published: October 2024

Production reference: 2111024

Published by Packt Publishing Ltd.
Grosvenor House
11 St Paul's Square
Birmingham
B3 1RB, UK.

ISBN 978-1-83546-357-4

www.packt.com

To my loving friends and family

– Donald A. Tevault

Contributors

About the author

Donald A. Tevault, but you can call him Donnie. He started with Linux in 2006, and has been working with it ever since. In that time, Donnie has created training documentation for Linux administration, bash scripting, and Nagios administration. He has served as the Linux consultant for an Internet of Things security firm, and operates the BeginLinux Guru channel on YouTube. Donnie's other books include Mastering Linux Security and Hardening and Linux Service Management Made Easy with systemd.

I'd like to thank the team at Packt Publishing for guiding this book through to completion, and my tech reviewer Jason for his invaluable suggestions.

About the reviewer

Jason Willson has been working in the Tech industry for over 20 years since his first job at the help desk at his alma mater, Grove City College. He was first introduced to Linux in 2007 at a startup in Boston and has worked with it professionally and personally ever since. He's used command line and shell scripting techniques for a variety of tasks relating to Data Analysis, Systems Administration, and DevOps. He currently works as a DevOps Engineer at Carnegie Mellon University. In addition to reviewing this book, he has also reviewed another book published by Packt titled Linux Command Line and Shell Scripting Techniques by Vedran Dakic.

I'd like to thank the incredible Linkedin community for making this connection possible with Packt Publishing. I'd also like to thank all the coworkers, classmates, and mentors (personal, professional, and academic) who helped to shape me into who I am today. And last but not least, I'd like to thank my amazing wife Eva, who has been a constant support to me in reviewing this book despite such a hectic work schedule.

Join our community on Discord!

Read this book alongside other users, Linux experts, and the author himself.

Ask questions, provide solutions to other readers, chat with the author via Ask Me Anything sessions, and much more. Scan the QR code or visit the link to join the community.

https://packt.link/SecNet

Table of Contents

Preface   **xxiii**

Chapter 1: Getting Started with the Shell   **1**

Understanding Shells 1

Finding Help with Shell Commands 4

   Understanding Manual Pages • 4

   Understanding Info Pages • 7

   Getting to Know the Linux Documentation Project • 7

   Using Your Favorite Search Engine • 7

Using a Text Editor to Create Shell Scripts 8

   Text-mode Editors • 8

   GUI Text Editors • 10

Understanding Compiled versus Interpreted Programming 11

Understanding root and sudo Privileges 12

Summary 12

Questions 12

Further Reading 13

Answers 14

Chapter 2: Interpreting Commands   **15**

Understanding the Structure of a Command 15

   Using Command Options • 16

     Hands-on Lab – Practice With Command Options • 16

   Using Command Arguments • 18

Executing Multiple Commands at Once 20

   Running Commands Interactively • 20

   Using Command Sequences • 21

Chaining Commands with a Semi-Colon • 21

Conditional Command Execution with Double Ampersands • 22

Conditional Command Execution with Double Pipes • 22

Using the find Utility • 22

Performing Multiple Actions with find • 30

Hands-on Lab – Using find to Perform Other Commands • 31

Running Commands Recursively 33

Hands-on Lab – Using Commands with Recursion • 33

Understanding the Command History 35

Escaping and Quoting 39

Escaping Metacharacters • 39

Quoting • 41

Summary 42

Questions 42

Further Reading 43

Answers 44

Chapter 3: Understanding Variables and Pipelines 45

Understanding Environmental Variables 45

Understanding Programming Variables 48

Understanding Pipelines 49

Summary 51

Questions 51

Further Reading 52

Answers 52

Chapter 4: Understanding Input/Output Redirection 55

Introduction to Input/Output Redirection 55

Understanding stdout 57

Preventing File Overwrites • 57

Using the File Descriptor • 58

Understanding stdin 58

Understanding stderr 60

Understanding tee 63

Hands-on Lab – Pipes, Redirectors, and find 64

Summary 66

Questions 66

Further Reading 67

Answers 67

Chapter 5: Customizing the Environment 69

Technical Requirements 69

Reviewing the Environmental Variables 69

Understanding Shell Sessions 71

Understanding the Configuration Files 72

    bash Global Configuration Files on Fedora • 72

    Users' Configuration Files on Fedora • 74

    bash Global Configuration Files on Debian • 76

    Users' Configuration Files on Debian • 76

    Setting the Default Editor on Debian • 77

Setting Shell Options from the Command-line 78

Understanding Aliases 81

Summary 86

Questions 86

Further Reading 87

Answers 87

Chapter 6: Text-Stream Filters — Part 1 89

Technical Requirements 89

Introduction to Text-Stream Filters 90

Using cat 91

Using tac 96

Using cut 98

Using paste 100

Using join 102

Using sort 105

Summary 118

Questions 118

Further Reading 119

Answers 119

Chapter 7: Text Stream Filters — Part 2 121

Technical Requirements 122

Using expand 122

Using unexpand 124

Using nl 125

Using head 133

Using tail 136

Using Head And Tail Together 137

Using od 138

Using uniq 143

Using wc 147

Using fmt 149

Using split 151

Using tr 154

Using xargs 162

Using pr 166

Printing from the Command-line 172

Summary 174

Questions 174

Further Reading 175

Answers 175

Chapter 8: Basic Shell Script Construction   177

Technical Requirements 178

Understanding Basic Shell Script Construction 178

Hands-on Lab – Counting Logged-in Users • 180

Performing Tests 182

Using the test Keyword • 182

Enclosing a test Condition Within Square Brackets • 183

Using an if...then Construct • 184

Using Other Types of Tests • 184

Understanding Subshells 186

Hands-on Lab – Testing Conditions 186

Understanding Scripting Variables 188

Creating and Deleting Variables • 188

Understanding Variables and Shell Levels • 188

Understanding Case Sensitivity • 189

Understanding Read-Only Variables • 190

Understanding Array Variables 190

Hands-on Lab – Using Arrays • 191

Understanding Variable Expansion 194

Substituting a Value for an Unset Variable • 194

Substituting a Value for a Set Variable • 195

Assigning a Value to a Variable • 196

Displaying an Error Message • 197

Using Variable Offsets • 198

Matching Patterns • 200

Understanding Command Substitution 201

Understanding Decisions and Loops 204

The if. .then Construct • 204

The do. . while construct • 206

The for..in Construct • 208

The for Construct • 209

Using break • 210

Using continue • 211

The until Construct • 212

The case Construct • 213

Using Positional Parameters • 216

Understanding Exit Codes 219

Standard Shell Exit Codes • 219

User-defined Exit Codes • 222

More Information About echo 223

Looking at Some Real-World Examples 224

Hands-on Lab: Using if..then • 224

Hands-on Lab – Parsing an Apache Access Log • 226

Hands-on Lab – Beta Testing a Hard Drive • 228

Summary 229

Questions 230

Further Reading 231

Answers 231

Chapter 9: Filtering Text with grep, sed, and Regular Expressions

Chapter 9: Filtering Text with grep, sed, and Regular Expressions   233

Technical Requirements 233

Understanding Regular Expressions 234

Literals and Metacharacters • 234

Understanding sed **236**

Understanding sed Portability Issues • 236

Installing gsed on FreeBSD • 237

Installing gsed on macOS • 237

Installing gsed on OpenIndiana • 238

Substitution with sed • 239

Example 1: Modifying an Office Memo • 239

Example 2: Modifying a List of Hollywood Actors • 242

Example 3: Modifying Lists of Cars • 244

Example 4: Performing a Whole-Word Substitution • 247

Deletion with sed • 249

Example 1: Deleting Items from a List • 249

Example 2: Deleting Blank Lines • 252

Appending and Inserting with sed • 253

Example 1: Appending Lines of Text • 253

Example 2: Performing Multiple Operations at Once • 255

Example 3: Inserting Lines of Text • 256

Changing with sed • 256

Example 1: Changing Edsel to Studebaker • 256

Example 2: Changing Entire Lines of Text • 257

Other Miscellaneous sed tricks • 258

Example 1: Using the q Command • 258

Example 2: Using the w Command • 258

Example 3: Using the r Command • 259

Using sed program files • 260

Example 1: Appending Lines in a Text File • 260

Example 2: Changing Lines in a Text File • 261

Example 3: Substituting Text • 262

Example 4: Copying Lines from One File to Another • 263

Compound Scripts in sed Program Files • 263

Using sed in Shell Scripts • 265

Understanding grep **267**

Basic Searches with grep • 267

More Advanced Searches with grep • 269

Example 1: Searching for Whole Words • 269

Even More Advanced Searches with grep • 273

Example 1: Auditing Source Code Files • 273

Example 2: Searching for Social Security Numbers • 274

Example 3: Using the ^ Metacharacter • 275

Using Extended Regular Expressions with grep • 275

Example 1: Basic Search with Extended Syntax • 275

Example 2: Searching for Consecutive Duplicate Words • 276

Example 3: Searching for Words that Begin with a Certain Letter • 277

Example 4: Searching for Words with Digits • 278

Using Fixed-strings Regular Expressions with grep • 279

Using RegEx Helper Programs 280

RegexBuddy and RegexMagic • 280

Regex101 • 281

Looking at Some Real-World Examples 281

Modifying Multiple Files at Once • 281

Searching Through Apache Webserver Logs for Cross-site Scripting Attacks • 281

Automating Third-party Repository Installations • 283

Filling Empty Fields in a .csv File • 284

Summary 286

Questions 286

Further Reading 287

Answers 287

Chapter 10: Understanding Functions **289**

Technical Requirements 289

Introduction to Functions 289

Defining a Function 291

Using Functions in Shell Scripts 293

Creating and Calling Functions • 293

Passing Positional Parameters to Functions • 294

Passing Values from a Function • 296

Creating Function Libraries 299

Looking at Some Real-World Examples 301

Checking Network Connectivity • 301

Using the CoinGecko API • 303

Hands-on Lab – Creating the coingecko.sh Script • 303

Summary 307

Questions 307

Further Reading 308

Answers 308

Chapter 11: Performing Mathematical Operations   309

Technical Requirements 309

Performing Integer Math with Expressions 309

   Using the expr Command • 310

   Using echo with Math Expressions • 312

Performing Integer Math with Integer Variables 314

Performing Floating Point Math with bc 315

   Using bc in Interactive Mode • 316

   Using bc Program Files • 320

   Using bc in Shell Scripts • 323

Summary 328

Questions 328

Further Reading 329

Answers 329

Chapter 12: Automating Scripts with here Documents and expect   331

Technical Requirements 331

Using here Documents 331

   Creating here Documents with Static Data • 333

   Creating here documents with Dynamic Data • 339

   Using Functions in here Documents • 341

Automating Responses with expect 346

   Security Implications with expect • 349

Summary 350

Questions 350

Further Reading 351

Answers 352

Chapter 13: Scripting with ImageMagick   353

Technical Requirements 353

Converting Non-standard Filename Extensions 354

Installing ImageMagick 355

   Displaying Images • 356

   Viewing Image Properties • 358

Resizing and Customizing Images 359

Batch-processing Image Files 364

Using Fred's ImageMagick Scripts 364

Summary 365

Questions 366

Further Reading 366

Answers 367

Chapter 14: Using awk — Part 1　369

Introducing awk 369

Understanding Patterns and Actions 371

Obtaining Input from Text Files 372

    Looking for Human Users • 373

    Parsing Webserver Access Logs • 375

    Using Regular Expressions • 386

Obtaining Input from Commands 388

Summary 394

Questions 394

Further Reading 395

Answers 396

Chapter 15: Using awk — Part 2　397

Technical Requirements 397

Basic awk Script Construction 397

Using Conditional Statements 399

Using a while Construct and Setting Variables 401

    Summing Numbers in a Line • 401

    Finding the CPU Generation • 403

Using for loops and Arrays 407

Using Floating Point Math and printf 409

Working with Multi-Line Records 413

Summary 415

Questions 415

Further Reading 416

Answers 416

Chapter 16: Creating User Interfaces with yad, dialog, and xdialog   419

Technical Requirements 419

Creating a Graphical User Interface with yad 420

  The yad Basics • 420

  Creating Data Entry Forms • 420

  Creating a Drop-down List • 424

  Using the yad File Manager • 425

    Creating a File Checksum Utility • 426

    Creating a GUI Front-end for ImageMagick • 428

  Programming Form Buttons • 431

  Some Final Thoughts about yad • 432

Creating User Interfaces with dialog and xdialog 433

  The dialog Basics • 433

  The xdialog Basics • 435

  Automatically Choosing Either dialog or xdialog • 437

  Adding Widgets • 439

  Creating an SSH Login Interface • 442

Summary 445

Questions 445

Further Reading 446

Answers 446

Chapter 17: Using Shell Script Options with getops   447

Technical Requirements 447

Understanding the Need for getopts 447

Understanding getopt versus getopts 448

Using getopts 449

Looking at Real-world Examples 453

  The Modified Coingecko Script • 453

  The Tecmint Monitor Script • 454

Summary 457

Questions 457

Further Reading 458

Answers 458

Chapter 18: Shell Scripting for Security Professionals 459

Technical Requirements 459

Simple Scripts for Auditing 460

Identifying an Operating System • 460

A Simple Port-scanning Script • 462

Auditing the root User Account • 467

Creating the root Account Auditing Script for Linux and OpenIndiana • 467

Modifying the root Account Auditing Script for Use on FreeBSD • 473

Creating a User Activity Monitoring Script • 476

Creating Simple Firewall Scripts 478

Creating an IP Address Blocking Script for Red Hat Distros • 478

Hands-on Lab: Create the Script with an Array and a for loop • 478

Hands-on Lab: Creating the Script with xargs • 480

Searching for Existing Security-related Scripts 482

Summary 484

Questions 484

Further Reading 485

Answers 485

Chapter 19: Shell Script Portability 487

Technical Requirements 487

Running bash on Non-Linux Systems 488

Using env to Set the bash Environment • 488

Creating a Symbolic Link to bash • 489

Understanding POSIX compliance 490

Understanding the Differences Between Shells 491

Understanding Bashisms 492

Using Portable Tests • 492

Making Portable Arrays • 495

Understanding Portability Problems with echo • 497

Testing Scripts for POSIX Compliance 499

Creating Scripts on a POSIX-compliant Shell • 499

Using checkbashisms • 501

Using shellcheck • 504

Specifying a Shell with the -s Option • 506

Hands-on Lab – Using -s to Scan Function Libraries • 507

Using shall • 511

Summary 513

Questions 513

Further Reading 514

Answers 515

Chapter 20: Shell Script Security   517

Technical Requirements 517

Controlling Access to Your Scripts 518

Assigning sudo Privileges • 518

Hands-on Lab – Configuring sudo • 518

Using an Access Control List • 521

Hands-on Lab – Setting an ACL for Horatio on Linux • 521

Hands-on Lab – Setting an ACL for Horatio on FreeBSD 14 • 524

Hands-on Lab – Setting an ACL for Horatio on OpenIndiana • 526

Obfuscating Plain-Text Scripts • 528

Installing shc • 528

Hands-on Lab – Using shc • 529

Hands-on Lab – Creating Untraceable Executables • 532

Decrypting shc Binaries • 536

Understanding SUID and SGID Considerations 539

Avoiding Sensitive Data Leakage 543

Securing Temporary Files • 543

Understanding the /tmp/ Directory • 543

The Wrong Way to Create Temporary Files • 544

The Right Way to Create Temporary Files • 545

Using Passwords in Shell Scripts • 548

Hands-on Lab – Encrypting Passwords • 548

Understanding Command Injection with eval 555

Using eval on the Command-line • 555

Using eval Safely • 556

Using eval Dangerously • 557

Using Alternatives to eval • 559

Using Command Substitution • 559

Evaluating if eval is Necessary • 560

Understanding Path Security 562

Attack Scenario 1: Compromising the User's Account • 563

Attack Scenario 2: Social Engineering • 564

Summary 565

Questions 565

Further Reading 566

Answers 567

Chapter 21: Debugging Shell Scripts   569

Technical Requirements 569

Understanding Common Scripting Errors 570

Not Enough Quoting • 570

Filenames with Blank Spaces • 570

Problems with Unset Variables • 571

Creating a Wild Loop • 575

Using Shell Script Debugging Tools and Techniques 577

Using echo Statements • 577

Using xtrace for Debugging • 581

Checking for Undefined Variables • 583

Checking for Errors with the -e Option • 585

Understanding the Problems with set -e and -e • 587

Using bash Debugger • 589

Installing bashdb on Linux • 590

Installing bashdb on FreeBSD • 590

Installing on macOS • 590

Debugging a Script with bashdb • 591

Getting Help with bashdb • 593

Summary 594

Questions 594

Further Reading 595

Answers 596

Chapter 22: Introduction to Z Shell Scripting   599

Technical Requirements 599

Introducing zsh 600

Installing zsh 600

Understanding the Unique Features of zsh Scripting 601

Differences in Variable Expansion • 602

Substituting Values • 602

Substituting Substrings • 603

Translating Between Upper and Lower Case • 604

Extended File Globbing • 606

Understanding zsh Arrays • 614

Enhanced Math Capabilities • 616

Using zsh Modules 618

Using the mathfunc Module • 618

The datetime Module • 620

Summary 622

Questions 622

Further Reading 623

Answers 623

Chapter 23: Using PowerShell on Linux   625

Technical Requirements 625

Installing PowerShell on Linux and macOS 626

Installing PowerShell on Linux via a snap Package • 626

Installing PowerShell on Fedora • 627

Installing PowerShell on macOS • 627

Invoking PowerShell • 627

Reasons for Linux and Mac Admins to Learn PowerShell 627

Working with Mixed Operating System Environments • 627

PowerShell Commands Can Be Simpler • 628

Enhanced Builtin Math Capabilities • 630

Differences Between PowerShell Scripting and Traditional Linux/Unix Scripting 632

Using Filename Extensions and the Executable Permission • 632

PowerShell is Object-oriented • 632

PowerShell Uses Cmdlets • 633

Using Aliases on PowerShell • 633

Viewing the Available PowerShell Commands 636

Getting Help with PowerShell Commands 638

Real-World Cross-Platform PowerShell Scripts 639

The write-marquee.ps1 Script • 639

The check-cpu.ps1 Script • 641

Summary 645

Further Reading 645

Other Books You May Enjoy 649

Index 653

Preface

Welcome to *The Ultimate Linux Shell Scripting Guide!* This book, which is ideal for both Linux beginners and more advanced Linux administrators, will guide you through the shell script creation process. We'll begin with basic command-line usage and will progress through more advanced concepts in every succeeding chapter. You'll see how to build scripts that can help you automate repetitive administrative tasks, as well as many other cool things. We'll primarily concentrate on bash scripting throughout most of the book. Later, we'll show you how to make your scripts portable so that they can run on legacy Unix systems that can't run bash. After chapters on shell script debugging and shell script security, we'll wrap up with introductions to the Z Shell and PowerShell.

Who this book is for

This book is appropriate for anyone who needs to master the concepts of shell scripting. Linux beginners can benefit, because it can help them master the concepts that will be covered on the CompTIA Linux+/Linux Professional Institute exam. More advanced Linux administrators can benefit because it will show them the more advanced concepts that they need to build really useful, practical shell scripts.

What this book covers

Chapter 1, Getting Started with the Shell, this chapter covers the basics of operating system shells that can be found on Linux and Unix-like systems. The reader will need to know these principles in order to understand principles that will be presented in later chapters.

Chapter 2, Interpreting Commands, there are five things that an operating system shell will do for us. These include interpreting commands, setting variables, enabling pipelines, allowing input/output redirection, and allowing customization of the user's working environment. In this chapter, we'll look at how shells interpret a user's commands.

Chapter 3, Understanding Variables and Pipelines, in this chapter, we'll look at the next two things that an operating system shell does for us, which is to allow us to set variables and use command pipelines. There's not that much to say about either of these topics, which is why we're combining them both into one chapter.

Chapter 4, Understanding Input/Output Redirection, in this chapter, we'll look at how to send the text output of a command to somewhere other than the terminal, which is the default output device. We'll then look at how to make a command bring in text from somewhere other than the keyboard, which is the default input device.

Finally, we'll look at how to send error messages to somewhere other than the terminal.

Chapter 5, Customizing the Environment, in this chapter, we'll look at the various configuration files for the various shell environments. We'll look at how to customize these configuration files, and how to set certain environmental options from the command-line.

Chapter 6, Text Stream Filters – Part 1, many times, an administrator will need to write a shell script that will retrieve text information from an external source, format it, and create a report. In this chapter, we'll introduce the concept of text stream filters, which can help with this process. Also, knowing about these text stream filters can help you pass certain Linux certification exams, such as the LPI/Linux+ exam. We will then show you how to use several of these filters.

Chapter 7, Text Stream Filters – Part 2, in this chapter, we'll continue our exploration of text stream filters.

Chapter 8, Basic Shell Script Construction, in this chapter, we'll explain about the basic structure of a shell script, and will use some of the text stream filters from the previous chapters to create simple scripts. We'll also look at some basic programming constructs that are common to all programming languages, and show you how to use them.

Chapter 9, Filtering Text with grep, sed, and Regular Expressions, in this chapter, you'll learn about the concept of regular expressions, and how to use them with grep and sed to filter or manipulate text. These techniques can not only help you find certain text, but can also help automate the creation of reports and the editing of multiple text files at once.

Chapter 10, Understanding Functions, functions are an important part of every programming language, because they make it easy for a programmer to reuse a block of code in numerous programs, or in numerous places within one single program. The programmer can pass parameters to a function, have the function operate on those parameters, and pass back the results to the main program.

Chapter 11, Performing Mathematical Operations, the various operating system shells all have means of performing mathematical operations either from the command-line, or from within a shell script. In this chapter, we'll look at how to perform operations with both integer and floating point math.

Chapter 12, Automating Scripts with here Documents and expect, although it's easy to have a shell script pull data out of a separate text file, it's sometimes handier to store the data within the shell script itself. We'll do that using a "here" document. In this chapter, you'll learn how to create and use "here" documents. You'll also see how to automate certain scripts with the expect utility.

Chapter 13, Scripting with ImageMagick, imageMagick is a text-mode program that is used to edit, manipulate, and view graphical image files. In this chapter, you'll learn how to automate the processing of images by using ImageMagick commands within shell scripts.

Chapter 14, Using awk–Part 1, this chapter covers awk, which is a tool that can extract specific text from text files, and automate the creation of reports and databases. Since awk is a full-blown programming language in its own right, we won't be covering it in depth here. Instead, we'll give you enough information so that you can create awk "one-liners" that can be used within shell scripts.

Chapter 15, Using awk–Part 2, this is a continuation of the previous chapter, in which we'll cover the more advanced concepts of scripting with awk.

Chapter 16, Creating User Interfaces with yad, dialog, and xdialog, so far, we've only looked at shell scripts that run strictly from the command-line. And indeed, that's how most people use them, and is what most people think about when they think about shell scripts. But, it's also possible to create shell scripts that offer a user interface. In this chapter, we'll use yad to create graphical user interfaces, and dialog to create ncurses-style interfaces.

Chapter 17, Using Shell Script Options with getopts, often, an administrator will need to pass both arguments and options to a shell script. Passing arguments, the objects upon which a script will operate, is easy. To also pass options, which modify how the script will operate, requires another type of operator. In this chapter, you'll learn how to use getopts to pass options to a script.

Chapter 18, Shell Scripting for Security Professionals, in this chapter, you'll learn how to either create shell scripts or search for existing shell scripts that can help security administrators perform their jobs. We'll also look at how to modify or improve existing shell scripts to meet specific needs of security administrators.

Chapter 19, Shell Script Portability, large organizations, such as large government agencies or large corporations, might have a diverse mix of Linux, Unix, and Unix-like machines. Sometimes, it's handy to write shell scripts that can automatically detect the type of system on which they're running, and run the appropriate code for each type of system. In this chapter, we'll look at several methods for enhancing script portability.

Chapter 20, Shell Script Security, scripting errors can cause a script to inadvertently cause the exposure of sensitive data, or to allow someone to perform unauthorized activities on a system. In this chapter, we'll look at ways to help the reader write shell scripts that are as secure as they possibly can be.

Chapter 21, Debugging Shell Scripts, shell scripts can have bugs, the same as with any other programming language. Sometimes, the bugs are easy to find, and sometimes they're not. In this chapter, we'll look at various methods that can help a busy administrator debug shell scripts that aren't working properly.

Chapter 22, Introduction to Z Shell Scripting, the Z Shell, or zsh, is an alternate shell that can be used in place of bash. It's mainly used in the same manner as bash, but it also has enhancements that bash doesn't have. In this chapter, we'll look at these enhancements, and also at some scripting tricks that you can't do with bash.

Chapter 23, Using PowerShell on Linux, powerShell was created by Microsoft for use on Windows operating systems back in 2006. In 2016, Microsoft announced that they had open-sourced PowerShell, and were making it available for Linux and macOS, as well as for Windows. In this chapter, we'll look at how PowerShell can be beneficial for Linux administrators, how to install it, and how to use it.

To get the most out of this book

Since the book begins with the very basics of Linux and Unix command-line usage, the reader really just needs to be comfortable with the idea of setting up VirtualBox and installing Linux, FreeBSD, and OpenIndiana virtual machines.

VirtualBox is a free download that you can get from here: https://www.virtualbox.org/

To run VirtualBox, you'll need a machine with a CPU that is capable of virtualization. Most modern CPUs have that capability, with the exception of certain Intel Core i3 and Core i5 models. (That's because they lack the hardware acceleration that's required for virtualization.) Also, you'll have to ensure that virtualization is enabled in your computer's BIOS.

For the demos, we'll be using Fedora, Debian, Ubuntu, FreeBSD, and OpenIndiana virtual machines. Here's where you can download the installation images:

- Fedora: `https://fedoraproject.org/`
- Debian: `https://www.debian.org/`
- Ubuntu: `https://ubuntu.com/`
- FreeBSD: `https://www.freebsd.org/`
- OpenIndiana: `https://openindiana.org/`

In all cases, you'll need to create a normal user account that has full sudo privileges. That happens automatically with Ubuntu and OpenIndiana during installation. With Debian and Fedora, that will happen automatically if you omit creating a root user password during installation.

For FreeBSD, things are a bit different. That's because the FreeBSD installer will have you create a password for the root user, and sudo won't be installed. So, here's the procedure for installing FreeBSD.

1. When you get to the installer section that has you create your own user account, you'll see:

    1. Login group is your_username. Invite your_username into other groups.
    2. Respond by typing wheel, in order to add yourself to the wheel group.

2. After the installation has completed, log into the root user account, using the password that you created during installation.

3. Install the sudo package by doing:

```
pkg install sudo
```

4. Configure sudo so that members of the wheel group have full sudo privileges. Begin by entering the command:

```
visudo
```

5. Scroll down to where you see this line:

```
# %wheel ALL=(ALL:ALL) ALL
```

    - Remove the # and the leading blank space from in front of this line.
    - Save the file and exit.

6. Log out from the root user's account, and log back in with your own account.

    When you need to perform an administrative command, you can now use sudo, as you would on any Linux distro.

Next, you'll need to install bash on FreeBSD.

Since bash doesn't come installed on FreeBSD by default, you'll need to install it yourself. Here's the procedure:

1. Install bash with this command:

```
sudo pkg install bash
```

2. Create a symbolic line to the bash executable, like this:

```
sudo ln -s /usr/local/bin/bash /bin/bash
```

Download the example code files

The code bundle for the book is hosted on GitHub at https://github.com/PacktPublishing/The-Ultimate-Linux-Shell-Scripting-Guide.git. We also have other code bundles from our rich catalog of books and videos available at https://github.com/PacktPublishing/. Check them out!

Download the color images

We also provide a PDF file that has color images of the screenshots/diagrams used in this book. You can download it here: https://packt.link/gbp/9781835463574.

Conventions used

There are a number of text conventions used throughout this book.

CodeInText: Indicates code words in text, database table names, folder names, filenames, file extensions, pathnames, dummy URLs, user input, and Twitter handles. For example: "Add the new functions to the /etc/bashrc file."

```
donnie@opensuse:~> git clone https://github.com/PacktPublishing/The-Ultimate-
Linux-Shell-Scripting-Guide.git
```

Bold: Indicates a new term, an important word, or words that you see on the screen. For instance, words in menus or dialog boxes appear in the text like this. For example: " First, let's see how many processes are in either the **Running** state or the **Zombie** state."

Warnings or important notes appear like this.

Tips and tricks appear like this.

Get in touch

Feedback from our readers is always welcome.

General feedback: Email feedback@packtpub.com and mention the book's title in the subject of your message. If you have questions about any aspect of this book, please email us at questions@packtpub.com.

Errata: Although we have taken every care to ensure the accuracy of our content, mistakes do happen. If you have found a mistake in this book, we would be grateful if you reported this to us. Please visit http://www.packtpub.com/submit-errata, click **Submit Errata**, and fill in the form.

Piracy: If you come across any illegal copies of our works in any form on the internet, we would be grateful if you would provide us with the location address or website name. Please contact us at copyright@packtpub.com with a link to the material.

If you are interested in becoming an author: If there is a topic that you have expertise in and you are interested in either writing or contributing to a book, please visit http://authors.packtpub.com.

Leave a Review!

Thank you for purchasing this book from Packt Publishing—we hope you enjoy it! Your feedback is invaluable and helps us improve and grow. Once you've completed reading it, please take a moment to leave an Amazon review; it will only take a minute, but it makes a big difference for readers like you.

https://packt.link/r/1835463576

Scan the QR code below to receive a free ebook of your choice.

https://packt.link/NzOWQ

Download a free PDF copy of this book

Thanks for purchasing this book!

Do you like to read on the go but are unable to carry your print books everywhere?

Is your eBook purchase not compatible with the device of your choice?

Don't worry, now with every Packt book you get a DRM-free PDF version of that book at no cost.

Read anywhere, any place, on any device. Search, copy, and paste code from your favorite technical books directly into your application.

The perks don't stop there, you can get exclusive access to discounts, newsletters, and great free content in your inbox daily.

Follow these simple steps to get the benefits:

1. Scan the QR code or visit the link below:

https://packt.link/free-ebook/9781835463574

2. Submit your proof of purchase.
3. That's it! We'll send your free PDF and other benefits to your email directly.

1
Getting Started with the Shell

Before we can talk about shell scripting, we need to know what a shell is and what kinds of shells are available for Linux, Unix, and Unix-like operating systems. We'll also talk about other important topics that will help get you started in the wide, wonderful world of shell scripting.

Topics in this chapter include:

- Understanding shells
- Finding help with shell commands
- Using a text editor
- Understanding compiled versus interpreted programming
- Understanding root and sudo privileges

If you're ready, let's get started on this important journey. And, always remember to have some fun along the way.

Understanding Shells

So, you're scratching your head and saying, "What is a shell, and why should I care?" Well, a shell is a program that acts as an intermediary between the user and the operating system kernel. A user types commands into the shell, which passes them into the kernel for processing. The output is then presented to the user via the computer **terminal**, which can also referred to as the **screen**. The most common shell on Linux systems is **bash**, but the **Z shell (zsh)** has been gaining popularity in recent years. (I'll explain why in *Chapter 22, Using the Z Shell.*) You'll find bash as the default shell on most Linux distros and certain Unix-like distros such as OpenIndiana, and zsh as the default on Kali Linux.

If you are brand new to the wild, wonderful world of Linux and its Unix or Unix-like cousins, you might be wondering what a *distro* is. Well, unlike Windows and macOS, which are proprietary and controlled by a single company, Linux and its cousins are primarily open source software, which means that anyone can take the source code and create their own implementations, or *distributions*. Red Hat Enterprise Linux, Fedora, and Ubuntu are examples of Linux distributions, and OpenIndiana and FreeBSD are examples of Unix-like distributions. But, we hard-core geeks rarely utter the word *distribution*, and instead just say *distro*, for short.

Also, the reason that I differentiate between Unix and Unix-like distros has to do with legal reasons that date back to the 1980s. This involves a rather complicated mess that I would rather not go into here. Suffice it to say that the creators of distros such as FreeBSD are not allowed to refer to their creations as Unix, even though they are mostly functionally equivalent. But, they can say that their creations are *Unix-like*.

The newest versions of macOS also have zsh set as the default shell. Fortunately, much of what you'll learn about bash also works on zsh. The main difference is that zsh has a few cool features that bash doesn't have. (Again, I'll explain all about that in *Chapter 22*.) **PowerShell**, which originally was only available for Microsoft Windows operating systems, has also been available for Linux and macOS since 2016. PowerShell is a whole different animal, but you might find it quite useful, as you should see when we get to *Chapter 23, Using PowerShell on Linux*.

It's common to hear people refer to bash as the *bash shell*. But, bash is short for *Bourne Again Shell*. So, when you say *bash shell*, you're really saying *Bourne Again Shell Shell*, which is a bit awkward. This is the same as when people talk about going to the *ATM machine* to withdraw some money. What they're really saying is that they're going to the *Automatic Teller Machine Machine*, which is also awkward.

And, don't even get me started on the people who talk about *hot water heaters*. I mean, if the water is already hot, why heat it?

On the other hand, if you find that you still need to say *bash shell* so that people will know what you're talking about, I'll understand and won't condemn you for it. In fact, you might even see me do that on occasion.

The coolest thing about modern operating system shells is that they're much more than just an interface tool. They're also full-blown programming environments with many of the same programming constructs as more complex programming languages, such as Pascal, C, or Java. Systems administrators can make their jobs much easier by using shell scripts to automate complex, repetitive tasks.

When you log into a text-mode Linux or Unix server, you'll be presented with a black screen and some text, which looks like this:

```
Debian GNU/Linux 12 debian12 tty1

debian12 login: donnie
Password:
Linux debian12 6.1.0-18-amd64 #1 SMP PREEMPT_DYNAMIC Debian 6.1.76-1 (2024-02-01) x86_64

The programs included with the Debian GNU/Linux system are free software;
the exact distribution terms for each program are described in the
individual files in /usr/share/doc/*/copyright.

Debian GNU/Linux comes with ABSOLUTELY NO WARRANTY, to the extent
permitted by applicable law.
Last login: Mon Mar 11 17:01:16 EDT 2024 from 192.168.0.16 on pts/0
donnie@debian12:~$ echo $SHELL
/bin/bash
donnie@debian12:~$
```

Figure 1.1: Plain bash on a text-mode Debian Linux machine

This is the unadorned, plain-jane shell. Machines with desktop environments installed will interface with the shell via a **terminal emulator**, which will look something like this:

Figure 1.2: A terminal emulator that interfaces with bash on an OpenIndiana machine

The name of the terminal emulator will differ from one desktop environment to the next, but all do the same job. The advantage of using a terminal emulator is that you'll have the luxury of using scroll bars, customizing the display, and using copy-and-paste for the command-line.

In any case, you can see which shell you're using by typing:

```
donnie@fedora:~$ echo $SHELL
/bin/bash
donnie@fedora:~$
```

In this case, you see that you're using bash.

Finding Help with Shell Commands

It doesn't matter how much of an expert you think you are, there will still be times when you'll need to look up some bit of information. With Linux, Unix, and Unix-like operating systems, there are several options for that.

Understanding Manual Pages

Manual pages, or **man pages** for short, have been built into Unix-like operating systems since almost forever. To use a man page, just enter man, followed by the name of the command, configuration file, or system component for which you seek information. For example, you could find out how to use the ls command like this:

```
man ls
```

Most of the time, the man command will open a man page in the less pager. (Some Unix implementations might use the more pager instead, but I haven't found any recent ones that do.) Either way, you'll be able to scroll through the man page or perform key word searches within the page to find the information that you seek.

The man pages are divided into sections that each correspond to a different category. On most Unix-like and Linux systems, there are eight main categories, more commonly referred to as *sections*, which are as follows:

Section number	Purpose
1	This section contains information about commands that can be used by any unprivileged user.
2	This section contains information about system calls, which are mainly of interest to software developers.
3	In this section, you'll find information about library functions, which will also mainly be of interest to software developers.
4	If you've ever wanted to find information about the device files in the /dev/ directory, this is the place to look. This section also contains information about device drivers.
5	Here you'll find information about the various configuration and system files on your system.

6	This is for information about games and screensavers. There's normally not much here.
7	This is for information about miscellaneous things that don't fit neatly into any of the other categories.
8	This is for information about administrative commands and system daemons.

Table 1.1: Describing the man page sections

You'll see the subdirectories that contain these man page files in the /usr/share/man/ directory. You also might see some subdirectories with names like man0p, man5p, or man8x. These subdirectories contain certain special-purpose man pages, which will differ on different Linux distros.

A lot of times, you won't need to think about these sections, because the man command will pull up the proper man page for you. Other times, you will need to pay attention to these sections, because many key words for which you'll search can be found in multiple sections. For example, here on the Fedora workstation that I'm using to write this, there are two man pages for printf. There are two ways to find them. First, you can use the man -aw command, like this:

```
[donnie@fedora ~]$ man -aw printf
/usr/share/man/man1/printf.1.gz
/usr/share/man/man3/printf.3.gz
[donnie@fedora ~]$
```

You can also use the whatis command, like this:

```
[donnie@fedora ~]$ whatis printf
printf (1)              - format and print data
printf (3)              - formatted output conversion
[donnie@fedora ~]$
```

Note that whatis is a synonym for man -f. You'll get the same results with either command, but my own preference is to use whatis.

So, we have a printf man page in Section 1, which means that we have a normal user command that's called printf. We also see a printf man page in Section 3, which means that there's a library function that's called printf. If you enter man printf, you'll see the man page from Section 1. You'll see that in the first line of the man page, which will look like this:

```
PRINTF(1)              User Commands              PRINTF(1)
```

If you instead want to see the man page from Section 3, you'll need to specify that in your command, like this:

```
man 3 printf
```

To broaden your search for all man pages that contain printf in either the title or the description of the man page, even if it's embedded into another text string, use either apropos or man -k, like this:

```
[donnie@fedora ~]$ apropos printf
asprintf (3)          - print to allocated string
BIO_printf (3ossl)    - formatted output to a BIO
BIO_snprintf (3ossl)  - formatted output to a BIO
BIO_vprintf (3ossl)   - formatted output to a BIO
BIO_vsnprintf (3ossl) - formatted output to a BIO
curl_mprintf (3)      - formatted output conversion
dprintf (3)           - formatted output conversion
tpm2_print (1)        - Prints TPM data structures
fprintf (3)           - formatted output conversion
fwprintf (3)          - formatted wide-character output conversion
printf (1)            - format and print data
printf (3)            - formatted output conversion
. . .
[donnie@fedora ~]$
```

Again, either command will give you the same output, but my own preference has always been to use apropos.

Most of the time, your Linux system does a good job of keeping the man page index updated. Once in a while though, you'll need to do it manually, like this:

```
[donnie@fedora ~]$ sudo mandb
[sudo] password for donnie:
Purging old database entries in /usr/share/man...
Processing manual pages under /usr/share/man...
Purging old database entries in /usr/share/man/ca...
Processing manual pages under /usr/share/man/ca...

. . .

. . .

Processing manual pages under /usr/local/share/man...
0 man subdirectories contained newer manual pages.
0 manual pages were added.
0 stray cats were added.
0 old database entries were purged.
[donnie@fedora ~]$
```

Okay, that about does it for the man page system. Let's talk about the info system.

Understanding Info Pages

The **info page** system is newer, and was invented by Richard M. Stallman as part of the **GNU Project**. The unique part about it is that each info page contains hyperlinks that can lead you to additional pages of information. For example, to obtain information about the info system, enter `info info`. This info page contains a menu, which looks something like this:

```
* Menu:


* Stand-alone Info::            What is Info?
* Invoking Info::               Options you can pass on the command line.
* Cursor Commands::             Commands which move the cursor within a node.
. . .

., . .
* Variables::                   How to change the default behavior of Info.
* Colors and Styles::           Customize the colors used by Info.
* Custom Key Bindings::         How to define your own key-to-command bindings.
* Index::                       Global index.
```

Each underlined item you see is a **hyperlink** to another page. With your cursor keys, move the cursor to the hyperlink that you want to see, and hit the *Enter* key. To see an info page for a specific command, such as `ls`, just do this:

```
info ls
```

If you need help with navigating through the info pages, just hit the H key to bring up a navigation menu.

And, that's about it for the info pages. Let's talk about on-line documentation.

Getting to Know the Linux Documentation Project

The Linux Documentation Project has been around since almost forever, and is an invaluable resource. The best part about it is the **Guides** section, where you'll find free-of-charge, full-length books about Linux and bash that you can download in a variety of formats. They're all quite old, with the newest one having been last updated in 2014. For the *Bash Guide for Beginners* book and the *Advanced Bash-Scripting* book that you'll find there, that doesn't matter. The concepts in those two books are eternal, and haven't really changed over the years. To see these books, go to `https://tldp.org/guides.html`.

Using Your Favorite Search Engine

If all else fails, just use your favorite search engine to find what you need to know about either scripting in general, or scripting on a particular operating system. You'll find plenty of help, such as blog posts, YouTube videos, and official documentation. There are plenty of Linux-specific websites that offer help on various things, and it's quite simple to find them.

Next, let's talk about text editors.

Using a Text Editor to Create Shell Scripts

To create your shell scripts, you'll need a text editor that's designed for Linux and Unix systems. You have plenty of choices, and which one you choose will depend upon several criteria:

- Are you editing on a text-mode machine or on a desktop machine?
- What features do you need?
- What is your own personal preference?

Text-mode Editors

Text-mode text editors can be used on machines that don't have a graphical user interface installed. The two most common text-mode text editors are nano and vim. The nano editor is installed by default on pretty much every Linux distro, and is quite easy to use. To use it, just type nano, followed by the name of the file that you want to either edit or create. At the bottom of the screen, you'll see the list of available commands. To invoke a command, press the *CTRL* key, followed by the letter key that corresponds to the desired command.

The downside of using nano is that it doesn't have the full range of features that you might want in a programmers' text editor. You can see here that the implementation of nano on my Fedora workstation has color-coding for the syntax, but it doesn't automatically format the code.

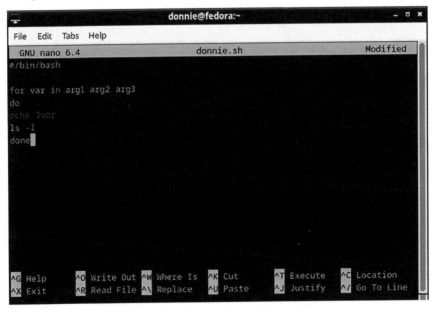

Figure 1.3: The nano text editor on my Fedora workstation

Note that on other Linux distros, nano might not even have color-coding.

My favorite text-mode editor is vim, which has features that would make almost any programmer happy. Not only does it have color-coded syntax highlighting, but it also automatically formats your code with proper indentations, as you see here:

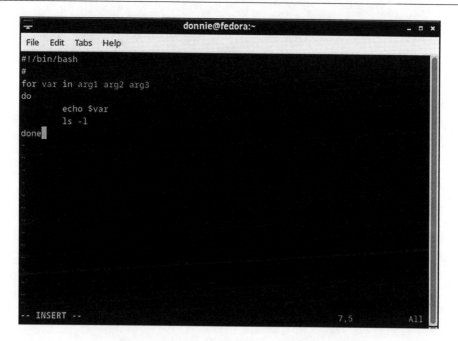

Figure 1.4: The vim text editor on my Fedora workstation

In reality, indentation isn't needed for bash scripting, because bash scripts work fine without it. However, the indentation does make code easier for humans to read, and having an editor that will apply proper indentation automatically is quite handy. Additionally, vim comes with a powerful search-and-replace feature, allows you to split the screen so that you can work on two files at once, and can be customized with a fairly wide selection of plug-ins. Even though it's a text-mode editor, you can use the right-click menu from your mouse to copy and paste text if you're remotely logged in to your server from a desktop machine or if you're editing a local file on your desktop machine.

The older vi text editor is normally installed on most Linux distros by default, but vim often isn't. On some distros, the vim command will work, even if vim isn't actually installed. That's because the vim command on them might be pointing to either vim-minimal or even to the old vi. At any rate, to install full-fledged vim on any Red Hat-type of distro, such as RHEL, Fedora, AlmaLinux, or Rocky Linux, just do:

```
sudo dnf install vim-enhanced
```

To install vim on Debian or Ubuntu, do:

```
sudo apt install vim
```

As much as I like vim, I do have to tell you that some users are a bit put off from using it, because they believe that it's too hard to learn. That's because the original version of vi was created back in the Stone Age of Computing, before computer keyboards had cursor keys, backspace keys, or delete keys. The old vi commands that you used to have to use instead of these keys have been carried over to the modern implementations of vim.

So, most `vim` tutorials that you'll find will still try to teach you all of those old keyboard commands.

Figure 1.5: This photo of me was taken during the Stone Age of Computing, before computer keyboards had cursor keys, backspace keys, or delete keys.

However, on the current versions of `vim` that you'll install on Linux and modern Unix-like distros such as FreeBSD and OpenIndiana, the cursor keys, backspace key, and delete key all work as they do on any other text editor. So, it's no longer necessary to learn all of those keyboard commands that you would have had to learn years ago. I mean, you'll still need to learn a few basic keyboard commands, but not as many as you had to before.

GUI Text Editors

If you're using a desktop machine, you can still use either `nano` or `vim` if you desire. But, there's also a wide range of GUI-type editors available if you'd rather use one of them. Some sort of no-frills text editor, such as `gedit` or `leafpad`, is probably already installed on your desktop system. Some slightly fancier programmer's editors, such as `geany`, `kwrite`, and `bluefish`, are available in the normal repositories of most Linux distros and some Unix-like distros. Your best bet is to play around with different editors to see what you like. Here's an example of `kwrite` with color-coded syntax highlighting enabled:

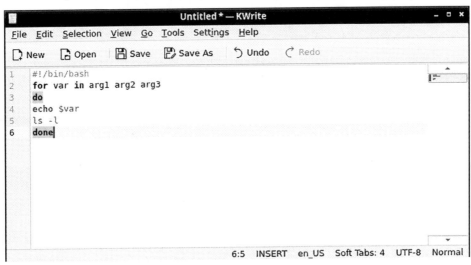

Figure 1.6: The Kwrite text editor.

If you're a Windows user, you'll never want to create or edit a shell script on your Windows machine with a Windows text editor such as Notepad or Wordpad, and then transfer the script to your Linux machine. That's because Windows text editors insert an invisible carriage return character at the end of each line. You can't see them, but your Linux shell can, and will refuse to run the script. Having said that, you might at times encounter scripts that someone else created with a Windows text editor, and you'll need to know how to fix them so that they'll run on your Linux or Unix machine. That's easy to do, and we'll look at that in *Chapter 7, Text Stream Filters-Part 2*.

That's about it for our overview of text editors for Linux. Let's move on and talk about compiled versus interpreted programming languages.

Understanding Compiled versus Interpreted Programming

Compiled programming consists of writing program code in a text editor, and then using a compiler to convert the text file into an executable binary file. Once that's done, users of the program won't be able to easily view the source code of the program. With **interpreted programming**, the program runs directly from a text file, without having to compile it first.

Compiled programming languages, such as C, C++, or Fortran, are good for when you need maximum performance from your programs. However, they can be fairly hard to learn, especially when it comes to the lower-level functions such as working with files. Interpreted languages might not offer quite as high a level of performance, but they are generally quite flexible, and generally easier to learn. Interpreted languages in general also offer a higher degree of portability between different operating systems. Shell scripting falls into the category of interpreted languages.

Here are some reasons why you might consider using an interpreted language:

- When you are looking for a simple solution.
- When you need a solution that is portable. If you pay attention to portability concerns, you can write one script that will work on different Linux distros, as well as on Unix/Unix-like systems. That can come in handy if you're working in a large corporation with a large network of mixed operating systems. (You might even find some larger corporations that are still running legacy Unix systems, such as AIX, HPUX, or SUNOS, alongside more modern implementations of Linux, BSD, or macOS.)

And, here are some reasons why you might consider using a compiled language:

- When the tasks require intensive use of system resources. This is especially true when speed is extremely important.
- When you are using math operations that require heavy number crunching.
- When you need complex applications.

- When your application has many sub-components with dependencies.
- When you want to create proprietary applications, and prevent users from viewing the application source code.

When you think about it, pretty much every example of productivity, server, gaming, or scientific software falls into one or more of these categories, which means that they really should be built with compiled languages for best performance.

Okay, let's now talk about sudo.

Understanding root and sudo Privileges

Some of the things you'll do in this course will require you to have administrative privileges. While it's possible and convenient to just log into the root command prompt, that's something that I like to discourage as much as possible. For best security, and to get used to what you'd be doing in an enterprise setting, your best bet is to use sudo.

Modern Linux distros allow you to add yourself to an administrators' group as you install the operating system. (That's the wheel group on Red Hat-type systems, and the sudo group on Debian/Ubuntu-type systems.) To run a command that requires administrative privileges, just do something like this:

```
sudo nftables list ruleset
```

You'll then be asked to enter the password for your own user account, rather than the one for the root user account.

That's about all we need to say about this topic, so let's summarize and move on to the next chapter.

Summary

In this chapter, I've laid a bit of the groundwork for what's to come in the following chapters. We looked at what an operating system shell is, and why we would use one. Then, we looked at the various ways to find help, did a high-level overview of Linux text editors, and wrapped up with a discussion of compiled versus interpreted programming and a brief mention of why we want to use sudo to run administrative commands.

In the next chapter, we'll begin looking at the various things that an operating system shell does for us. I'll see you there.

Questions

1. What is the most widely-used shell for Linux systems?

    a. zsh

    b. bash

    c. korn

    d. csh

2. What will happen if you create a Linux shell script on a Windows computer with a Windows text editor, such as Notepad or Wordpad?

    a. The script will run fine on a Linux machine.

    b. Your Windows machine will just shut down in protest of the fact that you're using it to create Linux scripts.

    c. The script won't run on a Linux machine, because Windows text editors insert an invisible carriage return character at the end of each line.

    d. Former Microsoft CEO Steve Ballmer will visit you and explain why Linux is a cancer.

3. 3. In which section would you find the man pages for administrative commands?

    a. 1

    b. 3

    c. 5

    d. 6

    e. 8

4. Which of the following statements is true?

    a. Interpreted programming languages are good for programs that perform heavy-duty math problems.

    b. Compiled programming languages are generally better than interpreted languages for any large, complex programs.

    c. Examples of interpreted programming languages include C, C++, and Fortran.

    d. There's no difference in performance between interpreted and compiled programming languages.

5. True or False: To run administrative commands, it's best to just log into the root user account.

Further Reading

- 22 Best Linux Text Editors for Coding: `https://phoenixnap.com/kb/best-linux-text-editors-for-coding`
- Ballmer: "Linux is a Cancer": `https://www.theregister.com/2001/06/02/ballmer_linux_is_a_cancer/`
- Microsoft once called Linux a cancer, and that was a big mistake: `https://www.zdnet.com/article/microsoft-once-called-linux-a-cancer-and-that-was-a-big-mistake/`
- VIM tutorial for Beginners: `https://linuxconfig.org/vim-tutorial`
- Distrowatch.com: `https://distrowatch.com/`
- The Linux Documentation Project: `https://tldp.org/`
- LinuxQuestions.org: `https://www.linuxquestions.org/`
- Linux man pages: `https://linux.die.net/man/`

Answers

1. b
2. c
3. e
4. b
5. False. It's better to use sudo from your own user account.

Join our community on Discord!

Read this book alongside other users, Linux experts, and the author himself.

Ask questions, provide solutions to other readers, chat with the author via Ask Me Anything sessions, and much more. Scan the QR code or visit the link to join the community.

`https://packt.link/SecNet`

2

Interpreting Commands

To fulfill its job as the interface between the user and the operating system kernel, a shell has to perform five different functions. These functions include interpreting commands, setting variables, enabling input/output redirection, enabling pipelines, and allowing customization of a user's working environment. In this chapter, we'll look at how bash and zsh interpret commands. As an added bonus, much of what we'll cover in the next few chapters will also help you prepare for certain Linux certification exams, such as the Linux Professional Institute or CompTIA Linux+ exams.

Topics in this chapter include:

- Understanding the structure of a command
- Executing multiple commands at once
- Running commands recursively
- Understanding the command history
- Escaping and quoting

To follow along, you can use pretty much any Linux distro that you desire, as long as it's running with either bash or zsh. Your best bet is to use a virtual machine instead of your production workstation, in case you accidentally delete or change something that you shouldn't.

Understanding the Structure of a Command

A handy thing to know for both real-life and any certification exams that you may take, is the structure of a command. Commands can consist of up to three parts, and there's a certain order for the parts. Here are the parts and the order in which you'll normally place them:

- The command itself
- Command options
- Command arguments

If you plan to take a Linux certification exam, you'll definitely want to remember this ordering rule. Later on though, we'll see that some commands don't always follow this rule.

Using Command Options

There are two general types of **option switches:**

- **Single-letter options:** For most commands, a single-letter option is preceded by a single dash. Most of the time, two or more single-letter options can be combined with a single dash.

- **Whole-word options:** For *most* commands, a whole word option is preceded by two dashes. Two or more whole-word options must be listed separately, because they can't be combined with a single pair of dashes.

To show you what we mean, check out this hands-on lab.

Hands-on Lab — Practice With Command Options

In this lab, we'll be working with the humble `ls` utility. Options and arguments are optional for this utility, so we'll get to see the different configurations for the command in this hands-on practice.

1. Let's issue the naked `ls` command in order to see the files and directories that are in our current directory.

```
[donnie@fedora ~]$ ls
4-2_Building_an_Alpine_Container.bak       Public
4-2_Building_an_Alpine_Container.pptx      pwsafe.key
addresses.txt                                                          python_
container
alma9_default.txt                                               rad-bfgminer
alma9_future.txt                                                   ramfetch
alma_link.txt                                                         read.
me.first
. . .

. . .
pCloudDrive                                                        yad-form.sh
 Pictures
[donnie@fedora ~]$
```

2. Now, let's add a single-letter option. We'll use the `-l` option to show the files and directories with some of their characteristics.

```
[donnie@fedora ~]$ ls -l
total 40257473
-rw-r--r--.  1 donnie donnie     754207 Apr  5 16:13  4-2_Building_an_
Alpine_Container.bak
-rw-r--r--.  1 donnie donnie     761796 Apr  8 14:49  4-2_Building_an_
Alpine_Container.pptx
-rw-r--r--.  1 donnie donnie        137 Apr  2 15:05  addresses.txt
-rw-r--r--.  1 donnie donnie       1438 Nov  2  2022  alma9_default.txt
. . .
```

```
. . .
-rwxr--r--.  1 donnie donnie          263 May 16 15:42  yad-form.sh
[donnie@fedora ~]$
```

3. Use the `ls` command with the `-a` option to see any hidden files or directories. (Hidden files or directories have names that begin with a period.)

```
[donnie@fedora ~]$ ls -a
.
.pcloud
..                                          pCloudDrive
4-2_Building_an_Alpine_Container.bak        Pictures
4-2_Building_an_Alpine_Container.pptx        .pki
addresses.txt                                                       .podman-
desktop
alma9_default.txt                                                    .profile
. . .
. . .
.mozilla
.Xauthority
Music
.xscreensaver
NetRexx                                                             .xsession-
errors
nikto                                                                   yad-
form.sh
[donnie@fedora ~]$
```

4. Next, let's combine the two options, so that we can see the characteristics of both the hidden and unhidden files and directories:

```
[donnie@fedora ~]$ ls -la
total 40257561
drwx------.  1 donnie donnie       2820 Jul 25 13:53  .
drwxr-xr-x.  1 root   root           12 Aug  9 2022  ..
-rw-r--r--.  1 donnie donnie        137 Apr  2 15:05     addresses.
txt
-rw-------.  1 donnie donnie      15804 Jul 24 17:53  .bash_history
-rw-r--r--.  1 donnie donnie         18 Jan 19 2022      .bash_
logout
-rw-r--r--.  1 donnie donnie        194 Apr  3 12:11      .bash_
profile
-rw-r--r--.  1 donnie donnie        513 Apr  3 12:11      .bashrc
. . .
```

```
. . .
-rw-r--r--.    1 donnie donnie              9041 Feb  4 12:57
.xscreensaver
-rw-------.    1 donnie donnie                 0 Jul 25 13:53
.xsession-errors
-rwxr--r--.    1 donnie donnie               263 May 16 15:42      yad-form.sh
[donnie@fedora ~]$
```

In the preceding examples, the donnie donnie part indicates that the files and directories belong to user donnie and are associated with the donnie group. In this example, we're using a whole-word option, --author, preceded by two dashes, to view some extra information. Let's use this --author switch and the -1 switch together to see who authored these files:

```
[donnie@fedora ~]$ ls -l --author
total 40257473
-rw-r--r--.  1 donnie donnie donnie         137 Apr  2 15:05      addresses.txt
-rw-r--r--.  1 donnie donnie donnie        1438 Nov  2 2022      alma9_default.
txt
-rw-r--r--.  1 donnie donnie donnie        1297 Nov  2 2022      alma9_future.txt
. . .

. . .
rwxr--r--.  1 donnie donnie donnie         263 May 16 15:42  yad-form.sh
[donnie@fedora ~]$
```

So, it appears that that Donnie character also created the files in the first place. (Oh, that's me, isn't it?)

Using Command Arguments

An argument is an object upon which a command will operate. For the ls command, an argument would be the name of a file or directory. For example, let's say that we want to see the details of just a certain file. We can do something like this:

```
[donnie@fedora ~]$ ls -l yad-form.sh
-rwxr--r--. 1 donnie donnie 263 May 16 15:42 yad-form.sh
[donnie@fedora ~]$
```

We can use the * **wildcard** to see details of all files of a certain type, like so:

```
[donnie@fedora ~]$ ls -l *.sh
-rwxr--r--. 1 donnie donnie 116 May 16 15:04 root.sh
-rwxr--r--. 1 donnie donnie 263 May 16 15:42 yad-form.sh
[donnie@fedora ~]$
```

If you're not familiar with the concept of wildcards, think of them as a way to perform pattern-matching. In the above example, the * wildcard is used to match one or more characters. For this reason, the `ls -l *.sh` command allows us to see all files with the .sh filename extension. You can also use this wildcard in other ways. For example, to see all filenames and directory names that begin with the letter w, just do this

```
donnie@opensuse:~> ls -ld w*
drwxrwxr-x 1 donnie users     22 Mar  5  2022 windows
-rw-r--r-- 1 donnie users 82180 Dec  7  2019 wingding.ttf
drwxr-xr-x 1 donnie users    138 Mar 11  2023 wownero-x86_64-
linux-gnu-v0.11
donnie@opensuse:~>
```

For more information about wildcards, check out the reference in the *Further Reading* section.

In this case, we're looking at all files whose names end in .sh.

You're not always limited to specifying just one argument. In this example, we're looking at three different files:

```
[donnie@fedora ~]$ ls -l missing_stuff.txt yad-form.sh Dylan-My_Back_Pages-tab.odt
-rw-r--r--. 1 donnie donnie 29502 Mar  7 18:30 Dylan-My_Back_Pages-tab.odt
-rw-r--r--. 1 donnie donnie   394 Dec  7  2022 missing_stuff.txt
-rwxr--r--. 1 donnie donnie   263 May 16 15:42 yad-form.sh
[donnie@fedora ~]$
```

Use the -ld option to view the characteristics of a directory without viewing the contents of the directory, like so:

```
[donnie@fedora ~]$ ls -ld Downloads/
drwxr-xr-x. 1 donnie donnie 8100 Aug  4 12:37 Downloads/
[donnie@fedora ~]$
```

Although you can actually change the order in which options and arguments appear in many commands, it's bad practice to do so. To avoid confusion and to prepare yourself for any Linux certifications exams that you might take, just follow the ordering rule that I've presented here. That is, the command itself, command options, and lastly, the command arguments.

That about does it for the command structure part. Let's move on to see how to execute multiple commands at once.

Executing Multiple Commands at Once

From either the command-line or from within shell scripts, it's handy to know how to combine multiple commands into one single command. In this section, I'll demonstrate three ways to do that which are:

- Running commands interactively
- Using command sequences
- Using the `find` utility

Running Commands Interactively

This is a form of shell-script programming, except that you're just executing all commands from the command-line, instead of actually writing, saving, and executing a script.   Here, you are creating a **for loop** – with each command of the loop on its own separate line – to perform a directory listing three times.

```
[donnie@fedora ~]$ for var in arg1 arg2 arg3
> do
> echo $var
> ls
> done
. . .
. . .
[donnie@fedora ~]$
```

At the end of each line, you'll hit the *Enter* key. But, nothing will happen until you type the done command on the final line. The for loop will then run three times, once for each of the three listed arguments. Each time that it runs, the value of an argument gets assigned to the var variable, and the echo command prints the currently-assigned value. The output will look something like this:

```
arg1
  4-2_Building_an_Alpine_Container.bak      Public
  4-2_Building_an_Alpine_Container.pptx     pwsafe.key
arg2
  4-2_Building_an_Alpine_Container.bak      Public
  4-2_Building_an_Alpine_Container.pptx     pwsafe.key
arg3
  4-2_Building_an_Alpine_Container.bak      Public
  4-2_Building_an_Alpine_Container.pptx     pwsafe.key
```

Next, hit the up arrow key on your keyboard, and you'll see the for loop that you just executed If you try this with bash, you'll see that the individual commands are separated by semi-colons, like so:

```
[donnie@fedora ~]$ for var in arg1 arg2 arg3; do echo $var; ls; done
```

On zsh, pressing the up arrow key will cause the command components to appear on their own separate lines, as you see here:

```
donnie@opensuse:~> for var in arg1 arg2 arg3
do
echo $var
ls
done
```

Either way, the for loop will run again when you hit the *Enter* key.

 If you're still a bit unclear about how for loops work, have no fear. We'll look at them in greater detail once we start actually creating shell scripts.

Using Command Sequences

Command sequences are another type of programming structure that you'll find very useful. Here, I'm demonstrating how to use them from the command-line so that you can grasp the basic concepts. In the upcoming chapters, I'll show you examples of how to use them in shell scripts.

Chaining Commands with a Semi-Colon

You can also use the semi-colon to separate stand-alone commands that you want to execute from the same command entry. If you wanted to cd to a certain directory and then look at its contents, you could enter each command on its own line. Or, you could enter them both on the same line. This process is called **command chaining**, which looks like this:

```
[donnie@fedora ~]$ cd /var ; ls
account   cache   db      ftp      kerberos   local   log   nis   preserve   spool   yp
adm       crash   empty   games    lib        lock    mail  opt   run        tmp
[donnie@fedora var]$
[donnie@fedora ~]$ cd /far ; ls
bash: cd: /far: No such file or directory
 4-2_Building_an_Alpine_Container.bak       Public
 4-2_Building_an_Alpine_Container.pptx      pwsafe.key
 addresses.txt                                                         python_container
 alma9_default.txt                                                     rad-bfgminer
 . . .
 . . .
[donnie@fedora ~]$
```

The first command failed because I tried to cd into a non-existent directory. But, the second command still executed, which listed the files in my home directory.

Conditional Command Execution with Double Ampersands

You can also instruct bash or zsh to only execute the second command if the first command successfully completes. Just separate the commands with && instead of with a semi-colon, like this:

```
[donnie@fedora ~]$ cd /var && ls
account  cache   db      ftp     kerberos  local  log   nis  preserve  spool  yp
adm      crash   empty   games   lib       lock   mail  opt  run       tmp
[donnie@fedora var]$
```

What if the first command doesn't run successfully? Note here that the second command doesn't execute:

```
[donnie@fedora ~]$ cd /far && ls
bash: cd: /far: No such file or directory
[donnie@fedora ~]$
```

Conditional Command Execution with Double Pipes

If you want bash or zsh to execute the second command only if the first command *doesn't* run successfully, just separate the commands with ||. (This is a pair of pipe characters, which you'll find on the same key as the backslash.) To illustrate, let's again make a slight typo while trying to change directories.

```
[donnie@fedora ~]$ ce /var || echo "This command didn't work."
bash: ce: command not found
This command didn't work.
[donnie@fedora ~]$
[donnie@fedora ~]$ cd /var || echo "This command didn't work."
[donnie@fedora var]$
```

For a more practical example, try changing to a directory, creating it if it doesn't exist, and then changing to it after it's been successfully created.

```
[donnie@fedora ~]$ cd mydirectory || mkdir mydirectory && cd mydirectory
bash: cd: mydirectory: No such file or directory
[donnie@fedora mydirectory]$
```

You'll still get an error message saying that the directory you tried to access doesn't exist. But, look at the command prompt, and you'll see that the directory has been created, and that you're now in it.

Using the find Utility

We'll now take a short intermission from our discussion of running multiple commands in order to introduce the find utility, which is truly the Cool-Mac Daddy of all search utilities. After this introduction, I'll use find to show you more ways to run multiple commands at once.

Also, it would behoove us to mention that find isn't just good for command-line searches. It's also excellent for use within shell scripts, as you'll see much later.

If you're as old as I am, you might remember the Windows XP search pooch, which pranced around on your screen every time you did a file search from the Windows XP graphical search utility. It was cute, but it didn't add to your search power. With the Linux find utility, you can perform powerful searches on just about any criterion you can think of, and then--from the same command-line entry--invoke another utility to do whatever you need to do with the search results. I won't try to discuss every option there is for find, since there are so many. Rather, I'll give you an overview of what you can do with find, and let you read its man page for the rest. (Just enter man find at the command-line to read about all of its options.)

In order to perform the most basic of searches, you'll need to specify two things:

- **The search path:** You can perform a search in either a specific path, or the entire filesystem. Since find is inherently recursive, the search will automatically extend to all of the subdirectories that are beneath of the directory that you specify. (Of course, you can also add command switches that limit the depth of the search.)
- **What you're searching for:** There are a lot of ways that you can specify this. You can search for files of a specific name, and decide whether to make the search case-sensitive. You can also use wildcards, or search for files with certain characteristics or that are of a certain age. Or, you can combine multiple criteria for even more specific searches. The main thing that limits you is your own imagination.

So now, let's say that you want to search the entire filesystem for all files whose names end in .conf. You'll want to use either the -name or the -iname switch in front of the file description that you want to search for. Otherwise, you'll get a jumbled up mess of every directory listing that you've searched, with the information you're looking for mixed in. For case-sensitive searches, use -name, and for case-insensitive searches, use -iname. In this case, we'll use -iname, since we want to make the search case-insensitive.

I know, I've told you previously that most whole-word option switches are preceded by a pair of dashes. The find utility is an exception to the rule, because its whole-word option switches are preceded by only a single dash.

Also, be aware that searching through an entire filesystem on a production server with very large drives can take a long time. It's sometimes necessary to do that, but it's best to confine your searches to specific directories whenever possible.

If you include a wildcard character with a search criterion, you'll need to enclose that search criterion in quotes. That will keep the shell from interpreting the wildcard character as an ambiguous file reference. For example, to perform a case-insensitive search through the current working directory and all of its subdirectories for all files with names ending with a .conf filename extension, I would do this:

```
[donnie@fedora ~]$ find -iname '*.conf'
././.cache/containers/short-name-aliases.conf
```

```
./.config/lxsession/LXDE/desktop.conf
./.config/pcmanfm/LXDE/desktop-items-0.conf
./.config/pcmanfm/LXDE/pcmanfm.conf
./.config/lxterminal/lxterminal.conf
./.config/Trolltech.conf
. . .
. . .
./tor-browser/Browser/TorBrowser/Data/fontconfig/fonts.conf
./rad-bfgminer/example.conf
./rad-bfgminer/knc-asic/RPi_system/raspi-blacklist.conf
./something.CONF
[donnie@fedora ~]$[donnie@fedora ~]$
```

By using the -iname option, I was able to find files with names that ended in either .conf or .CONF. If I had used the -name option instead, I would only have found files with names that end in .conf.

Normally, you would specify the search path as the first component of the find command. In the GNU implementation of find that's included on Linux-based operating systems, omitting the search path will cause find to search through the current working directory, as we've just seen. Unfortunately, that trick doesn't work for Unix/Unix-like operating systems, such as FreeBSD, macOS, or OpenIndiana. For those operating systems, you'll always need to specify a search path. To make find search through the current working directory, just use a dot to specify the search path. So, on my FreeBSD virtual machine, the command looks like this:

```
donnie@freebsd-1:~ $ find . -iname '*.conf'
./anotherdir/yetanother.conf
./anotherthing.CONF
./something.conf
donnie@freebsd-1:~ $
```

 Okay, I know. You're wondering why I'm mentioning FreeBSD, macOS, and OpenIndiana in what's supposed to be a Linux book. Well, it's because sometimes, we'll want to create shell scripts that work on multiple operating systems, rather than just on Linux. If you include the dot in this command, it will still work on your Linux machines, and will also work on your Unix/Unix-like machines.

You can also specify search paths that aren't your current working directory. For example, you can remain within your own home directory and search through the entire filesystem like this:

```
[donnie@fedora ~]$ find / -iname '*.conf'
```

Of course, this will take much longer than it does to just search through one directory. Also, you'll encounter errors because your normal user account won't have permission to go into every directory. To search through all directories on the filesystem, just preface the command with sudo, like this:

```
[donnie@fedora ~]$ sudo find / -iname '*.conf'
```

You can perform searches with more than one search criterion. If you separate the criteria with a space, it will be the same as placing an and operator between them. Here, we'll use the `-mtime -7` switch to find all of the `.conf` files that were modified within the last seven days, and the `-ls` switch at the end to show detailed information about the files:

```
[donnie@fedora ~]$ sudo find / -iname '*.conf' -mtime -7 -ls

      18       4 -rw-r--r--   1 root     root           328 Jul 24 17:50 /boot/
loader/entries/81085aed13d34626859063e7ebf29da5-6.4.4-100.fc37.x86_64.conf
  3321176      4 -rw-r--r--   1 donnie   donnie         467 Jul 24 16:14 /home/
donnie/.config/pcmanfm/LXDE/pcmanfm.conf
     370       4 -rw-r--r--   1 donnie   donnie        3272 Jul 19 16:21 /home/
donnie/.config/Trolltech.conf
. . .

. . .
4120762      8 -rw-r--r--   2 root           root            7017
Jul 21 14:43 /var/lib/flatpak/app/com.notepadqq.Notepadqq/x86_64/stable/
a049a1963430515aa15d950212fc1f0db7efb703a94ddd1f1d316b38ad12ec72/files/lib/
node_modules/npm/node_modules/request/node_modules/http-signature/node_modules/
jsprim/node_modules/verror/jsl.node.conf
[donnie@fedora ~]$
```

To search for `.conf` files that were modified more than seven days ago, replace the `-7` with `+7`, like this:

```
[donnie@fedora ~]$ sudo find / -iname '*.conf' -mtime +7 -ls
```

It's also possible to create more advanced searches by creating compound expressions. It works like Algebra, in that expressions are evaluated from left to right unless you group some of the terms with parentheses. But, with that, there are a couple of minor catches.

Since the parenthesis symbols have a special meaning in bash and zsh, you'll want to precede them with a backslash so that bash and zsh won't interpret them the wrong way. You'll also need to leave a space between the parenthesis symbols and the terms that they're enclosing.

Let's say that we now want to look for all of the `.conf` files in the `/etc/` directory that were either modified within the last seven days, or that were accessed more than 30 days ago. We'll use the `-atime` switch to set the access time criterion. The or operator is represented by `-o`.

```
[donnie@fedora ~]$ sudo find /etc -iname '*.conf' \( -mtime -7 -o -atime +30 \)
[sudo] password for donnie:
/etc/UPower/UPower.conf
/etc/X11/xinit/xinput.d/ibus.conf
/etc/X11/xinit/xinput.d/xcompose.conf
/etc/X11/xinit/xinput.d/xim.conf
. . .
```

```
. . .
/etc/appstream.conf
/etc/whois.conf
/etc/nfsmount.conf
[donnie@fedora ~]$
```

There are several subdirectories in /etc/ that require root privileges to enter, so I used sudo again, as I did before. Adding the -ls option at the end of the command would show the timestamps on the files, which would tell me which of the two search criteria applies to each specific file.

If you want to find files that belong to only a certain user, you can do that with the -user switch. Add a second criterion to find only files of a certain type that belong to a certain user. Here, I'm searching through the whole filesystem for all .png graphics files that belong to me:

```
[donnie@fedora ~]$ sudo find / -user donnie -iname '*.png'
/home/donnie/.cache/mozilla/firefox/xgwvyw2p.default-release/
thumbnails/9aa3453b0b6246665eb573e58a40fe7c.png
/home/donnie/.cache/mozilla/firefox/xgwvyw2p.default-release/
thumbnails/96c0e5aa4c2e735c2ead0701d2348dd6.png
. . .
. . .
/home/donnie/rad-bfgminer/vastairent.png
find: '/run/user/1000/doc': Permission denied
find: '/run/user/1000/gvfs': Permission denied
/tmp/.org.chromium.Chromium.IpK3VA/pcloud1_16.png
find: '/tmp/.mount_pcloudWz4ji1': Permission denied
[donnie@fedora ~]$
```

Even with full sudo privileges, there are still a couple of directories where I'm not allowed to access. But, that's okay.

You can use the -group switch to find files that belong to a certain group. Here, I'm looking through my own home directory for either files or directories that are associated with the nobody group.

```
[donnie@fedora ~]$ sudo find -group nobody -ls
   3344421      0 drwxr-xr-x   1 nobody    nobody        0 Jul 25 18:36 ./share
   3344505      0 -rw-r--r--   1 donnie    nobody        0 Jul 25 18:38 ./
somefile.txt
[donnie@fedora ~]$
```

Note that I'm still using sudo here, because even in my own home directory there are some directories that find won't access without it. (These are the directories that contain information about Docker containers.)

Conversely, you can use the -nogroup switch to find files that don't belong to any group that's listed in the /etc/group file.

```
[donnie@fedora ~]$ sudo find -nogroup
./.local/share/containers/storage/
overlay/994393dc58e7931862558d06e46aa2bb17487044f670f310dffe1d24e4d1eec7/diff/
etc/shadow
./.local/share/containers/storage/overlay/
ded7a220bb058e28ee3254fbba04ca90b679070424424761a53a043b93b612bf/diff/etc/
shadow
./.local/share/containers/storage/
overlay/8e012198eea15b2554b07014081c85fec4967a1b9cc4b65bd9a4bce3ae1c0c88/diff/
etc/shadow
./.local/share/containers/storage/
overlay/7cd52847ad775a5ddc4b58326cf884beee34544296402c6292ed76474c686d39/diff/
etc/shadow
[donnie@fedora ~]$
```

In the Linux/Unix world, everything on the system is represented by a file. Normal users of a system will usually just encounter regular files and directories, but there are many other types of files that will be of interest to a system administrator. The various file types include:

- **Regular files:** These are the types of files that a normal user would routinely access. Graphics files, video files, database files, spreadsheet files, text files, and executable files are all examples of regular files.

- **Directories:** It seems strange that a directory is a type of file, but that's just how it is in the Linux and Unix worlds.

- **Character devices:** A character device either accepts or supplies a serial stream of data. A sound card or a terminal would be represented by a character device file. You'll find these files in the /dev/ directory.

- **Block devices:** A block device file represents devices that can be accessed in a random manner. Examples include hard drives, solid-state drives, and drive partitions. You'll also find these files in the /dev/ directory.

- **Named pipes:** These devices take the output from one system process and supply it as the input to another system process, thus enabling inter-process communication.

- **Sockets:** These are the same as named pipes, except that they can send and receive file descriptors as part of the communications stream. Also, unlike named pipes, sockets can allow two-way data exchange between two processes.

- **Symbolic links:** This type of file simply points to either a regular file or directory. This allows users to either access files and directories from multiple places in the filesystem, or to access them by different names.

You can tell what type a file is by doing an ls -l command. The first character in the output for each file is known as the **file mode string**. This file mode string designates the file type. For example, let's look at what's in my home directory:

```
[donnie@fedora ~]$ ls -l
```

```
total 137972
-rw-r--r--.        1 donnie donnie        12111206 Feb 18 13:41 dnf_list.txt
drwxr-xr-x. 15 donnie donnie                  4096 Jul 27 16:39 orphaned_files
drwxr-xr-x.    2 donnie donnie                   6 Jul 29 16:53 perm_demo
-rw-r--r--.        1 donnie donnie             643 Mar 26 15:53 sample.json
[donnie@fedora ~]$
```

Lines that begin with a - represent a regular file, and lines that begin with a d represent a directory. The various file types are represented as follows:

File mode string	File type
-	Regular file
d	Directory
c	Character device
b	Block device
p	Named pipe
s	Socket
l	Symbolic link

Table 2.1: File type designators

There may be times when you'll need to locate all files of a certain type. You can do that with the -type option, like so:

```
[donnie@fedora ~]$ sudo find / -type p -ls
    545    0 prw-------  1 root     root            0 Jul 31 15:20 /run/
initctl
    542    0 prw-------  1 root     root            0 Jul 31 15:20 /run/
dmeventd-client
    541    0 prw-------  1 root     root            0 Jul 31 15:20 /run/
dmeventd-server
      6    0 p---------  1 donnie   donnie          0 Jul 31 15:29 /run/
user/1000/systemd/inaccessible/fifo
   1228    0 prw-------  1 root     root            0 Jul 31 15:21 /run/
systemd/inhibit/2.ref
   1193    0 prw-------  1 root     root            0 Jul 31 15:21 /run/
systemd/inhibit/1.ref
   1324    0 prw-------  1 root     root            0 Jul 31 15:29 /run/
systemd/sessions/3.ref
   1311    0 prw-------  1 root     root            0 Jul 31 15:29 /run/
systemd/sessions/1.ref
      8    0 p---------  1 root     root            0 Jul 31 15:20 /run/
systemd/inaccessible/fifo
```

```
    112     0 prw-------    1 root       root           0 Jul 31 15:20 /var/lib/
nfs/rpc_pipefs/gssd/clntXX/gssd
   [donnie@fedora ~]$
```

As you see, I'm using the `-type p` option to search for all named pipe files.

Now, let's consider the previous example in which we searched for all files that end with a `.conf` filename extension:

```
[donnie@fedora ~]$ sudo find / -iname '*.conf'
```

This command only found regular files because they're the only types of files on the system that have the `.conf` filename extension. But, let's now say that we want to search through the `/etc/` directory to find all subdirectories with the `conf` text string in their names. If we don't specify a file type, we'll see regular files, symbolic links, and directories:

```
[donnie@fedora ~]$ sudo find /etc -name '*conf*' -ls
   329486      4 -rw-r--r--    1 root       root         351 Jul 27 07:02 /etc/
dnf/plugins/copr.conf
   329487      4 -rw-r--r--    1 root       root          30 Jul 27 07:02 /etc/
dnf/plugins/debuginfo-install.conf
  8480155      4 -rw-r--r--    1 root       root          93 May 18 04:27 /etc/
dnf/protected.d/dnf.conf
 . . .
25325169      0 lrwxrwxrwx    1 root       root          43 Jul 29 18:19 /etc/
crypto-policies/back-ends/bind.config -> /usr/share/crypto-policies/DEFAULT/
bind.txt
 25325172      0 lrwxrwxrwx    1 root       root          45 Jul 29 18:19 /etc/
crypto-policies/back-ends/gnutls.config -> /usr/share/crypto-policies/DEFAULT/
gnutls.txt
 . . .
5430579       0 drwxr-xr-x    2 root       root          25 Sep 19  2022 /etc/
reader.conf.d
  8878157     0 drwxr-xr-x    3 root       root          27 Dec  8  2022 /etc/
pkgconfig
  8927250     0 drwxr-xr-x    2 root       root          83 Nov 16  2022 /etc/
krb5.conf.d
 . . .
[donnie@fedora ~]$
```

We'll use the `-type d` option to narrow things down:

```
[donnie@fedora ~]$ sudo find /etc -name '*conf*' -type d -ls
 17060336      0 drwxr-xr-x    2 root       root          41 Dec  8  2022 /etc/
fonts/conf.d
```

```
   25430579         0 drwxr-xr-x    2 root       root          25 Sep 19  2022 /etc/
reader.conf.d
    8878157         0 drwxr-xr-x    3 root       root          27 Dec  8  2022 /etc/
pkgconfig
    8927250         0 drwxr-xr-x    2 root       root          83 Nov 16  2022 /etc/
krb5.conf.d
   25313333         0 drwxr-xr-x    2 root       root           6 Feb  1 17:58 /etc/
security/pwquality.conf.d
   25395980         0 drwxr-xr-x    2 root       root          30 Dec  8  2022 /etc/
X11/xorg.conf.d
   17060487         0 drwxr-xr-x    2 root       root           6 Aug  9  2022 /etc/
pm/config.d
 . . .

 . . .
   16917753         0 drwxr-xr-x    2 root       root          33 Jul 29 18:11 /etc/
containers/registries.conf.d
[donnie@fedora ~]$
```

Cool. We now only see the directories, which is exactly what we want.

As I said before, there are a lot of options that you can use with the find utility. (Enter man find to see them all.)

Now, with the introduction to find out of the way, let's look at how to use find to perform multiple actions with one command.

Performing Multiple Actions with find

Our next trick contains a bit of a twist. We'll use find's -exec and -ok option switches to make find perform some sort of action on each file that it finds. First, find finds the files. Then, it causes another command to run that will take some sort of action on the files. Here's how it works.

The -exec and -ok switches tell the shell to perform a second command only if the first command produces valid output. It then uses the output of the first command (find) as arguments for the second. The difference between the two switches is that -exec causes the desired action to automatically execute on each file without prompting the user. The -ok switch will cause the action to stop after each file that find finds, asking the user whether or not to proceed with the action for that file. Here, we're searching the entire filesystem for all .zip files that are more than 30 days old, and copying them to the /home/donnie/ directory. (Note that I'm still using sudo so that I can access all directories.)

```
[donnie@fedora ~]$ sudo find / \( -mtime +30 -iname '*.zip' \) -exec cp {} /
home/donnie \;
```

The {} after the cp command tells bash or zsh, "Take the results from the find command, and put them here as the arguments". Note that this command sequence has to end with a semi-colon. But, since the semi-colon has special meaning for bash and zsh, you must precede it with a backslash so that bash and zsh will interpret it correctly.

Also, note that you must have a blank space after the first parenthesis, and another blank space before the backslash that precedes the last parenthesis.

Now, suppose that you only want to copy over some of the files that you find. Just replace the -exec switch with the -ok switch. It works the same as -exec, but it will ask permission before performing an operation on a file. You'll have to enter either *y* or *n* before continuing to the next file.

The same principle also works for removing files.

```
[donnie@fedora ~]$ sudo find / \( -mtime +30 -iname '*.zip' \) -ok rm {} \;
```

Let's now suppose that Vicky, Cleopatra, Frank, and Goldie are all creating graphics for some sort of project. They're supposed to place the graphics files into the graphics subdirectory that each of them have in their own home directory. Sometimes they forget though, and place the files into their top-level home directories, as we see in the following diagram:

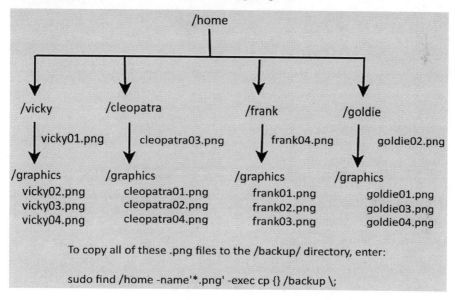

Figure 2.1: Some of these graphics files are in the wrong place.

Now, let's get a bit of hands-on practice with this.

Hands-on Lab — Using find to Perform Other Commands

For this lab, use a Fedora, Debian, or Ubuntu virtual machine. (I'll provide instructions for all of them.)

Let's say that we want to copy everyone's graphics files into a common backup directory.

1. First, create the /backup directory, like this:

```
[donnie@fedora ~]$ sudo mkdir /backup
```

For our present purposes, just leave ownership and permissions settings as they are.

2. Next, create user accounts for Vicky, Cleopatra, Frank, and Goldie, and assign a password to each account. On Fedora, the commands would look like this:

```
donnie@fedora:~$ sudo useradd frank
donnie@fedora:~$ sudo passwd frank
```

On either Debian or Ubuntu, use the interactive adduser command, which both creates the user account and sets the password. It looks like this:

```
donnie@debian12:~$ sudo adduser goldie
```

3. Log into each user's account, create a graphics directory in each user's home directory, and then create some fake graphics files. Here are the commands to do that:

```
goldie@fedora:~$ touch goldie02.png
goldie@fedora:~$ mkdir graphics
goldie@fedora:~$ cd graphics/
goldie@fedora:~/graphics$ touch {goldie01.png,goldie03.png,goldie04.png}
goldie@fedora:~/graphics$
```

The touch command is actually meant to be used by programmers for purposes that I won't go into here. But, it's also handy for situations like this, when you just need to create some fake files for testing purposes. By enclosing a comma-separated list of filenames within a pair of curly braces, you can create multiple files with just one single command. To verify that, let's peek into the graphics directory:

```
goldie@fedora:~/graphics$ ls -l
total 0
-rw-r--r--. 1 goldie goldie 0 Mar 23 13:27 goldie01.png
-rw-r--r--. 1 goldie goldie 0 Mar 23 13:27 goldie03.png
-rw-r--r--. 1 goldie goldie 0 Mar 23 13:27 goldie04.png
goldie@fedora:~/graphics$
```

4. For this step, you'll need to log back into your own user account. You want to be sure to get all of the graphics files, even if they're in the users' top-level home directories, and copy them into the /backup/ directory. Your command and results would look like this:

```
[donnie@fedora ~]$ sudo find /home -name '*.png' -exec cp {} /backup \;
[donnie@fedora ~]$ ls -l /backup/
total 0
-rw-r--r--. 1 root root 0 Jul 28 15:40 cleopatra01.png
-rw-r--r--. 1 root root 0 Jul 28 15:40 cleopatra02.png
-rw-r--r--. 1 root root 0 Jul 28 15:40 cleopatra03.png
```

```
-rw-r--r--. 1 root root 0 Jul 28 15:40 cleopatra04.png
-rw-r--r--. 1 root root 0 Jul 28 15:40 frank01.png
-rw-r--r--. 1 root root 0 Jul 28 15:40 frank02.png
-rw-r--r--. 1 root root 0 Jul 28 15:40 frank03.png
-rw-r--r--. 1 root root 0 Jul 28 15:40 frank04.png
-rw-r--r--. 1 root root 0 Jul 28 15:40 goldie01.png
-rw-r--r--. 1 root root 0 Jul 28 15:40 goldie02.png
-rw-r--r--. 1 root root 0 Jul 28 15:40 goldie03.png
-rw-r--r--. 1 root root 0 Jul 28 15:40 goldie04.png
-rw-r--r--. 1 root root 0 Jul 28 15:40 vicky01.png
-rw-r--r--. 1 root root 0 Jul 28 15:40 vicky02.png
-rw-r--r--. 1 root root 0 Jul 28 15:40 vicky03.png
-rw-r--r--. 1 root root 0 Jul 28 15:40 vicky04.png
[donnie@fedora ~]$
```

What I've shown you here just barely scratches the surface of what you can do with find. To see the complete list of search criteria that you can specify, open the find man page and scroll down to the TESTS section.

We'll look at some more find examples a bit later. For now though, let's look at how to create recursive commands.

Running Commands Recursively

We've already shown you that the find utility is inherently recursive. That is, it will automatically search through the subdirectories of your specified search path without you having to tell it to. Most Linux commands aren't that way, however. If you want them to work recursively, you'll have to tell them to. For the most part, this is done with either the -R switch or the -r switch. (Some commands use −R, and some use −r. Something that you'll eventually see for yourself is that there's not a lot of consistency in how the different commands work with option switches.) Let's see how it all works with a hands-on lab.

 The examples in this section involve using the numeric method to set file and directory permissions. For anyone who's not familiar with how to do that, I've provided a reference in the *Further Reading* section.

Hands-on Lab — Using Commands with Recursion

In this lab, you'll be using the recursive option for the ls and chmod utilities. Let's dig in.

First, let's create a new directory with a set of nested subdirectories, like this:

```
[donnie@fedora ~]$ sudo mkdir -p /perm_demo/level1/level2/level3/level4
[donnie@fedora ~]$
```

Next, we want to look at the permissions settings for the entire nest of directories. So, let's do this:

```
[donnie@fedora ~]$ ls -l /perm_demo/
total 0
drwxr-xr-x. 3 root root 20 Jul 29 17:09 level1
[donnie@fedora ~]$
```

Well now, that doesn't help, does it? All we can see is just the first level subdirectory.

Let's try adding the -R option to see if that helps:

```
[donnie@fedora ~]$ ls -lR /perm_demo/
/perm_demo/:
total 0
drwxr-xr-x. 3 root root 20 Jul 29 17:09 level1

/perm_demo/level1:
total 0
drwxr-xr-x. 3 root root 20 Jul 29 17:09 level2

/perm_demo/level1/level2:
total 0
drwxr-xr-x. 3 root root 20 Jul 29 17:09 level3

/perm_demo/level1/level2/level3:
total 0
drwxr-xr-x. 2 root root 6 Jul 29 17:09 level4

/perm_demo/level1/level2/level3/level4:
total 0
[donnie@fedora ~]$
```

This is much better, because we now see the permissions settings for all four of the nested subdirectories. But, we see that the permissions settings aren't what we want. With the 755 permission setting that we currently have, we're allowing the user to have read/write/execute access, while the group and others have read/execute access. What we really want is for the user and the group to both have read/write/execute access, and for others to have no access at all. We'll do that by using chmod to change the permissions settings to 770. The -R switch will allow us to change the settings for the top-level directory, as well as all four of the nested subdirectories.

Recursively set the correnct permissions setting with this command:

```
[donnie@fedora ~]$ sudo chmod -R 770 /perm_demo/
[donnie@fedora ~]$
```

Now that you've removed access for others, you'll need to use sudo to view the permissions settings:

```
[donnie@fedora ~]$ sudo ls -lR /perm_demo/
/perm_demo/:
total 0
drwxrwx---. 3 root root 20 Jul 29 17:09 level1

/perm_demo/level1:
total 0
drwxrwx---. 3 root root 20 Jul 29 17:09 level2

/perm_demo/level1/level2:
total 0
drwxrwx---. 3 root root 20 Jul 29 17:09 level3

/perm_demo/level1/level2/level3:
total 0
drwxrwx---. 2 root root 6 Jul 29 17:09 level4

/perm_demo/level1/level2/level3/level4:
total 0
[donnie@fedora ~]$
```

You see that the permissions setting is now 770 for the entire nest, which means that we have achieved extreme coolness.

> **Tip**
>
> You might, at some point, be called upon to create a shell script that will automatically compile and install a program. The ability to create nested directories and recursively change permissions settings on them will come in quite handy when writing those kinds of scripts.

There are several other utilities that also have the recursive feature. (You'll encounter some of them as you go through this book.) The slight catch is that for some of them the recursive option switch is -r, and for other it's -R. But, that's okay. When in doubt, just consult the man page for the utility that you need to use.

Now that we've covered recursion, let's have a history lesson.

Understanding the Command History

Whenever you work with the command-line, there will be times when you'll have to enter some commands more than once. If you've just entered a command that's long and complex, you may not exactly be thrilled at the prospect of having to type it in all over again. Not to worry, though. For this, bash and zsh give you the ability to recall and/or edit commands that you've previously entered. There are a few ways to do this.

Whenever you enter a command, it gets stored in memory until you exit the shell session. The command will then get added to a file that's specified by the HISTFILE variable. Usually, this is the .bash_history file on bash, and the .histfile file on zsh. You'll find these stored in each user's home directory. To verify that, you can use the echo command, like this:

```
[donnie@fedora ~]$ echo $HISTFILE
/home/donnie/.bash_history
[donnie@fedora ~]$
```

On zsh, you'll see this:

```
donnie@opensuse:~> echo $HISTFILE
/home/donnie/.histfile
donnie@opensuse:~>
```

The number of commands that get saved to either the .bash_history file or the .histfile is set by the HISTSIZE variable in the /etc/profile file. (Both bash and zsh reference the same file.) You can use grep to search for that line without having to open the file, like so:

```
[donnie@fedora ~]$ grep HISTSIZE /etc/profile
HISTSIZE=1000
export PATH USER LOGNAME MAIL HOSTNAME HISTSIZE HISTCONTROL
[donnie@fedora ~]$
```

You can also use echo to see the setting:

```
[donnie@fedora ~]$ echo $HISTSIZE
1000
[donnie@fedora ~]$
```

Either way, we see that the system is set up to store the last 1,000 user commands in the .bash_history file.

More often than not, you'll probably use the up and down arrow keys on your keyboard to call up previously entered commands. If you keep pressing the up arrow key, you'll scroll through the list of previous commands, starting with the last one entered. If you go past the command that you want, you can use the down arrow key to get back to it. When you finally do get to the command that you want to repeat, you can either press the *Enter* key to enter it as is, or edit it and then press *Enter*.

You can also use the ! in various ways to recall past commands. For example, entering !! will execute the last command that you entered, as you see here:

```
[donnie@fedora ~]$ ls -l *.txt
-rw-r--r--. 1 donnie donnie 12111206 Feb 18 13:41 dnf_list.txt
-rw-r--r--. 1 donnie donnie     2356 Jul 29 18:46 md5sumfile.txt
-rw-r--r--. 1 donnie donnie     2356 Jul 29 18:49 newmd5sums.txt
[donnie@fedora ~]$ !!
ls -l *.txt
```

```
-rw-r--r--. 1 donnie donnie 12111206 Feb 18 13:41 dnf_list.txt
-rw-r--r--. 1 donnie donnie     2356 Jul 29 18:46 md5sumfile.txt
-rw-r--r--. 1 donnie donnie     2356 Jul 29 18:49 newmd5sums.txt
[donnie@fedora ~]$
```

Use the ! followed by a text string to execute the last executed command that begins with that string. Let's say that I want to repeat the last grep command that I did, like this:

```
[donnie@fedora ~]$ !grep
grep HISTSIZE /etc/profile
HISTSIZE=1000
export PATH USER LOGNAME MAIL HOSTNAME HISTSIZE HISTCONTROL
[donnie@fedora ~]$
```

Use !? followed by a string to execute the last executed command that contains that string, like this:

```
[donnie@fedora ~]$ echo "The fat cat jumped over the skinny dog."
The fat cat jumped over the skinny dog.
[donnie@fedora ~]$ !?skinny
echo "The fat cat jumped over the skinny dog."
The fat cat jumped over the skinny dog.
[donnie@fedora ~]$
```

Now, for the coolest part of all. First, let's view the history list, like so:

```
[donnie@fedora ~]$ history
    1  sudo dnf -y upgrade
    2  sudo shutdown -r nowj
    3  sudo shutdown -r now
    4  cd /usr/share
 . . .
 . . .
  478  echo "The fat cat jumped over the skinny dog."
  479  clear
       [donnie@fedora ~]$
```

To execute a command from this list, enter ! followed by the command number. For example, to perform the echo command again, enter !478, like so:

```
[donnie@fedora ~]$ !478
echo "The fat cat jumped over the skinny dog."
The fat cat jumped over the skinny dog.
[donnie@fedora ~]$
```

Of all of the history tricks that I've shown you, this last one is the most useful one for me. But wait, here's yet one more trick that you might find useful. That is, you can display the command history along with timestamps that show when each command has been executed. On bash, just do this:

```
donnie@opensuse:~> HISTTIMEFORMAT="%d/%m/%y %T " history
```

The output will look something like this:

```
 49   22/03/24 14:02:29 ./start_mining.sh
 50   22/03/24 14:02:29 vim start_mining.sh
 51   22/03/24 14:02:29 ./start_mining.sh
 52   22/03/24 14:02:29 cd
 53   22/03/24 14:02:29 cd Downloads/
 54   22/03/24 14:02:29 ls
. . .
. . .
1046  23/03/24 12:03:53 clear
1047  23/03/24 12:05:37 HISTTIMEFORMAT="%d/%m/%y %T " history
donnie@opensuse:~>
```

What's happening here is that we're configuring the HISTTIMEFORMAT environmental variable to display the timestamp in our desired format, and then running the history command.

This is somewhat easier on zsh, because zsh allows us to use history with the -f option switch, like so:

```
donnie@opensuse:~> zsh
donnie@opensuse:~> history -f
   17   3/23/2024 11:58   echo $HISTFILE
   18   3/23/2024 11:58   cd /etc
   19   3/23/2024 11:58   ls
   20   3/23/2024 11:58   less zprofile
. . .
. . .
 31   3/23/2024 11:58   echo $HISTFILE
 32   3/23/2024 11:58   exit
donnie@opensuse:~>
```

Note that running history -f on bash will give you an error message, like this one:

```
donnie@opensuse:~> history -f
bash: history: -f: invalid option
history: usage: history [-c] [-d offset] [n] or history -anrw [filename] or
history -ps arg [arg...]
donnie@opensuse:~>
```

All right, let's move on to the next topic.

Escaping and Quoting

Whenever you type anything on the command-line or into a shell script, you'll be using a mix of normal alphanumeric text and non-alphanumeric characters. Some of these characters have special meanings within the shell, and will cause the shell to perform in some special way. Sometimes, you'll want the shell to interpret these special characters as normal text, instead of as something with a magical power. To do that, you can either **escape** or **quote** the special characters.

There are two general classes of characters that can be interpreted by the shell from within a shell command. These are:

- **Normal characters:** bash and zsh interpret these characters literally. In other words, they have no special meaning to the shell.

- **Metacharacters:** These characters have special meanings for bash and zsh. You could say that a metacharacter provides some sort of special instruction to these shells.

Here's a space-separated list of metacharacters that can be used in either shell scripts or shell commands:

```
&  ;  |  *  ?  '  "  `  [  ]  (  )  $  <  >  {  }  #  /  \  !  ~
```

I'd rather not try to explain what each one does right now, because many of them can perform multiple functions, depending upon the context of the command. But, we've already seen some of them in action, and we'll see the rest of them in action as we progress through this book.

Escaping Metacharacters

We've already seen some of these metacharacters in action in the previous examples. To further demonstrate, let's look at the humble * metacharacter, which can be used as a wildcard. Let's first do a directory listing of all of the .conf files in the /etc/ directory, like so:

```
[donnie@fedora ~]$ ls /etc/*.conf
/etc/anthy-unicode.conf   /etc/libaudit.conf        /etc/rsyncd.conf
/etc/appstream.conf       /etc/libuser.conf         /etc/rsyslog.conf
/etc/asound.conf          /etc/locale.conf          /etc/sestatus.conf
. . .
. . .
/etc/ld.so.conf                     /etc/resolv.conf
[donnie@fedora ~]$
```

You see that I've just listed all files with filenames that end with a `.conf` filename extension. Now, let's place a `\` in front of the `*`, like this:

```
[donnie@fedora ~]$ ls /etc/\*.conf
ls: cannot access '/etc/*.conf': No such file or directory
[donnie@fedora ~]$
```

Placing the `\` in front of the `*` caused the shell to interpret the `*` literally, instead of as a metacharacter. Instead of looking for all files with `.conf` at the end of their filenames, we're now looking for just one specific file with the filename, `*.conf`. No such file exists, so `ls` returned an error message.

In our `find` example where we performed a compound search, we had to place a `\` in front of each parenthesis character so that the shell would interpret them correctly. Here's what that looked like:

```
[donnie@fedora ~]$ sudo find / \( -mtime +30 -iname '*.zip' \)
/home/donnie/Downloads/Roboto_Condensed.zip
/home/donnie/Downloads/Bungee_Spice.zip
. . .
. . .
/home/donnie/dosbox/turboc/SAMPLES/simpwn18/SWTCPPRJ.ZIP
/home/donnie/dosbox/turboc/SAMPLES/simpwn18/SWH.ZIP
/home/donnie/dosbox/turboc/SAMPLES/simpwn18/SIMPWIN.ZIP
/home/donnie/dosbox/turboc/SAMPLES/simpwn18/SWTC.ZIP
/home/donnie/dosbox/turbocplusplus/TC/TC.zip
[donnie@fedora ~]$
```

Now, let's try it without the `\` characters:

```
[donnie@fedora ~]$ sudo find / ( -mtime +30 -iname '*.zip' )
bash: syntax error near unexpected token `('
[donnie@fedora ~]$
```

This time, I get an error message, because `bash` doesn't understand what I'm trying to do.

Now, just for fun, try this pair of commands on your own machine and note the difference in output:

```
echo I won $300.
echo I won \$300.
```

I guess that I should mention that when you place a `\` in front of a metacharacter so that the shell will interpret the metacharacter literally, it's called **escaping** the metacharacter. This is something that you'll use extensively for either normal shell commands or shell scripting.

Okay, let's look at another way to make the shell interpret metacharacters literally.

Quoting

You sometimes might have to quote a text string when performing a shell command or writing a shell script. This simply involves surrounding the text string with either a pair of double quotes (") or a pair of single quotes ('). If you surround a text string with a pair of single quotes, the shell will interpret any metacharacters that are within the quotes as normal, literal characters. If you surround a text string with a pair of double quotes, the shell will interpret most, but not all, metacharacters as normal, literal characters. To show how that works, let's create a programming variable that we'll call name, and assign to it the value charlie, like so:

```
[donnie@fedora ~]$ name=charlie
[donnie@fedora ~]$
```

Next, we'll try to echo back the value of name, using a pair of single quotes:

```
[donnie@fedora ~]$ echo '$name'
$name
[donnie@fedora ~]$
```

You see that the single quotes cause the shell to interpret the $ as a literal character. Now, let's see what happen if we use a pair of double quotes:

```
[donnie@fedora ~]$ echo "$name"
charlie
[donnie@fedora ~]$
```

This time, we see the variable's actual value, because the $ is one of the metacharacters that the double quotes won't treat as a literal character.

 We'll cover the topic of programming variables more in depth later. So for now, don't stress out if you don't fully understand the concept.

For reference, here's the complete list of metacharacters that won't get interpreted as literal characters by surrounding them with double quotes:

- "
- \
- `
- $

To clarify, the list consists of the double quote character, the backslash, the back-tick, and the dollar sign. (For now, don't worry about what all of these metacharacters do. We'll cover them all in due time.)

For all other metacharacters, it doesn't matter whether you use double quotes or single quotes. Let's look at this example that uses a wildcard character:

```
[donnie@fedora ~]$ echo '*.txt'
*.txt
[donnie@fedora ~]$ echo "*.txt"
*.txt
[donnie@fedora ~]$
```

Either way, the result is the same. Both times, the * gets treated as a literal character. To use the * as an actual metacharacter, just omit the quotes, like so:

```
[donnie@fedora ~]$ echo *.txt
addresses.txt alma9_default.txt alma9_future.txt alma_link.txt centos7scan_
modified.txt centos7scan.txt dnf_list.txt finances.txt missing_stuff.txt
password_for_RHEL_VM.txt rpmfusion.txt somefile.txt temp.txt test.txt text.txt
ubuntuscan_modified.txt ubuntuscan.txt withL3.txt withoutL3.txt
[donnie@fedora ~]
```

Okay, that pretty much does it for escaping and quoting, as well as for the whole chapter. Let's summarize and move on.

Summary

We've covered some important basics in this chapter. We started by describing the structure and the components of a shell command, and how to perform multiple actions with just one single command. Then, we looked at the find utility, and the cool things that you can do with it. We then looked at how to run commands recursively, and wrapped up with a discussion about escaping and quoting.

In the next chapter, we'll talk about variables and pipelines. I'll see you there.

Questions

1. Which of the following sets of metacharacters would cause the second command to run only if the first command runs successfully?

    a. ||
    b. &&
    c. |
    d. &

2. You want to run a command that contains the $ metacharacter, but you want the shell to interpret the metacharacter literally. How would you do that? (Choose two.)

    a. Precede the metacharacter with a /.
    b. Surround the text string that contains the metacharacter with a pair of single quotes.
    c. Precede the metacharacter with a \.

     d.   Surround the text string that contains the metacharacter with a pair of double quotes.

     e.   It's not possible.

3. You're using `find` to search for files on a FreeBSD system. To search through the current working directory, what must you do on FreeBSD that you don't have to do on Linux?

     a.   Use a dot to designate the search path.

     b.   Nothing. The commands are performed the same way on both systems.

     c.   This isn't possible on a FreeBSD system.

     d.   Use `sudo`.

4. You want to create a nested directory structure with one single `mkdir` command. How would you do that?

     a.   Use the `-r` option to make `mkdir` run recursively.

     b.   Use the `-R` option to make `mkdir` run recursively.

     c.   Use the `-P` option.

     d.   Use the `-p` option.

5. You want to automatically perform an action on every file that `find` finds, without being prompted. Which `find` option would you use to do that?

     a.   `-ok`

     b.   `-exec`

     c.   `--exec`

     d.   `--ok`

Further Reading

- Linux File Permissions Explained: `https://www.redhat.com/sysadmin/linux-file-permissions-explained`

- How to Use Bash Wildcards for Globbing?: `https://www.shell-tips.com/bash/wildcards-globbing/#gsc.tab=0`

- How to Recursively Search Directory Names in Linux: `https://www.howtogeek.com/devops/how-to-recursively-search-directory-names-in-linux/`

- Find Command in Linux: `https://linuxize.com/post/how-to-find-files-in-linux-using-the-command-line/`

- 10 Ways to Use the Linux find Command: `https://www.redhat.com/sysadmin/linux-find-command`

- What are Linux Metacharacters? Everything You Need to Know: `https://www.makeuseof.com/what-are-linux-metacharacters/`

- 6 Linux metacharacters I love to use on the command line: `https://opensource.com/article/22/2/metacharacters-linux`

- How to Use Your Bash History in the Linux or MacOS Terminal: `https://www.howtogeek.com/44997/how-to-use-bash-history-to-improve-your-command-line-productivity/`
- Navigating Bash History Ctrl+r: `https://lornajane.net/posts/2011/navigating-bash-history-with-ctrlr`
- How to Find When a Command is Executed in Linux: `https://ostechnix.com/find-when-a-command-is-executed-in-linux/`
- Escape Quotes in Bash: `https://linuxsimply.com/bash-scripting-tutorial/quotes/escape-quotes/`

Answers

1. b
2. b and c
3. a
4. d
5. b

Join our community on Discord!

Read this book alongside other users, Linux experts, and the author himself.

Ask questions, provide solutions to other readers, chat with the author via Ask Me Anything sessions, and much more. Scan the QR code or visit the link to join the community.

`https://packt.link/SecNet`

3

Understanding Variables and Pipelines

In the previous chapter, you saw how the shell interprets users' commands, and you saw various examples of how to craft your commands. In this chapter, I'll tell you about variables and pipelines.

The ability to create variables and assign values to them is an important part of any programming environment. As you would expect, both bash and zsh have this capability. In the first part of this chapter, we'll cover the basics about environmental variables and programming variables.

In the second part of the chapter, we'll cover how to use pipelines. Pipelines are very simple, and you might have already used them at some point. So, I promise to make this write-up both short and sweet. (Actually, there's not a lot to say just yet about either of these topics, which is why I'm combining both of them into one chapter.)

Topics in the chapter include:

- Understanding environmental variables
- Understanding programming variables
- Understanding pipelines

If you're ready, let's get started.

Understanding Environmental Variables

Environmental variables control the configuration and functioning of the operating system shell. When you install either a Linux or Unix/Unix-like operating system such as FreeBSD or OpenIndiana, you'll find that a default set of environmental variables has already been defined at both the global and user levels.

To see the list of environmental variables and their settings, use the env command, like so:

```
[donnie@fedora ~]$ env
SHELL=/bin/bash
```

```
IMSETTINGS_INTEGRATE_DESKTOP=yes
COLORTERM=truecolor
XDG_CONFIG_DIRS=/etc/xdg/lxsession:/etc/xdg
HISTCONTROL=ignoredups
. . .
. . .
MAIL=/var/spool/mail/donnie
OLDPWD=/etc/profile.d
_=/bin/env
[donnie@fedora ~]$
```

The complete list of environmental variables is very extensive. Fortunately, you don't need to memorize what each and every item does for you. Most of the ones that you do need to know are self-explanatory.

Instead of viewing the entire list, you can also view the value of a specific item. Just use the echo command, and precede the variable name with a $, like so:

```
[donnie@fedora ~]$ echo $USER
donnie
[donnie@fedora ~]$ echo $PATH
/home/donnie/.local/bin:/home/donnie/bin:/home/donnie/.cargo/bin:/usr/local/
bin:/bin:/usr/bin:/usr/local/sbin:/usr/sbin:/sbin
[donnie@fedora ~]$ echo $EDITOR
/usr/bin/nano
[donnie@fedora ~]$
```

Here we see that I (donnie) am the current logged-in user, what my path setting is, and what my default editor is. You would view the value of any other environmental variable the same way.

An important thing to note is that the names of all environmental variables always consist of all up-per-case letters. Nothing in either the operating system or the shell prevents the use of lower-case letters, but there is a very good reason for not using them. It's just that variable names are case-sensitive. Best practice dictates using nothing but upper-case letters for environmental variable names and either all lower-case letters or a mix of upper and lower-case letters for programming variable names. This will prevent you from accidentally overwriting the value of an environmental variable. (I'll show you more about that in the next section.)

As I mentioned before, environmental variables are configured at both the global and user levels. Variable settings at the global level affect all users of bash and zsh. For bash, you'll find most of these global settings in the /etc/profile file, the /etc/bashrc file, and various files in the /etc/profile.d/ directory. For zsh, you'll find these settings in the /etc/zprofile, /etc/zshrc, and /etc/zshenv files. (Note that zsh also references the same /etc/profile file that bash references.) If you were to open one of these files at this point, you likely won't understand much of what's going on in them. That's okay, because for now that doesn't matter. But, you'll easily be able to find where the environmental variables are set, because the variable names are all in upper-case letters.

Now, let's say you don't like a particular setting. For example, let's say that you want to customize your command-line prompt to your own liking. Here on my Fedora workstation, my bash prompt looks like this:

```
[donnie@fedora ~]$
```

The format of the prompt is determined by the PS1 environmental variable. We can see the PS1 settings like this:

```
[donnie@fedora ~]$ echo $PS1
[\u@\h \W]\$
[donnie@fedora ~]$
```

Here's the breakdown of what you've just seen:

- [: This is a literal character, which is the first thing we see in the prompt.
- \u: This causes the current user's username to appear.
- @: This is another literal character.
- \h: This causes the first component of the machine's hostname to appear.
- \W: This causes the name of the current working directory to appear. Note that the upper-case W doesn't cause the entire pathname to appear.
-]: This is another literal character.
- \$: This causes the $ to show for all normal users, and the # to appear for the root user.

A while ago, I said that we can use the \ to force the shell to interpret a metacharacter as a literal character. Here though, we see another use for the \. When configuring the PS1 parameters, the \ indicates that we're about to use a **macro** command. (Think of a macro as a command that runs when you perform some simple action, such as hitting a specific key or clicking on a specific button.)

Now, let's say that we want the entire path of the current working directory to appear, along with the current date and time. To do that, we'll replace the \W with \w, and add the \d and \t macros, like this:

```
[donnie@fedora ~]$ export PS1="[\d \t \u@\h \w]\$"
[Wed Aug 09 18:14:26 donnie@fedora ~]$
```

Note that I had to surround the new parameter within a pair of quotes so that the shell would interpret the metacharacters properly. Also, note what happens when I cd into a down-level directory:

```
[Wed Aug 09 18:14:26 donnie@fedora ~]$cd /etc/profile.d/
[Wed Aug 09 18:29:15 donnie@fedora /etc/profile.d]$
```

Substituting the /w for the /W causes the entire path of the current working directory to show up.

When you configure the PS1 parameter from the command-line, the new settings will disappear as soon as you either log out from the machine or close the terminal window. To make the setting permanent, just edit the .bashrc file that's in your home directory. Add the export PS1="[\d \t \u@\h \w]$ " line to the end of the file, and you'll see the new prompt the next time you either log into the machine or open a new terminal window.

There are still a lot more ways to customize the command prompt that I haven't shown you. For a more complete list, see the reference that I provided in the *Further Reading* section. Also, note that I've only covered how to do this with bash, because zsh uses different command prompt parameters. (I'll show you all about that in *Chapter 22, Using the Z Shell*.)

I can read your mind, and can see that you're wondering what environmental variables have to do with shell scripting. Well, it's just that sometimes you'll need to have your script perform a specific action that depends upon the value of a specific environmental variable. For example, let's say that you only want the script to run for the root user, and not for any unprivileged user. Since we know that the user identification number for the root user is 0, we can write code that allows the script to run if the UID variable is set to 0, and to prevent the script from running if the UID is set to anything other than 0.

And by the way, I apologize if it seems a bit creepy that I can read your mind.

That does it for our introduction to environmental variables. Let's now take a quick look at programming variables.

Understanding Programming Variables

Sometimes, it's necessary to define variables to use in your scripts. You can define, view, and unset these variables as needed for your programming needs. Note that although the system will allow you to create programming variable names with all upper-case letters, it's considered bad form to do so. Best practice is to always name your programming variables with lower-case letters, so that you won't risk accidentally overwriting the value of an environmental variable with the same name. (Of course, you won't cause any long-term damage by overwriting an environmental variable. But, why risk overwriting an environmental variable that you might need to use later in your script?)

To show how this all works, let's create some programming variables from the command-line, and view the assigned values. First, we'll create the car variable and assign to it the value Ford, like this:

```
[donnie@fedora ~]$ car=Ford
[donnie@fedora ~]$ echo $car
Ford
[donnie@fedora ~]$
```

To view the value of a variable, use echo, and precede the name of the variable with a $, just as we did with the environmental variables. Now, let's open a child shell with the bash command, to see if we can still view the value of this car variable, and then exit back to the parent shell, like this:

```
[donnie@fedora ~]$ bash
[donnie@fedora ~]$ echo $car

[donnie@fedora ~]$ exit
```

```
exit
[donnie@fedora ~]$
```

We can't see the value of car this time, because we didn't **export** the variable. Exporting the variable will permit a child shell to access the variable. As you might have guessed, we'll use the export command to do this, like so:

```
[donnie@fedora ~]$ export car=Ford
[donnie@fedora ~]$ echo $car
Ford
[donnie@fedora ~]$ bash
[donnie@fedora ~]$ echo $car
Ford
[donnie@fedora ~]$ exit
exit
[donnie@fedora ~]$
```

This time, we see that the value of car now shows up in the child shell.

We'll be working with variables throughout the rest of this book, so you'll be learning a lot more about how to use them. For now though, this quick introduction is enough.

Next, let's do some plumbing.

Understanding Pipelines

A **pipe** will take the output of one command and use it as the input for another command. It's represented by the | symbol, which is on the same key as the backslash. You'll often invoke a simple **pipeline** from the command-line for various purposes. But, you can also create very complex, multi-stage pipelines for your shell scripts.

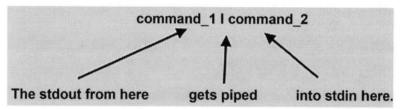

Figure 3.1: Creating a pipeline. Note that stdout is short for Standard Output, and stdin is short for Standard Input.

To see how this can be useful, let's say that you want to look at a listing of all files in a certain directory. But, there are so many files that the output would scroll off of the screen where you'd never be able to see it. You can solve the problem by taking the output of the ls command and using it as the input for the less command. It would look something like this:

```
[donnie@fedora ~]$ ls -l | less
```

The ls -l listing will open in the less pager, so that you can scroll through the output or perform searches for particular text strings.

Now, let's say that I only want to see files with the text string alma in their filenames. That's easy enough. I'll just pipe the ls -l output into grep, like so:

```
[donnie@fedora ~]$ ls -l | grep alma
-rw-r--r--.  1 donnie donnie         1438 Nov  2  2022 alma9_default.txt
-rw-r--r--.  1 donnie donnie         1297 Nov  2  2022 alma9_future.txt
-rw-r--r--.  1 donnie donnie           81 Jan 11  2023 alma_link.txt
[donnie@fedora ~]$
```

Now, let's say that I don't want to see the filenames, but I do want to know how many files there are. I'll just add another pipe stage, like so:

```
[donnie@fedora ~]$ ls -l | grep alma | wc -l
3
[donnie@fedora ~]$
```

The wc -l command counts the number of lines in the output, which in this case tells us how many files I have that contain the text string alma in their filenames.

If you're not familiar with grep, just understand for now that it's a utility that can search for either specific text strings or for text patterns. It can search through text files without you having to open them, or it can search for text strings or patterns in the output that you would pipe into it from another command.

Okay, I've shown you some simple examples of how to create pipelines from the command-line. Now, I want to show you something that I hope you'll *never* do. This involves using the cat utility.

One thing that you can do with cat is to dump the contents of a text file to your screen. It's mainly useful for viewing small files, as you see here:

```
[donnie@fedora ~]$ cat somefile.txt
This is just some file that I created to demonstrate cat.
[donnie@fedora ~]$
```

If you use cat to view a large file, the output will scroll off of the screen where you might not be able to view it. I have seen cases where somebody would still use cat to dump the file, and then pipe the output into less, like so:

```
[donnie@fedora ~]$ cat files.txt | less
```

I've also seen people pipe cat output into grep to search for a text string, like this:

```
[donnie@fedora ~]$ cat files.txt | grep darkfi
drwxr-xr-x.  1 donnie donnie          414 Apr  3 12:41 darkfi
[donnie@fedora ~]$
```

Both of these examples work, but it requires less typing to just use either `less` or `grep` without `cat`, like so:

```
[donnie@fedora ~]$ less files.txt
. . .
. . .
[donnie@fedora ~]$ grep darkfi files.txt
drwxr-xr-x.  1 donnie donnie           414 Apr  3 12:41 darkfi
[donnie@fedora ~]$
```

In other words, although piping `cat` output into other utilities does work, it's less efficient than just directly using the other utilities, and can make your scripts a bit less efficient and a bit harder to read. And, as a real-life lover of cats, it always bothers me to see someone engaging in `cat` abuse.

What I've shown you here is just scratching the surface of what you can do with pipelines. A major reason why Linux and Unix administrators need to create shell scripts is to automate the extraction and formatting of information from either text files or the output of certain programs. Doing that often requires very long, complex, multi-stage pipelines with a different extraction or formatting utility at each stage. Before you can start doing that, you'll need to learn how to use these utilities, which you'll begin doing in *Chapter 6, Text Stream Filters – Part 1*. And, before we can get to that, we need to cover a few more basic functions of `bash` and `zsh`.

Summary

Although this chapter has been rather short, we covered a good bit of important information. We began by looking at environmental variables, showing how to modify one of them, and explaining why you might need to use environmental variables in your shell scripts. Next, we covered programming variables, explaining how to create and export them. Finally, we did a bit of plumbing work by creating some pipelines.

In the next chapter, we'll cover the concept of input/output redirection. I'll see you there.

Questions

1. Which of the following metacharacters allows you to view the assigned value of a variable?

    a. `*`

    b. `%`

    c. `$`

    d. `^`

2. Which of the following statements is true?

    a. It's perfectly correct to use either all upper-case or all lower-case letters to create your programming variable names.

    b. Variable names are not case-sensitive.

    c.   You should always use upper-case letters to create the names of programming variables.

    d.   You should always use lower-case letters to create the names of programming variables.

3. How would you cause a child shell to recognize a variable that you created in the parent shell?

    a.   In the child shell, import the variable from the parent shell.

    b.   In the parent shell, use the `export` keyword when creating the variable.

    c.   You can't, because the parent shell and child shell are isolated from each other.

    d.   The child shell and the parent shell always share variables by default.

4. Which of these metacharacters would you use to take the output of one command and use it at the input of another command?

    a.   `$`

    b.   `|`

    c.   `&`

    d.   `%`

Further Reading

- How to Change/Set up bash custom prompt (PS1) in Linux: `https://www.cyberciti.biz/tips/howto-linux-unix-bash-shell-setup-prompt.html`
- How to Count Files in a Directory in Linux?: `https://www.linuxjournal.com/content/how-count-files-directory-linux`

Answers

1. c

2. d

3. b

4. b

Join our community on Discord!

Read this book alongside other users, Linux experts, and the author himself.

Ask questions, provide solutions to other readers, chat with the author via Ask Me Anything sessions, and much more. Scan the QR code or visit the link to join the community.

`https://packt.link/SecNet`

Leave a Review!

Thank you for purchasing this book from Packt Publishing—we hope you enjoy it! Your feedback is invaluable and helps us improve and grow. Once you've completed reading it, please take a moment to leave an Amazon review; it will only take a minute, but it makes a big difference for readers like you.

Scan the QR code below to receive a free ebook of your choice.

`https://packt.link/NzOWQ`

4

Understanding Input/Output Redirection

In the previous chapter, we discussed how to use variables and pipelines in a shell. This time, we'll look at how to send the text output of a command to somewhere other than the terminal, which is the default output device. We'll then look at how to make a command bring in text from somewhere other than the keyboard, which is the default input device. Finally, we'll look at how to send error messages to somewhere other than the terminal.

Topics in this chapter include:

- Understanding `stdout`
- Understanding `stdin`
- Understanding `stderr`
- Understanding `tee`

Okay, let's get started.

Introduction to Input/Output Redirection

In order to extract information from different sources and format it for presentation, we'll often need to use various utilities that are collectively known as **text stream filters**. When you work with text-stream filtering utilities, it only makes sense that you would need a way to feed them some sort of input. It also makes sense that you would need a way to see the output, and to see error messages if something goes wrong. For these purposes, we have `stdin`, `stdout`, and `stderr`.

- `stdin`: This is short for *standard input*. By default, `stdin` comes from the keyboard. However, by using pipes or redirectors, you can also obtain `stdin` from either a file or from the output of another command.

- stdout : This is short for *standard output*. By default, stdout gets sent to your computer screen. You can use pipes to have stdout become the stdin for another command, or you can use redirectors to save the stdout as a file on a storage device. If you don't want to see any output at all, just use redirectors to send stdout to the proverbial *bit bucket*.
- stderr: As you may have guessed, this is short for *standard error*. If a command doesn't execute properly, you'll receive an error message. By default, the message shows up on the screen. However, you can use pipes or redirectors to change stderr's destination, just the same as you can with stdout.

I've told you before that everything on a Linux, Unix, or Unix-like systems such as FreeBSD or Open-Indiana is represented by a file. stdin, stdout, and stderr are represented on a Linux system by files in the /proc/ filesystem. In the /dev/ directory, there are symbolic links that point to these files, as we see here:

```
[donnie@fedora ~]$ cd /dev
[donnie@fedora dev]$ ls -l std*
lrwxrwxrwx. 1 root root 15 Aug 11 13:29 stderr -> /proc/self/fd/2
lrwxrwxrwx. 1 root root 15 Aug 11 13:29 stdin -> /proc/self/fd/0
lrwxrwxrwx. 1 root root 15 Aug 11 13:29 stdout -> /proc/self/fd/1
[donnie@fedora dev]$
```

Note that the lowest-level subdirectory where these files are found is fd, which stands for **file descriptor**. So, these files that represent stdin, stdout, and stderr are collectively known as file descriptors.

I'm not going to delve into the nitty-gritty details of how this works, because it's not really necessary. The only part of this that you really need to know is the ID numbers of the file descriptors, which are as follows:

- 0: This is for stdin.
- 1: This is for stdout.
- 2: This is for stderr.

Remembering the numbers of these file descriptors, which are the same across all Linux, Unix/Unix-like systems, will help you understand some concepts that I'll present later in this chapter.

Here's what you can do with redirectors:

- Direct a command to obtain its input (stdin) from someplace other than the keyboard.
- Have a command send its output (stdout) to someplace other than the computer screen.
- Have a command send its error messages (stderr) to somplace other than the computer screen.

There are several operator symbols that you'll use with redirectors. Most are easy to understand, but you may find that the ones associated with stderr are a bit confusing. Not to worry though, because I'm here to help. Let's start by taking a look at the stdout family of operators, which consists of >, >|, and >>.

Understanding stdout

Let's say that you want to look at the listing of files that are in a certain directory. Instead of piping the ls output into less, you want to create a text file of this listing so that you can print it later. Here's a graphical representation of how it works:

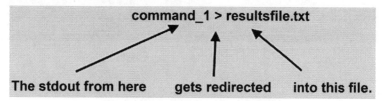

Figure 4.1: How stdout works

Here's what it looks like in practice, where I'm sending output from the ls command to the filelist. txt file:

```
[donnie@fedora ~]$ ls > filelist.txt
[donnie@fedora ~]$
```

As you can see, this is fairly simple. You can take pretty much any command that normally sends its output to the computer screen, and have it sent to a text file instead. There is one thing that you have to be careful with, though. If you redirect a command's output to a file that already exists, you will overwrite it, and all previous information in that file will be lost. There are three ways to prevent this from happening.

Preventing File Overwrites

In this section, I'll show you two ways to prevent overwriting existing files, which are:

- Ensure that an existing file with same name as the file that you want to create doesn't already exist.
- Set the noclobber option.

Let's look at both of these methods.

The first way to prevent accidentally overwriting an important file is the most obvious. That is, before you redirect output to a file, make sure that a file of that name doesn't already exist. Later, I'll show you how trivial it is to write shell script code that will check for this.

The second way is to set the noclobber option for your shell environment, like so:

```
[donnie@fedora ~]$ set -o noclobber
[donnie@fedora ~]$
```

You can set this option either from the command-line or from within a shell script. With this option set, bash and zsh will issue an error message if you try to use a redirector to overwrite a file, as you see here:

```
[donnie@fedora ~]$ ls -la > filelist.txt
```

```
bash: filelist.txt: cannot overwrite existing file
[donnie@fedora ~]$
```

However, if you really want to overwrite a file with this option set, you can do so by making a slight modification to the redirection command. Just use >| for your operator instead of just a plain >, like so:

```
[donnie@fedora ~]$ ls -la >| filelist.txt
[donnie@fedora ~]$
```

There was no error message this time, which means that I really did overwrite the file.

 Be aware that when you set the noclobber option, it's not a permanent setting. It will go away as soon as you exit from your bash or zsh session. (This includes when you close your terminal emulator window.) Also be aware that the noclobber option will not prevent you from losing your files by overwriting them with the mv or cp commands. It also won't stop you from deleting them with the rm command.

Using the File Descriptor

I told you just a bit ago that the file descriptor for stdout is the number 1. If you really wanted to, you could include this file descriptor in any of the commands that I've shown you, which would look something like this:

```
[donnie@fedora ~]$ ls 1> filelist.txt
[donnie@fedora ~]$
```

"What's the advantage of this?", you're wondering. Well, in this case, there is none. Leave out the 1, and things will work just as well. But, in a few pages, we'll be talking about stderr. That's where the file descriptor ID numbers *will* come in handy.

Okay, that's enough about getting things out. Now, let's get some things in.

Understanding stdin

This will be a bit easier, since only one operator symbol is involved. Here's the graphical representation:

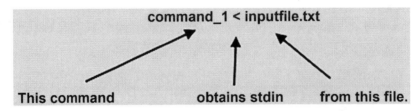

Figure 4.2: How stdin works

For our example, we'll briefly look at the tr utility. (We'll give tr a more in-depth explanation in *Chapter 7, Text Stream Filters-Part 2*. For now, let's just say that it's a utility that *translates* things.) By default, tr would take its stdin from the keyboard.

One thing you can do is to type a text string in all lower-case, and have `tr` echo it back to you in all upper-case. Hit the *Enter* key after you've typed the `tr  [:lower:]  [:upper:]` command, and hit it again after you've typed your line of text. When the upper-case line comes up, hit *Ctrl-d* to exit `tr`. It should look something like this:

```
[donnie@fedora ~]$ tr [:lower:] [:upper:]
i only want to type in all upper-case letters.
I ONLY WANT TO TYPE IN ALL UPPER-CASE LETTERS.
[donnie@fedora ~]$
```

If you need for `tr` to take its input from a file, just add the appropriate redirector operator and the filename, like so:

```
[donnie@fedora ~]$ tr [:lower:] [:upper:] < filelist.txt
15827_ZIP.ZIP
2023-08-01_15-23-31.MP4
2023-08-01_16-26-12.MP4
2023-08-02_13-57-37.MP4
21261.ZIP
. . .
. . .
YAD-FORM.SH
ZONEINFO.ZIP
[donnie@fedora ~]$
```

This won't change the original file. It will only cause the file contents to be displayed on screen in all upper-case letters. If you want to save this converted output to another file, just add one of the `stdout` operators and a new filename, like this:

```
[donnie@fedora ~]$ tr [:lower:] [:upper:] < filelist.txt > filelist_2.txt
[donnie@fedora ~]$
```

When you use this trick, you'll always need to specify a new filename for the output. If you use this trick to try to just modify the original file, you'll end up with nothing but a file with no contents. So, entering this would be a bad thing:

```
[donnie@localhost ~]$ tr [:lower:] [:upper:] < filelist.txt >
filelist.txt
[donnie@localhost ~]$
```

Of course, you could also use the `>>` operator in this trick to append the new information to the original file, like so:

```
     [donnie@localhost ~]$ tr [:lower:] [:upper:] < testfile.txt
>> testfile.txt
     [donnie@localhost ~]$
```

The stdin and stdout operators are fairly easy to understand. The stderr operator isn't hard, but some aspects of it can be a bit tricky. So, before getting started, sit back, take a deep breath and relax. Ready? Good, let's go.

Understanding stderr

The redirector operators for stderr are 2> and 2>>. If you're wondering why, it's because of the file descriptor ID numbers that we looked at a few pages ago. The ID number for stderr just happens to be 2. As always, here's the graphical representation:

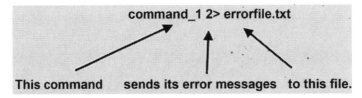

Figure 4.3: How stderr works

If you run a command and something goes wrong, it will output an error message via stderr. By default, this message will get sent to the computer screen. Also by default, stderr messages get mixed in with stdout messages. So, if your command outputs both good data and error messages, you'll have to scroll through the output messages on your screen to separate the two. Fortunately, you can use redirectors to change that behavior. To show how this works, let's take another look at the find utility that we discussed in *Chapter 2, Interpreting Commands*.

If you're logged on to a computer as a normal user and you use find to search through an entire file system, you'll get error messages when find tries to access directories that you don't have permission to access. You'll also get good output, but note how the good is mixed in with the bad in this example:

```
[donnie@fedora ~]$ find / -name README
find: '/boot/loader/entries': Permission denied
find: '/boot/lost+found': Permission denied
find: '/boot/efi': Permission denied
find: '/boot/grub2': Permission denied
find: '/dev/vboxusb': Permission denied
/home/donnie/.cache/go-build/README
 . . .
 . . .
/home/donnie/Downloads/lynis/README
/home/donnie/Downloads/lynis/extras/README
/home/donnie/Downloads/lynis/plugins/README
[donnie@fedora ~]$
```

If you append a 2> redirector and a filename to this command, you can send the error messages to a text file so that you can just look at the good data on the screen. Here's how that looks:

```
[donnie@fedora ~]$ find / -name README 2> find_error.txt
/home/donnie/.cache/go-build/README
/home/donnie/.local/share/containers/storage/
overlay/994393dc58e7931862558d06e46aa2bb17487044f670f310dffe1d24e4d1eec7/diff/
etc/profile.d/README
/home/donnie/.local/share/containers/storage/
overlay/63ba8d57fba258ed8ccaec2ef1fd9e3e27e93f7f23d0683bd83687322a68ed29/diff/
etc/fonts/conf.d/README
. . .
. . .
/home/donnie/Downloads/lynis/README
/home/donnie/Downloads/lynis/extras/README
/home/donnie/Downloads/lynis/plugins/README
[donnie@fedora ~]$
```

You can combine redirectors to have stdout sent to one text file, and stderr sent to another text file, like this:

```
[donnie@fedora ~]$ find / -name README > find_results.txt 2> find_error.txt
[donnie@fedora ~]$
```

If you don't want to see any error messages at all, just send stderr to the /dev/null device, which is known in some circles as the infamous *bit bucket*. Anything sent there will never see the light of day. Here's how that looks:

```
[donnie@fedora ~]$ find / -name README 2> /dev/null
/home/donnie/.cache/go-build/README
/home/donnie/.local/share/containers/storage/
overlay/994393dc58e7931862558d06e46aa2bb17487044f670f310dffe1d24e4d1eec7/diff/
etc/profile.d/README
/home/donnie/.local/share/containers/storage/
overlay/63ba8d57fba258ed8ccaec2ef1fd9e3e27e93f7f23d0683bd83687322a68ed29/diff/
etc/fonts/conf.d/README
. . .
. . .
/home/donnie/Downloads/lynis/README
/home/donnie/Downloads/lynis/extras/README
/home/donnie/Downloads/lynis/plugins/README
[donnie@fedora ~]$
```

If you want to send the good data to the bit bucket so that you'll see nothing but error messages, you can use this command:

```
[donnie@fedora ~]$ find / -name README > /dev/null
find: '/boot/loader/entries': Permission denied
find: '/boot/lost+found': Permission denied
find: '/boot/efi': Permission denied
find: '/boot/grub2': Permission denied

. . .

. . .

find: '/var/tmp/systemd-private-075495f99a0e4571a4507a921ef61dab-chronyd.
service-vVTD10': Permission denied
find: '/var/tmp/systemd-private-075495f99a0e4571a4507a921ef61dab-ModemManager.
service-CG1GeZ': Permission denied
[donnie@fedora ~]$
```

You can also append error messages to an existing file with the 2>> operator, like so:

```
[donnie@fedora ~]$ cd /far 2> error.txt
[donnie@fedora ~]$ cat error.txt
bash: cd: /far: No such file or directory
[donnie@fedora ~]$ cd /fat 2>> error.txt
[donnie@fedora ~]$ cat error.txt
bash: cd: /far: No such file or directory
bash: cd: /fat: No such file or directory
[donnie@fedora ~]$
```

So far, so good. Now, as promised, we'll look at the part that can be a bit confusing. Well, actually, it's not *that* confusing. It's just that we're going to use a bit of shorthand that takes a bit of getting used to.

Let's say that you want to send both stdout and stderr to the same place. Does that mean that you have to enter the destination twice, with two different redirectors? Thanks to this bit of shorthand, the answer is *No*. Here's how it works.

If you want both stderr and stdout to go to the same text file, just enter your command with the regular stdout operator and destination. Then, at the end, append 2>&1. If you need a way to help understand this, just remember that stderr is File Descriptor ID 2, and stdout is File Descriptor ID 1. So, you can read this as, stderr *(ID 2) goes to the same place as* stdout *(ID 1)*.

To have both stderr and stdout of a find operation sent to the same text file, you can enter:

```
[donnie@fedora ~]$ find / -name README > find_results.txt 2>&1
[donnie@fedora ~]$
```

There may be times when you wouldn't want any output from either stderr or stdout. For example, if you needed to run a backup job in the background, you wouldn't want any screen output to mess up the text file that you're editing in the foreground. (You also wouldn't need to save any of the output to a text file.) For this, you can enter something like this:

```
[donnie@fedora ~]$ find \( -iname '*.txt' -mtime -1 \) -exec cp {} /backup/ \;
> /dev/null 2>&1
[donnie@fedora ~]$
```

(Note that I've set the permissions on the /backup/ directory so that I can write to it with my normal user privileges.)

I think that that about does it for stderr. And now, as a no-extra-cost bonus, I'll show you how to send your output to both the screen and a text file at the same time.

Understanding tee

The tee command is rather unique, because it's not really a normal redirector. Rather, it's a utility that can take output from a command and send it to both the screen and to a file at the same time. So, instead of using it with a redirector symbol as we've been doing, you'll send it its input via a pipe.

If you need to see a command's output on the screen and also save it as a text file, pipe the output of the command through the tee utility, like this:

```
[donnie@fedora ~]$ ps a | tee ps.txt
    PID TTY      STAT   TIME COMMAND
    972 tty1     Ss+    0:00 -bash
   1005 pts/0    Ss     0:00 -bash
   1076 pts/0    R+     0:00 ps a
   1077 pts/0    S+     0:00 tee ps.txt
[donnie@fedora ~]$ ls -l ps.txt
-rw-r--r--. 1 donnie donnie 181 Aug 12 17:29 ps.txt
[donnie@fedora ~]$
```

Note that you don't have to use the stdout operator (>) with this command. The name of the text file is used as the argument for tee.

If you run another command with the same filename, the first file that you created will get overwritten. (Of course, you can prevent that by setting the noclobber option, as I showed you just a while ago.) If you want to append output to an existing file, you can use the -a option, like this:

```
[donnie@fedora ~]$ ps a | tee -a ps.txt
    PID TTY      STAT   TIME COMMAND
    972 tty1     Ss+    0:00 -bash
   1005 pts/0    Ss     0:00 -bash
   1087 pts/0    R+     0:00 ps a
```

```
    1088 pts/0      S+      0:00 tee -a ps.txt
[donnie@fedora ~]$
```

There's another use for tee that you definitely need to know about. It's just that at times, you might have to create a shell script that will automatically create or update a configuration file in the /etc/ directory. It seems logical that you would use echo and either the > or >> operator to accomplish that. But, look what happens when I try that:

```
[donnie@fedora ~]$ sudo echo "This is a new setting." > /etc/someconfig.cfg
-bash: /etc/someconfig.cfg: Permission denied
[donnie@fedora ~]$ sudo echo "This is a new setting." >| /etc/someconfig.cfg
-bash: /etc/someconfig.cfg: Permission denied
[donnie@fedora ~]$ sudo echo "This is a new setting." >> /etc/someconfig.cfg
-bash: /etc/someconfig.cfg: Permission denied
[donnie@fedora ~]$
```

As you see, the shell doesn't allow me to redirect output into a file in the /etc/ directory, even when I use sudo privileges. (Okay, you can do this if you actually log into the root user's shell, but let's say that we don't want to do that.) The solution is to use tee, as you see here:

```
[donnie@fedora ~]$ echo "This is a new setting." | sudo tee /etc/someconfig.cfg
This is a new setting.
[donnie@fedora ~]$ ls -l /etc/someconfig.cfg
-rw-r--r--. 1 root root 23 Aug 12 17:47 /etc/someconfig.cfg
[donnie@fedora ~]$
```

When running this from the command-line, I have to precede the tee command with sudo. If you put a command like this in a shell script, you'll be able to omit the sudo, because you'll be running the entire script with sudo privileges.

Now, as cool as tee sounds, there is one slight catch. That is, tee always sends both good output and error messages to the screen, but it only sends good output to the designated file.

So far, it's been pretty easy for you to follow along in your own shell as I've explained things. Now that things are getting a bit more complex, let's tie things together a bit by doing an actual hands-on lab.

Hands-on Lab – Pipes, Redirectors, and find

For this assignment, you'll be working with pipes and redirectors. To see the full effect of this exercise, you'll need to be logged in as a normal user, and *not* as root.

1. Enter the following, noting that you're deliberately typing the name of a non-existent directory in order to generate an error message.

    ```
    find /far -iname '*'
    ```

2. Note the output, and then enter:

```
find /far -iname '*' 2> error.txt
cat error.txt
```

3. Create a listing of files and see how many there are, by entering:

```
find / -iname '*.txt' > filelist.txt 2> error_2.txt
find / -iname '*.txt' 2> /dev/null | wc -l
less filelist.txt
less error_2.txt
```

 If you're logged on as a normal user instead of as root, this should generate some error messages about the fact that you don't have permission to look in certain directories. The list of .txt files will be written to the filelist.txt file, and the error messages will be written to the error_2.txt file .

4. Search for README files by entering:

```
find / -name README > files_and_errors.txt 2>&1
less files_and_errors.txt
```

This time, the 2>&1 that's appended to the end of the command caused the error messages and the file list to both go to the same file.

5. For the next operation, you'll send the file list to both the screen and to a file. Enter:

```
find / -name README | tee filelist_2.txt
less filelist_2.txt
```

Note that both the file list and the error messages will print on the screen, but that only the file list will go to the file.

6. Create a simulated backup directory, like so:

```
sudo mkdir /backup
sudo chown your_user_name:your_user_name /backup
```

7. Copy all of the .txt files that you created within the last day to the /backup/ directory, and send all screen output to the /dev/null device:

```
find \( -iname '*.txt' -mtime -1 \) -exec cp {} /backup/ \; > /dev/null
2>&1
```

8. View the files in the /backup/ directory:

```
ls -l /backup
```

End of lab

Well, that's pretty much it for this chapter. Let's summarize and move on.

Summary

In this chapter, we looked at the concept of Input/Output redirection. It's a simple concept, really. It just means that we either take input from somewhere other than the keyboard, or we send output to somewhere other than the terminal screen. We looked at the redirection operators, how to use them, and some of the pitfalls of using them incorrectly.

In the next chapter, we'll look at ways to modify your shell environment. I'll see you there.

Questions

1. What is the file descriptor number for `stdin`?

    a. 0
    b. 1
    c. 2
    d. 3

2. Which of the following operators is for `stdin`?

    a. `>`
    b. `>>`
    c. `<`
    d. `<<`

3. What will happen if you run this command?

    ```
    tr [:lower:] [:upper:] < filelist.txt > filelist.txt
    ```

    a. The `filelist.txt` file will get overwritten with updated output.
    b. The output of `tr` will be appended to the end of the file.
    c. You'll receive a warning message.
    d. The contents of the `filelist.txt` file will be wiped out, and you'll be left with just an empty file.

4. What is the default `stdin` device?

    a. keyboard
    b. terminal
    c. mouse
    d. a named pipe

5. Which of these operators would you use to send `stderr` and `stdout` to the same place?

    a. `2>1&`
    b. `2>&1`

    c.   2&1

    d.   2>1

Further Reading

- Five ways to use redirect operators in Bash: `https://www.redhat.com/sysadmin/redirect-operators-bash`

- How to manipulate files with with shell redirection and pipelines in Linux: `https://www.redhat.com/sysadmin/linux-shell-redirection-pipelining`

- How to redirect shell command output: `https://www.redhat.com/sysadmin/redirect-shell-command-script-output`

Answers

1. a
2. c
3. d
4. a
5. b

Join our community on Discord!

Read this book alongside other users, Linux experts, and the author himself.

Ask questions, provide solutions to other readers, chat with the author via Ask Me Anything sessions, and much more. Scan the QR code or visit the link to join the community.

`https://packt.link/SecNet`

5

Customizing the Environment

In this chapter, we'll look at the various configuration files for the bash shell environment. We'll look at how to customize these configuration files, and how to set certain environmental options from the command-line.

Topics in this chapter include:

- Reviewing the environmental variables
- Understanding the configuration files
- Setting shell options from the command line

I'm sticking with bash for now, but in *Chapter 22, Understanding the Z Shell*, I'll explain how zsh is set up.

If you're raring and ready, let's get going.

Technical Requirements

For this chapter, you'll need one Fedora virtual machine and one Debian virtual machine. I won't be providing a Hands-On Lab in this chapter. Instead, I'll just invite you to follow along on your virtual machines as you read through the chapter.

Reviewing the Environmental Variables

In *Chapter 3, Understanding Variables and Pipelines*, I introduced the concept of environmental variables. In this chapter, I'd like to expand on that topic.

We've already seen that environmental variables can be used to help customize and control your shell environment. Here's a table of some of the more common environmental variables:

Environmental Variable	Purpose
USER	The username of the person who is currently logged into the system.
UID	The User ID number of the logged-in user.

`EUID`	The Effective User ID number of the user who's running a certain process.
`MAIL`	This defines the path to the mail spool of the logged in user.
`SHELL`	The path to the shell that is currently in use.
`PWD`	The current working directory. (PWD stands for "Print Working Directory".)
`OLDPWD`	The previous working directory.
`HOSTNAME`	The hostname of the computer.
`PATH`	A colon-delimited list of directories in which the system looks when you type an executable program name. This variable gets built in several configuration files, such as `/etc/profile` and the `.bashrc` file that resides in the user's home directory.
`HOME`	This holds the path for the current user's home directory. Some programs will use this variable to determine where to find configuration files or determine the default location to store files.
`PS1`	The primary shell prompt.
`PS2`	The secondary shell prompt.
`TERM`	This specifies the current terminal type. You'll probably see it set as either `xterm` or some form of `xterm` for non-login sessions and login sessions from a remote GUI terminal emulator, and just `Linux` for login sessions at the local console. (I'll explain the types of sessions in the next section.) The system needs to know which terminal type is in use so that it will know how to move the cursor and display text effects in text-mode programs.
`DISPLAY`	This variable allows you to have multiple displays running from the same computer. If you're only running one display, you'll see a returned value of `:0`. (That means, the first display on the current computer.)
`EDITOR`	This sets the default text editor that you want to use for system administrative functions such as `systemctl edit` and `crontab -e`. Your best choices are generally either `nano` or `vim`.

Table 5.1: The more common environmental variables

The slightly tricky part about this is that environmental variables aren't always exactly the same across all Linux distros. For example, the `EDITOR` variable is defined here on my Fedora workstation, but it's not used at all on any Debian or Ubuntu distros. Instead, Debian and Ubuntu use another mechanism for setting the default editor, which we'll look at in a bit.

Now, before I can fully explain the `bash` configuration files, I need to explain the different types of shell sessions.

Understanding Shell Sessions

Any time you initiate interaction with a shell, you're creating a **shell session**. Shell sessions can be classified in the following ways:

- **Interactive shells:** When you sit down at a computer and enter commands on the command-line, you're working with an interactive shell.

- **Non-interactive shells:** When a shell session is invoked from within a shell script, you're working with a non-interactive shell.

- **Login shells:** If you log into a Linux machine that's running in text mode, without a graphical interface, you're working with a login shell. You can also work with a login shell on a desktop machine by invoking a *Ctrl-Alt-Function_Key* sequence to switch away from the desktop interface to a text mode terminal. (You can use function keys F1 through F6 for this.) Or, you can invoke the `bash -l` command in the normal terminal emulator to open a child `bash` session in login mode. The final way to initiate a login shell session is to log into a machine remotely via Secure Shell. Regardless of whether the remote machine is of a text-mode or GUI-mode variety, your remote session will be of the login shell type.

- **Non-login shells:** Any time you open a terminal emulator on a desktop Linux machine, you're working with a non-login shell.

So, what does all this mean? Well, the difference between interactive and non-interactive shells is fairly obvious, so I won't talk more about that. But, I would like to point out two different ways to know whether you're working with a login shell or a non-login shell.

The first way is to use the `shopt` command, like so:

```
[donnie@fedora ~]$ shopt login_shell
login_shell         off
[donnie@fedora ~]$
```

The `shopt` command can be used to set various configuration options for a `bash` session. Here though, I'm using it without any option switches to just view the `login_shell` setting. You see here that the `login_shell` setting is `off`, which means that I'm in a non-login shell here on my Fedora workstation. On my text mode Fedora Server virtual machine, the `shopt` output looks like this:

```
[donnie@fedora-server ~]$ shopt login_shell
login_shell        on
[donnie@fedora-server ~]$
```

As you see, the `login_shell` parameter is `on`.

The second way to tell if you're in a login shell is to use the `echo $0` command, like this:

```
[donnie@fedora ~]$ echo $0
bash
[donnie@fedora ~]$
```

The $0 argument is what's known as a **positional parameter**. I'll provide in-depth coverage of positional parameters in *Chapter 8, Basic Shell Script Construction*, so don't stress out about them just yet. All you need to know for now is that the echo $0 command shows the name of the script or executable that's currently in use.

In this case, we're in a bash session, which means that the bash executable is in use. But, how do we know whether or not we're using a login shell? Well, it's just that the bash output is not preceded by a dash, which means that we're not in a login shell. To show the difference, here's what you'll see on the text-mode Fedora Server virtual machine:

```
[donnie@fedora-server ~]$ echo $0
-bash
[donnie@fedora-server ~]$
```

The -bash output indicates that I'm in a login shell.

Even from afar, I can read your mind. (Yes, I know that that's creepy.) I know that you're wondering why you need to know about these different types of shell sessions. Well, it's just that there are several different bash configuration files. The type of shell session you're using determines which configuration files the session accesses. So, now that you know about the different types of shell sessions, we can look at these configuration files.

Understanding the Configuration Files

As we've already seen, you can set environmental variables from the command-line. But, any variables you set in this manner will only last for the duration of the command-line session. When you log out of the system or close the terminal emulator window, any environmental changes that you've made from the command-line will be lost.

What if we want to make these changes permanent? There are several configuration files that we can edit to save our changes. Some are global and will affect all users, while others will only affect an individual user. The slightly tricky part is that the files differ from one Linux distro to the next. Let's start by looking at the bash configuration files on Fedora. After that, we'll move on to Debian.

bash Global Configuration Files on Fedora

As we've already seen, there are global configuration files in the /etc/ directory, and users' configuration files in each user's own home directory. For the global configuration, we have these two files:

- /etc/profile
- /etc/bashrc

The /etc/profile file sets up the environment for anyone who opens a bash login shell session, and is executed as soon as a user logs in. Go ahead and open it and look through it. What you'll see is a somewhat complex shell script that performs the following functions:

- It defines the default PATH setting for both the root user and every non-root user who's using a login shell.

- It defines the various environmental variables that are associated with each logged-in user. These include the UID, EUID, USER, LOGNAME, and MAIL variables.
- It sets the machine's HOSTNAME.
- It sets the HISTSIZE variable, which defines how many past commands will be held in each user's command history.
- After having done all of the above, it reads in the various configuration scripts in the /etc/profile.d/ directory. Most of these scripts define system-wide behaviors for certain system utilities. There's also a script that sets the default EDITOR for system utilities that automatically open a text editor.

 Of course, at this point I don't expect you to completely understand what's going on in this profile file. However, what you see in this file is the kind of stuff that we'll be covering throughout the remainder of this book. Once you've gone through all of that, you'll be able to come back and have a better understanding of exactly what this file is doing.

The other global configuration file is the /etc/bashrc file, which affects non-login shell sessions. It does a few different things for us, but for our present purposes just know that this is where the PS1 variable is defined for interactive sessions, and that it defines the PATH setting for users who are using a non-login shell.

In addition to these two main files, there are also supplementary configuration files in the /etc/profile.d/ directory, as you see here:

```
[donnie@fedora profile.d]$ ls
bash_completion.sh  colorxzgrep.sh   gawk.csh  sh.local
colorgrep.csh            colorzgrep.csh    gawk.sh   vim-default-editor.csh
colorgrep.sh             colorzgrep.sh     lang.csh  vim-default-editor.sh
colorls.csh              csh.local             lang.sh       which2.csh
colorls.sh               debuginfod.csh    less.csh   which2.sh
colorxzgrep.csh     debuginfod.sh     less.sh
[donnie@fedora profile.d]$
```

Each of these files contains supplementary configuration information for the shell environment. In general, each file does either one of these two things for us:

- Creating aliases for certain other commands. (We'll cover aliases in just a bit.)
- Defining environmental variables that aren't already defined in the /etc/profile or /etc/bashrc files.

For a simple example of the second function, let's look at the definition for the EDITOR variable. On the server version of Fedora it will be in the /etc/profile.d/vim-default-editor.sh file, and on the workstation version of Fedora it will be in the /etc/profile.d/nano-default-editor.sh file. Here's what the server version looks like:

```
# Ensure vim is set as EDITOR if it isn't already set
```

```
if [ -z "$EDITOR" ]; then
    export EDITOR="/usr/bin/vim"
fi
```

Again, I don't expect you to fully understand what's going on with this just yet. So for now, the simple explanation is that if the EDITOR environmental variable hasn't yet been set, then it will be set it to /usr/bin/vim. (On the workstation edition of Fedora, EDITOR will be set to /usr/bin/nano.)

There may be times when an administrator needs to alter the default environmental settings that have been defined in either /etc/profile or /etc/bashrc. You could do that by editing the /etc/profile or the /etc/bashrc file, but that's not recommended. Instead, just place the new settings in the /etc/profile.d/sh.local file. Currently, there's nothing in that file except for an explanatory comment, as we see here:

```
#Add any required envvar overrides to this file, it is sourced from /etc/
profile
```

Okay, that about does it for the global configuration files on Fedora. Let's now look at the users' own configuration files.

Users' Configuration Files on Fedora

Shell configuration files in the users' home directories are considered as hidden files, because their filenames begin with a dot. To see them, you'll need to use the -a option with ls, like so:

```
[donnie@fedora ~]$ ls -la
total 20
drwx------. 3 donnie donnie  111 Aug 26 16:28 .
drwxr-xr-x. 3 root   root     20 Aug 19 18:15 ..
-rw-------. 1 donnie donnie 1926 Aug 26 15:51 .bash_history
-rw-r--r--. 1 donnie donnie   18 Feb  5  2023 .bash_logout
-rw-r--r--. 1 donnie donnie  141 Feb  5  2023 .bash_profile
-rw-r--r--. 1 donnie donnie  492 Feb  5  2023 .bashrc
-rw-------. 1 donnie donnie   37 Aug 26 16:28 .lesshst
drwx------. 2 donnie donnie   48 Aug 21 14:13 .ssh
[donnie@fedora ~]$
```

Only three of these files are of concern to us, which are:

- .bash_logout: This file is currently empty, except for an explanatory comment. Any commands that you place in this file will be executed either upon logging out of an interactive login shell session, or when the exit function is invoked at the end of a shell script. Among other things, you could use this to automatically clean up temporary files or to perform an automatic backup of files in a user's home directory when the user exits the shell session.

- .bash_profile: This file is only used for login shell sessions. So, if you open a terminal emulator on your desktop machine, anything that's in this file will have no effect. If you look at the contents of this file, you'll see that the only thing it does by default is to cause the .bashrc file to be read in.

- .bashrc: This is the main bash configuration file for the user level, which directly affects non-login shell sessions. Since the .bash_profile file causes the .bashrc file to be read in for login shell sessions, anything you place into .bashrc affects both login and non-login sessions.

So, how does this work in practice? Well, let's say that you need to add the /opt/ directory to your working PATH. Currently, the PATH looks like this:

```
[donnie@fedora-server ~]$ echo $PATH
/home/donnie/.local/bin:/home/donnie/bin:/usr/local/bin:/usr/bin:/usr/local/
sbin:/usr/sbin
[donnie@fedora-server ~]$
```

To add the /opt/ directory, open the .bashrc file in your text editor, and look for this stanza:

```
if ! [[ "$PATH" =~ "$HOME/.local/bin:$HOME/bin:" ]]
then
    PATH="$HOME/.local/bin:$HOME/bin:$PATH"
fi
```

Change it so that it looks like this:

```
if ! [[ "$PATH" =~ "$HOME/.local/bin:$HOME/bin:" ]]
then
    PATH="$HOME/.local/bin:$HOME/bin:$PATH:/opt:"
fi
```

Log out and then log back in. Your PATH setting should now look like this:

```
[donnie@fedora-server ~]$ echo $PATH
/home/donnie/.local/bin:/home/donnie/bin:/usr/local/bin:/usr/bin:/usr/local/
sbin:/usr/sbin:/opt:
[donnie@fedora-server ~]$
```

You can now place executable scripts or binary executable files in the /opt/ directory, and run them without having to specify the entire path.

To make a permanent change to your command prompt setting so that it will also show the current date and time, place this line at the end of the .bashrc file:

```
export PS1="[\d \t \u@\h \w] \$ "
```

Log out and log back in. Your command prompt should now look like this:

```
[Tue Aug 29 17:13:55 donnie@fedora-server ~] $
```

So, that's all pretty cool, right? For even more coolness, let's move on to the Debian configuration files.

bash Global Configuration Files on Debian

On Debian, things are somewhat different. The /etc/profile file is still there, but it's radically different from the one on Fedora. Go ahead and look at it on your own virtual machine. You'll see that all it does is define the PATH and PS1 variables and read in any supplementary files that are in the /etc/profile.d/ directory. If the session is an actual bash session instead of an sh session, then it will also read in the /etc/bash.bashrc file. Also, you'll see that Debian uses a method for defining PATH that's radically different from the method that's used on Fedora.

Instead of the /etc/bashrc file that Fedora uses, Debian uses the /etc/bash.bashrc file. This file does the following things for us:

- It checks the size of the window in which the bash session is running, so that the correct number of lines and columns can be displayed after the user enters a command.
- It defines the PS1 variable.
- If a user enters a command that bash can't find, it invokes the command_not_found_handle function if the command-not-found software package isn't installed.

At the top of the bash.bashrc file, you'll see that it's invoked for interactive shell sessions, and that it will also get invoked for login shell sessions if the profile file sources it. We've already seen that the profile file does source it, so we know that bash.bashrc does run for both login and non-login interactive sessions.

 When a configuration file reads in information from another configuration file, we say that the first file is **sourcing** the second file.

Unlike on Fedora, the /etc/profile.d/ directory doesn't do much for us by default. The only thing you'll see there is the bash_completion.sh script. As you'll see in a moment, the aliases that are defined in the /etc/profile.d/ directory on Fedora are defined in the users' configuration files on Debian.

Users' Configuration Files on Debian

In each user's home directory on a Debian system, we have these bash configuration files:

- .bash_logout: This is the same as the .bash_logout file on Fedora, except that it contains a command that will clear the screen upon logout from a login session.
- .profile: This replaces the .bash_profile that's on Fedora, and serves the same purpose.
- .bashrc: It does the same things as the .bashrc file on Fedora, and more besides. It also defines some of the environmental variables that are defined globally on Fedora, and it also defines some of the aliases that are defined in the /etc/profile.d/ directory on Fedora.

As I've already told you, I don't expect you to read through any of these configuration files and completely understand what they're doing. That's why I've only shown you a few small snippets of these files instead of trying to explain each one in detail. After you've completely gone through this book, you'll have gained a better understanding of them.

 I should also point out that every family of Linux distros has its bash configuration files set up differently. I can't cover all of them, but you can probably figure out what's going on with them from what I've told you here.

Setting the Default Editor on Debian

Oh, dear, I almost forgot to show you how to change the default editor for Debian, since we can't do it by setting an environmental variable. So, let's look at that now.

On a Debian system, the default editor is defined by a pair of symbolic links, as you see here:

```
donnie@debian:~$ ls -l /usr/bin/editor
lrwxrwxrwx 1 root root 24 Jan 18  2023 /usr/bin/editor -> /etc/alternatives/
editor
donnie@debian:~$ cd /etc/alternatives/
donnie@debian:/etc/alternatives$ ls -l editor
lrwxrwxrwx 1 root root 9 Jan 18  2023 editor -> /bin/nano
donnie@debian:/etc/alternatives$
```

The editor symbolic link in the /usr/bin/ directory points to the editor symbolic link in the /etc/alternatives/ directory, which in turn points to the nano executable that's in the /bin/ directory. This tells us that nano is set as the default editor. To change the default editor on a Debian machine, you'll first need to ensure that the editor that you want to use is installed. Then, use the update-alternatives utility, like so:

```
donnie@debian:~$ sudo update-alternatives --config editor
[sudo] password for donnie:
There are 3 choices for the alternative editor (providing /usr/bin/editor).

  Selection    Path                 Priority   Status
------------------------------------------------------------
* 0            /bin/nano             40        auto mode
  1            /bin/nano             40        manual mode
  2            /usr/bin/vim.basic    30        manual mode
  3            /usr/bin/vim.tiny     15        manual mode
Press <enter> to keep the current choice[*], or type selection number: 2
update-alternatives: using /usr/bin/vim.basic to provide /usr/bin/editor
(editor) in manual mode
donnie@debian:~$
```

I've chosen the number 2 option to set vim as the default editor. Let's see how that changed the symbolic link in the /etc/alternatives/ directory:

```
donnie@debian:~$ ls -l /etc/alternatives/editor
lrwxrwxrwx 1 root root 18 Sep  2 15:26 /etc/alternatives/editor -> /usr/bin/
vim.basic
donnie@debian:~$
```

Very cool. This allows me to use my favorite editor.

Okay, now that we've seen the configuration files, let's look at another way to customize a shell session.

Setting Shell Options from the Command-line

In addition to using environmental variables to modify your shell session, you can also use **shell options**. You would use the set command to set shell options from either the command-line or from within your shell scripts. You can also use it from the command-line to just view the options that are set.

 You can use either the Fedora or the Debian virtual machine for this section. With only one minor exception that concerns a man page, everything will be the same on both of them.

To begin, let's invoke the set command without any options or arguments, like so:

```
[donnie@fedora-server ~]$ set
BASH=/bin/bash
BASHOPTS=checkwinsize:cmdhist:complete_
fullquote:expand_aliases:extglob:extquote:force_
fignore:globasciiranges:globskipdots:histappend:interactive_comments:login_
shell:patsub_replacement:progcomp:promptvars:sourcepath

. . .

. . .
quote_readline ()
{
    local ret;
    _quote_readline_by_ref "$1" ret;
    printf %s "$ret"
}
[donnie@fedora-server ~]$
```

What you'll see is a complete list of environmental variables and **shell functions** that are active for this shell session. (I'll tell you more about shell functions in *Chapter 10, Understanding Functions*.)

Use the set -o command to just see the list of shell options that are active, like this:

```
[donnie@fedora-server ~]$ set -o
```

```
allexport              off
braceexpand            on
emacs                  on
errexit                off
errtrace               off
functrace              off
hashall                on
histexpand             on
history                on
 . . .

 . . .
xtrace                 off
[donnie@fedora-server ~]$
```

I won't go over what each and every one of these options does, but I will tell you how to find out what they do. The only catch is that there's a bit of a trick to it. That is, there's no man page that's specifically for the set command. When you do man set on your Fedora machine, you'll actually pull up the bash man page. On Debian, you'll have to do man bash, because man set won't work at all. The reason for this is that the set command is built into the bash executable, and doesn't have its own executable. Once you have the bash man page up, you'll need to search through it to find the explanation of the set command and all of its options. For now, let's look at a couple of the more useful options and how to set them.

In *Chapter 4, Understanding Input/Output Redirection*, I told you how the noclobber option can help prevent you from accidentally overwriting an important file. By default, noclobber is off, as you see here:

```
[donnie@fedora-server ~]$ set -o | grep noclobber
noclobber              off
[donnie@fedora-server ~]$
```

The way you turn options on and off is completely counterintuitive. You'll use the set -o command to turn an option on and the set +o command to turn an option off, which is the exact opposite of what you'd think it would be. (I have no idea why someone decided to do things this way. But, whatever, right?) So, let's say that we want to turn the noclobber option on. Here's what that looks like:

```
[donnie@fedora-server ~]$ set -o noclobber
[donnie@fedora-server ~]$ set -o | grep noclobber
noclobber              on
[donnie@fedora-server ~]$
```

Now, let's turn it back off:

```
[donnie@fedora-server ~]$ set +o noclobber
[donnie@fedora-server ~]$ set -o | grep noclobber
```

```
noclobber               off
[donnie@fedora-server ~]$
```

For some options, such as `noclobber`, you can use a shorthand notation. So, to minimize keystrokes while turning `noclobber` on or off just do this:

```
[donnie@fedora-server ~]$ set -C
[donnie@fedora-server ~]$ set -o | grep noclobber
noclobber               on
[donnie@fedora-server ~]$ set +C
[donnie@fedora-server ~]$ set -o | grep noclobber
noclobber               off
[donnie@fedora-server ~]$
```

In this example, the `-C` replaces `-o noclobber`, and `+C` replaces `+o noclobber`.

Another option that you might find useful is the `allexport` option. To see how you might use it, let's set a programming variable from the command-line, and then try to use it in a child shell. Here's what that looks like:

```
[donnie@fedora-server ~]$ car="1958 Edsel Corsair"
[donnie@fedora-server ~]$ echo $car
1958 Edsel Corsair
[donnie@fedora-server ~]$ bash
[donnie@fedora-server ~]$ echo $car
[donnie@fedora-server ~]$ exit
exit
[donnie@fedora-server ~]$
```

As you see, once I opened a child shell with the `bash` command, the value of `car` is no longer available to me. One way to fix that is to precede the variable definition with `export`, like so:

```
[donnie@fedora-server ~]$ export car="1958 Edsel Corsair"
[donnie@fedora-server ~]$ bash
[donnie@fedora-server ~]$ echo $car
1958 Edsel Corsair
[donnie@fedora-server ~]$ exit
exit
[donnie@fedora-server ~]$
```

This time, the value of `car` is available to me in the child shell. The problem with this method is that I would have to remember to precede each variable definition I create with `export`. It would be easier just to set the `allexport` option so that every variable I create will be exported automatically. Here's how that works:

```
[donnie@fedora-server ~]$ set -o allexport
```

```
[donnie@fedora-server ~]$ set -o | grep allexport
allexport             on
[donnie@fedora-server ~]$ car="1964 Ford Galaxie"
[donnie@fedora-server ~]$ bash
[donnie@fedora-server ~]$ echo $car
1964 Ford Galaxie
[donnie@fedora-server ~]$ exit
exit
[donnie@fedora-server ~]$
```

This time, the car variable got exported automatically so that its value is available in the child shell. When you're done with allexport, you can turn it off, like so:

```
[donnie@fedora-server ~]$ set +o allexport
[donnie@fedora-server ~]$ set -o | grep allexport
allexport             off
[donnie@fedora-server ~]$
```

The -a shorthand notation is also available for allexport, which looks like this:

```
[donnie@fedora-server ~]$ set -a
[donnie@fedora-server ~]$ set -o | grep allexport
allexport             on
[donnie@fedora-server ~]$ set +a
[donnie@fedora-server ~]$ set -o | grep allexport
allexport             off
[donnie@fedora-server ~]$
```

And now, my shell option settings are back to their default values.

Keep in mind that any options that you set will return to normal when you exit from the shell session.

Okay, that does it for shell options, at least for now. In *Chapter 21, Debugging Shell Scripts*, I'll show you a couple of more cool tricks that you can do with them. With all this out of the way, let's move on to the final section of this chapter.

Understanding Aliases

If you ever watch any crime dramas on television, you might see some criminal who uses more than one name. Of course, only one of those names is the criminal's real name. All of the other names are fake names, or aliases, that the criminal uses to prevent being found by the police. In the world of operating system shells, **aliases** are quite useful and have nothing to do with criminal activity. In fact, you're already using them without realizing it.

Think of an alias as a command that you can use in place of another command. For example, let's say that you're one of those poor souls who's stuck using Windows most of the time, and who only occasionally gets the chance to work with Linux.

Now, let's say that every time you get on a Linux machine, you instinctively always type in Windows commands, as you're doing here:

```
[donnie@fedora-server ~]$ ls
[donnie@fedora-server ~]$ ls -a
.  ..  .bash_history  .bash_logout  .bash_profile  .bashrc  .lesshst  .ssh
.viminfo
[donnie@fedora-server ~]$ cls
-bash: cls: command not found
[donnie@fedora-server ~]$
```

Yeah, that `cls` command that you always use on Windows doesn't work so well on Linux, does it? There's an easy fix to that, though. Just create an alias that points to the `clear` command, like so:

```
[donnie@fedora-server ~]$ alias cls=clear
[donnie@fedora-server ~]$
```

Once you do this, you'll be able to clear the screen with either the `cls` command or the `clear` command. Note that in this case, I didn't have to surround the alias definition with quotes because it doesn't contain any blank spaces or special symbols. Creating an alias that has blank spaces or special characters in its definition would look something like this:

```
donnie@fedora-server:~$ alias lla='ls -la --color=auto'
donnie@fedora-server:~$ lla
total 12680
drwx------. 14 donnie donnie     4096 Mar 30 17:02 .
drwxr-xr-x. 11 root   root        137 Mar 23 13:10 ..
-rwxr--r--.  1 donnie donnie       46 Mar 30 14:08 awk_kernel.awk
-rw-------.  1 donnie donnie    26137 Mar 30 13:58 .bash_history
-rw-------.  1 donnie donnie        0 Dec 29 18:11 .bash_history-01492.tmp
-rw-------.  1 donnie donnie        0 Dec 29 18:11 .bash_history-01790.tmp
-rw-r--r--.  1 donnie donnie       18 Sep 27  2022 .bash_logout
-rw-r--r--.  1 donnie donnie      141 Sep 27  2022 .bash_profile
-rw-r--r--.  1 donnie donnie      492 Sep 27  2022 .bashrc
drwxr-xr-x.  3 donnie donnie       24 Nov 22 16:57 .cache
drwx------.  3 donnie donnie       17 Mar 26  2023 .config
drwxr-xr-x.  3 donnie donnie     4096 Dec 26 16:42 csvquote
-rw-r--r--.  1 donnie donnie 12827862 Dec 18 14:01 dnf_list.txt
-rwxr--r--.  1 donnie donnie      514 Mar 30 14:08 factorial2.sh
-rwxr--r--.  1 donnie donnie      228 Mar 30 14:08 factorial.sh
-rw-r--r--.  1 donnie donnie        0 Mar 30 14:08 filelist.txt
drwxr-xr-x.  3 donnie donnie       17 Dec 20 15:00 go
-rw-r--r--.  1 donnie donnie        0 Mar 30 14:08 graphic1.png
-rw-r--r--.  1 donnie donnie        0 Mar 30 17:02 graphic2.png
-rw-------.  1 donnie donnie      116 Aug 14  2023 .histfile
drwxr-xr-x.  3 donnie donnie       33 Mar 26  2023 .kube
-rw-------.  1 donnie donnie      138 Mar 30 13:58 .lesshst
```

Figure 5.1: Using my new lla alias on Fedora

Coolness, it works.

To see the list of all active aliases, just use the alias command without any options or arguments, like this:

```
[donnie@fedora-server ~]$ alias
alias cls='clear'
alias egrep='egrep --color=auto'
alias fgrep='fgrep --color=auto'
alias grep='grep --color=auto'
alias l.='ls -d .* --color=auto'
alias ll='ls -l --color=auto'
alias lla='ls -la --color=auto'
alias ls='ls --color=auto'
alias which='(alias; declare -f) | /usr/bin/which --tty-only --read-alias
--read-functions --show-tilde --show-dot'
. . .

. . .
alias zgrep='zgrep --color=auto'
[donnie@fedora-server ~]$
```

As you see, they're listed in alphabetical order. On Fedora, several aliases have already been globally-defined in a set of scripts in the /etc/profile.d/ directory. For an example, let's look in the /etc/profile.d/colorls.sh script. Most of the script is rather complex, consisting of commands that define the color scheme that will be used with the ls aliases. At the bottom, you'll find the actual aliases, which look like this:

```
alias ll='ls -l --color=auto' 2>/dev/null
alias l.='ls -d .* --color=auto' 2>/dev/null
alias ls='ls --color=auto' 2>/dev/null
```

Here, we see that:

- The ll alias replaces the ls -l --color=auto command
- The l. alias replaces the ls -d .* --color=auto command
- The ls alias replaces the ls --color=auto command.

To see how these aliases work, create a few files and directories in the home directory of your Fedora virtual machine, like this:

```
[donnie@fedora-server ~]$ touch somefile.sh anyfile.txt graphic1.png
[donnie@fedora-server ~]$ mkdir somedir
[donnie@fedora-server ~]$ chmod u+x somefile.sh
[donnie@fedora-server ~]$
```

When you do a plain `ls` command, you'll see that the plain text file shows up in either black or white letters, depending upon whether you're using a black or a white background for your terminal. The directory shows up in blue letters, the graphic file shows up in magenta letters, and the executable script shows up in green letters. The `ll` alias performs the same function as the `ls -l` command, again with color coding, as you see here:

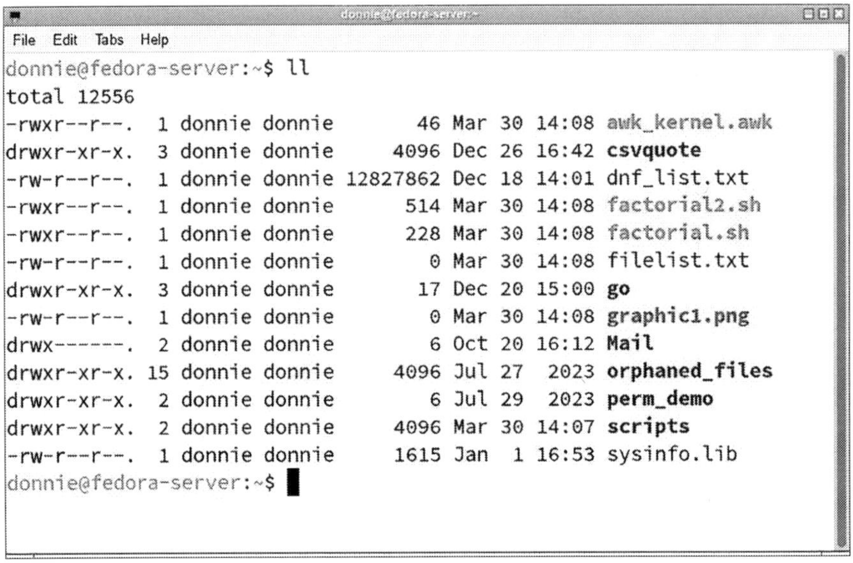
donnie@fedora-server:~
File Edit Tabs Help
donnie@fedora-server:~$ ll
total 12556
-rwxr--r--. 1 donnie donnie 46 Mar 30 14:08 awk_kernel.awk
drwxr-xr-x. 3 donnie donnie 4096 Dec 26 16:42 csvquote
-rw-r--r--. 1 donnie donnie 12827862 Dec 18 14:01 dnf_list.txt
-rwxr--r--. 1 donnie donnie 514 Mar 30 14:08 factorial2.sh
-rwxr--r--. 1 donnie donnie 228 Mar 30 14:08 factorial.sh
-rw-r--r--. 1 donnie donnie 0 Mar 30 14:08 filelist.txt
drwxr-xr-x. 3 donnie donnie 17 Dec 20 15:00 go
-rw-r--r--. 1 donnie donnie 0 Mar 30 14:08 graphic1.png
drwx------. 2 donnie donnie 6 Oct 20 16:12 Mail
drwxr-xr-x. 15 donnie donnie 4096 Jul 27 2023 orphaned_files
drwxr-xr-x. 2 donnie donnie 6 Jul 29 2023 perm_demo
drwxr-xr-x. 2 donnie donnie 4096 Mar 30 14:07 scripts
-rw-r--r--. 1 donnie donnie 1615 Jan 1 16:53 sysinfo.lib
donnie@fedora-server:~$

Figure 5.2: Using the ll alias on Fedora

Finally, the `l.` alias shows you the files and directories whose names begin with a dot, again with color coding. It looks something like this:

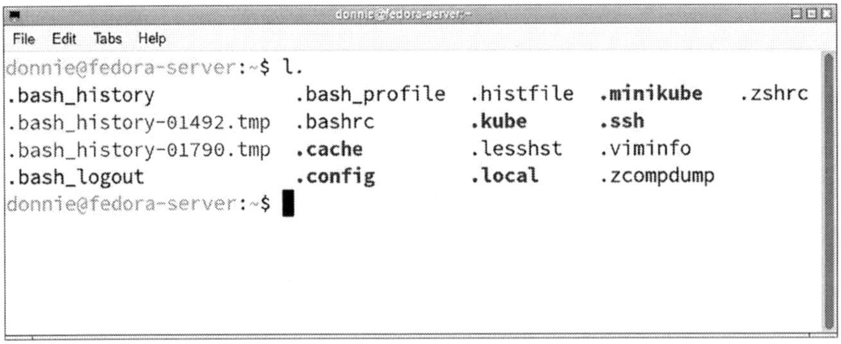
donnie@fedora-server:~
File Edit Tabs Help
donnie@fedora-server:~$ l.
.bash_history .bash_profile .histfile .minikube .zshrc
.bash_history-01492.tmp .bashrc .kube .ssh
.bash_history-01790.tmp .cache .lesshst .viminfo
.bash_logout .config .local .zcompdump
donnie@fedora-server:~$

Figure 5.3: Using the l. alias on Fedora

The Debian developers have done things differently. Instead of defining aliases at the global level, the Debian folk just define them at the user level. You'll find the list of defined aliases in the `.bashrc` file that's in every user's home directory. Only one is enabled by default, but you can easily enable any or all of the others by removing the # symbol from in front of them.

On the Fedora machine, there's a `which` alias that replaces the `which` command. This alias shows you not only where the executable file for a command is, it also shows you if there's an alias for that command. Here's what that looks like:

```
[donnie@fedora-server ~]$ which ls
alias ls='ls --color=auto'
    /usr/bin/ls
[donnie@fedora-server ~]$
```

There's no `which` alias on Debian, so you can't use `which` to see if there are any aliases for other commands. Here's what the Debian output looks like:

```
donnie@debian:~$ which ls
/usr/bin/ls
donnie@debian:~$
```

It's important to note that if you have an alias that has the same name as the actual underlying command, the alias always takes precedence. There are two ways to override that so that you can directly invoke the executable file for a command. The first way is to just specify the entire path to that executable, like this:

```
[donnie@fedora-server ~]$ /usr/bin/ls
anyfile.txt  somedir  somefile.sh
[donnie@fedora-server ~]$
```

The second way is to precede the command with a backslash, like this:

```
[donnie@fedora-server ~]$ \ls
anyfile.txt  somedir  somefile.sh
[donnie@fedora-server ~]$
```

You'll now see the `ls` output without any color-coding. Let's try it again with `which`, like this:

```
[donnie@fedora-server ~]$ /usr/bin/which ls
/usr/bin/ls
[donnie@fedora-server ~]$
```

This time, `which` only shows the location of the executable file, and ignores the alias. If you need to disable an alias, use the `unalias` command, like this:

```
[donnie@fedora-server ~]$ which which
alias which='(alias; declare -f) | /usr/bin/which --tty-only --read-alias
--read-functions --show-tilde --show-dot'
    /usr/bin/which
[donnie@fedora-server ~]$ unalias which
[donnie@fedora-server ~]$ which which
```

```
/usr/bin/which
[donnie@fedora-server ~]$
```

In this case, the alias is only disabled temporarily, until you close the shell session. If you use `unalias` for any aliases that you've created from the command-line, that alias will be disabled permanently.

The last thing I'll say about aliases is that any alias you set at the command-line will disappear when you exit the shell session. To make them permanent on either Debian or Fedora, just place them in the `.bashrc` file that's in your home directory.

All right, that pretty much wraps things up for this chapter. Let's summarize and move on.

Summary

In this chapter, we've completed laying the groundwork for the chapters to come. We explained the different types of shell sessions, and then looked at the configuration files that affect the shell environment at both the global and user levels. Then, we looked at how to set shell options and how to create and use aliases.

Now that you know the basics of how a shell operates, you're ready to tackle some meatier issues, like how to use text-stream filters. We'll start with that in the next chapter. I'll see you there.

Questions

1. Which two of the following commands turn on the `noclobber` option? (Choose two.)

    a. `set +o noclobber`

    b. `set -o noclobber`

    c. `set -C`

    d. `set +C`

2. On a Fedora machine, which of the following user-level configuration files will only affect a login shell session?

    a. `profile`

    b. `.bash_profile`

    c. `.bash.bashrc`

3. You've just opened a terminal emulator on your desktop Linux machine. What type of shell session are you using? (Choose two.)

    a. non-interactive

    b. login

    c. interactive

    d. non-login

Further Reading

- How to List Environmental Variables on Linux: `https://www.howtogeek.com/842780/linux-list-environment-variables/`
- Types of Linux Shell Sessions: `https://www.automationdojos.com/types-of-linux-shell-sessions/`
- Linux set Command & How to Use it (9 examples): `https://phoenixnap.com/kb/linux-set`

Answers

1. b and c
2. c
3. c and d

Join our community on Discord!

Read this book alongside other users, Linux experts, and the author himself.

Ask questions, provide solutions to other readers, chat with the author via Ask Me Anything sessions, and much more. Scan the QR code or visit the link to join the community.

`https://packt.link/SecNet`

6

Text-Stream Filters — Part 1

This is the first of two chapters in which I introduce the concept of text-stream filters. We'll look at what they are and how to use them from the command-line. In the following chapters, I'll present some examples of how these filter utilities can be used in shell scripts.

There are two reasons why you should learn about these various utilities. First, they're very helpful if you need to create shell scripts that can automate the creation of different types of documents, such as reports. The second reason is that they are covered on certain Linux certification exams, such as the CompTIA Linux+/Linux Professional Institute exams.

Topics in this chapter include:

- Introduction to text-stream filters
- Using cat
- Using tac
- Using cut
- Using paste
- Using join
- Using sort

Okay, let's get cracking, shall we?

Technical Requirements

Use any of your Linux virtual machines for this chapter, because these filter utilities work the same on all of them. Or, if you just happen to be running either Linux or macOS on your host machine, feel free to use it instead of a virtual machine. There's no hands-on lab, so feel free to try out all the commands on your own machine as you go through the chapter.

You'll be working with a lot of text files in both this chapter and the next one. For your convenience, I've placed the files in the GitHub repository. If you're using Linux, the best way to retrieve them is to install git on your system with your distro's normal package manager.

Then, use the following command to download the files:

```
donnie@opensuse:~> git clone https://github.com/PacktPublishing/The-Ultimate-
Linux-Shell-Scripting-Guide.git
```

Then, `cd` into the `The-Ultimate-Linux-Shell-Scripting-Guide` directory that the `git` command created, where you'll find subdirectories for the various chapters.

If you're on a Mac, you'll need to open the App Store and install the `Xcode` package in order to use `git`. Then, use the command that I've just shown you to download the files.

I've also included a few examples of how some of these utilities work on FreeBSD and OpenIndiana. You can create a FreeBSD and an OpenIndiana virtual machine if you like, but it's not strictly necessary just yet.

Introduction to Text-Stream Filters

As either a Linux systems administrator or an office worker who uses Linux on the desktop, you'll probably have a certain number of text files that you need to work with. You may even get tasked with extracting data from these files and presenting the data effectively.

Or, you might need to extract data from utilities that show the status of your Linux system or from within scripts that automatically scrape the web for some specific information. The **text-stream filter utilities** that I present in this topic can help make these jobs easier. Once you learn them, you may even find that you can extract and display data with them more quickly than you could with text editors or word processors.

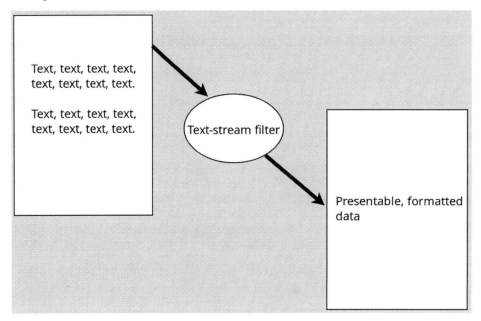

Figure 6.1: The basic concept of text-stream filters

With only one exception, you won't use these utilities to modify the original text file. You'll use them either to view the selected data on-screen, pipe the selected data to another utility, or use a redirector to create or append the selected data to another text file.

Using cat

The cat utility has nothing to do with our feline friends. It's used to either view, create, or join multiple text files together. (In fact, the term cat is short for *catenate*, which is a fancy way of saying "to join two things together, end-to-end".)

I said in the introduction that Mac users can perform the demos in this chapter on their Macs. Now though, I have to add a bit of a caveat. That's because there are at least three versions of cat, which all have different sets of option switches. I'll point out the differences as we go along.

Sometimes, you'll need to write scripts that are portable across various different operating systems. So, it's important that you know about these little idiosyncrasies.

By default, stdin for cat is the keyboard, and stdout is the computer screen. If you just type cat at the command prompt, you'll be able to type in text and make it echo back to you as soon as you hit *Enter*. It will keep doing this until you press *Ctrl-d* to end it. Here's what it looks like:

```
[donnie@fedora ~]$ cat
Hi there!
```

I haven't hit *Enter* yet. Watch what happens when I do:

```
[donnie@fedora ~]$ cat
Hi there!
Hi there!
```

This is the only line I want to enter, so I'll exit out of cat with *Ctrl-d*:

```
[donnie@fedora ~]$ cat
Hi there!
Hi there!
[donnie@fedora ~]$
```

Of course, this by itself isn't terribly useful. But, you can use cat with the stdout redirector to create simple text files. When you're through typing the message, hit *Enter* once more to get to a blank line, and then press *Ctrl-d* to exit. It should look something like this:

```
[donnie@fedora ~]$ cat > newtext.txt
Hi there! I'm using cat to create a
text file. I hope that it turns out well.
[donnie@fedora ~]$
```

Once you've created your file you can use cat to display it. It's not like the less utility though, because cat simply dumps everything in the file onto the display screen without pagination. You don't need to use a stdin redirector with cat, because cat is designed to use arguments instead of stdin redirectors. Anyway, here's what this looks like:

```
[donnie@fedora ~]$ cat newtext.txt
Hi there! I'm using cat to create a
text file. I hope that it turns out well.
[donnie@fedora ~]$
```

Now, use cat to create a second file, like so:

```
[donnie@fedora ~]$ cat > newtext_2.txt
I'm going to catenate this file to the first
file, just to see if it actually works.
[donnie@fedora ~]$
```

Here's where the catenate part comes in. Invoke cat again, but use the names of both of your new files as arguments, like so:

```
[donnie@fedora ~]$ cat newtext.txt newtext_2.txt
Hi there! I'm using cat to create a
text file. I hope that it turns out well.
I'm going to catenate this file to the first
file, just to see if it actually works.
[donnie@fedora ~]$
```

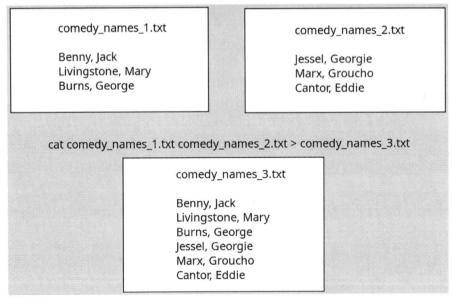

Figure 6.2: Directing the contents of two files into a third file.

This time, you'll see both of your files displayed as if they were one single file.

Now, add a stdout redirector to create a new file by combining the first two, like this:

```
[donnie@fedora ~]$ cat newtext.txt newtext_2.txt > newtext_3.txt
[donnie@fedora ~]$ cat newtext_3.txt
Hi there! I'm using cat to create a
text file. I hope that it turns out well.
I'm going to catenate this file to the first
file, just to see if it actually works.
[donnie@fedora ~]$
```

It's important to understand that you need to create a third text file when you do this. That's because if you were to redirect the output of the two original files into either one of the two original files, you would completely obliterate the contents of that destination file. The only thing you'd have left would be the contents of the second file. In fact, let me show you:

```
[donnie@fedora ~]$ cat newtext.txt newtext_2.txt > newtext.txt
[donnie@fedora ~]$ cat newtext.txt
I'm going to catenate this file to the first
file, just to see if it actually works.
[donnie@fedora ~]$
```

As you see, the text that was in the original newtext.txt file no longer exists.

There are several display options that you can use with cat. To see how to use them, create another text file. This time, add some tabs and a whole bunch of empty lines. It will look something like this:

```
[donnie@fedora ~]$ cat > newtext_4.txt
    I'm now adding tabs, spaces, and blank lines, to see if some
  of the options will work.




    Hopefully, they will.



    I hope.
[donnie@fedora ~]$
```

At the beginning of the of the options will work line I inserted a few blank spaces. I began all of the other lines by hitting the *Tab* key once.

Let's say that we don't need so many consecutive blank lines. That's no problem. I'll just use the -s option to squeeze them out, like so:

```
[donnie@fedora ~]$ cat -s newtext_4.txt
    I'm now adding tabs, spaces, and blank lines, to see if some
  of the options will work.
    Hopefully, they will.
    I hope.
[donnie@fedora ~]$
```

It looks better, doesn't it?

On Linux, FreeBSD, and macOS, you can see where all of the tabs are by using the -t option, like this:

```
[donnie@fedora ~]$ cat -t newtext_4.txt
^II'm now adding tabs, spaces, and blank lines, to see if some
  of the options will work.
^IHopefully, they will.
^II hope.
[donnie@fedora ~]$
```

You see that all of the tabs now show up as ^I characters.

On OpenIndiana you'll need to combine the -t and the -v options to see the tab characters, because using the -t option alone won't show you anything. Here's how it looks on OpenIndiana:

```
donnie@openindiana:~$ cat -tv test.txt
Testing, testing.
^IMore testing.
^I^IYet more testing.
Testing yet again,
^Iand again.
^I^I^IDone.
donnie@openindiana:~$
```

If you want to see where the end of each line is, use the -e option, like this:

```
[donnie@fedora ~]$ cat -e newtext_4.txt
    I'm now adding tabs, spaces, and blank lines, to see if some$
  of the options will work.$
$
$
$
$
    Hopefully, they will.$
$
```

```
$
    I hope.$
[donnie@fedora ~]$
```

On OpenIndiana you'll need to combine the -e and the -v options, because using the -e option alone won't show you anything. Here's how it looks on OpenIndiana:

```
donnie@openindiana:~$ cat -ev test.txt
    I'm now adding tabs, spaces, and blank lines, to see if some$
  of the options will work.$
$
$
$
$
    Hopefully, they will.$
$
$
    I hope.$
donnie@openindiana:~$
```

As you see, the end of each line is marked by a $.

On Linux only, you can see both where the tabs are and where the end of each line is by using the -A option, like so:

```
[donnie@fedora ~]$ cat -A newtext_4.txt
^II'm now adding tabs, spaces, and blank lines, to see if some$
  of the options will work.$
$
$
$
$
^IHopefully, they will.$
$
$
^II hope.$
[donnie@fedora ~]$
```

Note that the -A option only works on the Linux version of cat. It does not work on OpenIndiana, FreeBSD, or macOS.

Also, note that if script portability is a concern, you can use cat -tv as well as cat -ev on Linux machines, even though the -v option isn't necessary on Linux.

The -b option will number all non-blank lines for you, like this:

```
[donnie@fedora ~]$ cat -b newtext_4.txt
     1               I'm now adding tabs, spaces, and blank lines, to see if some
     2        of the options will work.
     3               Hopefully, they will.
     4               I hope.
[donnie@fedora ~]$
```

Or, use the -n option to have all lines numbered, like this:

```
[donnie@fedora ~]$ cat -n newtext_4.txt
     1               I'm now adding tabs, spaces, and blank lines, to see if some
     2        of the options will work.
     3
     4
     5
     6
     7               Hopefully, they will.
     8
     9
    10               I hope.
[donnie@fedora ~]$
```

That's it for cat, so let's look at tac.

Using tac

tac--cat spelled backwards--displays one or more files at a time in reverse order. To see how it works, we'll first create two text files that will look like this:

```
[donnie@fedora ~]$ cat > testfile_1.txt
one
two
three
four
five
six
[donnie@fedora ~]$ cat > testfile_2.txt
seven
eight
nine
ten
eleven
```

```
twelve
[donnie@fedora ~]$
```

Let's use cat to view both of the files at once:

```
[donnie@fedora ~]$ cat testfile_1.txt testfile_2.txt
one
two
three
four
five
six
seven
eight
nine
ten
eleven
twelve
[donnie@fedora ~]$
```

You can use tac to view one file in reverse order:

```
[donnie@fedora ~]$ tac testfile_1.txt
six
five
four
three
two
one
[donnie@fedora ~]$
```

Or, view two or more files in reverse order:

```
[donnie@fedora ~]$ tac testfile_1.txt testfile_2.txt
six
five
four
three
two
one
twelve
eleven
ten
nine
```

```
eight
seven
[donnie@fedora ~]$
```

Note that the contents of the first file is displayed first, followed by the contents of the second file.

And, of course, you can use the stdout redirector to create a new text file, like this:

```
[donnie@fedora ~]$ tac testfile_1.txt testfile_2.txt > testfile_3.txt
[donnie@fedora ~]$
```

You would think that tac would use the same options as cat, but it doesn't. None of the options for cat can be used for tac.

That's it for tac. Next up is cut.

Using cut

As its name implies, this handy utility is used to cut and display selected information from a text file. Think of it as something that will take a vertical slice of a text file and send it to the output of your choice. There are two ways to specify where you want to begin and end the slice. You can specify it either by specifying the starting and ending characters, or by specifying the fields.

To specify your slice by fields, you'll need to use both the -d and -f switches. The -d switch will specify the delimiter, the character that separates the fields. That's so that cut will know where each field begins and ends. The -f switch will specify which fields you want to look at. In this diagram, you see that I used cut to extract the user name and real name--fields 1 and 5--from the /etc/passwd file.

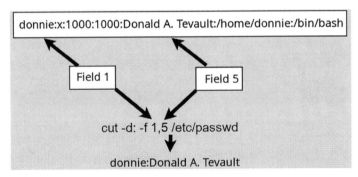

Figure 6.3: Using cut to view fields 1 and 5 of the passwd file

Since the fields in this file are separated by colons, I used -d: for the delimiter switch.

The other method for specifying the slice is the character method. With this method, you select the beginning and the ending characters of the lines of text that you want to display. In the next diagram, you see that I've saved a listing of files in my current directory to filelist.txt.

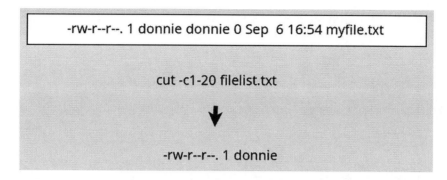

Figure 6.4: Using cut to view the first 20 characters

I've decided that I only want to look at the first 20 characters of the lines of text in this file, so I used the
`-c` switch appended with the appropriate character numbers. (Note that you can type the command
as either `cut -c1-20 filelist.txt` or as `cut -c 1-20 filelist.txt`. The blank space between the
`-c` and the first number is optional.) To further illustrate how this works, let me show you what the
output of cutting an actual multi-line file looks like:

```
[donnie@fedora ~]$ cut -c 1-20 filelist.txt
total 2109597
drwxr-xr-x  1 donnie
-rw-r--r--  1 donnie
-rw-r--r--  1 donnie
-rw-r--r--  1 donnie
. . .

. . .
drwxr-xr-x  1 donnie
-rwxr--r--  1 donnie
-rwxr--r--  1 donnie
-rwxr--r--  1 donnie
[donnie@fedora ~]$
```

You see that cut operates on every line in the file. Also, you see that the entire first line prints out because it consists of fewer than 20 characters. (The same thing happens when you use the field method.)

Of course, with both of the above examples, you have the option of using a `stdout` redirector to save
the extracted information to a text file. For example, you could do something like this:

```
[donnie@fedora ~]$ cut -d: -f 1,5 /etc/passwd > passwd_cut.txt
[donnie@fedora ~]$ cut -c1-20 myfile.txt > filelist_cut.txt
[donnie@fedora ~]$
```

As with most of the text-stream filter utilities, you can either pipe the output from cut into another utility, or pipe another utility's output into cut. In the previous example, I really didn't need to save the ls -l output to a text file. I could have just piped the ls -l output into cut, like this:

```
[donnie@fedora ~]$ ls -l myfile.txt | cut -c1-20
-rw-r--r--. 1 donnie
[donnie@fedora ~]$
```

Add on a stdout redirector, and you can also save this to a text file, like so:

```
[donnie@fedora ~]$ ls -l myfile.txt | cut -c1-20 > filelist_cut.txt
[donnie@fedora ~]$
```

That's it for cut. Now, let's do some pasting.

Using paste

Instead of joining two or more files together end-to-end as cat does, paste joins them together side-by-side. This is handy when you have two or more files of columnar data, and you want to look at all of the data in one display. Go ahead and create the two text files that you see in the following diagram Then try out the paste command that you see in the diagram.

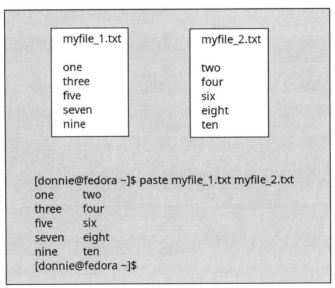

Figure 6.5: Pasting two files together with paste

There are two options that you can use with paste. The serial option, set with the -s switch, allows you to view the columns of data horizontally. Pasting the myfile_1.txt and myfile_2.txt with the -s option looks like this:

```
[donnie@fedora ~]$ paste -s myfile_1.txt myfile_2.txt
one  three  five   seven  nine
```

```
two  four   six     eight   ten
[donnie@fedora ~]$
```

The delimiter option, set by the -d switch, allows you to change how the columns are separated. If you leave out the -d switch, the columns of the pasted display will be separated by tabs, as you see in the preceding examples. To replace the tabs with something else, just place the desired replacement after the -d switch. Here, I'm using a set of double-quotes with a space in between to replace each tab with a normal space:

```
[donnie@fedora ~]$ paste -d" " myfile_1.txt myfile_2.txt
one two
three four
five six
seven eight
nine ten
[donnie@fedora ~]$
```

Now, here's a really cool trick that you can use to impress your friends. First, create four new text files as follows:

```
[donnie@fedora ~]$ cat > number_1.txt
one
1
uno
[donnie@fedora ~]$ cat > number_2.txt
two
2
dos
[donnie@fedora ~]$
[donnie@fedora ~]$ cat > number_3.txt
three
3
tres
[donnie@fedora ~]$ cat > number_4.txt
four
4
cuatro
[donnie@fedora ~]$
```

Now, put them all together with paste. This time, place the +, -, and = signs between the quotes after the -d, like this:

```
[donnie@fedora ~]$ paste -d"+-=" number_3.txt number_2.txt number_1.txt
number_4.txt
```

```
three+two-one=four
3+2-1=4
tres+dos-uno=cuatro
[donnie@fedora ~]$
```

As you see, the three arithmetic operators got placed in the appropriate places. (Oh, and in case you're wondering, uno, dos, tres, and cuatro are Spanish for 1, 2, 3, and 4.)

 This really is more than just a crazy party trick. I'll show you a practical use for this in *Chapter 11, Performing Mathematical Operations*.

Okay, now that we've pasted some files together, let's join some together.

Using join

Here's another handy utility you can use to combine two text files. (Unlike the other utilities we've looked at, you can use join for two text files, but no more than two.) To see how it works, take a look at the following diagram with its text files about famous Hollywood actors from a by-gone era. Then, go ahead and create the files, with tabs between the two columns of each file. Then, run the command that's shown in the diagram.

Figure 6.6: Joining two files together with join

As you see, the join utility replaces the tabs that were between the columns with blank spaces.

Note that in each of the two input files, the first field is the same. (In this case, it's the last name of each actor.) In the output, the first field--which we'll call the **key field**--is only listed once. The information for each actor's last name--the key field--is obtained from both of the two input files.

The thing to remember here is that you have to have one field that is identical in both input files. It doesn't have to be the first field, as we'll illustrate in the next example.

You can use the -j switch to use another field, if you so desire. You can see this with the following two lists of numbers:

```
[donnie@fedora ~]$ cat > num_1.txt
1    one
3    three
4    four
7    seven
5    five
[donnie@fedora ~]$ cat > num_2.txt
uno         one
tres        three
cuatro      four
siete       seven
cinco       five
[donnie@fedora ~]$
```

Now, let's join them:

```
[donnie@fedora ~]$ join -j 2 num_1.txt num_2.txt
one 1 uno
three 3 tres
four 4 cuatro
seven 7 siete
five 5 cinco
[donnie@fedora ~]$
```

Here, the second field is identical in each input file, so I used the -j 2 option to designate that field as the key field.

You can pipe the output of join into other utilities for customized output. If you want to number the lines of the output, pipe it into cat with the -n option, like so:

```
[donnie@fedora ~]$ join -j 2 num_1.txt num_2.txt | cat -n
     1    one 1 uno
     2    three 3 tres
     3    four 4 cuatro
     4    seven 7 siete
```

```
     5       five 5 cinco
[donnie@fedora ~]$
```

It's rather common these days for people to create spreadsheet files in **Comma Separated Values** (**csv**) format, rather than in a spreadsheet program's native format. The advantages of this are that the files can be created in any plain-text editor, and that the files can be read by any spreadsheet program. You can make join work with these files by using the -t switch to specify that the fields are separated by commas instead of by tabs. To see how that works, copy the actorfile_1.txt and actorfile_2.txt files to corresponding .csv files, like so:

```
[donnie@fedora ~]$ cp actorfile_1.txt actorfile_1.csv
[donnie@fedora ~]$ cp actorfile_2.txt actorfile_2.csv
[donnie@fedora ~]$
```

Next, edit the two .csv files to replace the tabs with commas. The first file will look like this:

```
[donnie@fedora ~]$ cat actorfile_1.csv
Benny,Jack
Allen,Fred
Ladd,Alan
Hitchcock,Alfred
Robinson,Edgar
[donnie@fedora ~]$
```

The second file will look like this:

```
[donnie@fedora ~]$ cat actorfile_2.csv
Benny,comedy
Allen,comedy
Ladd,adventure
Hitchcock,mystery
Robinson,drama
[donnie@fedora ~]$
```

Now, watch what happens when I try to use join in the normal way:

```
[donnie@fedora ~]$ join actorfile_1.csv actorfile_2.csv
join: actorfile_1.csv:2: is not sorted: Allen,Fred
join: actorfile_2.csv:4: is not sorted: Hitchcock,mystery
join: input is not in sorted order
[donnie@fedora ~]$
```

It doesn't work, because join thinks that there's only one field in each file. To make it work, I'll need to use the -t switch to specify the comma as my field separator, like so:

```
[donnie@fedora ~]$ join -t, actorfile_1.csv actorfile_2.csv
Benny,Jack,comedy
```

```
Allen,Fred,comedy
Ladd,Alan,adventure
Hitchcock,Alfred,mystery
Robinson,Edgar,drama
[donnie@fedora ~]$
```

Cool, that looks much better. And of course, you can always redirect the output into a third .csv file that you can import into any spreadsheet program.

There are still more possibilities for how you can use join, which you can see in the join man page. Combine the power of join with the power of the next utility that we're about to cover, and you'll have the makings of an easy-to-use utility for creating simple databases.

Using sort

This is a versatile utility that you can use by itself, or in conjunction with other utilities. You can use it to sort either one file, or multiple files together.

There are lots of options for different purposes. You can choose how to format your output, how you want the data sorted, and what fields you want to use for the sort. You can even perform sorts on two or more fields at once, with the primary sort on one field and secondary sorts on others.

There are a lot of ways that you can use sort. As I've said before, the only limitation is your own imagination. To start, look at the following diagram. Create the text file on your own machine and then run the commands that you see:

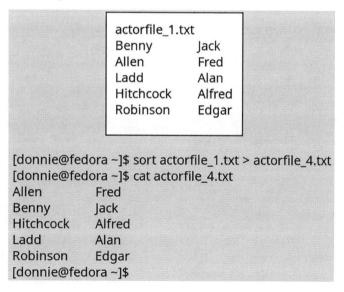

Figure 6.7: Sorting the actorfile_1.txt file

What you see in the above diagram is the simplest of sorts. By default, sorts are case-sensitive and are performed on each entire line of the input file.

In the next example, I'll show you two options at once. The first is the -k option, which allows you to sort the input file on a particular field. The second is the -o option, which allows you to save the output to a text file. Of course, you can still do that with a redirector. But, unlike the redirector, the -o option allows you to save the sorted output back to the original input file without wiping out its contents.

Before I show you that, I'm going to copy the actorfile_1.txt file over to the actorfile_5.txt file, so that I can use the actorfile_1.txt file again later:

```
[donnie@fedora ~]$ cp actorfile_1.txt actorfile_5.txt
[donnie@fedora ~]$
```

Now, let's see how this works:

```
[donnie@fedora ~]$ sort -k2 actorfile_5.txt -o actorfile_5.txt
[donnie@fedora ~]$ cat actorfile_5.txt
Ladd            Alan
Hitchcock       Alfred
Robinson        Edgar
Allen           Fred
Benny           Jack
[donnie@fedora ~]$
```

As you see, the original input file is now sorted according to the actors' first names.

Let's say that you need a list of actresses to go along with your list of actors, and that the list looks something like this:

```
[donnie@fedora ~]$ cat > actorfile_6.txt
MacLaine        Shirley
Booth           Shirley
Stanwick        Barbara
Allen           Gracie
[donnie@fedora ~]$
```

Sort the actorfile_1.txt file and the actorfile_6.txt file together, like this:

```
[donnie@fedora ~]$ sort actorfile_1.txt actorfile_6.txt
Allen           Fred
Allen           Gracie
Benny           Jack
Booth           Shirley
Hitchcock       Alfred
Ladd            Alan
MacLaine        Shirley
Robinson        Edgar
```

```
Stanwick          Barbara
[donnie@fedora ~]$
```

After you view the results on screen, save the results to a new file, like this:

```
[donnie@fedora ~]$ sort actorfile_1.txt actorfile_6.txt -o actorfile_7.txt
[donnie@fedora ~]$
```

You can also pipe this through the tee utility, so that you can see the output on screen and save it to a file at the same time.

```
[donnie@fedora ~]$ sort actorfile_1.txt actorfile_6.txt | tee actorfile_8.txt
Allen             Fred
Allen             Gracie
Benny             Jack
Booth             Shirley
Hitchcock         Alfred
Ladd              Alan
MacLaine          Shirley
Robinson          Edgar
Stanwick          Barbara
[donnie@fedora ~]$ ls -l actorfile_8.txt
-rw-r--r--. 1 donnie donnie 130 Sep  6 19:02 actorfile_8.txt
[donnie@fedora ~]$
```

There are a few other options that could help you out in special situations. To demonstrate, create the file fruit.txt, which will look like this:

```
[donnie@fedora ~]$ cat > fruit.txt
Peach
Peach
apricot
peach
Apricot
[donnie@fedora ~]$
```

You see that there are some duplicate entries. Let's see what a normal sort would look like:

```
[donnie@fedora ~]$ sort fruit.txt
apricot
Apricot
peach
Peach
Peach
[donnie@fedora ~]$
```

Since you only need one entry for each fruit, use the `-u` option to get rid of duplicate entries, like this:

```
[donnie@fedora ~]$ sort -u fruit.txt
apricot
Apricot
peach
Peach
[donnie@fedora ~]$
```

That looks somewhat better. But, do you really need to have the fruit names repeated in both upper-case and lower-case? If not, then add the `-f` switch to make `sort` look at all letters as if they were uppercase, like so:

```
[donnie@fedora ~]$ sort -uf fruit.txt
apricot
Peach
[donnie@fedora ~]$
```

Some older Linux books may tell you that text files with a mixture of upper-case and lower-case letters in the sorted fields won't sort properly unless you use the `-f` switch.

For example, the name "MacLeod" would have come before the name "Mack" because the upper-case L would have been placed before the lower-case k. The `-f` switch would have forced `sort` to place the list items in proper alphabetical order, regardless of case. However, with the newer Linux distros, this is no longer a problem. The `-f` switch still has its uses, as you see in the above example. But, this problem that those other Linux books tell you about no longer exists.

For our next demonstration, create a file with a list of numbers.

```
[donnie@fedora ~]$ cat > numbers.txt
1
5
10
78
78034
10053
[donnie@fedora ~]$
```

Here's what you'll get when you try to sort the list:

```
[donnie@fedora ~]$ sort numbers.txt
1
10
10053
```

```
5
78
78034
[donnie@fedora ~]$
```

That's probably not what you want. To make it sort in proper numerical order, use the -n switch, like so:

```
[donnie@fedora ~]$ sort -n numbers.txt
1
5
10
78
10053
78034
[donnie@fedora ~]$
```

Add the -r switch to sort the file in reverse order:

```
[donnie@fedora ~]$ sort -nr numbers.txt
78034
10053
78
10
5
1
[donnie@fedora ~]$
```

This time, just for fun, create a text file with some decimals and negative numbers, as well as some positive numbers:

```
[donnie@fedora ~]$ cat > numbers_2.txt
-68
57
2.6
1.24
10000
14
1.4
8
80
8.2
.8
-87
[donnie@fedora ~]$
```

Now, let's see how this sorts out without any option switches:

```
[donnie@fedora ~]$ sort numbers_2.txt
10000
1.24
1.4
14
2.6
57
-68
.8
8
80
8.2
-87
[donnie@fedora ~]$
```

As before, add the -n switch to sort the list in proper numerical order:

```
[donnie@fedora ~]$ sort -n numbers_2.txt
-87
-68
.8
1.24
1.4
2.6
8
8.2
14
57
80
10000
[donnie@fedora ~]$
```

For our next example, let's create a file list of used automobiles. We'll list the make, model, year, mileage (in thousands), and the selling price. (If you're not here with me in the United States, just pretend that the miles are really kilometers.) Here's what the list looks like:

```
[donnie@fedora ~]$ cat > autos.txt
plymouth        satellite    1970    154     600
plymouth        fury         1970    73      2500
plymouth        breeze       1996    116     4300
chevy           malibu       2000    60      3000
ford            mustang 1965    45      10000
```

```
volvo              s80          1998    102     9850
ford               thunderbird  2003    15      3500
chevy              malibu       1999    50      3500
bmw                325i         1985    115     450
bmw                325i         1985    60      1000
honda              accord       2001    30      6000
ford               taurus       2004    10      17000
toyota             rav4         2002    180     750
chevy              impala       1985    85      1550
ford               explorer     2003    25      9500
jeep               wrangler     2003    54      1600
edsel              corsair 1958 47      750
ford               galaxie 1964 128     60
[donnie@fedora ~]$
```

We'll first do a normal sort, like so:

```
[donnie@fedora ~]$ sort autos.txt
bmw                325i         1985    115     450
bmw                325i         1985    60      1000
chevy              impala       1985    85      1550
chevy              malibu       1999    50      3500
chevy              malibu       2000    60      3000
edsel              corsair 1958 47      750
ford               explorer     2003    25      9500
ford               galaxie 1964 128     60
ford               mustang 1965 45      10000
ford               taurus       2004    10      17000
ford               thunderbird  2003    15      3500
honda              accord       2001    30      6000
jeep               wrangler     2003    54      1600
plymouth           breeze       1996    116     4300
plymouth           fury         1970    73      2500
plymouth           satellite    1970    154     600
toyota             rav4         2002    180     750
volvo              s80          1998    102     9850
[donnie@fedora ~]$
```

By default, a sort operation will start with the first column of a file, and go through each entire row until it runs out of non-unique entries. Here, we see that everything sorts properly until it gets to the year column. (We'll fix that in a moment.)

Whenever there is more than one car of a certain make, the sort will continue to the model column. When there is more than one of a given model, the sort will continue on to the year column. The mileage column is considered in the sort as well, even though it may not look like it in this example. That's because of the problem with numerical sorting that I showed you a couple of pages ago.

In order to sort numbers in numerical order instead of machine-sort order, you have to use the -n switch. We can do that by using the -k switch to specify the individual columns that we want to sort, like so:

```
[donnie@fedora ~]$ sort -k1,3 -k4n autos.txt
bmw             325i        1985    60      1000
bmw             325i        1985    115     450
chevy           impala      1985    85      1550
chevy           malibu      1999    50      3500
chevy           malibu      2000    60      3000
edsel           corsair 1958    47      750
ford            explorer    2003    25      9500
ford            galaxie 1964    128     60
ford            mustang 1965    45      10000
ford            taurus      2004    10      17000
ford            thunderbird 2003    15      3500
honda           accord      2001    30      6000
jeep            wrangler    2003    54      1600
plymouth        breeze      1996    116     4300
plymouth        fury        1970    73      2500
plymouth        satellite   1970    154     600
toyota          rav4        2002    180     750
volvo           s80         1998    102     9850
[donnie@fedora ~]$
```

The -k1,3 option means to sort on fields one through three. (In other words, sort on the make, model, and year fields.) The -k4n option means to also sort on the fourth (the mileage) field in numerical order.

Note that you can specify sort options for individual fields. Also note that the price column will never be considered in this sort, since no line entries are completely identical up through the mileage column.

Next, let's sort our autos list first by both manufacturer and then by price. For this, you would have to sort on fields one and five. Since we already know that we need the -n switch for column five to sort properly, we'll go ahead and add it in, like so:

```
[donnie@fedora ~]$ sort -k 1 -k5n autos.txt
bmw             325i        1985    115     450
bmw             325i        1985    60      1000
chevy           impala      1985    85      1550
chevy           malibu      1999    50      3500
chevy           malibu      2000    60      3000
```

edsel	corsair 1958	47	750	
ford	explorer	2003	25	9500
ford	galaxie 1964	128	60	
ford	mustang 1965	45	10000	
ford	taurus	2004	10	17000
ford	thunderbird	2003	15	3500
honda	accord	2001	30	6000
jeep	wrangler	2003	54	1600
plymouth	breeze	1996	116	4300
plymouth	fury	1970	73	2500
plymouth	satellite	1970	154	600
toyota	rav4	2002	180	750
volvo	s80	1998	102	9850
[donnie@fedora ~]$				

Whenever you specify two or more -k switches, sort will perform its operation in more than one pass. For the first pass, it will sort on the field specified with the first -k switch. Sorts on the remaining specified fields will be performed in subsequent passes.

 Here, we see that sort ignored the second -k switch. That's because the first -k switch didn't specify an end point for its sort. So, sort evaluated each entire line on the first pass, and decided that a second pass wasn't needed.

Now, let's specify an endpoint for the first -k switch to see if that makes a difference.

[donnie@fedora ~]$ sort -k1,1 -k5n autos.txt				
bmw	325i	1985	115	450
bmw	325i	1985	60	1000
chevy	impala	1985	85	1550
chevy	malibu	2000	60	3000
chevy	malibu	1999	50	3500
edsel	corsair 1958	47	750	
ford	galaxie 1964	128	60	
ford	thunderbird	2003	15	3500
ford	explorer	2003	25	9500
ford	mustang 1965	45	10000	
ford	taurus	2004	10	17000
honda	accord	2001	30	6000
jeep	wrangler	2003	54	1600
plymouth	satellite	1970	154	600
plymouth	fury	1970	73	2500
plymouth	breeze	1996	116	4300

```
toyota              rav4            2002    180     750
volvo               s80             1998    102     9850
[donnie@fedora ~]$
```

The -k1,1 option means that we want the first pass to sort on the first—and only the first—field of our file. By adding that end point, our sort works as we want it to.

You don't have to start with the first field for your sorts. For this next example, we'll sort first by field three (year), and then by field one (make).

```
[donnie@fedora ~]$ sort -k3 -k1 autos.txt
edsel               corsair         1958    47      750
ford                galaxie         1964    128     60
ford                mustang         1965    45      10000
plymouth            satellite       1970    154     600
plymouth            fury            1970    73      2500
bmw                 325i            1985    115     450
bmw                 325i            1985    60      1000
chevy               impala          1985    85      1550
plymouth            breeze          1996    116     4300
volvo               s80             1998    102     9850
chevy               malibu          1999    50      3500
chevy               malibu          2000    60      3000
honda               accord          2001    30      6000
toyota              rav4            2002    180     750
ford                thunderbird     2003    15      3500
ford                explorer        2003    25      9500
jeep                wrangler        2003    54      1600
ford                taurus          2004    10      17000
[donnie@fedora ~]$
```

Again, you can see what happens when you don't specify an end point for your first sort field. So, let's try this again.

```
[donnie@fedora ~]$ sort -k3,3 -k1 autos.txt
edsel               corsair         1958    47      750
ford                galaxie         1964    128     60
ford                mustang         1965    45      10000
plymouth            fury            1970    73      2500
plymouth            satellite       1970    154     600
bmw                 325i            1985    115     450
bmw                 325i            1985    60      1000
chevy               impala          1985    85      1550
plymouth            breeze          1996    116     4300
```

```
volvo            s80            1998   102   9850
chevy            malibu         1999   50    3500
chevy            malibu         2000   60    3000
honda            accord         2001   30    6000
toyota           rav4           2002   180   750
ford             explorer       2003   25    9500
ford             thunderbird    2003   15    3500
jeep             wrangler       2003   54    1600
ford             taurus         2004   10    17000
[donnie@fedora ~]$
```

Okay, so it still didn't work. Everything is still sorted correctly by year, but not by make. We're not the ones to give up here, so let's try it one more time.

```
[donnie@fedora ~]$ sort -b -k3,3 -k1 autos.txt
edsel            corsair        1958   47    750
ford             galaxie        1964   128   60
ford             mustang        1965   45    10000
plymouth         fury           1970   73    2500
plymouth         satellite      1970   154   600
bmw              325i           1985   115   450
bmw              325i           1985   60    1000
chevy            impala         1985   85    1550
plymouth         breeze         1996   116   4300
volvo            s80            1998   102   9850
chevy            malibu         1999   50    3500
chevy            malibu         2000   60    3000
honda            accord         2001   30    6000
toyota           rav4           2002   180   750
ford             explorer       2003   25    9500
ford             thunderbird    2003   15    3500
jeep             wrangler       2003   54    1600
ford             taurus         2004   10    17000
[donnie@fedora ~]$
```

Note how in four out of the five fields, the text strings are of different lengths. Theoretically, the extra blank spaces in the lines with shorter text strings should have adversely affected all of the sort operations that we've performed. For some reason, however, only this last sort operation was affected. By adding the -b switch, we're telling sort to ignore the extra blank spaces.

Okay, maybe you don't have a collection of antique automobiles. But, you might have lists of other items that you'll need to sort in various ways. Keep in mind that you can use the techniques that I've presented here for any type of list that you might have.

All right, that's enough for the vintage automobiles. Let's now look at sorting lists of months. First, let's create the list, like so:

```
[donnie@fedora ~]$ cat > dates.txt
Dec  2023
jan  2023
Oct  2023
Sep  2022
Feb  2022
mar  2023
may  2022
[donnie@fedora ~]$
```

Now, use the -M switch to sort the list by month:

```
[donnie@fedora ~]$ sort -M dates.txt
jan  2023
Feb  2022
mar  2023
may  2022
Sep  2022
Oct  2023
Dec  2023
[donnie@fedora ~]$
```

As you see, the -M switch isn't case-sensitive.

Now, use the techniques you've learned in the previous examples to sort first by year, and then by month, like so:

```
[donnie@fedora ~]$ sort -k2,2 -k1M dates.txt
Feb  2022
may  2022
Sep  2022
jan  2023
mar  2023
Oct  2023
Dec  2023
[donnie@fedora ~]$
```

And finally, as promised, I'll now show you how to use join and sort together to somewhat emulate a simple relational database program. Let's first take a peek at the input files, which are the same ones that we used before. First, we have actorfile_1.txt:

```
[donnie@fedora ~]$ cat actorfile_1.txt
```

```
Benny           Jack
Allen           Fred
Ladd            Alan
Hitchcock       Alfred
Robinson        Edgar
[donnie@fedora ~]$
```

The second input file is `actorfile_2.txt`, which looks like this:

```
[donnie@fedora ~]$ cat actorfile_2.txt
Benny           comedy
Allen           comedy
Ladd            adventure
Hitchcock       mystery
Robinson        drama
[donnie@fedora ~]$
```

Now, we'll join them together and feed the results through `sort`. (Again, note how `join` turns the tabs in the input into normal spaces.)

```
[donnie@fedora ~]$ join actorfile_1.txt actorfile_2.txt | sort
Allen Fred comedy
Benny Jack comedy
Hitchcock Alfred mystery
Ladd Alan adventure
Robinson Edgar drama
[donnie@fedora ~]$
```

Okay, this doesn't look so great, because `join` doesn't maintain proper column alignment. Let's fix that by piping the output into the `column -t` command, like this:

```
donnie@fedora:~$ join actorfile_1.txt actorfile_2.txt | sort | column -t
Allen           Fred            comedy
Benny           Jack            comedy
Hitchcock       Alfred          mystery
Ladd            Alan            adventure
Robinson        Edgar           drama
donnie@fedora:~$
```

We can use the techniques we've already learned to sort by category, and then by last name.

```
[donnie@fedora ~]$ join actorfile_1.txt actorfile_2.txt | sort -b -k3,3 -k1
Ladd Alan adventure
Allen Fred comedy
Benny Jack comedy
```

```
Robinson Edgar drama
Hitchcock Alfred mystery
[donnie@fedora ~]$
```

As you see, there's a lot to this topic, but don't let that discourage you. With a little practice, you'll be sorting with the pros.

Okay, that just about wraps things up for this chapter. Let's summarize and move on.

Summary

As a Linux systems administrator, a developer, or even an office clerk who uses Linux, you might need to extract and format data from either text files or the output of system commands. In this chapter you learned about various text-stream filters and how they can be useful for helping you do this. There are plenty more filters left to cover, which we'll do in the next chapter. I'll see you there.

Questions

1. Which of the following utilities would you use to join two or more files together side-by-side?

    a. join

    b. cat

    c. tac

    d. paste

2. Which two of the following utilities can you use together to create simple databases? (Choose two.)

    a. paste

    b. sort

    c. join

    d. cat

3. Which of the following commands would properly save the output of the cat operation?

    a. cat file1.txt file2.txt > file1.txt

    b. cat file1.txt file2.txt > file2.txt

    c. cat file1.txt file2.txt > file3.txt

4. You want sort to sort on Field 1, and only Field 1, of your file. What would your command look like?

    a. sort -F1 myfile.txt

    b. sort -F1,1 myfile.txt

    c. sort -k1 myfile.txt

    d. sort -k1,1 myfile.txt

5. Which of the following option switches would you use with cat to eliminate duplicate blank lines?

    a. `-d`

    b. `-s`

    c. `-o`

    d. `-u`

Further Reading

- Linux Professional Institute Exam 101 Objectives: `https://www.lpi.org/our-certifications/exam-101-objectives`

- How to Use the join Command on Linux: `https://www.howtogeek.com/542677/how-to-use-the-join-command-on-linux/`

- sort Command Examples: `https://linuxhandbook.com/sort-command/`

Answers

1. d
2. b and c
3. c
4. d
5. b

Join our community on Discord!

Read this book alongside other users, Linux experts, and the author himself.

Ask questions, provide solutions to other readers, chat with the author via Ask Me Anything sessions, and much more. Scan the QR code or visit the link to join the community.

`https://packt.link/SecNet`

7

Text Stream Filters – Part 2

In this chapter, we'll continue our look at various text-stream filters. As you go through this chapter, I challenge you to use your imagination. Instead of thinking of these filter utilities as something you have to learn because I said so, or because you need to learn them for a Linux certification exam, try to imagine the ways in which each of these utilities can help you format your own text files and reports. Trust me, you'll never know when one or more of these utilities could come in handy.

Here are the topics that we'll cover in this chapter:

- Using expand
- Using unexpand
- Using nl
- Using head
- Using tail
- Using head and tail together
- Using od
- Using uniq
- Using wc
- Using fmt
- Using split
- Using tr
- Using xargs
- Using pr
- Printing from the Command-line

They're not hard to master, but there is a lot to cover. So if you're ready, let's get started.

Technical Requirements

Use either of your virtual machines, because things will work the same on either of them. Or, if your host machine is running either Linux or macOS, feel free to use it instead of a virtual machine. I won't be providing an actual hands-on lab, so feel free to follow along on your own machine as you read through the chapter. And, as before, you can download the text files that you'll need from the GitHub repository.

Using expand

There may be times when a text document that you create with columnar data just won't display correctly under certain circumstances. It may be because you separated the columns with tabs instead of with spaces. Sometimes, tabs won't display correctly, and you'll need to replace them with spaces.

To look at this, create the expand.txt text file. There will be three columns of data with two tabs between each column. The file will look like this:

```
[donnie@fedora ~]$ cat > expand.txt
one             two             three
four            five            six
seven           eight           nine
[donnie@fedora ~]$
```

Now, expand the file and note the output. It should look like this:

```
[donnie@fedora ~]$ expand expand.txt
one                     two             three
four                    five            six
seven                   eight           nine
[donnie@fedora ~]$
```

Since I still have this creepy habit of reading your mind, I know that you're wondering what's really going on, since the expanded output looks the same as the original file. This is where looks can be deceiving. When you expanded the file, each tab that you placed between the columns was replaced by a number of blank spaces. The number of spaces varies from line-to-line, depending upon how many characters are in each text string. That way, the columns will still all line up evenly.

> Actually, expand replaces each whole tab character with eight spaces. But when you have text strings of varying lengths, it doesn't appear to do that. That's because expand adjusts the number of blank spaces it inserts to keep all of the columns lined up. If you have a text file with more than one tab between the columns and with varying length text strings, all but one of the tabs will be replaced by exactly eight spaces.

If you want to prove this, save the expanded output to a new file, and then open the new file with your favorite text editor. In my case, I'll use vim, like so:

```
[donnie@fedora ~]$ expand expand.txt > expand_2.txt
[donnie@fedora ~]$ vim expand_2.txt
```

Now, move your cursor to the blank area between two of the columns. Move to the left or right between the columns, and you'll see that you'll only move one space at a time. Close this file, and open the original file. When you move the cursor between the columns of this file, you'll see that it moves by the length of a tab, instead of by just one space.

There are two options that you can use with expand. The first is the -t option. This lets you set the number of spaces you want to use in place of the tabs, instead of using the default of eight. Here, we want to replace each tab with only two blank spaces.

```
[donnie@fedora ~]$ expand -t2 expand.txt
one     two     three
four    five    six
seven   eight   nine
[donnie@fedora ~]$
```

With only two spaces replacing each tab, expand failed to keep the columns properly aligned. Feel free to experiment with other -t values to see how things turn out.

With the -i switch, you can instruct expand to only replace tabs that are at the beginning of each line. Subsequent tabs in each line will remain unaltered. To see how it works, copy the expand_1.txt file to the expand_1a.txt file, like so:

```
donnie@fedora:~$ cp expand_1.txt expand_1a.txt
donnie@fedora:~$
```

Open expand_1a.txt in your text editor, and insert one tab at the beginning of line 1, two tabs at the beginning of line 2, and three tabs at the beginning of line 3. The edited file should now look like this:

```
donnie@fedora:~$ cat expand_1a.txt
    one     two     three
        four    five    six
            seven   eight   nine
donnie@fedora:~$
```

Using the -i option, expand this file into the expand_1b.txt file, like so:

```
donnie@fedora:~$ expand -i expand_1a.txt > expand_1b.txt
donnie@fedora:~$
```

Open expand_1b.txt in your text editor, and verify that only the tabs that preceded each line were replaced with blank spaces.

Guess what? That's all I have to say about expand. Now, let's go in the opposite direction.

Using unexpand

Now that I've told you what expand does, do I really need to tell you what unexpand does? That's right, you guessed it. unexpand removes the blank spaces from between columns, and replaces them with tabs. There are a couple of slight catches, though. By default, unexpand only operates on spaces that are at the beginning of a line. That's just the opposite of how expand works with tabs. So, if you want to replace all spaces in a line with tabs, you'll need to use the -a switch. The second catch is that by default, unexpand only works if it sees eight consecutive blank spaces. Any grouping of fewer than eight consecutive blank spaces won't get converted to tabs. (You can change that behavior with the -t switch, as you'll see in a few moments.)

I'll demonstrate by unexpanding the expand_2.txt file that I've just created in the expand section, using the -a option, like so:

```
[donnie@fedora ~]$ unexpand -a expand_2.txt
one             two           three
four            five          six
seven           eight         nine
[donnie@fedora ~]$
```

Again, you can't really tell the difference. To see the difference, save the results to a new file, like so:

```
[donnie@fedora ~]$ unexpand -a expand_2.txt > unexpand.txt
[donnie@fedora ~]$
```

Open the new file in your favorite text editor. Now, when you move your cursor between the columns, you'll see that it jumps by the length of a tab, instead of by just one space. In other words, it's now just like the original file that I expanded in the previous section.

 This works because when I used expand to create the expand_2.txt file, the tabs between the columns were all replaced by eight or more blank spaces.

Now, I told you before that by default, unexpand only operates on the blank spaces that are at the beginning of a line. To see that, open the expand_3.txt file, which will look like this:

```
donnie@fedora:~$ cat expand_3.txt
        one         two       three
    four        five    six
  seven         eight           nine
donnie@fedora:~$
```

It's rather ugly because nothing is in alignment, but in this case that's what we want. The first line is preceded by eight blank spaces, the second line is preceded by four blank spaces, and the third line is preceded by two blank spaces. Between the columns are varying numbers of blank spaces.

Next, create the unexpand_2.txt file by unexpanding the expand_3.txt file, like so:

```
donnie@fedora:~$ unexpand expand_3.txt > unexpand_2.txt
donnie@fedora:~$
```

Open the unexpand_2.txt file in your text editor and verify that only the eight blank spaces at the beginning of the first line were replaced by a tab. Close the file and repeat the command with the -t4 option, like this:

```
donnie@fedora:~$ unexpand -t4 expand_3.txt > unexpand_2.txt
donnie@fedora:~$
```

This time, you should see that the blank spaces at the beginning of both lines 1 and 2 have been replaced by tabs. Try this again with the -t2 option, and you'll see that the blank spaces that precede all three lines are replaced by tabs. Finally, run these commands again with the -a option to perform a global replacement of the blank spaces.

I have to confess that for a long time, I never thought that I would use either expand or unexpand for anything. But, I was wrong. Several years ago, a former client tasked me with teaching a Kali Linux course. The book that I was using had a shell script that was supposed to automatically extract the IP address from the output of the ifconfig command. The script didn't work though, because after the author wrote the book someone changed the ifconfig code so that the output would be formatted differently.

I had to modify the script to make it work, and I used either expand or unexpand as part of the fix. (That was long ago, so I don't remember which one I used. But, that doesn't matter.) So, it goes to show that you just never know. (Yes, I am a poet.)

Okay, enough of expanding and unexpanding. Let's do some numbering.

Using nl

The nl utility is used for numbering lines of a text file. It's easy to use, and there are only a few options that you need to remember. Let's start by creating a file with ten consecutive lines, like so:

```
[donnie@fedora ~]$ cat > lines.txt
This is line one.
This is line two.
This is line three.
This is line four.
This is line five
This is line six
This is line seven.
This is line eight.
This is line nine.
This is line ten.
[donnie@fedora ~]$
```

Let's number the lines in the file, like so:

```
[donnie@fedora ~]$ nl lines.txt
     1 This is line one.
     2 This is line two.
     3 This is line three.
     4 This is line four.
     5 This is line five
     6 This is line six
     7 This is line seven.
     8 This is line eight.
     9 This is line nine.
    10 This is line ten.
[donnie@fedora ~]$
```

Now, let's create another file just like this one, except that we'll insert a few blank lines.

```
[donnie@fedora ~]$ cat > lines_2.txt
This is line one.

This is line two.

This is line three.
This is line four.
This is line five.


This is line six.

This is line seven.
This is line eight.
This is line nine.


This is line ten.
[donnie@fedora ~]$
```

Again, we'll number this file without specifying any options.

```
[donnie@fedora ~]$ nl lines_2.txt
     1 This is line one.

     2 This is line two.
```

```
      3 This is line three.
      4 This is line four.
      5 This is line five.



      6 This is line six.


      7 This is line seven.
      8 This is line eight.
      9 This is line nine.



     10 This is line ten.
[donnie@fedora ~]$
```

If you don't specify any options, only the non-blank lines will be numbered. Use the -b switch with the appropriate options to change that behavior. With the a option, you can number all lines, including the blanks. (By the way, the -b switch stands for **body**. In other words, this switch sets the way in which nl numbers lines in the body of the file. In just a moment, I'll show you how this comes into play.)

```
[donnie@fedora ~]$ nl -ba lines_2.txt
      1 This is line one.
      2
      3 This is line two.
      4
      5 This is line three.
      6 This is line four.
      7 This is line five.
      8
      9
     10 This is line six.
     11
     12 This is line seven.
     13 This is line eight.
     14 This is line nine.
     15
     16
     17 This is line ten.
[donnie@fedora ~]$
```

The -bt option causes nl to only number non-empty lines in the text file body, while the -bn option tells nl not to number lines at all in the text file body. This may sound a bit strange to you, since the first option defines what is already default behavior, and the second option seems to defeat the whole purpose of using nl. I'll clarify all of this in just a moment.

When you create a text file, you can use a special set of delimiters to define a header, a body, and a footer that will be used by nl.

As you can see in the following diagram, you do this by placing the appropriate series of backslashes and colons at the start of each section.

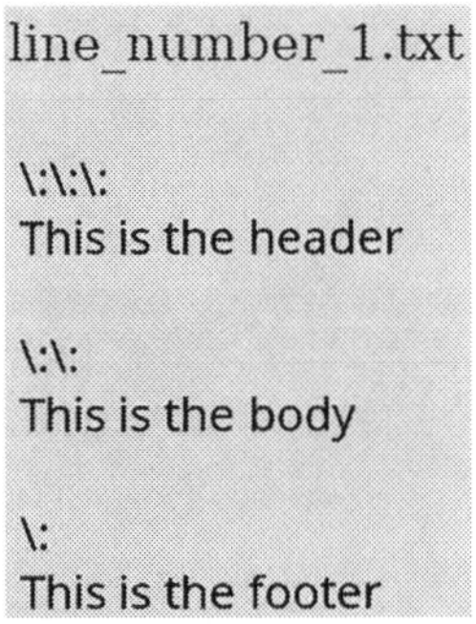

line_number_1.txt

\:\:\:
This is the header

\:\:
This is the body

\:
This is the footer

Figure 7.1: The header, body, and footer sections of a text file

Three of each character defines the header, two of each defines the body, and one of each defines the footer. The nl utility allows you to number each of these sections in its own way. Put this to the test by creating your own three-section text file, which will look like this:

```
[donnie@fedora ~]$ cat > line_number_1.txt
\:\:\:
This is the file header.
\:\:
This is the body of the file.
There's not a lot to say, so I'll
close it.
\:
This is the footer.
[donnie@fedora ~]$
```

When using nl without specifying any options, only the non-blank lines in the body will get numbered, as you see here:

```
[donnie@fedora ~]$ nl line_number_1.txt
         This is the file header.

     1    This is the body of the file.
     2    There's not a lot to say, so I'll
```

```
     3       close it.

         This is the footer.
[donnie@fedora ~]$
```

To number lines in the header and footer, you would use the -h and the -f switches. The options that go with those switches are the same as the ones that go with the -b switch. So, to number all lines in the header as well as the non-blank lines in the body, you would use the -ha option, like so:

```
[donnie@fedora ~]$ nl -ha line_number_1.txt
     1       This is the file header.
     2
     1       This is the body of the file.
     2       There's not a lot to say, so I'll
     3       close it.

         This is the footer.
[donnie@fedora ~]$
```

To number only non-blank lines in the header and non-blank lines in the body, use the -ht option, like so:

```
[donnie@fedora ~]$ nl -ht line_number_1.txt
     1       This is the file header.

     1       This is the body of the file.
     2       There's not a lot to say, so I'll
     3       close it.

         This is the footer.
[donnie@fedora ~]$
```

Next, let's number all lines in the footer, like so:

```
[donnie@fedora ~]$ nl -fa line_number_1.txt
         This is the file header.

     1       This is the body of the file.
     2       There's not a lot to say, so I'll
     3       close it.

     1       This is the footer.
[donnie@fedora ~]$
```

This time, the footer got numbered, but the header didn't. In both cases, the non-blank lines in the body got numbered, even though I didn't specify for nl to do that. To prevent nl from numbering lines in the body while numbering all lines in both the header and footer, include the -bn option, like this:

```
[donnie@fedora ~]$ nl -bn -ha -fa line_number_1.txt
     1      This is the file header.
     2

       This is the body of the file.
       There's not a lot to say, so I'll
       close it.


     1      This is the footer.
[donnie@fedora ~]$
```

You can also have nl search for lines that contain a certain text string, and number only those lines. For this, you would use the p option. Let's take our first text file, which we'll call lines.txt, and number only the line that contains the word seven. (Note that you can't have a space between the p and the string for which you're searching.) It will look something like this:

```
[donnie@fedora ~]$ nl -bpseven lines.txt
       This is line one.
       This is line two.
       This is line three.
       This is line four.
       This is line five
       This is line six
     1      This is line seven.
       This is line eight.
       This is line nine.
       This is line ten.
[donnie@fedora ~]$
```

Now, let's create a file that's a tad bit more realistic. We'll even go all out and give it header, body, and footer.

```
[donnie@fedora ~]$ cat > macgruder.txt
\:\:\:
This is the file outlining the strategy
for the MacGruder Corporation account.
\:\:
It is vitally important to maintain close
working relations with the IT gurus at
the MacGruder Corporation. This account
represents our company's best opportunity
```

```
in ages to make a huge sale of servers,
desktop computers, routers, and software
services. We must give full attention
to the needs and wants of the MacGruder
Corporation.
\:
This document contains sensitive
information about the MacGruder
Corporation.
[donnie@fedora ~]$
```

Now, number every line in the body that contains the word MacGruder, like this:

```
[donnie@fedora ~]$ nl -bpMacGruder macgruder.txt
       This is the file outlining the strategy
       for the MacGruder Corporation account.

       It is vitally important to maintain close
       working relations with the IT gurus at
    1     the MacGruder Corporation. This account
       represents our company's best opportunity
       in ages to make a huge sale of servers,
       desktop computers, routers, and software
       services. We must give full attention
    2     to the needs and wants of the MacGruder
       Corporation.

       This document contains sensitive
       information about the MacGruder
       Corporation.
[donnie@fedora ~]$
```

If you specify for nl to only number the MacGruder lines for the header and/or the footer without specifying anything for the body, nl will also number all non-blank body lines by default, as you see here:

```
[donnie@fedora ~]$ nl -hpMacGruder -fpMacGruder macgruder.txt
       This is the file outlining the strategy
    1     for the MacGruder Corporation account.

    1     It is vitally important to maintain close
    2     working relations with the IT gurus at
    3     the MacGruder Corporation. This account
    4     represents our company's best opportunity
```

```
     5          in ages to make a huge sale of servers,

     6          desktop computers, routers, and software

     7          services. We must give full attention

     8          to the needs and wants of the MacGruder

     9          Corporation.


        This document contains sensitive

     1          information about the MacGruder

        Corporation.
[donnie@fedora ~]$                                      /
```

Include the -bn option to only number the MacGruder lines in the header and/or footer, like this:

```
[donnie@fedora ~]$ nl -bn -hpMacGruder -fpMacGruder macgruder.txt
        This is the file outlining the strategy

     1          for the MacGruder Corporation account.


        It is vitally important to maintain close

        working relations with the IT gurus at

        the MacGruder Corporation. This account

        represents our company's best opportunity

        in ages to make a huge sale of servers,

        desktop computers, routers, and software

        services. We must give full attention

        to the needs and wants of the MacGruder

        Corporation.


        This document contains sensitive

     1          information about the MacGruder

        Corporation.
[donnie@fedora ~]$
```

And now, you're wondering when you would ever create a text file with these nl-style headers and footers. Well, the answer is--drum-roll, please--I have no idea. After some rather extensive research, I've not found any other utility that displays these headers and footers as actual headers and footers. In fact, the utilities I've found that convert text files to other formats can insert their own headers and footers, but they'll display the nl-style headers and footers as just part of the normal document.

However, nl is still useful for times when you need to insert line numbers into files that consist of nothing but a body. Also, if you plan to take a Linux certification exam, you'll need to know about the header, body, and footer concept of nl-style text files, because you just might see some questions about it.

The man page for nl is seriously deficient, so you'll instead want to consult the info page for more nl information and options. The command to run for that is:

```
[donnie@fedora ~]$ info nl
```

That does it for nl. Let's move on ahead.

Using head

If you only want to view a certain number of lines from the beginning of a text file, use the head utility. To demonstrate, I'll be showing you files that are here on my Fedora workstation. If you don't have the same exact files on your own machine, feel free to use others.

 By default, head displays the first ten lines of a file. I'll show you in just a bit how to change that.

Let's start by entering the /var/log/ directory, and looking at the first ten lines of the boot.log file, like this:

```
[donnie@fedora ~]$ cd /var/log
[donnie@fedora log]$ sudo head boot.log
[  OK  ] Finished logrotate.service - Rotate log files.
[FAILED] Failed to start vmware.ser… starts and stops VMware services.
See 'systemctl status vmware.service' for details.
        Starting vmware-USBArbitra…s and stops the USB Arbitrator....
[  OK  ] Started rsyslog.service - System Logging Service.
[  OK  ] Started chronyd.service - NTP client/server.
[  OK  ] Started vmware-USBArbitrat…rts and stops the USB Arbitrator..
        Starting livesys-late.serv…ate init script for live image....
[  OK  ] Started livesys-late.servi… Late init script for live image..
[  OK  ] Started dbus-broker.service - D-Bus System Message Bus.
[donnie@fedora log]$
```

Use the -n switch to change the number of lines that you want to see. To only see the first five lines, enter this:

```
[donnie@fedora log]$ sudo head -n5 boot.log
[  OK  ] Finished logrotate.service - Rotate log files.
[FAILED] Failed to start vmware.ser… starts and stops VMware services.
See 'systemctl status vmware.service' for details.
        Starting vmware-USBArbitra…s and stops the USB Arbitrator....
[  OK  ] Started rsyslog.service - System Logging Service.
[donnie@fedora log]$
```

In this case, the -n is optional. You'll get the same results by running the command like this:

```
[donnie@fedora log]$ sudo head -5 boot.log
```

The dash in front of the number means that the number is an option. It doesn't mean that the number is negative. But, as you'll see in a moment, some commands will require you to use the -n.

You can choose to view the first lines from more than one file at the same time by including multiple filenames in your command. Here, we're looking at the first five lines of the boot.log file and the cron file.

```
[donnie@fedora log]$ sudo head -n5 boot.log cron
[sudo] password for donnie:
==> boot.log <==
[  OK  ] Finished logrotate.service - Rotate log files.
[FAILED] Failed to start vmware.ser… starts and stops VMware services.
See 'systemctl status vmware.service' for details.
         Starting vmware-USBArbitra…s and stops the USB Arbitrator....
[  OK  ] Started rsyslog.service - System Logging Service.
==> cron <==
Sep  9 17:36:05 fedora crond[2062]: (CRON) INFO (Shutting down)
Sep 11 15:27:58 fedora crond[2038]: (CRON) STARTUP (1.6.1)
Sep 11 15:27:58 fedora crond[2038]: (CRON) INFO (Syslog will be used instead of
sendmail.)
Sep 11 15:27:58 fedora crond[2038]: (CRON) INFO (RANDOM_DELAY will be scaled
with factor 85% if used.)
Sep 11 15:27:58 fedora crond[2038]: (CRON) INFO (running with inotify support)
[donnie@fedora log]$
```

Use the -q option to enable quiet mode. That way, when you view lines from more than one file at a time, you won't see the header lines for the files. (This could come in handy if you're running head from within a shell script.)

Also, note how you can combine options with only one dash. In this case, use of the -n is mandatory if you want to set the number of lines that you want to see. Here's what it looks like:

```
[donnie@fedora log]$ sudo head -qn5 boot.log cron
[  OK  ] Finished logrotate.service - Rotate log files.
[FAILED] Failed to start vmware.ser… starts and stops VMware services.
```

```
See 'systemctl status vmware.service' for details.
        Starting vmware-USBArbitra…s and stops the USB Arbitrator....
[  OK  ] Started rsyslog.service - System Logging Service.
Sep  9 17:36:05 fedora crond[2062]: (CRON) INFO (Shutting down)
Sep 11 15:27:58 fedora crond[2038]: (CRON) STARTUP (1.6.1)
Sep 11 15:27:58 fedora crond[2038]: (CRON) INFO (Syslog will be used instead of
sendmail.)
Sep 11 15:27:58 fedora crond[2038]: (CRON) INFO (RANDOM_DELAY will be scaled
with factor 85% if used.)
Sep 11 15:27:58 fedora crond[2038]: (CRON) INFO (running with inotify support)
[donnie@fedora log]$
```

Use the -n option with a negative number to see all but the last n lines of a file. If you want to see all but the last 20 lines of the boot.log file, enter this:

```
[donnie@fedora log]$ sudo head -n-20 boot.log
```

Again, in this case, use of the -n is mandatory.

You can look at a number of either bytes, kilobytes, or megabytes from the beginning of a file with the -c option. Here, we're looking at the first 30 bytes of the boot.log file:

```
[donnie@fedora log]$ sudo head -c30 boot.log
[  OK  ] Finished [donnie@fedora log]$
```

You see that the -c option has a slight quirk to it. For some reason, the newline command isn't issued, and your new command prompt will end up on the same line as your output.

Now, let's look at the first two kilobytes of boot.log by placing a k after the 2, like this:

```
[donnie@fedora log]$ sudo head -c2k boot.log
```

To view the first two megabytes of this file, you would have placed an m after the 2, like this:

```
[donnie@fedora log]$ sudo head -c2m boot.log
```

 If you're wondering why a c is used to denote the number of bytes, it's because c stands for *character*. One character just happens to be one byte in size. So, when you tell head or tail how many bytes you want to see, you're really telling it how many characters you want to see.

That's all for head. Let's move back to the tail.

Using tail

As you may have guessed, `tail` allows you to view lines from the end of a file. By default, it will display the last ten lines. Let's take another look at the boot.log file:

```
[donnie@fedora log]$ sudo tail boot.log
[  OK  ] Reached target remote-fs-p…eparation for Remote File Systems.
[  OK  ] Reached target remote-fs.target - Remote File Systems.
         Starting rpc-statd-notify.…- Notify NFS peers of a restart...
         Starting systemd-user-sess…vice - Permit User Sessions...
[  OK  ] Started rpc-statd-notify.s…m - Notify NFS peers of a restart.
[  OK  ] Finished systemd-user-sess…ervice - Permit User Sessions.
[  OK  ] Started atd.service - Deferred execution scheduler.
[  OK  ] Started crond.service - Command Scheduler.
         Starting plymouth-quit-wai… until boot process finishes up...
         Starting plymouth-quit.ser… Terminate Plymouth Boot Screen...
[donnie@fedora log]$
```

To specify the number of lines or bytes that you want to see, just use the same options that you used for head. There are however, a few options that head doesn't have. For example, if you place a + in front of a number, you'll be able to start your display from a certain line. Here, I've decided to view everything from line 33 to the end of the file.

```
[donnie@fedora log]$ sudo tail -n+33 boot.log
```

Note that the -n is mandatory for this.

You can use the same trick to start the display at two kilobytes into the file, like this:

```
[donnie@fedora log]$ sudo tail -c+2k boot.log
```

 If you're wondering why a c is used to denote the number of bytes, it's because *c* stands for *character*. One character just happens to be one byte in size. So, when you tell head or tail how many bytes you want to see, you're really telling it how many characters you want to see.

The last option for tail is the -f option, which stands for *follow*. This option provides a running, changing display of a log file. For example, to view the last ten lines of the secure log file here on my Fedora machine, with the display changing as new events are added, I would enter:

```
[donnie@fedora log]$ sudo tail -f secure
```

When you're through, just hit *Ctrl-c* to exit.

This could come in handy if you suspect that some nefarious activity may be taking place on your system, because it allows you to constantly monitor for security events as they pop up. Or, if you need to troubleshoot something, use this option to monitor your normal system log.

For our next trick, let's see about using head and tail together.

Using Head And Tail Together

You've seen how to use head to view lines from the beginning of a file, and how to use tail to view lines from the end of a file.

That's all well and good, but what if you want to view selected lines from somewhere in the middle of a file? That's easy. Just use head and tail together. Here's how it works.

Let's say that you want to view lines 11 through 20 of a file with 39 lines. Just enter:

```
[donnie@fedora log]$ sudo head -n20 boot.log | tail
```

You can use nl to prove that you're really seeing lines 11 through 20, like so:

```
[donnie@fedora log]$ sudo nl -ba boot.log | head -n20 | tail
    11      [  OK  ] Started rtkit-daemon.servi…timeKit Scheduling Policy
Service.
    12      [  OK  ] Started avahi-daemon.service - Avahi mDNS/DNS-SD Stack.
    13      [  OK  ] Started abrtd.service - ABRT Daemon.
    14      [  OK  ] Started switcheroo-control… Switcheroo Control Proxy
service.
    15      [  OK  ] Started abrt-journal-core.… ABRT coredumpctl message
creator.
    16      [  OK  ] Started abrt-oops.service - ABRT kernel log watcher.
    17      [  OK  ] Started abrt-xorg.service - ABRT Xorg log watcher.
    18      [  OK  ] Started alsa-state.service…nd Card State (restore and
store).
    19      [  OK  ] Reached target sound.target - Sound Card.
    20      [  OK  ] Started upower.service - Daemon for power management.
[donnie@fedora log]$
```

You can make a lot of other combinations besides this one. (Again I say, you're only limited by your own imagination.) If you want to look at lines 10 through 15 of boot.log, enter this:

```
[donnie@fedora log]$ sudo head -n15 boot.log | tail -n6
```

Again, you can use nl to prove that you're looking at the correct lines, like so:

```
[donnie@fedora log]$ sudo nl -ba boot.log | head -n15 | tail -n6
    10      [  OK  ] Started dbus-broker.service - D-Bus System Message Bus.
    11      [  OK  ] Started rtkit-daemon.servi…timeKit Scheduling Policy
Service.
    12      [  OK  ] Started avahi-daemon.service - Avahi mDNS/DNS-SD Stack.
    13      [  OK  ] Started abrtd.service - ABRT Daemon.
```

```
    14        [  OK  ] Started switcheroo-control… Switcheroo Control Proxy
service.
    15        [  OK  ] Started abrt-journal-core.… ABRT coredumpctl message
creator.
[donnie@fedora log]$
```

And, that does it for head and tail. Let's now have some real fun by doing some octal dumping.

Using od

The **octal dump** (od) utility has a lot of options, and it would require quite a few pages to fully explore them. But, unless you're a hard-core programmer, you'll probably have need for only a very few of these options.

If you take a Linux certification exam, you may see a question or two about od. However, you probably won't see any questions that cover od in any amount of depth. So for now, I'll just cover the basics.

The name of this utility is a bit misleading. It does, by default, display file contents as octal byte-code. But, that's not all that it does. By using the appropriate option switches, you can also use od to display file contents in several other formats. od is normally used to display the contents of binary files, but you can also use it to display non-printing characters in normal text files.

You can display the contents of an entire file, or limit the amount of the file contents that you want to display. If you choose to display an entire file, you may want to either pipe the output into less, or redirect the output to a new text file. Let's start by looking at part of the od output from the echo binary file:

```
[donnie@fedora ~]$ od /bin/echo
0000000 042577 043114 000402 000001 000000 000000 000000 000000
0000020 000003 000076 000001 000000 030020 000000 000000 000000
0000040 000100 000000 000000 000000 104450 000000 000000 000000
0000060 000000 000000 000100 000070 000015 000100 000040 000037
0000100 000006 000000 000004 000000 000100 000000 000000 000000
0000120 000100 000000 000000 000000 000100 000000 000000 000000
.  .  .
.  .  .
```

Note how the left column starts at zero, and increments by 20 (octal) from one line to the next. Think of this column as the address column. The addresses can be used to mark and later find some particular data within the file. The rest of each line represents the actual data.

To view the file in other formats, use the -t switch with the appropriate option. For example, you can view the echo binary in hexadecimal format like this:

```
[donnie@fedora ~]$ od -tx /bin/echo
0000000 464c457f 00010102 00000000 00000000
0000020 003e0003 00000001 00003010 00000000
```

```
0000040 00000040 00000000 00008928 00000000
0000060 00000000 00380040 0040000d 001f0020
0000100 00000006 00000004 00000040 00000000
0000120 00000040 00000000 00000040 00000000

.   .   .

.   .   .
```

Note how the first column remained the same. Only the other columns changed.

If you're a normal user, you may not need od for much else besides viewing non-printing characters in text files. You may need, for example, to find new-line or carriage return characters. For this, you can use the -tc option and look for characters that are preceded with a backslash. In the example that we're about to examine, \n represents newline characters, and \r represents carriage return characters.

I'll be performing the demos with a Project Gutenberg ebook file that's titled, *How to Speak and Write Correctly*. You can download it from here: https://www.gutenberg.org/cache/epub/6409/pg6409.txt

Or, you can also just get it from the Github repository. Either way, the filename will be pg6409.txt.

Now, let's look at the first ten lines of our file, like this:

```
[donnie@fedora ~]$ od -tc pg6409.txt | head
0000000 357 273 277   T   h   e       P   r   o   j   e   c   t       G
0000020   u   t   e   n   b   e   r   g       e   B   o   o   k       o
0000040   f       H   o   w       t   o       S   p   e   a   k       a
0000060   n   d       W   r   i   t   e       C   o   r   r   e   c   t
0000100   l   y  \r  \n               \r  \n   T   h   i   s       e
0000120   b   o   o   k       i   s       f   o   r       t   h   e
0000140   u   s   e       o   f       a   n   y   o   n   e       a   n
0000160   y   w   h   e   r   e       i   n       t   h   e       U   n
0000200   i   t   e   d       S   t   a   t   e   s       a   n   d  \r
0000220  \n   m   o   s   t       o   t   h   e   r       p   a   r   t
[donnie@fedora ~]$
```

You see that there are multiple \n and \r characters in this file. But, what does that mean? First, it means that the file was created with a Windows-based text editor, such as Notepad or Wordpad. For some bizarre reason, Windows text editors insert both newline characters (\n) and carriage return characters (\r) at the end of each line.

Unix and Linux text editors only insert a newline character at the end of each line. If you're on a Unix or Linux machine and just want to read a text file that has carriage return characters, everything will work just fine. But, if you want to search for something in the text file, the carriage return characters might prevent the search from performing correctly.

Also, Unix and Linux operating systems won't correctly read shell scripts or configuration files if they contain any carriage returns.

You can use the -ta option to view non-printable characters by their official ASCII names, like this:

```
[donnie@fedora ~]$ od -ta pg6409.txt | head
0000000 o   ;   ?   T   h   e   sp  P   r   o   j   e   c   t   sp  G
0000020 u   t   e   n   b   e   r   g   sp  e   B   o   o   k   sp  o
0000040 f   sp  H   o   w   sp  t   o   sp  S   p   e   a   k   sp  a
0000060 n   d   sp  W   r   i   t   e   sp  C   o   r   r   e   c   t
0000100 l   y   cr  nl  sp  sp  sp  sp  cr  nl  T   h   i   s   sp  e
0000120 b   o   o   k   sp  i   s   sp  f   o   r   sp  t   h   e   sp
0000140 u   s   e   sp  o   f   sp  a   n   y   o   n   e   sp  a   n
0000160 y   w   h   e   r   e   sp  i   n   sp  t   h   e   sp  U   n
0000200 i   t   e   d   sp  S   t   a   t   e   s   sp  a   n   d   cr
0000220 nl  m   o   s   t   sp  o   t   h   e   r   sp  p   a   r   t
[donnie@fedora ~]$
```

This time, the newlines and carriage returns are represented by nl and cr instead of by \n and \r.

If you want to begin the display from somewhere other than the beginning of the file, use the -j switch. For example, if you want to begin viewing from address 0000640, enter:

```
[donnie@fedora ~]$ od -ta -j0000640 pg6409.txt | head
0000640 e   d   sp  S   t   a   t   e   s   ,   cr  nl  y   o   u   sp
0000660 w   i   l   l   sp  h   a   v   e   sp  t   o   sp  c   h   e
0000700 c   k   sp  t   h   e   sp  l   a   w   s   sp  o   f   sp  t
0000720 h   e   sp  c   o   u   n   t   r   y   sp  w   h   e   r   e
0000740 sp  y   o   u   sp  a   r   e   sp  l   o   c   a   t   e   d
0000760 cr  nl  b   e   f   o   r   e   sp  u   s   i   n   g   sp  t
0001000 h   i   s   sp  e   B   o   o   k   .   cr  nl  cr  nl  T   i
0001020 t   l   e   :   sp  H   o   w   sp  t   o   sp  S   p   e   a
0001040 k   sp  a   n   d   sp  W   r   i   t   e   sp  C   o   r   r
0001060 e   c   t   l   y   cr  nl  cr  nl  cr  nl  A   u   t   h   o
[donnie@fedora ~]
```

If you want to read in only a certain portion of the file, use the -N switch. Here, I'm reading in the first 0000640 bytes worth of our text file:

```
[donnie@fedora ~]$ od -ta -N0000640 pg6409.txt
0000000 o   ;   ?   T   h   e   sp  P   r   o   j   e   c   t   sp  G
0000020 u   t   e   n   b   e   r   g   sp  e   B   o   o   k   sp  o
0000040 f   sp  H   o   w   sp  t   o   sp  S   p   e   a   k   sp  a
. . .
. . .
```

```
0000600 sp  y   o   u   sp  a   r   e   sp  n   o   t   sp  l   o   c
0000620 a   t   e   d   sp  i   n   sp  t   h   e   sp  U   n   i   t
0000640
[donnie@fedora ~]$
```

Finally, let's combine these two options. Let's start at address `0000400` and read in `0000640` bytes worth of the file, like so:

```
[donnie@fedora ~]$ od -ta -j0000400 -N0000640 pg6409.txt
0000400 a   w   a   y   sp  o   r   sp  r   e   -   u   s   e   sp  i
0000420 t   sp  u   n   d   e   r   sp  t   h   e   sp  t   e   r   m
0000440 s   cr  nl  o   f   sp  t   h   e   sp  P   r   o   j   e   c
. . .
. . .
0001160 0   0   4   sp  [   e   B   o   o   k   sp  #   6   4   0   9
0001200 ]   cr  nl  sp  sp  sp  sp  sp  sp  sp  sp  sp  sp  sp  sp
0001220 sp  sp  sp  M   o   s   t   sp  r   e   c   e   n   t   l   y
0001240
[donnie@fedora ~]$
```

Keep in mind that the numbers in the address column are in octal format. That's why you need to use something like `0000640` in the addressing options. If you were to use `640` instead, **od** would look at it as a decimal number, and would give you different results from what you expected.

```
donnie@fedora:~$ od -ta -j400 -N640 pg6409.txt
0000620 a   t   e   d   sp  i   n   sp  t   h   e   sp  U   n   i   t
0000640 e   d   sp  S   t   a   t   e   s   ,   cr  nl  y   o   u   sp
0000660 w   i   l   l   sp  h   a   v   e   sp  t   o   sp  c   h   e
. . .
. . .
0001740 E   sp  W   A   T   E   R   S   cr  nl  cr  nl  cr  nl  cr  nl
0001760 cr  nl  T   H   E   sp  C   H   R   I   S   T   I   A   N   sp
0002000 H   E   R   A   L   D   cr  nl  B   I   B   L   E   sp  H   O
0002020
donnie@fedora:~$
```

As you see, this isn't what you want.

Here's an example of how you might be able to use **od**. Suppose that you have a couple of text files that you need to **cat** together, but they just don't line up correctly. To demonstrate, create a text file that has tabs at the beginning of several lines, like so:

```
[donnie@fedora ~]$ cat > alignment_1.txt
```

```
This is line one.
This is line two.
        This is line three.
            This is line four.
                    This is line five.
[donnie@fedora ~]$
```

Create a second file just like it, except without the tabs, like so:

```
[donnie@fedora ~]$ cat > alignment_2.txt
This is line one.
This is line two.
This is line three.
This is line four.
This is line five.
[donnie@fedora ~]$
```

Now, pretend that you don't know about the tabs that are in the first file. Furthermore, pretend that it's such a large file that you haven't been able to look through it in order to notice the tabs. With that in mind, try to cat the two files together, like this:

```
[donnie@fedora ~]$ cat alignment_1.txt alignment_2.txt
This is line one.
This is line two.
    This is line three.
            This is line four.
                This is line five.
This is line one.
This is line two.
This is line three.
This is line four.
This is line five.
[donnie@fedora ~]$
```

So now, you're scratching your head, wondering why things aren't lining up correctly. A quick way to find out what's going on would be to pipe the output through od with the -ta switch, like this:

```
[donnie@fedora ~]$ cat alignment_1.txt alignment_2.txt | od -ta
0000000 T   h   i   s   sp  i   s   sp  l   i   n   e   sp  o   n   e
0000020 .   nl  T   h   i   s   sp  i   s   sp  l   i   n   e   sp  t
0000040 w   o   .   nl  ht  T   h   i   s   sp  i   s   sp  l   i   n
0000060 e   sp  t   h   r   e   e   .   nl  ht  ht  T   h   i   s   sp
0000100 i   s   sp  l   i   n   e   sp  f   o   u   r   .   nl  ht  ht
0000120 ht  T   h   i   s   sp  i   s   sp  l   i   n   e   sp  f   i
```

```
0000140 v e   . nl  T   h   i   s  sp  i   s  sp  l   i   n   e
0000160 sp o   n   e   . nl  T   h   i   s  sp  i   s  sp  l   i
0000200 n e  sp  t   w   o   . nl  T   h   i   s  sp  i   s  sp
0000220 l i   n   e  sp  t   h   r   e   e   . nl  T   h   i   s
0000240 sp i   s  sp  l   i   n   e  sp  f   o   u   r   . nl  T
0000260 h i   s  sp  i   s  sp  l   i   n   e  sp  f   i   v   e
0000300 . nl
[donnie@fedora ~]$
```

All of the ht instances you see indicate the presence of a hard tab, which gives you a clue about how to fix the alignment issues. You can also od each file separately to find where you need to edit.

There are still more od options that you might find useful. To see them, consult either the od man page or the od info page.

In real life, you can use od to help troubleshoot problems with either shell scripts or Linux/Unix configuration files. Remember that if scripts or configuration files contain any carriage return characters, the operating system won't be able to read them. Also, Linux operating systems have begun making more extensive use of .yaml files in recent years. In addition to the carriage return problem, .yaml files also require that each line be indented in a specific way. Using od can help determine if each line is indented with the correct number of tabs or spaces.

Next, let's look at something that's uniquely different.

Using uniq

Use the uniq utility with files that have consecutive, identical lines. Its default behavior is to only show one copy of any line that is duplicated. Let's begin by creating the fruit.txt file, like so:

```
[donnie@fedora ~]$ cat > fruit.txt
Peach
Peach
peach
apricot
Apricot
peach
Apricot
[donnie@fedora ~]$
```

Using uniq without any options gives you this:

```
[donnie@fedora ~]$ uniq fruit.txt
Peach
peach
```

```
apricot
Apricot
peach
Apricot
[donnie@fedora ~]$
```

This got rid of the duplicates that were identical in case. But you still have some consecutive words that are the same, except for case. Use the -i switch to make this operation case-insensitive, like this:

```
[donnie@fedora ~]$ uniq -i fruit.txt
Peach
apricot
peach
Apricot
[donnie@fedora ~]$
```

Of the two duplicate pairs, whichever word was on top was the one that stayed. In the Peach pair, the upper-case Peach was on top, so it stayed. In the Apricot pair, the lower-case apricot was on top, so it stayed.

You can get a count of how many consecutive duplicate lines there are with the -c switch. Combine it with the -i switch to make the count case-insensitive. Here's how that works:

```
[donnie@fedora ~]$ uniq -c fruit.txt
      2 Peach
      1 peach
      1 apricot
      1 Apricot
      1 peach
      1 Apricot
[donnie@fedora ~]$ uniq -ic fruit.txt
      3 Peach
      2 apricot
      1 peach
      1 Apricot
[donnie@fedora ~]$
```

The -u switch allows you to only display lines that aren't repeated. You can also make this case-insensitive by combining it with the -i switch. Here's what that looks like:

```
[donnie@fedora ~]$ uniq -u fruit.txt
peach
apricot
Apricot
peach
```

```
Apricot
[donnie@fedora ~]$ uniq -iu fruit.txt
peach
Apricot
[donnie@fedora ~]$
```

Use the -d switch to show one copy of each line that is repeated, and to not show any line that isn't repeated. Again, you can combine this with the -i switch, like so:

```
[donnie@fedora ~]$ uniq -d fruit.txt
Peach
[donnie@fedora ~]$ uniq -id fruit.txt
Peach
apricot
[donnie@fedora ~]$
```

You can also have uniq perform its comparisons on partial lines, instead of whole lines. To demo this, create a file of two sets of statements. Have some of the statements differ in only the first word, like so:

```
[donnie@fedora ~]$ cat > newfile.txt
The cat is sitting under the table.
Katelyn cat is sitting under the table.
Mr. Gray, the tomcat, is on the couch.
Mr. Gray, the tomcat, is on the couch.
Mister Gray, the tomcat, is on the couch.
[donnie@fedora ~]$
```

A default uniq operation would yield this:

```
[donnie@fedora ~]$ uniq newfile.txt
The cat is sitting under the table.
Katelyn cat is sitting under the table.
Mr. Gray, the tomcat, is on the couch.
Mister Gray, the tomcat, is on the couch.
[donnie@fedora ~]$
```

Use the -f switch to tell uniq to ignore fields in its comparison. In this case, a field is a word in a sentence. The number after the -f tells uniq how many fields to ignore. For now, let's make uniq ignore the first word, like so:

```
[donnie@fedora ~]$ uniq -f1 newfile.txt
The cat is sitting under the table.
Mr. Gray, the tomcat, is on the couch.
[donnie@fedora ~]$
```

You can use the `-c` switch in the same manner, except that it would have `uniq` skip a number of characters, instead of fields. This could be handy if you have lines with leading blank spaces.

If you want `uniq` to end its comparisons before it gets to the end of the lines, use the `-w` switch. The number after the `-w` tells `uniq` how many characters into the line to perform its comparison. If a `-c` or a `-f` switch is specified, the count doesn't begin until after the `-c` or `-f` switch is satisfied.

To demo this, create yet another text file that will look like this:

```
[donnie@fedora ~]$ cat > newfile_2.txt
Mr. Gray is on the couch.
Mr. Gray is on the back of the couch.
Mister Gray is on the back of the couch.
[donnie@fedora ~]$
```

This time, we want our comparison to begin on the second word of each sentence, and to end on the 14th character of the comparison. Here's how that works:

```
[donnie@fedora ~]$ uniq -f1 -w14 newfile_2.txt
Mr. Gray is on the couch.
[donnie@fedora ~]$
```

Okay, easy enough so far, right?

For the next demo, create a pair of files so that you can use `join` and `uniq` together. First, create the `actorfile_9.txt` file, which will look like this:

```
[donnie@fedora ~]$ cat > actorfile_9.txt
Wayne       John
Allen       Gracie
Allen       Fred
Price       Vincent
Davis       Bette
[donnie@fedora ~]$
```

Next, create the `actorfile_10.txt` file, which will look like this:

```
[donnie@fedora ~]$ cat > actorfile_10.txt
Wayne           drama
Allen           comedy
Allen           comedy
Price           horror
Davis           drama
[donnie@fedora ~]$
```

Join the two files together to see what happens:

```
[donnie@fedora ~]$ join actorfile_9.txt actorfile_10.txt
```

```
Wayne John drama
Allen Gracie comedy
Allen Gracie comedy
Allen Fred comedy
Allen Fred comedy
Price Vincent horror
Davis Bette drama
[donnie@fedora ~]$
```

Notice that when the key field is the same on two consecutive lines, join thinks that it has to list each of those lines twice in the combined output. You can take care of that by piping the output through uniq, like so:

```
[donnie@fedora ~]$ join actorfile_9.txt actorfile_10.txt | uniq
Wayne John drama
Allen Gracie comedy
Allen Fred comedy
Price Vincent horror
Davis Bette drama
[donnie@fedora ~]$
```

Okay, that's it for uniq. Let's now do some counting.

Using wc

This easy-to-use utility gives you a quick way to count the number of lines, words, and/or bytes in a text file. So, if you're typing a document that can only contain a certain number of words, you don't have to sit there and manually try to count the words as you scroll the document up your screen. Just use wc, instead.

The default output for wc shows you the number of lines, followed by the number of words, and then by the number of bytes. Finally, it shows the name of the input file. Here's how that looks:

```
[donnie@fedora ~]$ wc actorfile_1.txt
 5 10 67 actorfile_1.txt
[donnie@fedora ~]$
```

So, the actorfile_1.txt file contains five lines, ten words, and 67 bytes.

If you specify more than one file, wc will tell give you information for each individual file, and the total for all of the files, which looks like this:

```
[donnie@fedora ~]$ wc actorfile_1.txt actorfile_2.txt macgruder.txt
   5   10   67 actorfile_1.txt
   5   10   77 actorfile_2.txt
  19   77  510 macgruder.txt
  29   97  654 total
```

```
[donnie@fedora ~]$
```

Use the -l (that's a lower-case L) switch if you only want to see the number of lines in your files. Here's how that looks:

```
[donnie@fedora ~]$ wc -l actorfile_1.txt
5 actorfile_1.txt
[donnie@fedora ~]$
```

The -w switch shows the number of words in a file, like this:

```
[donnie@fedora ~]$ wc -w actorfile_1.txt
10 actorfile_1.txt
[donnie@fedora ~]$
```

Use the -c switch to show only the number of bytes, like so:

```
[donnie@fedora ~]$ wc -c actorfile_1.txt
67 actorfile_1.txt
[donnie@fedora ~]$
```

To see the numbers of characters in a file, use -m, like this:

```
[donnie@fedora ~]$ wc -m actorfile_1.txt
67 actorfile_1.txt
[donnie@fedora ~]$
```

Theoretically, the -c and the -m outputs should be identical as you see above, because one character is one byte in size. However, the outputs might differ slightly for large text files, as you see here:

```
[donnie@fedora ~]$ wc -c pg6409.txt
282605 pg6409.txt
[donnie@fedora ~]$ wc -m pg6409.txt
282419 pg6409.txt
[donnie@fedora ~]$
```

I have no idea of why that is, because I've never found any explanation about it.

The last switch is the -L switch, which shows you the length of the longest line in your input file, like this:

```
[donnie@fedora ~]$ wc -L pg6409.txt
87 pg6409.txt
[donnie@fedora ~]$
```

You can combine wc with other utilities. Suppose that you have a text file that contains a lot of duplicate lines. Combine wc with uniq to see how eliminating the blank lines would affect the size of the pg6409.txt file that you downloaded from Project Gutenberg, like so:

```
[donnie@fedora ~]$ wc pg6409.txt
```

```
   6019   45875 282605 pg6409.txt
[donnie@fedora ~]$ uniq pg6409.txt | wc
   5785    45875   282137
[donnie@fedora ~]$
```

You see that `uniq` has reduced the number of lines, but the word count remains the same. This tells us that all of the duplicate lines are blank lines. The byte-count has also gone down, because even empty spaces count as characters, which are one byte in size.

If you're a systems administrator, you can use `wc` to help with your security audits. If you know how many users are supposed to be authorized for your system, you can periodically check the number of lines in the `/etc/passwd` file. (Remember, each line represents one user.) This gives you a good way to recognize if a user has been added behind your back.

All righty, we're through counting. It's time now to do some formatting.

Using fmt

The `fmt` utility works by attempting to make all non-blank lines in a text file the same length. Its default action is to set a target length of 75 characters for each line. However, you can change that if your file is either too narrow or too wide to display properly. The slight catch is that it doesn't work well with every file. If your file has things like tables, indices, or tables of contents, `fmt` can mess up their formatting. (That's ironic, considering that `fmt` is short for *format*.) You would then have to go back and manually edit them to make them look right.

> I should point out for all of these examples to work on a virtual machine, you'll need to have the virtual machine window set to a wider-than-default width. You can do that by opening the Virtualbox **View** menu for the virtual machine, and selecting the **Scaled Mode** option. That will allow you to resize the virtual machine window to suit your needs.
>
> Another option is to just remotely log into the virtual machine from your host machine's terminal. You'll then be able to resize the terminal window as you desire.

We'll start by looking at an excerpt from the `pg6409.txt` ebook file that you've already downloaded from the Project Gutenberg site. Here's what the unformatted excerpt file looks like:

```
donnie@fedora:~$ cat excerpt.txt
It is the purpose of this book, as briefly and concisely as possible, to
direct the reader along a straight course, pointing out the mistakes he
must avoid and giving him such assistance as will enable him to reach the
goal of a correct knowledge of the English language. It is not a Grammar
in any sense, but a guide, a silent signal-post pointing the way in the
right direction.
donnie@fedora:~$ 
```

Figure 7.2: The unformatted text

I've decided that that's a bit too wide, so I'll use fmt with its default target setting of 75 characters per line, like so:

```
donnie@fedora:~$ fmt excerpt.txt
It is the purpose of this book, as briefly and concisely as possible,
to direct the reader along a straight course, pointing out the mistakes
he must avoid and giving him such assistance as will enable him to reach
the goal of a correct knowledge of the English language. It is not a
Grammar in any sense, but a guide, a silent signal-post pointing the
way in the right direction.
donnie@fedora:~$ 
```

Figure 7.3: Using fmt with the default width

It still seems a bit too wide. So, let's use the -w switch to narrow it down to a width of 60 characters, like so:

```
donnie@fedora:~$ fmt -w60 excerpt.txt
It is the purpose of this book, as briefly and concisely
as possible, to direct the reader along a straight course,
pointing out the mistakes he must avoid and giving him
such assistance as will enable him to reach the goal of
a correct knowledge of the English language. It is not a
Grammar in any sense, but a guide, a silent signal-post
pointing the way in the right direction.
donnie@fedora:~$ 
```

Figure 7.4: Setting a width of 60 characters

On second thought, let's try it with a line width of 90 characters, like this:

```
donnie@fedora:~$ fmt -w90 excerpt.txt
It is the purpose of this book, as briefly and concisely as possible, to direct the
reader along a straight course, pointing out the mistakes he must avoid and giving
him such assistance as will enable him to reach the goal of a correct knowledge of the
English language. It is not a Grammar in any sense, but a guide, a silent signal-post
pointing the way in the right direction.
donnie@fedora:~$ 
```

Figure 7.5: Setting a width of 90 characters

The -u switch ensures that you always have one space between each word, and two spaces between each sentence, which looks like this:

```
donnie@fedora:~$ fmt -u excerpt.txt
It is the purpose of this book, as briefly and concisely as possible,
to direct the reader along a straight course, pointing out the mistakes
he must avoid and giving him such assistance as will enable him to reach
the goal of a correct knowledge of the English language. It is not a
Grammar in any sense, but a guide, a silent signal-post pointing the
way in the right direction.
donnie@fedora:~$ 
```

Figure 7.6: Using the -u option

Use the -s switch if you want to make long lines shorter, but you don't want to make short lines longer. (Note that you can use a single dash to combine switches.) Here's how that looks:

```
[donnie@fedora ~]$ fmt -sw60 excerpt.txt
It is the purpose of this book, as briefly and concisely
as possible, to
direct the reader along a straight course, pointing out
the mistakes he
must avoid and giving him such assistance as will enable
him to reach the
goal of a correct knowledge of the English language. It
is not a Grammar
in any sense, but a guide, a silent signal-post pointing
the way in the
right direction.
[donnie@fedora ~]$
```

Yeah, the -s doesn't work so well with this particular file, and I've never really found a use for it myself. But, that doesn't mean that you'll never find a use for it.

Once you've finally decided that you like what you see, use a redirector to save the output to a new file, like this:

```
[donnie@fedora ~]$ fmt -uw80 excerpt.txt > formatted_excerpt.txt
[donnie@fedora ~]$
```

Now that we've had enough of formatting, let's do some splitting.

Using split

You can use split to break one large text file into two or more smaller ones. By default, it takes a large file and splits it into smaller files of 1,000 lines each. (Of course, the last file may be smaller.) Also by default, the names of these new small files will be xaa, xab, xac, and so on. Let's begin by looking at the line-count of the public-domain ebook file that you downloaded from Project Gutenberg, like so:

```
[donnie@fedora ~]$ wc -l pg6409.txt
6019 pg6409.txt
[donnie@fedora ~]$
```

Since there are 6,019 lines in this file, split will break it into six files of 1,000 lines each, and one file of only 19 lines. Here's how it works:

```
[donnie@fedora ~]$ split pg6409.txt
[donnie@fedora ~]$ ls -l x*
-rw-r--r--. 1 donnie donnie 38304 Sep 15 17:31 xaa
-rw-r--r--. 1 donnie donnie 48788 Sep 15 17:31 xab
```

```
-rw-r--r--. 1 donnie donnie 42676 Sep 15 17:31 xac
-rw-r--r--. 1 donnie donnie 42179 Sep 15 17:31 xad
-rw-r--r--. 1 donnie donnie 54845 Sep 15 17:31 xae
-rw-r--r--. 1 donnie donnie 55021 Sep 15 17:31 xaf
-rw-r--r--. 1 donnie donnie   792 Sep 15 17:31 xag
[donnie@fedora ~]$
```

To verify that this works, use wc to perform a line-count of each file:

```
[donnie@fedora ~]$ wc -l xaa xab xac xad xae xaf xag
  1000 xaa
  1000 xab
  1000 xac
  1000 xad
  1000 xae
  1000 xaf
    19 xag
  6019 total
[donnie@fedora ~]$
```

Use the -a option to change the length of the new filenames. The following command will give you a five-character suffix for the filenames.

```
[donnie@fedora ~]$ split -a5 pg6409.txt
[donnie@fedora ~]$ ls -l xaaa*
-rw-r--r--. 1 donnie donnie 38304 Sep 15 17:37 xaaaaa
-rw-r--r--. 1 donnie donnie 48788 Sep 15 17:37 xaaaab
-rw-r--r--. 1 donnie donnie 42676 Sep 15 17:37 xaaaac
-rw-r--r--. 1 donnie donnie 42179 Sep 15 17:37 xaaaad
-rw-r--r--. 1 donnie donnie 54845 Sep 15 17:37 xaaaae
-rw-r--r--. 1 donnie donnie 55021 Sep 15 17:37 xaaaaf
-rw-r--r--. 1 donnie donnie   792 Sep 15 17:37 xaaaag
[donnie@fedora ~]$
```

You can also change the filename prefix from x to whatever you want. Just add the desired prefix to the end of the command, like this:

```
[donnie@fedora ~]$ split -a5 pg6409.txt pg6409.txt
[donnie@fedora ~]$ ls -l pg6409.txt*
-rw-r--r--. 1 donnie donnie 282605 Sep 13 17:39 pg6409.txt
-rw-r--r--. 1 donnie donnie  38304 Sep 15 17:40 pg6409.txtaaaaa
-rw-r--r--. 1 donnie donnie  48788 Sep 15 17:40 pg6409.txtaaaab
-rw-r--r--. 1 donnie donnie  42676 Sep 15 17:40 pg6409.txtaaaac
-rw-r--r--. 1 donnie donnie  42179 Sep 15 17:40 pg6409.txtaaaad
```

```
-rw-r--r--. 1 donnie donnie  54845 Sep 15 17:40 pg6409.txtaaaae
-rw-r--r--. 1 donnie donnie  55021 Sep 15 17:40 pg6409.txtaaaaf
-rw-r--r--. 1 donnie donnie    792 Sep 15 17:40 pg6409.txtaaaag
[donnie@fedora ~]$
```

If you don't want to use letters for the filename suffixes, use the -d option to use numeric prefixes. (Again, notice how you can combine switches with only a single dash.) Do it like this:

```
[donnie@fedora ~]$ split -da5 pg6409.txt pg6409.txt
[donnie@fedora ~]$ ls -l pg6409.txt0000*
-rw-r--r--. 1 donnie donnie 38304 Sep 15 17:42 pg6409.txt00000
-rw-r--r--. 1 donnie donnie 48788 Sep 15 17:42 pg6409.txt00001
-rw-r--r--. 1 donnie donnie 42676 Sep 15 17:42 pg6409.txt00002
-rw-r--r--. 1 donnie donnie 42179 Sep 15 17:42 pg6409.txt00003
-rw-r--r--. 1 donnie donnie 54845 Sep 15 17:42 pg6409.txt00004
-rw-r--r--. 1 donnie donnie 55021 Sep 15 17:42 pg6409.txt00005
-rw-r--r--. 1 donnie donnie   792 Sep 15 17:42 pg6409.txt00006
[donnie@fedora ~]$
```

But, what if 1,000 lines is too long for your files? Then, use the -l switch to change it to something else. Here, I'm creating files of 400 lines each:

```
[donnie@fedora ~]$ split -da5 -l400 pg6409.txt pg6409.txt
[donnie@fedora ~]$
```

Note that whenever you use two or more option switches that each take a numeric option, you have to use a separate dash for each option.

You can use the -b switch to create files that are a specific number of bytes in size. Here, I'm breaking the file into chunks of 900 bytes each:

```
[donnie@fedora ~]$ split -da5 -b900 pg6409.txt pg6409.txt
[donnie@fedora ~]$
```

Add either a k or an m after the numeric option for the -b switch, and you can specify either kilobytes or megabytes, instead of the default bytes. In this example, I'm going back in time and pretending that I have to divide the file into two parts so that I can store it on two old-fashioned 180-Kbyte floppy disks:

```
[donnie@fedora ~]$ split -da5 -b180k pg6409.txt pg6409.txt
[donnie@fedora ~]$ ls -l pg6409.txt000*
-rw-r--r--. 1 donnie donnie 184320 Sep 15 17:55 pg6409.txt00000
-rw-r--r--. 1 donnie donnie  98285 Sep 15 17:55 pg6409.txt00001
[donnie@fedora ~]$
```

I'll wrap up the split write-up by making a confession, in order to unburden my soul. As I hinted in the previous paragraph, the original purpose of split was to split up text files that are too large to store on a single old-fashioned floppy disk.

In the modern age, we have hard drives and solid-state drives that have multiple Terabytes of capacity, and USB memory sticks that have multiple Gigabytes of capacity. So, you'll likely find that split isn't as useful as it used to be. But, do keep it in mind if you plan to take a Linux certification exam, because you just might see some questions about it.

Okay, we've had enough of splitting, so let's do some translating.

Using tr

You can use tr for a variety of translation chores. (After all, tr does stand for *translate*.) Rather than translating from one language to another, tr translates from one character to another, from a range of characters to another, or from one class of characters to another. You can also delete selected characters from a file or eliminate duplicate characters.

Compared to the utilities that we've looked at so far, there's a big difference with how tr operates. The other utilities that we've looked at so far can get their input from arguments that you would supply on the command-line. So, you don't need to use the stdin redirector with them. The tr utility can't use arguments, so you'll either have to use a stdin redirector or pipe its input in from another command.

For the first example, create the file translation.txt, and use tr to change every occurrence of a single character. Make the file look like this:

```
[donnie@fedora ~]$ cat > translation.txt
Let's translate all of the a's into A's.
[donnie@fedora ~]$
```

Now, let's do the actual translation, like so:

```
[donnie@fedora ~]$ tr 'a' 'A' < translation.txt
Let's trAnslAte All of the A's into A's.
[donnie@fedora ~]$
```

After the tr, I placed two text strings within single quotes. The first string represents what I want to find and change. The second string represents what we want the first string to become. In this case, I want to change all lower-case a's into upper-case A's.

You can translate multiple characters by either listing them individually or by specifying ranges of characters. In this next example, I've chosen to convert a's to A's and l's to L's.

```
[donnie@fedora ~]$ cat > translation_2.txt
Let's translate all of the a's into A's
and all of the l's into L's.
[donnie@fedora ~]$
[donnie@fedora ~]$ tr 'al' 'AL' < translation_2.txt
Let's trAnslAte ALL of the A's into A's
And ALL of the L's into L's.
[donnie@fedora ~]$
```

Separate the characters with a dash to specify a range of characters, like so:

```
[donnie@fedora ~]$ cat > translation_3.txt
Let's now convert everything from
a through l to A through L.
[donnie@fedora ~]$
[donnie@fedora ~]$ tr 'a-l' 'A-L' < translation_3.txt
LEt's now ConvErt EvErytHInG From
A tHrouGH L to A tHrouGH L.
[donnie@fedora ~]$
```

You can specify more than one range, like this:

```
[donnie@fedora ~]$ cat > translation_4.txt
Let's now convert everything from
a through l to A through L, and
everything from u through z to
U through Z.
[donnie@fedora ~]$
[donnie@fedora ~]$ tr 'a-lu-z' 'A-LU-Z' < translation_4.txt
LEt's noW ConVErt EVErYtHInG From
A tHroUGH L to A tHroUGH L, AnD
EVErYtHInG From U tHroUGH Z to
U tHroUGH Z.
[donnie@fedora ~]$
```

Other types of conversion are also possible. Here, I'm converting the letters a through e to the numbers 1 through 5:

```
[donnie@fedora ~]$ cat > translation_5.txt
Let's now convert a through e to
1 through 5.
Are we ready?
[donnie@fedora ~]$
[donnie@fedora ~]$ tr 'a-e' '1-5' < translation_5.txt
L5t's now 3onv5rt 1 through 5 to
1 through 5.
Ar5 w5 r514y?
[donnie@fedora ~]$
```

As is the case with many of these utilities, tr gives you multiple ways to perform certain operations. For example, to convert all lower-case letters in a file to upper-case letters, you can specify the ranges 'a-z' and 'A-Z' in your command, like this:

```
[donnie@fedora ~]$ cat > translation_6.txt
```

```
Let's now convert all lower-case letters
into upper-case letters.
[donnie@fedora ~]$
[donnie@fedora ~]$ tr 'a-z' 'A-Z' < translation_6.txt
LET'S NOW CONVERT ALL LOWER-CASE LETTERS
INTO UPPER-CASE LETTERS.
[donnie@fedora ~]$
```

You can also use character classes to perform this conversion. A **character class** consists of the name of a type of characters placed within the square bracket and colon characters. For example, the character class for lower-case characters is represented by [:lower:], and the character class for upper-case letters is represented by [:upper:]. So, the preceding command could be typed in like this:

```
[donnie@fedora ~]$ tr [:lower:] [:upper:] < translation_6.txt
LET'S NOW CONVERT ALL LOWER-CASE LETTERS
INTO UPPER-CASE LETTERS.
[donnie@fedora ~]$
```

Here's a table of the rest of the character classes.

Class Name	What It Means
[:alnum:]	Letters and digits. (In other words, alphanumeric.)
[:alpha:]	Letters
[:blank:]	Whitespace
[:cntrl:]	Control characters
[:digit:]	Digits
[:graph:]	All printable characters except for spaces
[:lower:]	All lower-case letters
[:print:]	All printable characters, including spaces
[:punct:]	All punctuation characters
[:space:]	Either veritcal or horizontal whitespace
[:upper:]	All upper-case letters
[:xdigit:]	Hexadecimal digits

Table 7.1: Character classes

This looks easy enough, right? Unfortunately though, there's a bit of a catch. Watch what happens when I try to translate digits to hexadecimal digits:

```
[donnie@fedora ~]$ tr [:digit:] [:xdigit:] < numbers.txt
tr: when translating, the only character classes that may appear in
```

```
string2 are 'upper' and 'lower'
[donnie@fedora ~]$
```

The answer to this dilemma is in the tr man page, where it says that "while translating, [:lower:] and [:upper:] may be used in pairs to specify case conversion". Granted, it doesn't say that *only* [:lower:] and [:upper:] can be used in pairs, but that is the implication. However, you can use these other character classes in other types of tr operations, which we'll get to in just a bit.

If you want to delete certain characters from a text stream, use the -d switch. In this example, I'll delete all vowels from the text.

 Note that with the -d switch, you only need to specify one text string or character class.

Here's how that looks:

```
[donnie@fedora ~]$ cat > translation_7.txt
I will now show you how to delete
all vowels from a text stream. Are
you really ready for this?
[donnie@fedora ~]$
[donnie@fedora ~]$ tr -d 'aeiouAEIOU' < translation_7.txt
 wll nw shw y hw t dlt
ll vwls frm  txt strm. r
y rlly rdy fr ths?
[donnie@fedora ~]$
```

Add the -c switch, and you can make tr operate on everything except what you specify. Here, I'll remove all the consonants, punctuation, spaces, and newline characters. That is, I'll remove everything that isn't a vowel. Prepare to be amazed at what you're about to see:

```
[donnie@fedora ~]$ cat > translation_8.txt
I'll now show you how to delete
everything except for vowels from
a text stream.
[donnie@fedora ~]$
[donnie@fedora ~]$ tr -dc 'aeiouAEIOU' < translation_8.txt
Iooouooeeeeeieeooeoaeea[donnie@fedora ~]$
```

When I say that this removes everything but the vowels, I do mean *everything*, including the invisible newline characters. This explains why all of the vowels are on one line, and why the command prompt is now on the same line as the output.

You can do the same things by specifying character classes instead of characters or ranges of characters. In this example, I'm removing everything except for lower-case letters:

```
[donnie@fedora ~]$ tr -dc [:lower:] < translation_9.txt
histimewellremoveeverythingthatalowercaseletter[donnie@fedora ~]$
```

This time, let's remove all of the non-printable control characters, like this:

```
[donnie@fedora ~]$ cat > translation_10.txt
Now, let's remove
all of the
control characters.
[donnie@fedora ~]$
[donnie@fedora ~]$ tr -d [:cntrl:] < translation_10.txt
Now, let's removeall of thecontrol characters.[donnie@fedora ~]$
```

Of course, the only control characters in this file are newline characters, but that's okay. If you have a file that also contained other types of control characters, and you only want to delete all of the newline characters, just do this:

```
[donnie@fedora ~]$ cat > translation_11.txt
Now,
I just want to
delete the
newline characters.
[donnie@fedora ~]$
[donnie@fedora ~]$ tr -d '\n' < translation_11.txt
Now,I just want todelete the newline characters.[donnie@fedora ~]$
```

If you have sequential occurrences of a given character or character class, you can use the -s switch to replace them with only a single occurrence. Here's how that looks:

```
[donnie@fedora ~]$ cat > translation_12.txt
Take a look at the poor
yellow dog. The poor little
pooch isn't as peppy as he
used to be.
[donnie@fedora ~]$
[donnie@fedora ~]$ tr -s [:alpha:] < translation_12.txt
Take a lok at the por
yelow dog. The por litle
poch isn't as pepy as he
used to be.
[donnie@fedora ~]$
```

If you specify two strings with the -s switch, tr will first replace the characters in the first string with the characters in the second string. Then, it will squeeze out the resultant consecutive characters. As before, prepare to be amazed at what you'll see here:

```
[donnie@fedora ~]$ cat > translation_13.txt
tennessee
[donnie@fedora ~]$
[donnie@fedora ~]$ tr -s 'tnse' 'srne' < translation_13.txt
serene
[donnie@fedora ~]$
```

So, I turned *tennessee* into *serene*. (Perform this trick at your next party in case you need to liven things up a bit.)

You can combine tr with other text-stream utilities, which would look something like this:

```
[donnie@fedora ~]$ sort autos.txt | tr [:lower:] [:upper:] | head
BMW            325I         1985   115     450
BMW            325I         1985   60      1000
CHEVY          IMPALA       1985   85      1550
CHEVY          MALIBU       1999   50      3500
CHEVY          MALIBU       2000   60      3000
EDSEL          CORSAIR 1958 47     750
FORD           EXPLORER     2003   25      9500
FORD           GALAXIE 1964 128    60
FORD           MUSTANG 1965 45     10000
FORD           TAURUS       2004   10      17000
[donnie@fedora ~]$
```

Here's a more practical use for tr. Let's say that you've been given a text file of columnar data that you need to format for printing. But, the columns are all separated with a single space and nothing lines up correctly, as you see here:

```
[donnie@fedora ~]$ cat > spaces.txt
one two
three four
five six
seven eight
nine ten
[donnie@fedora ~]$ cat spaces.txt
one two
three four
five six
seven eight
```

```
nine ten
[donnie@fedora ~]$
```

 You can't use unexpand to replace the spaces with tabs, because you need at least two spaces between the columns for unexpand to work.

In this case, you can use tr to replace the spaces with tabs. (Note that there is a blank space between the first set of single quotes. So yes, you can quote spaces.)

```
[donnie@fedora ~]$ tr ' ' '\t' < spaces.txt
one         two
three       four
five        six
seven       eight
nine        ten
[donnie@fedora ~]$
```

Even if you do have more than one space between the columns, unexpand still might not be the best choice. Here, I've placed two spaces between the columns:

```
[donnie@fedora ~]$ cat > spaces_2.txt
one   two
three   four
five   six
seven   eight
nine   ten
[donnie@fedora ~]$
```

I'll use unexpand with the -t2 switch so that it will only take two spaces to make a tab, like so:

```
[donnie@fedora ~]$ unexpand -t2 spaces_2.txt
one         two
three           four
five        six
seven           eight
nine        ten
[donnie@fedora ~]$
```

That's somewhat better, but things still look a bit ragged. So, I'll use tr to replace the spaces with tabs, like this:

```
[donnie@fedora ~]$ tr ' ' '\t' < spaces_2.txt
one                 two
```

```
three              four
five               six
seven              eight
nine               ten
[donnie@fedora ~]$
```

Much nicer, eh? But, since there were originally two spaces between columns, I now have two tabs between columns. I only want one tab between columns, so I'll use the `-s` switch to squeeze out the excess tabs, like this:

```
[donnie@fedora ~]$ tr -s ' ' '\t' < spaces_2.txt
one        two
three      four
five       six
seven      eight
nine       ten
[donnie@fedora ~]$
```

For the final example, consider the Project Gutenberg file that I showed you earlier. Remember that it contains carriage return characters, indicating that it was created on a Windows computer. Here's how that looks:

```
[donnie@fedora ~]$ od -c pg6409.txt | head
0000000 357 273 277   T   h   e       P   r   o   j   e   c   t       G
0000020   u   t   e   n   b   e   r   g       e   B   o   o   k       o
0000040   f       H   o   w       t   o       S   p   e   a   k       a
0000060   n   d       W   r   i   t   e       C   o   r   r   e   c   t
0000100   l   y  \r  \n          \r  \n   T   h   i   s       e
0000120   b   o   o   k       i   s       f   o   r       t   h   e
0000140   u   s   e       o   f       a   n   y   o   n   e       a   n
0000160   y   w   h   e   r   e       i   n       t   h   e       U   n
0000200   i   t   e   d       S   t   a   t   e   s       a   n   d  \r
0000220  \n   m   o   s   t       o   t   h   e   r       p   a   r   t
[donnie@fedora ~]$
```

As I pointed out before, each `\r` represents a carriage return. Now, let's pretend that this is a Linux configuration file, and that we need to strip out the carriage returns so that Linux will properly read it. Save the output to a new file, like so:

```
[donnie@fedora ~]$ tr -d '\r' < pg6409.txt > pg6409_stripped.txt
[donnie@fedora ~]$
```

Did it work? Let's see:

```
[donnie@fedora ~]$ od -c pg6409_stripped.txt | head
0000000 357 273 277   T   h   e       P   r   o   j   e   c   t       G
```

```
0000020 u     t     e     n     b     e     r     g           e     B     o     o     k           o
0000040 f           H     o     w           t     o           S     p     e     a     k           a
0000060 n     d           W     r     i     t     e           C     o     r     r     e     c     t
0000100 l     y     \n                      \n    T     h     i     s           e     b     o
0000120 o     k           i     s           f     o     r           t     h     e           u     s
0000140 e           o     f           a     n     y     o     n     e           a     n     y     w
0000160 h     e     r     e           i     n           t     h     e           U     n     i     t
0000200 e     d           S     t     a     t     e     s           a     n     d     \n    m     o
0000220 s     t           o     t     h     e     r           p     a     r     t     s           o
[donnie@fedora ~]$
```

I don't see any carriage returns, so it worked just fine.

 In reality, most people just use the `dos2unix` utility to strip out the carriage returns. But, if you plan to take any Linux certification exams, you might also want to know how to do it with `tr`.

The next utility we'll look at will make you want to talk like a pirate.

Using xargs

It's fitting that I'm writing this on *International Talk Like a Pirate Day*, because when you pronounce the name of this utility just right, it really does sound like something that a pirate would say. So, all together now, in your best pirate voice. . .

Xaaaaarrrrrgs!

Okay, enough silliness. Let's get to work.

Seriously, `xargs` is a handy utility that can be used in a few different ways. Since the current topic is text-stream filters though, we'll only look at it in that context for the time being. Later on, I'll show you other uses for it.

`xargs` doesn't work by itself, and is always used with another utility. Its purpose is to take output from one source and use it as arguments for the other command. It works somewhat like the `-exec` option with `find`, but with a few differences. That is, `xargs` can be used with other utilities besides `find`, it has more options, and it's more efficient. Let's look at a few examples.

If you want to sort multiple files, you can list them all on the command-line when you invoke `sort`. To demo this, let's review the `actorfile_1.txt` file and the `actorfile_6.txt` file that I already had you create:

```
[donnie@fedora ~]$ cat actorfile_1.txt
Benny          Jack
Allen          Fred
Ladd           Alan
```

```
Hitchcock            Alfred
Robinson             Edgar
[donnie@fedora ~]$ cat actorfile_6.txt
MacLaine             Shirley
Booth                Shirley
Stanwick             Barbara
Allen                Gracie
[donnie@fedora ~]$
```

Now, let's sort them together, like so:

```
[donnie@fedora ~]$ sort actorfile_1.txt actorfile_6.txt
Allen                Fred
Allen                Gracie
Benny                Jack
Booth                Shirley
Hitchcock            Alfred
Ladd                 Alan
MacLaine             Shirley
Robinson             Edgar
Stanwick             Barbara
[donnie@fedora ~]$
```

That works fine if you only have two files to sort. But, what if you have a whole bunch of files that you want to sort? And, what if you need to update those files on a regular basis and sort them again after each update? Listing every file in a sort command would soon become tiresome and a bit unwieldy. To simplify the job, you can either write a shell script with the names of all of the files, or use xargs with a list of all the files. Since we haven't yet looked at writing shell scripts, let's look at xargs.

First, create a file with a list of the files that you want to sort, like so:

```
[donnie@fedora ~]$ cat > xargs_sort.txt
actorfile_1.txt actorfile_6.txt
[donnie@fedora ~]$
```

As you see, the filenames can all be on the same line, with only a single space between them. Or, if you prefer, you can place each filename on its own line. Either way works equally well.

Now, use xargs and sort to read in the list of files, and then to sort the actual files, like so:

```
[donnie@fedora ~]$ xargs sort < xargs_sort.txt
Allen                Fred
Allen                Gracie
Benny                Jack
Booth                Shirley
Hitchcock            Alfred
```

```
Ladd            Alan
MacLaine        Shirley
Robinson        Edgar
Stanwick        Barbara
[donnie@fedora ~]$
```

As I said, this would be handy if you have a lot of files that you have to update and sort on a frequent basis. Just build the list of the files that you need to sort, so that you don't always have to type the names of all of the files.

Let's now create a file with a list of names, and use xargs to feed the list into the echo command, like this:

```
[donnie@fedora ~]$ cat > howdy.txt
Jack,
Jane,
Joe,
and John.
[donnie@fedora ~]$
[donnie@fedora ~]$ xargs echo "Howdy" < howdy.txt
Howdy Jack, Jane, Joe, and John.
[donnie@fedora ~]$
```

Pretty slick, eh? (I know that you're just dying to show this trick at your next party.) But, there's more.

You can use the -i switch and a set of curly braces to place the arguments wherever you want in the output string.

 Note that for this example to work properly, each name will have to be on its own line in the input file. That's because -i also causes the command to invoke once for each line in the input file.

Anyway, here's how it works:

```
[donnie@fedora ~]$ cat > xargs_test.txt
Frank
Goldie
Vicky
[donnie@fedora ~]$
[donnie@fedora ~]$ xargs -i echo "Howdy {}.  Are you busy for lunch?" < xargs_
test.txt
Howdy Frank.  Are you busy for lunch?
Howdy Goldie.  Are you busy for lunch?
Howdy Vicky.  Are you busy for lunch?
[donnie@fedora ~]$
```

If we use the -n num switch, we can tell xargs to execute the associated command once for every *num* lines of input.

```
[donnie@fedora ~]$ cat howdy.txt
Jack,
Jane,
Joe,
and John.
[donnie@fedora ~]$
[donnie@fedora ~]$ xargs -n1 echo "Howdy" < howdy.txt
Howdy Jack,
Howdy Jane,
Howdy Joe,
Howdy and
Howdy John.
[donnie@fedora ~]$
```

That didn't work out so well, so let's try with -n2 to see if it makes a difference.

```
[donnie@fedora ~]$ xargs -n2 echo "Howdy" < howdy.txt
Howdy Jack, Jane,
Howdy Joe, and
Howdy John.
[donnie@fedora ~]$
```

That looks much better.

Finally, we can use the -1 num switch to determine the number of lines we want for our output. Here, we're creating two lines of output.

```
[donnie@fedora ~]$ cat howdy.txt
Jack,
Jane,
Joe,
and John.
[donnie@fedora ~]$
[donnie@fedora ~]$ xargs -l2 echo "Howdy" < howdy.txt
Howdy Jack, Jane,
Howdy Joe, and John.
[donnie@fedora ~]$
```

That's about it for now. There are still other uses for xargs, which I'll cover a bit later. Next, let's add some final polish to your important text files.

Using pr

You've been working hard, using various text-stream filters to extract meaningful data from your text files, and creating formatted reports. Now, it's time to make that hard work pay off by committing your work to paper. Sure, you can print your files without using pr. But for a nice professional look, pr can give you just the right finishing touch.

With pr, you can effortlessly prepare your files for printing by breaking them into pages, and by adding headers and page numbers. In that regard, it's better than using a regular text editor. In fact, it's almost like using a mini word processor. It also gives you other formatting options that text editors won't give you. (You'll see some examples in just a few moments.)

Once you've used pr to perform your final formatting, you can print directly from the command-line by either piping pr's output into the lpr utility, or by invoking lpr with your filename as an argument. (I'll tell you more about lpr in just a bit.) There are a few reasons why you want to know how to do that.

If you work with a Linux or Unix server that doesn't have a GUI installed, you will need to know how to print from the command-line, because text-mode text editors don't include a print function. Also, if you know how to print from the command-line, you'll be able to set up batch jobs that can print multiple files at once, and automate your printing by setting print jobs up with either a cron job or a systemd timer. That could come in handy if you need to automatically print log files or reports on a nightly basis.

By default, pr breaks your files into single-spaced pages of 66 lines each. It also places the file's last modification date and time, the filename, and the page number into the header of every page, which is followed by a trailer of blank lines. With the appropriate switches however, all of this can be changed. Let's start by looking at an example of pr's default behavior. Here's an excerpt from the public-domain e-book, *How to Speak and Write Correctly*:

```
donnie@fedora:~$ pr excerpt_2.txt


2024-04-30 16:02                    excerpt_2.txt                    Page 1



It is very easy to learn how to speak and write correctly, as for all
purposes of ordinary conversation and communication, only about 2,000
different words are required. The mastery of just twenty hundred words,
the knowing where to place them, will make us not masters of the English
language, but masters of correct speaking and writing. Small number, you
will say, compared with what is in the dictionary! But nobody ever uses
all the words in the dictionary or could use them did he live to be the
age of Methuselah, and there is no necessity for using them.
```

Figure 7.7: Using pr with default settings

What I can't show you due to book formatting concerns is that there are a lot of blank lines after the last line of text. That's because pr recognizes that this short excerpt doesn't fill the page.

You can use the -h option to replace the filename with a header of your choice, like so:

```
donnie@fedora:~$ pr -h "How to Speak and Write Correctly" excerpt_2.txt


2024-04-30 16:02          How to Speak and Write Correctly          Page 1


It is very easy to learn how to speak and write correctly, as for all
purposes of ordinary conversation and communication, only about 2,000
different words are required. The mastery of just twenty hundred words,
the knowing where to place them, will make us not masters of the English
language, but masters of correct speaking and writing. Small number, you
will say, compared with what is in the dictionary! But nobody ever uses
all the words in the dictionary or could use them did he live to be the
age of Methuselah, and there is no necessity for using them.
```

Figure 7.8: Setting a custom header with pr

If you don't need to place headers in your output but still need to use pr's other features, use the -t switch to omit the header, like this:

```
donnie@fedora:~$ pr -t excerpt_2.txt
It is very easy to learn how to speak and write correctly, as for all
purposes of ordinary conversation and communication, only about 2,000
different words are required. The mastery of just twenty hundred words,
the knowing where to place them, will make us not masters of the English
language, but masters of correct speaking and writing. Small number, you
will say, compared with what is in the dictionary! But nobody ever uses
all the words in the dictionary or could use them did he live to be the
age of Methuselah, and there is no necessity for using them.
donnie@fedora:~$ 
```

Figure 7.9: Using the -t option

The -d option will double-space your output:

```
donnie@fedora:~$ pr -d excerpt_2.txt


2024-04-30 16:02                        excerpt_2.txt                        Page 1


It is very easy to learn how to speak and write correctly, as for all

purposes of ordinary conversation and communication, only about 2,000

different words are required. The mastery of just twenty hundred words,

the knowing where to place them, will make us not masters of the English

language, but masters of correct speaking and writing. Small number, you

will say, compared with what is in the dictionary! But nobody ever uses

all the words in the dictionary or could use them did he live to be the

age of Methuselah, and there is no necessity for using them.
```

Figure 7.10: Using the -d option

Use the -o option with a number to set the left margin. (The number represents the number of spaces to indent the left margin.) Here, I'm setting a margin of eight spaces:

```
donnie@fedora:~$ pr -o8 excerpt_2.txt


     2024-04-30 16:02                   excerpt_2.txt                   Page 1


     It is very easy to learn how to speak and write correctly, as for all
     purposes of ordinary conversation and communication, only about 2,000
     different words are required. The mastery of just twenty hundred words,
     the knowing where to place them, will make us not masters of the English
     language, but masters of correct speaking and writing. Small number, you
     will say, compared with what is in the dictionary! But nobody ever uses
     all the words in the dictionary or could use them did he live to be the
     age of Methuselah, and there is no necessity for using them.
```

Figure 7.11: Setting the left margin

As I've already said, the default page length is 66 lines. You can change that with the -l option. To set a page length of 80 lines, enter:

```
[donnie@fedora ~]$ pr -l80 excerpt_2.txt
```

By default, pr separates pages by inserting multiple newline characters at the end of each page. Use the -f option to insert a single form-feed character between pages, instead. If you need to insert line numbers, use the -n option. Here, I'm combining both of these options with a single dash:

```
donnie@fedora:~$ pr -fn excerpt_2.txt


2024-04-30 16:02                    excerpt_2.txt                    Page 1


    1    It is very easy to learn how to speak and write correctly, as for all
    2    purposes of ordinary conversation and communication, only about 2,000
    3    different words are required. The mastery of just twenty hundred words,
    4    the knowing where to place them, will make us not masters of the English
    5    language, but masters of correct speaking and writing. Small number, you
    6    will say, compared with what is in the dictionary! But nobody ever uses
    7    all the words in the dictionary or could use them did he live to be the
    8    age of Methuselah, and there is no necessity for using them.

donnie@fedora:~$ █
```

Figure 7.12: Using form feeds and adding line numbers

To work with a range of pages, just place a + in front of the first page number, and prefix the last page number with a colon. Here, I've chosen to look at pages 10 through 12 of the full pg6409.txt file:

```
[donnie@fedora ~]$ pr +10:12 pg6409.txt
2023-09-13 17:39                    pg6409.txt                    Page 10
_Thou_, _He_, _She_, and _It_, with their plurals, _We_, _Ye_ or _You_
and _They_.
. . .

. . .
[donnie@fedora ~]$
```

If you omit the last page number, you'll see everything from the first page until the end of the file. Here, I'm looking at everything from page 103 until the end:

```
[donnie@fedora ~]$ pr +103 pg6409.txt
2023-09-13 17:39                    pg6409.txt                    Page 103
1.A. By reading or using any part of this Project Gutenberg™
electronic work, you indicate that you have read, understand, agree to
. . .

. . .
[donnie@fedora ~]$
```

I've saved the columns and merge options until last, because they're the trickiest to use.

The columns option allows you to output your text in multiple columns. You set it by using a - fol-lowed by a number. The trick is, that you'll first have to format your text so that it's not too wide for the columns. Here's what you get if you try to output our sample text as a two-column page:

```
donnie@fedora:~$ pr -2 excerpt_2.txt


2024-04-30 16:02                     excerpt_2.txt                    Page 1



It is very easy to learn how to spe language, but masters of correct sp
purposes of ordinary conversation a will say, compared with what is in
different words are required. The m all the words in the dictionary or
the knowing where to place them, wi age of Methuselah, and there is no
```

Figure 7.13: The first attempt at using two columns

You can see that that's not real useful, because too much got left out. The easiest way to handle this is to change the line width with fmt, and then pipe the output to pr, like so:

```
donnie@fedora:~$ fmt -w35 excerpt_2.txt | pr -2


2024-04-30 16:21                                                     Page 1



It is very easy to learn how            of the English language, but
to speak and write correctly,           masters of correct speaking and
as for all purposes of ordinary         writing. Small number, you will
conversation and communication,         say, compared with what is in the
only about 2,000 different words        dictionary! But nobody ever uses
are required. The mastery of            all the words in the dictionary or
just twenty hundred words,              could use them did he live to be
the knowing where to place              the age of Methuselah, and there
them, will make us not masters          is no necessity for using them.
```

Figure 7.14: Combining fmt and pr

Of course, you might have to experiment with the line-width until you get what you want.

You'll have the same problem with the merge option. Here, I'm using the -m switch to show two files side-by-side:

```
donnie@fedora:~$ pr -m excerpt.txt excerpt_2.txt


2024-04-30 16:23                                               Page 1



It is the purpose of this book, as  It is very easy to learn how to spe
direct the reader along a straight  purposes of ordinary conversation a
must avoid and giving him such assi  different words are required. The m
goal of a correct knowledge of the  the knowing where to place them, wi
in any sense, but a guide, a silent  language, but masters of correct sp
right direction.                     will say, compared with what is in
                                     all the words in the dictionary or
                                     age of Methuselah, and there is no
```

Figure 7.15: First attempt at merging two files

Again, you see that the lines are too wide to fit properly in two columns. The best way to handle this is to narrow the lines with fmt, but save the output to two intermediate files. Then, use pr to merge the two new files. Here what that process looks like:

```
[donnie@fedora ~]$ fmt -w35 excerpt.txt > excerpt_fmt.txt
[donnie@fedora ~]$ fmt -w35 excerpt_2.txt > excerpt_2_fmt.txt
```

```
donnie@fedora:~$ pr -m excerpt_fmt.txt excerpt_2_fmt.txt


2024-04-30 16:27                                               Page 1



It is the purpose of this book,     It is very easy to learn how
as briefly and concisely as         to speak and write correctly,
possible, to direct the reader      as for all purposes of ordinary
along a straight course, pointing   conversation and communication,
out the mistakes he must avoid      only about 2,000 different words
and giving him such assistance      are required. The mastery of
as will enable him to reach the     just twenty hundred words,
goal of a correct knowledge of      the knowing where to place
the English language. It is not a   them, will make us not masters
Grammar in any sense, but a guide,  of the English language, but
a silent signal-post pointing the   masters of correct speaking and
way in the right direction.         writing. Small number, you will
                                    say, compared with what is in the
                                    dictionary! But nobody ever uses
                                    all the words in the dictionary or
                                    could use them did he live to be
                                    the age of Methuselah, and there
                                    is no necessity for using them.
```

Figure 7.16: Merging the two formatted files

Once you have everything looking good on-screen, you're ready to redirect your pr output into a new text file, and then print it.

Printing from the Command-line

As I've already mentioned a few times, it is possible to print text files from the command-line. (Actually, you can also print PostScript files, .pdf files, image files, and a few other types of document files from the command line. For now though, we're only interested in printing text files.) To do this, your Linux, Unix, or Unix-like machine needs to have the following two things installed on it:

- **Common Unix Printing Software** (**CUPS**): This is normally installed by default on desktop implementations of Linux, but not on text-mode server implementations of Linux.
- **The proper driver for your printer**: CUPS includes a wide-range of printer drivers that are ready to go. However, your particular printer might not be included. If that's the case, you'll need to obtain the proper driver from the printer manufacturer and follow their instructions for installing it.

Installing CUPS is generally quite easy, because it's included in the repositories of most Linux distros. On any type of Red Hat-style machine, such as Fedora, AlmaLinux, Rocky Linux, Oracle Linux, or RHEL, just do:

```
sudo dnf install cups
```

On Debian or any of its derivatives, you'll need two packages. To install them, just do:

```
sudo apt install cups cups-bsd
```

Next, you'll need to find out if CUPS includes the driver for your printer. Do that with the lpinfo -m command on a Red Hat-type system, and with the sudo lpinfo -m command on a Debian-type system.

You can pipe the output into less if you want to scroll through the whole list. Or, pipe it into grep if you want to search for a specific printer manufacturer, which will look something like this:

```
donnie@debian:~$ sudo lpinfo -m | grep -i brother
donnie@debian:~$
```

So, the Debian implementation of CUPS doesn't include drivers for any Brother printer. But, as you see here, CUPS on my Fedora workstation has quite a wide selection of Brother printer drivers:

```
[donnie@fedora ~]$ lpinfo -m | grep -i brother
gutenprint.5.3://brother-dcp-1200/expert Brother DCP-1200 - CUPS+Gutenprint
v5.3.4
gutenprint.5.3://brother-dcp-1200/simple Brother DCP-1200 - CUPS+Gutenprint
v5.3.4 Simplified
gutenprint.5.3://brother-dcp-8045d/expert Brother DCP-8045D - CUPS+Gutenprint
v5.3.4
gutenprint.5.3://brother-dcp-8045d/simple Brother DCP-8045D - CUPS+Gutenprint
v5.3.4 Simplified
```

```
.  .  .

.  .  .
gutenprint.5.3://brother-mfc-9600/expert Brother MFC-9600 - CUPS+Gutenprint
v5.3.4
gutenprint.5.3://brother-mfc-9600/simple Brother MFC-9600 - CUPS+Gutenprint
v5.3.4 Simplified
MFC7460DN.ppd Brother MFC7460DN for CUPS
lsb/usr/MFC7460DN.ppd Brother MFC7460DN for CUPS
[donnie@fedora ~]$
```

The only catch was that the Fedora workstation didn't have the drivers for my Brother MFC7460DN printer, so I had to download the driver from the Brother website and install it myself. (The driver that I installed is represented by the last two items in this list.) The lpstat -p -d command shows me the status of my printer, as you see here:

```
[donnie@fedora ~]$ lpstat -p -d
printer MFC7460DN is idle.   enabled since Tue 19 Sep 2023 06:17:03 PM EDT
system default destination: MFC7460DN
[donnie@fedora ~]$
```

Cool. It's ready to go.

Once you've set everything up, you're ready to print with either lp or lpr. (They're two different utilities that both do the same thing, but with different option switches. To make things simple, I'm just going to show you lpr.) To print to a specific printer, do something like this:

```
[donnie@fedora ~]$ lpr -P MFC7460DN somefile.txt
```

The -P option directs the print job to the desired printer. If you don't want to always have to specify a printer, you can set a default printer, like this:

```
[donnie@localhost ~]$ lpoptions -d MFC7460DN
```

(Note that this will require sudo privileges on a Debian-type system.)

Once you've assigned a default printer, you can run a print job like this:

```
[donnie@fedora ~]$ lpr somefile.txt
```

If you have multiple files that you need to print out, there's no need to issue multiple lpr commands. Instead, just place the names of the files that you want to print into a separate text file, and then use xargs to read the list. That will look something like this:

```
[donnie@fedora ~]$ xargs lpr < print_list.txt
[donnie@fedora ~]$
```

Easy, right? Well, there are actually a lot more print options that you can use with either `lp` or `lpr`, but for now we'll just go with the basics. To see a complete tutorial on printing with `lp` and `lpr`, your best bet is to pull up a web browser on a Linux desktop machine, and navigate to `http://localhost:631`. In addition to the tutorial, you'll see that you can also perform certain administrative functions from the web interface.

All right, I think that will do for this chapter. Let's wrap things up and move on.

Summary

In this chapter, I showed you a lot more utilities that you can use to format text files as either you or your employer might require. Finally, at the end, I showed you the basics of setting up a printer on a text-mode server.

The beauty of all this is that you can create shell scripts that will automatically obtain information from various sources, create properly-formatted text files, and then print them. You can even have the scripts run automatically by creating either a `cron` job or a `systemd` timer.

Oh, but I haven't shown you how to create a shell script, have I? That's okay, because that will be the subject of the next chapter. I'll see you there.

Questions

1. Which two of the following commands would you use to see if a text file contains carriage return characters? (Select two.)

    a. `od -tx filename.txt`

    b. `od -tc filename.txt`

    c. `od -ta filename.txt`

    d. `od -td filename.txt`

2. You've created a text file that contains a list of other text files. And now, you want to sort all of the files that are contained in that list, and save the output to one new file. Which of the following commands would you use for that?

    a. `sort sort_list.txt > combined_sorted.txt`

    b. `xargs sort sort_list.txt > combined_sorted.txt`

    c. `xargs sort < sort_list.txt > combined_sorted.txt`

    d. `sort < sort_list.txt > combined_sorted.txt`

3. Which of the following commands will number all lines in the body of a text file?

    a. `nl -a file.txt`

    b. `nl file.txt`

    c. `nl -bn file.txt`

    d. `nl -ba file.txt`

4. Which utility would you most likely use for the final step of preparing a text file for printing?

    a. `fmt`

    b. `pr`

    c. `lp`

    d. `lpr`

5. Which of the following commands would you use to verify that the driver for your printer is installed on your computer?

    a. `lpinfo -m`

    b. `lpstat -p -d`

    c. `lpr -i`

    d. `lp -i`

Further Reading

- nl Command in Linux with Examples: `https://linuxconfig.org/nl`
- head Command in Linux (5 Essential Examples: `https://linuxhandbook.com/head-command/`
- Using od to See How Text isFormatted: `https://bash-prompt.net/guides/od/`
- wc Command in Linux with Examples: `https://www.geeksforgeeks.org/wc-command-linux-examples/`
- tr Command in Linux with Examples: `https://linuxize.com/post/linux-tr-command/`
- How to use the Linux tr Command: `https://www.howtogeek.com/886723/how-to-use-the-linux-tr-command/`
- Talk Like a Pirate Day: `https://nationaltoday.com/talk-like-a-pirate-day/`
- How to Use the xargs Command on Linux: `https://www.howtogeek.com/435164/how-to-use-the-xargs-command-on-linux/`
- How I use the Linux fmt command to format text: `https://opensource.com/article/22/7/fmt-trivial-text-formatter`
- pr command in Linux: `https://www.geeksforgeeks.org/pr-command-in-linux/`
- Master the Linux "pr" Command: A Comprehensive Guide: `https://hopeness.medium.com/master-the-linux-pr-command-a-comprehensive-guide-b166865c933e`

Answers

1. b and c
2. c
3. d
4. b
5. a

Join our community on Discord!

Read this book alongside other users, Linux experts, and the author himself.

Ask questions, provide solutions to other readers, chat with the author via Ask Me Anything sessions, and much more. Scan the QR code or visit the link to join the community.

https://packt.link/SecNet

8

Basic Shell Script Construction

Yeah, I know. You're dying to start creating some shell scripts, but haven't been able to do that yet. So, in this chapter, we'll look at the basics of shell script construction. We'll then wrap things up by looking at some shell scripts that are both practical and useful.

Many of the techniques that I'm presenting in this chapter work for any shell, but I'll also present some that might only work on bash. So, just to keep things simple though, I'll be sticking with bash for now. In *Chapter 22, Using the zsh Shell*, I'll show you techniques that are specific to zsh. In *Chapter 19, Shell Script Portability*, I'll show you techniques that will work on a wide variety of shells.

The topics that you'll see in this chapter include:

- Understanding basic shell script construction
- Performing tests
- Understanding subshells
- Understanding scripting variables
- Understanding array variables
- Understanding variable expansion
- Understanding command substitution
- Understanding decisions and loops
- Understanding positional parameters
- Understanding exit codes
- More information about echo
- Looking at some real-world examples

All right, if you're ready, let's jump in.

Technical Requirements

Use any Linux distro that has bash installed. If you're a Mac user, you'll want to use one of your Linux virtual machines, because some of the scripts use commands that won't work on macOS. Feel free to follow along on your local machine as you go through this chapter, but also be aware that I will provide some actual hands-on labs.

I've also included one hands-on exercise that uses a FreeBSD virtual machine. Create the FreeBSD virtual machine and install both sudo and bash, as I showed you in the book's *Preface*.

Also, as I explained in the *Preface*, you can download the scripts from the Github repository by doing:

```
git clone https://github.com/PacktPublishing/The-Ultimate-Linux-Shell-
Scripting-Guide.git
```

Understanding Basic Shell Script Construction

The first thing you'll need to do when creating a shell script is to define which shell you want to use to interpret the script.

 You might have a particular reason for choosing one shell over another. That's something we'll talk about in *Chapter 19, Shell Script Portability*, and *Chapter 22, Using the Z Shell*.

You'll define the shell to use as the interpreter in the **shebang line**, which is the first line of the script. It will look something like this:

```
#!/bin/bash
```

Normally of course, a line that begins with the # sign would indicate a comment that would be ignored by the shell. The shebang line--and please don't ask me why it's called that--is an exception to that rule. In addition to defining a specific shell that you want to use, such as /bin/bash or /bin/zsh, you can also define the generic /bin/sh shell to make your scripts more portable, so that they'll run on a wider variety of shells and operating systems. Here's how that looks:

```
#!/bin/sh
```

This generic sh shell is supposed to make it so that you can run your scripts on different systems that might or might not have bash installed. But, it's also problematic because the various shells that sh represents aren't fully compatible with each other. Here's the breakdown of how it works:

- On FreeBSD and possibly other **Berkeley Software Distribution** (BSD)-type systems, the sh executable is the old-school Bourne shell, which is the ancestor of the Bourne Again Shell (bash).
- On Red Hat-type systems, sh is a symbolic link that points to the bash executable. Be aware that bash can use certain programming features that the other shells in this list can't use. (I'll explain more about this in *Chapter 19, Shell Script Portability*.)

- On Debian/Ubuntu-type systems, sh is a symbolic link that points to the dash executable. dash stands for **Debian Almquist Shell**, which is a faster, more lightweight implementation of bash.

- On Alpine Linux, sh is a symbolic link that points to ash, which is a lightweight shell that's part of the busybox executable. (On Alpine, bash is not installed by default.)

- On OpenIndiana, which is a **Free Open Source Software** fork of Oracle's Solaris operating system, sh is a symbolic link that points to the ksh93 shell. This shell, which is also known as the Korn shell, is somewhat, but not completely, compatible with bash. (It was created by a guy named David Korn, and has nothing to do with any vegetable.)

- On macOS, sh is a symbolic link that points to bash. (Curiously, zsh is the default login shell on macOS, but bash is still installed by default and is available for use.)

Be aware that using #!/bin/sh in your scripts can be problematic. That's because the various shells on the various operating systems that #!/bin/sh represents aren't fully compatible with each other. So, let's say that you're creating a script on a Red Hat machine, on which sh points to bash. There's a real possibility that the script won't run on either a Debian or a FreeBSD machine, on which sh points to dash and Bourne shell, respectively. For that reason, we'll concentrate on bash for now, and will just use #!/bin/bash as our shebang line. And, as I mentioned before, we'll talk more about this topic in *Chapter 19, Shell Script Portability*.

A shell script can be as simple or as complex as your needs dictate. It can be just one or more normal Linux/Unix commands put together in a list, to be performed sequentially. Or, you can have scripts that can approach the complexity of programs written in a higher-level programming language, such as C.

Let's start by taking a look at a very simple, one-command script.

```
#!/bin/bash
rsync -avhe ssh /var/www/html/course/images/ root@192.168.0.22:/var/www/html/
course/images/
```

This is a simple one-line script that I used to use to back up my images directory on one computer to a backup directory on a Debian computer. It uses rsync, with its appropriate options, to synchronize the two directories via a Secure Shell (ssh) session. (Although I normally don't like to allow the root user to do ssh logins, in this case it's necessary. Obviously, I would only do this on a local network, and would never do it across the Internet.) Appropriately, I named the script rsync_with_debian. Before I could run the script, I had to add the executable permission, like this:

```
chmod u+x rsync_with_debian
```

On the second line of this rsync_with_debian script, right after the shebang line, you see the exact same command that I would have typed on the command-line if I didn't have the script. So, you see, I've greatly simplified things by creating a script.

To make this script available to all users on the system, place it in the /usr/local/bin/ directory, which should be in everyone's PATH setting.

Before going further, let's reinforce what you've just learned with a hands-on lab.

Hands-on Lab — Counting Logged-in Users

This lab will help you create a shell script that shows how many users are logged in, and then modify it so that only unique users are listed. (This script uses some of the text stream filters that you learned about in the previous two chapters.)

1. On one of your Linux virtual machines, create three additional user accounts. On your Fedora virtual machine, do it like this, except choose your own user names:

    ```
    sudo useradd vicky
    sudo passwd vicky
    ```

    On a Debian virtual machine, do it like this:

    ```
    sudo adduser vicky
    ```

2. At the local terminal of the virtual machine, obtain its IP address, like this:

    ```
    ip a
    ```

3. Open four terminal windows on your host machine. Using the IP address of your own virtual machine, log into your own account from one window, and then log into each of the other accounts from the other windows. The commands will look something like this:

    ```
    ssh vicky@192.168.0.9
    ```

4. From the terminal window where you're logged in, view all of the users who are currently logged in, like this:

    ```
    who
    ```

    You should see five users, because your own account will show up once for the local terminal log-in, and once for the remote ssh log-in.

5. Create the logged-in.sh script, and make it look like this:

    ```
    #!/bin/bash
    users="$(who | wc -l)"
    echo "There are currently $users users logged in."
    ```

    I'm using the concept of **command substitution** to assign the output of the who | wc -l command to the value of the users scripting variable. (I'll tell you more about command substitution later, so don't stress out about it just yet.)

6. Make the script executable, like this:

    ```
    chmod u+x logged-in.sh
    ```

7. Now, run the script, like this:

```
./logged-in.sh
```

The output should look like this:

```
There are currently 5 users logged in.
```

The problem here is that there are really only four users, because your own username is counted twice. So, let's fix that.

8. Modify the `logged-in.sh` script so that it now looks like this:

```
#!/bin/bash
users="$(who | wc -l)"
echo "There are currently $users users logged in."
echo
uniqusers="$(who | cut -d" " -f1 | sort | uniq | wc -l)"
echo "There are currently $uniqusers unique users logged in."
```

The variable `uniqusers` is created by all of the commands that are piped to each other inside the (). The cut operation is delimited by a blank space (-d" ") and the first field (-f1) is what you will cut from the output of `who`. That output is piped to `sort` and then to `uniq`, which will only send the names of unique users to the `wc -l` command.

9. Run the script again, and the output should look like this:

```
There are currently 5 users logged in.
There are currently 4 unique users logged in.
```

10. Make one last modification to the script to list the names of the unique users who are logged in. The completed script will look like this:

```
#!/bin/bash
users="$(who | wc -l)"
echo "There are currently $users users logged in."
echo
uniqusers="$(who | cut -d" " -f1 | sort | uniq | wc -l)"
echo "There are currently $uniqusers unique users logged in."
echo
listusers="$(who | cut -d" " -f1 | sort | uniq)"
echo "These users are currently logged in: \n$listusers "
```

11. Run the script again, and you should get output that looks something like this:

```
There are currently 5 users logged in.
There are currently 4 unique users logged in.
These users are currently logged in:
```

```
cleopatra
donnie
frank
vicky
```

Congratulations! You've just created your first shell script. Now, let's do some testing.

Performing Tests

There will be times when your scripts will need to test for a certain condition before making a decision on which action to take. You might need to check for the existence of a certain file or directory, whether certain permissions are set on a file or directory, or for a myriad of other things. There are three ways to perform a test, which are:

- Use the keyword test followed by a test condition, with another command joined to it with either a && or a || construct.
- Enclose the test condition within a set of square brackets.
- Use an if. . .then construct

Let's start by looking at the test keyword.

Using the test Keyword

For our first example, let's test to see whether a certain directory exists, and then create it if it doesn't. Here's how that works:

```
[donnie@fedora ~]$ test -d graphics || mkdir graphics
[donnie@fedora ~]$ ls -ld graphics/
drwxr-xr-x. 1 donnie donnie 0 Sep 26 15:41 graphics/
[donnie@fedora ~]$
```

Now, let's put that into the test_graphics.sh script:

```
#!/bin/bash
cd
pwd
test -d graphics || mkdir graphics
cd graphics
pwd
```

Let's run this script to see what we get:

```
[donnie@fedora ~]$ ./test_graphics.sh
/home/donnie
/home/donnie/graphics
[donnie@fedora ~]$
```

As you may have guessed, the -d operator stands for *directory*. The || construct causes the mkdir command to run if the graphics directory doesn't exist. And of course, if the directory already exists, it won't get created again. This is a good safety measure that can prevent you from accidentally overwriting any existing files or directories. (I'll show you a chart with more test operators in just a moment.)

Now, let's look at the second way to perform a test.

Enclosing a test Condition Within Square Brackets

The second way to perform a test is to enclose the test condition within a pair of square brackets, like so:

```
[ -d graphics ]
```

First, note how you must have a blank space after the first bracket and before the second one. This tests for the existence of the graphics directory, just as the test -d construct did. Now, let's put that into the test_graphics_2.sh script, like so:

```
#!/bin/bash
cd
pwd
[ -d graphics ] || mkdir graphics
cd graphics
pwd
```

Running this script will give you the exact same output as the first script. Now, let's put a twist on things. Modify the test_graphics_2.sh script so that it looks like this:

```
#!/bin/bash
cd
pwd
[ ! -d graphics ] && mkdir graphics
cd graphics
pwd
```

The ! is a negation operator, which makes the affected operator do the opposite of what it's supposed to do. In this case, the ! causes the -d operator to check for the *absence* of the graphics directory. To make this work properly, I also had to change the || operator to the && operator. (Also, note that there must be a blank space between the ! and the -d.)

You can also test for numerical values, like this:

```
[ $var -eq 0 ]
```

You see that I'm calling up the value of the variable var, and testing to see if it is equal (-eq) to 0. Instead of using a negation (!) here to see if the variable is *not* equal to 0, use the -ne operator. Let's see how that looks in the test_var.sh script:

```
#!/bin/bash
```

```
var1=0
var2=1
[ $var1 -eq 0 ] && echo "$var1 is equal to zero."
[ $var2 -ne 0 ] && echo "$var2 is not equal to zero."
```

Now, let's run it:

```
[donnie@fedora ~]$ ./test_var.sh
0 is equal to zero.
1 is not equal to zero.
[donnie@fedora ~]$
```

The third way to perform a test is to use an if. . .then construct, which we'll briefly talk about next.

Using an if. . .then Construct

Using an if. . .then construct is handy when you have more complex test conditions. Here's the most basic example, in the form of the test_graphics_3.sh script:

```
#!/bin/bash
cd
pwd
if [ ! -d graphics ]; then
        mkdir graphics
fi
cd graphics
pwd
```

This construct begins with the if statement, and ends with the fi statement. (That's if spelled backwards.) Place a semi-colon after the test condition, followed by the keyword then. After that, specify the action that you want to perform, which in this case is mkdir graphics. Although indenting the action block isn't necessary in shell scripting, as it is in other languages, it does help make the script more readable.

Of course, there's a lot more to if. . .then constructs than just this. Not to worry though, because I'll show you more about them in the *Understanding Decisions and Loops* section. Before we get there though, I want to show you some more concepts that you can use to fancy up your if. . .then constructs.

Now, let's look at the various other types of tests that you can do.

Using Other Types of Tests

There are a lot more kinds of tests that you can do, including text string comparisons, numerical comparisons, whether files or directories exist and what permissions are set on them. Here's a chart of the more popular tests, along with their operators:

Operator	Test
-b filename	True if a block device file with the specified filename exists.
-c filename	True if a character device file with the specified filename exists.
-d directory_name	True if a directory with the specified directory name exists.
-e filename	True if any type of file with the specified filename exists.
-f filename	True if a regular file with the specified filename exists.
-g filename	True if a file or directory has the SGID permission set.
-G filename	True if a file exists and is owned by the Effective Group ID
-h filename	True if the file exists and it's a symbolic link
-k filename	True if the file or directory exists and has the sticky bit set
-L filename	True if the file exists and it's a symbolic link. (This is the same as -h.)
-p filename	True if the file exists and it's a named pipe
-O filename	True if the file exists and it's owned by the Effective UID
-r filename	True if the file exists and it's readable
-S filename	True if the file exists and it's a socket
-s filename	True if the file exists and it's non-zero bytes in size
-u filename	True if the file exists and it has the SUID bit set
-w filename	True if the file exists and it's writable
-x filename	True if the file exists and it's executable
file1 -nt file2	True if file1 is newer than file2
file1 -ot file2	True if file1 is older than file2
-z string	True if the length of the text string is 0
-n string	True if the length of the text string is not 0
string1 == string2	True if the two text strings are identical
string1 != string2	True if the two text strings are not identical
string1 < string2	True if string1 comes before string2 in alphabetical order
string1 > string2	True if string1 comes after string2 in alphabetical order
integer1 -eq integer2	True if the two integers are equal
integer1 -ne integer2	True if the two integers are not equal

`integer1 -lt` `integer2`	True if `integer1` is less than `integer2`
`integer1 -gt` `integer2`	True if `integer1` is greater than `integer2`
`integer1 -le` `integer2`	True if `integer1` is less than or equal to `integer2`
`integer1 -ge` `integer2`	True if `integer1` is greater than or equal to `integer2`
`-o optionname`	True if a shell option is enabled

I know, that's a lot of stuff, isn't it? But, that's okay. If you don't want to memorize all of this, just keep this chart handy for ready reference.

Next up, let's talk about subshells.

Understanding Subshells

When you perform a test using the `[ $var -ne 0 ]` construct, the test will invoke a **subshell**. To prevent a test from invoking a subshell, use this construct, instead:

```
[[ $var -ne 0 ]]
```

This can make your script run somewhat more efficiently, which might or might not be a huge deal for your particular script.

> This `[[. . .]]` type of construct is also necessary when you perform tests that require matching a pattern to a regular expression. (Matching regular expressions won't work within a `[. . .]` construct.)
>
> The downside of this `[[. . .]]` construct is that you can't use it on certain non-bash shells, such as dash, ash, or Bourne. (You'll see that in *Chapter 19, Shell Script Portability*.)
>
> Of course, you don't know what regular expressions are just yet, and that's okay. I'll show you all about them in *Chapter 9, Filtering Text with grep, sed, and Regular Expressions*.

At any rate, you can always try your scripts with subshells and without subshells, to see which works better for you.

We've now looked at all three methods to perform testing. So, how about a bit of practice with a hands-on lab?

Hands-on Lab – Testing Conditions

For this step, download the `tests-test.sh` script from the Github repository. (It's a rather long script that I can't reproduce here, due to book formatting considerations.) Open the script in your text editor, and examine how it's constructed. The first thing you'll see is that it's checking for the existence of the `myfile.txt` file, like this:

```
#!/bin/bash
[ -f myfile.txt ] && echo "This file exists." || echo "This file does not
exist."
```

After that, you'll see the command to create the file if it doesn't exist, like this:

```
echo "We will now create myfile.txt if it does not exist, and make it with only
read permissions for $USER."
[ -f myfile.txt ] || touch myfile.txt
```

Next, you'll see the command to set 400 as the permissions setting, which means that the user has permission to read the file, and that nobody has permission to write to it. Then, we want to verify that all write permissions have been removed. Here's how that looks:

```
chmod 400 myfile.txt
ls -l myfile.txt
echo
echo "We will now see if myfile.txt is writable."
[ -w myfile.txt ] && echo "This file is writable." || echo "This file is not
writable."
```

After several more permissions settings manipulations and tests for them, you'll see this stanza that tests for the existence of a directory, and creates it if it doesn't exist:

```
[ -d somedir ] || echo "somedir does not exist."
[ -d somedir ] || mkdir somedir && echo "somedir has just been created."
ls -ld somedir
```

The final thing you'll see is the stanza that tests for the noclobber option, sets it, and then tests for it again.

After you've finished reviewing the script, run it to see what happens.

For bonus points, retype the script into your own script file. Why? Well, a dirty little secret is that if you type code in yourself, it will help you better understand the concepts.

For the next step, create the tests-test_2.sh script with the following contents:

```
#!/bin/bash
echo "We will now compare text strings."
string1="abcd"
string2="efgh"
[[ $string1 > $string2 ]] && echo "string1 comes after string2 alphabetically."
|| echo "string1 comes before string2 alphabetically."
echo
echo "We will now compare numbers."
num1=10
num2=9
```

```
[[ $num1 -gt $num2 ]] && echo "num1 is greater than num2." || echo "num1 is
less than num2."
```

Make the script file executable and then run it to view the results. Change the values of the string1, string2, num1, and num2 variables and then run the script again and view the results.

End of lab.

Next, let's take a closer look at variables.

Understanding Scripting Variables

I've already told you a bit about scripting variables, and you've already seen them in use. But, there's a bit more to the story.

Creating and Deleting Variables

As you've already seen, it's sometimes either necessary or more convenient to define variables in your scripts. You can also define, view, and unset variables from the command-line. Here's an example:

```
[donnie@fedora ~]$ car=Ford
[donnie@fedora ~]$ echo $car
Ford
[donnie@fedora ~]$ unset car
[donnie@fedora ~]$ echo $car
[donnie@fedora ~]$
```

Here, I've defined the variable car, and set its value to Ford. The first echo command shows the assigned value. The second echo command verifies that I've successfully cleared the variable with unset.

Understanding Variables and Shell Levels

When you place a shebang line, such as #!/bin/bash or #!/bin/sh, at the start of your script, a new non-interactive child shell will be invoked every time you run the script. When the script finishes, the child shell terminates. The child shell inherits any variables that are exported from the parent shell. But, the parent shell won't inherit any variables from the child shell. To demonstrate, let's set the car variable to Volkswagen in the parent shell, like so:

```
[donnie@fedora ~]$ export car="Volkswagen"
[donnie@fedora ~]$ echo $car
Volkswagen
[donnie@fedora ~]$
```

Next, create the car_demo.sh script, like so:

```
#!/bin/bash
echo \$car is set to $car
export car=Toyota
echo "The $car is very fast."
echo \$car is set to $car
```

Make the file executable and then run the script. The output should look like this:

```
[donnie@fedora ~]$ ./car_demo.sh
$car is set to Volkswagen
The Toyota is very fast.
$car is set to Toyota
[donnie@fedora ~]$
```

Note how the Volkswagen value of car was inherited from the parent shell. That's because I used the export command to make sure that this value would be available to the child shell that the script invokes. Let's try this again, except this time, I won't export the variable:

```
[donnie@fedora ~]$ unset car
[donnie@fedora ~]$ car=Studebaker
[donnie@fedora ~]$ ./car_demo.sh
$car is set to
The Toyota is very fast.
$car is set to Toyota
[donnie@fedora ~]$
```

To make this work, I first had to unset the car variable. In addition to clearing out the value of car, it also cleared out the export. When I ran the script this time, it couldn't find the value of car that I set in the parent shell.

So, why is this important? It's just that you may, at times, find yourself writing scripts that will call another script, which will effectively open another child shell. If you want variables to be available to a child shell, you have to export them.

Understanding Case Sensitivity

Variable names are case sensitive. So, a variable named car is completely different from variables named Car or CAR.

Environmental variables have names with all upper-case letters, and it's best practice for programming variable names to be in either all lower-case letters or mixed-case letters. Amazingly, Linux and Unix shells don't enforce that rule for programming variables. But, it is best practice, because it helps prevent you from accidentally overwriting the value of an important environmental variable.

Sad to say, there are shell scripting tutorials on the web in which the authors have you create programming variable names with all upper-case letters. In fact, I just came across one such tutorial. For the most part, the author has you create variables with names that don't conflict with any environmental variables. In one spot though, the author has you create the USER variable and assign a value to it. Of course, USER is already the name of an environmental variable, so assigning a new value to it will overwrite what its value should be. The lesson here is that there are a lot of good tutorials on the web, but there are also a lot that give out wrong information.

Understanding Read-Only Variables

You've just seen that when you declare a variable in the normal way, you can either unset it or give it a new value. You can also make a variable read-only, which prevents the variable from being either redefined or unset. Here's how that works:

```
[donnie@fedora ~]$ car=Nash
[donnie@fedora ~]$ echo $car
Nash
[donnie@fedora ~]$ readonly car
[donnie@fedora ~]$ unset car
bash: unset: car: cannot unset: readonly variable
[donnie@fedora ~]$ car=Hudson
bash: car: readonly variable
[donnie@fedora ~]$
```

With the read-only property set, the only way that I can either change or get rid of car is to close the terminal window.

Well, this is the only way that you can get rid of a read-only variable if you don't have root user privileges. If you do have root user privileges, you can use the **GNU bash Debugger** (gbd) to get rid of it. But, that's beyond the scope of this chapter. (We'll look at gbd in *Chapter 21, Debugging Shell Scripts*.)

Okay, this is all great if all you need is to define some individual variables. But, what if you need a whole list of variables? Well, this is where arrays come in handy. Let's look at that next.

Understanding Array Variables

An array allows you to collect a list into one variable. The easy way to create an array variable is to assign a value to one of its indices, like so:

```
name[index]=value
```

Here, name is the name of the array, and index is the position of the item in the array. (Note that index must be a number.) value is the value that's set for that individual item in the array.

The numbering system for arrays begins with 0. So, name[0] would be the first item in the array. To create an indexed array, use declare with the -a option, like so:

```
[donnie@fedora ~]$ declare -a myarray
[donnie@fedora ~]$
```

Next, let's create the list that will be inserted into the array, like so:

```
[donnie@fedora ~]$ myarray=(item1 item2 item3 )
[donnie@fedora ~]$
```

You can view the value of any individual item in the array, but there's a special way to do it. Here's what it looks like:

```
[donnie@fedora ~]$ echo ${myarray[0]}
item1
[donnie@fedora ~]$ echo ${myarray[1]}
item2
[donnie@fedora ~]$ echo ${myarray[2]}
item3
[donnie@fedora ~]$
```

Note how I had to surround the myarray[x] construct with a pair of curly braces.

To view the whole list of array items, use either a * or an @ in place of the index number, like so:

```
[donnie@fedora ~]$ echo ${myarray[*]}
item1 item2 item3
[donnie@fedora ~]$ echo ${myarray[@]}
item1 item2 item3
[donnie@fedora ~]$
```

To just count the number of array items, insert a # in front of the array name, like this:

```
[donnie@fedora ~]$ echo ${#myarray[@]}
3
[donnie@fedora ~]$ echo ${#myarray[*]}
3
[donnie@fedora ~]$
```

Okay, that covers the basics of arrays. Let's do something a bit more practical with a hands-on lab.

Hands-on Lab — Using Arrays

1. To see how arrays are built, create the ip.sh script with the following contents:

```
#!/bin/bash
echo "IP Addresses of intruder attempts"
```

```
declare -a ip
ip=( 192.168.3.78 192.168.3.4 192.168.3.9 )
echo "ip[0] is ${ip[0]}, the first item in the list."
echo "ip[2] is ${ip[2]}, the third item in the list."
echo "****************************"
echo "The most dangerous intruder is ${ip[1]}, which is in ip[1]."
echo "****************************"
echo "Here is the entire list of IP addresses in the array."
echo ${ip[*]}
```

2. Make the file executable and run it.

```
chmod u+x ip.sh
./ip.sh
```

3. Create the /opt/scripts/ directory to store data files that your scripts will need to access, like this:

```
sudo mkdir /opt/scripts
```

4. In the /opt/scripts/ directory, create the banned.txt file. (Note that in this directory, you'll need to use sudo when opening your text editor.) Add to it the following contents:

```
192.168.0.48
24.190.78.101
38.101.148.126
41.206.45.202
58.0.0.0/8
59.107.0.0/17
59.108.0.0/15
59.110.0.0/15
59.151.0.0/17
59.155.0.0/16
59.172.0.0/15
```

5. In your own home directory, create the attackers.sh script, which will build an array of banned IP addresses from a list in a text file. Add the following contents:

```
#!/bin/bash
badips=$(cat /opt/scripts/banned.txt)
declare -a attackers
attackers=( $badips )
echo "Here is the complete list: "
echo ${attackers[@]}
echo
```

```
echo "Let us now count the items in the list."
num_attackers=${#attackers[*]}
echo "There are $elements IP addresses in the list."
echo
echo "attackers[2] is ${attackers[2]}, which is the third address in the
list."
exit
```

6. Set the executable permission and run the script, like so:

```
chmod u+x attackers.sh
./attackers.sh
```

7. Modify the script so that the elements 0, 5, and 8 are printed to screen, and rerun the script. (You've already seen how to do it.)

End of Lab

A few words of explanation about this attackers.sh script are in order. First, in the second line, I'm using command substitution with the cat command to assign the contents of the banned.txt script to the badips variable. (I know, I keep showing you examples of command substitution, but I haven't fully explained it yet. Don't worry though, I'll do that in a bit.) However, this still isn't an array. I've created that separately in the declare -a line. In the attackers= line, I called back the value of the badips variable, which I then used to build the attackers array. Alternatively, I could have skipped using the intermediate variable and built the array directly from the cat command substitution, as I did in this attackers_2.sh script:

```
#!/bin/bash
declare -a badips
badips=( $(cat /opt/scripts/banned.txt) )
echo "Here is the complete list: "
echo ${badips[@]}
echo
echo "Let us now count the items in the list."
elements=${#badips[*]}
echo "There are $elements IP addresses in the list."
echo
echo "badips[2] is ${badips[2]}, which is the third address in the list."
exit
```

Either way works, but this way is a bit more streamlined.

 In a real-life scenario, you could add code that will automatically invoke a firewall rule that will block all of the addresses in the banned.txt file. But, that requires using techniques that I haven't yet shown you. So, we'll just have to get that later.

Next, let's expand some variables.

Understanding Variable Expansion

Variable expansion, which is also called **parameter expansion**, allows the shell to test or modify values of a variable to be used in a script, using special modifiers enclosed in curly braces and preceded by a $ (${variable}). If this variable is not set in bash it will be expanded to a null string. The best way to begin is to show you a few simple examples.

Substituting a Value for an Unset Variable

First, I'll define the cat variable with the name of my 16-year old gray kitty. Then, I'll perform a test to see if cat really has a set value, like this:

```
[donnie@fedora ~]$ cat=Vicky
[donnie@fedora ~]$ echo ${cat-"This cat variable is not set."}
Vicky
[donnie@fedora ~]$
```

Next, I'll unset the value of cat, and perform the test again. Watch what happens:

```
[donnie@fedora ~]$ unset cat
[donnie@fedora ~]$ echo ${cat-"This cat variable is not set."}
This cat variable is not set.
[donnie@fedora ~]$
```

So, what happened? Well, the - between cat and "This cat variable is not set." tests to see whether or not the cat variable has an assigned value. If the variable has no assigned value, then the text string that comes after the - is substituted for the variable's value. However, the substituted value is not actually *assigned* to the variable, as you see here:

```
[donnie@fedora ~]$ echo $cat
[donnie@fedora ~]$
```

Now, assign a null value to cat, and try this again:

```
donnie@fedora:~$ cat=
donnie@fedora:~$ echo ${cat-"This cat variable is not set."}
donnie@fedora:~$
```

This time, we just get a blank line as output, because the cat variable is set. It's just that it's set to a null value. Let's try this again, using : - instead of - , like so:

```
donnie@fedora:~$ echo ${cat:-"This cat variable is not set."}
This cat variable is not set.
donnie@fedora:~$
```

This works because placing a : in front of the - causes variables that have been set with a null value to be treated as unset variables.

Okay, that does it for unset variables. Sometimes though, we might need to work with variables that do have set values, as you'll see next.

Substituting a Value for a Set Variable

You can go the opposite way by substituting a value for a variable that *does* have an assigned value, like this:

```
[donnie@fedora ~]$ car="1958 Edsel Corsair"
[donnie@fedora ~]$ echo ${car+"car is set and might or might not be null"}
car is set and might or might not be null
[donnie@fedora ~]$
```

In this case, the + construct causes the following text string to be substituted for the variable's assigned value. Note that since there are no special characters in this text string that need to be escaped, the quotes are optional. However, best practice dictates using quotes anyway, just to be safe. Also note that this substitution did not change the actual assigned value of the car variable, as you see here:

```
[donnie@fedora ~]$ echo $car
1958 Edsel Corsair
[donnie@fedora ~]$
```

As you just saw with the – operator, the + operator treats variables with a null value as being set. If you want to treat variables with null values as unset, then use the :+ operator. If you create a variable and leave it with a null value, it will look something like this:

```
[donnie@fedora ~]$ computer=
[donnie@fedora ~]$ echo ${computer:+"computer is set and is not null"}
[donnie@fedora ~]$
```

You see that with a null value, there's no output from the echo command. Now, since I just happen to be using a Dell computer, let's set the value of computer to Dell, as you see here:

```
[donnie@fedora ~]$ computer=Dell
[donnie@fedora ~]$ echo ${computer:+"computer is set and might or might not be null"}
computer is set and might or might not be null
[donnie@fedora ~]$
```

As I've already indicated, the operators that we've just looked at will substitute a value for a variable, depending upon whether the value has an assigned value. But, they won't actually change the value of the variable. But, we might at times need to change a variable's value, as we'll see next.

Assigning a Value to a Variable

This next trick actually will assign a value to an unset variable, using the = and := operators. Let's begin by assigning a value to the town variable:

```
donnie@fedora:~$ unset town
donnie@fedora:~$ echo $town
donnie@fedora:~$ echo ${town="Saint Marys"}
Saint Marys
donnie@fedora:~$ echo $town
Saint Marys
donnie@fedora:~$
```

Now, let's see if we can assign a different value to town:

```
donnie@fedora:~$ echo ${town="Kingsland"}
Saint Marys
donnie@fedora:~$ echo $town
Saint Marys
donnie@fedora:~$
```

As you've seen before, using this operator without a preceding : causes a variable with a null value to be treated as a set variable. Here's how that looks:

```
donnie@fedora:~$ unset town
donnie@fedora:~$ town=
donnie@fedora:~$ echo ${town="Saint Marys"}
donnie@fedora:~$
```

To show how using the := operator works, let's create the armadillo variable with a null value, and then assign to it a default value, like so:

```
[donnie@fedora ~]$ armadillo=
[donnie@fedora ~]$ echo ${armadillo:=Artie}
Artie
[donnie@fedora ~]$ echo $armadillo
Artie
[donnie@fedora ~]$
```

Artie is the tentative name that I've given to the armadillo who's recently begun visiting my back yard at night. But, I don't yet know if the armadillo is a boy or a girl, so I don't yet know if Artie is an appropriate name. If I find out that it's a girl, I might want to change the name to Annie. So, let's try the preceding exercise again, but with armadillo set to Annie. Then, we'll see if we can use our variable expansion to change it to Artie, like so:

```
[donnie@fedora ~]$ armadillo=Annie
[donnie@fedora ~]$ echo ${armadillo:=Artie}
```

```
Annie
[donnie@fedora ~]$ echo $armadillo
Annie
[donnie@fedora ~]$
```

You see that since the armadillo variable already had the Annie assigned as its value, the echo ${armadillo:=Artie} command had no effect, other than to show the value that I had already assigned.

Now, what if you don't want to substitute a variable's value, but just want to see an error message? Let's look at that.

Displaying an Error Message

You won't always want to perform either a value substitution or a value assignment for an unset variable. Sometimes, you might just want to see an error (stderror) message if the variable is unset. Do that with the :? construct, like this:

```
[donnie@fedora ~]$ dog=
[donnie@fedora ~]$ echo ${dog:?The dog variable is unset or null.}
bash: dog: The dog variable is unset or null.
[donnie@fedora ~]$
```

Let's try that again with a dog named Rastus, which was the name of an English Shepard that my Grandma had when I was a kid. It will look like this:

```
[donnie@fedora ~]$ dog=Rastus
[donnie@fedora ~]$ echo ${dog:?The dog variable is unset or null.}
Rastus
[donnie@fedora ~]$
```

I know, you're thinking that this looks just like the first example, where I substituted a message for the value of the unset cat variable with a -. Well, you're kind of right. It's just that the - substitutes a value that shows up as stdout, while the :? substitutes a message that shows up as stderr. Another difference is that if you use :? in a shell script with an unset variable, it will cause the script to exit.

Try that by creating the ex.sh script with the following contents:

```
#!/bin/bash
var=
: ${var:?var is unset, you big dummy}
echo "I wonder if this will work."
```

So far, I've been showing you how to use echo to both perform the variable expansion and show the results. This particular construct allows you to just test the variable without echoing the results, by using a : instead of echo. Now when I run this script, you'll see that it exits before the final echo command can execute, as you see here:

```
[donnie@fedora ~]$ ./ex.sh
```

```
./ex.sh: line 3: var: var is unset, you big dummy
[donnie@fedora ~]$
```

Wait a minute! Did I just call myself a big dummy? Oh, well. Anyway, let's change the script so that var has an assigned value, as you see in this ex_2.sh script:

```
#!/bin/bash
var=somevalue
: ${var:?"var is unset, you big dummy"}
echo "I wonder if this will work with a value of "$var"."
```

The script now runs to completion, as you see here:

```
donnie@fedora:~$ ./ex_2.sh
I wonder if this will work with a value of somevalue.
donnie@fedora:~$
```

So to reiterate, using the : in place of the echo prevents the ${var:?"var is unset, you big dummy"} construct from printing out the value of the variable. We can change that behavior by changing the : back to an echo, as you see here in ex_3.sh:

```
#!/bin/bash
var=somevalue
echo ${var:?"var is unset, you big dummy"}
echo "I wonder if this will work with a value of "$var"."
```

Now, let's see the results of that change:

```
donnie@fedora:~$ ./ex_3.sh
somevalue
I wonder if this will work with a value of somevalue.
donnie@fedora:~$
```

This time, the value of var does print out.

As you've just seen with the - and the + operators, preceding the ? with a : causes the operator to treat a variable that was created with a null value as unset. Leaving out the : causes the operator to treat variables that were created with a null value as set.

Now, let's change gears by looking at variable offsets.

Using Variable Offsets

The last type of variable expansion that I'll show you involves the substitution of just a subset of a text string. This involves using a **variable offset**, and is a bit more difficult to understand unless you can see an example.

When you set a variable it will have a set size, or number of characters. The `${variable:offset}` construct uses the offset, or number of characters from the specified location. So, if the offset is 4 it will omit the first four characters, and will only echo all of the characters after the fourth character. The addition of a length parameter with the `${variable:offset:length}` construct allows you to also determine how many characters that you want to use. To begin, let's create the text variable with a value of MailServer, like so:

```
[donnie@fedora ~]$ text=MailServer
[donnie@fedora ~]$ echo $text
MailServer
[donnie@fedora ~]$
```

Now, let's say that we only want to see the text that comes after the fourth letter. Use an offset, like this:

```
[donnie@fedora ~]$ echo ${text:4}
Server
[donnie@fedora ~]$
```

Cool, it works. Now, let's say that we want to see just the first four letters. Use an offset and length, like this:

```
[donnie@fedora ~]$ echo ${text:0:4}
Mail
[donnie@fedora ~]$
```

This means that we're starting after position 0, and are viewing only the first four letters.

You can also extract text from somewhere in the middle of the text string, like so:

```
[donnie@fedora ~]$ echo ${text:4:5}
Serve
[donnie@fedora ~]$
```

Here, I'm starting after the fourth character, and am extracting the next five characters.

For something a bit more practical, let's set the location variable with the name of a US city and state, along with its associated zip code. (That's *postal code* for anyone who isn't here in the US.) Then, let's say that we want to extract the zip code portion of the text string, like so:

```
[donnie@fedora ~]$ location="Saint Marys GA 31558"
[donnie@fedora ~]$ echo "Zip Code: ${location:14}"
Zip Code:  31558
[donnie@fedora ~]$
```

Instead of setting the offset by counting from the beginning of the text string, I could also have used a negative number to just extract the last part of the text string. Since the zip code is five digits long, I could use a -5, like this:

```
[donnie@fedora ~]$ echo "Zip Code: ${location: -5}"
```

```
Zip Code: 31558
[donnie@fedora ~]$
```

To ensure that this always works properly, be sure to always leave a blank space between the : and the -. Also, since city names will always vary in length, this would be a better option if you need to extract zip codes from a whole list of locations.

That's it for offsets. So now, let's match some patterns.

Matching Patterns

The next variable expansion trick involves matching patterns. Let's start by creating the `pathname` variable, like so:

```
[donnie@fedora ~]$ pathname="/var/lib/yum"
[donnie@fedora ~]$
```

Now, let's say that I want to strip the lowest level directory from this path. I'll do that with a % and an *, like so:

```
[donnie@fedora ~]$ echo ${pathname%/yum*}
/var/lib
[donnie@fedora ~]$
```

The % tells the shell to omit the final part of the string that matches the pattern. In this case, the * at the end isn't necessary, because yum just happens to be at the end of the `pathname`. So, you'll get the same result without it. But, if you want to omit the lowest two levels of `pathname`, you will need to use the * so that the pattern will match properly. Here's what I'm talking about:

```
[donnie@fedora ~]$ echo ${pathname%/lib}
/var/lib/yum
[donnie@fedora ~]$ echo ${pathname%/lib*}
/var
[donnie@fedora ~]$
```

 You see that without the *, the pattern matching didn't work. With the *, the matching worked just fine. So, even when the * isn't absolutely necessary, it's best to include it, just to be sure.

On the other hand, you might at times just want to extract the names of the lower level directories. To do that, just replace the % with a #, like so:

```
[donnie@fedora ~]$ echo ${pathname#/var}
/lib/yum
[donnie@fedora ~]$ echo ${pathname#/var/lib}
/yum
```

```
[donnie@fedora ~]$
```

Let's wrap this section up with one final trick. This time, I'll match a pattern and then substitute something else. First, I'll create the string variable, like so:

```
[donnie@fedora ~]$ string="Hot and Spicy Food"
[donnie@fedora ~]$ echo $string
Hot and Spicy Food
[donnie@fedora ~]$
```

That's good, except that I've decided that I don't want blank spaces between the words. So, I'll substitute an _ character, like so:

```
[donnie@fedora ~]$ echo ${string/[[:space:]]/_}
Hot_and Spicy Food
[donnie@fedora ~]$
```

That didn't work out so well, because it only replaced the first blank space. To perform a global replacement, I'll need to add an extra forward slash after `string`, like this:

```
[donnie@fedora ~]$ echo ${string//[[:space:]]/_}
Hot_and_Spicy_Food
[donnie@fedora ~]$
```

This looks much better. But, what's really going on here? Well, we're using a `/pattern_to_be_replaced/` construct to perform the substitution. Whatever you place between the two forward slashes is what you want to replace. You can specify an individual character, a character class, or some other pattern that you want to replace. At the end, between the last forward slash and the closing curly brace, place the character that you want to substitute.

There's still a bit more to the variable expansion business, but I've shown you the most practical examples. If you want to see more, you'll find a reference in the *Further Reading* section.

Okay, now that we've substituted some patterns, let's move on to substituting commands.

Understanding Command Substitution

In the *Counting Logged-in Users* and *Using Arrays* Hands-on Labs, I've shown you some examples of **command substitution** in action, but I haven't yet fully explained it. It's about time that I do.

Command substitution is an extremely handy tool that you will use extensively. I mean, really. You can do some very cool stuff with it. It involves taking the output from a shell command and either using it in another command, or assigning it as the value of some variable. You'll place the command from which you'll be taking output within a `$( )` construct. Here's a very simple example:

```
[donnie@fedora ~]$ echo "This machine is running kernel version $(uname -r)."
This machine is running kernel version 6.5.5-200.fc38.x86_64.
[donnie@fedora ~]$
```

You see how the output of the uname -r command, which shows the version of the current running Linux kernel, is substituted for the command substitution construct.

Now, let's create the `command_subsitution_1.sh` script, and make it look like this:

```
#!/bin/bash
[[ ! -d Daily_Reports ]] && mkdir Daily_Reports
cd Daily_Reports
datestamp=$(date +%F)
echo "This is the report for $datestamp" > daily_report_$datestamp.txt
```

Here's the breakdown. In the second line, I'm testing for the absence of the `Daily_Reports` directory. If it's not there, then I'll create it. In the fourth line, I'm using command substitution to create the `datestamp` variable with the current date as its assigned value. The current date is returned by the `date +%F` command, and will be in the year-month-day format (2023-10-03). In the final line, I'm echoing a message that contains today's date into a file that contains today's date in its filename. Here's what that looks like:

```
[donnie@fedora ~]$ ls -l Daily_Reports/
total 4
-rw-r--r--. 1 donnie donnie 34 Oct  3 15:30 daily_report_2023-10-03.txt
[donnie@fedora ~]$ cat Daily_Reports/daily_report_2023-10-03.txt
This is the report for 2023-10-03
[donnie@fedora ~]$
```

Is that slick, or is that slick? Trust me, you'll be doing this sort of thing a lot if you need to create scripts that will automatically generate reports.

Tip

There are many different formatting options that you can use with the `date` command. To see them all, just view the `date` man page.

But, we're missing an important element here. What if today's report has already been created? Do you want to overwrite it?

No, in this case, I don't. So, let's create the `command_substitution_2.sh` script to test for the absence of today's report before creating another one. It involves adding just a teeny bit of extra code, like this:

```
#!/bin/bash
[[ ! -d Daily_Reports ]] && mkdir Daily_Reports
cd Daily_Reports
datestamp=$(date +%F)
[[ ! -f daily_report_$datestamp.txt ]] && echo "This is the report for
$datestamp" > daily_report_$datestamp.txt || echo "This report has already been
done today."
```

That last command that looks like three lines is really just one line that wraps around on the printed page.

Now, prepare to be amazed at what happens when I run this new, modified script:

```
[donnie@fedora ~]$ ./command_substitution_2.sh
This report has already been done today.
[donnie@fedora ~]$
```

Just for fun, let's look at some other cool examples.

Let's create a script, which we'll call am_i_root_1.sh, which will look like this:

```
#!/bin/bash
test $(whoami) != root && echo "You are not the root user."
test $(whoami) == root && echo "You are the root user."
```

The whoami command returns the name of the user who's running the command. Here's what that looks like when I run it first without sudo, and then with sudo:

```
[donnie@fedora ~]$ whoami
donnie
[donnie@fedora ~]$ sudo whoami
root
[donnie@fedora ~]$
```

As you see, running whoami with sudo shows that I'm the root user. The first command uses the != operator to test if the user is *not* the root user. The second command uses the == operator to test if the user *is* the root user. Now, let's run the script to see what happens:

```
[donnie@fedora ~]$ ./am_i_root_1.sh
You are not the root user.
[donnie@fedora ~]$ sudo ./am_i_root_1.sh
[sudo] password for donnie:
You are the root user.
[donnie@fedora ~]$
```

It works, which means that we have achieved coolness. But, we can be even more cool by streamlining things a bit. Modify the script so that it looks like this:

```
#!/bin/bash
test $(whoami) != root && echo "You are not the root user." || echo "You are
the root user."
```

Instead of two commands in this script, I now have only one. But either way, the output is identical.

Instead of placing your command within a $( ) construct, you can also surround it with a pair of backticks, like this:

```
[donnie@fedora ~]$ datestamp=`date +%F`
[donnie@fedora ~]$ echo $datestamp
2023-10-03
[donnie@fedora ~]$
```

That works, but it's a deprecated method that I don't recommend. The biggest problem with it is that if your command contains any special characters that the shell might interpret incorrectly, you'll have to be sure to escape them with a backslash. With the newer $( ) construct, you don't have to worry so much about that. I'm only mentioning this method because you might still see other people's scripts that use it.

That does it for the command substitution business. Now, we need to make some decisions.

Understanding Decisions and Loops

So far, I've been showing you a lot of programming techniques and constructs that are specific to shell scripting. In this section, I'll show you some constructs that are common to most all programming languages. I'll begin by showing you another way to make decisions.

The if. .then Construct

Although the && and || decision constructs work for simple scripts, you might want to use if . . then constructs for anything more complex, such as when you would need to test for multiple conditions at once. For the first example, create the am_i_root_2.sh script, which will look like this:

```
#!/bin/bash
if [ $(id -u) == 0 ]; then
        echo "This user is root."
fi
if [ $(id -u) != 0 ]; then
        echo "This user is not root."
        echo "This user's name is $(id -un)."
fi
```

 Note that each decision stanza begins with if and ends with fi. (Yes, that's if spelled backwards.) Also note that with bash shell scripting, indentation isn't required, as it is in certain other programming languages. But, it does make the code much more readable.

Instead of using the whoami command this time, I'm using the id command, which offers more options than whoami. (See the man pages for both commands for details.) As far as the rest of it goes, rather than trying to explain it all in detail, I'll just let you study this script to see how everything works. That will be easier for me, and less boring for you. And besides, I have faith in you.

Now, let's see what happens when I run this script:

```
[donnie@fedora ~]$ ./am_i_root_2.sh
This user is not root.
This user's name is donnie.
[donnie@fedora ~]$
[donnie@fedora ~]$ sudo ./am_i_root_2.sh
This user is root.
[donnie@fedora ~]$
```

When you're testing for more than one condition for the same decision, it would be more proper to use one if .. then .. elif construct, rather than two if .. then constructs. This can add a bit more clarity to your code, so that anyone who reads it can make a bit more sense of it. Let's create the am_i_root_3.sh script to showcase this technique. Make it look like this:

```
#!/bin/bash
if [ $(id -u) == 0 ]; then
        echo "This user is root."
elif [ $(id -u) != 0 ]; then
        echo "This user is not root."
        echo "This user's name is $(id -un)."
fi
```

The elif keyword in this script is short for else if. Other than that, everything is pretty much the same as it was before in the previous script. When you run it, you'll get the same output as you got for the previous script. Also, note that you can test for multiple conditions with more than one elif stanza.

Alternatively, you could also use an if .. then .. else construct. Create the am_i_root_4.sh script, which will look like this:

```
#!/bin/bash
if [ $(id -u) == 0 ]; then
        echo "This user is root."
else
        echo "This user is not root."
        echo "This user's name is $(id -un)."
fi
```

Using else can be handy, because it defines a default action to take if the conditions in any of the if or elif stanzas aren't fulfilled. For example, take a look at this script that detects which operating system your machine is running:

```bash
#!/bin/bash
os=$(uname)
if [[ $os == Linux ]]; then
        echo "This machine is running Linux."
elif [[ $os == Darwin ]]; then
        echo "This machine is running macOS."
elif [[ $os == FreeBSD ]]; then
        echo "This machine is running FreeBSD."
else
        echo "I don't know this $os operating system."
fi
```

You see that this script can detect Linux, macOS, or FreeBSD. If the machine isn't running any of those three operating systems, the else statement at the end displays the default message. Another thing to note is that you'll need to place a semi-colon and a then keyword at the end of each if or elif statement, but you don't need to place them after an else statement.

Here's how that looks when I run the script on an OpenIndiana machine:

```
donnie@openindiana:~$ ./os-test.sh
I don't know this SunOS operating system.
donnie@openindiana:~$
```

Of course, if I wanted to, I could insert another elif stanza to test for SunOS.

That about covers it for if. .then. Let's now do something while waiting for something else.

The do. . while construct

This construct will continuously execute a set of commands while a certain condition is true. Here's an example:

```bash
#!/bin/bash
x=10
while [[ $x -gt 0 ]]; do
        x=$(expr $x - 1)
        echo $x
done
```

This while_demo.sh script starts by assigning a value of 10 to the x variable. As long as the value of x remains greater than 0, it will subtract 1 from this value and assign the new value to x, using the expr $x-1 command. It then echos the new value. The output looks like this:

```
[donnie@fedora ~]$ ./while_demo.sh
9
8
7
6
5
4
3
2
1
0
[donnie@fedora ~]$
```

Note that in this while_demo.sh script, you can use a bit of shorthand for decrementing the value of x by 1 for each loop. Just replace the x=$(expr $x - 1) line with:

```
((x--))
```

This is the same type of construct that you might be used to seeing in C or C++ language programs. However, this construct is not portable, which means that it works fine on bash, but not on other shells. So, if you need to make your script so that it will run on Bourne shell, dash, or ash, you'll need to avoid this construct and instead stick with the x=$(expr $x - 1) construct.

You could also use a while loop to read a text file, line-by-line. Here's the very simple read_file.sh script that reads the /etc/passwd file:

```
#!/bin/bash
file=/etc/passwd
while read -r line; do
        echo $line
done < "$file"
```

As you see, I start by creating the file variable with /etc/passwd as its assigned value. The while line defines the variable line, and the read -r command assigns values to the line variable. On each pass of the while loop, the read -r command reads one line of the file, assigns the contents of the line to the line variable, and then echos the contents of the line to stdout. When all lines of the file have been read, the loop terminates. At the end, you see that I'm using a stdin redirector to make the while loop read the file. Normally, read breaks long lines into shorter lines and terminates each part of the long line with a backslash. The -r option disables that behavior.

There may be times when you'll want to create an infinite loop that never stops until you tell it to. (There might also be times when you'll create an infinite loop by accident, but that's a whole different story. For now, let's assume that you want to do it on purpose.) To demonstrate, create the `infinite_loop.sh` script, and make it look like this:

```
#!/bin/bash
while :
do
        echo "This loop is infinite."
        echo "It will keep going until you stop it."
        echo "To stop it, hit Ctrl-c."
        sleep 1
done
```

It's a rather useless script, which does nothing but echo some messages. The `sleep 1` command causes a one-second delay between each iteration of the loop. Here's what happens when I run this script:

```
[donnie@fedora ~]$ ./infinite_loop.sh
This loop is infinite.
It will keep going until you stop it.
To stop it, hit Ctrl-c.
This loop is infinite.
It will keep going until you stop it.
To stop it, hit Ctrl-c.
^C
[donnie@fedora ~]$
```

There are still a few other tricks that we can do with `while..do`, but this will do it for now. Let's now look at `for..in`.

The for..in Construct

The `for . . in` construct will process a list, and perform a command for each item in the list. In this `car_demo_2.sh` script, the `for` line creates the `cars` variable. Here's what it looks like:

```
#!/bin/bash
for cars in Edsel Ford Nash Studebaker Packard Hudson
do
        echo "$cars"
done
echo "That's all, folks!"
```

Each time that the loop iterates, the `in` keyword takes a name of a classic car from the list, and assigns it to `cars` as its value. The loop ends when it reaches the end of the list. Here's what happens when I run the script:

```
[donnie@fedora ~]$ ./car_demo_2.sh
Edsel
Ford
Nash
Studebaker
Packard
Hudson
That's all, folks!
[donnie@fedora ~]$
```

That's easy enough, so let's try another one. This time, create the list_demo.sh script, like this:

```
#!/bin/bash
for filename in *
do
        echo "$filename"
done
```

This loop just does an ls-style listing of the files in your current directory. I'm using the * wildcard to tell for to read in all of the filenames, regardless of how many files there are. In the echo line, I have to surround $filename with a pair of double quotes in case any filenames contain blank spaces. Here's what happens when I run it:

```
[donnie@fedora ~]$ ./list_demo.sh
15827_zip.zip
2023-08-01_15-23-31.mp4
2023-08-01_16-26-12.mp4
2023-08-02_13-57-37.mp4
. . .
. . .
xargs_test.txt
yad-form.sh
zoneinfo.zip
[donnie@fedora ~]$
```

The reason this works is that if you do echo * from the command-line, you'll see a jumbled-up listing of files in the directory. The for..in loop causes echo to list each filename on its own line.

Okay, we've just looked at for..in. Let's now look at for.

The for Construct

This is similar to the for . . in construct, except for where it gets its list. With for, the user will enter the list as arguments when calling the script. Let's create the car_demo_3.sh script to demonstrate this:

```
#!/bin/bash
```

```
for cars
do
        echo "$cars"
done
```

The cars variable gets created in the for line, but there's no list of cars. So, where does the list come from? It comes from arguments that the user enters on the command-line when he or she invokes the script. Instead of using classic car names this time, let's use a list of modern car names, like so:

```
[donnie@fedora ~]$ ./car_demo_3.sh Toyota Volkswagen Subaru Honda
Toyota
Volkswagen
Subaru
Honda
[donnie@fedora ~]$
```

Next, let's look at the break command.

Using break

Use the break command to further control how you want for..in and while..do loops to operate. To see how this works, create the break_demo.sh script and make it look like this:

```
#!/bin/bash
j=0
while [[ $j -lt 5 ]]
do
        echo "This is number: $j"
        j=$((j + 1))
        if [[ "$j" == '2' ]]; then
                echo "We have reached our goal: $j"
                break
        fi
done
echo "That's all, folks!"
```

The while line tells the script to run as long as the value of j is less than 5. The j=$((j + 1)) construct on the sixth line is a mathematical operator, with increments the value of j by 1 on each iteration of the loop. The if..then construct that starts on the seventh line defines what should happen when the value of j is equal to 2. The break command then terminates the loop. Here's how it looks:

```
[donnie@fedora ~]$ ./break_demo.sh
This is number: 0
This is number: 1
We have reached our goal: 2
```

```
That's all, folks!
[donnie@fedora ~]$
```

As I've indicated for the while_demo.sh script, you can replace the j=$((j + 1)) construct with:

```
((j++))
```

However, ((j++)) is bash-specific, and might not work on other non-bash shells.

You can also express this as j=$(expr j + 1), which is also portable, and is the form that I showed you in the while_demo.sh script.

(I'll show you more about performing math in shell scripts in *Chapter 11, Performing Mathematical Operations*.)

Just for fun, delete the break command from the script and run it again. You should now see this:

```
[donnie@fedora ~]$ ./break_demo.sh
This is number: 0
This is number: 1
We have reached our goal: 2
This is number: 2
This is number: 3
This is number: 4
That's all, folks!
[donnie@fedora ~]$
```

This time, the loop keeps running past the number 2.

Now that we've taken a break, let's continue.

Using continue

The continue command also modifies how for..in and while..do loops operate. This time, create the for_continue.sh script, and make it look like this:

```
#!/bin/bash
for cars in Pontiac Oldsmobile Buick Chevrolet Ford Mercury
do
        if [[ $cars == Buick || $cars == Mercury ]]; then
                continue
        fi
```

```
        echo $cars
done
```

On each iteration of the for loop, a different classic car name gets assigned as the value of cars. The if..then stanza determines if the value of cars is either Buick or Mercury. The continue command within the if..then stanza causes the loop to skip over those two car names, so that the echo command won't list them. You also see another use for the || construct here. When used within a test operation, the || acts as an or operator. Here's what the output looks like:

```
[donnie@fedora ~]$ ./for_continue.sh
Pontiac
Oldsmobile
Chevrolet
Ford
[donnie@fedora ~]$
```

Next, let's try this with a while..do loop. Create the while_continue.sh script, like this:

```
#!/bin/bash
j=0
while [[ $j -lt 6 ]]
do
        j=$((j + 1))
        [[ $j -eq 3 || $j -eq 6 ]] && continue
        echo "$j"
done
```

This time, we just want to skip over numbers 3 and 6. Here's the output:

```
[donnie@fedora ~]$ ./while_continue.sh
1
2
4
5
[donnie@fedora ~]$
```

Okay, enough of that. Let's look at the until construct.

The until Construct

The until loop will continue until a certain condition is met. You can use it for a variety of things, such as playing a guessing game. See how it works by creating the secret_word.sh script, like this:

```
#!/bin/bash
secretword=Donnie
word=
```

```
echo "Hi there, $USER!"
echo "Would you like to play a guessing game?"
echo "If so, then enter the correct secret word"
echo "to win a special prize."
echo
echo
until [[ "$word" = "$secretword" ]]
do
        echo -n "Enter your guess.   "
        read word
done
echo "Yay!  You win a pat on the back!"
```

So, I've set the secretword to Donnie. (Hey, that's me!) I then set word to a null value. The until loop will run until I enter the correct value for secretword. (In this case, read pauses the script until you enter your guess.) It works like this:

```
[donnie@fedora ~]$ ./secret_word.sh
Hi there, donnie!
Would you like to play a guessing game?
If so, then enter the correct secret word
to win a special prize.
Enter your guess.  Vicky
Enter your guess.  Cleopatra
Enter your guess.  Donnie
Yay!  You win a pat on the back!
[donnie@fedora ~]$
```

Cool, right? I mean, this is yet another trick that you can perform at your next party.

All right, let's move on to the next one.

The case Construct

The case construct provides a way to avoid using an if..then..else construct. It allows users to enter a text string, then evaluate that string and provide the option that the string indicates. Here's the basic structure of case:

```
case $variable in
  match_1)
     commands_to_execute
     ;;
  match_2)
    commands_to_execute
     ;;
```

```
   match_3)
     commands_to_execute
       ;;
 *)  Optional Information
     commands_to_execute_for_no_match
       ;;
 esac
```

The case statement is matched against a number of values until a match is found. When a match is found, the commands are executed until the double semicolons (;;) are reached. Then, the commands after the esac line are executed.

If there is no match, then the commands between the *) and the double semicolons are executed. The *) acts the same way as the else in an if ...then construct, in that they both provide a default action in case none of the tested conditions are met.

Just for fun, try this out by creating the term_color.sh script, which will look like this:

```
#!/bin/bash
echo -n "Choose Background Color for Terminal(b-black,g-grey): "
read color
case "$color" in
b)
   setterm -background black -foreground white
   ;;
g)
   setterm -background white -foreground black
   ;;
*)
   echo "I do not understand"
   ;;
esac
exit
```

This script allows you to change the background color of your terminal. (And yes, I know that I've set the g option to white. That's because when you run this script and choose the g option, the background will look more gray than white.) Running the script looks like this:

```
[donnie@fedora ~]$ ./term_color.sh
Choose Background Color for Terminal(b-black,g-grey): g
[donnie@fedora ~]$
```

Run the script in your own terminal, choose the g option, and you should see the background of the command prompt turn gray. (Or, if your terminal is already set up with a white background, choose the b option, instead.) To see the background for the whole terminal turn gray, just type clear.

For even more fun, edit the script to add another option. First, make the echo line at the top look like this:

```
echo -n "Choose Background Color for Terminal(b-black,g-grey,y-yellow): "
```

Then, add the y option after the g option. This new option will look like this:

```
y)
    setterm -background yellow -foreground red
    ;;
```

To see something that's hideously ugly, run the script again and choose the y option. (Don't worry though, because the setting isn't permanent.) Here's how using the various options will look:

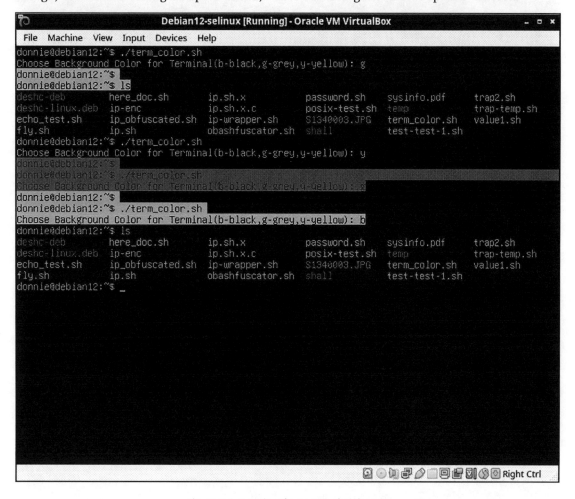

Figure 8.1: Running the term_color.sh script

Okay, you've already seen how to use for to enter arguments when you invoke your scripts. Now, let's look at another way.

Using Positional Parameters

When you run a shell script, you can also enter command-line parameters that will be used within the script. The first parameter that you enter will be designated as $1, the second will be designated as $2, and so on. ($9 is as high as you can go.) The $0 parameter is reserved for the name of the script.

To see how this works, create the position_demo.sh script, which will look like this:

```
#!/bin/bash
# position_demo
echo "I have a cat, whose name is $1."
echo "I have another cat, whose name is $2."
echo "I have yet another cat, whose name is $3."
echo
echo
echo "The script that I just ran is $0"
```

To invoke the script, enter three names after the name of the script, like this:

```
[donnie@fedora ~]$ ./position_demo.sh Vicky Cleopatra Lionel
I have a cat, whose name is Vicky.
I have another cat, whose name is Cleopatra.
I have yet another cat, whose name is Lionel.
The script that I just ran is ./position_demo.sh
[donnie@fedora ~]$
```

In the output, the $1, $2, and $3 variables will be expanded to the names that I entered on the command-line. The $0 variable will be expanded to the full path and name of the script.

There are three special positional parameters that you can use to enhance your scripts. Here's the list:

- $#: This shows the number of parameters that you've entered.
- $@: This lists all of the parameters that you've entered, with each one on a separate line.
- $*: This lists all of the parameters that you've entered on a single line, with a blank space between each one.

One cool thing that you can do with the $# parameter is error-checking. To see what I mean, run the position_demo.sh script again, but only enter one name as an argument. You should see something like this:

```
[donnie@fedora ~]$ ./position_demo.sh Vicky
I have a cat, whose name is Vicky.
I have another cat, whose name is .
I have yet another cat, whose name is .
The script that I just ran is ./position_demo.sh
[donnie@fedora ~]$
```

As you see, it gave me no warning about the fact that I didn't list the correct number of names. Let's modify things a bit to take care of that. Create the position_demo_2.sh script, and make it look like this:

```bash
#!/bin/bash
# position_demo
if [[ $# -ne 3 ]]; then
        echo "This script requires three arguments."
        exit 1
fi
echo "I have a cat, whose name is $1."
echo "I have another cat, whose name is $2."
echo "I have yet another cat, whose name is $3."
echo
echo
echo "The script that I just ran is $0"
```

Run this script with all three names, and you'll get the same output that you got with the first script. Then, run it again with only one name, and you should see this:

```
[donnie@fedora ~]$ vim position_demo_2.sh
[donnie@fedora ~]$ ./position_demo_2.sh Vicky
You entered 1 argument(s).
This script requires two arguments.
[donnie@fedora ~]$
```

That looks much better.

To introduce our next trick, take a look at the output of the date command, without specifying any formatting options, like this:

```
[donnie@fedora ~]$ date
Fri Oct  6 03:24:39 PM EDT 2023
[donnie@fedora ~]$
```

You see seven fields in the output, which are:

- Day of week
- Month
- Date
- Time
- AM or PM
- Timezone
- Year

Now, create the `position_demo_3.sh` script, which will treat each field of the date output as a positional parameter. Make it look like this:

```
#!/bin/bash
set $(date)
echo $*
echo "Day, First Argument: $1"
echo "Month, Second Argument: $2"
echo "Date, Third Argument: $3"
echo "Time, Fourth and Fifth Arguments: $4, $5"
echo "Time Zone, Sixth Argument: $6"
echo "Year, Seventh Argument: $7"
echo "$2 $3, $7"
```

On the second line, you see another use for the `set` command that you haven't yet seen. The first time you saw `set`, it was with the `-o` option to set shell options. This time, I'm using it without any options and with `$(date)` as an argument. Here's what the bash man page says about using `set` in this manner:

> *Without options, display the name and value of each shell variable in a format that can be reused as input for setting or resetting the currently-set variables.*

In this case, `set` is taking the output of `$(date)` and formatting it in a way that allows the individual fields to be used as positional parameters.

On the third line, you see where the real magic happens. The `$*` positional parameter lists all fields of `$(date)` on a single line. The rest of the `echo` commands just output a text string, followed by the value of the specified field or fields. Here's what it looks like:

```
[donnie@fedora ~]$ ./position_demo_3.sh
Fri Oct 6 03:46:28 PM EDT 2023
Day, First Argument: Fri
Month, Second Argument: Oct
Date, Third Argument: 6
Time, Fourth and Fifth Arguments: 03:46:28, PM
Time Zone, Sixth Argument: EDT
Year, Seventh Argument: 2023
Oct 6, 2023
[donnie@fedora ~]$
```

It works as it should, and looks pretty cool. Add this to the list of tricks to try at your next party.

I think that that about covers it for positional parameters. Let's now look at exit codes.

Understanding Exit Codes

You've already seen some examples of using the exit command, which can either terminate a script normally or cause it to terminate early upon an error condition. What I haven't explained yet, is about **exit codes**. There are two general classes of exit codes, which are:

- **Standard shell exit codes:** Each shell has its own defined set of exit codes. (To keep things simple, I'll just talk about bash exit codes in this chapter.)
- **User-defined exit codes:** You can also define your own exit codes for different purposes.

Let's talk about standard exit codes first.

Standard Shell Exit Codes

When a program or script runs successfully, it returns an exit code of 0. Otherwise, the exit code will be a non-0 number from 1 to 255. To demonstrate, use find to search through the /etc/ directory for the passwd file, like so:

```
[donnie@fedora ~]$ find /etc -name passwd
find: '/etc/audit': Permission denied
find: '/etc/cups/ssl': Permission denied
. . .
. . .
/etc/pam.d/passwd
find: '/etc/pki/rsyslog': Permission denied
find: '/etc/polkit-1/localauthority': Permission denied
find: '/etc/polkit-1/rules.d': Permission denied
. . .
. . .
find: '/etc/credstore.encrypted': Permission denied
/etc/passwd
[donnie@fedora ~]$
```

You see that find found the file, but we also have a lot of Permission denied errors due to the fact that there are directories that I can't enter with my normal user privileges. Now, verify the exit code, like this:

```
[donnie@fedora ~]$ echo $?
1
[donnie@fedora ~]$
```

The ? is a special variable that returns the exit code for the previous command that was just run. In this case, the exit code is 1, which tells me that there was some kind of error condition. The specific error was that find couldn't enter certain directories to perform its search. So, let's try this again with sudo, like so:

```
[donnie@fedora ~]$ sudo find /etc -name passwd
```

```
[sudo] password for donnie:
/etc/pam.d/passwd
/etc/passwd
[donnie@fedora ~]$ echo $?
0
[donnie@fedora ~]$
```

This time I get exit code 0, which means that there were no error conditions.

Most of the time, you'll see either 0 or 1 as the exit code. The complete list of codes that you might see include the following:

- 1   General errors
- 2   Misuse of shell builtins
- 126   Cannot invoke requested command
- 127   Command not found
- 128   Invalid argument to exit
- 128+n   Fatal error signal n
- 130   Script terminated by *Ctrl-c*

It's possible to demonstrate some of the other codes. Start by creating the exit.sh script, like so:

```
#!/bin/bash
exit n
```

Right away, you can see the error. The exit command requires a numerical argument, and won't work with an alphabetical argument. But, we're going to pretend that we don't see the error, and try to run it anyway. Here's what you'll get:

```
[donnie@fedora ~]$ ./exit.sh
./exit.sh: line 2: exit: n: numeric argument required
[donnie@fedora ~]$ echo $?
2
[donnie@fedora ~]$
```

The 2 exit code indicates that I misused a **shell builtin**.

A **shell builtin** is just a command that doesn't have its own executable program file, because it's built into the bash executable program file. One would think that I would get a 128 code, since I provided an invalid argument to exit, but that's not how it works. (In fact, I'm really not sure what I would have to do to get a 128 code. But, that's okay.) To see the complete list of shell builtins, just view the builtins man page.

A 126 code normally means that you don't have permission to run a command. For example, let's say that I forgot to set the executable permission on a script, as you see here:

```
[donnie@fedora ~]$ ls -l somescript.sh
```

```
-rw-r--r--. 1 donnie donnie 0 Oct  7 16:26 somescript.sh
[donnie@fedora ~]$
```

Watch what happens when I try to run this script:

```
[donnie@fedora ~]$ ./somescript.sh
bash: ./somescript.sh: Permission denied
[donnie@fedora ~]$ echo $?
126
[donnie@fedora ~]$
```

You can generate a 127 code by trying to execute a command that doesn't exist, like this:

```
[donnie@fedora ~]$ donnie
bash: donnie: command not found
[donnie@fedora ~]$ echo $?
127
[donnie@fedora ~]$
```

Obviously, my name is not a command.

The 128+n code means that some sort of fatal error condition occurred. The n signifies another digit that's added to 128. For example, if you start a command and *Ctrl-c* out of it before it completes, you'll get a code of 128+2, which equals 130. (The 2 in this case indicates the specific fatal condition.)

You can use standard exit codes within a shell script to make it handle different conditions. To see that, create the netchk.sh script, as follows:

```
#!/bin/bash
if [[ $# -eq 0 ]]; then
        site="google.com"
else
        site="$1"
fi
ping -c 2 $site > /dev/null
if [[ $? != 0 ]]; then
        echo $(date +%F) . . . Network Failure!
        logger "Could not reach $site."
else
        echo $(date +%F) . . . Success!
        logger "$site is reachable."
fi
```

This script expects you to invoke it with a hostname, domain name, or an IP address as an argument. In the first if..then construct at the top, you see that if you don't enter an argument, the script will default to using google.com as the argument. \

Otherwise, it will use the argument that you specified. It will then try to ping the specified site. If the ping is successful, the exit code will be 0. Otherwise, it will be something other than 0.

In the second `if..then` construct, you see that if the exit code is not 0, it will echo a `Network Failure` message and send an entry to the system log file, which on the Fedora machine is `/var/log/messages`. Otherwise, it will echo a `Success` message. Here's how that looks:

```
[donnie@fedora ~]$ ./netchk.sh
2023-10-07 . . . Success!
[donnie@fedora ~]$ ./netchk.sh www.donnie.com
ping: www.donnie.com: Name or service not known
2023-10-07 . . . Network Failure!
[donnie@fedora ~]$
```

There's not much else to say about the standard exit codes. So, let's say a few words about user-defined exit codes.

User-defined Exit Codes

You can specify your own exit codes simply by specifying a numerical argument for `exit`. This is handy for whenever you might need to pass some specific exit code to an external program. The Nagios network monitoring tool is a great example.

Nagios is a tool that can monitor pretty much every type of device on your network. It can monitor various types of servers, workstations, routers, switches, and even printers. What makes it so cool is that it's modular, which means that it works with plug-ins. If you need to monitor a particular device and find that there's no plug-in that will do the job, you can just write your own. You can write plug-ins in a variety of programming languages, which includes shell scripting.

You can install a Nagios monitoring agent on a server or workstation that you want to monitor, and create a shell script that generates exit codes that Nagios expects to see. To understand how it works, check out this code snippet from a larger script:

```
#!/bin/bash
os=$(uname)
quantity=$(cut -f3 -d: /etc/passwd | grep -w 0 | wc -l)
if [ $os == Linux ]; then
        if [ $quantity -gt 1 ]; then
                echo "CRITICAL.  There are $quantity accounts with UID 0."
                exit 2
        else
                echo "OKAY.  There is only one account with UID 0."
                exit 1
        fi
```

This script is looking at the /etc/passwd file to see if there is more than one user with a UID of 0. That's important, because UID 0 is what gives a user account root user powers. So, on any Linux system, you never want to see more than one user account with UID 0. In the if..then construct, you see that if the script finds more than one UID 0 account, it will generate an exit code of 2. Otherwise, it will generate an exit code of 1.

This exit code and its corresponding echo command get passed to the Nagios monitoring agent. The monitoring agent will then pass the output from the echo command to the Nagios server, which will display the message on the Nagios dashboard. (You'll see the entire script in just a few moments, when you get to the *Looking at Some Real-World Examples* section.)

That's about it for exit codes. Let's now take a closer look at echo.

More Information About echo

You've already seen the most simple way to use echo, which is to either display a message on the screen or send text into a text file. What you haven't seen yet is echo's various formatting options.

If you use it with the -n switch, you'll prevent it from creating a new line at the end of the text output, like this:

```
[donnie@fedora ~]$ echo -n "The fat cat jumped over the skinny dog."
The fat cat jumped over the skinny dog.[donnie@fedora ~]$
```

Use it with the -e switch, and you'll be able to use some backslash options. For example, to insert a vertical tab into a line of text, use the -e switch with the \v option, like this:

```
[donnie@fedora ~]$ echo -e "The fat cat jumped\v over the skinny dog."
The fat cat jumped
                   over the skinny dog.
[donnie@fedora ~]$
```

To insert a horizontal tab, use the \t option, like this:

```
[donnie@fedora ~]$ echo -e "The fat cat jumped\t over the skinny dog."
The fat cat jumped      over the skinny dog.
[donnie@fedora ~]$
```

If you want to insert a backslash into the text, just use two consecutive backslashes, like this:

```
[donnie@fedora ~]$ echo -e "The fat cat jumped over the thin\\skinny dog."
The fat cat jumped over the thin\skinny dog.
[donnie@fedora ~]$
```

You're not limited to just echoing text messages. You can also use a wildcard character to show a list of files that you have in the current directory, like this:

```
[donnie@fedora ~]$ echo *
```

```
1 15827_zip.zip 18.csv 2023-08-01_15-23-31.mp4 2023-08-01_16-26-12.mp4 2023-
08-02_13-57-37.mp4 2023-10-25_price.txt 21261.zip 4-2_Building_an_Alpine_
Container.bak 4-2_Building_an_Alpine_Container.pptx 46523.zip 48986.zip 50645.
zip 54586.zip 70604.zip access_log_parse.sh access_log_parse.txt actorfile_10.
txt actorfile_11.txt actorfile_1.txt actorfile_2.txt actorfile_4.txt
actorfile_5.txt actorfile_6.txt actorfile_7.txt actorfile_8.txt actorfile_9.
txt add_fields.awk add-repos.sh addresses.txt alignment_1.txt alignment_2.txt
alma9_default.txt alma9_future.txt alma_link.t
. . .

. . .
donnie@fedora:~$
```

You can also echo a message along with the file list, like so:

```
[donnie@fedora ~]$ echo -e "These are my files:\n" *
These are my files:

 15827_zip.zip 2023-08-01_15-23-31.mp4 2023-08-01_16-26-12.mp4
. . .

. . .
test.txt yad-form.sh zoneinfo.zip
[donnie@fedora ~]$
```

With a bit of imagination, you'll be able to use these echo formatting options to enhance the appearance of your screen output and text documents.

 Sadly, as cool as these formatting options for echo are, they don't work well on certain non-bash shells, such as dash. In *Chapter 19—Shell Script Portability*, I'll show you how to fix that by using printf instead of echo.

That's about it for echo. Let's move on to the real world.

Looking at Some Real-World Examples

In this section, I'll show you some practical, real-life things that you can do with some of the techniques that we've covered so far. Actually, rather than just showing you, I'll let you get your hands dirty with some cool hands-on labs.

Hands-on Lab: Using if..then

This is absolutely a real-life example. Several years ago, I created this script as a plug-in for the Nagios network monitoring system. The scenario was that we wanted to make sure that malicious hackers haven't added a rogue UID 0 account to the /etc/passwd file on Linux and FreeBSD machines. That's because any account with a UID setting of 0 in the passwd file has full root privileges, and we don't want any unauthorized accounts to have root privileges.

The problem is that on Linux machines there's only supposed to be one user account with UID 0, and on FreeBSD there are two accounts with UID 0. (One UID 0 account is named toor, which has bash set as the default shell. The other UID 0 account is root, which has csh set as the default shell.) So, we needed a script that will work on both operating systems. (Note that you'll be altering the passwd file for this lab, so you'll want to do this on a virtual machine, and not on a real production machine.)

Note that the exit 1 and exit 2 status codes that you'll see are what Nagios expects to see to indicate either OKAY or CRITICAL. Also note that you can add more elif stanzas if you want to check other UNIX or UNIX-like operating systems. (In fact, you'll see that I've just now added code to check macOS and OpenIndiana.) With the introduction out of the way, let's get to the procedure.

1. Unfortunately, the script is too long to reproduce in the book. So, go to the Github repository and download the UID-0_check.sh script. Transfer it to a Linux virtual machine. Open the script in your text editor, and examine the code.

2. Run the script to see the results. You should see this message:

```
[donnie@fedora ~]$ ./UID-0_check.sh
OKAY.  There is only one account with UID 0.
[donnie@fedora ~]$
```

3. **WARNING: Again I say, do this on a virtual machine, not on your production workstation.**

   On a Linux virtual machine, create another user account, using the appropriate user-creation command for your Linux distro. Open the /etc/passwd file in your text editor, and change the UID number for the new user to 0.

   This UID field is the third field in each line of the passwd file. For example, you see here that Vicky's UID is 1001:

```
vicky:x:1001:1001::/home/vicky:/bin/bash
```

   Changing her UID to 0 will make the line look like this:

```
vicky:x:0:1001::/home/vicky:/bin/bash
```

4. Save the file and run the script again. You should now see a message that looks like this:

```
[donnie@fedora ~]$ ./UID-0_check.sh
CRITICAL.  There are 2 accounts with UID 0.
[donnie@fedora ~]$
```

5. Delete the new user account.

6. Create a FreeBSD virtual machine and install sudo and bash as I showed you in the *Preface* chapter. Transfer the UID-0_check.sh script to it, and repeat Steps 3 through 5. This time, you should see that 2 accounts are OKAY, and that 3 accounts are CRITICAL. This will give you a chance to see how the elif [$os == FreeBSD]; then stanza at the bottom of the script can correctly detect which operating system you're running, so that it can run the correct code.

End of lab

Hands-on Lab – Parsing an Apache Access Log

In this lab, I'll show you how much power a one-command shell script can have. Building up that one command can be a bit tricky though, so I'll show you how to build it one step at a time, ensuring that each step works properly before continuing to the next step. If you're ready, let's dig in.

1. Set up a Fedora Server virtual machine with Bridged networking. (You'll need Bridged networking so that you can access the machine from other machines on your network.)

2. Install and activate the Apache webserver, like this:

    ```
    sudo dnf install httpd
    sudo systemctl enable --now httpd
    ```

3. Open Port 80 on the virtual machine's firewall, like this:

    ```
    sudo firewall-cmd --permanent --add-service=http
    sudo firewall-cmd --reload
    ```

4. From as many other machines on your network as possible, open a web browser and navigate to the virtual machine's IP address. The URL that you enter should look something like this:

    ```
    http://192.168.0.10
    ```

    Note that you can access this from either physical machines or other virtual machines that are on the same network. Also, note that there's no need to set up your own web page, because the default *Fedora Webserver Test Page* will work fine for your needs.

5. View the Apache access log, like this:

    ```
    sudo less /var/log/httpd/access_log
    ```

    Note how each line begins with the IP address of each machine that accessed this website. Here's an example:

    ```
    192.168.0.25 - - [06/Oct/2023:16:44:15 -0400] "GET /poweredby.png
    HTTP/1.1" 200 5714 "http://192.168.0.10/" "Mozilla/5.0 (Windows NT 10.0;
    Win64; x64; rv:109.0) Gecko/20100101 Firefox/118.0"
    ```

6. You see that the source IP address is in the first field, and that the fields are separated by blank spaces. So, one way that we can see just the list of source IP addresses is to use cut, and to specify a blank space as the delimiter to view just the first field. The command and its output would look something like this:

    ```
    [donnie@fedora-server ~]$ sudo cut -d" " -f1 /var/log/httpd/access_log
    ::1
    192.168.0.16
    192.168.0.16
    192.168.0.27
    . . .
    ```

```
.  .  .
192.168.0.25
192.168.0.25
192.168.0.9
192.168.0.8
192.168.0.8
192.168.0.8
192.168.0.8
[donnie@fedora-server ~]$
```

With only one exception, you see the list of IPv4 addresses of the machines that accessed this server. The one exception is the IPv6 address at the top of the list, which is the localhost address of the Fedora Server machine. (You likely won't see this IPv6 address, unless you access the page from within the virtual machine itself.)

7. So far, so good. You've successfully isolated the first field. Let's now add the second part, which will sort the output so that the uniq filter will work properly in the next step. Here's what that looks like:

```
sudo cut -d" " -f1 /var/log/httpd/access_log | sort
```

By using sort without the -n option, the list doesn't get sorted in proper numerical order. But for this step, that doesn't matter.

8. The next step is to eliminate duplicate IP addresses from the output, and to also count how many there are of each in the source file. Here's how that looks:

```
[donnie@fedora-server ~]$ sudo cut -d" " -f1 /var/log/httpd/access_log |
sort | uniq -c
      1 ::1
     11 192.168.0.16
      4 192.168.0.25
      4 192.168.0.27
      4 192.168.0.8
      1 192.168.0.9
[donnie@fedora-server ~]$
```

9. We'll now do a reverse numerical sort on the number of times that each IP address occurs, like so:

```
[donnie@fedora-server ~]$ sudo cut -d" " -f1 /var/log/httpd/access_log |
sort | uniq -c | sort -nr
     11 192.168.0.16
      4 192.168.0.8
      4 192.168.0.27
      4 192.168.0.25
```

```
     1 192.168.0.9
     1 ::1
[donnie@fedora-server ~]$
```

10. Now that you know that the command works properly, create the `ipaddress_count.sh` script, and make it look like this:

```
#!/bin/bash
cut -d" " -f1 /var/log/httpd/access_log | sort | uniq -c | sort -nr
```

Be aware that you'll need to use sudo to run this script.

11. Finally, let's fancy things up a bit. Add some code to save the results to a text file with a time-stamp in its filename. It should look like this:

```
#!/bin/bash
timestamp=$(date +%F)
echo "These addresses have accessed this webserver as of $timestamp." >
ipaddress_list_$timestamp.txt
cut -d" " -f1 /var/log/httpd/access_log | sort | uniq -c | sort -nr >>
ipaddress_list_$timestamp.txt
```

Of course, there are other available programs that do a more comprehensive job of parsing your webserver log files. But, this script is handy for a quick analysis of who is accessing your server.

End of lab

Let's move on to the final lab.

Hands-on Lab – Beta Testing a Hard Drive

The final example involves an experience that I had quite a few years ago. That's when the good folk at Western Digital invited me to participate in a beta test of a new model hard drive. All I really had to do was to keep the drive running for the whole four-month test period, and then collect log data from the drive's BIOS at the end of the test period. But, I went a bit beyond that by writing a shell script that automatically collected drive performance data on a daily basis. As before, do this on your Fedora Server virtual machine.

1. To collect drive performance data, you'll need to install a couple of packages, like this:

```
sudo dnf install sysstat smartmontools
```

2. Start the sysstat service and ensure that it's active, like this:

```
sudo systemctl start sysstat
systemctl status sysstat
```

3. You'll use the sar component of the sysstat package to collect your data. But, it will be a few minutes before any sar data become available. While you're waiting, generate some hard drive activity by doing a system update, like so:

```
sudo dnf -y upgrade
```

4. View the sar man page and take note of the different types of data that can be collected with the various sar option switches. You'll be seeing several of those options in the shell script.

   This is another one of those scripts that's too large to reproduce in the book. So, download the hard_drive.sh script from the Github repository. Open it in your text editor and study it. I've covered all of the concepts that I've used in this script, so you should be able to figure out what it's doing.

5. The last command in the script is a smartctl command, which requires sudo privileges. So, you'll need to use sudo to run the script, like so:

```
sudo ./hard_drive.sh
```

   Be patient, because this takes a few minutes to run. Also, be aware that the virtual drive of your virtual machine isn't smartmontools-aware, which means that you'll see some warning messages in your report.

6. When the script has finished running, look at the generated report in the Drive_Reports directory.

7. Feel free to run this script on your Linux host machine. It should run on most any Linux distro, as long as you have the sysstat and smartmontools packages installed, and the sysstat service is running.

End of Lab

All right, that wraps it up for this chapter. Let's summarize and move on.

Summary

We covered an incredible amount of ground in this chapter, and I hope that I haven't overwhelmed you. What I wanted to do was to provide you with a comprehensive overview of the concepts and techniques that you would use to build a usable shell script. We started with some techniques that are unique to shell scripting, and followed up with techniques that are common to most all programming languages.

And really, that's one of the coolest things about learning shell scripting. It's much easier to learn than higher-level languages such as C, Java, or Rust, but it's still extremely useful. And, as you learn shell scripting, you also learn about the constructs and concepts that also apply to the higher-level languages. So, if you ever plan to learn another programming language, learning shell scripting first can help you prepare for it.

But, even with all that we've covered, we're not done yet. In the next chapter, I'll present a few more ways to filter and manipulate text. I'll see you there.

Questions

1. Which of the following snippets represents the *most preferred* way to perform command substitution?

    a. `` `command` ``

    b. `%(command)`

    c. `"command"`

    d. `$(command)`

2. You need to create an array of names. How would you do that?

    a. `set array=names`

        `names=( Vicky Frank Cleopatra Katelyn )`

    b. `array=names`

        `names=( Vicky Frank Cleopatra Katelyn )`

    c. `array names`

        `names=( Vicky Frank Cleopatra Katelyn )`

    d. `declare names`

        `names=( Vicky Frank Cleopatra Katelyn )`

    e. `declare -a names`

        `names=( Vicky Frank Cleopatra Katelyn )`

3. How would you view the exit code of a command that you just ran?

    a. `echo $#`

    b. `echo $?`

    c. `echo $$`

    d. `echo $!`

4. You want to create a loop that will read a list of names, and then echo the names into another text file. But, you want to skip two of the names. Which of the following commands would make your script do that?

    a. `break`

    b. `skip`

    c. `continue`

    d. `stop`

5. You want to compare two numerical values to see if they're equal. which of the following operators would you use?

    a. =

    b. -eq

    c. ==

    d. -ne

Further Reading

- What is the Bash Shebang and How to Use It: `https://www.rosehosting.com/blog/what-is-the-bash-shebang/`
- An Introduction to Parameter Expansion in bash: `https://opensource.com/article/17/6/bash-parameter-expansion`
- Shell Parameter Expansion (Bash Reference Manual): `https://www.gnu.org/software/bash/manual/html_node/Shell-Parameter-Expansion.html`
- Introduction to if: `https://tldp.org/LDP/Bash-Beginners-Guide/html/sect_07_01.html`
- Bash while Loop: `https://linuxize.com/post/bash-while-loop/`
- How to Find Most Used Disk Space Directories and Files in Linux: `https://www.tecmint.com/find-top-large-directories-and-files-sizes-in-linux/`
- Standard Exit Status Codes in Linux: `https://www.baeldung.com/linux/status-codes`
- How to Use the sar Command on Linux: `https://www.howtogeek.com/793513/how-to-use-the-sar-command-on-linux/`

Answers

1. d
2. e
3. b
4. c
5. b

Join our community on Discord!

Read this book alongside other users, Linux experts, and the author himself.

Ask questions, provide solutions to other readers, chat with the author via Ask Me Anything sessions, and much more. Scan the QR code or visit the link to join the community.

`https://packt.link/SecNet`

9

Filtering Text with grep, sed, and Regular Expressions

So far, we've looked at how to perform file searches with find, and at how to use text-stream filter utilities to extract and present data from text files and program output streams. In this chapter we'll be looking at two other utilities, sed and grep, that will allow you to supercharge both your searches and your text manipulations. Before that though, you need to understand about Regular Expressions.

Topics in this chapter include:

- Understanding Regular Expressions
- Understanding sed
- Understanding grep
- Using RegEx Buddy
- Using RegEx101
- Looking at some real-world examples

If you're ready, let's get started.

Technical Requirements

Use any of your Linux virtual machines or your Linux host machine.

Also, as always, you can grab the scripts and text files from Github, like so:

```
git clone https://github.com/PacktPublishing/The-Ultimate-Linux-Shell-
Scripting-Guide.git
```

Understanding Regular Expressions

When you worked with the text-stream filters in *Chapter 6, Text Stream Filters Part 1* and *Chapter 7, Text Stream Filters Part 2*, you were manipulating simple text strings. That is, you were working with alphabetic characters, numbers, and the control characters that allow you to place tabs, spaces, and newlines into your text files. **Regular Expressions**, which you'll sometimes see shortened to either **regexp** or **regex**, can include text strings, or even be a text string. They can also include special characters, collectively called **metacharacters**, which give such awesome power to the tools that understand them. In fact, you can think of Regular Expressions as a sort of programming language, with text strings as the words and metacharacters as the punctuation. Rather than just enabling you to search for simple text strings, regular expressions allow you to search for patterns. For example, if you need to search through a file for all telephone numbers or all credit card numbers, you can create a regular expression that searches for text strings that match those patterns.

 I need to clarify something that's a bit confusing. *Regular Expressions*, always written in the plural form and with upper-case letters beginning each word, is the name of the pattern-matching language. That's different from a *regular expression*, which is a pattern-matching construct that you would build with the *Regular Expressions* language.

Understand, though, that the topic of Regular Expressions is a huge one, and is a topic about which whole books are written. For now, I'll just give you the basics that you need to understand how to use them with grep and sed. Let's begin by looking at the two general types of characters that you would use in a regular expression.

Literals and Metacharacters

There are two types of characters that you'll use in regular expressions. **Literals** are any character which is to be taken literally. In other words, literals are anything that you want to treat as just plain text. **Metacharacters** give you the ability to modify your pattern-matching according to your needs. You can, for example, use metacharacters to find a text pattern that occurs at either the beginning or end of a line, while leaving the pattern alone if it occurs somewhere else in the line. You can also use metacharacters to perform different types of wild-card pattern-matching.

There are three types of metacharacters, which are:

- **Positional anchors:** These define where in either a file or a line that you would want to find a match.

- **Character sets:** These define either a range or a specific type of literal character that you want to match. In other words, if you want to find a text string that contains nothing but lower-case letters, you don't have to list each lower-case letter in your regular expression. Instead, just use the lower-case letter character set.

- **Modifiers:** Mainly, these metacharacters allow you to define how many of any literal character or string of literal characters that you want to match at a time. The other modifiers are the or operator and the grouping operator.

The **positional anchors,** are as you see in the following table:

Positional anchor	Description
^	This allows you to match a pattern that occurs at the beginning of a line. You would always place it to the left of the pattern that you want to match, like this: ^pattern
$	This allows you to match a pattern that occurs at the end of a line. You would always place it to the right of the pattern that you want to match, like this: pattern$
\<pattern\>	This pair of symbols marks word boundaries. For example, if you were to search for the pattern *and,* use of this metacharacter would only match with the whole word *and,* instead of with any word that contains the text string *and.*

The following table explains the about the various **character sets.**

Character set examples	Description
[abc] [a-z] [:lower:] [:digit:]	This should already be familiar to you. This defines either a set of characters or a range of characters to match in a pattern. You can also use the same character classes that you used with the text-stream filters.
[^abc] [^a-z]	In the previous table, I showed you how the ^ can be used as a positional anchor. But, when used as the first character of a character set, the ^ acts as a negation operator. So, while [abc] matches everything with an a, b, or c in it, [^abc] matches everything without an a, b, or c in it.

The final type of metacharacters consists of the **modifiers,** as you see in this table:

Basic modifier	Extended modifier	Description
*	*	Wild-card to match zero or more of the single character or single-character regular expression that precedes it. Note that this behavior is different from what you're used to seeing with * in normal command-line operations, in commands such as ls -l *.txt.
\?	?	Wild-card to match zero or one instance of the preceding single character or regular expression.
\+	+	A wild-card that must have a match. Matches one or more instances of the preceding single character or regular expression.

\{n\}	{n}	Matches *n* occurrences of the preceding single character or regular expression.
\{n,\}	{n,}	Matches at least *n* occurrences of the preceding single character or regular expression.
|	|	It's called an **alternation**, but think of it as an or operator.
\(regex\)	(regex)	This symbolizes grouping. It matches the regex that's within the parentheses, but it can be modified as a whole. It can also be used in back-references.

Don't worry about the difference between the **Basic Modifiers** and **Extended Modifiers** just yet. I'll cover that when we get to the *Understanding grep* section.

As I said before, the topic of Regular Expressions is quite vast and complex. I don't have space to give a complete tutorial on the subject, so I'll instead just provide examples of using various regular expressions in the sed and grep sections.

You can find some more information on regular expressions by looking at the regex man page, which is in section 7 of the man pages. (Just don't expect to become a regex expert by reading it.) View the proper man page by doing:

```
man 7 regex
```

Now that I've introduced you to Regular Expressions and regular expressions, allow me to introduce you to a utility that uses them.

Understanding sed

sed, short for **Stream Editor**, is an extremely powerful utility, and is another subject on which whole books are written. The goal here is to help you learn the basics for now, and to whet your appetite to learn more later.

If you've ever had to error-check or edit large text documents, you'll appreciate the power of sed. For simple jobs, a one-line command, known as a **sed script**, might be all you need. For more complex jobs, such as when you might need to make multiple changes at a time to one or more documents, you can write lengthy program files and execute them with sed. The only limitation is your own imagination. But, before we can talk about the cool things you can do with sed, we need to take a brief intermission to talk about sed portability issues.

Understanding sed Portability Issues

If you need to work with non-Linux operating systems, you'll encounter two different implementations of sed. Linux operating systems use the GNU implementation, and the BSD implementation is used on macOS, the BSD distros, and OpenIndiana.

BSD stands for **Berkeley Software Distribution,** and GNU is a recursive acronym that stands for **GNU is not Unix.**

The difference is that the GNU implementation has really cool, advanced features that the BSD implementation lacks. So, many of the examples that I'm about to show you in this section—specifically the append (a), insert (i), and change (c) commands, as well as any command that uses a regular expression—won't work on the BSD implementation. Fortunately though, there's an easy fix for all of these operating systems. Just install the gsed package, and then create a sed alias that points to the gsed executable. Here are the directions for the various operating systems.

Installing gsed on FreeBSD

On FreeBSD, install gsed like this:

```
donnie@freebsd14:~ $ sudo pkg install gsed
```

Then, edit the .shrc file that's in your home directory, adding the following line to the alias section:

```
alias sed='/usr/local/bin/gsed'
```

Log out of the terminal and then log back in again. Verify that the alias has taken effect by doing:

```
donnie@freebsd14:~ $ type sed
sed is an alias for /usr/local/bin/gsed
donnie@freebsd14:~ $
```

Installing gsed on macOS

Installing gsed on macOS is just as easy, but you'll first need to install the Homebrew system.

You'll find directions on how to install Homebrew at: https://brew.sh/

Then, install gsed by doing:

```
macmini@MacMinis-Mac-mini ~ % brew install gsed
```

Add the alias to the .zprofile file that's in your home directory, by adding this line:

```
alias sed='/usr/local/bin/gsed'
```

Close your terminal window and then open it again. Then, verify that the alias has taken effect:

```
macmini@MacMinis-Mac-mini ~ % type sed
```

```
sed is an alias for /usr/local/bin/gsed
macmini@MacMinis-Mac-mini ~ %
```

Installing gsed on OpenIndiana

OpenIndiana doesn't have gsed in its normal software repository. So, you'll need to install a third-party repository to get it. First, open Firefox on your OpenIndiana machine and navigate to: http://buildfarm.opencsw.org/opencsw/official/

Download the the pkgutil.pkg file that you'll see there.

Install the package by doing:

```
donnie@openindiana:~$ sudo pkgadd -d ./pkgutil.pkg
```

This will install pkgutil into the /opt/csw/bin/ directory, as you see here:

```
donnie@openindiana:/opt/csw/bin$ ls -l
total 209
-rwxr-xr-x   1 root     bin         106397 Nov 12  2013 pkgutil
donnie@openindiana:/opt/csw/bin$
```

This directory isn't in your PATH, so you'll need to fix that. The easiest way is to create a symbolic link in the /usr/sbin/ directory, like so:

```
donnie@openindiana:/opt/csw/bin$ sudo ln -s /opt/csw/bin/pkgutil /usr/sbin/
pkgutil
Password:
donnie@openindiana:/opt/csw/bin$ which pkgutil
/usr/sbin/pkgutil
donnie@openindiana:/opt/csw/bin$
```

Next, install the gsed package, like this:

```
donnie@openindiana:~$ sudo pkgutil -i gsed
```

Finally, you're ready to create the alias. On OpenIndiana, you'll need to create it in two different files. To enable the alias when you open a terminal on the local machine, you'll need to add it to the .bashrc file in your home directory, like so:

```
alias sed='/usr/bin/gsed'
```

To enable the alias when you login remotely via ssh, you'll need to create the .bash_profile file in your home directory, and add the same alias line to it.

Now that you've installed gsed and created an alias on your non-Linux system, you'll be able to run any sed command you want from the command-line. Unfortunately, this won't work if you place any sed commands into your shell scripts, because shell scripts don't read the .bashrc, .shrc, .bash_profile, or .zprofile files that contain the alias. That's okay for now, because I'll show you how to deal with that later. First though, I need to show you how to use the various sed commands.

Now that that's done, let's look at how to actually use sed. There are several different sed functions that you need to know. Let's start with the substitute function.

Substitution with sed

In the diagram below, you see the breakdown of a typical sed substitution script.

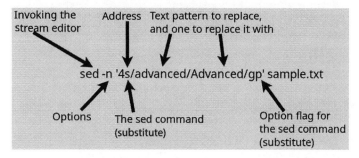

Figure 9.1: A typical sed substitution script

Now, let's look at some specific examples.

Example 1: Modifying an Office Memo

Let's begin with a simple office memo. Create the tom.txt file, as you see here:

```
Memo:  tom tinker
    We regret to inform you that tom
    Tinker will no longer be working
    with us.  Tom tinker is leaving to
    embark on his own business venture.
    We wish tom tinker well.  Good-bye, tom.
cc: tom Tinker
```

You can see that the document has a few problems. The most obvious is that proper names aren't always capitalized. We need a way to automate the process of making these corrections.

It's possible to make all corrections at once, but first, let's just look at how to replace *tom* with *Tom*. Do it like this:

```
[donnie@fedora ~]$ sed 's/tom/Tom/' tom.txt
Memo:  Tom tinker
    We regret to inform you that Tom
    Tinker will no longer be working
    with us.  Tom tinker is leaving to
    embark on his own business venture.
    We wish Tom tinker well.  Good-bye, tom.
cc: Tom Tinker
[donnie@fedora ~]$
```

The first thing you see within the single quotes is the letter s. That's what tells sed to perform a substitution. Next, you see the two patterns that you're working with. The first is the pattern that you're replacing, and the second is what you're using as the replacement. After you close the expression with another single quote, list the text file that you want to modify. (Note that you don't need a stdin redirector.)

Now, this did work for the most part, but we still have one lower-case *tom* in the last line of the body. That's because by default, the s command for sed will only replace the first occurrence of a pattern in a given line. To fix this, use the s command with its global (g) option. That way, every occurrence of a pattern in any given line will be replaced. Here is what that looks like:

```
[donnie@fedora ~]$ sed 's/tom/Tom/g' tom.txt
Memo:  Tom tinker
    We regret to inform you that Tom
    Tinker will no longer be working
    with us.  Tom tinker is leaving to
    embark on his own business venture.
    We wish Tom tinker well.  Good-bye, Tom.
cc: Tom Tinker
[donnie@fedora ~]$
```

This works much better. But, we still have lower-case surnames to replace. Let's combine two commands to replace both the first and last names at once, like this:

```
[donnie@fedora ~]$ sed 's/tom/Tom/g ; s/tinker/Tinker/g' tom.txt
Memo:  Tom Tinker
    We regret to inform you that Tom
    Tinker will no longer be working
    with us.  Tom Tinker is leaving to
    embark on his own business venture.
    We wish Tom Tinker well.  Good-bye, Tom.
```

```
cc: Tom Tinker
[donnie@fedora ~]$
```

All you have to do is create two separate sed scripts, and combine them with a semi-colon. You can place both scripts within only one set of single quotes.

By default, sed will read in the text file that you want to modify, and send the entire modified file to stdout.

What if you only want to see the lines that actually got modified?

For that, you would use the -n switch as the sed option, and the p switch as the s command option. First, let's look at what happens when you use only one of these switches at a time. Here's what happens if you use -n without the p:

```
[donnie@fedora ~]$ sed -n 's/tom/Tom/g ; s/tinker/Tinker/g' tom.txt
[donnie@fedora ~]$
```

Without the p switch for the s command, the -n switch will suppress all output, which isn't what we want. This is because the -n switch is the *quiet* switch, which negates sed's default behavior of passing the processed file to stdout.

Next, let's try it with just the p and without the -n, which will look like this:

```
[donnie@fedora ~]$ sed 's/tom/Tom/g ; s/tinker/Tinker/gp' tom.txt
Memo:   Tom Tinker
Memo:   Tom Tinker
    We regret to inform you that Tom
    Tinker will no longer be working
    with us.  Tom Tinker is leaving to
    with us.  Tom Tinker is leaving to
    embark on his own business venture.
    We wish Tom Tinker well.  Good-bye, Tom.
    We wish Tom Tinker well.  Good-bye, Tom.
cc: Tom Tinker
[donnie@fedora ~]$
```

Without the -n option, the p option for the s command will cause sed to print its default output, in addition to printing the modified lines a second time. (Actually, we see here that two lines were printed a third time, since more than one replacement was done in each.) This is because without the quiet switch (-n), sed once again defaults to printing out the processed file. Then, the p option for the s command causes all modified lines to print out again.

Now, to see only the modified lines, let's combine the options, like this:

```
[donnie@fedora ~]$ sed -n 's/tom/Tom/gp ; s/tinker/Tinker/gp' tom.txt
Memo:   Tom tinker
Memo:   Tom Tinker
```

```
        We regret to inform you that Tom
        with us.  Tom Tinker is leaving to
        We wish Tom tinker well.  Good-bye, Tom.
        We wish Tom Tinker well.  Good-bye, Tom.
cc: Tom Tinker
[donnie@fedora ~]$
```

So the lesson here is that you must use -n and p together, because using just one of them won't give
you what you want.

Wait though, you're not through yet. It seems that your boss is a bit of a practical joker. So, he tells you
to replace the last *Tinker* with *Stinker*. As he turns to leave, he winks and says, "Yeah, that'll get him".
Here's where the addressing option comes in handy.

Since you know that the last *Tinker* is the last word in the last line of the file, you can direct sed to only
replace that occurrence by placing the *end-of* metacharacter ($), in the address. Here's how that looks:

```
[donnie@fedora ~]$ sed 's/tom/Tom/g ; s/tinker/Tinker/g ; $s/Tinker/Stinker/'
tom.txt
Memo:  Tom Tinker
        We regret to inform you that Tom
        Tinker will no longer be working
        with us.  Tom Tinker is leaving to
        embark on his own business venture.
        We wish Tom Tinker well.  Good-bye, Tom.
cc: Tom Stinker
[donnie@fedora ~]$
```

Okay, let's move on to our next example.

Example 2: Modifying a List of Hollywood Actors

There are still plenty of other ways to perform substitutions with sed. To demonstrate, create the
actorsfile_11.txt file with the following list of Hollywood actors:

```
Jessel          George
Marx            Groucho
Cantor          Eddie
Allen           Fred
Burns           George
Wayne           John
Price           Vincent
Besser          Joe
Greenstreet     Sidney
Conrad          William
```

You've decided that you want to replace Groucho Marx with his brother Zeppo. Search for all lines that begin with Marx, and make the replacement only on those lines, like this:

```
[donnie@fedora ~]$ sed '/^Marx/s/Groucho/Zeppo/' actorfile_11.txt
Jessel          George
Marx            Zeppo
Cantor          Eddie
Allen           Fred
Burns           George
Wayne           John
Price           Vincent
Besser          Joe
Greenstreet     Sidney
Conrad          William
[donnie@fedora ~]$
```

In this example, you used a regular expression for an address. That is, you placed the literal string *Marx* within the default sed delimiters (the forward slashes), then preceded it with the ^ metacharacter. That causes the substitute command to look for only the occurrence of *Marx* at the beginning of a line. Note again how this address immediately precedes the s command. You don't need to use the global option for the s command, because you already know that there's only one occurrence of a given word in each line.

You've now decided that you need to replace Joe Besser with Joe DeRita. (That's appropriate, because in real life the Three Stooges really did replace Joe Besser with Joe DeRita, after Joe Besser left to care for his ailing wife.) This time, you want to search for lines that end with *Joe*, and make the replacement only on those lines, like this:

```
[donnie@fedora ~]$ sed '/Joe$/s/Besser/DeRita/' actorfile_11.txt
Jessel          George
Marx            Groucho
Cantor          Eddie
Allen           Fred
Burns           George
Wayne           John
Price           Vincent
DeRita          Joe
Greenstreet     Sidney
Conrad          William
[donnie@fedora ~]$
```

This time, you used the $ metacharacter in the address to tell s to look at the end of the lines. Note how you had to place this metacharacter at the end of the literal string.

Okay, enough of actors. Let's look at some classic cars.

Example 3: Modifying Lists of Cars

You can also replace individual characters. Create the `cars_2.txt` file with the following contents:

```
[donnie@fedora ~]$ cat > cars_2.txt
edsel
Edsel
Edsel
desoto
desoto
Desoto
Desoto
nash
Nash
nash
Hudson
hudson
hudson
[donnie@fedora ~]$
```

In this file, you see that you need to capitalize the names of some of the listed cars. For now, let's just concentrate on capitalizing *Desoto*. If you tell sed to replace every *d* with a *D*, you'll get this:

```
[donnie@fedora ~]$ sed 's/d/D/' cars_2.txt
eDsel
EDsel
EDsel
Desoto
Desoto
Desoto
Desoto
nash
Nash
nash
HuDson
huDson
huDson
[donnie@fedora ~]$
```

That's not what you want. But, you know that there is a lower-case *desoto* only in lines four and five. So, you can tell sed to replace the lower-case *d* in only those two lines, like this:

```
[donnie@fedora ~]$ sed '4,5s/d/D/' cars_2.txt
edsel
```

```
Edsel
Edsel
Desoto
Desoto
Desoto
Desoto
nash
Nash
nash
Hudson
hudson
hudson
[donnie@fedora ~]$
```

 Note that the comma between the two line numbers means *lines four through five*, not *lines four and five*.

You can tell sed to search for *desoto* at the beginning of a line, like this:

```
[donnie@fedora ~]$ sed '/^desoto/s/d/D/' cars_2.txt
edsel
Edsel
Edsel
Desoto
Desoto
Desoto
Desoto
nash
Nash
nash
Hudson
hudson
hudson
[donnie@fedora ~]$
```

Insert the -n and p switches if you only want to see the lines that changed, like so:

```
[donnie@fedora ~]$ sed -n '/^desoto/s/d/D/p' cars_2.txt
Desoto
Desoto
[donnie@fedora ~]$
```

There are three ways to save your modifications. You can use the stdout redirector to create a new file, like this:

```
[donnie@fedora ~]$ sed -n '/^desoto/s/d/D/p' cars_2.txt > cars_cap.txt
[donnie@fedora ~]$
```

You can use the w switch with the s command to save to a new file, like this:

```
[donnie@fedora ~]$ sed '/^desoto/s/d/D/w newcarsfile.txt' cars_2.txt
edsel
Edsel
Edsel
Desoto
Desoto
Desoto
Desoto
nash
Nash
nash
Hudson
hudson
hudson
[donnie@fedora ~]$
```

The only catch with this is that even though the w switch shows the entire contents of the modified file on screen, it only saves the modified lines to a new file, as you see here:

```
[donnie@fedora ~]$ cat newcarsfile.txt
Desoto
Desoto
[donnie@fedora ~]$
```

The final way to save your modifications is to use the -i switch to modify the original file, like so:

```
[donnie@fedora ~]$ sed -i '/^desoto/s/d/D/' cars_2.txt
[donnie@fedora ~]$
```

Unlike when you use the w switch, the -i saves the entire modified file, as you see here:

```
[donnie@fedora ~]$ cat cars_2.txt
edsel
Edsel
Edsel
Desoto
```

```
Desoto
Desoto
Desoto
nash
Nash
nash
Hudson
hudson
hudson
[donnie@fedora ~]$
```

If you want to create a backup of the original file before it gets modified, just put the suffix that you want to append to the backup filename after the -i switch, like so:

```
[donnie@fedora ~]$ sed -i.bak '/^desoto/s/d/D/' cars_2.txt
[donnie@fedora ~]
```

Note that you can't have a blank space between the -i and the .bak. Verify that the operation worked, like this:

```
[donnie@fedora ~]$ ls -l cars_2.txt.bak
-rw-r--r--. 1 donnie donnie 82 Oct 11 13:58 cars_2.txt.bak
[donnie@fedora ~]$
```

Next, let's do some whole-word substitutions.

Example 4: Performing a Whole-Word Substitution

What if you have a pattern that can be part of other words, but you only want to perform substitutions on the pattern if it's a whole word unto itself? To illustrate, create the ing.txt file with this somewhat corny story:

```
It began raining just as the
baseball team began their spring
training.  Meanwhile, Susan began
singing as she was playing the
piano.  Just being alive was great,
and Michael was thinking about how
he was going to begin working on
his new novel.  Writing was like
a tonic to him.  It was just like
acting out all of his fantasies.
I think I've used ing enough in this
story to illustrate my point about ing.
So, ing away, and then ing some more.
```

Now, let's say that you want to replace the word *ing* with the word *ING*. Try this command to see what you get:

```
[donnie@fedora ~]$ sed 's/ing/ING/g' ing.txt
It began rainING just as the
baseball team began their sprING
trainING.  Meanwhile, Susan began
sINGING as she was playING the
piano.  Just beING alive was great,
and Michael was thinkING about how
he was goING to begin workING on
his new novel.  WritING was like
a tonic to him.  It was just like
actING out all of his fantasies.
I think I've used ING enough in this story to illustrate my point about ING.
So, ING away, and then ING some more.
```

You really only wanted to replace the whole word *ing* with *ING*, but ended up replacing the *ing*'s that show up in other words, also. Here's where you need to use word boundaries, like so:

```
[donnie@fedora ~]$ sed 's/\<ing\>/ING/g' ing.txt
It began raining just as the
baseball team began their spring
training.  Meanwhile, Susan began
singing as she was playing the
piano.  Just being alive was great,
and Michael was thinking about how
he was going to begin working on
his new novel.  Writing was like
a tonic to him.  It was just like
acting out all of his fantasies.
I think I've used ING enough in this
story to illustrate my point about ING.
So, ING away, and then ING some more.
```

All you had to do was to place the string that you wanted to replace inside of a of \< \> construct.

As you look at the metacharacter chart that I presented a few pages back, you may think, "Hey, I've discovered another way to do this. I can just use a wild-card character". Indeed, in this case, it would work, as you see here:

```
[donnie@fedora ~]$ sed 's/ \+ing/ ING/g' ing.txt
It began raining just as the
baseball team began their spring
training.  Meanwhile, Susan began
```

```
singing as she was playing the
piano.  Just being alive was great,
and Michael was thinking about how
he was going to begin working on
his new novel.  Writing was like
a tonic to him.  It was just like
acting out all of his fantasies.
I think I've used ING enough in this
story to illustrate my point about ING.
So, ING away, and then ING some more.
```

Here, you used the \+ metacharacter to replace all *ing*'s that are preceded by one or more blank spaces. (Note that I left a space between the first forward slash and the \+ metacharacter in the s command. I also had to leave a blank space before the *ING* in order to also leave a space in the output.) However, in this case, this isn't the most elegant solution, since it won't work in all cases. To illustrate, create the ing_2.txt file, and make it look like this:

```
I'm writing yet another story about
the suffix ing.  I hope that this
ing story will help illustrate our point.
```

Perform the previous command again, and you should get this:

```
[donnie@fedora ~]$ sed 's/ \+ing/ ING/g' ing_2.txt
I'm writing yet another story about
the suffix ING.  I hope that this
ing story will help illustrate our point.
[donnie@fedora ~]$
```

The *ing* in the last line didn't get replaced, because it's at the beginning of a line. Therefore, no blank spaces can precede it. Wild-card metacharacters are handy devices, and do have legitimate uses. But here, we find that they're not the best solution.

That covers it for substitution. Let's now do some deletions.

Deletion with sed

You can use the d command to perform deletions. This is simpler than the substitution process, since all you really need is an address and the d command. We'll begin by deleting some items from a list.

Example 1: Deleting Items from a List

Let's take another look at our cars_2.txt file, and try to delete all references to Edsel. (We want to forget that the Edsel was ever made, as Ford Motor Company has tried to do ever since 1960.) First, as a reminder, here's what the original file looks like:

```
[donnie@fedora ~]$ cat cars_2.txt
```

```
edsel
Edsel
Edsel
Desoto
Desoto
Desoto
Desoto
nash
Nash
nash
Hudson
hudson
hudson
[donnie@fedora ~]$
```

Well, it's not exactly original, because I forgot that I had modified it to capitalize all of the *desoto*'s. But, that doesn't matter. To delete all references to the Edsel, try this:

```
[donnie@fedora ~]$ sed '/edsel/d' cars_2.txt
Edsel
Edsel
Desoto
Desoto
Desoto
Desoto
nash
Nash
nash
Hudson
hudson
hudson
[donnie@fedora ~]$
```

This command only deleted the lower-case *edsel*. But, I need a way to delete all references to Edsel. Fortunately, you can use a regular expression to specify multiple characters in the address, like this:

```
[donnie@fedora ~]$ sed '/[eE]dsel/d' cars_2.txt
Desoto
Desoto
Desoto
Desoto
```

```
nash
Nash
nash
Hudson
hudson
hudson
[donnie@fedora ~]$
```

All you had to do was to put both *e* and *E* within brackets, and use that for the first character of the address.

If you want to delete everything except for references to *Edsel*, use an ! to invert the command. Now, you'd think that you'd want to put the inversion character in front of the address that you're searching for, but that isn't the case. Instead, place the inversion character in front of the command character itself. So, in this case, you would place the exclamation point in front of the d, like this:

```
[donnie@fedora ~]$ sed '/[eE]dsel/!d' cars_2.txt
edsel
Edsel
Edsel
[donnie@fedora ~]$
```

 You've just seen an example of how things aren't always implemented consistently across the various shell scripting tools. A while ago, you saw that the ^ is the inversion operator for Regular Expressions. Here, you see that the ! is the inversion operator for sed commands. You've also seen that the ^ can also be used to indicate the beginning of a line. So yeah, things can get a bit confusing.

You can also choose a range of line numbers for the address. This time, let's delete all references to Nash, which happen to be in lines eight through ten, like this:

```
[donnie@fedora ~]$ sed '8,10d' cars_2.txt
edsel
Edsel
Edsel
Desoto
Desoto
Desoto
Desoto
Hudson
hudson
hudson
[donnie@fedora ~]$
```

Place an exclamation point in front of the d to delete everything except for lines eight through ten, like this:

```
[donnie@fedora ~]$ sed '8,10!d' cars_2.txt
nash
Nash
nash
[donnie@fedora ~]$
```

That does it for the classic cars. Next, I'll show you what to do if your file has too many blank lines.

Example 2: Deleting Blank Lines

For our last deletion trick, here's how you can delete blank lines from a file. Just make an address with the start-of-line metacharacter (^) right next to the end-of-line metacharacter ($). Start by creating the blank_lines.txt file, like this:

```
One non-blank line.



Another non-blank line.



Yet another non-blank line.

And one last non-blank line.
```

Now, perform the deletion, with ^$ as the regular expression, like this:

```
[donnie@fedora ~]$ sed '/^$/d' blank_lines.txt
One non-blank line.
Another non-blank line.
Yet another non-blank line.
And one last non-blank line.
[donnie@fedora ~]$
```

 Note the difference between this and the way we previously used the *end-of* metacharacter in the substitution script. Since we're using two metacharacters together to form a regular expression, we have to place them between two forward slashes.

Now, for the next trick.

Appending and Inserting with sed

The a command for the Linux implementation of sed is used to append a line of text after another line of text. Let's see how it works.

Example 1: Appending Lines of Text

You can use that feature to add some model names to the cars list. Add the *Ambassador* model for the Nash line, like this:

```
[donnie@fedora ~]$ sed '/[nN]ash/aAmbassador' cars_2.txt
edsel
Edsel
. . .

. . .
nash
Ambassador
Nash
Ambassador
nash
Ambassador
Hudson
hudson
hudson
[donnie@fedora ~]$
```

That's good, but you can make it better. Start by indenting the model names. Do that by adding a preceding tab, like this:

```
[donnie@fedora ~]$ sed '/[nN]ash/a\\tAmbassador' cars_2.txt
edsel
Edsel
. . .

. . .
nash
        Ambassador
Nash
        Ambassador
nash
        Ambassador
Hudson
hudson
hudson
[donnie@fedora ~]$
```

Note that I can only show a partial output here, due to book formatting constraints.

The control character for a tab is \t. Note though, that you had to add another backslash so that sed would properly recognize it.

You can do the same thing by using a line address. Let's append a model name to line six, like so:

```
[donnie@fedora ~]$ sed '6a\\tFiredome' cars_2.txt
edsel
Edsel
Edsel
Desoto
Desoto
Desoto
        Firedome
Desoto
nash
Nash
nash
Hudson
hudson
hudson
```

But, that doesn't cover all of the *Desoto*'s. Let's append the model name to lines four through seven, like this:

```
[donnie@fedora ~]$ sed '4,7a\\tFiredome' cars_2.txt
edsel
Edsel
Edsel
Desoto
     Firedome
Desoto
     Firedome
Desoto
     Firedome
Desoto
     Firedome
```

```
nash
. . .
[donnie@fedora ~]$
```

Now, let's combine some operations. Start by editing the cars_2.txt file so that it once again has some lower-case *desoto*'s. It should look like this:

```
edsel
Edsel
Edsel
desoto
desoto
Desoto
desoto
nash
Nash
nash
Hudson
hudson
hudson
```

But, you're not limited to just performing one operation at a time. So, let's see how we can combine operations.

Example 2: Performing Multiple Operations at Once

You'll add a model to both the Edsel and Desoto lines, and delete every make that isn't capitalized. Note that you can't just place everything within one set of quotes, or use a semi-colon to separate the operations. For this, you have to give every operation its own set of quotes, and precede every operation with the -e switch. That's because these operations are sequential, which means that the first operation must run to completion before the second one can begin. Here's how it looks:

```
[donnie@fedora ~]$ sed -e '6a\\tFiredome' -e '/Edsel/a\\tCorsair' -e
'/^[a-z]/d' cars_2.txt
Edsel
    Corsair
Edsel
    Corsair
Desoto
    Firedome
Nash
Hudson
[donnie@fedora ~]$
```

Now that we've looked at appending text, let's see how to insert text.

Example 3: Inserting Lines of Text

The i command works the same way, except that it will insert a line of text before another line of text, like this:

```
[donnie@fedora ~]$ sed -e '/Edsel/i1958' -e '/^[[:lower:]]/d' cars_2.txt
1958
Edsel
1958
Edsel
Desoto                                       /
Nash
Hudson
[donnie@fedora ~]$
```

As a bonus, I've also shown you another way to get rid of all car names that begin with a lower-case letter.

That's it for this trick. Let's move on to the next one.

Changing with sed

You would use the c command to change a string of text. (You can also change text with the s command, but this is a bit shorter to type.) Let's see how it's done.

Example 1: Changing Edsel to Studebaker

As before, you'll work with the cars_2.txt file. Begin by changing *Edsel* and *edsel* to *Studebaker*, like so:

```
[donnie@fedora ~]$ sed '/[eE]dsel/cStudebaker' cars_2.txt
Studebaker
Studebaker
Studebaker
desoto
desoto
Desoto
desoto
nash
Nash
nash
Hudson
hudson
hudson
[donnie@fedora ~]$
```

You can also specify the change to make by line numbers. Here's what happens when you use the *edsel* and *Edsel* line numbers as the address:

```
[donnie@fedora ~]$ sed '1,3cStudebaker' cars_2.txt
Studebaker
desoto
desoto
Desoto
desoto
nash
Nash
nash
Hudson
hudson
hudson
[donnie@fedora ~]$
```

You see that this worked a bit differently than before. Instead of making the change to each line separately, as happened with the other commands, here the command tells sed to replace the range of lines as a group.

I know this looks amazing, but you haven't seen anything yet. Check out this next amazing trick.

Example 2: Changing Entire Lines of Text

For an even better example, create the cars_4.txt file, like this:

```
donnie@fedora:~$ cat cars_4.txt
1958 Edsel Corsair
1949 Oldsmobile 88
1959 Edsel Ranger
1960 Edsel Ranger
1958 Edsel Bermuda
1964 Ford Galaxie
1954 Nash Ambassador
donnie@fedora:~$
```

Now, prepare to be amazed when you run this sed command:

```
donnie@fedora:~$ sed '/[eE]dsel/c1963 Studebaker Avanti' cars_4.txt
1963 Studebaker Avanti
1949 Oldsmobile 88
1963 Studebaker Avanti
1963 Studebaker Avanti
1963 Studebaker Avanti
1964 Ford Galaxie
1954 Nash Ambassador
donnie@fedora:~$
```

So now, you see the biggest difference between the s and the c sed commands. Instead of just replacing the text string or pattern that you specify, the c command replaces the entire line in which the text string or pattern is found. In this case, every entire line that contains the text string *Edsel* was replaced with *1963 Studebaker Avanti*. Cool, right?

Other Miscellaneous sed tricks

We're not done yet. Here are a few more cool tricks that you can do with sed.

Example 1: Using the q Command

The q command causes sed to behave just like the head utility. It tells sed to read in the designated number of lines, and then quit. If you want to show the first ten lines of our public domain e-book, enter this:

```
[donnie@fedora ~]$ sed '10q' pg6409.txt
The Project Gutenberg eBook of How to Speak and Write Correctly

This ebook is for the use of anyone anywhere in the United States and
most other parts of the world at no cost and with almost no restrictions
whatsoever. You may copy it, give it away or re-use it under the terms
of the Project Gutenberg License included with this ebook or online
at www.gutenberg.org. If you are not located in the United States,
you will have to check the laws of the country where you are located
before using this eBook.
[donnie@fedora ~]$
```

If you want to view selected lines from somewhere in the middle of a large file, you may find that sed is easier to use than the head/tail combination. Here's how you can look at lines 1,005 through 1,010 of our e-book file:

```
[donnie@fedora ~]$ sed -n '1005,1010p' pg6409.txt
           Present                    Perfect
        To be loved              To have been loved
                      PARTICIPLES
[donnie@fedora ~]$
```

 Note that the p that I used here isn't quite the same as the p option for the *substitute* command. This print command is a separate command unto itself. Still though, it has to be used together with the -n option for sed to get the results that you want.

Example 2: Using the w Command

Use the w command to write selected lines of text to a new file. You can use a regular expression as an address, as you did above for the p command, or you can use line numbers, like this:

```
[donnie@fedora ~]$ sed '11,13whudson_cars.txt' cars_2.txt
edsel
Edsel
Edsel
desoto
desoto
Desoto
desoto
nash
Nash
nash
Hudson
hudson
hudson
[donnie@fedora ~]$
```

If the preceding command looks a bit confusing, you can insert some spaces to make it more clear, like this:

```
[donnie@fedora ~]$ sed '11,13 w hudson_cars.txt' cars_2.txt
```

Although you see the the contents of the entire file on screen, only the selected content gets saved in your new file, as you see here:

```
[donnie@fedora ~]$ cat hudson_cars.txt
Hudson
hudson
hudson
[donnie@fedora ~]$
```

The output will be the same as it was before. And, this demonstrates something that can be a bit confusing about sed. In some places of a sed script, blank spaces are optional. In other places, such as in a previous example when I showed you how to use the -i option with a filename suffix for the backup file, you can't use a blank space. As I said before, there's not always a lot of consistency with this stuff.

Example 3: Using the r Command

The r command will read a selected file and append it to the specified place in the file you're working with. To see this, create the cars_3.txt file, like this:

```
Packard
Kaiser
Frazer
```

Now, insert the cars_3.txt file after the second line of the cars_2.txt file, like this:

```
[donnie@fedora ~]$ sed '2rcars_3.txt' cars_2.txt
```

```
edsel
Edsel
Packard
Kaiser
Frazer
Edsel
desoto
desoto
Desoto
. . .

. . .
hudson
[donnie@fedora ~]$
```

Again, if this is confusing to read, then use the optional spaces, like so:

```
[donnie@fedora ~]$ sed '2 r cars_3.txt' cars_2.txt
```

Either way works equally well.

Using sed program files

If you have complex jobs that you perform on a regular basis, such as having to make multiple edits to either one or more documents at a time, you can create program files. Then, invoke sed with the -f switch to read the scripts from the file. Let's look at a few examples

Example 1: Appending Lines in a Text File

To see how this works, create the myfile_3.txt file, which will look like this:

```
This here is line one.
And here is the second line.
The third.
Line four.
This is the fifth sentence.
Six
This here is line seven.
Eighth and final.
```

Next, create the demo_append.txt file, which will serve as the sed program file. Make it look like this:

```
2a\
I'll place this line after line two.
```

Invoke the program file, like this:

```
[donnie@fedora ~]$ sed -f demo_append.txt myfile_3.txt
```

```
This here is line one.
And here is the second line.
I'll place this line after line two.
The third.
Line four.
This is the fifth sentence.
Six
This here is line seven.
Eighth and final.
[donnie@fedora ~]$
```

Note how I broke the single script in the program file into two lines. To make that work, I had to place a backslash at the end of the first line to let sed know that the script would continue on the next line. I'll show you in a few moments why that is important.

Now, let's try a program file that will insert some lines. This time, I'll use a text string for the address. Create the demo_insert.txt program file, like this:

```
/This/i\
I'll insert this line before all lines that contain "This".
```

Invoke the program, and you'll see this:

```
[donnie@fedora ~]$ sed -f demo_insert.txt myfile_3.txt
I'll insert this line before all lines that contain "This".
This here is line one.
And here is the second line.
The third.
Line four.
I'll insert this line before all lines that contain "This".
This is the fifth sentence.
Six
I'll insert this line before all lines that contain "This".
This here is line seven.
Eighth and final.
[donnie@fedora ~]$
```

Example 2: Changing Lines in a Text File

Now, let's change lines four through six to something else. Create the demo_change.txt file, like so:

```
4,6c\
Let's replace lines\
four through six\
to something else.
```

Note that I again have to use backslashes to show that the script continues on the next line. Run the program, and you'll see this:

```
[donnie@fedora ~]$ sed -f demo_change.txt myfile_3.txt
This here is line one.
And here is the second line.
The third.
Let's replace lines
four through six
to something else.
This here is line seven.
Eighth and final.
[donnie@fedora ~]$
```

Example 3: Substituting Text

Next, let's create the demo_sub.txt program file that will substitute *sentence* for *line*, and that will only send the modified lines to stdout. Make it look like this:

```
s/line/sentence/p
```

Invoke the program file, like this:

```
[donnie@fedora ~]$ sed -nf demo_sub.txt myfile_3.txt
This here is sentence one.
And here is the second sentence.
This here is sentence seven.
[donnie@fedora ~]$
```

Note that I had to invoke the program with the -n option of sed, because I used the p option inside the program file.

Try this again, except this time, use the write option to send the changed output to a new file. Create the demo_write.txt program file, like this:

```
s/line/sentence/w new_myfile.txt
```

Invoke the program and view the new file, like this:

```
[donnie@fedora ~]$ sed -nf demo_write.txt myfile_3.txt
[donnie@fedora ~]$ cat new_myfile.txt
This here is sentence one.
And here is the second sentence.
This here is sentence seven.
[donnie@fedora ~]$
```

Example 4: Copying Lines from One File to Another

Finally, create the demo_write_2.txt program file, which will copy selected lines from one file to another file. Make it look like this:

```
4,7w new_2_myfile.txt
```

Invoke it, and view the results, like this:

```
[donnie@fedora ~]$ sed -nf demo_write_2.txt myfile_3.txt
[donnie@fedora ~]$ cat new_2_myfile.txt
Line four.
This is the fifth sentence.
Six
This here is line seven.
[donnie@fedora ~]$
```

That's it for the simple program files. Let's now compound things a bit.

Compound Scripts in sed Program Files

So far, I've only shown you program files with one single sed script. You can also have program files with two or more scripts. Begin by creating the demo_compound.txt program file, which will look like this:

```
1,3s/Edsel/Packard/
2,4s/Packard/Lasalle/
3d
```

Now, create the riding.txt file, which will look like this:

```
Let's go for a ride in my Edsel.
Let's go for a ride in my Edsel.
Let's go for a ride in my Edsel.
Let's go for a ride in my Edsel.
```

Invoke the program file, like this:

```
[donnie@fedora ~]$ sed -f demo_compound.txt riding.txt
Let's go for a ride in my Packard.
Let's go for a ride in my Lasalle.
Let's go for a ride in my Edsel.
[donnie@fedora ~]$
```

Here's the breakdown:

- This program first had sed replace *Edsel* with *Packard* in lines one through three.
- In lines two through four, it had sed replace *Packard* with *Lasalle*.
- Finally, the last script deleted line three. Note that you didn't have to use backslashes here, since none of the scripts carried over on to the next line.

To see a second example, create the demo_compound_2.txt program file, like this:

```
2a\
No, I'd rather ride in the Hudson Hornet with the Twin-H Power Six.\
He'd rather ride in the Pierce-Arrow.
3p
```

Invoke the program, like this:

```
[donnie@fedora ~]$ sed -f demo_compound_2.txt riding.txt
Let's go for a ride in my Edsel.
Let's go for a ride in my Edsel.
No, I'd rather ride in the Hudson Hornet with the Twin-H Power Six.
He'd rather ride in the Pierce-Arrow.
Let's go for a ride in my Edsel.
Let's go for a ride in my Edsel.
Let's go for a ride in my Edsel.
[donnie@fedora ~]$
```

This time, you have one script that appends two additional lines after line two, and a second script that causes line three to print a second time.

Just for fun, do the same thing again, except this time delete the second line. Create the demo_compound_3.txt program file, like this:

```
2a\
No, I'd rather ride in the Hudson Hornet with the Twin-H Power six.\
He'd rather ride in the Pierce-Arrow.
2d
```

Run the program, like this:

```
[donnie@fedora ~]$ sed -f demo_compound_3.txt riding.txt
Let's go for a ride in my Edsel.
No, I'd rather ride in the Hudson Hornet with the Twin-H Power six.
He'd rather ride in the Pierce-Arrow.
Let's go for a ride in my Edsel.
Let's go for a ride in my Edsel.
[donnie@fedora ~]$
```

Even though you deleted the second line, you were still able to append the new lines to it.

Let's wrap up the sed discussion with something really fancy. Create the tab.txt program file, like this:

```
2,4s/^./\t&/
8c\
```

```
This really is the last line.
1d
```

You'll be amazed when you run this program. Here's what you'll see:

```
[donnie@fedora ~]$ sed -f tab.txt myfile_3.txt
    And here is the second line.
    The third.
    Line four.
This is the fifth sentence.
Six
This here is line seven.
This really is the last line.
[donnie@fedora ~]$
```

The first script adds a tab to the beginning of every non-blank line. (The ^. combination means to look for every line that begins with a non-blank character. The & after the tab character prevents sed from replacing the first character of each line with the tab. Instead, it just inserts the tab before the first character.) The second script changes the text in line eight. Finally, the third script deletes line one.

Using sed in Shell Scripts

Using sed in shell scripts is easy, if you only intend to run your scripts on Linux systems. For example, you can do something like this sed_test_0.sh script:

```
#!/bin/bash
sed '/[Ee]dsel/i1958' cars_2.txt
```

Here's how it looks when I run it on my Fedora workstation:

```
donnie@fedora:~$ ./sed_test_0.sh
1958
edsel
1958
Edsel
1958
Edsel
desoto
. . .
. . .
Hudson
hudson
hudson
donnie@fedora:~$
```

But, this won't work with the default implementation of sed that comes with FreeBSD, OpenIndiana, or macOS. In fact, here's what the above script gives me on a FreeBSD machine:

```
donnie@freebsd14:~ $ ./sed_test_0.sh
sed: 1: "/[Ee]dsel/i1958": command i expects \ followed by text
donnie@freebsd14:~ $
```

According to the error message, I should be able to make this work by preceding *1958* with a backslash. But, I tried it, and it still doesn't work.

As I mentioned in the *Understanding sed Portability Issues* section a few pages back, the implementation of sed that comes with most non-Linux systems lacks the capabilities of the Linux implementation. Specifically, the non-Linux implementation of sed lacks the ability to use the append (a), insert (i), and change (c) commands, as well as the ability to deal with regular expressions. So, you'll need to install gsed on your non-Linux systems and create an alias in your shell configuration files if you want to experience the full power of sed on your non-Linux machines. The second problem is that your shell scripts won't read the shell configuration files that are in your home directory. That in turn means that they won't find the sed alias that you created in those configuration files. Here's one solution for fixing that, in the sed_test_1.sh script:

```
#!/bin/bash
if [[ $(uname) == "Darwin" || $(uname) == "FreeBSD" || $(uname) == "SunOS" ]];
then
        gsed="gsed"
elif [[ $(uname) == "Linux" ]]; then
        gsed="sed"
else
        echo "I don't know that OS."
fi
$gsed '/[Ee]dsel/i1958' cars_2.txt
```

So, we want to invoke sed on our Linux machines, but we want to invoke gsed on everything else. To accomplish that, I'm using $(uname) to obtain the name of the operating system. In the first if statement, I'm using the || construct as an or operator. That way, I can test for Darwin, FreeBSD, or SunOS with just this one if statement. Then, I'm creating the gsed variable, and assigning either gsed or sed, as appropriate, as its value. Finally, in the $gsed line at the bottom, I'm calling back the value of the gsed variable to invoke either the gsed or the sed command. Does it work? Let's see what it does on FreeBSD:

```
donnie@freebsd14:~ $ ./sed_test_1.sh
1958
edsel
1958
Edsel
1958
```

```
Edsel
.  .  .
.  .  .
hudson
hudson
donnie@freebsd14:~ $
```

Oh, yeah. It works like a champ. I've also tested this on macOS, Linux, and OpenIndiana, and it works properly on all of them.

 I know, I've never before shown you that you can use a variable with a command as its assigned value. But, you see here that it's a handy little trick that you might find very useful.

And, this pretty much covers our discussion of sed. But, there's still a lot to learn about sed. As I've said before, it's another one of those topics about which whole books have been written. This will give you a good start, and will give you more than enough to pass the sed section of an introductory Linux certification exam.

Next, let's talk about grep.

Understanding grep

I've already shown you some fancy ways to search for files on your system. But, what if you need to search for something that's *in* a file? What if you don't know exactly what you're looking for? Worse yet, what if you don't even know which file to look in? Not to worry, grep is here to help.

grep, short for *Global Regular Expression Print*, is a powerful command-line utility that comes packaged with just about every Unix or Unix-derived operating system. (This includes Linux and macOS.) There's also an available version for Windows.

You can direct grep to search through one file or many. You can also pipe in output from some other utility so that you'll see only the information that you want to see. And, the fact that grep can use regular expressions allows you to perform searches even when you only have an approximate idea of what you're searching for.

grep isn't hard, but is does require a bit of practice. If you're ready, let's get started.

Basic Searches with grep

I've already shown you some examples of using grep in *Chapter 7, Text Stream Filters Part 2* and *Chapter 8, Basic Shell Script Construction*, but that's okay. I'd still like to start with the basics and provide an explanation of how to use it. I'll begin the demos with some text files that you've already created.

The most basic way to use grep is to search for a text string within a single file, like so:

```
[donnie@fedora ~]$ grep 'Edsel' cars_2.txt
```

```
Edsel
Edsel
[donnie@fedora ~]$
```

Here, I listed the text string that I want to find, and then listed the name of the file that contains the text string. I surrounded the search term with a pair of single quotes, but I didn't need to in this case. I only need the quotes if the search term contains characters that the shell will interpret incorrectly. (I most always use the single quotes, due to force-of-habit.)

By default, grep is case-sensitive. Use the -i switch to make it case-insensitive, like this:

```
[donnie@fedora ~]$ grep -i 'Edsel' cars_2.txt
edsel
Edsel
Edsel
[donnie@fedora ~]$
```

If you need to see which lines of the file contain the search term, use the -n switch, like this:

```
[donnie@fedora ~]$ grep -in 'Edsel' cars_2.txt
1:edsel
2:Edsel
3:Edsel
[donnie@fedora ~]$
```

You can use a wild-card to search through multiple files at once, like this:

```
[donnie@fedora ~]$ grep -in 'Edsel' cars*
cars_2.txt:1:edsel
cars_2.txt:2:Edsel
cars_2.txt:3:Edsel
cars_2.txt.bak:1:edsel
cars_2.txt.bak:2:Edsel
cars_2.txt.bak:3:Edsel
cars_2.txtbak:1:edsel
cars_2.txtbak:2:Edsel
cars_2.txtbak:3:Edsel
cars.txt:1:edsel
cars.txt:2:Edsel
cars.txt:3:Edsel
[donnie@fedora ~]$
```

Note how the filenames are now included in the output.

The -v switch means inverse. Use it to show all lines that *don't* have the specified search term, like this:

```
[donnie@fedora ~]$ grep -inv 'Edsel' cars*
```

```
cars_2.txt:4:desoto
cars_2.txt:5:desoto
cars_2.txt:6:Desoto
cars_2.txt:7:desoto
cars_2.txt:8:nash
cars_2.txt:9:Nash
cars_2.txt:10:nash
. . .
. . .
cars.txt:11:Hudson
cars.txt:12:hudson
cars.txt:13:hudson
[donnie@fedora ~]$
```

The -c switch shows a count of how many times a search pattern is in a file, but it doesn't show the lines where the search pattern was found. It looks like this:

```
[donnie@fedora ~]$ grep -ic 'edsel' cars*
cars_2.txt:3
cars_2.txt.bak:3
cars_2.txtbak:3
cars_3.txt:0
cars_cap.txt:0
cars.txt:3
[donnie@fedora ~]$
```

In these examples, I've been showing you how to combine the grep option switches with just a single -. Of course, you can just use one option at a time, if that fits your needs.

Okay, so these were fairly simple examples, and you're saying, "Hey, when do we get to the good stuff?" Well, hang on, it's coming.

More Advanced Searches with grep

Here are a few more cool grep optons.

Example 1: Searching for Whole Words

By default, grep doesn't search for whole words. So, if you search for the text string *and*, it will display lines that contain the words *land*, *hand*, *sand*, along with the word *and*. Let's look at that by searching through our public-domain e-book for the text string *noun*. (It's a very long output, so I'll only show part of it.) I'll make it a case-sensitive search, like this:

```
[donnie@fedora ~]$ grep 'noun' pg6409.txt
Noun, Adjective, Pronoun, Verb, Adverb, Preposition, Conjunction and
_Gender_ has the same relation to nouns that sex has to individuals, but
```

```
_Case_ is the relation one noun bears to another or to a verb or to a
An _Article_ is a word placed before a noun to show whether the latter is
An _Adjective_ is a word which qualifies a noun, that is, which shows
some distinguishing mark or characteristic belonging to the noun.
A _Pronoun_ is a word used for or instead of a noun to keep us from
repeating the same noun too often. Pronouns, like nouns, have case,
number, gender and person. There are three kinds of pronouns, _personal_,
of speech in properly pronouncing them.
. . .

. . .
[donnie@fedora ~]$
```

This search returned not only lines that contain the word *noun*, but also lines that contain *nouns, pronouns, Pronouns,* and *Pronoun*. One line has the word *pronouncing*. If you want to search for the word *noun*, and only the word *noun*, then you'll have to add the -w switch, like this:

```
[donnie@fedora ~]$ grep -w 'noun' pg6409.txt
_Case_ is the relation one noun bears to another or to a verb or to a
An _Article_ is a word placed before a noun to show whether the latter is
An _Adjective_ is a word which qualifies a noun, that is, which shows
some distinguishing mark or characteristic belonging to the noun.
A _Pronoun_ is a word used for or instead of a noun to keep us from
repeating the same noun too often. Pronouns, like nouns, have case,
An _Article_ is a word placed before a noun to show whether the noun is
thing but indicates the noun in its widest sense; thus, _a_ man means any
_Number_ is that inflection of the noun by which we indicate whether it
_Gender_ is that inflection by which we signify whether the noun is the
. . .

. . .
[donnie@fedora ~]$
```

You've narrowed the search considerably. (You'll still see some *Pronouns* in here, but only because they were on the same line as a *noun*.)

Example 2: Making Searches Case-Insensitive

Now, add the -i switch to make the search case-insensitive, like so:

```
[donnie@fedora ~]$ grep -iw 'noun' pg6409.txt
Noun, Adjective, Pronoun, Verb, Adverb, Preposition, Conjunction and
Interjection. Of these, the Noun is the most important, as all the others
are more or less dependent upon it. A Noun signifies the name of any
_Case_ is the relation one noun bears to another or to a verb or to a
An _Article_ is a word placed before a noun to show whether the latter is
An _Adjective_ is a word which qualifies a noun, that is, which shows
```

```
some distinguishing mark or characteristic belonging to the noun.
A _Pronoun_ is a word used for or instead of a noun to keep us from
repeating the same noun too often. Pronouns, like nouns, have case,
An _Article_ is a word placed before a noun to show whether the noun is
thing but indicates the noun in its widest sense; thus, _a_ man means any
NOUN

. . .
[donnie@fedora ~]$
```

Add the ^ metacharacter to the left of the search pattern, and grep will only display the lines where the search pattern appears at the beginning, like this:

```
[donnie@fedora ~]$ grep -iw '^noun' pg6409.txt
Noun, Adjective, Pronoun, Verb, Adverb, Preposition, Conjunction and
NOUN
[donnie@fedora ~]$
```

Just for curiosity, count how many times the whole word *noun* shows up in this document by using the -c switch, like so:

```
[donnie@fedora ~]$ grep -iwc 'noun' pg6409.txt
33
[donnie@fedora ~]$
```

Now, will it make a difference if I omit the -i switch to make this case-sensitive? Let's see:

```
donnie@fedora:~$ grep -wc 'noun' pg6409.txt
29
donnie@fedora:~$
```

So, we have a total of 33 case-insensitive *noun* strings, and 29 that are case-sensitive. This tells me that there are four *noun* strings with at least one upper-case letter.

Example 3: Dealing with Carriage Returns

Here's a realistic scenario that you just might encounter at some point in your Linux career. It's one that could cause you a good bit of consternation until you finally figure it out.

You've just seen how to perform a case-insensitive search for every occurrence of the word *noun* at the start of a line. You found one *NOUN* on a line by itself. It would make sense then that you would also find that line by performing a case-insensitive search for *noun* at the end of lines. So now, give it a try:

```
[donnie@fedora ~]$ grep -iw 'noun$' pg6409.txt
[donnie@fedora ~]$
```

Wait a minute. Why didn't it find anything? We know that there's one to be found. Well, here's a clue.

A few chapters back, I told you that I downloaded this file from the Project Gutenberg web site. So, there's a good possibility that the file was created with either a DOS or Windows text editor.

That's significant because DOS and Windows text editors place a carriage return character at the end of each line in text files, where Unix and Linux text editors just use newline characters. If grep sees a newline character during a search, it will just ignore it. However, it won't ignore a carriage return. Now, let's test our theory. I'll start by showing you how to use another Regular Expressions metacharacter.

If you place a dot in a search pattern, it means that you'll accept the presence of any single character in that position, as long as the rest of the pattern can make a proper match. So, place a dot at the end of your search pattern. Then, pipe the output into the od -c command, like this:

```
[donnie@fedora ~]$ grep -iw 'noun.$' pg6409.txt | od -c
0000000   N   O   U   N  \r  \n                            /
0000006
[donnie@fedora ~]$
```

Yeah, there's the problem. The \r is the carriage return control character. Not to worry, though. Just use tr with the -d option to get rid of those pesky rascals. Save the converted output to a new file, like this:

```
[donnie@fedora ~]$ tr -d '\r' < pg6409.txt > linux_pg6409.txt
[donnie@fedora ~]$
```

Verify that the carriage returns are gone and that the grep search now works correctly, by performing the searches without the dot in the pattern. It should look like this:

```
[donnie@fedora ~]$ grep -iw 'noun$' linux_pg6409.txt | od -c
0000000   N   O   U   N  \n
0000005
[donnie@fedora ~]$ grep -iw 'noun$' linux_pg6409.txt
NOUN
[donnie@fedora ~]$
```

Now when you feed the search output through od, you'll see that the carriage return character is gone. Then, when you try the original search, you get just what you're supposed to get.

But, you're not done yet. What if there's a *noun* at the end of a line that's also the end of a sentence? Then, the *noun* would be followed by a period, and the search as you've just performed it wouldn't pick it up. Let's go back a few steps, and perform the search with our dot metacharacter again, like so:

```
[donnie@fedora ~]$ grep -iw 'noun.$' linux_pg6409.txt
some distinguishing mark or characteristic belonging to the noun.
_s_ and these phrases are now idioms of the language. All plural nouns
verb, _summons_, a noun.
[donnie@fedora ~]$
```

Now that the carriage return character is gone, this search now finds *noun.* and *nouns.* But, you don't want to find *nouns.* You only want to find the singular *noun.* I'll show you how by introducing another metacharacter, like this:

```
[donnie@fedora ~]$ grep -iw 'noun\.\?$' linux_pg6409.txt
some distinguishing mark or characteristic belonging to the noun.
NOUN
verb, _summons_, a noun.
[donnie@fedora ~]$
```

By placing a backslash in front of the dot, you've turned the dot metacharacter into a common period. The \? tells grep to try to find a match for the character that precedes it, but that it's okay if it doesn't find a match. So here, you're telling grep to perform a case-insensitive search for the whole word *noun* at the ends of lines, with or without the period. (Are you beginning to see how much fun that Regular Expressions can be?)

Okay, you've seen some cool stuff, but you're still not done. So, let's move on.

Even More Advanced Searches with grep

You can combine grep with other utilities for even more advanced searches. Here's how.

Example 1: Auditing Source Code Files

To demo this, use either your Fedora Server or your Debian virtual machine, so that you can install a package that you might not want to install on your Linux workstation, if that's what you're using. On Fedora Server, install the `cairo-devel` package, like this:

```
[donnie@fedora-server ~]$ sudo dnf install cairo-devel
```

If you'd rather use the Debian virtual machine, install the `libghc-cairo-dev` package, like this:

```
donnie@debian:~$ sudo apt install libghc-cairo-dev
```

Next, look through the source code files in the /usr/include/cairo/ directory, looking for lines that have the string #include, like this:

```
[donnie@fedora-server ~]$ grep -ihr '#include' /usr/include/cairo/* | sort |
uniq -c
      1 #include "cairo-deprecated.h"
      1 #include "cairo-features.h"
      9 #include "cairo.h"
      1 #include <cairo.h>
      1 #include "cairo-version.h"
      1 #include <fontconfig/fontconfig.h>
      1 #include <ft2build.h>
      1 #include FT_FREETYPE_H
      2 #include <stdio.h>
      1 #include <X11/extensions/Xrender.h>
      2 #include <X11/Xlib.h>
      1 #include <xcb/render.h>
```

```
     1 #include <xcb/xcb.h>
[donnie@fedora-server ~]$
```

If you don't want to show the filenames where the text strings are found, use the -h switch. Then feed the lines through sort, which in turn will feed the lines through uniq. That way, you'll end up with sorted output, and all duplicate lines will be eliminated.

Also, by using the -c switch with uniq, we'll find out how many times each particular line was duplicated.

Example 2: Searching for Social Security Numbers

Here's a more complex example of how to use a regular expression for your search. First, create the ssn.txt file with a list of names, birth dates, and US Social Security numbers, like this:

```
Knockwurst,     Ronald J.       899-98-1247
Born 28 April 1954
Liverwurst,     Alex            988-45-7898
Born 1 Feb 1933
Saurbraten,     Alicia          978-98-6987
Born 5 Apr 1956
Hassenfeffer,   Gerald          999-87-1258
Born 10 Jan 1961
```

 Note that these are all fictitious, so we're not violating anyone's privacy here. Also, I have no idea why I chose German foods for the surnames. Perhaps I was hungry?

Then, construct a grep command that will only show lines that contain Social Security numbers, like this:

```
[donnie@fedora ~]$ grep '[0-9]\{3\}-[0-9]\{2\}-[0-9]\{4\}' ssn.txt
Knockwurst, Ronald J.       899-98-1247
Liverwurst, Alex            988-45-7898
Saurbraten, Alicia          978-98-6987
Hassenfeffer,       Gerald          999-87-1258
[donnie@fedora ~]$
```

Here, each instance of [0-9] means that you're searching for any digit. The numbers that are surrounded by the backslashes and curly braces mean that you want to find a certain number of consecutive digits. So, the [0-9]\{3\} construct means that you're hunting for three consecutive digits. There are three of those groupings in this regular expression, all separated by a hyphen.

Example 3: Using the ^ Metacharacter

Here's one more example before we move on to the next topic. This is an example of how the ^ metacharacter can have two different meanings, depending on its placement in the regular expression. See how that works in the following grep command:

```
[donnie@fedora ~]$ grep '^[^a-zA-Z]' pg6409.txt | less
```

In this command, the '^[^a-zA-Z]' regular expression means to look for all lines that do *not* begin with a letter. That's because outside of the square bracket, the ^ means to only look for a match at the beginning of a line. Inside the square brackets, in front of the designated search term, it means to display everything that *doesn't* match that term.

Of course, you'll also see a lot of consecutive blank lines, since blank lines don't start with a letter. If you don't need to see all of those blank lines, just feed the grep output into uniq, like this:

```
[donnie@fedora ~]$ grep '^[^a-zA-Z]' pg6409.txt | uniq | less
```

Be sure to scroll through the output of both of these two commands, and note the difference.

All right, let's move on to see if we can extend things a bit.

Using Extended Regular Expressions with grep

As you saw on the regular expressions metacharacter charts a few pages back in the *Understanding Regular Expressions* section, there are two forms of command syntax for grep. What I've shown you so far is the *basic* syntax. The other form is the *extended* syntax. Here are two differences between the two:

- Basic syntax requires the use of a backslash in front of certain metacharacters, but extended syntax doesn't.
- Extended syntax requires that you either use egrep instead of grep, or grep with the -E option switch. (Be aware that although egrep still works for now, it's considered as obsolete and might cease to work in the future. So, you should always use grep -E, instead.)

Okay, here are some examples.

Example 1: Basic Search with Extended Syntax

Let's take another look at a previous example. Here's the command with normal, basic syntax:

```
[donnie@fedora ~]$ grep -iw 'noun\.\?$' linux_pg6409.txt
some distinguishing mark or characteristic belonging to the noun.
NOUN
verb, _summons_, a noun.
[donnie@fedora ~]$
```

Here's the exact same command with extended syntax:

```
[donnie@fedora ~]$ grep -E -iw 'noun\.?$' linux_pg6409.txt
some distinguishing mark or characteristic belonging to the noun.
NOUN
verb, _summons_, a noun.
[donnie@fedora ~]$
```

Okay, it's not a big deal here, because using the extended syntax only eliminated one backslash that I had to type. But, if you have a grep command that requires you to escape lots of characters with basic syntax, the extended syntax could considerably cut down on the typing.

Example 2: Searching for Consecutive Duplicate Words

The next example is just a bit more complex. You're looking through the /etc/services file for all lines that contain consecutive duplicate words, like so:

```
[donnie@fedora ~]$ grep -Ei '\<([a-z]+) +\1\>' /etc/services
http           80/tcp          www www-http      # WorldWideWeb HTTP
http           80/udp          www www-http      # HyperText Transfer Protocol
nextstep       178/tcp         NeXTStep NextStep      # NeXTStep window
nextstep       178/udp         NeXTStep NextStep      # server
[donnie@fedora ~]$
```

Here's the breakdown:

- The \<. . .\> construct represents a word boundary. The pattern that's inside this construct will match a single word, and only a single word.

- The [a-z] means that we're looking for a single alphabetic character. Of course, you see nothing but lower-case letters here, which would normally mean that this would only match lower-case letters. But, the i in the grep -Ei command makes this case-insensitive.

- The + at the end of [a-z] is called a **repeat character**. This means that we want to match one or more of whatever character or set of characters precedes it. In this case, we want to match a pattern that contains only the set of characters that's between the two square brackets.

- Placing the [a-z]+ within a pair of parentheses indicates that we want to evaluate this part of the regular expression before we evaluate the second part.

- Finally, the +\1 in the second part of the regular expression means that we want to find an additional second match to the pattern that's described in the first part. In other words, we want to find all lines in the /etc/services file that contain two consecutive identical words.

Now, make the search case-sensitive by leaving out the -i option, like so:

```
[donnie@fedora ~]$ grep -E '\<([a-z]+) +\1\>' /etc/services
http           80/tcp          www www-http      # WorldWideWeb HTTP
http           80/udp          www www-http      # HyperText Transfer Protocol
[donnie@fedora ~]$
```

Example 3: Searching for Words that Begin with a Certain Letter

Next, look through the /etc/ directory for all files and directories with names that begin with either a *p* or a *q*, like this:

```
[donnie@fedora ~]$ ls /etc/ | grep -E '^[pq]'
pam.d
paperspecs
passwd
. . .
. . .
purple
qemu-ga
[donnie@fedora ~]$
```

Try that again, except this time look for files and directories that have *p* or *q* as the first letter, and that also have *p* as the second letter, like so:

```
[donnie@fedora ~]$ ls /etc/ | grep -E '^[pq]p+'
ppp
[donnie@fedora ~]$
```

Now, list all files and directories in the /etc/ directory with names that begin with *se* and have the optional third letter of *r*, like this:

```
[donnie@fedora ~]$ ls /etc/ | grep -E '^ser?'
security
selinux
services
sestatus.conf
setroubleshoot
[donnie@fedora ~]$
```

Try this again, but this time *require* that the file and directory names have *r* as the third letter. (I'm not going to show you how this time, but I will give you a hint. Just look at the previous example.)

In this next example, I'm going to show you a bit of shorthand. List all files and directories in the /etc/ directory that use non-alphanumeric characters in their names, like this:

```
[donnie@fedora ~]$ ls /etc/ | grep -E '\W'
anthy-unicode.conf
appstream.conf
asound.conf
at.deny
bash_completion.d
. . .
```

```
. . .
vmware-vix
whois.conf
xattr.conf
yum.repos.d
[donnie@fedora ~]$
```

You see the file and directory names that contain characters such as dots, underscores, and hyphens. Any file or directory name that doesn't have any of these non-alphanumeric characters won't show up. The \W in this example is just shorthand for [^_[:alnum:]]. The ^ indicates an inversion, which causes grep to search for the non-alphanumeric characters.

Using a lower-case *w* (\w) would replace [_[:alnum:]], which would cause grep to search for all alpha-numeric characters.

Example 4: Searching for Words with Digits

Next, search through /etc/ for all files and directories with a numeric digit in their names, like this:

```
[donnie@fedora ~]$ ls /etc/ | grep -E '[[:digit:]]'
dbus-1
grub2.cfg
grub2-efi.cfg
ImageMagick-7
. . .
. . .
tpm2-tss
udisks2
X11
[donnie@fedora ~]$
```

For the final example, use the alternator operator to create an either/or type of regular expression, like so:

```
[donnie@fedora ~]$ ls /etc/ | grep -E '(cron|yum)'
anacrontab
cron.d
cron.daily
cron.deny
cron.hourly
cron.monthly
crontab
cron.weekly
yum.repos.d
[donnie@fedora ~]$
```

The | in the (cron|yum) construct acts as an or operator, which allows grep to search for directories and filenames that contain either *cron* or *yum*. (By the way, if you're doing this on a Debian machine instead of a Fedora machine, just replace *yum* with *apt*.)

That's it for extended grep. Let's turn our attention to fixed-strings.

Using Fixed-strings Regular Expressions with grep

Either fgrep or grep -F will interpret any patterns you feed it as literal expressions. So, if you follow either grep -F or fgrep with a regular expression, you'll actually be searching for that regular expression, instead of the parsed pattern. For example, let's copy the ssn.txt file that we used earlier to ssn_2.txt, and add a line. The new file will look like this:

```
Knockwurst,      Ronald J.        899-98-1247
Born 28 April 1954
Liverwurst,      Alex             988-45-7898
Born 1 Feb 1933
Saurbraten,      Alicia           978-98-6987
Born 5 Apr 1956
Hassenfeffer,    Gerald           999-87-1258
Born 10 Jan 1961
'[0-9]\{3\}-[0-9]\{2\}-[0-9]\{4\}'
```

This new last line is the regular expression that you'll use to search through the file. Using grep with no options, as you saw before, will yield a list of lines that contain Social Security numbers, as you see here:

```
[donnie@fedora ~]$ grep '[0-9]\{3\}-[0-9]\{2\}-[0-9]\{4\}' ssn_2.txt
Knockwurst,      Ronald J.        899-98-1247
Liverwurst,      Alex             988-45-7898
Saurbraten,      Alicia           978-98-6987
Hassenfeffer,    Gerald           999-87-1258
[donnie@fedora ~]$
```

But, look what happens if you use either fgrep or grep -F:

```
[donnie@fedora ~]$ grep -F '[0-9]\{3\}-[0-9]\{2\}-[0-9]\{4\}' ssn_2.txt
'[0-9]\{3\}-[0-9]\{2\}-[0-9]\{4\}'
[donnie@fedora ~]$
```

With either fgrep or grep -F, the regular expression is interpreted as just another text string.

As is the case with egrep, fgrep is considered as obsolete and might cease to work in the somewhat near future. So, your best bet is to get used to using grep -E and grep -F, instead of egrep and fgrep. (The main reason I mention them at all is because you might find other tutorials that mention them.)

Now that you've seen some regular expressions in use, let's look at how to simplify the process of creating them.

Using RegEx Helper Programs

Okay, now that you've seen so many examples, you can now create regular expressions to do whatever you need to be done.

What?! *No*, you say?

Don't feel bad. I've told you already that Regular Expressions is quite complex, and is something about which entire books have been written. That's where a helper program can come in handy. Let's look at some examples.

RegexBuddy and RegexMagic

RegexBuddy and RegexMagic are a pair of helper programs that are published by the *Just Great Software* company. The difference between them is that RegexBuddy is mainly a point-and-click interface for building your own regular expressions. There is a library of pre-built regular expressions that you can use, but to build anything else you'll still need to know something about the Regular Expressions language.

RegexMagic is great for Regular Expressions beginners, because all you need to do is to enter some sample text and mark the areas that you want to convert to a regular expression. RegexMagic then generates the regular expression for you.

There are really only two slight drawbacks to RegexBuddy and RegexMagic. First, they're both closed-source, commercial programs, so you'll need to pay for them. But, the price is quite reasonable, at only US $39.95 each. (You can get a discount if you buy them both in a bundle.)

The second slight drawback is that they're only written for the Windows operating system. However, you'll be glad to know that they both run fine under WINE on Linux machines. (In fact, I have them both installed here on this Fedora workstation.) The RegexBuddy and RegexMagic websites even give you directions on how to install these programs under WINE.

WINE is a recursive acronym that stands for *WINE is Not an Emulator*. It's a translation layer that converts Windows executable code to Linux executable code, and is included in the repositories for pretty much every Linux distro.

Also, please know that I have no financial arrangements with the folk at Just Great Software, so I don't receive any compensation for telling you about their products.

To check out these cool products, just visit their websites. You can find RegexBuddy here: `https://www.regexbuddy.com/index.html`

And, you can find RegexMagic here: `https://www.regexmagic.com/`

Now, let's check out a free tool.

Regex101

If you prefer to use a free-of-charge tool, you might want to check out Regex101. It's web-based, so there's nothing to download or to install. It doesn't have the bells and whistles that RegexBuddy and RegexMagic have, but there's enough there to get you started. Signing in to an account is optional, but there are benefits to doing so. Note that you won't be creating an account, but will instead be signing in via either your Google or Github account.

You can check out Regex101 here: `https://regex101.com/`

I think that we've covered enough theory. Let's move on to the real world.

Looking at Some Real-World Examples

I have some cool case studies on how to use sed, grep, and regular expressions in real life. So, read on and enjoy!

Modifying Multiple Files at Once

If you have more than one file that you need to modify in the same manner, you can have sed do them all in one command, just by using a * wildcard in the filename. Quite a few years ago I assisted a website maintainer in migrating a set of PHP-based websites from a CentOS 5 server to a CentOS 6 server. To make the sites work with the newer PHP version, she needed to add a line of new code to each .php file. That could have been a bit problematic, because she had about 2,000 files to modify, which is more than you'd want to edit manually. I suggested that she use sed to modify all files at once, and she knew immediately what I was talking about. (I jogged her memory by making the suggestion.)

Searching Through Apache Webserver Logs for Cross-site Scripting Attacks

About 15 years ago, a security worker buddy of mine called me with an urgent plea for help. His boss at the credit union where he worked had handed him a USB memory stick with four Gigabyes--Yes, four *Gigabytes*!--worth of compressed Apache access logs, and told him to look through them for signs of **cross-site scripting attacks**. What's a poor security admin to do in a case like this?

Cross-site scripting, often abbreviated as **XSS**, is used by malicious hackers to steal information or to manipulate websites. I know that this name is confusing, and that it doesn't give you an accurate picture of what XSS attacks really do. It would be more accurate to call this type of attack a **Javascript injection attack**, because that's how it really works.

When an attacker finds a website that's vulnerable to this type of attack, he or she can use an attack tool, such as ones that are part of Kali Linux, to perform his or her dirty deeds. Or at least, that's how it is nowadays. When my buddy called me up 15 years ago, it was still possible to perform an XSS attack with a simple web browser. All an attacker had to do was to append some special Javascript code to the end of a website's URL, like this:

```
https://www.mybigbank.com/<BR SIZE="&{alert('XSS')}">
```

It's no longer possible to perform an XSS attack with a web browser, because modern versions of all web browsers now sanitize their input. So now, the Javascript in the URL no longer has any effect.

But, I digress.

After my buddy called me, I set up a machine with an Apache webserver, and then performed some XSS attacks against it from another machine. I discovered that log file entries that were the result of an XSS attack had a % pattern in the GET portion, like this:

```
192.168.0.252 - - [05/Aug/2009:15:16:42 -0400] "GET /%27%27;!-%22%3CXSS%3E=&{()
} HTTP/1.1" 404 310 "-" "Mozilla/5.0 (X11; U; Linux x86_64; en-US; rv:1.9.0.12)
Gecko/2009070812 Ubuntu/8.04 (hardy) Firefox/3.0.12"
```

The GET /%27%27 part is what tells us that this is from an XSS attack. No log file entries that were the result of normal website access had this pattern.

There were also a couple of other variations on this pattern, and the first thing I had to do was to create the regular expressions that I needed to match all of them. The regular expressions that I created were GET /%, GET /.%, and GET /.=%. (The dot is a wildcard, which tells the script to search for any character in that position.) Next, I created the script, using the find utility to find and read all of the Apache log files. Here's the script that I created:

```
#!/bin/bash
inputpath=$1
output_file=$2
if [ -f $output_file ]; then
        echo "This file already exists.  Choose another filename."
        exit;
fi
find $inputpath -iname '*.gz' -exec zcat {} \; | grep 'GET /%' > $output_file
find $inputpath -iname '*.gz' -exec zcat {} \; | grep 'GET /.%' >> $output_file
find $inputpath -iname '*.gz' -exec zcat {} \; | grep 'GET /.=%' >> $output_
file
less $output_file
exit
```

The first thing you see is that I'm using positional parameter $1 to designate the mount point of the USB memory stick, and positional parameter $2 to designate the filename of the report file. The if.. then construct is a safety feature that prevents the user from overwriting an existing file. The command to invoke the script would have looked something like this:

```
./cross-site-search /media/PATRIOT/ ~/cross-site-search-results.txt
```

Linux system log files are normally always compressed with gzip, and the filenames will end with a .gz. So, I had find search for all .gz files on the memory stick, read them with zcat, and pipe the output into grep. Finally, I had the report automatically open in less.

Fortunately, my buddy was able to verify that this script actually does work. The previous autumn, the credit union had hired a penetration testing outfit to test security, with XSS attacks being part of the test. The script found all instances of the pen tester's attack, so everyone was happy.

Automating Third-party Repository Installations

The next real-world script that I'll show you is, sadly, one that you won't be able to run. That's because I created it sometime in either 2010 or 2011, when I was creating training documentation and plug-ins for the Nagios monitoring system. My client and I were doing everything with CentOS 5 and CentOS 6 at the time, which are now both obsolete.

This scenario is part of a larger scenario that involved automatically downloading and compiling Nagios Core source code on a CentOS server. One of the prerequisites was to install the RPMForge and EPEL third-party software repositories. At that time, installing a third-party repository on CentOS also required you to configure the priorities of each of the repositories, in order to prevent having one repository overwrite packages that had been installed from another repository. Since my client and I were constantly having to perform new Nagios installations, I wrote a script to help automate the process. The script is too large to reproduce here, so I'll invite you to download the add-repos.sh script from Github. However, I will reproduce a few snippets here to explain things.

At the top of the script, you see this if..then..else construct:

```
if [ $(uname -m) == x86_64 ]; then
        rpm -Uvh http://pkgs.repoforge.org/rpmforge-release/rpmforge-
release-0.5.3-1.el6.rf.x86_64.rpm
else
        rpm -Uvh http://pkgs.repoforge.org/rpmforge-release/rpmforge-
release-0.5.3-1.el6.rf.i686.rpm
fi
```

At that time, the computer industry was still transitioning from 32-bit to 64-bit CPUs. So, the maintainer of the now defunct RPMForge repository offered separate installation packages for each. (I wanted to completely make the break to 64-bit, but my client insisted on still supporting 32-bit.) This construct automatically detects which flavor of CentOS is installed, and then downloads and installs the appropriate RPMForge package.

Next is the line that installs the packages for the EPEL repository and for setting the repository priorities. It looks like this:

```
yum install -y epel-release yum-plugin-priorities
```

The final step is to use sed to automatically set the priorities for each section of the various repository configuration files. Here's a snippet from one of those files:

```
[base]
name=CentOS-$releasever - Base
mirrorlist=http://mirrorlist.centos.org/?release=$releasever&arch=$basearch&repo
```

```
=os&infra=$infra
#baseurl=http://mirror.centos.org/centos/$releasever/os/$basearch/
gpgcheck=1
gpgkey=file:///etc/pki/rpm-gpg/RPM-GPG-KEY-CentOS-6
```

Other sections of the file were named [updates], [extras], [centosplus], and [contrib]. (To see the whole file, download the CentOS-Base.repo file from GitHub.) The other configuration files were also divided into sections with different names. The goal was to use sed to automatically append a priority= line just under the [section_name] line of every section of every file.

Here's what those sed scripts look like:

```
sed -i '/\[base\]/apriority=1' /etc/yum.repos.d/CentOS-Base.repo
sed -i '/\[updates\]/apriority=1' /etc/yum.repos.d/CentOS-Base.repo
sed -i '/\[extras\]/apriority=1' /etc/yum.repos.d/CentOS-Base.repo
sed -i '/\[centosplus\]/apriority=2' /etc/yum.repos.d/CentOS-Base.repo
sed -i '/\[contrib\]/apriority=2' /etc/yum.repos.d/CentOS-Base.repo
sed -i '/\[rpmforge\]/apriority=10' /etc/yum.repos.d/rpmforge.repo
sed -i '/\[rpmforge-extras\]/apriority=11' /etc/yum.repos.d/rpmforge.repo
sed -i '/\[rpmforge-testing\]/apriority=11' /etc/yum.repos.d/rpmforge.repo
sed -i '/\[epel\]/apriority=12' /etc/yum.repos.d/epel.repo
sed -i '/\[epel-debuginfo\]/apriority=13' /etc/yum.repos.d/epel.repo
sed -i '/\[epel-source\]/apriority=13' /etc/yum.repos.d/epel.repo
```

You see that each sed script appends the proper priorities settings to their proper places. The result would have looked something like this:

```
[base]
priority=1
name=CentOS-$releasever - Base
. . .
. . .
```

And now, let's look at one final real-life scenario.

Filling Empty Fields in a .csv File

If you ever have to work with columnar data, you might find yourself having to work with **Comma Separated Value** (.csv) files. As the name suggests, these are files with rows of data, with the same number of fields in each row. The fields are all separated by commas, like so:

```
donnie@fedora:~$ cat inventory_2.csv
Kitchen spatula,$4.99,Housewares,Sale Over
Raincoat,$36.99,Clothing,On Sale!
Claw hammer,$7.99,Tools,On Sale Next Week
donnie@fedora:~$
```

The beauty of .csv files is that you can use a normal plain-text editor to create them. Then, you can open them up in any spreadsheet program, like this:

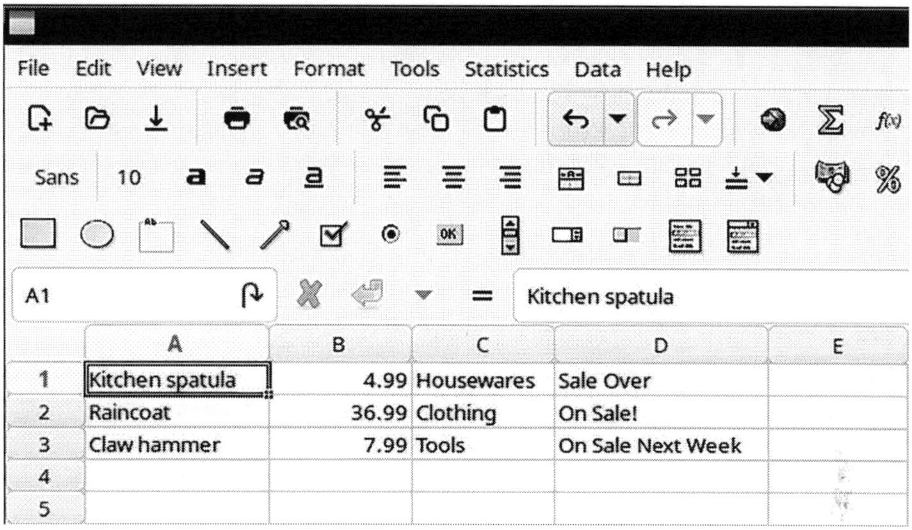

Figure 9.2: Opening a .csv file as a spreadsheet

At times, you might encounter a .csv file that contains empty fields, like this one:

```
donnie@fedora:~$ cat myfile.csv
1,2,3,4,5,6,7
,,,,,,
1,,,4,5,,
,2,3,4,5,,
donnie@fedora:~$
```

You see that the commas are there, but there are no values in the fields between them. Opening this file in a spreadsheet program would look like this:

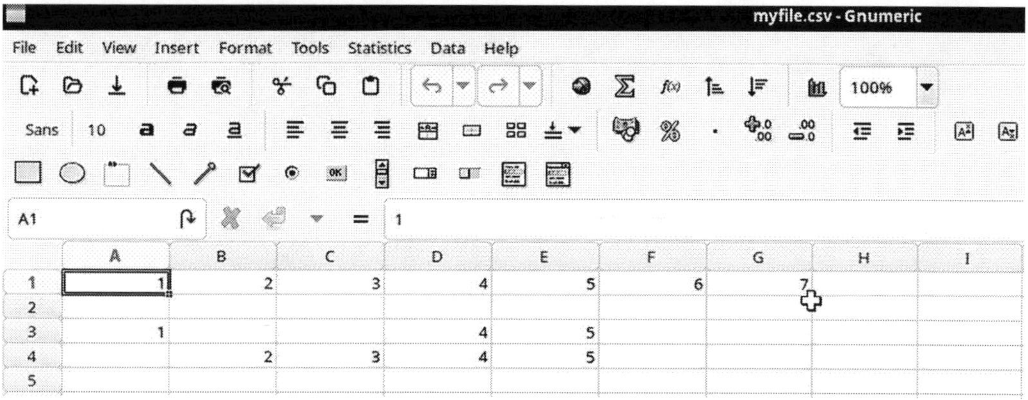

Figure 9.3: Opening a .csv file with empty fields

Okay, that doesn't look like a complete disaster, but you want something that looks better. So, you need to find an easy way to place values in all of the empty fields. You might want to insert some value as just a placeholder, or you might want to insert some text that explains why the fields are empty. Either way, sed makes that easy.

But, I have to confess that someone else has already created a solution for this, and I can't really improve upon it. So, rather than try to explain the solution myself, I'll invite you to visit the author's original article that contains the solution, which is here: `https://linuxconfig.org/how-to-fill-all-empty-valued-cells-within-a-csv-file-with-sed-and-bash-shell`

Okay, that covers it for this chapter. Let's wrap this baby up and move on.

Summary

As always, we've covered lots of ground in this chapter. I first gave you a basic explanation of Regular Expressions, regular expressions, sed, and grep. Then, I showed you how to use regular expressions with both sed and grep. I also showed you some cool tools that can help simplify the process of creating regular expressions. Finally, I showed you some real-live scenarios in which I actually used these concepts for my own scripts.

The next chapter will be about functions. I'll see you there.

Questions

1. Which of the following is the preferred method for using grep with extended syntax?

    a. `Egrep`

    b. `egrep`

    c. `grep -e`

    d. `grep -E`

2. Which of the following are the two general types of characters that are used in regular expressions? (Choose two.)

    a. digits

    b. alphabetic

    c. literals

    d. numbers

    e. metacharacters

3. When creating a regular expression, which of the following would you use as an or operator?

    a. `or`

    b. `-o`

    c. `-or`

    d. `|`

    e. `?`

4. What are the three types of metacharaters in Regular Expressions? (Choose three.)

    a. Literals

    b. Positional anchors

    c. Numbers

    d. Character sets

    e. Modifiers

5. Which option switch would you use with sed to save changes to the source file?

    a. `-o`

    b. `-i`

    c. `-s`

    d. `-n`

Further Reading

- Regex Tutorial—How to write regular expressions?: `https://www.geeksforgeeks.org/write-regular-expressions/`
- Regular Expressions.info: `https://www.regular-expressions.info/`
- Learn Regex: A Beginner's Guide: `https://www.sitepoint.com/learn-regex/`
- A Practical Guide to Regular Expressions: `https://www.freecodecamp.org/news/practical-regex-guide-with-real-life-examples/`
- Regex Cheat Sheet and Quick Reference: `https://quickref.me/regex.html`
- How to Use the sed Command on Linux: `https://www.howtogeek.com/666395/how-to-use-the-sed-command-on-linux/`
- How to Use sed to Find and Replace String in Files: `https://linuxize.com/post/how-to-use-sed-to-find-and-replace-string-in-files/`
- How to Use the grep Command on Linux: `https://www.howtogeek.com/496056/how-to-use-the-grep-command-on-linux/`
- How to use the Linux grep command: `https://opensource.com/article/21/3/grep-cheat-sheet`

Answers

1. d
2. c and e
3. d
4. b, d, and e
5. b

Join our community on Discord!

Read this book alongside other users, Linux experts, and the author himself.

Ask questions, provide solutions to other readers, chat with the author via Ask Me Anything sessions, and much more. Scan the QR code or visit the link to join the community.

https://packt.link/SecNet

Leave a Review!

Thank you for purchasing this book from Packt Publishing—we hope you enjoy it! Your feedback is invaluable and helps us improve and grow. Once you've completed reading it, please take a moment to leave an Amazon review; it will only take a minute, but it makes a big difference for readers like you.

Scan the QR code below to receive a free ebook of your choice.

https://packt.link/NzOWQ

10

Understanding Functions

Functions are an important component of pretty much every modern programming language. They're simply blocks of code that each perform one specific task. The cool thing about them is that they allow programmers to reuse code. That is, one block of code can be called either from within a program in various places, or it can be called by various different programs from function libraries. In this chapter, I'll show you the basics about using functions in shell scripts.

Topics in this chapter include:

- Introduction to functions
- Defining a function
- Using functions in shell scripts
- Creating function libraries
- Looking at some real-world examples

If you're ready, let's get started.

Technical Requirements

Use any of your Linux virtual machines or your Linux host machine.

Also, as always, you can grab the scripts and text files from Github, like so:

```
git clone https://github.com/PacktPublishing/The-Ultimate-Linux-Shell-
Scripting-Guide.git
```

Introduction to Functions

As I've mentioned above, a function is a block of programming code that performs a specific task. What makes functions so cool is that they really cut down on the amount of code that you have to type. Instead of having to type in the same code every time you want to perform a task, you can just call the function, instead. This cuts down on the size of your scripts, and makes typing the script much less prone·to error.

Also, after a function has been called the first time, it resides in system memory, which can enhance the performance of your scripts.

You can create functions that accept parameters from the main program, that return values to the main program, or that might do some stand-alone task that doesn't involve either passing parameters or passing values. Learning to create functions is easy, because for the most part you're just using the same coding techniques that I've already shown you. I mean, yeah, there are some new things that you'll have to learn, but there's really nothing hard about any of it.

If you're running Linux on your workstation, you're already using a lot of functions without realizing it. To see the functions that your system is running, just run a `declare -F` command, like so:

```
[donnie@fedora ~]$ declare -F
declare -f __expand_tilde_by_ref
declare -f __fzf_comprun
declare -f __fzf_defc
. . .

. . .
declare -f gawkpath_prepend
declare -f quote
declare -f quote_readline
[donnie@fedora ~]$
```

These functions are loaded into system memory by the shell every time you log into your computer, and are used by the various utilities that make up the `bash` ecosystem.

Running `declare` with a lower case `-f` also shows you the code for each function. You can also list the name of a function to only see the code for it, like this:

```
[donnie@fedora ~]$ declare -f __expand_tilde_by_ref
__expand_tilde_by_ref ()
{
    if [[ ${!1-} == \~* ]]; then
        eval $1="$(printf ~%q "${!1#\~}")";
    fi
}
[donnie@fedora ~]$
```

To see where these functions are defined, you'll need to enter debugger mode and then use a `declare -F` command, like this:

```
[donnie@fedora ~]$ bash --debugger
[donnie@fedora ~]$ declare -F __expand_tilde_by_ref
__expand_tilde_by_ref 1069 /usr/share/bash-completion/bash_completion
[donnie@fedora ~]$
```

So, you see that this function is defined on line number 1069 of the `bash_completion` function library file that's in the `/usr/share/bash-completion/` directory. Go ahead and peek into that file, and you'll see that many functions are defined in it. When you're through with debugger mode, just type `exit`.

You can also obtain information about a function with the `type` command, like so:

```
[donnie@fedora ~]$ type quote
quote is a function
quote ()
{
    local quoted=${1//\'/\'\\\'\'};
    printf "'%s'" "$quoted"
}
[donnie@fedora ~]$
```

Now that you know what functions are, let's see if we can define some.

Defining a Function

You can define a function in the following places:

- On the command-line
- In a shell script
- In a function library
- In a shell configuration file

Defining a function from the command-line can be useful if you need to do any quick testing or experimentation with new code. Here's what it looks like:

```
[donnie@fedora ~]$ howdy() { echo "Howdy, world!" ; echo "How's it going?"; }
[donnie@fedora ~]$ howdy
Howdy, world!
How's it going?
[donnie@fedora ~]$
```

The name of this function is `howdy`, and the `()` tells the shell that this is a function. The code for the function is within the pair of curly braces. The function consists of two `echo` commands, which are separated by a semi-colon. Note that you need to place another semi-colon at the end of the final command. You also need to have one blank space between the first curly brace and the first command, and the final semi-colon and the closing curly brace.

Some tutorials that you'll find might tell you that you can begin the function with the keyword `function`, as you see here:

```
[donnie@fedora ~]$ function howdy() { echo "Howdy, world!" ; echo "How's it
going?"; }
[donnie@fedora ~]$ howdy
```

```
Howdy, world!
How's it going?
[donnie@fedora ~]$
```

But, creating functions without the function keyword works well, so there's no real reason to use it.

 Be aware that using the function keyword is a really bad idea, because it's not portable. I mean, it works on bash, zsh, and ash, but it doesn't work on ksh, dash, or Bourne Shell. Even where you can use the function keyword, it serves no real purpose. So, your best bet is to just never use it.

Any functions that you define on the command line will be ephemeral and will disappear as soon as you close the terminal. So, you'll want to commit them to a file to make them permanent. Also, any functions that you define on the command-line will not be visible in a bash --debug session, because they don't get exported to a child shell.

There's no difference in how you would create a function in shell scripts, function library files, and shell configuration files. But, there a couple of different methods for how you structure your functions.

The first method is to place the entire function on a single line, with or without the preceding function keyword. This would look exactly as it would if you were to create a function on the command-line. Since you've already seen that, I'll say no more about it.

The other method is to structure your functions in a multi-line format, as you would do in other programming languages such as C or Java. This is really your best bet, because it makes your code much more readable and less prone to error. A quick way to see how that looks is to view the single-line howdy function that I just created on the command-line with declare -f, like so:

```
[donnie@fedora ~]$ declare -f howdy
howdy ()
{
    echo "Howdy, world!";
    echo "How's it going?"
}
[donnie@fedora ~]$
```

The declare -f command automatically converts the function that I entered on the command-line into multi-line format. If I wanted to, I could just copy and paste this into a shell script file. In fact, I think I will copy it into a new howdy_func.sh script. Here's what it will look like:

```
#!/bin/bash
howdy ()
{
    echo "Howdy, world!";
    echo "How's it going?"
}
```

As before, the preceding `function` keyword is optional. I've chosen to omit it, since it serves no function and isn't compatible with some non-bash shells.

Okay, this all looks good, but watch what happens when I run the script:

```
[donnie@fedora ~]$ ./howdy_func.sh
[donnie@fedora ~]$
```

Nothing happens, which isn't good. I'll show you why in the next section.

Using Functions in Shell Scripts

You'll be amazed at how functions can make your shell scripts so much more *functional*. (Yeah, I know. That really was a bad pun.) Read on to see how to make that happen.

Creating and Calling Functions

When you place a function inside a shell script, the function code won't get executed until you call the function. Let's modify the `howdy_func.sh` script to make that happen, like this:

```
#!/bin/bash
howdy ()
{
    echo "Howdy, world!";
    echo "How's it going?"
}
howdy
```

You see that all I had to do was to place the name of the function outside of the function code block. Also, note that the function definition must come before the function call. Otherwise, the shell will never be able to find the function. Anyway, when I run the script now, it works fine:

```
[donnie@fedora ~]$ ./howdy_func.sh
Howdy, world!
How's it going?
[donnie@fedora ~]$
```

I should also point out that the first curly brace can be on a line by itself as you see above, or it can be on the same line as the function name, like this:

```
#!/bin/bash
howdy() {
        echo "Howdy, world!"
        echo "How's it going?"
}
howdy
```

I personally prefer this way for a simple reason. It's just that my preferred text editor is `vim`, and placing the first curly brace on the same line as the function name causes `vim` to activate its automatic indenting feature.

The ability to reuse code is one of the coolest features about functions. Instead of having to type the same code in every place where you need to perform a certain task, just type it once and call it from wherever you need to. Let's make another slight modification to the `howdy_func.sh` script, like so:

```
#!/bin/bash
howdy ()
{       ⁄
    echo "Howdy, world!";
    echo "How's it going?"
}
howdy
echo
echo "Let's do some more stuff and then"
echo "we'll call the function again."
echo
howdy
```

Here's what running the modified script looks like:

```
[donnie@fedora ~]$ ./howdy_func.sh
Howdy, world!
How's it going?
Let's do some more stuff and then
we'll call the function again.
Howdy, world!
How's it going?
[donnie@fedora ~]$
```

So, I called the function twice, and it got executed twice. How cool is that? But, it gets even better.

Passing Positional Parameters to Functions

You can also pass positional parameters into a function, the same as you can pass them into a shell script. To do that, call the function with a value that you want to pass as a positional parameter, as you see here in this `greet_func.sh` script:

```
#!/bin/bash
greetings() {
        echo "Greetings, $1"
}
greetings Donnie
```

You see the `$1` positional parameter in the function. When I call the function, I'm passing the value Donnie into the function. Here's what happens when I run the script:

```
[donnie@fedora ~]$ ./greet_func.sh
Greetings, Donnie
[donnie@fedora ~]$
```

You can also pass the positional parameter into the script as you normally would, and then pass it into the function, as you see here:

```
#!/bin/bash
greetings() {
        echo "Greetings, $1"
}
greetings $1
```

Here's what happens when I run this script:

```
[donnie@fedora ~]$ ./greet_func2.sh Frank
Greetings, Frank
[donnie@fedora ~]$
```

That's good, but it only works with one parameter. Any additional names that you pass in as parameters won't show up in the output. You can fix that by defining additional parameters, like this:

```
#!/bin/bash
greetings() {
        echo "Greetings, $1 $2"
}
greetings $1 $2
```

And, that's fine if you know that you'll always want to pass in a specified number of parameters. If you don't want to limit yourself like this, use the `$@` as the positional parameter. That way, you can pass in however many parameters you want each time that you run the script. Here's what it looks like:

```
#!/bin/bash
greetings() {
        echo "Greetings, $@"
}
greetings $@
```

Let's see what it looks like when I pass in four names:

```
[donnie@fedora ~]$ ./greet_func4.sh Vicky Cleopatra Frank Charlie
Greetings, Vicky Cleopatra Frank Charlie
[donnie@fedora ~]$
```

That looks good. But, I can still fancy it up a bit, like this:

```
[donnie@fedora ~]$ ./greet_func4.sh Vicky, Cleopatra, Frank, "and Charlie"!
Greetings, Vicky, Cleopatra, Frank, and Charlie!
[donnie@fedora ~]$
```

Pretty slick, eh? What's even more slick is having a function pass values back to the main program.

Passing Values from a Function

Okay, here's where I need to pause for a moment and clarify something for the veterans of other programming languages. Unlike what you may be used to with other languages, a shell scripting function cannot *directly* return a value to its caller, which is normally the main body of the program.

 Okay, there is a return command that you can use in a function, but it's not the same as the return command in other languages. In shell scripts, the only thing that you can pass with return is just the exit status of a command.

You can create a function that will return a value, but you have to do it with either a **global variable** or a combination of a **local variable** and command substitution. Another difference is that in other languages, variables are local by default, and you have to specify which variables are to be global. In shell scripting, it's just the opposite. Shell scripting variables are global by default, and you have to specify which variables are to be local.

Now, for those of you who aren't veterans of other programming languages, allow me to explain the difference between local and global variables.

A global variable can be accessed from anywhere in a script, even if you defined it within a function. For example, look at the valuepass function in this value1.sh script:

```
#/bin/bash
valuepass() {
        textstring='Donnie is the great BeginLinux Guru'
}
valuepass
echo $textstring
```

Here's what happens when I run the script:

```
donnie@debian12:~$ ./value1.sh
Donnie is the great BeginLinux Guru
donnie@debian12:~$
```

In this script, you see that the function does nothing except to define the global textstring variable and set its value. The value of textstring is available outside of the function, which means that after calling the function, I can then echo back the value of textstring.

Now, let's define `textstring` as a local variable in the `value2.sh` script, like so:

```
#/bin/bash
valuepass() {
        local textstring='Donnie is the great BeginLinux Guru'
}
valuepass
echo $textstring
```

Watch what happens when I run the script this time:

```
donnie@debian12:~$ ./value2.sh
donnie@debian12:~$
```

There's no output this time, because the local variable isn't accessible outside of the function. Or, more accurately, the local variable isn't *directly* accessible outside of the function. There are ways to make the function pass the value of a local variable to an external caller, which I'll show you in just a few moments.

First though, I want answer a question that I know you're anxious to ask. That is, if we can use a global variable to pass a value outside of a function, why do we need local variables? Well, it's just that if you use nothing but global variables in your functions, you could turn your script into a debugging nightmare. That's because if you accidentally create a variable outside of the function with the same name as a global variable that's inside of the function, you would overwrite the value of the variable from within the function.

By using only local variables inside of functions, you avoid that problem. If you have an external variable that has the same name as a local variable that's in a function, the external variable won't overwrite the internal variable's value. To demo this, let's create the `value3.sh` script, like so:

```
#/bin/bash
valuepass() {
        textstring='Donnie is the great BeginLinux Guru'
}
valuepass
echo $textstring
textstring='Who is the great BeginLinux Guru?'
echo $textstring
```

You see that I've set the `textstring` variable in the function back to a global variable, and I've defined the variable again outside of the function. Here's what happens when I run the script now:

```
donnie@debian12:~$ ./value3.sh
Donnie is the great BeginLinux Guru
Who is the great BeginLinux Guru?
donnie@debian12:~$
```

The second echo $textstring command used the new value of textstring, which overwrote the previous value. That's fine if that's what you want to happen, but it usually isn't what you want to happen.

One way to have a function pass a value with a local variable is to call the function from within a command substitution construct. To demo that, create the value4.sh script, like so:

```
#!/bin/bash
valuepass() {
        local textstring='Donnie is the great BeginLinux Guru'
        echo "$textstring"
}
result=$(valuepass)
echo $result
```

You see here that I've created the external result variable, and assigned to it the value that was obtained by the $(valuepass) command substitution.

Another method for obtaining a value from a function is to use a **result variable**. This involves passing the *name* of a variable into the function when you call it, and then assigning a value to that variable inside the function. Let's look at the value5.sh script to see how that works:

```
#/bin/bash
valuepass() {
        local __internalvar=$1
        local myresult='Shell scripting is cool!'
        eval $__internalvar="'$myresult'"
}
valuepass result
echo $result
```

The valuepass result command calls the function and passes the name of the result variable into the function, via the $1 positional parameter. Understand though, that result still doesn't have an assigned value, so the only thing that you're passing into the function is just the name of the variable, and nothing else.

> Up to this point, you've only seen positional parameters used to pass values into the script when you invoke the script. Here, you seen how positional parameters can also be used to pass values from the main body of a script into a function.

Inside the function, this variable name is represented by the $1 positional parameter. This variable name is assigned as the value of the local __internalvar variable. The next line assigns Shell scripting is cool! as the value of the local myresult variable. In the final line, the eval command sets the value of $myresult as the value of the $__internalvar variable.

Remember that the value of the __internalvar variable is result, which is the name of the variable that we passed into the function. Also, be aware that this is now a global variable, because I didn't specify the local keyword here. This means that its value can be passed back to the main body of the script.

So now, $__internalvar is really the result variable with Shell scripting is cool! as its assigned value.

Understand though, that you don't want the variable name that you pass into a function to be the same as the name of the local variable that's inside the function. Otherwise, the eval command won't be able to properly set the value of the variable. That's why I prefaced the name of the local variable with a pair of underscores, so that I can be sure to prevent having a variable with the same name outside of the function. (Of course, only one underscore would have sufficed, but the accepted convention is to use two underscores.)

Next, let's create some libraries.

Creating Function Libraries

For a convenient way to make your functions reusable, just place them into a function library. Then, from within your scripts, call the desired libraries with either a source command or a dot command. If you're the only one who will ever use the libraries, you can place them in your own home directory.

If you want to make them available for everyone, you can place them in a central location, such as in the /usr/local/lib/ directory.

For a simple demonstration, I've created the donnie_library file in the /usr/local/lib/ directory with two simple functions. It looks like this:

```
howdy_world() {
echo "Howdy, world!"
echo "How's it going?"
}
howdy_georgia() {
echo "Howdy, Georgia!"
echo "How's it going?"
}
```

(I live in the state of Georgia, which explains the second function.)

There's no need to set the executable permission on this file, because it only contains code that will be called in by an executable script.

Next, I created the library_demo1.sh script, which looks like this:

```
#!/bin/bash
```

```
source /usr/local/lib/donnie_library
howdy_world
```

You see that I used the source command to reference the donnie_library file. I then called the howdy_world function as I would normally do. Running the script looks like this:

```
[donnie@fedora ~]$ ./library_demo1.sh
Howdy, world!
How's it going?
[donnie@fedora ~]$
```

I also created the library_demo2.sh file, which looks like this:

```
#!/bin/bash
. /usr/local/lib/donnie_library
howdy_georgia
```

This time I replaced the source command with a dot, to show you that they both do the exact same thing.

Be aware that using the source keyword works on ash, ksh, zsh, and bash, but it doesn't work on certain other shells, such as dash or Bourne. If you need your scripts to run on as many shells as possible, you'll need to use the dot, and avoid using source.

I then called the second function in the library file. Running this script looks like this:

```
[donnie@fedora ~]$ ./library_demo2.sh
Howdy, Georgia!
How's it going?
[donnie@fedora ~]$
```

For something a bit more practical, let's add a network checking function, using a case..esac construct. Unfortunately, the donnie_library file is now too large to show you here in the book, but you can download it from the Github repository. Still though, I do want to point out one thing about this case..esac construct, which you see here:

```
network() {
site="$1"
case "$site" in
"")
        site="google.com"
;;
*)
        site="$1"
;;
esac
```

```
   . . .
   . . .
   }
```

 Note how for the first condition I used a `""` construct. The pair of double-quotes, with no blank space between them, means that no value has been passed in for the positional parameter. This also means that google.com will be used as the default site name.

Now, the library_demo3.sh script that uses this new function looks like this:

```
#!/bin/bash
. /usr/local/lib/donnie_library
network $1
```

Running the script without supplying an argument looks like this:

```
[donnie@fedora ~]$ ./libary_demo3.sh
2023-10-27 . . . Success! google.com is reachable.
[donnie@fedora ~]$
```

Here's how it looks when I supply a valid site name as the argument:

```
[donnie@fedora ~]$ ./libary_demo3.sh www.civicsandpolitics.com
2023-10-27 . . . Success! www.civicsandpolitics.com is reachable.
[donnie@fedora ~]$
```

And finally, here's what I get when I supply an invalid site name:

```
[donnie@fedora ~]$ ./libary_demo3.sh www.donnie.com
ping: www.donnie.com: Name or service not known
2023-10-27 . . . Network Failure for site www.donnie.com!
[donnie@fedora ~]$
```

I know, it's a crying shame that there's no website that's named after me. (I might have to correct that problem some day.)

And, guess what? That's really all I have to say about function libraries. Let's move on to the real world.

Looking at Some Real-World Examples

Here are a few cool examples of functions in action. Enjoy!

Checking Network Connectivity

This function is essentially the same as the one that I've just shown you in the previous section. The only real difference is that I'm using an if..then construct instead of the case..esac construct.

Also, I placed this function into the actual executable script. But, you can easily move it into a library file if you desire. (I can't show you the entire script here due to book formatting constraints, but you can download it from the Github repository. It's the `network_func.sh` file.) Anyway, here's the important part that I really want you to see:

```bash
#!/bin/bash
network() {
if [[ $# -eq 0 ]]; then
        site="google.com"
else
        site="$1"
fi
. . .

. . .

}
network
network www.civicsandpolitics.com
network donnie.com
```

You see that after I defined the `network()` function, I called it three different times. I first called it without a positional parameter, so that it would ping `google.com`. I then called it with another real website and then with a fake website as the positional parameter. Here's what I get when I run this new script:

```
[donnie@fedora ~]$ ./network_func.sh
2023-10-27 . . . Success for google.com!
2023-10-27 . . . Success for www.civicsandpolitics.com!
ping: donnie.com: Name or service not known
2023-10-27 . . . Network Failure for donnie.com!
[donnie@fedora ~]$
```

That part works. Let's now look in the system log file to see if the `logger` utility that's in the function actually made the appropriate log entries:

```
[donnie@fedora ~]$ sudo tail /var/log/messages
. . .

. . .
Oct 27 16:14:21 fedora donnie[38134]: google.com is reachable.
Oct 27 16:14:23 fedora donnie[38137]: www.civicsandpolitics.com is reachable.
Oct 27 16:14:23 fedora donnie[38140]: Could not reach donnie.com.
[donnie@fedora ~]$
```

Yeah, that part works too. So once again, we have achieved coolness. (Of course, you can also modify the script so that you can supply your own positional parameter as an argument. I'll leave it to you to do that.)

Be aware that I tested this script on a Fedora machine, which still uses the old-style `rsyslog` log files. If you try this on Debian, you'll need to install `rsyslog` yourself. By default, Debian 12 now only uses the `journald` logging system, and doesn't come with `rsyslog` installed.

Next, is a little something that I whipped up for myself.

Using the CoinGecko API

CoinGecko is a cool website where you can go to check on the prices and statistics of pretty much every cryptocurrency there is. It's fairly quick to use if you just need to check on one coin, but it can be fairly time-consuming if you need to check on multiple coins.

You can create a custom portfolio of coins, which is useful if you always want to see the same list of coins. But, it's not so useful if you always want to check on different lists of coins. So, you might like to streamline the process a bit. For that, you can create a shell script that uses the CoinGecko **Application Programming Interface (API)**.

To take full advantage of all of the CoinGecko API features, you'll need to become a paying customer, which is rather expensive. Fortunately, you don't need to do that for this demo. Instead, you'll just use CoinGecko's public API key, which is free-of-charge. To demo this, let's do a hands-on lab.

Hands-on Lab — Creating the coingecko.sh Script

To begin, take a look at CoinGecko's documentation page (`https://www.coingecko.com/api/documentation`), and follow these steps as mentioned below:

1. Scroll down the page, and you'll see a list of the various functions that you can perform with the public API. You can use the forms in the drop-down lists to create the code that you'll copy into a shell script. I've already created the `coingecko.sh` shell script that performs three of those functions, which you can download from the Github repository. Before you use it though, you'll need to ensure that the `curl` and `jq` packages are installed on your system. Anyway, here's how the script works.

2. At the top of the `gecko_api` function, I defined the `coin` and `currency` variables as positional parameters `$1` and `$2`. The `if [ -z $coin ]; then` line checks to see if the value of `coin` is zero length. If it is, it means that I haven't entered any arguments when I invoked the script. So, it will then echo a series of statements about how to invoke the script.

3. Next, you see this `elif` stanza:

```
elif [ $coin == list ]; then
        curl -X 'GET' \
"https://api.coingecko.com/api/v3/coins/list?include_platform=true" \
   -H 'accept: application/json' | jq | tee coinlist.txt
```

4. I copied this `curl` command from the CoinGecko documentation page, and pasted it into the script.

5. Then, I piped the output into the `jq` utility to convert the normal **json** output to **pretty json** format.

6. I then piped that output into `tee` in order to both view the output on screen and save it to a text file. Invoking the script with the `list` argument will download the entire list of coins that are supported by the API. The `elif` construct in the next stanza is the same as this `elif` construct, except that it will show a list of *versus currencies* that you can use for pricing the coins.

7. The `else` construct in the final stanza of the function requires you to enter both a coin and a versus currency as arguments. The original code from the documentation page contained the actual names of the coin and versus currency that I entered into the form on the documentation page. I changed them to the `$coin` and `$currency` variables, respectively. I then had to change the pair of single quotes that surround the URL with a pair of double quotes, so that the `$` in the variable names would be interpreted correctly.

8. Let's say that you want to check the price of Bitcoin in US dollars. First, open the `coinlist.txt` file that you created when you ran the `./coingecko list` command. Search for Bitcoin, and you'll find a stanza that looks like this:

```
{
    "id": "bitcoin",
    "symbol": "btc",
    "name": "Bitcoin",
    "platforms": {}
},
```

9. Next, open the `currency_list.txt` that you created when you ran the `./coingecko currencies` command. Scroll down until you find the versus currency that you want to use to price your particular coin or coins. Now, to view the price of your coin(s) in your desired currency, enter the `"id:"` value for the coin from the `coinlist.txt` file as the first argument, and the desired versus currency as the second argument, like this:

```
[donnie@fedora ~]$ ./coingecko.sh bitcoin usd
  % Total    % Received % Xferd  Average Speed   Time    Time     Time
Current

                                 Dload  Upload   Total   Spent    Left
Speed
100   157    0    157     0      0      876      0 --:--:-- --:--:-- --:--:-
-    872
{
  "bitcoin": {
    "usd": 34664,
    "usd_market_cap": 675835016546.567,
    "usd_24h_vol": 27952066301.047348,
    "usd_24h_change": 2.6519150329293883,
    "last_updated_at": 1698262594
```

```
      }
  }
[donnie@fedora ~]$
```

10. So, it looks like the current price of Bitcoin is $34664 US.

You can view multiple coins at a time by entering a comma-separated list, like this:

```
[donnie@fedora ~]$ ./coingecko.sh bitcoin,ethereum,dero usd
  % Total      % Received % Xferd  Average Speed   Time    Time     Time
Current
                                   Dload  Upload   Total   Spent    Left
Speed
100   471    0   471    0     0   3218      0 --:--:-- --:--:-- --:--:-
-  3226
{
  "bitcoin": {
    "usd": 34662,
    "usd_market_cap": 675835016546.567,
    "usd_24h_vol": 27417000940.815952,
    "usd_24h_change": 2.647099155664393,
    "last_updated_at": 1698262727
. . .

. . .

[donnie@fedora ~]$
```

11. If you're a trader, you might want to check the price of an altcoin in terms of some other versus currency, such as Bitcoin satoshis. Here, I'm checking the Bitcoin satoshi price of Dero:

```
[donnie@fedora ~]$ ./coingecko.sh dero sats
  % Total      % Received % Xferd  Average Speed   Time    Time     Time
Current
                                   Dload  Upload   Total   Spent    Left
Speed
100   161    0   161    0     0   746      0 --:--:-- --:--:-- --:--:-
-   748
{
  "dero": {
    "sats": 8544.47,
    "sats_market_cap": 106868665749.11504,
    "sats_24h_vol": 50996466.4091239,
    "sats_24h_change": -3.2533636291339687,
    "last_updated_at": 1698263552
  }
```

```
}
[donnie@fedora ~]
```

12. So, the current satoshi price of Dero is 8544.47 sats. (Of course, these prices will be different by the time you look at them.)

13. The top three lines of the output are from the curl command that the script used to download information about the coins. For some strange reason, bash considers this curl message as an error message, even though it really isn't. But, that's actually good, because you can prevent having to see this message by using a stderr redirector at the end of your command, like this:

```
donnie@fedora:~$ ./coingecko.sh dero sats 2>/dev/null
{
  "dero": {
    "sats": 3389.23,
    "sats_market_cap": 42965410638.71136,
    "sats_24h_vol": 112468964.13986385,
    "sats_24h_change": 2.81262920882357,
    "last_updated_at": 1718482347
  }
}
donnie@fedora:~$
```

14. Oh, I almost forgot about the most important part of the script, which is the command that calls the function:

```
gecko_api $1 $2
```

It asks for two positional parameters, but will work just fine if you just enter either list or currencies as a single argument.

15. Okay, this is good. But, what if you have a very long list of coins that you want to track, and you don't want to type that whole long list in every time that invoke this script? Well, that's easy. I'll just create the mycoins.sh script, which will call the coingecko.sh script. Here's how it looks:

```
#!/bin/bash
./coingecko.sh bitcoin,dero,ethereum,bitcoin-cash,bitcoin-cash-
sv,bitcoin-gold,radiant,monero usd 2>/dev/null
```

Of course, you can edit this script to add your own list of favorite coins.

16. For a variation on this theme, download the coingecko-case.sh script, too. It's the same script, but I built it with a case..esac construct instead of an if..then contruct.

That's about it for functions, at least for now. But, don't be too surprised if you see more throughout the rest of this book.

Now, let's wrap up and move on.

Summary

Functions are an important part of most every modern programming language. In this chapter I've shown you how to construct them, how to call them, and how to create function libraries that you can either use for yourself or share with other users.

In the next chapter, I'll show you how to perform mathematical operations with shell scripts. I'll see you there.

Questions

1. Which two of the following methods would you use to create a function? (Choose two.)

   a. `function function_name()`

   b. `function_name()`

   c. `declare -f function_name`

   d. `declare -F function_name`

2. You want to create a function that will pass the value of a variable back to the main program. Which of the following should you use to do that?

   a. A global variable

   b. A local variable

   c. A return statement

   d. A continue statement

3. You want to create a function that any user can use in his or her own scripts. What is the best way to do that?

   a. Create a function library file in a central location, and make it executable.

   b. Add the new functions to the `/etc/bashrc` file.

   c. Create a function library file in a central location, but don't make it executable.

   d. D. Create a function library file in your own home directory.

4. Which two of the following commands would you use to reference a function library in your shell scripts? (Choose two.)

   a. `load`

   b. `reference`

   c. `source`

   d. `.`

5. You want to see the list of functions that are loaded into memory, along with their associated source code. Which command would you use?

   a. `declare -f`

   b. `declare -F`

    c.   `debugger -f`

    d.   `debugger -F`

Further Reading

- Bash Functions: `https://linuxize.com/post/bash-functions/`
- Returning Values from Bash Functions: `https://www.linuxjournal.com/content/return-values-bash-functions`
- Bash Function & How to Use It {Variables, Arguments, Return}: `https://phoenixnap.com/kb/bash-function`
- Writing shell scripts-Lesson 15: Errors and Signals and Traps: `http://linuxcommand.org/lc3_wss0150.php`
- (Note that the author of this tutorial uses all upper-case letters for the names of scripting variables, which is something that I don't advocate. Other than that, it's a good tutorial.)
- Advance Bash Script Guide: `https://tldp.org/LDP/abs/html/abs-guide.html#FUNCTIONS`

Answers

1. a and b
2. b
3. c
4. c and d
5. a

Join our community on Discord!

Read this book alongside other users, Linux experts, and the author himself.

Ask questions, provide solutions to other readers, chat with the author via Ask Me Anything sessions, and much more. Scan the QR code or visit the link to join the community.

`https://packt.link/SecNet`

11

Performing Mathematical Operations

The various operating system shells all have means of performing mathematical operations either from the command-line, or from within a shell script. In this chapter, we'll look at how to perform operations with both integer and floating point math.

Topics in this chapter include:

- Performing integer math with expressions
- Performing integer math with integer variables
- Performing floating point math with bc

If you're ready, let's get started.

Technical Requirements

Use any of your Linux virtual machines for this. And, as always, you can download the scripts by doing:

```
git clone https://github.com/PacktPublishing/The-Ultimate-Linux-Shell-
Scripting-Guide.git
```

Performing Integer Math with Expressions

You can do integer math directly in bash, which is sometimes handy. But, bash doesn't have the capability of doing floating point math. For that, you'll need to use a separate utility, which we'll look at later.

If you ever try to use echo to perform math on the command-line, you'll find that it doesn't work. What you'll get will look something like this:

```
[donnie@fedora ~]$ echo 1+1
1+1
[donnie@fedora ~]$ echo 1 + 1
```

```
1 + 1
[donnie@fedora ~]$
```

This is because echo treats your math problem as just a normal text string. So, you'll need some other way to solve your math problems. Fortunately, there are a few different ways to do this.

Using the expr Command

The expr command is for evaluating expressions. These expressions can be normal text strings, regular expressions, or mathematical expressions. For now, I'll just talk about using it to evaluate math expressions. Here's an example of its basic usage:

```
[donnie@fedora ~]$ expr 1 + 1
2
[donnie@fedora ~]$
```

Note that you need a blank space between the operator and each operand, or else you'll get this:

```
[donnie@fedora ~]$ expr 1+1
1+1
[donnie@fedora ~]$
```

Without the blank spaces, expr just echos back whatever you type in.

You can use expr with the +, -, /, *, and % operators to perform addition, subtraction, division, multiplication, or modulus operations. (Modulus operations show you the remainder after a division operation.) Special care is needed for using the * operator, because a shell will interpret it as a wild card. So, when performing multiplication, you'll need to escape the * with a \, like so:

```
[donnie@fedora ~]$ expr 3 \* 3
9
[donnie@fedora ~]$
```

Without the backslash in front of the *, you will receive an error, which will look like this:

```
donnie@fedora:~$ expr 3 * 3
expr: syntax error: unexpected argument '15827_zip.zip'
donnie@fedora:~$
```

For more complex problems, the normal rules of math apply, as you see here:

```
[donnie@fedora ~]$ expr 1 + 2 \* 3
7
[donnie@fedora ~]$
```

The laws of math dictate that division and multiplication always take precedence over subtraction and addition. So, you see here that the 2 * 3 operation gets performed before adding 1. But, just as in normal math, you can change the order in which operations are performed by placing a pair of parentheses around the operation that you want to perform first. Here's what that looks like:

```
[donnie@fedora ~]$ expr \( 1 + 2 \) \* 3
9
[donnie@fedora ~]$
```

Notice how I had to escape each parenthesis symbol with a backslash, and leave a blank space between the (and the 1, and between the 2 and the \.

You can also use expr with variables. To demo that, create the math1.sh script, like this:

```
#!/bin/bash
val1=$1
val2=$2
echo "val1 + val2 = " ; expr $val1 + $val2
echo
echo "val1 - val2 = " ; expr $val1 - $val2
echo
echo "val1 / val2 = " ; expr $val1 / $val2
echo
echo "val1 * val2 = " ; expr $val1 \* $val2
echo
echo "val1 % val2 = " ; expr $val1 % $val2
```

Running the script with 88 and 23 as the input values looks something like this:

```
[donnie@fedora ~]$ ./math1.sh 88 23
val1 + val2 =
111
val1 - val2 =
65
val1 / val2 =
3
val1 * val2 =
2024
val1 % val2 =
19
[donnie@fedora ~]$
```

Remember that expr can only work with integers. So, any results that involve a decimal get rounded up or down to the nearest integer.

And of course, you can also use expr with command substitution, as you see here in this math2.sh script:

```
#/bin/bash
result1=$(expr 20 \* 8)
result2=$(expr \( 20 + 4 \) / 8)
```

```
echo $result1
echo $result2
```

That's all there is to it for expr. Next, let's take another look at echo.

Using echo with Math Expressions

I know, I just told you that you can't use echo to perform math. Well, you actually can, but there's a special way to do it. You'll just have to place your math problem within either a $(( )) construct or a $[ ] construct, like so:

```
[donnie@fedora ~]$ echo $((2+2))
4
[donnie@fedora ~]$ echo $[2+2]
4
[donnie@fedora ~]$
```

Both constructs give the same results, so—on bash at least—whichever you use is a matter of personal preference.

A very cool thing about these two constructs is that you don't have to use a $ to call back the values of any variables that are within them. Likewise, you don't have to escape the * character with a backslash. Here's the math3.sh script to show you that:

```
#!/bin/bash
val1=$1
val2=$2
val3=$3
echo "Without grouping: " $((val1+val2*val3))
echo "With grouping: "   $(((val1+val2)*val3))
```

You also see that in the second echo command, I surrounded val1+val2 with its own set of parentheses in order to give the addition operation precedence over the multiplication operation. Anyway, here's what happens when I run the script:

```
[donnie@fedora ~]$ ./math3.sh 4 8 3
Without grouping:  28
With grouping:  36
[donnie@fedora ~]$
```

If you find the use of nested parentheses too confusing, you might want to use the square bracket construct instead, like this:

```
#!/bin/bash
val1=$1
val2=$2
val3=$3
```

```
echo "Without grouping: " $[val1+val2*val3]
echo "With grouping: "  $[(val1+val2)*val3]
```

Either way, you'll get the same results.

 There is a catch to this, though. It's just that the square bracket construct doesn't work on certain other shells, such as /bin/sh on FreeBSD and OpenIndiana, and /bin/dash on Debian and its derivatives. So, to make your scripts more portable, you'll need to use the ((..)) construct for your math problems, even though it can get a bit confusing.

Here's a more practical example of using parentheses to change the precedence of operations. In this new_year.sh script, I'm calculating the number of weeks left until the New Year. I start by using the date +%j command to calculate the numbered day of the year. Here's the output of that command:

```
[donnie@fedora ~]$ date +%j
304
[donnie@fedora ~]$
```

I'm writing this on 31 October, which is the 304th day of the year 2023. I'll then subtract that result from the number of days in a year, and divide that by 7 to give me the final answer. Here's what the script looks like:

```
#!/bin/bash
echo "There are $[(365-$(date +%j)) / 7 ] weeks left until the New Year."
```

You see that I used the square bracket construct in order to avoid the confusion of having so many nested parentheses. But, as I said before, that won't work on certain other non-bash shells.

Here's what I get when I run the script:

```
[donnie@fedora ~]$ ./new_year.sh
There are 8 weeks left until the New Year.
[donnie@fedora ~]$
```

Of course, you might be reading this in 2024, 2028, or even 2032, which are all leap years with 366 days, but that's okay. That extra day won't matter with this particular math problem.

Okay, how about one more example of a script with math expressions? Create the math4.sh script, like this:

```
#!/bin/bash
start=0
limit=10
while [ "$start" -le "$limit" ]; do
  echo "$start... "
  start=$["$start"+1]
done
```

This script begins with the number 0 as the initial value of start. It then prints out the value of start, increments it by 1, and then prints the next value. The loop continues until the value of limit is reached. Here's what that looks like:

```
[donnie@fedora ~]$ ./math4.sh
0...
1...
2...
3...
4...
5...
6...
7...
8...
9...
10...
[donnie@fedora ~]$
```

This pretty much covers it for using math expressions. Let's now see about using a new type of variable.

Performing Integer Math with Integer Variables

Instead of using mathematical expressions, you can use **integer variables**.

You've already seen the kind of thing that doesn't work, which looks like this:

```
[donnie@fedora ~]$ a=1
[donnie@fedora ~]$ b=2
[donnie@fedora ~]$ echo $a + $b
1 + 2
[donnie@fedora ~]$
```

That's because by default, the values of variables are text strings, rather than numbers. To make this work, use the declare -i command to create integer variables, like this:

```
[donnie@fedora ~]$ declare -i a=1
[donnie@fedora ~]$ declare -i b=2
[donnie@fedora ~]$ declare -i result=a+b
[donnie@fedora ~]$ echo $result
3
[donnie@fedora ~]$
```

Here's how it look in the math5.sh script:

```
#!/bin/bash
declare -i val1=$1
```

```
declare -i val2=$2
declare -i result1=val1+val2
declare -i result2=val1/val2
declare -i result3=val1*val2
declare -i result4=val1-val2
declare -i result5=val1%val2
echo "Addition: $result1"
echo "Division: $result2"
echo "Multiplication: $result3"
echo "Subtraction: $result4"
echo "Modulus: $result5"
```

In the declare -i commands, you don't need to precede variable names with a $ to call their values. You also don't need to use command substitution to assign the results of a math operation to a variable. Anyway, here's how it looks when I run it:

```
[donnie@fedora ~]$ ./math5.sh 38 3
Addition: 41
Division: 12
Multiplication: 114
Subtraction: 35
Modulus: 2
[donnie@fedora ~]$
```

And, since this is integer math, any results that contain a decimal get rounded up or down to the nearest integer.

Sometimes, integer math is all you need. But, what if you need more? That's in the next section, so stay tuned.

Performing Floating Point Math with bc

The methods you've just seen for performing math operations from the shell all have two limitations. First, these methods can only work with integers. Secondly, when using these methods, you're limited to just basic math. Fortunately, the bc utility solves both of those problems. In fact, you'd need to be an expert mathematician to take full advantage of bc's features. (I don't fall into that category, but I can still show you the basics of using bc.)

You should find that bc is already installed on your Linux or Unix system, so you likely won't have to mess around with installing it.

There are three ways to use bc, which are:

- **Interactive mode**: You'll just open bc, and enter math commands on its own command-line.
- **Program files**: Create programs in the bc language, and use bc to execute them.
- **Pipe math problems into bc**: You can do this either from the shell command-line, or from within shell scripts.

Let's look at interactive mode first.

Using bc in Interactive Mode

You can start bc in interactive mode by entering bc at the command-line, like so:

```
[donnie@fedora ~]$ bc
bc 1.07.1
Copyright 1991-1994, 1997, 1998, 2000, 2004, 2006, 2008, 2012-2017 Free
Software Foundation, Inc.
This is free software with ABSOLUTELY NO WARRANTY.
For details type `warranty'.
```

Now, you just type a math problem at the bc command prompt. Let's start by dividing 3 by 4, like this:

```
3/4
0
```

You see that this gives us 0 as the result. But wait, isn't bc supposed to be floating point-capable? Well, it is, but you have to start it with the -l option to bring in the optional math libraries. So, let's type quit to shut it down and start over, like this:

```
[donnie@fedora ~]$ bc -l
bc 1.07.1
Copyright 1991-1994, 1997, 1998, 2000, 2004, 2006, 2008, 2012-2017 Free
Software Foundation, Inc.
This is free software with ABSOLUTELY NO WARRANTY.
For details type `warranty'.
3/4
.75000000000000000000
```

If you don't want to see this many decimal places, use the scale command. Let's say that you only want to see two decimal places. Just set it like this:

```
[donnie@fedora ~]$ bc -l
bc 1.07.1
Copyright 1991-1994, 1997, 1998, 2000, 2004, 2006, 2008, 2012-2017 Free
Software Foundation, Inc.
This is free software with ABSOLUTELY NO WARRANTY.
For details type `warranty'.
scale=2
3/4
.75
```

Now, let's do something a bit more practical, by solving some geometry problems. As you likely know, a triangle has three angles, and the number of degrees in all three angles always adds up to 180 degrees, as you see here:

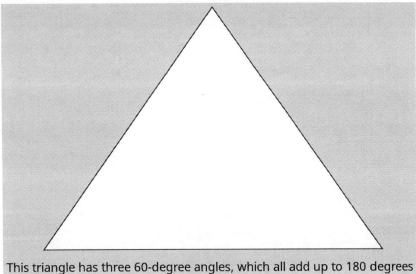

This triangle has three 60-degree angles, which all add up to 180 degrees

Figure 11.1: A triangle with three 60-degree angles

So, for example, you could have a triangle with a 40-degree angle, a 50-degree angle, and a 90-degree angle. At times though, you might only know the number of degrees in two of the angles, and will want to find the number of degrees for the third angle. You can do that by adding together the number of degrees for the two known angles, and subtracting the sum from 180. Here's what it looks like in bc interactive mode:

```
[donnie@fedora ~]$ bc -l
bc 1.07.1
Copyright 1991-1994, 1997, 1998, 2000, 2004, 2006, 2008, 2012-2017 Free
Software Foundation, Inc.
This is free software with ABSOLUTELY NO WARRANTY.
For details type `warranty'.
a=40
b=50
180-(a+b)
90
```

This also demonstrates how you can use variables in bc. This is handy, because if I want to run the calculation again on another set of values, I only have to type in the new variable assignments. Then, I'll just use the up-arrow key on the keyboard to get back to the formula.

Next, we'll look at a circle with a diameter of 25 and a radius of 12.5. (The unit-of-measure doesn't matter. It could be inches, centimeters, miles, or kilometers. It really doesn't matter.) To calculate the circumference of a circle, we need to multiply the circle's diameter by the value of pi (Π), like so:

```
[donnie@fedora ~]$ bc -l
bc 1.07.1
```

```
Copyright 1991-1994, 1997, 1998, 2000, 2004, 2006, 2008, 2012-2017 Free
Software Foundation, Inc.
This is free software with ABSOLUTELY NO WARRANTY.
For details type `warranty'.
pi=3.14159265358979323846
diameter=25
circumference=pi*diameter
print circumference
78.53981633974483096150
```

To calculate the area of a circle, multiply Π by the squared value of the radius, like this:

```
radius=12.5
area=pi*(radius^2)
print area
490.87385212340519350937
```

You see here that the ^ is used to denote an exponent, which in this case is 2. You also see that there's no echo command in the bc language. Instead, you'll use print.

You'll find many useful functions in the optional libraries, besides just the ability to deal with floating point math. For example, you can use the ibase and obase functions to convert numbers from one number system to another. Here, you see me converting a decimal number to a hexadecimal number:

```
[donnie@fedora ~]$ bc -l
bc 1.07.1
Copyright 1991-1994, 1997, 1998, 2000, 2004, 2006, 2008, 2012-2017 Free
Software Foundation, Inc.
This is free software with ABSOLUTELY NO WARRANTY.
For details type `warranty'.
obase=16
10
A
```

The obase=16 line tells bc that I want all numbers to be output in hexadecimal format. I don't have to use an ibase line to specify the input number system, because it already defaults to decimal. When I entered 10 as the number to convert, I got A as a result, which is the hexadecimal equivalent of decimal number 10. I can also convert from hexadecimal back to decimal, like this:

```
[donnie@fedora ~]$ bc -l
bc 1.07.1
Copyright 1991-1994, 1997, 1998, 2000, 2004, 2006, 2008, 2012-2017 Free
Software Foundation, Inc.
This is free software with ABSOLUTELY NO WARRANTY.
For details type `warranty'.
```

```
ibase=16
A
10
```

Again, since decimal is the default, I didn't have to specify it for the obase. (Well, I would have had to, if I hadn't closed and reopened bc after setting the obase to 16 for the previous example.)

Here's an example of setting both the ibase and the obase:

```
[donnie@fedora ~]$ bc -l
bc 1.07.1
Copyright 1991-1994, 1997, 1998, 2000, 2004, 2006, 2008, 2012-2017 Free
Software Foundation, Inc.
This is free software with ABSOLUTELY NO WARRANTY.
For details type `warranty'.
ibase=2
obase=16
1011101
10110
```

In this one, I chose to convert a binary number to hexadecimal.

You can also set the ibase and the obase to the same value in order to perform math in a different number system. Here's an example of how to perform binary math:

```
[donnie@fedora ~]$ bc -l
bc 1.07.1
Copyright 1991-1994, 1997, 1998, 2000, 2004, 2006, 2008, 2012-2017 Free
Software Foundation, Inc.
This is free software with ABSOLUTELY NO WARRANTY.
For details type `warranty'.
ibase=2
obase=2
101-1
100
101+101
1010
101/101
1.00000000000000000000000000000000000000000000000000000000000000000000\
0
```

Yeah, I wish that I would have had this back in the 1980s, when I had to learn binary math in my early computer classes. It would have made things so much easier. But seriously, note that in the division command, there are so many trailing zeros that a \ was used to continue them on the next line.

You can use a `scale=` command to change that, but you'll get some rather surprising results when using it in binary mode. Here's what I mean:

```
scale=2
101/101
1.0000000
scale=1
101/101
1.0000
```

I don't know why that is, but that's okay.

Tip

 Be aware that if you decide to convert a hexadecimal number to another format, the digits A through F must be typed in upper-case.

Other functions in the bc libraries include:

- s (x): The sine of x, in radians.
- c (x): The cosine of x, in radians.
- a (x): The arctangent of x, in radians.
- l (x): The natural logarithm of x.
- e (x): The exponential function of raising e to the value x.
- j (n,x): The Bessel function of integer order n of x.

For example, let's say that you need to find the natural logarithm of the number 80. Just do it like this:

```
[donnie@fedora ~]$ bc -l
bc 1.07.1
Copyright 1991-1994, 1997, 1998, 2000, 2004, 2006, 2008, 2012-2017 Free
Software Foundation, Inc.
This is free software with ABSOLUTELY NO WARRANTY.
For details type `warranty'.
l(80)
4.38202663467388161226
```

Okay, I think that that should cover it for interactive mode. Let's now look some bc programs.

Using bc Program Files

The main problem with using interactive mode is that as soon as you shut down bc, all of your work will disappear. One way to make your work permanent is to create a program file. Let's begin by creating the geometry1.txt file, which will look like this:

```
print "\nGeometry!\n"
print "Let's say that you want to calculate the area of a circle.\n"
print "Enter the radius of the circle: "; radius = read()
pi=3.14159265358979323846
area=pi*(radius^2)
print "The area of this circle is: \n"
print area
print "\n"
quit
```

You've already seen how to do the math, so I won't go over that again. But, I do want you to notice that the print command doesn't automatically insert a newline character at the end of lines. So, you'll have to do that yourself by adding a \n sequence at the end of your print commands. Also, notice on line 3 how I used the read() function to take the user's input and assign it to the radius variable. The last command must be quit, or else the program won't exit. To run this program, just type bc -1, followed by the name of the program file, like this:

```
[donnie@fedora ~]$ bc -l geometry1.txt
bc 1.07.1
Copyright 1991-1994, 1997, 1998, 2000, 2004, 2006, 2008, 2012-2017 Free
Software Foundation, Inc.
This is free software with ABSOLUTELY NO WARRANTY.
For details type `warranty'.
Geometry!
Let's say that you want to calculate the area of a circle.
Enter the radius of the circle: 20
The area of this circle is:
1256.63706143591729538400
[donnie@fedora ~]$
```

Tip

I cheated a bit here, by copying the value of Π from a website where it had already been calculated. If you'd rather calculate the value of Π yourself, you can do it with this formula:

```
pi=4*a(1)
```

The next example is a checkbook balancing program that I borrowed from the bc documentation page. Here's what it looks like:

```
scale=2
print "\nCheck book program\n!"
print "  Remember, deposits are negative transactions.\n"
print "  Exit by a 0 transaction.\n\n"
```

```
print "Initial balance? "; bal = read()
bal /= 1
print "\n"
while (1) {
  "current balance = "; bal
  "transaction? "; trans = read()
  if (trans == 0) break;
  bal -= trans
  bal /= 1
}
quit
```

Here, you see that the bc language has the same programming constructs that you've already seen in normal shell scripting. (In this case, you see a while loop.) The bc language implements them a bit differently, but that's okay. The next things to note are the scale=2 and the bal /= 1 lines. These two commands ensure that the program's output will always have two digits after the decimal point, even when you only enter an integer without any decimals. To show what I mean, open bc in interactive mode and type in these commands:

```
[donnie@fedora ~]$ bc
bc 1.07.1
Copyright 1991-1994, 1997, 1998, 2000, 2004, 2006, 2008, 2012-2017 Free
Software Foundation, Inc.
This is free software with ABSOLUTELY NO WARRANTY.
For details type `warranty'.
scale=2
bal=1000
print bal
1000
bal /= 1
print bal
1000.00
```

You see that before I invoked the bal /= 1 command, print bal only shows 1000, without any decimals. So, why does this work? Well, it's just that the bal /= 1 command is just a shorthand way of expressing a division by 1. In other words, it does the same thing that the bal=(bal/1) command does, except with less typing. In this case, we're dividing 1000 by 1, which still gives us 1000. But, because we set the scale to 2, printing any number that's a result of a math operation will now always show two decimal places.

The next thing to note in the program file is the bal -= trans line. The -= operator causes the balance to decrement by the amount of the financial transaction that's represented by trans. Now, I really don't know why the program's author did this, because it means that the user has to enter a positive number to reduce the balance, and a negative number to add to the balance.

Changing the line to bal += trans would make much more sense. That way a negative number would represent a debit, a positive number would represent a deposit, and all would be right with the world. Anyway, I digress.

Running the program looks like this:

```
[donnie@fedora ~]$ bc checkbook_bc
bc 1.07.1
Copyright 1991-1994, 1997, 1998, 2000, 2004, 2006, 2008, 2012-2017 Free
Software Foundation, Inc.
This is free software with ABSOLUTELY NO WARRANTY.
For details type `warranty'.
Check book program
!  Remember, deposits are negative transactions.
   Exit by a 0 transaction.
Initial balance? 1000
current balance = 1000.00
transaction?
```

Now, just enter your transactions, and then enter 0 to quit.

There's a lot more that you can do with bc program files, but I think you get the overall idea. Let's now look at using bc in normal shell scripts.

Using bc in Shell Scripts

The third and final way to use bc is to run bc commands from a normal shell environment. So, you can either run bc commands from the shell command-line, or place them into normal shell scripts. Here's an example:

```
[donnie@fedora ~]$ pi=$(echo "scale=10; 4*a(1)" | bc -l)
[donnie@fedora ~]$ echo $pi
3.1415926532
[donnie@fedora ~]$
```

Here, I'm using command substitution to assign a value to pi. Within the command substitution construct, I'm echoing a bc-style math formula into bc. The first thing you see is that I've set the scale to 10. The 4*a(1) means that I'm taking the arctangent of 1 and multiplying it by 4, which is one of the many formulas that you can use to approximate the value of pi (Π). (Remember that Π is an irrational number, which means that you will never find its exact value.)

Now, let's put this into the pi_bc.sh shell script, which looks like this:

```
#!/bin/bash
if [ -z $1 ]; then
        echo "Usage:"
        echo "./pi_bc.sh scale_value"
```

```
    else
            pi=$(echo "scale=$1; 4*a(1)" | bc -l)
            echo $pi
    fi
```

I've fancied things up a bit, by allowing you to specify your own scaling value when you invoke the script. You see that if you don't enter a scaling value, it will return a message that tells you to do so. Running the script looks like this:

```
[donnie@fedora ~]$ ./pi_bc.sh 20
3.14159265358979323844
[donnie@fedora ~]$
```

Of course, you can enter even larger scaling values if you'd like.

You can also use bc to create your own function libraries. For example, check out this baseconv.lib library file that I created in my /usr/local/lib/ directory:

```
        h2d() {
                h2dnum=$(echo "ibase=16; $input_num" | bc)
                }
        d2h() {
                d2hnum=$(echo "obase=16; $input_num" | bc)
                }
        o2h() {
                o2hnum=$(echo "obase=16; ibase=8; $input_num" | bc)
                }
        h2o() {
                h2onum=$(echo "obase=8; ibase=16; $input_num" | bc)
                }
```

The bc-func_demo.sh script that uses this library is too long to show here in its entirety. But, you can download it from the GitHub repository. For now, I'll just show you a few snippets and provide some explanation.

The top part of the script looks like this:

```
#!/bin/bash
. /usr/local/lib/baseconv.lib
until [ "$choice" = "q" ]; do
        echo "Choose your desired function from the following list: "
        echo "For hex to decimal, press \"1\"."
        echo "For decimal to hex, press \"2\"."
        echo "For octal to hex, press \"3\"."
        echo "For hex to octal, press \"4\"."
        echo "To quit, press \"q\"."
```

The first thing you see is that I'm sourcing the library file with the . /usr/local/lib/baseconv.lib command. After that, you see a construct that I've neglected to show you before. The until. .do construct will keep showing you a menu until you hit the *q* key. I mean, if you make any of the other choices, you'll be prompted to enter a number that you want to convert. When the conversion is done, the menu will pop right back up, and will stay there until you hit the *q*. The next bit of code is a case. .esac construct, which performs the task that you choose from the menu. Here's the first part of that:

```
read choice
        case $choice in
                1) echo "Enter the hex number that you would like to convert. "
                   read input_num
                   h2d
                   echo $h2dnum
                   echo
                   echo
                   ;;
```

Running the script looks like this:

```
[donnie@fedora ~]$ ./bc-func_demo.sh
Choose your desired function from the following list:
For hex to decimal, press "1".
For decimal to hex, press "2".
For octal to hex, press "3".
For hex to octal, press "4".
To quit, press "q".
2
Enter the decimal number that you would like to convert.
10
A
```

Below this, which is beyond the point where I can show you here, the menu re-appears, waiting for your next response.

Now, this does work, but it uses global variables to pass values from the functions back to the main script. I've already told you that this isn't the safest way of doing business, and that it's better to use a combination of local variables and command substitution. The modified library file is also too long to show here in its entirety, but here's a snippet:

```
        h2d() {
                local h2dnum=$(echo "ibase=16; $input_num" | bc)
                echo $h2dnum
                }
        d2h() {
                local d2hnum=$(echo "obase=16; $input_num" | bc)
```

```
        echo $d2hnum
        }
   o2h() {
        local o2hnum=$(echo "obase=16; ibase=8; $input_num" | bc)
        echo $o2hnum
        }
```

You can download this entire `baseconv_local.lib` file, as well as the `bc-func_local_demo.sh` script that uses it, from Github. The script is mostly the same as the previous one, except for the code in the `case. .esac` construct that invokes the functions. Here's a snippet:

```
read choice
      case $choice in
             1) echo "Enter the hex number that you would like to convert. "
                read input_num
                result=$(h2d)
                echo $result
                echo
                echo
                ;;
```

I've already explained this construction in *Chapter 10--Understanding Functions*, so I won't say anything more about it here.

The final example I'll show you uses one of the many text stream filters that you thought you'd never use. This involves using the `paste` command to help calculate the total combined market share for the various versions of the Windows operating system. To see what I mean, take a look at this `os_combined-ww-monthly-202209-202309-bar.csv` file that you can download from Github:

```
"OS","Market Share Perc. (Sept 2022 - Oct 2023)"
"Windows 11",17.21
"Windows 10",45.62
"Windows 7",3.5
"Windows 8.1",1.5
"Windows 8",1.3
"Windows XP",0.6
"OS X",17.66
"Unknown",6.55
"Chrome OS",3.15
"Linux",2.89
"Other",0.01
```

These market share stats are for the various desktop operating systems, as reported by the *Statcounter Global Stats* site.

Well, kind of. That's because many years ago when I first created this demo for a shell scripting class that I was teaching, the Statcounter people broke down the Windows share by its different versions, as you see here. Now though, they only list the overall Windows market share in this combined report, and break down the market share for the various versions of Windows in a separate Windows-only report. So, I had to doctor up this file a bit to recreate how the report used to be so that the demo can work. (But hey, whatever works, right?) The demo script for this is the report_os.sh script, which you can also download from Github.

The first echo command in the script is what adds the market share for all of the various versions of Windows together, in order to calculate the total combined market share for Windows. Here's how that looks:

```
echo "The market share for Windows is $(grep 'Win' $file | cut -d, -f2 | paste
-s -d+ | bc)%." > report_for_$(date +%F).txt
```

So, after I cut the second field out of all of the Windows lines, I use paste in serial mode, with the + as the paste field delimiter. I'll pipe all that into bc and then redirect the output to a text file with today's date in the filename.

The echo commands for the rest of the operating systems are more straightforward, since they don't require any math calculations. Here's the one for macOS:

```
echo "The market share for macOS is $(grep 'OS X' $file | cut -d, -f2)%." >>
report_for_$(date +%F).txt
```

Yes, I do know that Apple changed the name of their operating system to macOS. But, the Statcounter people still list it as OS X, so that's what I need for the search term in the script. Anyway, running the script looks like this:

```
[donnie@fedora ~]$ ./report_os.sh os_combined-ww-monthly-202209-202309-bar.csv
[donnie@fedora ~]$
```

The resultant report file looks like this:

```
The market share for Windows is 69.73%.
The market share for macOS is 17.66%.
The market share for Linux is 2.89%.
The market share for Chrome is 3.15%.
The market share for Unknown is 6.55%.
The market share for Others is 0.01%.
```

When I doctored the input file to have it list the various versions of Windows, I took care to ensure that the total Windows share still adds up to what it's supposed to be. So yes, as I'm writing this in October 2023, the total Windows market share really is 69.73%.

By the way, if you're interested in seeing more statistics about operating system usage, check out the Statcounter Global Stats site here: https://gs.statcounter.com/

I do believe that this about covers it for shell scripting math. Let's summarize and move on.

Summary

In this chapter, I've shown you several ways to perform math operations in bash, and even provided a couple of tips on how to ensure that your math scripts can run on non-bash shells. I started with the various methods of performing integer math, and then showed you various ways to use bc to perform floating point math. As I said before, you'd need to be a math expert to take full advantage of all of bc's features. But, even if you aren't, there's still a lot you can do with it. And, there are plenty of math tutorials online that can help. Just use your favorite search engine to find them.

In the next chapter, I'll show you how to use here documents. I'll see you there.

Questions

1. Which of the following methods would you used to perform integer math from the command-line?

    a.   echo 1+1

    b.   echo 1 + 1

    c.   echo $(bc 1+1)

    d.   expr 1+1

    e.   expr 1 + 1

2. You want to ensure that your shell script works on bash, as well as on non-bash shells. Which of the following commands could you use in your script?

    a.   echo $((1+2+3+4))

    b.   echo $[1+2+3+4]

    c.   echo $[[1+2+3+4]]

    d.   echo $(1+2+3+4)

3. You want to perform floating point math. Which of the following commands would you use?

    a.   bc

    b.   bc -f

    c.   bc -l

    d.   bc --float

4. You need to find the natural logarithm of 8. How would you do it?

    a. `expr log(8)`

    b. `echo [log(8)]`

    c. Use `l(8)` with `bc`

    d. Use `log(8)` with `bc`

5. Which of these commands would you use to find the approximate value of Π?

    a. `pi=$("scale=10; 4*a(1)" | bc -l)`

    b. `pi=$(echo "scale=10; 4*a(1)" | bc -l)`

    c. `pi=$(bc -l "scale=10; 4*a(1)" )`

    d. `pi=$(echo "scale=10; 4*arc(1)" | bc -l)`

Further Reading

- Bash Math Operations (Bash Arithmetic) Explained: `https://phoenixnap.com/kb/bash-math`
- bc Command Manual: `https://www.gnu.org/software/bc/manual/html_mono/bc.html`
- What is a good command-line calculator on Linux: `https://www.xmodulo.com/command-line-calculator-linux.html`
- Geometry Cheat Sheet: `https://s3-us-west-1.amazonaws.com/math-salamanders/Geometry/Geometry-Information-Pages/Geometry-Cheat-Sheets/geometry-cheat-sheet-4-2d-shapes-formulas.pdf`
- Mathematics LibreTexts: `https://math.libretexts.org/`
- Statcounter Global Stats: `https://gs.statcounter.com/`

Answers

1. e
2. a
3. c
4. c
5. b

Join our community on Discord!

Read this book alongside other users, Linux experts, and the author himself.

Ask questions, provide solutions to other readers, chat with the author via Ask Me Anything sessions, and much more. Scan the QR code or visit the link to join the community.

https://packt.link/SecNet

12

Automating Scripts with here Documents and expect

So, exactly where is *here*? Well, I suppose that it's just where I happen to be, or from your own perspective, wherever you happen to be. The bigger mystery, which nobody seems to have figured out, is why a very useful shell scripting construct has such a strange name.

A **here document**, which can also be called a **here script** or a **heredoc**, isn't really a document, and it has nothing to do with anyone's current location. But, as you shall soon see, it's extremely useful in a number of different ways, such as in automating your scripts.

The second automation method I'll show you is **expect**, which is a scripting environment with its own scripting language.

Topics in this chapter include:

- Using here Documents
- Automating responses with expect

All right, let's get ready to automate!

Technical Requirements

You can use any Linux virtual machine for this chapter. Also, as always, you can grab the script and text files from GitHub by doing:

```
git clone https://github.com/PacktPublishing/The-Ultimate-Linux-Shell-
Scripting-Guide.git
```

Using here Documents

A *here document* is a block of code that you place into a script to perform a certain task. Yeah, I know, I said the same thing about functions. But, *here documents* are completely different. They've been around since the early days of Unix, and can be used in various different programming languages.

Formatting note: The accepted Unix and Linux convention for writing out the term "here document" is to do so in all lower-case letters. That can get a bit confusing, though. So, to eliminate the confusion, I'll just italicize the term throughout the rest of this book, like this: *here document*.

Here documents work by providing another way to redirect input into a particular command. The code that performs this redirection is enclosed by a pair of **limit strings**, which look something like this:

```
command << _EOF_

. . .

Code to execute or data to display

. . .

_EOF_
```

The << sequence is a special type of redirector. It takes input from whatever code or text is between the two limit strings, which in this case are called _EOF_. It's traditional to use either _EOF_ or EOF as the limit strings, but you can actually use pretty much any text string you want, as long as they're the same at both the beginning and end of the code block, and also as long as they don't conflict with the names of any variables or functions. In fact, it can often help make the script more readable if you give descriptive names to your limit strings. (Some tutorials that you'll find use the term **token** instead of **limit string**, but it's still the same thing.)

Instead of using << as the redirector, you can also use <<-, like this:

```
command <<- _EOF_

. . .

Code to execute or data to display

. . .

_EOF_
```

Adding the dash prevents any leading tab characters from indenting any displayed text. (Leading spaces will still indent the text, but tabs won't. I'll explain more about this in just a bit.) This makes it so that you can indent the code in the script to make it more readable, without causing the output to be indented.

Here are some of the things that you can do with *here documents*:

- Display multi-line comments from a shell script.
- Create a simple look-up directory.
- Automate the creation of documents, such as web content files or reports.

Your *here documents* can work with either static or dynamic data. Let's start with the static ones, since they're the simplest.

Creating here Documents with Static Data

There may be times when you'll want your scripts to display some sort of a multi-line message when users invoke them. This message could be a help message, a copyright message, or a licensing message. You could do that with a series of echo commands, which would look something like this:

```
#!/bin/bash
echo "This software is released under the GNU GPL 3 license."
echo "Anyone who uses this software must respect the terms"
echo "of this license."
echo
echo "GNU GPL 3 is a license that aims to protect software freedom."
```

This works, but if you need to display a long message, typing in many individual echo commands can get a bit tedious. Using a *here document* to display the message can make things much easier. Here's how that looks in the here-doc1.sh script:

```
#!/bin/bash
cat << licensing
This software is released under the GNU GPL 3 license.
Anyone who uses this software must respect the terms
of this license.
GNU GPL 3 is a license that aims to protect software freedom.
licensing
```

In this case, I'm using licensing as the limit strings, instead of the more traditional _EOF_. This way, I can tell at a glance what the *here document* is doing for me. Here's what happens when I run the script:

```
[donnie@fedora ~]$ ./here-doc1.sh
This software is released under the GNU GPL 3 license.
Anyone who uses this software must respect the terms
of this license.
GNU GPL 3 is a license that aims to protect software freedom.
[donnie@fedora ~]$
```

As you see, the text that's between the two licensing strings gets redirected into the cat command, which then displays the text on screen.

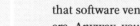 There may be times when you'll need to choose a license for any free-as-in-freedom software or shell scripts that you need to create. There are many free software licenses from which to choose, and you'll need to choose the one that best fits your needs. Basically though, you can classify the various licenses as either permissive or non-permissive. Permissive licenses, such as the MIT and BSD licenses, allow licensed code to be embedded into proprietary software, and don't require that the source code for the finished product be provided to the customer. (This is why Apple can include FreeBSD code in its proprietary OS X and macOS operating systems.) Non-permissive licenses, such as the various GNU Public Licenses, prohibit the use of licensed code in proprietary software, and require that software vendors make the source code of the finished product available to customers. Anyway, you can read all about the various free software licenses here: `https://opensource.org/licenses/`

By the way, MIT stands for Massachusetts Institute of Technology, BSD stands for Berkeley Software Distribution, and GNU is a recursive acronym that stands for GNU is not Unix.

There may be times when you'll want to indent the code in your *here documents* to make the script more readable. That's not the case with this `here-doc1.sh` script, but let's pretend that it is. Let's create the `here-doc1-tabs.sh` script, and make it look like this:

```
#!/bin/bash
cat << licensing
                This software is released under the GNU GPL 3 license.
        Anyone who uses this software must respect the terms
        of this license.
    GNU GPL 3 is a license that aims to protect software freedom.
licensing
```

This is the same as `here-doc1.sh`, except that I placed two tabs in front of the "This software. . ." line, one tab in front of the "Anyone who. . ." and ". . .of this license" lines, and three blank spaces in front of the "GNU GPL 3. . ." line. Watch what happens when I run this new script:

```
donnie@fedora:~$ ./here-doc1-tabs.sh
                This software is released under the GNU GPL 3 license.
        Anyone who uses this software must respect the terms
        of this license.
    GNU GPL 3 is a license that aims to protect software freedom.
donnie@fedora:~$
```

Now, let's say that we want to leave the tabs and the blank space in the script, but we don't want the tabs to show up in the output. All we have need to do is to change the `<<` to `<<-`, as you see here in the `here-doc1-tabs-dash.sh` script:

```
#!/bin/bash
cat <<- licensing
```

```
             This software is released under the GNU GPL 3 license.
        Anyone who uses this software must respect the terms
        of this license.
    GNU GPL 3 is a license that aims to protect software freedom.
licensing
```

Now, watch what happens when I run it:

```
donnie@fedora:~$ ./here-doc1-tabs-dash.sh
This software is released under the GNU GPL 3 license.
Anyone who uses this software must respect the terms
of this license.
    GNU GPL 3 is a license that aims to protect software freedom.
donnie@fedora:~$
```

This time, all of the lines that begin with tabs in the script now output text that is flush with the left margin. However, the line that begins with three blank spaces outputs text with three blank spaces.

 As I mentioned in the opening paragraph of this section, using `<<-` instead of `<<` prevents any leading tabs in your *here document* from showing up in the script's output. But, it allows any leading blank spaces to show up.

It's important to remember that you can't have any blank spaces in front of the closing limit string. If I were to insert a blank space in front of the closing `licensing` string in the `here-doc1.sh` script, I would get an error message that looks something like this:

```
[donnie@fedora ~]$ ./here-doc1.sh
./here-doc1.sh: line 10: warning: here-document at line 3 delimited by end-of-
file (wanted `licensing')
This software is released under the GNU GPL 3 license.
Anyone who uses this software must respect the terms
of this license.
GNU GPL 3 is a license that aims to protect software freedom.
 licensing
[donnie@fedora ~]$
```

Of course, this isn't what you want.

This `here-doc1.sh` script isn't very useful as-is, because the only thing it does is display a message. So normally, you'd place the rest of your code after the *here document*. One cool trick you can do is to place a `sleep` command and a `clear` command immediately after the *here document*, so that the opening message will display for a specified number of seconds before the main part of the script begins to execute.

Also, you're not limited to using this type of *here document* at the beginning of the script. You can place one anywhere in the script where you might need to impart some sort of information to a user.

Next, let's create a simple look-up directory with a list of phone numbers. Here's the `here-doc2.sh` script that does that:

```
#!/bin/bash
grep $1 <<directory
lionel          555-1234
maggie          555-2344
katelyn         555-4555
cleopatra       555-4818
vicky           555-1919
charlie         555-2020
frank           555-2190
goldie          555-8340
directory
exit
```

In this script, I'm passing a name as a positional parameter to the grep command. The phone directory entries are between the two `directory` limit strings. Note that in this script, I didn't place a blank space between the `<<` and the first limit string, as I did in the previous example. This just shows you that the blank space is optional, and that either way works. Anyway, here's what happens when I look up Lionel's phone number:

```
[donnie@fedora ~]$ ./here-doc2.sh lionel
lionel          555-1234
[donnie@fedora ~]$
```

If your *here document* includes any metacharacters that cause the shell to take some sort of action, you'll need to escape them with a backslash, as you see here in the `here-doc3.sh` script:

```
#!/bin/bash
grep $1 <<donations
lionel          \$5.00
maggie          \$2.50
katelyn         \$10.00
cleopatra       \$7.35
vicky           \$20.00
charlie         \$3.00
frank           \$8.25
goldie          \$9.05
donations
exit
```

Surrounding strings that contain special characters with quotes won't work, because *here documents* treat all quote symbols as literal characters.

This method of dealing with special characters works, but there's an easier way. Just place a backslash in front of the limit string, like this:

```
#!/bin/bash
grep $1 <<\donations
lionel          $5.00
maggie          $2.50
katelyn         $10.00
cleopatra       $7.35
vicky           $20.00
charlie         $3.00
frank           $8.25
goldie          $9.05
donations
exit
```

You can also surround the limit string with a pair of single quotes, like this:

```
#!/bin/bash
grep $1 <<'donations'
lionel          $5.00
maggie          $2.50
katelyn         $10.00
cleopatra       $7.35
vicky           $20.00
charlie         $3.00
frank           $8.25
goldie          $9.05
donations
exit
```

Although these latter two methods work well and are easier than having to escape every special character individually, they can mess you up if you need to use a $ to obtain the value of a variable. That's because everything will get treated as a literal string, even if you don't want that. To see how that works, let's look at the here-doc3-wrong.sh script:

```
#!/bin/bash
grep $1 <<\donations
lionel          $5.00
maggie          $2.50
katelyn         $10.00
```

```
cleopatra        $7.35
vicky            $20.00
charlie          $3.00
frank            $8.25
goldie           $9.05
$1
donations
exit
```

You see that I've placed a backslash in front of the opening donations limit string in order to escape all of the $ metacharacters. I've also placed a $1 on a line by itself, just before the closing donations limit string. What I want to happen is for the value of the $1 positional parameter to print out at the end of the output. But, watch what happens when I run this:

```
donnie@fedora:~$ ./here-doc3-wrong.sh lionel
lionel            $5.00
donnie@fedora:~$
```

Now, let's remove the backslash from in front of the opening limit string, and escape all of the $ metacharacters individually, except for the one that's in the positional parameter. This script should now look like this:

```
#!/bin/bash
grep $1 <<donations
lionel           \$5.00
maggie           \$2.50
katelyn          \$10.00
cleopatra        \$7.35
vicky            \$20.00
charlie          \$3.00
frank            \$8.25
goldie           \$9.05
$1
donations
exit
```

When I run the script now, the value of the $1 at the bottom should print out, like this:

```
donnie@fedora:~$ ./here-doc3-wrong.sh lionel
lionel            $5.00
lionel
donnie@fedora:~$
```

The lesson here is that even though some of our programming shortcuts can be very handy, it might not always be appropriate to use them.

That pretty much covers the static angle. Now, let's get dynamic.

Creating here documents with Dynamic Data

In addition to including normal data in *here documents*, you can also include the programming constructs and commands that you'd use normally. Then, just redirect the output into a dynamically-generated document. Here's the `here-doc4.sh` script, which shows a simple example of redirecting output into a `.html` file:

```
#!/bin/bash
title="System Information for $HOSTNAME"
current_date=$(date +%F)
cat <<- _system-info_ > sysinfo.html
<title>
$title
</title>
<body>
$(uname -opr) <br>
Updated on:  $current_date
</body>
_system-info_
```

To prove that it works, just open the resultant file in a web browser. The web page should look something like this:

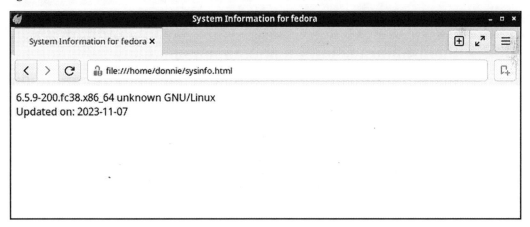

Figure 12.1: The web page that was generated by the here-doc4.sh script

Of course, I'm keeping things simple here by creating a very simple document with only a few simple HTML tags to format it. But, if you're clever with HTML coding, you can make the document as fancy as you want.

In case you're wondering, HTML stands for **Hypertext Markup Language.** Long ago, when the public Internet was brand new and I still had a full head of hair, the only way to create websites was to hand-code them in HTML. (Ah, yes. Those were the days.)

You can also create documents in other formats. For example, if you want to create a .pdf document, there are a couple of ways to do that. The simplest way is to install the appropriate pandoc packages from either your Linux or FreeBSD distro's repository. (It's also available for macOS, but you'll need to download the installer package from the Pandoc website.) The slight catch with this is that you'll also need to install a **PDF engine**, and some PDF engines aren't available for all distros. Your best bet is to stick with the **pdflatex engine**, because it's available for pretty much all Linux distros, as well as for FreeBSD and macOS. (Sadly, there are no pandoc or PDF engine packages available for OpenIndiana.) On your Fedora virtual machine, install pandoc and the pdflatex engine with this simple command:

```
[donnie@fedora ~]$ sudo dnf install pandoc-pdf
```

This same command will also install pandoc on Red Hat Enterprise Linux-type distros, but you'll first need to install the EPEL repository. On AlmaLinux and Rocky Linux, install EPEL like this:

```
[donnie@rocky ~]$ sudo dnf install epel-release
```

On Debian or Ubuntu-type distros, just do:

```
donnie@ubuntu2204:~$ sudo apt install pandoc texlive-latex-recommended
```

On FreeBSD do:

```
donnie@freebsd-1:~ $ sudo pkg install hs-pandoc texlive-full
```

 Note that for FreeBSD, I'm assuming that you've already installed the sudo package, added yourself to the wheel group, and have configured visudo. If you haven't, you can just log in as the root user for now, in order to perform the installation. Also, if you haven't done so already, be sure to install the bash package, and create a symbolic link to bash in the /bin/ directory, like this:

```
donnie@freebsd-1:~ $ sudo ln -s /usr/local/bin/bash /bin/bash
```

The here-doc scripts that I've shown you so far will work on the /bin/sh shell that FreeBSD uses by default, but I'll soon be showing you a script that will require actual bash.

For macOS, you'll need to download the Pandoc and MacTeX installers from their respective websites.

If you're running OpenIndiana, you're out of luck, because there are no pandoc or pdf engine packages available for it. That's okay though, because as you'll see in a few moments, I've made the upcoming demo script so that it will still run on it.

In any case, the installation of pandoc and the pdf engine packages takes a while, because a lot of dependencies also need to be installed. So, you might as well go grab your favorite beverage while you're waiting.

Once you have pandoc installed, on everything except for OpenIndiana, add the following lines to the end of your here-doc4.sh script:

```
pandoc -o sysinfo.pdf sysinfo.html
rm sysinfo.html
```

Now when you run the here-doc4.sh script, you'll end up with the sysinfo.pdf file as the result. You can either open the file in your favorite document viewer, or add a line of code to have the file automatically print out. Assuming that you've installed the appropriate printer drivers and have set a default printer, the command that you would add to the end of the script to do this would be:

```
lpr sysinfo.pdf
```

Tip

I showed you how to set up a default printer and use lpr in *Chapter 7, Text Stream Filters - Part 2*.

The reason I'm using HTML in this *here document* example is simply because HTML is so easy. If you're clever with any other document markup language, such as Postscript, Markdown, Troff or LaTeX, feel free to use one of them in place of HTML. In all cases, you can convert the resultant file to a .pdf file, if that's what you need. On the other hand, if you don't need anything this fancy, you could omit all markup language tags, and just save your output to a plain-text file. Then, use the appropriate text stream filters, such as fmt and pr, to prepare the file for print out. The possibilities are only limited by your own imagination.

Now that we've covered the basics, let's look at something that's a bit more complex.

Using Functions in here Documents

For this section, I created the sysinfo.lib file, which you can download from Github. Then, copy it to your /usr/local/lib/ directory. Finally, download the system-info.sh script from Github. I can't show you either the library file or the shell script in their entirety here, but I can show you some snippets and provide some explanation.

In this demo, you'll see what I had to do to make this script work on Linux, FreeBSD, macOS, and OpenIndiana.

The first two functions in the library, the show_uptime() and drive_space() functions, are quite easy. Each of them executes just one simple system information command and then adds some HTML tags, as you see here:

```
show_uptime() {
            echo "<h2>System uptime</h2>"
```

```
            echo "<pre>"
            uptime
            echo "</pre>"
    }
    drive_space() {
        echo "<h2>Filesystem space</h2>"
        echo "<pre>"
        df -P
        echo "</pre>"

    }
```

I used df -P in the drive_space() function so that the output would format properly on macOS. (The -P isn't needed for Linux, FreeBSD, or OpenIndiana, but it doesn't hurt anything to have it.)

Now, take a look at the home_space() function:

```
home_space() {
            echo "<h2>Home directory space by user</h2>"
            echo "<pre>"
            echo "Bytes Directory"
            if [ $(uname) = SunOS ]; then
                    du -sh /export/home/* | sort -nr
            elif [ $(uname) = Darwin ]; then
                    du -sh /Users/* | sort -nr
            else
                    du -sh /home/* | sort -nr
            fi
            echo "</pre>"

    }
```

This function uses the du utility to report the amount of drive space that each user's home directory is using. The slight problem is that OpenIndiana and macOS don't have users' home directories in the /home/ directory, as Linux and FreeBSD do. So, I included code that would determine where du is to look, as determined by the operating system.

Next are the open_files() and open_files_root() functions, which report the number of files that the apache and root users have open. Both functions are the same except for the specified user, so I'll just show you one of them here:

```
open_files_root() {
            echo "<h2>Number of open files for root</h2>"
            echo "<pre>"
            lsof -u root | wc -l
            echo "</pre>"

    }
```

You see that it's very simple, and just pipes the lsof -u output into wc -1 to count the number of open files for the specified user.

The next function is open_files_users(), which is a bit more complex. I once again need to take the difference in home directory locations into account, which you see here in the first half of the function:

```
open_files_users() {
        echo "<h2> Number of open files for normal users</h2>"
        if [ $(uname) = SunOS ]; then
            cd /export/home
        elif [ $(uname) = Darwin ]; then
            cd /Users
        else
            cd /home
        fi
```

The second half of the function is a *for* loop that reads the names of the users' home directories, and then uses those names in the lsof commands. But, there's another wrinkle here that we need to iron out. It's that if your Linux machine has the /home/ directory mounted on its own partition, and the partition is formatted with either the ext3 or ext4 filesystem, there will be a lost+found directory that's not a user's home directory. On macOS, you'll see a Shared directory that's also not a user's home directory. If you try to use either of these two directory names as an argument for lsof, you'll receive an error. So, I had to add some code to exclude those two directory names from being used, as you see here:

```
for user in *
        do
        if [[ $user != "lost+found" ]] && [[ $user != "Shared" ]]; then
                echo "There are $(lsof -u $(id -u $user) | wc -1) open files
for $user. "
                echo "<br>"
        fi
        done
        cd
    }
```

You see that I'm using the && sequence as an *and* operator so that I can place both test conditions into just one if..then construct. One reference that I found states that the *and* (&&) and *or* (||) operators work better with the [[..]] test construct than they do with the [..] test construct. However, I just tested the function both ways, and both work for me here. I've also shown you something that I don't remember having shown you before. That is, you can nest one command substitution construct within another command substitution construct, as you see in the first echo line.

Finally, there's the `system_info()` function, which again will work differently on different operating systems. That's because system information is in the `/etc/os-release` file on Linux and FreeBSD and in the `/etc/release` file on OpenIndiana. On macOS, there's no kind of release file at all, so I had to use another method. Anyway, here's the top portion of the function, which is for Linux and FreeBSD:

```
system_info() {
            # Find any release files in /etc
            if [ -f /etc/os-release ]; then
                    os=$(grep "PRETTY_NAME" /etc/os-release)
                    echo "<h2>System release info</h2>"
                    echo "<pre>"
                    echo "${os:12}"
                    echo "<br>"
                    uname -orp
                    echo "</pre>"
```

If the `/etc/os-release` file is present, the value of the os variable will be the `PRETTY_NAME` line from that file. The echo `"${os:12}"` line strips off the `PRETTY_NAME` part, so that only the actual version name of the Linux or FreeBSD distro is left. I then used the `uname -orp` command to show the system information that I want everyone to see. (I'll let you look in the uname man page to see what all of the option switches are doing.)

The next part of the function is for OpenIndiana, as you see here:

```
elif [ $(uname) = SunOS ]; then
                    echo "<h2>System release info</h2>"
                    echo "<pre>"
                    head -1 /etc/release
                    echo "<br>"
                    uname -orp
                    echo "</pre>"
```

The `/etc/release` file on OpenIndiana isn't the same as the `/etc/os-release` file on Linux and FreeBSD. So, I used the `head -1` command to read the first line of the file, which contains the version name of the distro.

The final portion of this function is for OS X/macOS, as you see here:

```
elif [ $(uname) = Darwin ]; then
                    echo "<h2>System release info</h2>"
                    echo "<pre>"
                    sw_vers
                    echo "<br>"
                    uname -sprm
                    echo "</pre>"
```

```
else
            echo "Unknown operating system"
}
```

Since there's no release file of any kind, I used the `sw_vers` command instead, which is only available on OS X and macOS. The output from this command looks like this:

```
Donald-Tevaults-Mac-Pro:~ donnie$ sw_vers
ProductName:    Mac OS X
ProductVersion: 10.14.6
BuildVersion:   18G9323
Donald-Tevaults-Mac-Pro:~
```

And yes, that is a very old version of the Mac operating system. But, the machine is a mid-2010 model Mac Pro, and this is the newest version that it will run. (Well, it can run a more recent version, but I'll have to perform some unnatural acts that aren't authorized by Apple in order to do it. This involves installing the OpenCore Legacy Patcher, which will modify the Mac's bootloader so that you can install a newer version of macOS. Be aware though that things can go wrong with this, which could render your Mac unbootable. Trust me, I know.)

I also had to use a different combination of option switches for uname, because macOS uses a different implementation of uname. (Again, look at the man page for uname on your Mac machine to see what the option switches are doing.)

That's it for the function library file. Now, we need to look at the `system_info.sh` script that uses this library. Here's the top part:

```
#!/bin/bash
# sysinfo_page - A script to produce an HTML file
. /usr/local/lib/sysinfo.lib
title="System Information for $HOSTNAME"
right_now=$(date +"%x %r %Z")
time_stamp="Updated on $right_now by $USER"
```

The shebang line, which we first talked about in *Chapter 8, Basic Shell Script Construction*, has to be #!/bin/bash, because some of the alternate shells that are referenced by #!/bin/sh aren't compatible with some of the programming constructs that I need to use. So, if you're running this script on either Alpine Linux or FreeBSD, you'll need to install bash.

The rest of this top portion just reads in the function library and sets up the variables that I'll use in the rest of the script. So, there's nothing hard there.

The next portion consists of the *here document*, which inserts the proper HTML tags and invokes several functions, as you see here:

```
cat <<- _system-info_ > sysinfo.html
    <html>
```

```
    <head>
        <title>
. . .
. . .
    $(home_space)
    $(open_files_root)
    $(open_files_users)
    </body>
    </html>
_system-info_
```

So again, there's nothing hard here.

The final portion of the script converts the .html output file to a .pdf file, if the pandoc package is installed. If it's not, then it will just leave the .html file alone. Here's how that looks:

```
if [[ -f /usr/local/bin/pandoc ]] || [[ -f /usr/bin/pandoc ]]; then
        pandoc -o sysinfo.pdf sysinfo.html
        rm sysinfo.html
fi
exit
```

As much as I'd like to always have a .pdf file, that's not possible on OpenIndiana. As I've mentioned before, pandoc isn't in the OpenIndiana repository. The only other .pdf creation tool I've seen for OpenIndiana is groff, but that involves using a whole different markup language.

When you run this script, you'll need to use your sudo privileges in order to access information about other users. Also, don't be alarmed if you get error messages about directories that the script can't access, because that happens even with sudo. For example, here on my Fedora workstation, the script can't access the pCloud directory that's in my home directory, because it's a mount point for a remote drive.

This is all I'll say about *here documents* for now. But, in *Chapter 20, Shell Script Portability*, I'll show you more about them, and will also show you more ways to make scripts run across a variety of operating systems and shells. For now though, let's look at what to expect next.

Automating Responses with expect

There may be times when you'll need to run a script that stops multiple times to prompt you for some sort of input. That can get a bit tedious after a while, especially if you need to run the script multiple times on multiple servers or workstations. Wouldn't it be nice to automate the responses? Well, with all due respect, you can with expect.

So, what is expect? Well, it's a programming environment, similar to what you have with bash. If you have an interactive shell script that *expects* certain responses, you can use expect to automatically send the correct responses. Let's begin with the simplest of examples. First, create the interactive_script. sh script, like so:

```
#!/bin/bash
echo "Hello. What is your name?"
read $reply
echo "What's your favorite operating system?"
read $reply
echo "How many cats to you have?"
read $reply
echo "How many dogs do you have?"
read $reply
```

When you run this script, it will pause at each read `$reply` command so that you can type in a response. Of course, that's not a big deal for this simple script. But now, pretend that you've written some sort of software testing script that's long and complex, and that requires the software tester to constantly enter responses. Unless you enjoy pain, and I doubt that you do, you probably don't want to be glued to your workstation, constantly entering responses for those long tests. So, your best bet is to automate the process, and your best bet for that is to use `expect`. You should find it already installed on a Mac, but for everything else you'll have to install it yourself.

Verify whether it's installed by doing:

```
which expect
```

If it's not installed, it should be in your distro's repository as the expect package. On FreeBSD, you'll need to take the additional step of creating a symbolic link, so that you won't have to modify your scripts to run on FreeBSD. Do it like this:

```
donnie@freebsd-1:~ $ sudo ln -s /usr/local/bin/expect /bin/expect
donnie@freebsd-1:~ $
```

Now that it's installed, create the `interactive_script.exp` companion script. The easiest way to do that is to use autoexpect, like this:

```
[donnie@fedora ~]$ autoexpect -f interactive_script.exp ./interactive_script.sh
autoexpect started, file is script.exp
Hello. What is your name?
Donnie
What's your favorite operating system?
Linux
How many cats do you have?
1
How many dogs do you have?
0
autoexpect done, file is script.exp
[donnie@fedora ~]$
```

As you see, autoexpect runs the original `interactive_script.sh` script, and prompts you for responses. The responses get saved to the `interactive_script.exp` script that you specified with the -f option. Note that if the original script is in your home directory, you'll need to precede its name with a ./ so that autoexpect can find it. The entire `interactive_script.exp` script is too long to show, so I'll show you some snippets, along with some explanation.

The first thing to note is that expect scripts have their own shebang line, which looks like this:

```
#!/bin/expect -f
```

The -f means that responses will be read from this file.

The next thing I want to show you is the spawn command, which looks like this:

```
spawn ./interactive_script.sh
```

When I run the expect script, it will automatically start the original shell script.

Next, let's look at how the expect script provides responses:

```
expect -exact "Hello. What is your name?\r
"
send -- "Donnie\r"
expect -exact "Donnie\r
What's your favorite operating system?\r
"
send -- "Linux\r"
expect -exact "Linux\r
How many cats to you have?\r
"
send -- "1\r"
expect -exact "1\r
How many dogs do you have?\r
"
send -- "0\r"
```

The expect commands duplicate the questions from the original shell script. By including the -exact option, the questions must be identical to the originals. The first expect command only asks for my name, and all of the others both send back the response and then pull in the next question. The \r at the end of each line provides a carriage return, so that the next response or question will show on a new line. (Note that this isn't the Windows-type of carriage return that can cause so much trouble in text files or configuration files.)

The very last line of the expect script looks like this:

```
expect eof
```

As you might expect, this indicates the End of File.

Another cool thing about autoexpect is that it automatically sets the executable permission on the script files that it generates. So, you won't have to do that yourself. Now, here's what happens when I run this expect script:

```
[donnie@fedora ~]$ ./interactive_script.exp
spawn ./interactive_script.sh
Hello. What is your name?
Donnie
What's your favorite operating system?
Linux
How many cats to you have?
1
How many dogs do you have?
0
[donnie@fedora ~]$
```

All of the questions got answered automatically, without me having to interact with the script at all.

Now, as cool as autoexpect is, there are some drawbacks. First, it only comes with the expect packages that are in the repositories for the various Linux distros. For some strange reason, it's not available for FreeBSD, OpenIndiana, or macOS. So, if you ever need to create an expect script for any of those operating systems, your best bet is to create it on a Linux machine, and then transfer it over to the non-Linux machine. Secondly, if you use it with a software installation script that uses curl or wget to download the software, the output from curl or wget that shows the status of the download will become part of the expect script. You'll need to remove all of that from the expect script by hand so that the script will work correctly. And lastly, you can't expect autoexpect to do everything. Sometimes, you'll just need to hand-code the expect scripts yourself.

Security Implications with expect

There are lots of ways to use expect, but in my own opinion, it's most useful for the automation of software testing or installation. Most other tutorials you'll find show you how to automate either ssh login sessions or scp file transfers, but you need to be careful if you use expect for anything like that. The problem is that the password of the destination machine will get stored in plain-text format in the expect script, which is also plain text. Making things even worse, is that some of these tutorials have you access the root user account of the destination machine like this.

Now, my own general rule is to never enable the root user account when setting up a server, as long as the operating system installer gives me that choice. When setting up something like FreeBSD, where that isn't a choice, I like to install and configure sudo as my first post-installation step, and then disable the root account. However, there are times when it's necessary to enable the root user account, as well as to use scp to transfer files to the root user's account. If that is ever necessary, it's more secure to disable password authentication on the server, and instead use key-based authentication.

Even then, I only feel comfortable accessing the root user account from within a tightly-controlled local network, rather than from across the Internet. Having said all this, if you still ever find it necessary to store plain-text ssh passwords in an expect script, be sure to store the script in a location that only you or trusted members of your team can access. (But hopefully though, you'll find another way to do things that won't require placing passwords into the expect scripts.)

The only other thing I'll say about expect is that it is a vast topic, and at least one entire book has been written about it. (I'll leave a link for it in the *Further Reading* section for anyone who might be interested.)

Okay, let's wrap this chapter up and move on.

Summary

In this chapter, I've shown you some cool tricks to help automate your scripts. I first showed you *here documents*, and how to use them in a few different ways. Then, I showed you expect, which is a whole scripting language unto itself. I showed you some ways to use expect, and then talked about some of its security implications.

In the next chapter, I'll show you some scripting tricks for ImageMagick. I'll see you there.

Questions

1. What is a here document?

    a. It shows your current location.

    b. It's a block of code for a specific purpose.

    c. It's a type of executable script.

    d. It's a block of static data.

2. Which of the following statements is true?

    a. A here document uses its own scripting language.

    b. A here document can only be used in bash scripts.

    c. A here document can be used with a variety of programming and scripting languages.

    d. A here document can only be used to display comments or other static data.

3. How do you define a here document?

    a. Place #!/bin/here in the script as the shebang line.

    b. Surround the entire here document with a pair of double quotes.

    c. Surround the entire here document with a pair of single quote.

    d. Surround the entire *here document* with a pair of limit strings.

4. Which of the following statements is true?

    a. You can use `autoexpect` for any situation, and then use the resultant `expect` scripts without any editing.

    b. The `expect` scripts that `autoexpect` creates might need to be hand-edited to make them work correctly.

    c. You can use `autoexpect` on any operating system, including Linux, FreeBSD, macOS, and OpenIndiana.

    d. You should never use `autoexpect` for anything.

5. What is one implication of using `expect`?

    a. When using `expect` to automate `ssh` logins or `scp` transfers, the password for the destination server will be stored in plain-text within the `expect` script.

    b. There are no implications.

    c. It's not very efficient.

    d. It's too hard to create an expect script.

Further Reading

- How to Use "Here Documents" in Bash on Linux: `https://www.howtogeek.com/719058/how-to-use-here-documents-in-bash-on-linux/`

- How to Create TXT Template Scripts in BASH: `https://www.maketecheasier.com/create-txt-template-scripts-bash/`

- Here Documents: `https://tldp.org/LDP/abs/html/here-docs.html`

- How to Use Heredoc in Shell Scripting: `https://www.tecmint.com/use-heredoc-in-shell-scripting/`

- Writing Shell Scripts-Lesson 3: Here scripts: `http://linuxcommand.org/lc3_wss0030.php`

- How to Use Here Document (heredoc) in Linux Shell Script: `https://linuxtldr.com/heredoc/`

- Linux expect Command with Examples: `https://phoenixnap.com/kb/linux-expect`

- Automate Input to Linux Scripts with the expect Command: `https://www.howtogeek.com/devops/automate-inputs-to-linux-scripts-with-the-expect-command/`

- Expect Command in Linux with Examples: `https://www.geeksforgeeks.org/expect-command-in-linux-with-examples/`

- Expect Command and How to Automate Shell Scripts like Magic: `https://likegeeks.com/expect-command/`

- Automating Responses to Scripts on Linux Using expect and autoexpect: `https://www.networkworld.com/article/969513/automating-responses-to-scripts-on-linux-using-expect-and-autoexpect.html`

- Exploring Expect: `https://amzn.to/3MSNqAV`

Answers

1. b
2. c
3. d
4. b
5. a

Join our community on Discord!

Read this book alongside other users, Linux experts, and the author himself.

Ask questions, provide solutions to other readers, chat with the author via Ask Me Anything sessions, and much more. Scan the QR code or visit the link to join the community.

`https://packt.link/SecNet`

13

Scripting with ImageMagick

ImageMagick is an awesome package of graphics manipulation tools. You can use these tools to perform many of the same jobs that you'd perform with GUI-type tools such as The GIMP and Adobe Photoshop. But, the ImageMagick tools are command-line tools, which allows you to use them in scripts in order to automate many types of jobs. These scripts can either be normal shell scripts, or scripts that use the ImageMagick scripting environment.

Topics in this chapter include:

- Converting non-standard filename extensions
- Installing ImageMagick
- Displaying images
- Viewing image properties
- Resizing and customizing images
- Batch-processing image files
- Using Fred's ImageMagick scripts

If you're ready, let's get started.

Technical Requirements

For this chapter, I'm using a desktop implementation of Fedora, because it comes with the newest version of ImageMagick. Debian 12 comes with an older version, but the commands and techniques that I present here also work on it.

Also, as always, you can download the scripts for this chapter by doing:

```
git clone https://github.com/PacktPublishing/The-Ultimate-Linux-Shell-
Scripting-Guide.git
```

Converting Non-standard Filename Extensions

Before I even get to ImageMagick, I need to address something that's a bit of a bugaboo with me. It's that Linux and Unix operating systems are all case-sensitive, while other operating systems aren't. So on Linux and Unix, `somegraphic.png` and `somegraphic.PNG` are two different files, while on Windows they both represent the same file. On Linux and Unix, it's more proper to use lower-case letters in filename extensions. If you're running a desktop implementation of either Linux or Unix, you might find that your GUI file manager won't automatically open your graphics files in the graphics file viewer if the filename extensions for those files consist of upper-case letters. This wouldn't be that big of a problem, except for the fact that certain Windows utilities and certain digital cameras always create graphics files with all upper-case letters in their filenames. Also, if you create a script to perform a batch operation on a whole directory full of images, having some filename extensions in upper-case letters and some in lower-case letters will mess you up. So, you'll want to rename those files to match the Linux/Unix convention. If you have a whole directory full of files to convert, you'll want to automate the process. So, check out this nifty `rename_extension.sh` script that can help you out:

```bash
#!/bin/bash
for file in *.JPG; do
        mv -- "$file" "${file%.JPG}.jpg"
done
```

As you see, this is just a simple `for` loop that searches for all files in the current directory that have the `.JPG` filename extension. The real magic is performed by the `mv` command that's within the loop. (Remember that `mv` can be used to rename files and directories, as well as to move them to other locations.) The `--` sequence marks the end of the `mv` options list, and prevents problems with any files with filenames that begin with a `-`. At the end of the line, you see a variable expansion construct that replaces `.JPG` with `.jpg` for all filenames. And here, I need to add a word of caution.

Always be sure that your variable substitution constructs are built with a pair of curly braces, and not with a pair of parentheses. If you accidentally use parentheses instead of curly braces, the script will delete all of the files it finds, which probably isn't what you want.

Anyway, let's test the script to see what happens. Here are the contents of my graphics directory before I run the script:

```
[donnie@fedora script_test]$ ls
rename_extension2.sh  S1180001.JPG  S1340001.JPG  S1340003.JPG
rename_extension.sh   S1180002.JPG  S1340002.JPG
[donnie@fedora script_test]$
```

Now, let's run the script and then view the directory contents:

```
[donnie@fedora script_test]$ ./rename_extension.sh
[donnie@fedora script_test]$ ls
```

```
rename_extension2.sh   S1180001.jpg   S1340001.jpg   S1340003.jpg
rename_extension.sh    S1180002.jpg   S1340002.jpg
[donnie@fedora script_test]$
```

If you don't want to deal with variable expansion or if you're using a shell that doesn't support it, you can instead use the basename utility, as you see here in the rename_extension2.sh script:

```
#!/bin/bash
for file in *.JPG; do
        mv -- $file "$(basename -- "$file" .JPG).jpg"
done
```

The basename utility works by stripping the directory path from a filename and, if specified, the filename extension as well. Here's how it works when I just want to strip away the directory path:

```
[donnie@fedora ~]$ basename Pictures/script_test/rename_extension.sh
rename_extension.sh
[donnie@fedora ~]$
```

And, here's how it works when I want to strip away both the directory path and the filename extension:

```
[donnie@fedora ~]$ basename Pictures/script_test/rename_extension.sh .sh
rename_extension
[donnie@fedora ~]$
```

Of course, this works with any filename extension, as you see here:

```
[donnie@fedora ~]$ basename Pictures/script_test/S1340001.JPG .JPG
S1340001
[donnie@fedora ~]$
```

For me, .JPG and .MP4 files are the biggest problems, because my little Panasonic camcorder/camera saves its files with these naming formats. If you ever need to work with screenshots from a Windows machine, you'll be working with .PNG files. It's an easy matter to adapt either of the two scripts that I've just shown you to convert any of these filename extensions to all lower-case letters.

Now, with these preliminaries out of the way, let's look at ImageMagick.

Installing ImageMagick

You'll find ImageMagick in the repositories of OpenIndiana and pretty much every Linux distro. You'll also find it in the repositories of FreeBSD and its desktop-oriented derivatives, such as GhostBSD and MidnightBSD. With only a couple of slight caveats, installation is quick and easy.

The first caveat concerns Debian. As you may already know, Debian tends to march to the beat of a different drummer, and is quite slow about getting up-to-date packages in its repositories.

So, if you're installing ImageMagick on Debian 12 or older, you'll get the older ImageMagick 6, rather than the current ImageMagick 7. (You might get version 7 if you switch to either Debian Testing or Debian Unstable, but I haven't confirmed that since I prefer to stick with the stable branch.)

The other caveat is that there's no consistency in how the various distros name the ImageMagick package. For example, the package name is `ImageMagick` on Fedora, `imagemagick` on Debian, OpenIndiana, and Alpine Linux, and `ImageMagick7` on FreeBSD and its desktop derivatives. In all cases though, just install it using your distro's normal package management tool.

If you're running either macOS or Windows, you'll find directions on how to install ImageMagick on them at the official ImageMagick website. (You'll find the link to the ImageMagick website in the *Further Reading* section.)

Now that you have ImageMagick installed, let's look at what we can do with it.

Displaying Images

To display an image, use the `display` command, like this:

```
donnie@fedora script_test]$ display S1180001.jpg
```

I know, you're wondering why I'm devoting a whole section of this chapter to just tell you that. Hang on, though, because there's more.

Once you've opened the image, you can click either the right or the left mouse button to bring up a menu. The left mouse button brings up a menu that performs many of the image manipulation functions that you can do from the command-line. Here's how it looks:

Figure 13.1: The ImageMagick left-click menu

The right-click menu is much simpler, as you see here:

Figure 13.2: The ImageMagick right-click menu

One thing you can do with the right-click menu is to display information about the image, which will look something like this:

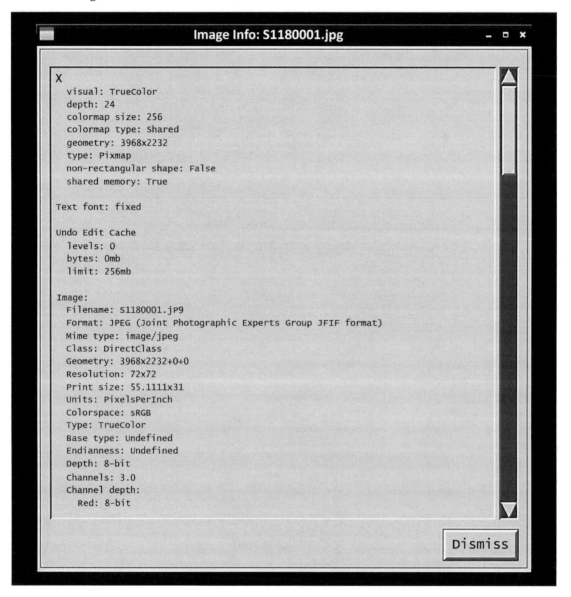

Figure 13.3: Displaying image information from the right-click menu

You can learn how to use these menus by just playing around with them to see what everything does. But, as cool as all this is, it still doesn't help us with shell scripting. So, we still need to see what we can do with ImageMagick from the command-line.

Viewing Image Properties

Use the `identify` command to view the properties of an image, like this:

```
[donnie@fedora script_test]$ identify S1180001.jpg
S1180001.jpg JPEG 3968x2232 3968x2232+0+0 8-bit sRGB 1.90756MiB 0.000u 0:00.000
[donnie@fedora script_test]$
```

To see more information, use the -verbose option, like this:

```
[donnie@fedora script_test]$ identify -verbose S1180001.jpg
Image:
  Filename: S1180001.jpg
  Permissions: rw-r--r--
  Format: JPEG (Joint Photographic Experts Group JFIF format)
  Mime type: image/jpeg
. . .
. . .
  Number pixels: 8.85658M
  Pixel cache type: Memory
  Pixels per second: 55.2201MP
  User time: 0.160u
  Elapsed time: 0:01.160
  Version: ImageMagick 7.1.1-15 Q16-HDRI x86_64 21298 https://imagemagick.org
[donnie@fedora script_test]$
```

One thing that we see about the above example is that it's quite large, at 3968x2232 pixels and 1.90756MiB in size. I don't need it to be that large, so let's see about making it smaller.

Resizing and Customizing Images

Let's say that I want to downsize my image to 1000x1000 pixels. I would do it like this:

```
[donnie@fedora script_test]$ convert -resize 1000x1000 S1180001.jpg S1180001_
small.jpg
[donnie@fedora script_test]$
```

By default, the convert command maintains the original aspect ratio of the image. So, the size of my downsized image is actually 1000x563 pixels, as you see here:

```
[donnie@fedora script_test]$ identify S1180001_small.jpg
S1180001_small.jpg JPEG 1000x563 1000x563+0+0 8-bit sRGB 328914B 0.000u
0:00.000
[donnie@fedora script_test]$
```

Instead of specifying the size by pixels, you can specify the desired size in terms of a percentage of the original size, like so:

```
[donnie@fedora script_test]$ convert -resize 20% S1180001.jpg S1180001_small2.
jpg
[donnie@fedora script_test]$
```

Now when I display the image, it will actually fit on my computer screen. Here's how it looks:

Figure 13.4: Goldie, sleeping in my bedroom window sill

You can apply a special effect to an image at the same time that you resize it. For example, let's turn this picture of Goldie into a charcoal drawing, like this:

```
[donnie@fedora script_test]$ convert -resize 15% -charcoal 2 S1180001.jpg
S1180001_charcoal.jpg
[donnie@fedora script_test]$
```

The -charcoal option requires you to specify a number to determine the strength of the effect. In this case I just used -charcoal 2, which gives me just the effect that I want. (I started with -charcoal 15, but that didn't look good at all.) Here's how it turned out:

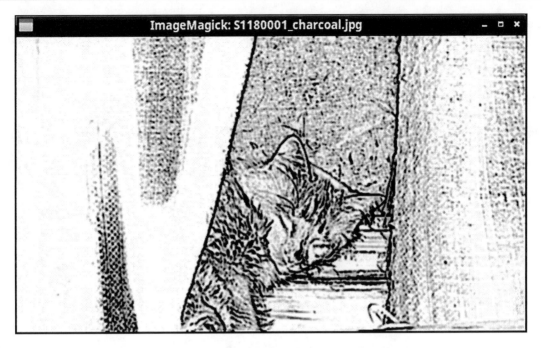

Figure 13.5: Goldie with the charcoal effect

 There's such a wide array of effects that you can apply to your images, that it's impossible for me to list them all here. To see the complete list, just view the convert man page.

One of the pleasant surprises about ImageMagick is that you can learn to do these sorts of things quite quickly, by consulting the magick and ImageMagick man pages, the ImageMagick website or the various tutorials that you'll find on the either the web or on YouTube. In fact, every time I've ever tried to do anything like this with a GUI-type program, such as GIMP or PhotoShop, it always took me forever to figure it out.

Something that's always bugged me about tablets and smart phones is that when you put them into selfie mode to take a picture of yourself, the picture is always reversed. So, let's say that I were to take a selfie of me playing guitar. I'm a right-handed guitarist, but a selfie taken with my smartphone would make me look like a left-handed guitarist. (Paul McCartney, the world's most famous living left-handed guitarist, would appear to be right-handed.) ImageMagick makes it easy to correct that, just by using convert with the -flop option, like so:

```
[donnie@fedora script_test]$ convert -flop S1180001_charcoal.jpg S1180001_
charcoal_flop.jpg
```

I don't have any selfies handy at the moment, so I instead flopped Goldie's picture. Here's how it turned out:

Figure 13.6: Goldie's picture, reversed

If you've ever made the mistake of holding your camera upside down while taking a picture, you can also reverse your pictures vertically by using the -flip option, like so:

```
donnie@fedora:~/Pictures/script_test$ convert -resize 15% -flip S1180001.jpg
S1180001_flip.jpg
donnie@fedora:~/Pictures/script_test$
```

Here's how it turned out:

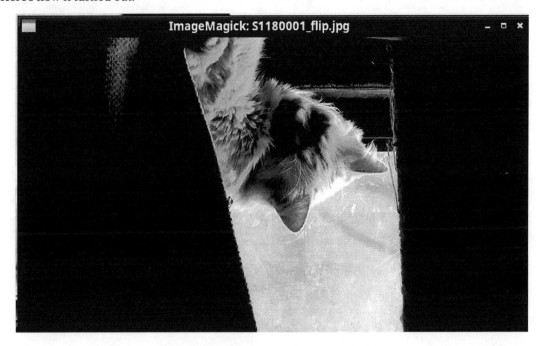

Figure 13.7: Goldie has been flipped upside-down

The last trick I'll show you is how to convert from one image format to another. Just use convert without any option switches, like so:

```
[donnie@fedora script_test]$ convert S1180001_small2.jpg S1180001_small2.png
[donnie@fedora script_test]$ ls -l *.png
-rw-r--r--. 1 donnie donnie 494190 Dec  4 17:19 S1180001_small2.png
[donnie@fedora script_test]$
```

So, I now have a .png file to go along with the .jpg file. To see all of the image formats that Image-Magick can work with, just do:

```
[donnie@fedora ~]$ identify -list format
```

You're not always limited to just working with existing image files. You can also create original text image files with a variety of special effects. For example, let's create a fancy image file of my name, like this:

```
[donnie@fedora Pictures]$ convert -size 320x115 xc:lightblue  -font Comic-
Sans-MS -pointsize 72 -fill Navy -annotate 0x0+12+55 'Donnie' -fill RoyalBlue
-annotate 0x130+25+80 'Donnie' font_slewed.jpg
[donnie@fedora Pictures]$
```

Of course, the font that you specify must be installed on your system. In this case, I'm using the infamous Comic Sans font that everybody loves to hate. (It's a Microsoft font, which I do have installed on this Fedora machine. I always install the full suite of Microsoft fonts on my Linux machines so that I can work with my publisher and my clients.) Also, note that you can't have blank spaces in the font names. Replace each blank space with a dash, and you should be good. To understand the rest of the command, look in the ImageMagick man pages for explanations of all of the options. Anyway, here's what my new image looks like:

Figure 13.8: The text image file that I created with ImageMagick

Pretty cool, right? It gets even more cool, when you look at the plethora of examples on the Font Effects page of the official ImageMagick documentation, which you can find here: `https://imagemagick.org/Usage/fonts/`

There's a whole lot more that you can do with ImageMagick, but this is enough for now. Let's now talk about using ImageMagick in shell scripts.

Batch-processing Image Files

Now, let's say that you have a whole directory full of image files that you need to manipulate all in the same way. Using a GUI-type graphics program will be quite tedious, because you'll only be able to work with one file at a time. With ImageMagick, just write a simple script to do the work for you. For example, let's look at the `resize.sh` script:

```
#!/bin/bash
for picture in *.jpg; do
        convert -resize 15% "$picture" "${picture%.jpg}_small.jpg"
done
```

As you see, it's really not that much different from the `rename_extension.sh` script that I've already shown you. Just a simple `for` loop and a bit of variable expansion is all you need. And of course, you can replace this `-resize` command with any other ImageMagick command you want.

Okay, this pretty much does it for the simple stuff. Let's move on to the more complex stuff.

Using Fred's ImageMagick Scripts

There's a lot you can do with the simple types of ImageMagick commands that I've just shown you. For simple projects, you might not need anything more complex. But, if you're a professional graphics artist, you might need more. You can create some awesome-looking images with awesome effects, but that might require using a very complex set of ImageMagick commands. Fortunately, there's a way to cheat, because someone else has already done this work for you.

Fred's ImageMagick Scripts are bash scripts that incorporate very complex sets of ImageMagick commands. As I'm writing this in December 2023, Mr. Fred Weinhaus has a total of 375 scripts that you can download from his site. They're free of charge for personal use, but Fred does request that you contact him to arrange for payment if you need to use them for your business. I can't even begin to describe all of the scripts and the effects that they can all create. So instead, I'll just encourage you to go to Fred's site and download some of the scripts for your own study. You can find Fred's site here:

```
http://www.fmwconcepts.com/imagemagick/
```

And, here's what the site looks like:

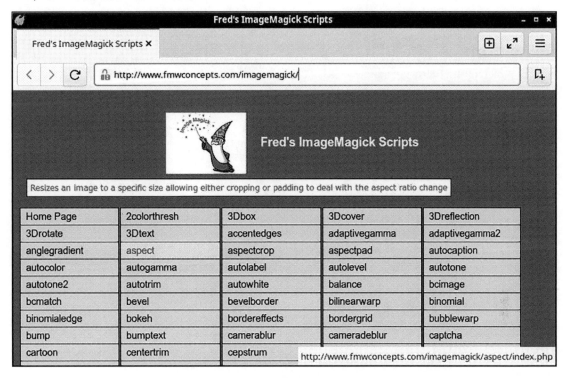

Figure 13.9: Fred's ImageMagick Scripts site

As you see in this graphic, you can get a description of what each script does by moving your cursor over the script name.

I believe that this about does it for an introduction to ImageMagick scripting. So, let's summarize and move on.

Summary

ImageMagick is a great tool for both casual and professional graphics artists. You can perform some simple image manipulations with some very simple commands, or you can create awesome effects with more complex commands.

In this chapter, I started by explaining how to automate the process of changing non-standard file-name extensions to the standard Linux/Unix format. I then explained how to install ImageMagick on a variety of operating systems. Next, I showed you how to display images, view image properties, and how to resize and customize images, all from the command-line. Finally, I showed you how to cheat a bit, by studying and trying out Fred's ImageMagick scripts.

Of course, there's still much more that you can do with ImageMagick than I can show you here. There are ImageMagick tutorials all over the place on the web, and you can easily find them with your favorite search engine. Better yet, go to YouTube, and search for ImageMagick tutorials there.

In the next chapter, I'll show you how to squawk with awk. I'll see you there.

Questions

1. Which of the following statements is false?

    a. There's not much you can do with ImageMagick, because it lacks a graphical user interface.

    b. It's sometimes easier to apply an effect with ImageMagick than it is with a GUI-type program.

    c. You can batch process a directory full of graphics files by placing ImageMagick commands into a shell script.

    d. ImageMagick is simple to use for simple tasks, but you can also perform more complex image manipulations with more complex scripts.

2. What are two methods that you can use to automate the process of changing filename extensions on a whole directory of graphics files?

    a. Use command substitution

    b. Use variable expansion

    c. Use command expansion

    d. Use the basename utility

3. Which ImageMagick command would you use to display image properties?

    a. show

    b. identify

    c. show_properties

    d. properties

Further Reading

- bash--How do I change the extension of multiple files?: https://unix.stackexchange.com/questions/19654/how-do-i-change-the-extension-of-multiple-files

- ImageMagick.org: https://imagemagick.org/

- Getting started with ImageMagick: https://opensource.com/article/17/8/imagemagick

- Getting Started with ImageMagick: `https://riptutorial.com/imagemagick`
- Manipulating Images with ImageMagick Command-line Tools: `https://www.baeldung.com/linux/imagemagick-edit-images`
- Fred's ImageMagick Scripts: `http://www.fmwconcepts.com/imagemagick/`

Answers

1. a
2. b and d
3. b

Join our community on Discord!

Read this book alongside other users, Linux experts, and the author himself.

Ask questions, provide solutions to other readers, chat with the author via Ask Me Anything sessions, and much more. Scan the QR code or visit the link to join the community.

`https://packt.link/SecNet`

14

Using awk – Part 1

In this chapter, I'll show you a bit about awk. It's a programming environment with a long and storied history that dates back to the 1970s, when it was invented by Alfred Aho, Peter Weinberger, and Brian Kernighan for use with the early Unix operating systems.

There are several ways in which you can use awk. It is a full-blown programming language, so you can use it to write very complex, stand-alone programs. You can also create simple awk commands that you can either run from the command-line or from within normal shell scripts. There's a lot to awk, and entire books have been written about it. The goal for this chapter is to show you how to use awk in normal shell scripts.

Topics in this chapter include:

- Introducing awk
- Understanding patterns and actions
- Obtaining input from text files
- Obtaining input from commands

If you're ready to squawk with awk, let's get started.

Introducing awk

awk is a pattern-scanning and text-processing utility that you can use to automate the process of creating reports and databases. With its built-in math functions, you can also use it to perform spreadsheet operations on text files of columnar, numerical data. The term awk comes from the names of its creators, Aho, Weinberger and Kernighan. The original version is now referred to as "old awk". Newer implementations, such as nawk and gawk, have more features and are somewhat easier to use.

The version of awk you have depends upon which operating system you're running. Most Linux operating systems run gawk, which is the GNU implementation of awk. There's most always an awk symbolic link that points to the gawk executable, as you see here on my Fedora workstation:

```
[donnie@fedora ~]$ awk --version
```

```
GNU Awk 5.1.1, API: 3.1 (GNU MPFR 4.1.1-p1, GNU MP 6.2.1)
Copyright (C) 1989, 1991-2021 Free Software Foundation.
This program is free software; you can redistribute it and/or modify
it under the terms of the GNU General Public License as published by
the Free Software Foundation; either version 3 of the License, or
(at your option) any later version.
. . .

. . .
[donnie@fedora ~]$ ls -l /bin/awk
lrwxrwxrwx. 1 root root 4 Jan 18  2023 /bin/awk -> gawk
[donnie@fedora ~]$
```

A notable exception is with Alpine Linux, which by default uses the lightweight awk implementation that's built into the busybox executable. However, both gawk and mawk, another awk implementation, are available for installation from the Alpine repositories. (I couldn't find a definitive answer for why mawk is called mawk. But, its author is Michael Brennan, so I'm guessing that it's supposed to stand for "Michael's awk".)

Unix and Unix-like operating systems, such as macOS, OpenIndiana, and the various BSD distros, use nawk, which is short for "new awk". You'll sometimes see this referred to as the "one true awk", partly because Brian Kernighan, one of the authors of the original awk, is one of its maintainers. However, gawk is available for installation for both FreeBSD and OpenIndiana, and mawk is available for FreeBSD.

So, what are the differences between these different awk implementations? Well, here's a quick rundown:

- busybox: The awk implementation that's built into busybox is super lightweight, and is ideal for low-resource embedded systems. This is why it's the default choice for Alpine Linux, which is also popular for embedded systems. Be aware though that it might not always have the features that you need for complex awk commands or scripts.
- nawk: As I've already mentioned, nawk is the default choice for most Unix and Unix-like systems such as FreeBSD, OpenIndiana, and macOS. But, the executable file you'll find on these systems is normally just awk, instead of nawk.
- mawk: This is supposed to be a faster version of awk, which was created by Mike Brennan.
- gawk: This implementation has features that the other implementations don't have. One major enhancement is the inclusion of **internationalization and localization** capabilities, which facilitates creating software for different languages and locales. It also includes TCP/IP networking capabilities and enhanced features for dealing with regular expressions.

Unless I state otherwise, I'll be showing you coding techniques that work the same on both nawk and gawk. So, let's get started.

Understanding Patterns and Actions

An awk **pattern** is simply the text or the regular expression upon which an **action** will operate. The source can be either a plain text file or the output of another program. To begin, let's dump the entire contents of the /etc/passwd file to the screen, like so:

```
[donnie@fedora ~]$ awk '{print $0}' /etc/passwd
root:x:0:0:root:/root:/bin/bash
bin:x:1:1:bin:/bin:/sbin/nologin
. . .

. . .
donnie:x:1000:1000:Donald A. Tevault:/home/donnie:/bin/bash
systemd-coredump:x:986:986:systemd Core Dumper:/:/usr/sbin/nologin
systemd-timesync:x:985:985:systemd Time Synchronization:/:/usr/sbin/nologin
clamupdate:x:984:983:Clamav database update user:/var/lib/clamav:/sbin/nologin
setroubleshoot:x:983:979:SELinux troubleshoot server:/var/lib/setroubleshoot:/
usr/sbin/nologin
[donnie@fedora ~]$
```

In this command, the {print $0} part is the action, which must be surrounded by a pair of single quotes. The $ designates which field to print. In this case, the $0 causes every field to print. Specifying a pattern would cause only the lines with that pattern to print. By not specifying a pattern this time, I caused every line to print. Now, let's say that I only want to show the line that contains a specific username. I'll just add the pattern, like this:

```
[donnie@fedora ~]$ awk '/donnie/ {print $0}' /etc/passwd
donnie:x:1000:1000:Donald A. Tevault:/home/donnie:/bin/bash
[donnie@fedora ~]$
```

The pattern needs to be enclosed within a pair of forward slashes, which in turn need to be within the pair of single quotes that also surround the action.

 awk operates on groups of information known as records. By default, each line in a text file is one record. For now, that's all we're going to deal with. However, you can also have files with multi-line records, which require special techniques to process. I'll show you that in the next chapter.

Since {print $0} is the default action, I could just omit that part and get the same result, like so:

```
[donnie@fedora ~]$ awk '/donnie/' /etc/passwd
donnie:x:1000:1000:Donald A. Tevault:/home/donnie:/bin/bash
[donnie@fedora ~]$
```

Next, let's just print out the first field of this line. Do it like this:

```
[donnie@fedora ~]$ awk '/donnie/ {print $1}' /etc/passwd
donnie:x:1000:1000:Donald
[donnie@fedora ~]$
```

The $1 designates that I want to print field number 1. But wait though, this still isn't right, because the command has actually printed fields 1 through 5. That's because the default field delimiter for awk is a blank space. Field 5, which contains my full name, has a blank space between the "Donald" and the "A." So, as far as awk is concerned, this is the beginning of the second field. To fix that, I'll use the -F: option to make awk recognize the colon as the field delimiter, like this:

```
[donnie@fedora ~]$ awk -F: '/donnie/ {print $1}' /etc/passwd
donnie
[donnie@fedora ~]$
```

Finally, I have the output that I want.

If you need to display more than one field, use a comma-separated list of field identifiers in the action, like this:

```
[donnie@fedora ~]$ awk -F: '/donnie/ {print $1, $7}' /etc/passwd
donnie /bin/bash
[donnie@fedora ~]$
```

So here, I'm displaying fields 1 and 7. (Note that the comma between the field numbers is what places a blank space between the fields in the output. Omitting the comma would cause the output to not have that blank space.)

You can also pipe the output of another program into awk, like this:

```
[donnie@fedora ~]$ cat /etc/passwd | awk -F: '/donnie/ {print $1}'
donnie
[donnie@fedora ~]$
```

Yeah, I know. It's usually bad form to pipe cat output into another utility, when you could just directly use the other utility. But for now, this serves to demonstrate the concept.

All of the demos that I've shown you thus far could also have been done with cat, grep, cut, or combinations thereof. So, you could be forgiven for wondering what the point is in using awk. Well, hang on, because you'll soon see that awk can do some awesome things that the other utilities can't do, or can't do as well. We'll begin by taking a closer look at how awk can process input from plain text files.

Obtaining Input from Text Files

As you might have already guessed, the default manner in which awk operates is to read a file line-by-line, searching for the specified pattern in each line. When it finds a line that contains the specified pattern, it will perform the specified action on that line. Let's begin by building upon the passwd file example that I showed you in the previous section.

Looking for Human Users

The /etc/passwd file contains a list of all users on the system. What I've always found curious is that system user accounts and normal human user accounts are all mixed together in the same file. But, let's say that as part of your administrator duties, you need to maintain a list of normal human users on each machine. One way to do that is to use awk to search through the passwd file for the **User ID Numbers (UIDs)** that correspond to human users. To find out what the UID numbers for normal users are, you can look in the /etc/login.defs file that's on most Linux systems. This file can be somewhat different on different Linux systems, so I'll just show you how it is on my Fedora machine. On lines 142 through 145, you see this:

```
# Min/max values for automatic uid selection in useradd(8)
#
UID_MIN                    1000
UID_MAX                   60000
```

So, to view all human user accounts on my system, I would search for all passwd file lines where field 3 (the UID field) contains a value that is greater than or equal to 1000 and less than or equal to 60000, like so:

```
donnie@fedora:~$ awk -F: '$3 >= 1000 && $3 <= 60000 {print $1, $7}' /etc/passwd
donnie /bin/bash
vicky /bin/bash
frank /bin/bash
goldie /bin/bash
cleopatra /bin/bash
donnie@fedora:~$
```

You can also redirect the output into a text file, by placing the output redirector within the action construct, like this:

```
donnie@fedora:~$ awk -F: '$3 >= 1000 && $3 <= 60000 {print $1, $7 > "users.
txt"}' /etc/passwd
donnie@fedora:~$ cat users.txt
donnie /bin/bash
vicky /bin/bash
frank /bin/bash
goldie /bin/bash
cleopatra /bin/bash
donnie@fedora:~$
```

In both examples, note how I'm using && as the and operator in the pattern portion of the command.

Of course, there's no need to type this whole long command every time you want to use it. Instead, just put it into a normal shell script, which I'll call user_list.sh. It will look something like this:

```
#!/bin/bash
awk -F: '$3 >= 1000 && $3 <= 60000 {print $1, $7 > "users.txt"}' /etc/passwd
```

That's good, but what if you need a comma-separated value (.csv) file that you can easily import into a spreadsheet? Well, I've got you covered. Just add a BEGIN section, where you would define the new field delimiter for the output, as well as the field delimiter for the input, like this:

```
donnie@fedora:~$ awk 'BEGIN {OFS = ","; FS = ":"}; $3 >= 1000 && $3 <= 60000
{print $1,$7 > "users.csv"}' /etc/passwd
donnie@fedora:~$ cat users.csv
donnie,/bin/bash
vicky,/bin/bash
frank,/bin/bash
goldie,/bin/bash
cleopatra,/bin/bash
victor,/bin/bash
valerie,/bin/bash
victoria,/bin/bash
donnie@fedora:~$
```

This might seem a bit strange, because when you define an input field delimiter in the awk action, you used the -F option. But, when you define an input field delimiter in the BEGIN section, you use the FS option. Likewise, you use OFS in the BEGIN section to define the output field delimiter. (In awk-speak, field delimiters are actually called **Field Separators**, which explains why these BEGIN options are called FS and OFS.)

The BEGIN section of an awk command or script is where you add any type of initialization code that you want to run before awk starts processing the input file. You can use it to define field separators, add a header to the output, or initialize global variables that you'll use later.

That's good, but I'd also like to see the users' UIDs. So, I'll just add field 3 to the mix, like this:

```
donnie@fedora:~$ awk 'BEGIN {OFS = ","; FS = ":"}; $3 >= 1000 && $3 <= 60000
{print $1,$3,$7 > "users.csv"}' /etc/passwd
donnie@fedora:~$ cat users.csv
donnie,1000,/bin/bash
vicky,1001,/bin/bash
frank,1003,/bin/bash
goldie,1004,/bin/bash
cleopatra,1005,/bin/bash
victor,1006,/bin/bash
valerie,1007,/bin/bash
victoria,1008,/bin/bash
donnie@fedora:~$
```

Now that I have my awk command the way I want it, I'll place it into the user_list2.sh shell script that will look like this:

```
#!/bin/bash
awk 'BEGIN {OFS = ","; FS = ":"}; $3 >= 1000 && $3 <= 60000 {print $1,$3,$7 >
"users.csv"}' /etc/passwd
```

You could write a program that does this same thing in some other programming language, such as Python, C, or Java. But, the program code would be quite complex and more difficult to get right. With awk, all it takes is just a simple single-line command.

Next, let's see how awk can help a busy webserver administrator.

Parsing Webserver Access Logs

Webserver access logs contain a lot of information that can help a website owner, a webserver administrator, or a network security administrator. There are a lot of fancy log-parsing tools that can build fancy reports that tell you everything that's going on, if that's what you need. But, there may be times when you'll want to quickly extract some specific data without taking the time to run some fancy tool. There are a few different ways to do that, and awk is one of the best.

To begin the scenario, you'll need a virtual machine with an active webserver installed. To keep things simple, I'll just install the Apache server and the PHP module on my Fedora Server virtual machine, like this:

```
donnie@fedora:~$ sudo dnf install httpd php
```

Next, enable and start the Apache service, like this:

```
donnie@fedora:~$ sudo systemctl enable --now httpd
```

To access the server from different machines, you'll need to open Port 80 on the firewall, like this:

```
donnie@fedora:~$ sudo firewall-cmd --add-service=http --permanent
donnie@fedora:~$ sudo firewall-cmd --reload
donnie@fedora:~$
```

Finally, in the `/var/www/html/` directory, create the `test.php` file, with the following contents:

```
<?php echo "<strong><center>This is the awk Test Page</strong></center>";
?>
```

 Reminder: To make this work, be sure to set your virtual machine up with Bridged Mode networking, so that other machines on your network can reach it. Also, be sure that the virtual machines that you use to access the webserver are also set up in Bridged Mode, so that each machine will have its own IP address in the access log file.

Now, from as many other machines as possible, access both the Fedora Webserver Test Page and the `test.php` page. Then, try to access a non-existent page. Your URLs should look something like this:

```
http://192.168.0.11
http://192.168.0.11/test.php
http://192.168.0.11/bogus.html
```

On the webserver virtual machine, open the `var/log/httpd/access_log` file in `less`, like this:

```
donnie@fedora:~$ sudo less /var/log/httpd/access_log
```

Note the structure of the file, and how it uses blank spaces as field delimiters for some fields and double quotes as field delimiters for other fields. For example, here's one entry from my own access file:

```
192.168.0.17 - - [18/Dec/2023:16:40:03 -0500] "GET /test.php HTTP/1.1" 200 59
"-" "Mozilla/5.0 (X11; SunOS i86pc; rv:120.0) Gecko/20100101 Firefox/120.0"
```

So, you see here that some fields are surrounded by double quotes, and others aren't. For now, let's look at the IP addresses that have accessed this machine, like so:

```
donnie@fedora:~$ sudo awk '{print $1}' /var/log/httpd/access_log | sort -V |
uniq
192.168.0.10
192.168.0.16
192.168.0.17
192.168.0.18
192.168.0.27
192.168.0.37
192.168.0.107
192.168.0.251
```

```
192.168.0.252
donnie@fedora:~$
```

As you see, I just piped the awk output into sort -V, which I then piped into uniq. Using the -V option for sort causes the IP addresses to be sorted in correct numerical order. You can't use the -n switch for this, because by default, sort treats the dots in the IP addresses as decimal points. The -V option overrides that behavior by doing what is called a **natural sort**.

This is good, except that I still don't know how many times the webserver was accessed from each IP address. I'll use uniq with the -c option to see that, which will look like this:

```
donnie@fedora:~$ sudo awk '{print $1}' /var/log/httpd/access_log | sort -V |
uniq -c
      6  192.168.0.10
     20 192.168.0.16
     12 192.168.0.17
      2  192.168.0.18
      4  192.168.0.27
     15 192.168.0.37
      6  192.168.0.107
     14 192.168.0.251
      6  192.168.0.252
donnie@fedora:~$
```

That's good, but I really want to create a .csv file, as I did for my list of users. I can't do that by defining the OFS parameter in the BEGIN section this time, because the count field isn't created until I pipe the output into uniq -c. So, I'll cheat a bit by installing the miller package, which is in the repositories for most Linux distros, as well as for FreeBSD. On a Mac, you should be able to install it with homebrew. Anyway, to create the .csv file, I'll just pipe the output from this awk command into the mlr utility, which is part of the miller package. Here's how that looks:

```
donnie@fedora:~$ sudo awk '{print $1}' /var/log/httpd/access_log | sort -V |
uniq -c | mlr --p2c cat > ip_list.csv
donnie@fedora:~$ cat ip_list.csv
6,192.168.0.10
27,192.168.0.16
12,192.168.0.17
2,192.168.0.18
4,192.168.0.27
15,192.168.0.37
6,192.168.0.107
14,192.168.0.251
6,192.168.0.252
donnie@fedora:~$
```

The `--p2c` option for `mlr` is what converts the output to `.csv` format. After that is `cat`, which is the `mlr` verb. You see that this `cat` just dumps the output to either the screen or to a file, the same as its `bash` cousin does.

I'm showing you how to create `.csv` files, because for historical reasons, `.csv` is the most popular format for plain-text data files, and your employer or clients might expect you to use them. However, as we'll see in a bit, this isn't always the best format. In certain circumstances, you might find that your best bet is to forget about `.csv` files, and instead save your data to **Tab Separated Value** (`.tsv`) files, which might look something like this:

```
donnie@fedora:~$ cat inventory.tsv
Kitchen spatula     $4.99        Housewares
Raincoat            $36.99       Clothing       On Sale!
Claw hammer         $7.99        Tools
donnie@fedora:~$
```

You can also import them into your favorite spreadsheet program, and in certain circumstances, they're much easier to deal with.

If you need a `.json` file instead of a `.csv` file, `mlr` can also do that for you. You'll just replace the `--p2c` option with the `--ojson` option, like this:

```
donnie@fedora:~$ sudo awk '{print $1}' /var/log/httpd/access_log | sort -V |
uniq -c | mlr --ojson cat > ip_list.json
donnie@fedora:~$ cat ip_list.json
{ "1": "      6 192.168.0.10" }
{ "1": "     27 192.168.0.16" }
{ "1": "     12 192.168.0.17" }
{ "1": "      2 192.168.0.18" }
{ "1": "      4 192.168.0.27" }
{ "1": "     15 192.168.0.37" }
{ "1": "      6 192.168.0.107" }
{ "1": "     14 192.168.0.251" }
{ "1": "      6 192.168.0.252" }
donnie@fedora:~$
```

There's a lot more that you can do with `mlr` than I can show you here. To learn more about it, consult either the `mlr` man page or the Miller Documentation web page. (You'll find a link to the Miller page in the *Further Reading* section.) As good as `mlr` is though, it does have one flaw. That is, it can't handle fields that contain blank spaces or commas. So, you won't be able to use it for every field in the Apache access log.

Now, let's say that we want to see which operating systems and browsers are accessing this server. The **User Agent** string that contains that information is in field 6, which is surrounded by a pair of double quotes. So, we'll have to use the double quote as the field delimiter, like this:

```
donnie@fedora:~$ sudo awk -F\" '{print $6}' /var/log/httpd/access_log | sort |
uniq
Lynx/2.8.9rel.1 libwww-FM/2.14 SSL-MM/1.4.1 OpenSSL/1.1.1t-freebsd
Lynx/2.9.0dev.10 libwww-FM/2.14 SSL-MM/1.4.1 GNUTLS/3.7.1
Lynx/2.9.0dev.12 libwww-FM/2.14 SSL-MM/1.4.1 GNUTLS/3.7.8
Mozilla/5.0 (Macintosh; Intel Mac OS X 10_14_6) AppleWebKit/605.1.15 (KHTML,
like Gecko) Version/14.1.2 Safari/605.1.15
. . .

. . .
Mozilla/5.0 (X11; Linux x86_64; rv:120.0) Gecko/20100101 Firefox/120.0
Mozilla/5.0 (X11; Linux x86_64; rv:45.0) Gecko/20100101 Firefox/45.0
Mozilla/5.0 (X11; SunOS i86pc; rv:120.0) Gecko/20100101 Firefox/120.0
Mozilla/5.0 (X11; Ubuntu; Linux x86_64; rv:109.0) Gecko/20100101 Firefox/113.0
donnie@fedora:~$
```

You can see here that I had to escape the double quote with a backslash, so that the shell won't misinterpret it.

Next, let's look for a specific User Agent. Let's say that we want to know how many users are using a Mac. Just add the pattern, like this:

```
donnie@fedora:~$ sudo awk -F\" '/Mac OS X/ {print $6}' /var/log/httpd/access_
log | sort | uniq -c
      8 Mozilla/5.0 (Macintosh; Intel Mac OS X 10_14_6) AppleWebKit/605.1.15
(KHTML, like Gecko) Version/14.1.2 Safari/605.1.15
      6 Mozilla/5.0 (Macintosh; Intel Mac OS X 10.14; rv:109.0) Gecko/20100101
Firefox/115.0
      6 Mozilla/5.0 (Macintosh; PPC Mac OS X 10.4; FPR10; rv:45.0)
Gecko/20100101 Firefox/45.0 TenFourFox/7450
      9 Mozilla/5.0 (Macintosh; U; PPC Mac OS X 10_4_11; en)
AppleWebKit/533.19.4 (KHTML, like Gecko) Version/4.1.3 Safari/533.19.4
donnie@fedora:~$
```

The entries for the Intel Mac are from my 2010-model Mac Pro, so they make sense. But, what's with that PPC business in lines 3 and 4 of the output? Well, that's also easily explained. Just for fun, I fired up my 21-year old eMac that's equipped with an old-school Motorola PowerPC G4 processor, and used it to access the test webserver. (I'm guessing that you'll never see any of those on your own network.)

You can also obtain this information with nothing but pure awk, without having to pipe the output into other utilities. Do that by building an **associative array**, which looks like this:

```
donnie@fedora:~$ sudo awk '{count[$1]++}; END {for (ip_address in count) print
```

```
ip_address, count[ip_address]}' /var/log/httpd/access_log
192.168.0.251 14
192.168.0.252 6
192.168.0.10 6
192.168.0.16 22
192.168.0.17 12
192.168.0.107 6
192.168.0.18 2
192.168.0.27 4
192.168.0.37 15
donnie@fedora:~$
```

Add a BEGIN section with an OFS definition, and you can create a .csv file. Here's how that looks:

```
donnie@fedora:~$ sudo awk 'BEGIN {OFS = ","}; {count[$1]++}; END {for (ip_
address in count) print ip_address, count[ip_address]}' /var/log/httpd/access_
log > ip_addresses.csv
donnie@fedora:~$ cat ip_addresses.csv
192.168.0.251,14
192.168.0.252,6
192.168.0.10,6
192.168.0.16,27
192.168.0.17,12
192.168.0.107,6
192.168.0.18,2
192.168.0.27,4
192.168.0.37,15
donnie@fedora:~$
```

Unlike the normal shell scripting arrays that you've seen previously, awk associative arrays use text strings, instead of numbers, as their indexes. Also, arrays in awk are defined on-the-fly, and don't have to be declared before you can use them. So here you see the count array, with whatever the respective values of field 1 are for the index values. The ++ operator, which assumes an initial value of 0, adds together the number of times each index string is found in the file. The first portion of this command, which ends at the semi-colon, processes the file line-by-line as awk normally does. The END keyword designates code that will run after the line-by-line processing has completed. In this case, you see a for loop that prints out a summary of unique IP addresses, along with how many times each one was found. Unfortunately, there's no easy way to sort the output with pure awk, but you can still pipe the output into sort, like this:

```
donnie@fedora:~$ sudo awk 'BEGIN {OFS = ","}; {count[$1]++}; END {for (ip_
address in count) print ip_address, count[i]}' /var/log/httpd/access_log | sort
-t, -V -k1,1 > ip_addresses.csv
```

```
donnie@fedora:~$ cat ip_addresses.csv
192.168.0.10,6
192.168.0.16,27
192.168.0.17,12
192.168.0.18,2
192.168.0.27,4
192.168.0.37,15
192.168.0.107,6
192.168.0.251,14
192.168.0.252,6
donnie@fedora:~$
```

To make this work, I'm using sort with the -t, option to define the comma as the field delimiter. (Yeah, I know. It would be nice if all Linux and Unix utilities used the same option switch to define field delimiters, but that's just not how the world works.)

Another difference with using pure awk is that the number of occurrences for each IP address is in the second column, rather than in the first column as you saw before. That's okay here, but it might not work so well for other fields. For example, let's change the command to look at the User Agents in field 6:

```
donnie@fedora:~$ sudo awk -F\" '{count[$6]++}; END { for (i in count) print i,
count[i]}' /var/log/httpd/access_log | sort
Lynx/2.8.9rel.1 libwww-FM/2.14 SSL-MM/1.4.1 OpenSSL/1.1.1t-freebsd 2
Lynx/2.9.0dev.10 libwww-FM/2.14 SSL-MM/1.4.1 GNUTLS/3.7.1 4
Lynx/2.9.0dev.12 libwww-FM/2.14 SSL-MM/1.4.1 GNUTLS/3.7.8 3
Mozilla/5.0 (Macintosh; Intel Mac OS X 10_14_6) AppleWebKit/605.1.15 (KHTML,
like Gecko) Version/14.1.2 Safari/605.1.15 8
. . .
. . .
Mozilla/5.0 (X11; Ubuntu; Linux x86_64; rv:109.0) Gecko/20100101 Firefox/113.0
6
donnie@fedora:~$
```

Yeah, it works, but having the number of occurrences in the second column for this makes the output somewhat less readable.

As I mentioned before, the .csv format isn't always your best choice for a plain-text data file. In fact, it's impossible to turn the output from field 6 into a proper .csv file that any spreadsheet program will properly display. That's because this field contains blank spaces and commas that make a spreadsheet program think that there are more fields in the .csv file than there really are.

So, the easiest solution is to surround the text in field 6 with a pair of double quotes and save the output to a .tsv file. Then, when you open the file in your spreadsheet, define the " as the field delimiter. Anyway, here's the command to create the .tsv file, without using an associative array:

```
donnie@fedora:~$ sudo awk 'BEGIN {FS="\""} {print "\"" $6 "\""}' /var/log/
```

```
httpd/access_log | sort | uniq -c | sort -k 1,1 -nr > user_agent.tsv
donnie@fedora:~$
```

By default, awk strips out the double quotes that surround field 6 in the original log file. So, to make
this work properly, I have to put them back into the final output file. In the action part, you see that
I'm printing a double quote both before and after $6. By omitting the commas that you might nor-
mally place between the various print elements, I'll ensure that there are no blank spaces between
the quotes and the text. Then, I'm just piping the output into sort, uniq, and sort again as I've shown
you before. Here's how the file looks:

```
donnie@fedora:~$ cat user_agent.tsv
     23 "Mozilla/5.0 (X11; Linux x86_64; rv:120.0) Gecko/20100101
Firefox/120.0"
      9 "Mozilla/5.0 (X11; SunOS i86pc; rv:120.0) Gecko/20100101 Firefox/120.0"
      9 "Mozilla/5.0 (Macintosh; U; PPC Mac OS X 10_4_11; en)
AppleWebKit/533.19.4 (KHTML, like Gecko) Version/4.1.3 Safari/533.19.4"
      8 "Mozilla/5.0 (Macintosh; Intel Mac OS X 10_14_6) AppleWebKit/605.1.15
(KHTML, like Gecko) Version/14.1.2 Safari/605.1.15"
      6 "Mozilla/5.0 (X11; Ubuntu; Linux x86_64; rv:109.0) Gecko/20100101
Firefox/113.0"
. . .
. . .
      3 "Lynx/2.9.0dev.12 libwww-FM/2.14 SSL-MM/1.4.1 GNUTLS/3.7.8"
      2 "Lynx/2.8.9rel.1 libwww-FM/2.14 SSL-MM/1.4.1 OpenSSL/1.1.1t-freebsd"
donnie@fedora:~$
```

If you prefer to use an associative array, you can do it like this:

```
donnie@fedora:~$ sudo awk -F\" '{count[$6]++}; END { for (ip_address in count)
printf "%s \"%s\"\n", count[ip_address], ip_address}' /var/log/httpd/access_log
| sort -nr > user_agent.tsv
donnie@fedora:~$ cat user_agent.tsv
     23 "Mozilla/5.0 (X11; Linux x86_64; rv:120.0) Gecko/20100101
Firefox/120.0"
      9 "Mozilla/5.0 (X11; SunOS i86pc; rv:120.0) Gecko/20100101 Firefox/120.0"
      9 "Mozilla/5.0 (Macintosh; U; PPC Mac OS X 10_4_11; en)
AppleWebKit/533.19.4 (KHTML, like Gecko) Version/4.1.3 Safari/533.19.4"
      8 "Mozilla/5.0 (Macintosh; Intel Mac OS X 10_14_6) AppleWebKit/605.1.15
(KHTML, like Gecko) Version/14.1.2 Safari/605.1.15"
      6 "Mozilla/5.0 (X11; Ubuntu; Linux x86_64; rv:109.0) Gecko/20100101
Firefox/113.0"
. . .
. . .
      3 "Lynx/2.9.0dev.12 libwww-FM/2.14 SSL-MM/1.4.1 GNUTLS/3.7.8"
```

```
        2 "Lynx/2.8.9rel.1 libwww-FM/2.14 SSL-MM/1.4.1 OpenSSL/1.1.1t-freebsd"
donnie@fedora:~$
```

Note how I had to surround the `printf` parameters with a pair of double quotes. The first `%s` parameter is for the count field, and the second `%s` parameter is for the user agent field. To add the double quotes in the proper places, I added a `\"` to both before and after the second `%s`. Using either the associative array method or the non-associative array method gives me the same results. Now, when I open the file in a spreadsheet program, I'll just define the double quote as the field delimiter. Here's how that looks on LibreOffice Calc:

Separator Options

◯ Fixed width   ⦿ Separated by

☐ Tab   ☐ Comma   ☐ Semicolon   ☐ Space   ☑ Other   ["|]

☐ Merge delimiters   ☐ Trim spaces   String delimiter: [" ▼]

Figure 14.1: Setting the field delimiter in LibreOffice Calc

 I know that I haven't fully explained `print` versus `printf` yet, but I will in the next chapter.

The `user_agent.tsv` file should now display properly, with the count in the first column and the User Agent string in the second column.

Next, let's count the number of times that each URL on the webserver was hit. I like having the count as the first field of output, so I'll again pipe the `awk` output into `uniq` and `sort`, like so:

```
donnie@fedora:~$ sudo awk '{print $7}' /var/log/httpd/access_log | sort | uniq
-c | sort -k1,1 -n
      1 /something.html
      1 /test
      1 /test.html
      1 /test/php
      1 /test.php?module=..../
      2 /test.
php?module=..../.....//.....//.....//.....//.....//.....//.....//.....//.....//.....//proc/
self/environ%0000
      2 /test.php?page=../../../../../../../../../../../../../../../proc/self/
environ%00
     11 /icons/poweredby.png
     11 /poweredby.png
     11 /report.html
     12 /favicon.ico
```

```
     17 /
     18 /test.php
donnie@fedora:~$
```

Using the blank space as the field delimiter means that the URL field is field 7. At the end, I'm piping the output into sort again so that the list will print out according to the number of hits for each URL. But actually, I'd like that to show the most popular URLs at the top of the list. So, I'll just add the -r option to sort in reverse, like this:

```
donnie@fedora:~$ sudo awk '{print $7}' /var/log/httpd/access_log | sort | uniq
-c | sort -k1,1 -nr
     18 /test.php
     17 /
     12 /favicon.ico
     11 /report.html
     11 /poweredby.png
     11 /icons/poweredby.png
      2 /test.php?page=../../../../../../../../../../../../../../../proc/self/
environ%00
      2 /test.
php?module=..../..//..../..//..../..//..../..//..../..//..../..//..../..//proc/
self/environ%0000
      1 /test.php?module=..../
      1 /test/php
      1 /test.html
      1 /test
      1 /something.html
donnie@fedora:~$
```

One thing we see is that someone tried to perform a directory traversal attack against me, as evidenced by the lines that begin with /test.php?page or /test.php?module. I'll show you more about that later in *Chapter 18, Shell Scripting for Security Professionals*.

That last field we'll look at is field 9, which is the **HTTP status code**. Again, we'll use the blank space as the field delimiter, like so:

```
donnie@fedora:~$ sudo awk '{print $9}' /var/log/httpd/access_log | sort | uniq
-c | sort -k1,1 -nr
     53 200
     17 404
     17 403
      2 304
donnie@fedora:~$
```

Here's the breakdown of what these codes mean:

- **200:** The 200 code means that users were able to access web pages normally, with no problems.

- **304:** The 304 code just means that when a user reloaded a page, nothing on the page had changed, so that it didn't need to be reloaded.

- **403:** The 403 code means that someone tried to access a page for which the user wasn't authorized.

- **404:** The 404 means that a user tried to access a page that doesn't exist.

Okay, all this is good. So now, let's put all this into the access_log_parse.sh script, which will look like this:

```bash
#!/bin/bash
#
timestamp=$(date +%F_%I-%M-%p)
awk 'BEGIN {FS="\""} {print "\"" $6 "\""}' /var/log/httpd/access_log | sort |
uniq -c | sort -k 1,1 -nr > user_agent_$timestamp.tsv
awk '{print $1}' /var/log/httpd/access_log | sort -V | uniq -c | sort -k1,1 -nr
>> source_IP_addreses_$timestamp.tsv
awk '{print $7}' /var/log/httpd/access_log | sort | uniq -c | sort -k1,1 -nr >
URLs_Requested_$timestamp.tsv
awk '{print $9}' /var/log/httpd/access_log | sort | uniq -c | sort -k1,1 -nr >
HTTP_Status_Codes_$timestamp.tsv
```

I've decided that I want to create a separate .tsv file for each function, and that I want to have a timestamp in each filename. The %F option for date prints the date in YEAR-MONTH-DATE format, which is fine. I could have used the %T option to print the time, but that would have placed colons in the filenames, which would require me to escape the colons every time I want to access one of these files from the command line. So, I instead used the %I-%M-%p combination, in order to replace the colons with dashes. (To see more formatting options, consult the date man page.) The rest of the script consists of the commands that you've already seen, so I won't repeat any of those explanations.

Of course, you can fancy up any of these scripts to meet your own desires and needs. Just use the techniques that I've shown you in previous chapters to add markup language tags to the output, and convert the output files to .html or .pdf format. For the multi-function script that I've just now shown you, you could add either if..then or case constructs that would allow you to choose the specific function that you want to run. And, don't feel bad if you need to refer back to the previous chapters to see how any of this is done. Trust me, I won't hold it against you.

So far, we've been parsing through the entire file to find what we want to see. Sometimes though, you might just want to view information from either a specific line or range of lines. For example, let's say that you just want to see line 10. Do it like this:

```
donnie@fedora:~$ sudo awk 'NR == 10' /var/log/httpd/access_log
```

```
192.168.0.16 - - [17/Dec/2023:17:31:20 -0500] "GET /test.php HTTP/1.0" 200 59
"-" "Lynx/2.9.0dev.10 libwww-FM/2.14 SSL-MM/1.4.1 GNUTLS/3.7.1"
donnie@fedora:~$
```

The NR variable represents the **Number of Record**. Since each record in the access_log file consists of only a single line, this is the same as defining the line number that you want to see. To see a range of lines, do something like this:

```
donnie@fedora:~$ sudo awk 'NR == 10, NR == 15 {print $1}' /var/log/httpd/
access_log
192.168.0.16
192.168.0.16
192.168.0.16
192.168.0.107
192.168.0.107
192.168.0.107
donnie@fedora:~$
```

Here, I'm looking at field 1 of lines 10 through 15. Of course, you could do the same thing by combining the tail, head, and cut utilities, but this is way easier.

> In this section, we've looked at FS, OFS, and NR. What I haven't told you yet is that these three constructs are variables that are built into awk. There are many more built-in variables, but I'd rather not overwhelm you by explaining all of them now. If you're interested in reading about all of them, just open the awk man page and scroll down to the **Built-in Variables** section.

The log parsing techniques that I've presented here can be used for any type of log file. To design your awk commands, look through the log files that you want to process and take note of how the fields are laid out in each line, and what information they contain.

Before we move on, let's look at a few other log-parsing techniques.

Using Regular Expressions

You can enhance your awk experience with regular expressions, just as you can with other text-manipulation utilities.

> If you need to, refer back to *Chapter 2, Text Stream Filters – Part 2* and *Chapter 9, Filtering Text with grep, sed, and Regular Expressions* to review the concepts of regular expressions and POSIX character classes.

For our first example, let's say that you need to search through the /etc/passwd file for all users whose usernames begin with a lower-case *v*. Just use a simple regular expression, which will look like this:

```
donnie@fedora:~$ awk '/^v/' /etc/passwd
vicky:x:1001:1001::/home/vicky:/bin/bash
victor:x:1006:1006::/home/victor:/bin/bash
valerie:x:1007:1007::/home/valerie:/bin/bash
victoria:x:1008:1008::/home/victoria:/bin/bash
donnie@fedora:~$
```

This works because the username field is the first field of every line. So, you don't need to do anything any fancier than just this. But, let's suppose you need to search for something in another field that begins with a certain character. For example let's say that you need to search through the Apache access log file for all HTTP status codes that are in the 400 range. Just do something like this:

```
donnie@fedora:~$ sudo awk '$9 ~ /^4/{print $9}' /var/log/httpd/access_log |
sort -n | uniq -c
     17 403
     20 404
donnie@fedora:~$
```

The $9 in the pattern means that you're looking for a certain pattern in field 9. The ~ means that you want something in that field to match whatever is within the following forward slashes. In this case, it's looking for anything in field 9 that begins with the number 4. In the output, you see that I've found both the 403 and the 404 status codes. And, if you need to, you can save the output to a .csv file, like so:

```
donnie@fedora:~$ sudo awk '$9 ~ /^4/{print $9}' /var/log/httpd/access_log |
sort -n | uniq -c | mlr --p2c cat > status_code.csv
donnie@fedora:~$ cat status_code.csv
17,403
20,404
donnie@fedora:~$
```

If you prefer, you can save it to a .tsv file by omitting the mlr --p2c cat portion, like so:

```
donnie@fedora-server:~$ sudo awk '$9 ~ /^4/{print $9}' /var/log/httpd/access_
log | sort -n | uniq -c > status_code.tsv
donnie@fedora-server:~$ cat status_code.tsv
      6 403
      4 404
donnie@fedora-server:~$
```

To see everything *except* for a certain pattern, use the !~ construct, like this:

```
donnie@fedora:~$ sudo awk '$9 !~ /^4/{print $9}' /var/log/httpd/access_log |
sort -n | uniq -c
     53 200
      2 304
donnie@fedora:~$
```

This allows us to see everything except for the 400 codes.

Next, let's say that we want to see all instances where someone used either the Safari or the Lynx web browsers. You could do this:

```
donnie@fedora:~$ sudo awk '/Safari|Lynx/' /var/log/httpd/access_log
```

However, that doesn't work, because it will include entries like this one:

```
192.168.0.27 - - [17/Dec/2023:17:43:40 -0500] "GET / HTTP/1.1" 403 8474 "-"
"Mozilla/5.0 (Windows NT 10.0; Win64; x64) AppleWebKit/537.36 (KHTML, like
Gecko) Chrome/120.0.0.0 Safari/537.36 Edg/120.0.0.0"
```

For some strange reason, Apache can't exactly identify the Microsoft Edge browser, so it reports it as several different possibilities, including Safari. To narrow that down, I'll exclude any users who are using Windows. (Safari used to be available for Windows, but the Windows version was discontinued in 2012.) Here's how that looks:

```
donnie@fedora:~$ sudo awk -F\" '$6 ~/Safari|Lynx/ && $6 !~ /Windows/' /var/log/
httpd/access_log
```

And here, you see something that's rather strange. It's that when you use an or or an and operator within a regular expression, you use either a single | or a single &. When you use an or or an and operator outside of a regular expression, you use either || or &&. I know, it's confusing, but that's just the way it is. Anyway, if you look through the output now, you'll see that there are no lines from the Windows users.

I know, this is just scratching the surface for what you can do with awk and regular expressions. If you ask real nicely, I might show you a few more examples in the next section, which will be about how to use awk to process information from other commands.

Obtaining Input from Commands

Let's start with something simple, by obtaining some basic process information. On the Fedora Server virtual machine that's running Apache, search for all ps aux output lines that contain the httpd pattern, like so:

```
donnie@fedora:~$ ps aux | awk '/httpd/ {print $0}'
root        1072  0.0  0.2  19108 10796 ?            Ss   14:36    0:01 /usr/sbin/
httpd -DFOREGROUND
```

```
apache      1111  0.0  0.1  19204  6788 ?          S     14:36   0:00 /usr/sbin/
httpd -DFOREGROUND
apache      1112  0.0  0.2 2158280 8448 ?          Sl    14:36   0:02 /usr/sbin/
httpd -DFOREGROUND
apache      1113  0.0  0.2 2420488 8592 ?          Sl    14:36   0:03 /usr/sbin/
httpd -DFOREGROUND
apache      1114  0.0  0.2 2158280 8448 ?          Sl    14:36   0:02 /usr/sbin/
httpd -DFOREGROUND
donnie      1908  0.0  0.0   9196  3768 pts/0      S+    17:13   0:00 awk /httpd/
{print $0}
donnie@fedora:~$
```

Next, let's say that we want to see all processes that are owned by the root user. That's also easy. Just do this:

```
donnie@fedora:~$ ps aux | awk '$1 == "root" {print $0}'
root           1  0.0  0.6  74552 27044 ?          Ss    14:26   0:05 /usr/lib/
systemd/systemd --switched-root --system --deserialize=36 rhgb
root           2  0.0  0.0      0     0 ?          S     14:26   0:00 [kthreadd]
root           3  0.0  0.0      0     0 ?          S     14:26   0:00 [pool_
workqueue_release]
. . .
. . .
root        1688  0.0  0.1  16332  6400 ?          S     16:53   0:00 systemd-
userwork: waiting...
donnie@fedora:~$
```

There's nothing really new here, because these awk commands are the same as you saw in the previous section. Indeed, pretty much all of the techniques that you can do with parsing log files also work here. So, let's not repeat any more of that.

The first step for parsing information from the ps utility is to see what the various fields are. The aux combination of options is what I find most useful for myself, simply because it displays the specific information that I most need to see. To see the ps header that shows the field names, I'll pipe the ps aux output into head -1, like this:

```
[donnie@fedora ~]$ ps aux | head -1
USER       PID  %CPU %MEM    VSZ   RSS TTY      STAT  START   TIME COMMAND
[donnie@fedora ~]$
```

Here's the breakdown of what all these fields represent:

- USER: The user that owns each particular process.
- PID: The **Process ID** number of each process.
- %CPU: The percentage of CPU resources that each process consumes.

- RSS: The **Resident Set Size** is the amount of actual physical, non-swapped memory that each process uses. (I know that this is out of order, but you'll soon see the reason.)

- %MEM: The ratio of the process's RSS to the amount of physical memory that's installed in the machine.

- VSZ: The **Virtual Set Size** is the amount of virtual memory that each process is using. (This is expressed in numbers of 1024-byte units.)

- TTY: This is the terminal which is controlling each process.

- STAT: This column holds the status code of each process.

- START: The starting time or date of each process.

- TIME: This is the cumulative CPU time for each process, in "[DD-]HH:MM:SS" format.

- COMMAND: The commands that started each process.

 Bear in mind that there are many options switches for ps, which all show different types of process data. There are also many ways to combine the switches in order to get all of the information you need, displayed in your preferred format. For now though, I'm just going to stick with ps aux, mainly because it's the most useful option combination for me. For more details, see the ps man page.

By default, ps commands always display this header along with the information that you want to see. So, you'll see this header if you pipe ps into an awk command that doesn't filter it out. For example, let's look at the processes that are not owned by the root user, like this:

```
donnie@fedora:~$ ps aux | awk '$1 != "root" {print $0}'
USER         PID %CPU %MEM    VSZ    RSS   TTY   STAT START   TIME COMMAND
systemd+     800  0.1     0.1         16240 7328  ?           Ss        14:27
0:13   /usr/lib/systemd/systemd-oomd
systemd+     801  0.0     0.4         27656 16236 ?           Ss        14:27
0:00   /usr/lib/systemd/systemd-resolved
. . .

. . .
donnie      1745  200     0.1          9888  4520  pts/0     R+        17:10
0:00   ps aux
donnie       746  0.0     0.0          9196  3804  pts/0     S+        17:10
0:00   awk $1 != "root" {print $0}
donnie@fedora:~$
```

That's fine most of the time. But, having that header there might mess you up if you need to save the information to a formatted text file. To fix this, let's use the **Number of Record** (NR) variable that I showed you in the previous section. Here's how that works:

```
donnie@fedora:~$ ps aux | awk 'NR > 1 && $1 != "root" {print $0}'
systemd+     800  0.1  0.1  16240  7328 ?          Ss    14:27   0:15 /usr/lib/
systemd/systemd-oomd
```

```
systemd+     801  0.0  0.4  27656 16236 ?         Ss    14:27   0:00 /usr/lib/
systemd/systemd-resolved
. . .
. . .
donnie      1765  250  0.1   9888  4620 pts/0     R+    17:26   0:00 ps aux
donnie      1766  0.0  0.0   9196  3780 pts/0     S+    17:26   0:00 awk NR > 1
&& $1 != "root" {print $0}
donnie@fedora:~$
```

The NR > 1 clause means that we only want to see records that come after record 1. In other words, we don't want to see the first line of output, which in this case would be the ps header.

Now that we know what each field is, we can create some useful one-liners to extract information. First, let's see how many processes are in either the **Running** state or the **Zombie** state. (A Zombie process is a dead process that hasn't yet been properly destroyed by its parent process. You can view the ps man page to learn more about them.) We know that the STAT column is field 8, so the command will look like this:

```
[donnie@fedora ~]$ ps aux | awk '$8 ~ /^[RZ]/ {print}'
donnie      2803 30.5  1.6 4963152 1058324 ?      Rl    14:00  70:12 /usr/lib64/
firefox/firefox
donnie      4383  1.9  0.4 3157216 307460 ?        Rl    14:03   4:18 /usr/
lib64/firefox/firefox -contentproc -childID 33 -isForBrowser -prefsLen 31190
-prefMapSize 237466 -jsInitLen 229864 -parentBuildID 20231219113315 -greomni /
usr/lib64/firefox/omni.ja -appomni /usr/lib64/firefox/browser/omni.ja -appDir /
usr/lib64/firefox/browser {d458c911-d065-4a3c-bdd5-9d06fc1d030d} 2803 true tab
donnie     46283  0.0  0.0      0     0 ?           R    17:50   0:00 [Chroot
Helper]
donnie     46315  0.0  0.0 224672  3072 pts/0      R+    17:50   0:00 ps aux
[donnie@fedora ~]$
```

It looks a bit jumbled up because the COMMAND field for the second process contains a very long string, but that's okay. You can still see that field 8 in every line begins with the letter R. (You'll rarely see any Zombie processes on your systems, so don't worry about not seeing any of them here. And no, Zombie processes don't go around looking for brains to steal.)

The w command shows you a list of all users who are logged into the system, and what they're doing. It looks like this:

```
donnie@fedora:~$ w
 17:37:44 up  3:11,  4 users,  load average: 0.03, 0.06, 0.02
 USER       TTY       LOGIN@   IDLE    JCPU     PCPU     WHAT
 donnie     tty1      17:31    5:51    0.06s    0.06s    -bash
 donnie     pts/0     15:29    0.00s   0.35s    0.06s    w
 vicky      pts/1     17:32    4:50    0.05s    0.05s    -bash
```

```
frank        pts/2        17:33    3:18      0.05s     0.05s      -bash
donnie@fedora:~$
```

You see that I'm logged in via `tty1`, which is the local terminal. I'm also logged in remotely via a `pts` terminal, along with Vicky and Frank. (Remember that `tty` terminals indicate that someone is logged in locally, while `pts` terminals indicate that someone is logged in remotely.) Now, let's use `ps` to see more information about the processes that the remote users are running, like this:

```
donnie@fedora:~$ ps aux | awk '$7 ~ "pts"'
donnie    1492   0.0   0.1   8480   5204 pts/0  Ss    15:29    0:00 -bash
vicky     1845   0.0   0.1   8348   4960 pts/1  Ss+   17:32    0:00 -bash
frank     1892   0.0   0.1   8348   5000 pts/2  Ss+   17:33    0:00 -bash
donnie    1936   200   0.1   9888   4640 pts/0  R+    17:37    0:00 ps aux
donnie    1937   0.0   0.0   9064   3908 pts/0  S+    17:37    0:00 awk $7 ~ "pts"
donnie@fedora:~$
```

A few moments ago, I showed you how to strip the header line out of the output if your `awk` command doesn't already strip it out. This time, the `awk` command does strip it out, but I've decided that I want to see it. To fix that, I'll do this:

```
donnie@fedora:~$ ps aux | awk '$7 ~ "pts" || $1 == "USER"'
USER    PID   %CPU  %MEM  VSZ   RSS  TTY    STAT START   TIME COMMAND
donnie 1492  0.0   0.1   8480 5204 pts/0 Ss    15:29  0:00   -bash
vicky  1845  0.0   0.1   8348 4960 pts/1 Ss+   17:32  0:00   -bash
frank  1892  0.0   0.1   8348 5000 pts/2 Ss+   17:33  0:00   -bash
donnie 2029  400   0.1   9888 4416 pts/0 R+    17:48  0:00   ps aux
donnie 2030  0.0   0.0   9064 3928 pts/0 S+    17:48  0:00   awk $7 ~ "pts" ||
$1 == "USER"
donnie@fedora:~$
```

Note here that I'm using two different methods of finding a pattern. The `$7 ~ "pts"` portion finds all lines that contain the `pts` text string in field 7. So, we see that `pts/0`, `pts/1`, and `pts/2` all match this search criterion. The `$1 == "USER"` portion is looking for an exact, whole-word match. To demonstrate, look at this `user.txt` file:

```
[donnie@fedora ~]$ cat user.txt
USER          donnie
USER1         vicky
USER2         cleopatra
USER3         sylvester
[donnie@fedora ~]
```

Using the `~` to search for all lines with `USER` in field 1 gives us this:

```
[donnie@fedora ~]$ awk '$1 ~ "USER" {print $1}' user.txt
USER
```

```
USER1
USER2
USER3
[donnie@fedora ~]$
```

Replacing the ~ with == gives us this:

```
[donnie@fedora ~]$ awk '$1 == "USER" {print $1}' user.txt
USER
[donnie@fedora ~]$
```

So you see that there is a big difference. Also, note that since I'm searching for a literal text string, I can surround the search term (USER) within either a pair of double quotes or a pair of forward slashes when using the ~. However, when using the ==, you'll need to use the double quotes, because using the double slashes shows you nothing.

And, with that bit of a digression out of the way, let's get back to our regularly scheduled program.

I've now decided that I want to see all processes with a virtual memory size (VSZ) of more than 500,000 bytes. VSZ information is in field 5, so my awk command looks like this:

```
donnie@fedora:~$ ps aux | awk '$5 > 500000 {print $0}'
USER    PID  %CPU %MEM VSZ       RSS  TTY  STAT START   TIME COMMAND
apache 1098 0.0  0.2   2420488 8628  ?    Sl   14:28   0:04 /usr/sbin/httpd
-DFOREGROUND
apache 1099 0.0  0.2   2223816 8248  ?    Sl   14:28   0:03 /usr/sbin/httpd
-DFOREGROUND
apache 1100  0.0 0.2   2158280 8232  ?    Sl   14:28   0:04 /usr/sbin/httpd
-DFOREGROUND
donnie@fedora:~$
```

But, that's more information than I really need. I just want to look at the relevant fields, and I've decided to place each field on its own line, along with a label. Here's how I'll do it:

```
donnie@fedora:~$ ps aux | awk 'NR > 1 && $5 > 500000 {print "USER:" "\t\t" $1
"\n" "PID:" "\t\t" $2 "\n" "VSZ:" "\t\t" $5 "\n" "COMMAND:" "\t" $11 "\n\n"}'
USER:            apache
PID:             1147
VSZ:             2354952
COMMAND:         /usr/sbin/httpd
USER:            apache
PID:             1148
VSZ:             2158280
COMMAND:         /usr/sbin/httpd
USER:            apache
PID:             1149
```

```
VSZ:            2158280
COMMAND:            /usr/sbin/httpd
donnie@fedora:~$
```

As noted before, NR > 1 prevents ps from printing the default header. In the action, the print command places a pair of tabs (\t\t) between USER, PID, VSZ, and their respective values. The COMMAND
label is longer, so it only requires one tab (\t) between it and its values. This ensures that all values in
the second column line up nice and neat. The newlines (\n) after the USER, PID, and VSZ values cause
the next field to print on a new line. After the COMMAND value, I placed two newlines (\n\n) so that there
would be a blank line between each record.

Next, let's turn this command into a function that we can add to the sysinfo.lib function library that
I showed you in *Chapter 10--Understanding Functions*. Our new VSZ_info() function looks like this:

```
VSZ_info() {
        echo "<h2>Processes with more than 500000 bytes VSZ
        size.</h2>"
        echo "<pre>"
        ps aux | awk 'NR > 1 && $5 > 500000 {print "USER:" "\t\t" $1 "\n"
"PID:" "\t\t" $2 "\n" "VSZ:" "\t\t" $5 "\n" "COMMAND:" "\t" $11 "\n\n"}'
        echo "</pre>"
}
```

Now, in the system_info.sh script that I also showed you in *Chapter 10*, you'll need to add $(VSZ_info)
to the end of the list of functions that the script calls. Now when you run the script, you'll see the
VSZ information at the end of the output file. (Both files are too long to reproduce here, but you can
download them from GitHub.)

Okay, that about wraps it up for the basics of using awk in shell scripts. Let's summarize and move on.

Summary

In this chapter, I introduced you to the sacred mysteries of using awk. We started by looking at the
numerous implementations of awk, and at how a basic awk command is constructed. Next, we saw
how to use awk to process information either from a text file or from another program. Then, we saw
how to run awk commands from within a normal shell script. Finally, we turned an awk command
into a function, and added it to our function library file.

In the next chapter, we'll look at how to create awk program scripts. I'll see you there.

Questions

1.   What are the two parts of an awk command? (Choose two.)

     a.   action

     b.   expression

     c.   pattern

    d.   command

    e.   E. order

2. What does `{print $0}` do in an awk command?

    a.   It prints the name of the script that you're running, because `$0` is the bash positional parameter that hold the name of the script.

    b.   It prints the value that was assigned to the `0` variable.

    c.   It prints all fields of a record.

    d.   It's an invalid command that doesn't do anything.

3. You want to perform an exact, whole-word match for all lines that contain a certain text string. Which of the following awk operators would you use?

    a.   `==`

    b.   `=`

    c.   `eq`

    d.   `~`

4. Where is the best place to define values for `FS` and `OFS`?

    a.   In the END section of an awk command.

    b.   You can't. They already have pre-defined values.

    c.   In the BEGIN section of an awk command.

    d.   In the action of an awk command.

5. How do you use regular expressions with awk?

    a.   Surround the regular expression with a pair of forward slashes.

    b.   Surround the regular expression with a pair of single quotes.

    c.   Surround the regular expression with a pair of double quotes.

    d.   Don't surround the regular expression with anything.

Further Reading

- The GNU awk Users' Guide: `https://www.gnu.org/software/gawk/manual/gawk.html`
- Awk by Example: `https://developer.ibm.com/tutorials/l-awk1/`
- awklang.org--The site for things related to the awk language: `http://www.awklang.org/`
- awk: One True awk: `https://github.com/onetrueawk/awk`
- Awk Scripts YouTube channel: `https://www.youtube.com/@awkscripts`
- Miller Documentation: `https://miller.readthedocs.io/en/latest/`
- The GAWK Manual-Useful "One-liners": `http://web.mit.edu/gnu/doc/html/gawk_7.html`
- How to Use awk in Bash Scripting: `https://www.cyberciti.biz/faq/bash-scripting-using-awk/`

- Advanced Bash Shell Scripting Guide-Shell Wrappers: `https://www.linuxtopia.org/online_books/advanced_bash_scripting_guide/wrapper.html`
- Awk: The Power and Promise of a 40-year-old Language: `https://www.fosslife.org/awk-power-and-promise-40-year-old-language`

Answers

1. a and c
2. c
3. a
4. c
5. a

Join our community on Discord!

Read this book alongside other users, Linux experts, and the author himself.

Ask questions, provide solutions to other readers, chat with the author via Ask Me Anything sessions, and much more. Scan the QR code or visit the link to join the community.

`https://packt.link/SecNet`

Leave a Review!

Thank you for purchasing this book from Packt Publishing—we hope you enjoy it! Your feedback is invaluable and helps us improve and grow. Once you've completed reading it, please take a moment to leave an Amazon review; it will only take a minute, but it makes a big difference for readers like you.

Scan the QR code below to receive a free ebook of your choice.

`https://packt.link/NzOWQ`

15

Using awk — Part 2

In this chapter, we'll continue the discussion about awk, but from a different perspective. In the previous chapter, I showed you the basics of creating one-line awk commands that you can use in your normal shell scripts. In this chapter, I'll show you a bit about how to write awk scripts in the awk language. Topics in this chapter include:

- Basic awk script construction
- Using conditional statements
- Using a while construct and setting variables
- Using for loops and arrays
- Using floating point math and printf
- Working with multi-line records

If you're ready, let's dig in.

Technical Requirements

You can use either a Fedora or Debian virtual machine for this. And, as always, you can grab the scripts by doing:

```
git clone https://github.com/PacktPublishing/The-Ultimate-Linux-Shell-
Scripting-Guide.git
```

Basic awk Script Construction

Let's begin with the simplest awk script that you can imagine, which we'll call awk_kernel1.awk. It looks like this:

```
/kernel/
```

As you've likely guessed, this script will look through a specified file to search for all lines that contain the text string kernel. You already know that {print $0} is the default action if no action is specified. So, this script will print out every line that contains the specified text string.

In actual awk scripts, there's no need to preface every command with awk, and there's no need to surround the commands with pairs of single quotes, as you have to do when embedding awk commands in normal shell scripts. I didn't put a shebang line into this script, so there's no need to set the executable permission. Instead, just invoke the script like this:

```
donnie@fedora:~$ sudo awk -f awk_kernel1.awk /var/log/messages
Jan 11 16:17:55 fedora kernel: audit: type=1334 audit(1705007875.578:35): prog-
id=60 op=LOAD
Jan 11 16:18:00 fedora kernel: msr: Write to unrecognized MSR 0x17f by mcelog
(pid: 856).
Jan 11 16:18:00 fedora kernel: msr: See https://git.kernel.org/pub/scm/linux/
kernel/git/tip/tip.git/about for details.
. . .

. . .
Jan 11 17:15:28 fedora kernel: fwupdmgr[1779]: memfd_create() called without
MFD_EXEC or MFD_NOEXEC_SEAL set
donnie@fedora:~$
```

Sure, that works. But, wouldn't you really rather have a stand-alone, executable script? That's easy enough to do. Just add the shebang line, like this:

```
#!/usr/bin/awk -f
/kernel/
```

Then, make the script executable, the same as you would do with normal bash scripts.

There are two things that I want you to notice about this shebang line. First, is that I'm using /usr/bin/ instead of /bin/ as the path to the awk executable. That's because I want to make this script portable, so that it will run on Linux, Unix, and Unix-like systems such as FreeBSD and macOS.

> The /bin/ path that you're used to seeing in shebang lines is an artifact that's been carried over from older Linux systems. On current Linux systems, /bin/ is a symbolic link that points to /usr/bin/. On older Linux systems, /bin/ and /usr/bin/ used to be two separate directories, which each contained two separate sets of program files. That's no longer the case. Nowadays, you'll find the awk executable in /usr/bin/ on all Linux systems.
>
> FreeBSD still uses separate /bin/ and /usr/bin/ directories with different sets of program files. But, awk is in /usr/bin/, and there's no symbolic link for it in /bin/. So, just use #!/usr/bin/awk, and you'll be good-to-go for most operating systems.

The second thing to notice is that I still have to invoke awk with the -f option, which causes awk to read the program file. If you leave out the -f, the script won't work.

Now that you've seen the basic structure of an awk script, let's look at some awk programming constructs.

Using Conditional Statements

You've already been using if constructs without even knowing it. That's because you don't have to explicitly declare them as such. The simple /kernel/ command that you just saw in the awk_kernel1. awk script means that if the *kernel* string is found on a line, then print that line. However, awk also offers the whole array of programming constructs that you would expect to see in other languages. For example, let's create the awk_kernel2.awk script, which will look like this:

```
#!/usr/bin/awk -f
{
        if (/kernel/) {
                print $0
        }
}
```

This is somewhat different from what you're used to seeing in bash scripts, because in awk there's no need to use then or fi statements. This is because awk uses C language syntax for its programming constructs. So, if you're used to programming in C, rejoice!

Also, note how you need to surround the pattern with a pair of parentheses, and how you have to surround the entire multi-line script with a pair of curly braces. At any rate, just specify the name and location of your log file when running the script, like this:

```
donnie@fedora:~$ sudo ./awk_kernel2.awk /var/log/messages
```

Now, you're probably wondering why anyone would want to do the extra typing to create a full-blown if construct when just typing /kernel/ will do the job. Well, it's so that you can create full-blown if. .else constructs, like this one in the awk_kernel3.awk script:

```
#!/usr/bin/awk -f
{
        if ($5 ~ /kernel/) {
                print "Kernel here in Field 5"
        }
        else if ($5 ~ /systemd/) {
                print "Systemd here in Field 5"
        }
        else {
                print "No kernel or systemd in Field 5"
        }
}
```

Now, let's see how many times each type of message shows up in the log file:

```
donnie@fedora:~$ sudo ./awk_kernel3.awk /var/log/messages | sort | uniq -c
  25795 Kernel here in Field 5
  38580 No kernel or systemd in Field 5
  35506 Systemd here in Field 5
donnie@fedora:~$
```

Cool, it works.

For our final `if` trick, let's create the `awk_kernel4.awk` script, like this:

```
#!/usr/bin/awk -f
{
        if ($5 ~ /kernel/) {
                print "Kernel here in Field 5 on line " NR
        }
        else if ($5 ~ /systemd/) {
                print "Systemd here in Field 5 on line " NR
        }
        else {
                print "No kernel or systemd in Field 5 on line " NR
        }
}
```

The Number of Records (NR) built-in variable causes the line numbers to print out along with the messages. There will be lots of output, so you might want to pipe it into `less`, like this:

```
donnie@fedora:~$ sudo ./awk_kernel4.awk /var/log/messages | less
```

Here's a sample of the output:

```
Kernel here in Field 5 on line 468
Systemd here in Field 5 on line 469
Systemd here in Field 5 on line 470
No kernel or systemd in Field 5 on line 471
No kernel or systemd in Field 5 on line 472
No kernel or systemd in Field 5 on line 473
No kernel or systemd in Field 5 on line 474
No kernel or systemd in Field 5 on line 475
No kernel or systemd in Field 5 on line 476
Systemd here in Field 5 on line 477
```

Okay, I think you get the idea. Other than the different syntax, it's really no different from using `if` in normal bash scripts. So, let's move on for a while.

Using a while Construct and Setting Variables

In this section, I'll show you two new concepts at once. You'll see how to use a while loop, and how to use awk programming variables. Let's begin with something simple.

Summing Numbers in a Line

In this scenario, we have a file with several lines of numbers. We want to add the numbers on each line and show the sum for each line. First, create the input file and make it look something like this numbers_fields.txt file:

```
38 87 389 3 3432
34 13
38976 38 198378 38 3
3878538 38
38
893 18 3 384 352 3892 10921 10 384
348 35 293
93 1 2
1 2 3 4 5
```

This looks like quite a challenging task because each line has a different number of fields. But, it's actually quite easy. Here's the add_fields.awk script that does the job:

```
#!/usr/bin/awk -f
{
addend=1
sum=0
while (addend <= NF) {
sum = sum + $addend
addend++
                                }
print "Line " NR " Sum is " sum
}
```

The first thing I've done is to initialize the addend and sum variables. The addend variable represents the field numbers. By initializing it to a value of 1, the script will always begin at the first field of every line. The sum variable is initialized to 0, for obvious reasons. The while (addend <= NF) line causes the while loop to execute until it reaches the last field in a line. (The built-in NF variable holds the number of fields in a given line.) In the next line, using $addend is the same as listing a field number, such as $1 or $2. So, as you might expect, $addend returns the value that's contained in a given field. By using a variable in place of a hard-coded field number, we can use the addend++ command in the next line to advance to the next field in a line. (This variable++ construct increments the value of the variable by 1, the same as it does in C.)

If you're a bit confused by this, allow me to clarify.

Unlike in normal shell scripting, in `awk`, you don't preface the name of a variable with a `$` to call back its value. In `awk`, the `$` is instead used to reference the number of a field. So, prefacing a variable name with a `$` in awk just means that you're referencing the field number that's been assigned to that variable.

After the `while` loop finishes, the script prints out its message, with the sum of all the numbers on a line. Then, it returns to the beginning of the script and keeps going until all lines in the file have been processed. Here's what the output looks like:

```
donnie@fedora:~$ ./add_fields.awk numbers_fields.txt
Line 1 Sum is 3949
Line 2 Sum is 47
Line 3 Sum is 237433
Line 4 Sum is 3878576
Line 5 Sum is 38
Line 6 Sum is 16857
Line 7 Sum is 676
Line 8 Sum is 96
Line 9 Sum is 15
donnie@fedora:~$
```

It works, so everything is cool. Now, let's fancy things up a bit. Let's add a line that will produce the average of the numbers on each line and format the output. Name the file `average_fields.awk`, and make it look like this:

```
#!/usr/bin/awk -f
{
addend=1
sum=0
while (addend <= NF) {
        sum = sum + $addend
        addend++
}
print "Line " NR "\n\t" "Sum: " sum "\n\t" "Average: " sum/NF
}
```

What's so cool about this is that I can use the `NF` built-in variable in math operations. In this case, I'm just dividing the sum of each line by the number of fields in each line. The output looks like this:

```
donnie@fedora:~$ ./average_fields.awk numbers_fields.txt
Line 1
    Sum:  3949
```

```
    Average: 789.8
Line 2
    Sum: 47
    Average: 23.5
. . .

. . .
Line 9
    Sum: 15
    Average: 3
donnie@fedora:~$
```

> If you're used to C programming, understand that there's a difference between how awk and C use variables. Unlike in C, it's not necessary to declare awk variables before you use them. But, it is sometimes necessary to initialize them to a certain value before you use them. Also, unlike in C, there's only one variable type in awk. All awk variables are of the string type, and all awk math operators automatically recognize numerical values that these variables might represent.

Next, let's look at something a bit more complex.

Finding the CPU Generation

Let's consider another scenario. You have an old server that's powered by an AMD Opteron CPU. You just tried to install Red Hat Enterprise Linux 9 (RHEL 9) on it, and you can't get it to work. What could be the problem?

Well, it's just that your trusty Opteron CPU is too old, which means that it lacks certain capabilities that newer CPUs have. Ever since AMD created the first 64-bit x86 CPUs in 2003, both AMD and Intel have kept adding new capabilities to their newer models. In 2020, representatives from Intel, AMD, Red Hat, and SUSE got together and defined the four generations of x86_64. Each successive generation has capabilities that aren't in the previous generations. Here's a list of when each generation was introduced:

- Generation 1: 2003
- Generation 2: 2009
- Generation 3: 2013 for Intel, 2015 for AMD
- Generation 4: 2017 for Intel, 2022 for AMD

Software that was created for a first generation x86_64 CPU will also run fine on the three newer generations. But, if you have a newer CPU, you can make things run faster by using software that was optimized for it. Of course, that means that it won't run on the older CPUs. So, if you're still running a first generation x86_64 CPU, you won't be able to run either RHEL 9 or any of its clones. (Rumor has it that RHEL 10, which should be out sometime in 2025, will require at least a third generation x86_64 CPU. You'll find a link to the rumor in the *Further Reading* section.) That's actually okay, because Red Hat's target customers are the large enterprises that upgrade their gear on a regular basis.

This makes it very unlikely that any of them still run any of these first generation machines. This doesn't really affect normal home users of desktop Linux, because very few home users use either RHEL or a RHEL clone for that purpose, and most non-RHEL distros still support the old machines. So, how do you know which generation your CPU is? That's easy. Just write a script.

To get an idea of how this works, look in the /proc/cpuinfo file, and scroll down to the flags section. What you'll see depends upon which generation of x86_64 CPU is in your machine. Here on my 2012-model Dell workstation with an Intel Xeon CPU that's of the second generation x86_64 variety, the flags section looks like this:

```
flags           : fpu vme de pse tsc msr pae mce cx8 apic sep mtrr pge mca
cmov pat pse36 clflush mmx fxsr sse sse2 ht syscall nx rdtscp lm constant_tsc
rep_good nopl xtopology nonstop_tsc cpuid tsc_known_freq pni pclmulqdq ssse3
cx16 sse4_1 sse4_2 x2apic popcnt aes xsave avx hypervisor lahf_lm pti md_clear
flush_l1d
```

On my vintage 2009-model Hewlett-Packard machine with a pair of first generation Opteron CPUs, the flags section looks like this:

```
flags           : fpu vme de pse tsc msr pae mce cx8 apic sep mtrr pge mca
cmov pat pse36 clflush mmx fxsr sse sse2 ht syscall nx mmxext fxsr_opt pdpe1gb
rdtscp lm 3dnowext 3dnow constant_tsc rep_good nopl nonstop_tsc cpuid extd_
apicid pni monitor cx16 popcnt lahf_lm cmp_legacy svm extapic cr8_legacy abm
sse4a misalignsse 3dnowprefetch osvw ibs skinit wdt hw_pstate vmmcall npt lbrv
svm_lock nrip_save
```

You see here that the second generation CPU in my Dell has newer capabilities, such as sse4_1, sse4_2, and a few others that aren't in the old Opterons. On a Linux system, you can create either a bash script or an awk script that will automatically parse the /proc/cpuinfo file to determine the generation to which your CPU belongs. Here's the x86_64_check.awk script, which I borrowed from a post on the StackExchange site:

```
#!/usr/bin/awk -f
BEGIN {
    while (!/flags/) if (getline < "/proc/cpuinfo" != 1) exit 1
    if (/cmov/&&/cx8/&&/fpu/&&/fxsr/&&/mmx/&&/syscall/&&/sse2/) level = 1
    if (level == 1 && /cx16/&&/lahf/&&/popcnt/&&/sse4_1/&&/sse4_2/&&/ssse3/)
level = 2
    if (level == 2 && /avx/&&/avx2/&&/bmi1/&&/bmi2/&&/f16c/&&/fma/&&/abm/&&/
movbe/&&/xsave/) level = 3
    if (level == 3 && /avx512f/&&/avx512bw/&&/avx512cd/&&/avx512dq/&&/
avx512vl/) level = 4
    if (level > 0) { print "CPU supports x86-64-v" level; exit level + 1 }
    exit 1
}
```

The first thing to note is that the whole script needs to be part of a BEGIN block. That's because we need to process the whole cpuinfo file at once, instead of just one line at a time as awk would normally do. The BEGIN block helps us out with that.

Then, note that this script uses a different style for the if constructs. Instead of formatting them in the C language style as I showed you before, the author instead placed each if construct on its own line. Each style works equally well, and I'll leave it to you to decide which one you like better. Anyway, here's the breakdown of how it all works.

- At the end of each of the first four if statements, the level variable is set to a new value.
- The first if statement looks for capabilities that are in the first generation, and then assigns 1 as the value of level.
- The second if statement verifies that the CPU contains level 1 capabilities, looks for another set of capabilities that are in second generation CPUs, and then assigns 2 as the value of level.
- The process repeats for the third and fourth if statements, in order to detect either third or fourth generation CPUs.
- Finally, the fifth if statement verifies that the value of level is greater than 0, prints out the message, and then exits the script with an exit code that's the value of level plus 1.
- The exit 1 line at the end causes the script to exit with exit code 1 if the script fails to run correctly for whatever reason. (The level + 1 command at the end of the fourth if statement prevents a successful run of the program from returning a 1 for the exit code. Remember, 1 is normally an exit code for a program that doesn't run correctly.)

An interesting thing about awk variables is that all of them are string variables, which greatly simplifies the coding process. If you assign the value of 1 to the level variable, the value is stored as a string instead of as an integer. But, when you use variables to perform math operations in awk, everything works correctly because awk automatically recognizes when a string is really a number. Also, unlike bash, awk can natively perform floating point math operations. So, you can perform math operations much easier and faster in awk than you can in either bash scripting or a normal programming language. To demonstrate this, let's run this script on my both of the workstations that I currently have running. Here's what it looks like on my old Opteron-powered Hewlett-Packard:

```
donnie@opensuse:~> ./x86-64-level_check.awk
CPU supports x86-64-v1
donnie@opensuse:~> echo $?
2
donnie@opensuse:~>
```

As expected, the script shows that this is a first generation x86_64 machine. The echo $? command shows the exit code, which was created by the level + 1 command in the script. Now, here's how it looks on my Xeon-powered Dell:

```
donnie@fedora:~$ ./x86-64-level_check.awk
CPU supports x86-64-v2
donnie@fedora:~$ echo $?
```

```
3
donnie@fedora:~$
```

So yeah, everything works fine.

Ah, but wait. We're not done yet, because I haven't yet explained the `while` construct. It's a bit tricky, so I saved it for last.

I've already shown you that in the `/proc/cpuinfo` file, the strings that you seek are in the stanza with the text string `flags` in the first field. But, the `while (!/flags/)` statement makes it appear that we're *not* looking for the `flags` stanza. (Remember that the `!` is a negation operator.) To understand what's really going on, view the entire `cpuinfo` file by entering `cat /proc/cpuinfo`. You'll see that the same set of information prints out once for every CPU core in your system. For example, my Dell workstation is running with an octo-core Xeon. Hyperthreading is enabled, which means that I have a total of 16 virtual CPU cores. So, running `cat /proc/cpuinfo` causes the same CPU information to print 16 times. You'll also see that several more stanzas of information print out after the `flags` stanza. To understand how this `while` loop works, run the following one-line `awk` command:

```
donnie@fedora:~$ awk 'BEGIN {while (!/flags/) if (getline <"/proc/cpuinfo" ==
1) print $0}'
processor   : 0
vendor_id   : GenuineIntel
. . .
. . .
wp          : yes
flags          : fpu vme de pse tsc msr pae mce cx8 apic sep mtrr pge
mca cmov pat pse36 clflush dts acpi mmx fxsr sse sse2 ss ht tm pbe syscall nx
pdpe1gb rdtscp lm constant_tsc arch_perfmon pebs bts rep_good nopl xtopology
nonstop_tsc cpuid aperfmperf pni pclmulqdq dtes64 monitor ds_cpl vmx smx
est tm2 ssse3 cx16 xtpr pdcm pcid dca sse4_1 sse4_2 x2apic popcnt tsc_
deadline_timer aes xsave avx lahf_lm epb pti ssbd ibrs ibpb stibp tpr_shadow
flexpriority ept vpid xsaveopt dtherm ida arat pln pts vnmi md_clear flush_l1d
donnie@fedora:~$
```

The `flags` stanza is actually just a single long line that wraps around on both your terminal and on the printed page. So, `awk` treats the `flags` line as a single record. The `while (!/flags/)` statement in this command causes `getline` to read the `cpuinfo` file until it encounters the first `flags` string. This means that the CPU information for only the first CPU core will show up, and any information that comes after the first `flags` line will not show up. (Yeah, it looks a bit confusing, but it makes total sense when you think about it.)

In the original script, the `if (getline < "/proc/cpuinfo" != 1) exit 1` that's within the `while` loop does two things for us. First, it uses the `!=1` parameter to check for the existence of the `cpuinfo` file. If `!=1`, which is the same as saying *not true*, evaluates to *true*, then the script will exit with exit code 1.

If the !=1 parameter evaluates to *false*, which would mean that the file exists, then getline, a built-in awk function, will read in the cpuinfo file. This way, if you run this script on an operating system that doesn't have a /proc/cpuinfo file, such as FreeBSD, it will gracefully exit.

Now, some of you might prefer using C-style syntax to make the script a bit more readable. Fortunately, that's easy to do. Changing the style makes the script too long to show here in its entirety, but I can show you a snippet:

```
#!/usr/bin/awk -f
BEGIN {
        while (!/flags/) {
                if (getline < "/proc/cpuinfo" !=1) {
                        exit 1
                        }
                }
. . .
. . .
if (level > 0) {
                { print "CPU supports x86-64-v" level; exit level + 1 }
        }
        exit 1
}
```

If you want to see the converted script in its entirety, just download the x86-64-level_check2.awk file from GitHub.

I believe that we're done with this script. Let's see what we can do with a for loop and an array.

Using for loops and Arrays

Certain languages, such as Spanish and French, have the concept of masculine and feminine nouns. For this demo, we'll work with a list of English nouns, their Spanish equivalents, and the gender designations for the Spanish nouns.

 Why is someone with a French last name creating a list of Spanish words? Well, it's just that despite my French ancestry, I chose to learn Spanish instead of French in high school. So, I do know some Spanish, but I don't know French. (I know, I'm weird.) Also, I realize that the Spanish word *camión* has an accent over the last syllable. Alas, inserting accents with an English-language keyboard isn't easily done in a plain-text file, at least not without messing up how the awk script works.

To begin, create the spanish_words.txt file, and make it look like this:

```
ENGLISH:SPANISH:GENDER
cat:gato:M
```

```
table:mesa:F
bed:cama:F
bus:camion:M
house:casa:F
```

As you see, we're using colons as field separators, and using either M or F to designate if a word is masculine or feminine. The first line is a header, so we'll need to take that into account when we process the file.

Next, create the `masc-fem.awk` script, like this:

```
#!/usr/bin/awk -f
BEGIN {FS=":"}
NR==1 {next}
$3 == "M" {masc[$2]=$1}
$3 == "F" {fem[$2]=$1}
END {
        print "\nMasculine Nouns\n----";
                for (m in masc)
                        {print m "--" masc[m]; count++}
        print "\nFeminine Nouns\n----";
                for (f in fem)
                        {print f "--" fem[f]; count2++}
        print "\nThere are " count " masculine nouns and " count2 " feminine
nouns."
}
```

In the BEGIN section, we're setting the : as the field separator. The `NR == 1 {next}` line means to ignore line 1 and move on to the next line. The next two lines build the `masc` and `fem` arrays. Any line that has an M in field 3 goes into the `masc` array, and any line that has an F in field 3 goes into the `fem` array. The END section contains code that will run after the code in the main body has finished building the arrays. The two `for` loops work the same as you saw with the normal shell scripting `for` loops, except that we're now using C language syntax. The first loop prints out the list of masculine nouns and uses the `count` variable to add up the total of masculine nouns. The second loop does the same for the feminine nouns, except that it uses the `count2` variable to total the number of feminine nouns. Running the script looks like this:

```
donnie@fedora:~$ ./masc-fem.awk spanish_words.txt
Masculine Nouns
----
gato--cat
camion--bus
Feminine Nouns
----
```

```
mesa--table
casa--house
cama--bed
There are 2 masculine nouns and 3 feminine nouns.
donnie@fedora:~$
```

And, that's all there is to it. Easy, right?

For our next trick, let's do some floating-point math.

Using Floating Point Math and printf

For some strange reason, you've found yourself working a job that requires you to keep track of weather-related statistics. Your boss has just sent you a text file that contains a list of temperatures. Some of the temperatures are Celsius temperatures, and some are Fahrenheit temperatures. Your assigned task is to convert the Fahrenheit temperatures to Celsius temperatures. You can do that the hard way by using a calculator to manually convert each Fahrenheit temperature, or you can write a script that will automate the process. You've decided that it would be easier to write a script. The list of temperatures is in the temps.txt file, which looks like this:

```
Temperature Celsius_or_Fahrenheit
32 F
212 F
-40 F
-14.7 F
24.6111 C
75.8 F
55.21 F
23.9444 C
29.8 F
104.34 F
98.6 F
23.1 C
```

The first three temperatures are checks to verify that the script works correctly. We know that 32 degrees F equals 0 degrees C, that 212 degrees F equals 100 degrees C, and finally that -40 degrees F equals -40 degrees C. If the script converts those three temperatures correctly, we can be reasonably sure that the rest of the temperatures are getting converted correctly.

 Be sure that you haven't inserted a blank line after the last temperature line, or else the script will insert non-sense information after the last actual line of output data.

There are two ways to express the conversion formula. Here's one way:

```
(($1-32)*5) / 9
```

Here's the other way:

```
($1-32)/1.8
```

The $1 represents the field that holds the original Fahrenheit temperature. So, we begin by subtracting 32 from the Fahrenheit value.

Either formula works equally well, so it really doesn't matter which one we use. Just for fun, I'll use the first method in the fahrenheit_to_celsius.awk script, which looks like this:

```
#!/usr/bin/awk -f
NR==1 ; NR>1{print ($2=="F" ? (($1-32)*5) / 9 : $1)"\t\t Celsius"}
```

As you see, it's just a simple one-liner. The NR==1 causes the header to print out, and the NR>1 ensures that the conversions are performed only on the lines that contain actual data. The combination of the ? and the : in the print action is known as a **ternary operator**. If the first term ($2=="F") evaluates to true, then the original value of field 1 will be replaced by the value that's between the ? and the :. In this case, the new value is derived from performing the conversion calculation. After the new temperature value on each line, we want to print out a pair of tabs, followed by the word Celsius. Here's what happens when I run the script:

```
donnie@fedora:~$ ./fahrenheit_to_celsius.awk temps.txt
Temperature Celsius_or_Fahrenheit
0               Celsius
100             Celsius
-40             Celsius
-25.9444             Celsius
24.6111         Celsius
24.3333         Celsius
12.8944         Celsius
23.9444         Celsius
-1.22222             Celsius
40.1889         Celsius
37              Celsius
23.1            Celsius
donnie@fedora:~$
```

That doesn't look so good, because some of the Celsius values are longer than the others, which causes the second column of those lines to not line up correctly. We'll fix this by using printf instead of print.

The printf command allows you to customize the output in ways that you can't do with print. It works pretty much the same way in awk as it does in C, so once again you C programmers can rejoice. Here's how the solution works in the fahrenheit_to_celsius2.awk script:

```
#!/usr/bin/awk -f
NR==1; NR>1{printf("%-11s %s\n",($2=="F" ? (($1-32)*5) / 9 : $1), "Celsius")}
```

The % signs in the printf command represent formatting directives. Let's take the %-11s directive, which formats the first field in each line. The - tells printf to left-justify the output. (By default, the output is right-justified.) The 11s tells printf to allocate 11 spaces for the first field of output. If the string in any given line is less than 11 characters long, then printf will pad the output with enough blank spaces to make up the difference. Finally, %s\n causes printf to print out the designated text string as the second field, followed by a newline. (Unlike print, printf doesn't automatically add a newline at the end of a line.) Anyway, here's the output:

```
donnie@fedora:~$ ./fahrenheit_to_celsius2.awk temps.txt
Temperature Celsius_or_Fahrenheit
0           Celsius
100         Celsius
-40         Celsius
-25.9444    Celsius
24.6111     Celsius
24.3333     Celsius
12.8944     Celsius
23.9444     Celsius
-1.22222    Celsius
40.1889     Celsius
37          Celsius
23.1        Celsius
donnie@fedora:~$
```

Yes, that looks much better. But, what if you don't need to see all of those decimal places? Easy, just use a different formatting directive for the first field, as you see here in the fahrenheit_to_celsius3. awk script:

```
#!/usr/bin/awk -f
NR==1; NR>1{printf("%.2f %s\n",($2=="F" ? (($1-32)*5) / 9 : $1), "Celsius")}
```

Here, I'm using %.2f to format the output as a floating point number with only two digits after the decimal point. Here's how the output looks:

```
donnie@fedora:~$ ./fahrenheit_to_celsius3.awk temps.txt
Temperature Celsius_or_Fahrenheit
0.00 Celsius
100.00 Celsius
-40.00 Celsius
-25.94 Celsius
24.61 Celsius
24.33 Celsius
```

```
12.89 Celsius
23.94 Celsius
-1.22 Celsius
40.19 Celsius
37.00 Celsius
23.10 Celsius
donnie@fedora:~$
```

The only slight catch is that now the second column doesn't line up correctly. You can't use two directives together for a single field, so we'll just have to live with it like this. That's okay though, because if
you decide to redirect this output into a file, you'll still be able to import it into a spreadsheet program.

With a slight change in the formula, you can also change Celsius temperatures to Fahrenheit. Here's
the `celsius_to_fahrenheit2.awk` script that does that:

```
#!/usr/bin/awk -f
NR==1; NR>1{printf("%-11s %s\n",($2=="C" ? (($1+32)*9) / 5 : $1),"Fahrenheit")}
```

And, here's the output:

```
donnie@fedora:~$ ./celsius_to_fahrenheit2.awk temps.txt
Temperature Celsius_or_Fahrenheit
32          Fahrenheit
212         Fahrenheit
-40         Fahrenheit
-14.7       Fahrenheit
101.9       Fahrenheit
75.8        Fahrenheit
55.21       Fahrenheit
100.7       Fahrenheit
29.8        Fahrenheit
104.34      Fahrenheit
98.6        Fahrenheit
99.18       Fahrenheit
donnie@fedora:~$
```

Next, let's say that we don't care about seeing the list of temperatures, and only want to see the average.
Well, here's the `average_temp.awk` script which does that:

```
#!/usr/bin/awk -f
BEGIN{temp_sum=0; total_records=0; print "Calculate the average temperature."}
$2=="F"{temp_sum += ($1-32) / 1.8; total_records += 1;}
$2=="C" {temp_sum += $1; total_records += 1}
END {average_temp = temp_sum/total_records; print "The average temperature is:
\n\t " average_temp " Celsius."}
```

This time, I decided to use the alternate formula for converting from Fahrenheit to Celsius. In both of the $2== lines, I'm using the += operator to sum the temperatures in the first field and to increment the total_records variable. Here's the output:

```
donnie@fedora:~$ ./average_temp.awk temps.txt
Calculate the average temperature.
The average temperature is:
     18.2421 Celsius.
donnie@fedora:~$
```

To verify that it's giving you accurate averages, play around with different temperature values in the temps.txt file to see what happens.

The final thing I'll say on this topic is that awk offers the full range of math operators, as well as a good selection of math functions. You can find out more by following the links in the *Further Reading* section.

Next, let's see what we can do with multi-line records.

Working with Multi-Line Records

So far, we've been using awk to parse text files in which each line is its own distinct record. Sometimes though, you might have to work with files that have each record spread across several lines. For example, look at this inventory.txt file:

```
Kitchen spatula
$4.99
Housewares
Raincoat
$36.99
Clothing
On Sale!
Claw hammer
$7.99
Tools
```

The first and third records each consist of three lines, and the second record consists of four lines. Each record is separated by a blank space. Now, let's say that we need to import this information into a spreadsheet. That won't work well with multi-line records, so we'll need to find an easy way to convert it into a spreadsheet-friendly format. Once again, awk to the rescue! Here's the inventory.awk script that helps us out:

```
#!/usr/bin/awk -f
BEGIN {
        FS="\n"
        RS=""
        ORS=""
```

```
}
{
        count=1
        while (count<NF) {
                print $count "\t"
                count++
        }
        print $NF "\n"
}
```

The BEGIN block defines the newline (\n) as the field separator, which means that each line in a record is its own field. The record separator (RS) and the output record separator (ORS) are each defined as a null value (""). The RS variable interprets the null value as a blank line, but the ORS variable doesn't. In this case, having ORS defined as a null value just prevents the print command in the while loop from adding a newline at the end of each field.

There's not much in the while loop that you haven't seen before. It just uses the count variable to hold the number of the field that's being processed. The value of this count variable gets incremented by 1 after each iteration of the while loop. You might think it strange that the loop parameter is defined as count<NF instead of count<=NF. I mean, wouldn't we want to process the last field in every record? Well, we do process that last field with the print $NF "\n" command that comes after the while loop. As I said, defining the OFS as "" prevents the print command from adding a newline character at the end of each field. So, in order to have each record on a separate line, we have to have a separate print command for the final field, and specify that it will add a newline at the end of the line. At any rate, here's how things look when I use the script to parse the inventory.txt file:

```
donnie@fedora:~$ ./inventory.awk inventory.txt
Kitchen spatula     $4.99          Housewares
Raincoat            $36.99         Clothing      On Sale!
Claw hammer         $7.99          Tools
donnie@fedora:~$
```

Of course, you can redirect the output into a .tsv file that you can open in your favorite spreadsheet program. If you'd rather use a .csv file, just replace the print $count "\t" line in the while loop with print $count ",". The output will then look like this:

```
donnie@fedora:~$ ./inventory.awk inventory.txt
Kitchen spatula,$4.99,Housewares
Raincoat,$36.99,Clothing,On Sale!
Claw hammer,$7.99,Tools
donnie@fedora:~$
```

The beauty of this script is that it doesn't matter how many fields you have in each record. The NF built-in variable keeps track of how many fields there are, and the while loop processes each record accordingly.

Okay, I think that this will pretty much wrap up our introduction to awk scripting. So, let's summarize and move on.

Summary

The awk scripting language is exceedingly useful for anyone who needs to extract meaningful data from plain-text files. I began this chapter by showing you the basic construction of an awk script. Then, I showed you how to use if and if..else to create conditional commands, how to use while loops, and how to parse text files with multi-line records. For the demos, I showed you various awk scripts that do the types of jobs that you might encounter in real life.

Unfortunately, there's no way that I can do complete justice with this presentation of awk. It's another of those topics about which entire books have been written, so the best I can do here is to just whet your appetite.

In the next chapter, we'll get back to the main topic of shell scripting, by looking at a couple of utilities that allow you to create user interfaces for your scripts. I'll see you there.

Questions

1. For the best portability, which of the following shebang lines should you place in your awk scripts?

    a.   `#!/bin/awk`

    b.   `#!/usr/bin/awk -f`

    c.   `#!/bin/awk -f`

    d.   `#!/usr/bin/awk`

2. Which of the following statements is true?

    a.   All awk programming variables must be declared before you use them.

    b.   There are various types of awk variables, such as integer, floating-point, and string.

    c.   All awk programming variables are string-type variables.

    d.   You must convert string-type variables to either integer or floating-point variables before using them in math operations.

3. Within an awk script, how would you define the comma as the field separator?

    a.   `-F=,`

    b.   `-F=","`

    c.   `FS=,`

    d.   `.FS=","`

4. You have a text file with several lines of numbers, with blank spaces between the numbers. Each line has a different number of numbers. You want to sum the numbers on each line. When you write an awk script to create these sums, how would you account for the fact that each line has a different number of fields?

    a. Create a variable array to hold the number of fields in each line, and use a `for` loop to build the array.

    b. Use the `NF` built-in variable.

    c. Use the `NR` built-in variable.

    d. You can only do this when each line has the same number of fields.

5. Which of the following `printf` directives would you use to ensure that a floating-point number always displays with four digits after the decimal point?

    a. `%.4f`

    b. `%4`

    c. `#4.f`

    d. `#4`

Further Reading

- How do I check if my CPU supports x86_v2?: `https://unix.stackexchange.com/questions/631217/how-do-i-check-if-my-cpu-supports-x86-64-v2`

- Exploring x86-64-v3 for Red Hat Enterprise Linux 10: `https://developers.redhat.com/articles/2024/01/02/exploring-x86-64-v3-red-hat-enterprise-linux-10`

- x86_64 Levels: `https://medium.com/@BetterIsHeather/x86-64-levels-944e92cd6d83`

- How the awk Command Made Me a 10x Engineer: `https://youtu.be/FbSpuZVb164?si=ri9cnjBh1sxM_STz`

- Ternary Operators: `https://www.tutorialspoint.com/awk/awk_ternary_operators.htm`

- printf Examples: `https://www.gnu.org/software/gawk/manual/html_node/Printf-Examples.html`

- Doing math with awk: `https://www.networkworld.com/article/942538/doing-math-with-awk.html`

- Numeric functions in awk: `https://www.gnu.org/software/gawk/manual/html_node/Numeric-Functions.html`

Answers

1. b
2. c
3. d
4. b
5. a

Join our community on Discord!

Read this book alongside other users, Linux experts, and the author himself.

Ask questions, provide solutions to other readers, chat with the author via Ask Me Anything sessions, and much more. Scan the QR code or visit the link to join the community.

`https://packt.link/SecNet`

16

Creating User Interfaces with yad, dialog, and xdialog

I know, you're thinking that shell scripting consists of nothing but entering boring, plain-text commands in a terminal. But, what if I told you that you can fancy up your scripts by adding a user interface? What if I told you that you can have a graphical interface for desktop systems or a non-graphical interface for text-mode servers? Well, you can, and I'm here to show you how.

Topics in this chapter include:

- Creating a graphical user interface with yad
- Creating user interfaces with dialog and xdialog

If you're ready, let's get started.

Technical Requirements

For yad and xdialog, you'll need to use a desktop implementation of Linux. It doesn't much matter which distro you use, as long as the yad and xdialog packages are in the repository. Just use your distro's normal package management tool to install them. (The yad and xdialog packages are also available for GhostBSD, which is FreeBSD with either the Mate or Xfce desktop environment. If you're on a Mac, you'll need to install yad or xdialog via Homebrew. Alas, neither one is available for OpenIndiana, and yad isn't available for any of the RHEL 9-type distros.)

For the dialog section, you can use either a desktop or a text-mode server implementation of Linux.

And, as always, you can grab the scripts by running:

```
git clone https://github.com/PacktPublishing/The-Ultimate-Linux-Shell-
Scripting-Guide.git
```

Okay, let's begin by looking at yad.

Creating a Graphical User Interface with yad

Yet Another Dialog, or **yad** for short, is a very cool program that allows you to add GUI-type interfaces to your shell scripts. There's a lot you can do with it, and I'd like to show you a few simple examples.

The yad Basics

In the yad man page, you'll see a list of pre-defined components that you can use in your yad scripts. For example, if you do yad `--file`, you'll open the file manager that looks like this:

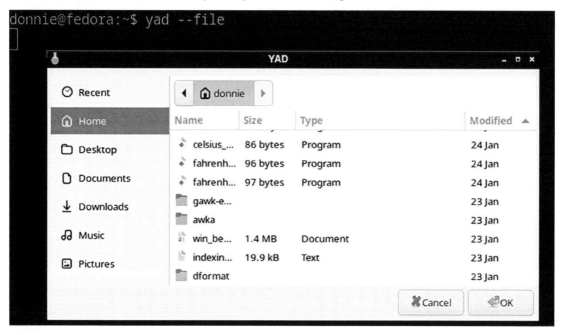

Figure 16.1: The yad file manager

As it is, this file manager won't do anything for you. If you click on a file and then click the **OK** button, the manager will close and the name of the file that you chose will print out on the command line, like this:

```
donnie@fedora:~$ yad --file
/home/donnie/win_bentley.pdf
donnie@fedora:~$
```

To make this useful, you'll need to add code that will perform some desired action upon the chosen file. Before we attempt something this complex though, let's begin with something that's a bit more simple.

Creating Data Entry Forms

Let's say that you're a collector of classic automobiles, and you need to create a simple database to keep track of your vast collection. We'll begin by testing the basic script, which looks like this:

```
#!/bin/bash
```

```
yad --title="Classic Autos" --text="Enter the info about your classic
auto:" --form --width=400 --field="Year":NUM --field="Make" --field="Model"
--field="Body Style" >> classic_autos.txt
```

That's a bit hard to read, though. So, let's make the yad-form-auto1.sh script a bit more readable, like this:

```
#!/bin/bash
yad --title="Classic Autos" --text="Enter the info about your classic auto:" \
        --form --width=400 \
        --field="Year":NUM \
        --field="Make" \
        --field="Model" \
        --field="Body Style" >> classic_autos.txt
```

This yad command is actually one long command. To make it more readable, I've broken it up over several lines, by adding a backslash after each option definition. You could leave out the backslashes and just place the entire command on one line, as you saw above, but this looks much better.

On the first line, I've placed both the --title and the --text definitions, which should be self-explanatory. The second line defines a form with a width of 400 pixels. Following that are the definitions for the data entry fields. Note that the Year field can only accept a numerical value, as indicated by the :NUM parameter. At the end, I'm redirecting the output into the classic_autos.txt file. (I'm using the >> operator so that I can add more than one auto to the file.) Here's how it looks when I run the script:

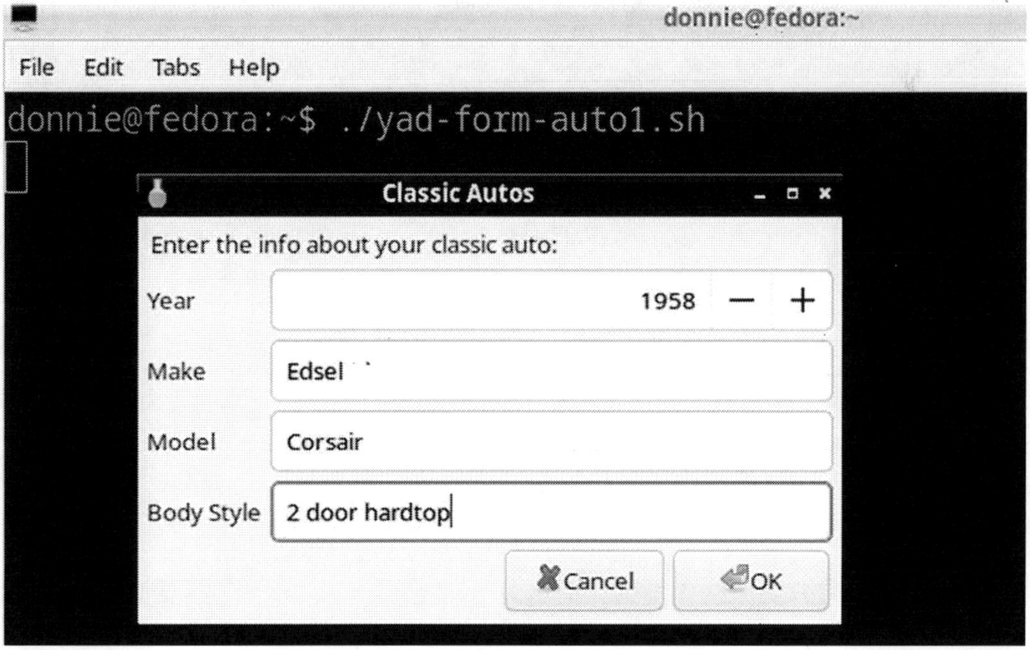

Figure 16.2: Running yad-form-auto1.sh

When I hit the **OK** button, the output will be saved to the classic_autos.txt file, which will look like this:

```
donnie@fedora:~$ cat classic_autos.txt
1958|Edsel|Corsair|2 door hardtop|
donnie@fedora:~$
```

By default, yad uses the | symbol as the output field separator. That's okay, because if you open this file in a spreadsheet program, you can set the | symbol as the field separator, and it will work just fine. But, you can change the field separator if you like. For example, if you want to create .csv files, just add the --separator="," parameter to the --form line.

One slight problem with this script is that every time you hit the **OK** button to create an entry in your text file, the script will exit. Each time you add an auto, you'll need to invoke the script again. Let's fix that with a while loop, as you see here in the yad-form-auto2.sh script:

```
#!/bin/bash
while :
do
yad --title="Classic Autos" --text="Enter the info about your classic auto:" \
        --form --width=400 \
        --field="Year":NUM \
        --field="Make" \
        --field="Model" \
        --field="Body Style" \
        --field="Date Acquired":DT >> classic_autos.txt
done
```

By using a : as the while condition, we're creating what's known as an infinite loop. In other words, this will never quit until you press **Ctrl-c**.

While I was at it, I added the Date Acquired field with the :DT option. This option causes a handy-dandy calendar to pop up whenever I click on the calendar icon. Here's how it looks:

Figure 16.3: The yad-form-auto2.sh script

This is good, but it's still not perfect. Due to using a : for the while condition, the only way to end this script is to **Ctrl-c** out of it, because the **Cancel** button won't do anything. To fix that, you need to understand that the **OK** button returns a 0 as the exit code, and the **Cancel** button returns a 1 as the exit code.

If you need to review the concept of exit codes, refer back to *Chapter 8, Basic Shell Script Construction.*

So, let's modify the `while` loop in this `yad-form-auto3.sh` script:

```bash
#!/bin/bash
while [ $? == 0 ]
do
yad --title="Classic Autos" --text="Enter the info about your classic auto:" \
        --form --width=400 \
        --field="Year":NUM \
        --field="Make" \
        --field="Model" \
        --field="Body Style" \
        --field="Date Acquired":DT >> classic_autos.txt
done
```

The `$? == 0` parameter retrieves the exit code and verifies that it's 0. This keeps the script running as long as you don't click on either the **Cancel** button or the **X** at the top corner of the window. (I forgot to mention that hitting the **X** returns an exit code of 252.)

Now, let's wrap this section up with one last modification.

Creating a Drop-down List

This time, we'll add a drop-down list for choosing the body style, and a free-form text box. Here's the `yad-form-auto4.sh` script to show you how it's done:

```bash
#!/bin/bash
bodystyles=$(echo "2 door hardtop,2 door sedan,4 door hardtop,4 door
sedan,station wagon,convertible,pickup truck,other")
while [ $? == 0 ]
do
yad --title="Classic Autos" --text="Enter the info about your classic auto:" \
        --form --width=400 --item-separator="," \
        --field="Year":NUM \
        --field="Make" \
        --field="Model" \
        --field="Body Style":CBE \
        --field="Date Acquired":DT >> classic_autos.txt \
        --field="Add any additional notes:":TXT \
        "" "" "" "$bodystyles" "Click on the calender icon"
done
```

The `bodystyles=` line, the `--item-separator` parameter in the `--form` line, and the `"" "" ""` line all work together to create the drop-down list. The `bodystyles=` defines the list of available body styles, separated by commas. This goes along with the `--item-separator` parameter, which ensures that the drop-down list appears with only one body style per line, instead of having all body styles on one line.

The :CBE parameter at the end of the --field="Body Style" line defines this field as a drop-down list with the option to edit it if you choose the **other** option. The last line in the while loop tells yad where to place the values of the bodystyles variable. We see that the Body Style field is the fourth field. So to represent the first three fields, which are blank by default, we place three pairs of double quotes ahead of the $bodystyles variable. The last item on the line places a line of text in the Date Acquired field. The final field definition is the free-form text box, as you see by the :TXT parameter. (The text box field comes after the drop-down list field, which means that you don't have to add another pair of double-quotes to be a placeholder.) Here's how it looks when I choose a body style:

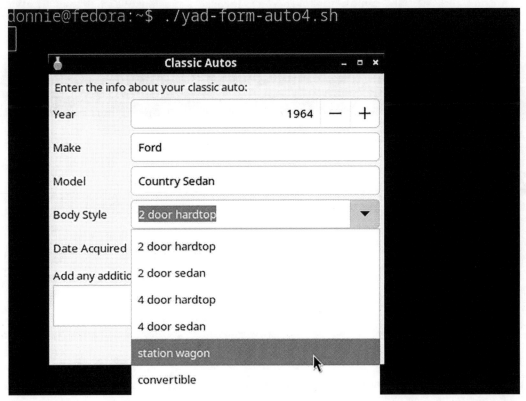

Figure 16.4: Using a drop-down list

Of course, you can adapt this script for pretty much any purpose. That can include keeping inventories of your own personal collections, store merchandise, or software licenses. (Let your imagination run wild.)

That wraps it up for this demo. Now, let's manage some files.

Using the yad File Manager

The easiest way to work with files is to create a variable, with its value assigned by a yad command substitution construct. Then, you can do whatever you want with the value of the variable. Let's see what we can do with that.

Creating a File Checksum Utility

For the first example, let's say that you want to create a list of files with their sha512 checksums. Here's the yad-file-checksum1.sh script that does just that:

```
#!/bin/bash
filetocheck=$(yad --file)
sha512sum $filetocheck >> file_checksums.txt
```

Clicking on a file assigns the name of that file to the filetocheck variable. We can then use the value of that variable as the argument for the sha512sum command.

Here's how it looks:

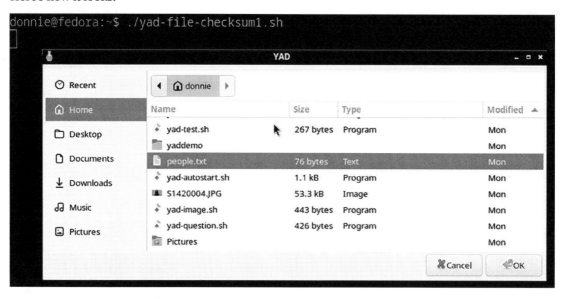

Figure 16.5: Opening a file with yad-file-checksum1.sh script

Clicking the **OK** button creates the file_checksum.txt file, which contains the SHA512 checksum of the people.txt file, which looks like this:

```
donnie@fedora:~$ cat file_checksums.txt
0aa501cc947b22c48c8b2bca0e2a9675fad58440133af8794d8e2b51160f72fa6851c6d76a8554
6938c23ff5bf70b841bd1099ca727b39a59f486348d3dcee50   /home/donnie/people.txt
donnie@fedora:~$
```

That's great, but as always, we can fancy things up a bit. In the yad-file-checksum2.sh script, we'll add a while loop so that the **Cancel** button will work, and also add the ability to choose multiple files. And, while we're at it, let's add a file preview feature. Here's how that looks:

```
#!/bin/bash
while [ $? == 0 ]
do
```

```
        filetocheck=$(yad --file --multiple --separator='\n' --add-preview
--width=800)
        sha512sum $filetocheck >> file_checksums.txt
done
```

The `--multiple` and the `--separator='\n'` options work together. Without the `--separator` option, the `--multiple` option will cause all filenames to appear as one long line, with filenames separated by a | symbol. This will cause the `sha512sum` utility to view that line as a single filename, which will cause an error. Placing a new line after each filename solves the problem. The `--add-preview` and the `--width` options should be self-explanatory, so I won't comment about them. At any rate, here's how the new script works:

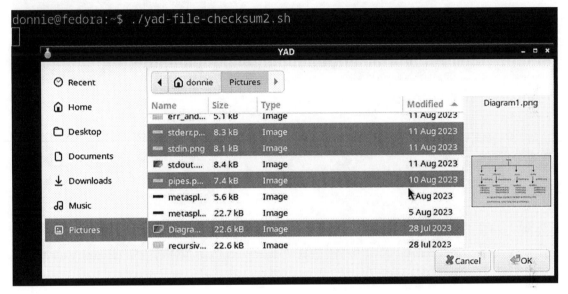

Figure 16.6: The file selector with the preview and multiple file options

You can select multiple non-consecutive files by holding down the **Ctrl** key, or multiple consecutive files by holding down the **Shift** key. The end result will be a text file that contains the SHA512 sum checks of all the selected files.

I have to confess that there's something weird going on with this script, and that it has me stumped. When you click on either the **Cancel** button or the **X** button, the dialog box will close down as it's supposed to do. But, for some strange reason the process doesn't end, which means that the terminal never returns to the command-prompt. I've tried performing every unnatural act I could think of to fix that, but to no avail. So, it appears that whenever you run this script, you'll just have to **Ctrl-c** out of it when you're done.

All right, let's move on to the next example.

Creating a GUI Front-end for ImageMagick

Next, let's see if we can create a GUI front-end for the ImageMagick program that we talked about back in *Chapter 13, Scripting with ImageMagick*. We'll begin with the `yad-image-resize1.sh` script, which looks like this:

```bash
#!/bin/bash
imageFile=$(yad --file --title="Select the image file" --width=800)
dialog=$(yad --title "Image Resize" --form --field="Resize parameter"
--field="Quality")
size=$(echo $dialog | awk 'BEGIN {FS="|" } { print $1 }')
quality=$(echo $dialog | awk 'BEGIN {FS="|" } { print $2 }')
convert "$imageFile" -resize "$size" -quality "$quality"% "$imageFile"
yad --title="Status" --width=300  --button="OK:0"  --text="All done. Yay!"
```

The first line creates the initial file selection window. It then assigns the filename of the selected file to the `imageFile` variable. Here's how this initial window looks:

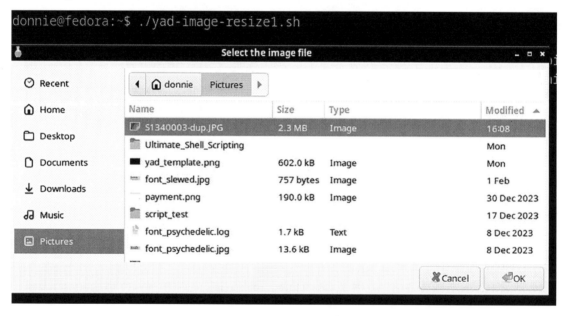

Figure 16.7: The initial file selection window for resizing images

The second line creates the **Image Resize** window that you'll use for entering the resize and quality parameters. When you enter your desired parameters, they'll get stored in the `dialog` variable as a single line, with the two parameters separated by a | symbol.

The next two lines create the `size` and `quality` variables, using the values that are stored in the `dialog` variable. We need a way to extract each individual parameter, and awk gives us a handy way to do it. Anyway, here's how the **Image Resize** window looks:

Figure 16.8: the Image Resize window

Next comes the `convert` line, which performs the actual resizing. You see that it's using values from the `size`, `quality`, and `imageFile` variables. When I click on the **OK** button, the resizing process will take place.

The final line creates the **Status** window, which shows that the process is complete. By default, yad windows have both a **Cancel** and an **OK** button. In this case, we only want the **OK** button, so we override the default behavior by explicitly creating an **OK** button with the `--button` option. Here's how this window looks:

Figure 16.9: The Status window

Look in your directory, and you should see that the image has indeed been resized.

To give credit where credit is due, I borrowed this script from a *Linux Magazine* article that was posted way back in 2012, and made a couple of minor tweaks to it. You'll find the link to the original article in the *Further Reading* section.

The major flaw with this script is that it overwrites the original graphics file with the resized version. Let's modify it so that it will save the resized version as a new file with a new filename. Here's the `yad-image-resize2.sh` script that does that:

```bash
#!/bin/bash
imageFile=$(yad --file --title="Select the image file" --width=800 --add-
preview)
```

```
newfilename=${imageFile%%.*}
suffix=${imageFile: -4}
dialog=$(yad --title "Image Resize" --form --field="Resize parameter"
--field="Quality")
size=$(echo $dialog | awk 'BEGIN {FS="|"} {print $1}')
quality=$(echo $dialog | awk 'BEGIN {FS="|"} {print $2}')
convert -resize "$size" -quality "$quality" "$imageFile" -delete 1
"$newfilename"_resized"$suffix"
yad --title="Status" --width=300  --button="OK:0"  --text="All done. Yay!"
```

To make this work, I created two new variables and used variable expansion to assign them their values. The newfilename=${imageFile%%.*} line grabs the first part of the imageFile filename, up to the the dot for the filename extension. For example, let's say that the value of imageFile is somegraphic. jpg. Using variable expansion to strip off the .jpg would result in assigning a value of somegraphic to the newfilename variable. The suffix variable uses the offset feature of variable expansion. In this case, the ${imageFile: -4} construct grabs the last four characters of the filename. This results in assigning a value of .jpg to the suffix variable.

The next thing to note is how I had to modify the convert command. (By the way, note that this convert command is quite long, and wraps around on the page.) All I did was to add the -delete 1 "$newfilename"_resized"$suffix" part to the end of the command that I had before. You've probably figured out that with our current example, this would create a new file with the filename, somegraphic_resized.jpg. But, you might be puzzled by the -delete 1 part. Well, it's just that under certain conditions, the convert command will create two output files, instead of just one, as you see here:

```
donnie@fedora:~/Pictures$ ls -l *dup*
-rw-r--r--. 1 donnie donnie 2324036 Feb 11 14:38 S1340003-dup.JPG
-rw-r--r--. 1 donnie donnie   29745 Feb 11 15:57 S1340003-dup_resized-0.JPG
-rw-r--r--. 1 donnie donnie  293424 Feb 11 15:57 S1340003-dup_resized-1.JPG
donnie@fedora:~/Pictures$
```

Adding the -delete 1 parameter just before the output filename parameter eliminates that problem, as you see here:

```
donnie@fedora:~/Pictures$ ls -l *dup*
-rw-r--r--. 1 donnie donnie 2324036 Feb 11 14:38 S1340003-dup.JPG
-rw-r--r--. 1 donnie donnie   29745 Feb 11 16:00 S1340003-dup_resized.JPG
donnie@fedora:~/Pictures$
```

The final modification I'll show you, which I'll put in yad-image-resize3.sh, causes the file manager to only display certain file types. Since we're dealing with graphics files, we only want the file manager to show us files with the .JPG, .jpg, .PNG, and .png filename extensions. We'll do that by just adding the --file-filter "Graphics files | *.JPG *.jpg *.PNG *.png") option to the imageFile= line that's at the top of the script. The new line now looks like this:

```
imageFile=$(yad --file --title="Select the image file" --width=800 --add-
preview --file-filter "Graphics files | *.JPG *.jpg *.PNG *.png")
```

Now that the line is quite long, let's make it more readable by breaking it up with backslashes, like so:

```
imageFile=$(yad --file --title="Select the image file" \
        --width=800 --add-preview \
        --file-filter "Graphics files | *.JPG *.jpg *.PNG *.png")
```

That looks much better, right?

All right, let's move on to our final example.

Programming Form Buttons

In this scenario, we're in a software developer's shop that's running a small fleet of Fedora Linux-powered workstations. We want to create a GUI-type setup utility that will simplify the process of setting up a new workstation. Furthermore, we want to carry this utility around on a USB memory stick so that we can either run it directly from the memory stick, or copy it to each workstation. Fortunately, that's easy with yad. Here's the yad-system-tool.sh script that does that:

```
#!/bin/bash
yad --title "System tools for a Fedora Workstation" --form --columns=3 \
        --width=540 --height=190 \
        --text="Tools for setting up Fedora or RHEL-type distros" \
        --field="<b>Update System</b>":FBTN "dnf -y upgrade" \
        --field="<b>Authoring and Publishing</b>":FBTN "dnf -y groupinstall
--with-optional 'Authoring and Publishing'" \
        --field="<b>Development Tools</b>":FBTN "dnf -y --with-optional
groupinstall 'Development Tools'" \
        --button=Exit:1
```

In this script, you see some options that you haven't seen before. The --columns=3 option in the first line means that we want to create a form with three buttons across on each row. On the second line, you see a --height option, as well as a --width option. In each of the --field lines, you see the :FBTN option, which defines the fields as programmable buttons. The <b> and </b> tags that surround the button text make the button text appear in bold type. The final portion of each --field line consists of the command that will run when you click on the button.

The first button is programmed to perform a system update with the dnf -y upgrade command. The -y causes the command to run without stopping to prompt the user about whether he or she really wants to do it. I had to use the -y option, because without it, the operation would abort at the prompt. The next two buttons each install a selected group of software packages. If you want to see what's in each of these groups, just run these two commands:

```
donnie@fedora:~$ sudo dnf group info "Authoring and Publishing"
donnie@fedora:~$ sudo dnf group info "Development Tools"
```

Since we're dealing with administrative commands in this script, we'll need to run it with sudo. Here's how it looks:

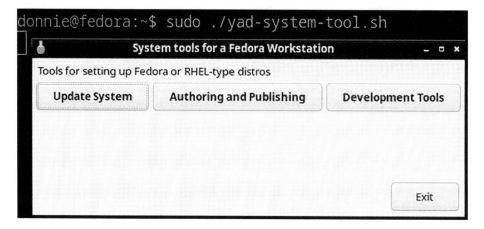

Figure 16.10: A yad form with programmable buttons

Now, just click on a button and watch what happens.

Adding more software installation choices is easy, by just adding more `--field` lines. If you want to see the list of software packages that are available on Fedora, just do:

```
donnie@fedora:~$ sudo dnf group list
```

I know, you're thinking that this type of chore would be more easily accomplished with a set of plain, text-mode scripts. And yeah, you're right. So, just think of this example as a template that you can use for your own purposes.

Also, I neglected to mention before that you'll need to manually install yad on each system that you want to administer with this script.

That wraps things up for this script, so let's move on.

Some Final Thoughts about yad

yad is a really cool program, and you can do a lot of really cool stuff with it. In fact, a person could probably write a whole book on nothing but yad. I can't do that at the moment, but I've hopefully given you enough to whet your appetite.

The main problem with yad is that for whatever reason, its creator has never written any real documentation for it, other than a very sparse man page. Fortunately, a lot of other people have taken up the challenge, and have created their own documentation and tutorials on both the web and on YouTube. (I'll link to some of these resources in the Further Reading section.)

Next, let's turn our attention to dialog and xdialog, which we can also use to create user interfaces for our scripts.

Creating User Interfaces with dialog and xdialog

Another slight problem with yad is that you can only use it on machines that have a desktop environment installed. But, many Linux, Unix, and Unix-like servers are set up with a full text-mode environment and don't have to use graphical desktops. Another slight problem with yad is that even on desktop-type operating systems, it's not always available for installation. However, if yad isn't available and you still need a GUI solution, you might be able to use xdialog, which is more universally available. Let's begin with a look at dialog, which can be used on text-mode machines.

The dialog Basics

dialog used to be installed by default on all Linux systems, but it no longer is. However, it's available for installation for pretty much every Linux distro. So, you can install it with your distro's normal package manager. On most Unix and Unix-like systems, such as OpenIndiana and FreeBSD, it still comes installed by default.

The basic dialog building blocks are known as **widgets**. Each widget has a set of parameters that you need to specify when you use it. For example, open the dialog man page and scroll down to the --msgbox paragraph, where you'll see this:

```
--msgbox text height width
```

So, this widget requires you to specify three parameters. (Unlike yad, specifying the dimensions of a dialog box isn't optional.) Let's see how that looks in the dialog-hello.sh script:

```
#!/bin/bash
dialog --title "Dialog message box" \
        --msgbox "\n Howdy folks!" 6 25
```

As you've seen before in the yad section, I used a backslash to break the command into two lines, which makes things a bit more readable. On the --msgbox line, we see the message text, the height as defined by the number of rows in the box, and the width as defined by the number of characters that fit on a line.

Running the script looks like this:

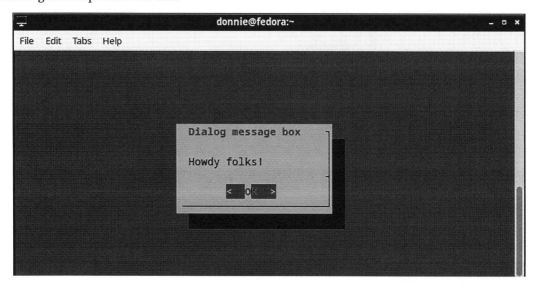

Figure 16.11: Running the dialog-hello.sh script

To close the window, just hit the **Enter** key, which activates the **OK** button by default. (On a desktop machine, you also have the option of clicking on the **OK** button with your mouse.) Once the window is closed, run the `clear` command to remove the blue background from your terminal.

By default, `dialog` windows always appear in the center of your terminal, and the blue background won't clear until you clear it yourself. Fortunately, you can change both behaviors. Here's a slightly modified version of our script, which places the window at the top left corner of the terminal:

```
#!/bin/bash
dialog --title "Dialog message box" \
        --begin 2 2 \
        --msgbox "\nHowdy folks!" 6 25
clear
```

Here's how that looks:

Figure 16.12: Placing the dialog box in the upper-left corner

The --begin option takes two parameters. The first one denotes the vertical position of the box, and the second one denotes the horizontal position. For example, by changing the line to --begin 15 2, the box would show up in the lower left corner. To place it into the upper right corner, you could change it to --begin 2 50. The clear command at the end will clear away the blue background when you hit the OK button.

Of course, this script isn't very useful, but that's okay. I'll show you some more useful concepts in just a bit. First though, allow me to say a few words about xdialog.

The xdialog Basics

If you need a GUI-type of user interface and yad isn't available for your desktop system, xdialog could be a good alternative. (I say could be, because neither yad nor xdialog is available for OpenIndiana.) It should be in the normal repository of your Linux or Unix-like distro, so just use your normal package manager to install it. The reason I can talk about both dialog and xdialog in the same section is because for the most part, code that's written for dialog can also run with xdialog.

There's one thing to look out for that could trip you up. For some strange reason, the package name is xdialog, in all lower-case letters. But, after it's installed, you'll need to invoke the program by typing Xdialog, with an upper-case X. (After I installed it, it took me a while to figure out why I couldn't get it to work.)

For the most part, changing a dialog script to run as a GUI-type program is a simple matter of changing all instances of dialog to Xdialog, as you see here:

```
#!/bin/bash
Xdialog --title "Dialog message box" \
        --begin 2 50 \
        --msgbox "\nHowdy folks!" 6 25
clear
```

Running the script on a desktop system gives you this:

```
donnie@fedora:~$ vim dialog-hello-temp.sh
donnie@fedora:~$ ./dialog-hello-temp.sh

                                          X  Di...ox  ∨  ∧  ✕

                                              ✓    OK
```

Figure 16.13: Running the script with xdialog

The first thing to note is that xdialog ignores the --begin option, and just places the box in the center of the terminal. There's also the fact that xdialog often requires you to create boxes with larger dimensions so that you can see everything. So, let's change that in the final xdialog-hello.sh script, like this:

```
#!/bin/bash
Xdialog --title "Dialog message box" \
        --begin 2 2 \
        --msgbox "\nHowdy folks!" 15 50
clear
```

As you see here, this makes things look much better:

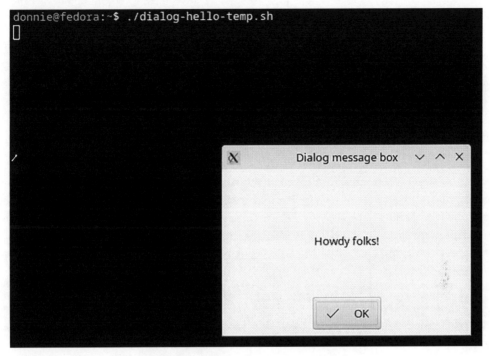

Figure 16.14: The improved xdialog script

With `xdialog`, the clear command at the end of the script is no longer necessary, but it doesn't hurt anything to leave it. In fact, we'll need it for the next demo.

Automatically Choosing Either dialog or xdialog

Now, here's something that's really cool. With only a few extra lines of code, you can make your script automatically detect whether it's running on a desktop or text-mode machine, and whether `xdialog` is installed. Here's the `xdialog-hello2.sh` script to show how it works:

```bash
#!/bin/bash
command -v Xdialog
if [[ $? == 0 ]] && [[ -n $DISPLAY ]]; then
        diag=Xdialog
else
        diag=dialog
fi
$diag --title "Dialog message box" \
        --begin 2 2 \
        --msgbox "\nHowdy folks!" 15 50
clear
```

There are several ways to detect if a program is installed. In *Chapter 12, Automating Scripts with here Documents and expect,* I showed you this method in the system_info.sh script:

```
if [[ -f /usr/local/bin/pandoc ]] || [[ -f /usr/bin/pandoc ]]; then
        pandoc -o sysinfo.pdf sysinfo.html
        rm sysinfo.html
fi
```

The pandoc executable that we needed is in the /usr/local/bin/ directory on FreeBSD, and in the /usr/bin/ directory on everything else. So, I set up this if..then construct to detect if the executable is in either place. That works, but I'd now like to show you an easier way.

In the xdialog-hello2.sh script, the command -v Xdialog command detects if the Xdialog executable file is present, regardless of which directory it's in. If it is, the command will return exit code 0. If it's not, the command will return exit code 1. To see how this works, go ahead and run this on the command line. Here's how it looks if the Xdialog executable isn't detected:

```
donnie@ubuntu2204:~$ command -v Xdialog
donnie@ubuntu2204:~$ echo $?
1
donnie@ubuntu2204:~$
```

And, here's how it looks if it is detected:

```
donnie@fedora:~$ command -v Xdialog
donnie@fedora:~$ echo $?
0
donnie@fedora:~$
```

In the next line, you see an if..then construct that checks for two things. First, it checks the exit code from the command command, and then it checks to see if a graphical desktop environment is installed. If the value of the DISPLAY environmental variable is of a non-zero length, then a desktop environment is installed. You can see how this works by running the echo $DISPLAY command yourself. Here's how it looks on a desktop machine:

```
donnie@fedora:~$ echo $DISPLAY
:0
donnie@fedora:~$
```

On a text-mode machine, you'll get no output at all, as you see here on this Ubuntu Server virtual machine:

```
donnie@ubuntu2204:~$ echo $DISPLAY
donnie@ubuntu2204:~$
```

For our purposes, we can say that the value of DISPLAY is zero characters long on this text-mode machine.

Now, let's take another look at our `if..then` statement:

```
if [[ $? == 0 ]] && [[ -n $DISPLAY ]]; then
        diag=Xdialog
else
        diag=dialog
fi
```

This means that if the exit code from the `command -v Xdialog` line is 0, and the value of the `DISPLAY` environmental variable is of a non-zero length, then the value of the `diag` variable becomes `Xdialog`. If either the `Xdialog` executable is missing or the value of `DISPLAY` is *not* a non-zero length, then the value of `diag` becomes `dialog`. What makes this even more cool is that this works the same on all Linux, Unix, or Unix-like systems. I've tested this script on FreeBSD, GhostBSD, DragonflyBSD, Open-Indiana, and on both desktop and text-mode implementations of Linux. On all of them, the script correctly detects everything that it's supposed to detect, and correctly chooses whether to run either `dialog` or `Xdialog`.

 Here's something that caused me a bit of consternation. I accidentally found out that the order in which you test for things sometimes matters. In the `if..then` construct of this script, I originally checked for the value of `DISPLAY` first, and then checked for the exit code of the `command` command. The script wouldn't run correctly like that, because the test for the `DISPLAY` value was setting the exit code to 0. When I reversed the order of the tests, everything began to work correctly.

Go ahead and try running this script on a variety of systems, just to see what happens.

Next, let's build on what we've already done by adding another widget.

Adding Widgets

You can add more functionality by adding more widgets. Take for example the `dialog-hello2.sh` script, which you can download from the Github repository. I can't show the entire file at once due to formatting constraints, so I'll show it to you a section at a time. Here's the top section:

```
#!/bin/bash
command -v Xdialog
if [[ $? == 0 ]] && [[ -n $DISPLAY ]]; then
        diag=Xdialog
else
        diag=dialog
fi
```

We've already seen this in the previous script, and I've already explained it. So, let's move on. Here's the next section:

```
$diag --title "Dialog message box" \
```

```
        --begin 2 2 \
        --msgbox "\n Hello world!" 20 50
$diag --begin 4 4 --yesno "Do you believe in magic?" 0 0
```

The first $diag line creates the initial message box in the top left corner, as specified by the --begin 2 2 option. The second $diag line creates a box with two buttons that are labeled as **Yes** and **No**. The --begin 4 4 option positions the yesno box just slightly lower and slightly more to the right of where the initial message box was. After --yesno, we see the text that we want the box to display and the height and width parameters. (Setting the height and width to 0 and 0 causes the box to size itself automatically.)

Next, we have a case..esac construct that assigns commands to the two buttons. Remember that when clicked, the **Yes** button returns exit code 0, and the **No** button returns exit code 1. Pressing the **Esc** key returns exit code 255. We can use these exit codes to trigger a desired command, as you see here:

```
case $? in
     0)
             clear
             echo "Cool!  I'm glad that you do." ;;
     1)
             clear
             echo "I'm sorry that you live such a dull life." ;;
     255)
             clear
             echo "You pressed the ESC key." ;;
esac
```

Okay, all this script does is display a message when you press a button. But, it does serve to demonstrate the concept, so it's all good.

You've already seen the initial message box, so I won't show that again. Instead, I'll show the yesno box that comes up next:

Figure 16.15: The yesno box

When I click the **Yes** button, I'll see the appropriate message, as you see here:

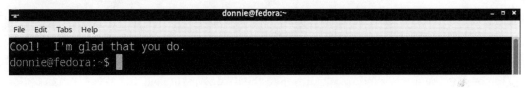

Figure 16.16: After clicking on the Yes button

And of course, this script runs equally well with xdialog on a machine that supports it.

Next, let's create something that will actually do some useful work for us.

Creating an SSH Login Interface

Let's say that you have a fleet of Linux, Unix, or Unix-like servers that you need to administer remotely via SSH. Trying to keep track of the server IP addresses is a confusing mess, so you've decided to simplify things. You've decided to create the xdialog-menu-test.sh to help you out. It's also too long to show here in its entirety, so I'll break it up into sections. Here's the top part:

```
#!/bin/bash
command -v Xdialog
if [[ $? == 0 ]] && [[ -n $DISPLAY ]]; then
        diag=Xdialog
else
        diag=dialog
fi
```

This is the same as it was in the previous script, so you already know about it. Here's the next section:

```
cmd=($diag --keep-tite --menu "Select options:" 22 76 16)
options=(1 "Remote SSH to Debian miner"
         2 "Remote SSH to Fedora miner"
         3 "Remote SSH to Fedora Workstation"
         4 "Remote SFTP to Fedora Workstation")
choices=$("${cmd[@]}" "${options[@]}" 2>&1 >/dev/tty)
```

The cmd= line creates a command within a pair of parentheses, and then assigns that command to the cmd variable array. This command, which will be invoked in the final line of the script, will build either a dialog or xdialog menu window. According to the dialog man page, the --keep-tite option is desirable when running the script in a graphical terminal emulator on a desktop machine, because it prevents the script from switching back and forth between the graphical terminal and the underlying shell terminal. After the --menu option, we see the text that is to be displayed, the height and width of the menu box, followed by the maximum number of menu entries that will be displayed at a time. (In this example, the user would need to scroll down to see past the first 16 menu entries.) The menu entries would be designated with a tag and an item string. For example, the first menu entry we see has a 1 as the tag, and **Remote SSH to Debian miner** as the item.

Next, we have the options stanza, which inserts all of the menu entries into an array. The choices= line uses the 2>&1> redirection operator to dump the contents of the array onto the terminal screen (/dev/tty). The @ in ${options[@]} is a form of variable expansion, because it allows an action to be carried out according to which menu item that a user chooses. The @ represents the index number of the array item that corresponds with a menu choice.

In *Chapter 8, Basic Shell Script Construction*, I showed you how to use either the * or the @ in place of a specific index number to show all elements in an array. In the cmd= line, each component of the `$diag --keep-tite --menu "Select options:" 22 76 16` command that's within the parentheses is a separate element of the cmd array. For this reason, we need to use either the * or the @ as the index for the cmd array in the choices= line at the bottom, so that the entire command will get invoked. The same thing is true for the list of options that get assigned to the options array in the options= line, as you'll see in a moment.

Now that we have a menu, we need to make it do something. That comes in the next section, which you see here:

```
for choice in $choices
do
    case $choice in
        1)
            ssh donnie@192.168.0.3
            ;;
        2)
            ssh donnie@192.168.0.12
            ;;
        3)
            ssh donnie@192.168.0.16
            ;;
        4)
            sftp donnie@192.168.0.16
            ;;
    esac
done
```

This is nothing that you haven't seen before. It's just a normal for loop that operates a case..esac construct. What is a bit different is that the value of the choices variable is the index number of the array item that corresponds with the chosen menu item. Each of the listed options in the options array consists of a number, followed by a complete phrase, such as 1 "Remote SSH to Debian miner". In this example, the number 1 represents element number 0 of the options array, and the following words in the phrase represent elements 1 through 5. In order for the options to properly display in the menu, you'll have to invoke the array with either * or @ in place of the index number. Here's the complete line where that happens:

```
choices=$("${cmd[@]}" "${options[@]}" 2>&1 >/dev/tty)
```

Since only one index value is ever assigned to choices, the for loop exits after its first run.

Now that everything is built, let's see if it works. Here's how it looks using xdialog on GhostBSD with the Mate desktop:

Figure 16.17: The xdialog-menu-test.sh script on GhostBSD

And, here's the exact same script on Fedora with dialog:

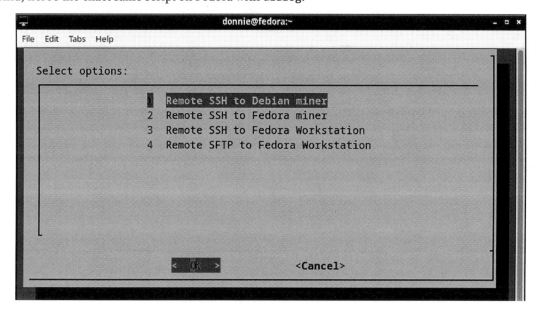

Figure 16.18: The xdialog-menu-test.sh script on Fedora with dialog

When you choose a menu item, the script will open a remote login prompt in the terminal, and then exit. That's okay, because if you want to connect to multiple remote servers at once, you'll need to open other terminals anyway.

Of course, you can fancy this script up to make it even more functional. For example, you can configure your SSH client to use different profiles or different encryption keys for different server sessions, and modify the commands in the menu accordingly. Or, you can use this as a template for something else altogether. As I keep saying, let your imagination run wild!

All right, I think that this about does it for yad, `dialog`, and `xdialog`. Let's wrap up and move on.

Summary

As always, we've covered a lot of ground in this chapter, and saw some cool stuff. We began with a discussion of yad, and how to use it to create graphical user interfaces for shell scripts. We then looked at how to use `dialog` to create user interfaces for text-mode environments, and `xdialog` for graphical environments. As an added bonus, you saw how to create scripts that will run with `xdialog` on machines that support it, and `dialog` on machines that don't.

These actually aren't the only three utilities that you can use to create user interfaces for your scripts. Other choices include `whiptail`, `cdialog`, and `zenity`. The good news is that once you've learned one, switching to another is fairly easy.

Now, you can do more with these utilities than I've been able to show you here. On the other hand, none of these utilities is suitable for creating anything that's really complex. For that, you'll need to learn a more complex programming language. Regardless, if all you need is a simple interface to make things easier for either yourself or for your users, these utilities can fill the bill.

In the next chapter, we'll look at how to run shell scripts with option switches. I'll see you there.

Questions

1. You want to create a graphical user interface for a shell script that will run on a wide variety of Linux, Unix, and Unix-like operating systems. Which of the follow utilities would you use for best availability?

    a. `zenity`

    b. `cdialog`

    c. `xdialog`

    d. `yad`

2. Which of the following statements is true about this code snippet?

```
command -v Xdialog
if [[ -n $DISPLAY ]] && [[ $? == 0 ]]; then
        diag=Xdialog
else
```

```
            diag=dialog
    fi
```

a. It's good code, and will work just fine.

b. It won't work, because it uses the wrong method to detect if the Xdialog executable is present.

c. It won't work, because it's not possible to detect if a certain executable is present.

d. It won't work, because having the [[-n $DISPLAY]] test come first ensures that $? always returns a value of 0.

Further Reading

- Dress Up Bash Scripts with YAD: https://www.linux-magazine.com/Online/Blogs/Productivity-Sauce/Dress-Up-Bash-Scripts-with-YAD

- YAD Guide: https://yad-guide.ingk.se/

- How to use ncurses widgets in shell scripts on Linux: https://linuxconfig.org/how-to-use-ncurses-widgets-in-shell-scripts-on-linux

- Designing Simple front ends with dialog/Xdialog: https://linuxgazette.net/101/sunil.html

- Adding dialog boxes to shell scripts: https://www.linux-magazine.com/Issues/2019/228/Let-s-Dialog

- Menu Driven Shell Script - Using Dialog Utility: http://web.archive.org/web/20120318060251/http://www.bashguru.com/2011/01/menu-driven-shell-script-using-dialog.html

- Xdialog Documentation: http://web.mit.edu/outland/share/doc/Xdialog-2.1.2/

Answers

1. c
2. d

Join our community on Discord!

Read this book alongside other users, Linux experts, and the author himself.

Ask questions, provide solutions to other readers, chat with the author via Ask Me Anything sessions, and much more. Scan the QR code or visit the link to join the community.

https://packt.link/SecNet

17

Using Shell Script Options with getops

Often, an administrator will need to pass both arguments and options to a shell script. That's easily done by passing positional parameters to the script, as we've seen in previous chapters. But, if you need to use normal Linux/Unix-style option switches, and you need to use arguments for certain options, then you'll need a helper program. In this chapter, I'll show you how to use getops to pass options, arguments, and options with arguments to a script.

Topics in this chapter include:

- Understanding the need for getopts
- Understanding getopt versus getopts
- Using getopts
- Looking at real-world examples

So, if you're ready, let's dig in.

Technical Requirements

You can use either your Fedora or your Debian virtual machine for this chapter. And, as always, you can grab the scripts by running:

```
git clone https://github.com/PacktPublishing/The-Ultimate-Linux-Shell-
Scripting-Guide.git
```

Understanding the Need for getopts

Before we do anything else, let's review the difference between **options** and **arguments**.

- Options modify the behavior of a program or script.
- Arguments are the objects upon which a program or script will act.

The simplest way to demonstrate the difference is with the humble `ls` command. If you want to see if a particular file is present, just use `ls` and the filename as an argument, like this:

```
donnie@fedora:~$ ls coingecko.sh
coingecko.sh
donnie@fedora:~$
```

If you want to see the details about the file, you'll need to add an option, like this:

```
donnie@fedora:~$ ls -l coingecko.sh
-rwxr--r--. 1 donnie donnie 842 Jan 12 13:11 coingecko.sh
donnie@fedora:~$
```

You see how the `-l` option modifies the behavior of the `ls` command.

You've already seen how to use normal positional parameters to pass options and arguments into a script. A lot of the time, this will work sufficiently well, and you won't need anything more. However, without some sort of helper utility, creating scripts that can properly parse a set of single-letter options that are combined with a single dash, or that have options with their arguments is very unwieldy. This is where getopts comes in. You can use it in a script to simplify the process. Before we talk about that though, I want to quickly cover something that might be a point of confusion for you.

Understanding getopt versus getopts

The getopt utility, which has its own executable file, has been around forever, since the early days of Unix. Its big advantage is that it can handle long options. In other words, in addition to feeding it single-letter options, such as `-a` or `-b`, you can also feed it whole-word options such as `--alpha` or `--beta`. And, that's it. That's really its only advantage.

It also has some disadvantages. The original implementation of getopt can't handle arguments that have blank spaces in their text strings. So, for example, if you need to work with a file that has a blank space in its filename, you can't specify that filename as an argument for a shell script that uses the original getopt. Also, the getopt syntax is a bit trickier than that of getopts, which makes getopts somewhat easier to use.

At some point in time, I'm not sure when, some random Linux developers decided to create a new implementation of getopt that would fix some of these deficiencies. (This is known as the **util-linux** implementation.) That would be great, except that it's still *only* in Linux. All of the Unix and Unix-like operating systems still have the original, unenhanced getopt. So, if you were to create a script on a Linux machine that uses the cool features of the enhanced getopt, you won't be able to run it on any Unix or Unix-like operating system, such as FreeBSD or OpenIndiana.

The newer getopts command, which is a shell builtin command that doesn't have its own executable, can work with arguments that contain blank spaces. The trade-off is that it can only work with single-letter options, and can't work with long options. The biggest advantage is that it's portable across Linux, Unix, and Unix-like operating systems, regardless of which shell you're using. So, if portability is one of your goals, your best bet is to just say *No* to getopt, and *Yes* to getopts.

For that reason, I'll only cover getopts in this chapter, and won't say anything more about the creaky old getopt.

With that out of the way, let's get down to the meat of the matter.

Using getopts

We'll begin with the getopts-demo1.sh script, which is the world's simplest getopts script. Here's how it looks:

```
#!/bin/bash
while getopts ab options; do
        case $options in
                a) echo "You chose Option A";;
                b) echo "You chose Option B";;
        esac
done
```

We're using a while loop to pass the chosen option or options into a case statement. The ab after the getopts command means that we're defining a and b as options that we can choose. (This list of allowable options is referred to as the **optstring**.) You can use any alpha-numeric character as an option. It's possible to use certain other characters as well, but it's not recommended. For reasons that will become clear later, you definitely *cannot* use either a ? or a : as an option. After the ab, you see options, which is just the name of the variable that we'll use in the case construct. (You can name the variable whatever you want.) Anyway, running the script looks like this:

```
donnie@fedora:~$ ./getopts-demo1.sh -a
You chose Option A
donnie@fedora:~$ ./getopts-demo1.sh -b
You chose Option B
donnie@fedora:~$
```

Okay, *big deal*, you're saying. We can do this sort of thing with just normal positional parameters. Ah, but here's something that you can't do with normal positional parameters:

```
donnie@fedora:~$ ./getopts-demo1.sh -ab
You chose Option A
You chose Option B
donnie@fedora:~$
```

So, you see how getopts allows you to combine options with a single dash, just as you're used to doing with normal Linux and Unix utilities. Something else that you can't do with normal positional parameters, at least not easily, is to have options that require their own arguments. Here's the getopts-demo2.sh script that shows how that's done:

```
#!/bin/bash
while getopts a:b: options; do
```

```
        case $options in
                a) var1=$OPTARG;;
                b) var2=$OPTARG;;
        esac
done
echo "Option A is $var1 and Option B is $var2"
```

When you place a colon after an allowable option in the optstring, you'll need to supply an argument for that option when you run the script. The argument for each option is stored in OPTARG, which is a variable that's built into the shell and that works with getopts. (Note that this variable name must consist of nothing but upper-case letters.) The while loop runs once for each option that is used, which means that the same OPTARG variable can be used for multiple option arguments. Just for fun, let's try this with my first name as the argument for the -a option, and my last name as the argument for the -b option. Here's how it looks:

```
donnie@fedora:~$ ./getopts-demo2.sh -a Donnie -b Tevault
Option A is Donnie and Option B is Tevault
donnie@fedora:~$
```

As it is now, the shell will return its own error message if you run the script with an invalid option, which looks like this:

```
donnie@fedora:~$ ./getopts-demo2.sh -x
./getopts-demo2.sh: illegal option -- x
Option A is  and Option B is
donnie@fedora:~$
```

In this case, the ./getopts-demo2.sh: illegal option -- x line is the error message that was generated by bash. You can suppress that error message by placing another colon at the beginning of the optstring. Optionally, you can add a \? choice to the case structure that will display your own custom error message for invalid choices, and a : choice to alert you if you try to run the script without supplying the required option arguments. Another problem is that if I don't supply the required option arguments, the final echo command still runs, when it really shouldn't. Anyway, here's how all of the fixes look in the getopts-demo3.sh script:

```
#!/bin/bash
while getopts :a:b: options; do
        case $options in
                a) var1=$OPTARG;;
                b) var2=$OPTARG;;
                \?) echo "I don't know the $OPTARG option";;
                :) echo "Both options require an argument.";;
        esac
done
[[ -z $var1 ]] || echo "Option A is $var1"
```

```
[[ -z $var2 ]] || echo "Option B is $var2"
```

Here's what happens when I run it with all of the necessary arguments:

```
donnie@fedora:~$ ./getopts-demo3.sh -a Donnie -b Tevault
Option A is Donnie
Option B is Tevault
donnie@fedora:~$
```

And here's how it looks if I either don't use all of the options or if I use an option without providing an argument:

```
donnie@fedora:~$ ./getopts-demo3.sh -a Donnie
Option A is Donnie
donnie@fedora:~$ ./getopts-demo3.sh -a
Both options require an argument.
donnie@fedora:~$ ./getopts-demo3.sh -a Donnie -b
Both options require an argument.
Option A is Donnie
donnie@fedora:~$
```

What we've done so far works perfectly with options that require arguments. In the getopts-demo4. sh script, I'll introduce two new concepts. You'll see how to require arguments for some options but not for others, and how to use non-option arguments. Here's how that looks:

```bash
#!/bin/bash
while getopts :a:b:c options; do
        case $options in
                a) var1=$OPTARG;;
                b) var2=$OPTARG;;
                c) echo "This option doesn't require an argument.";;
                \?) echo "I don't know the $OPTARG option";;
                :) echo "Both options require an argument.";;
        esac
done
[[ -z $var1 ]] || echo "Option A is $var1"
[[ -z $var2 ]] || echo "Option B is $var2"
shift $((OPTIND-1))
[[ -z $1 ]] || ls -l "$1"
```

The :a:b:c optstring, without a colon after the c, says that an argument is required for the -a and -b options, but not for the -c option. If any filenames are provided as non-option arguments, the last line at the bottom will perform an ls -1 command on those files. (Note that the [[-z $@]] structure will return an exit code of 0 if there are no non-option arguments. If there is a non-option argument, it will return an exit code of 1, which will trigger the ls -1 command.) But, here's the trick.

When you run this script, you'll need to specify the options and option arguments first. Then, at the end of the command, specify the filenames that will be the non-option arguments. Or, if you desire, just specify a non-option argument without using any of the options. The `shift $((OPTIND-1))` line is necessary to make the script recognize non-option arguments.

`OPTIND` is another variable that's built into the shell and that is meant to hold the number of `getopts` options that have been processed. The simplest way to understand what the `shift $((OPTIND-1))` command does is to think of it as a clearing mechanism. In other words, it clears away all of the `getopts` options that have been used and makes way for the non-option arguments. Another way to think of it is that it resets the positional parameter count back to `$1`. That way, you can access your non-option arguments the way you normally would, as you see on the final line. Also, note the `ls -l` `"$1"` command in the final line. This is a case where you absolutely *must* surround the positional parameter (`$1`, in this case) with a pair of double quotes. Otherwise, you'll get an error message if you try to access a file that has a blank space in its filename. Finally, note that you can list multiple positional parameters so that you can have multiple arguments, just as you've done before. Or, you can replace the `"$1"` parameter with `"$@"` so that you can use an unlimited number of non-option arguments.

So, running this script with no options, and with just a non-option argument, looks like this:

```
donnie@fedora:~$ ./getopts-demo4.sh "my new file.txt"
-rw-r--r--. 1 donnie donnie 0 Feb 25 13:00 'my new file.txt'
donnie@fedora:~$
```

If I were to remove the double quotes from around the positional parameter in the `ls -l` command, I would receive an error whenever I try to access a file with blank spaces in the filename. Here's how that looks:

```
donnie@fedora:~$ ./getopts-demo4.sh "my new file.txt"
ls: cannot access 'my': No such file or directory
ls: cannot access 'new': No such file or directory
ls: cannot access 'file.txt': No such file or directory
donnie@fedora:~$
```

So, remember to use those double quotes.

When I told you about the disadvantages of using `getopt`, I mentioned that the `getopt` syntax is trickier to use than that of `getopts`. If I were using `getopt` for these scripts, I would need to place one or more `shift` commands after each item in the `case` construct, so that the script would properly recognize the options. With `getopts`, this shifting is done automatically. The only place where I've had to use `shift` is in the `shift $((OPTIND-1))` command at the end. So you can see where `getopts` is much simpler.

Also, if you want to learn more about how to use `OPTIND` with `getops`, I've placed some references in the *Further Reading* section.

And really, this is pretty much it for the basic usage of `getopts`. So, let's move on.

Looking at Real-world Examples

Now that I've demonstrated the theory of using getopts, it's time to get down to business with a couple of real-world examples. Enjoy!

The Modified Coingecko Script

In *Chapter 10, Understanding Functions*, I showed you a pair of cool scripts that I created for my own use. To review, these scripts use the Coingecko API to automatically fetch information about cryptocurrencies.

The coingecko.sh script uses an if. .elif. .else construct to allow me to choose the function that I want to perform. In the coingecko-case.sh script, I use a case. .esac construct to achieve the same thing. Now, I present the third incarnation of the script, which uses getopts.

The coingecko-getopts.sh script is too large to reproduce here, so you'll need to grab it from GitHub. I do need to point out a few things about it, so I'll just show the relevant snippets here.

At the beginning of the script, I added the gecko_usage() function, which looks like this:

```
gecko_usage() {
        echo "Usage:"
        echo "To create a list of coins, do:"
        echo "./coingecko.sh -l"
        echo
        echo "To create a list of reference currencies, do:"
        echo "./coingecko.sh -c"
        echo
        echo "To get current coin prices, do:"
        echo "./coingecko.sh coin_name(s) currency"
}
```

Next, I deleted the coin=$1 and currency=$2 variable definitions from within the gecko_api() function, because we no longer need them.

Then, I added an error-checking option to the existing case structure, modified the **Usage** option to call the gecko_usage() function, and then surrounded it with a while loop, which looks like this:

```
while getopts :hlc options; do
        case $options in
                h)
                        gecko_usage
1)
        curl -X 'GET' \
        "https://api.coingecko.com/api/v3/coins/list?include_platform=true" \
         -H 'accept: application/json' | jq | tee coinlist.txt
        ;;
```

```
.  .  .
.  .  .
\?) echo "I don't know this $OPTARG option"
                        ;;
            esac
            done
```

 Remember to install the jq package, as I showed you in *Chapter 10*.

At first, I also had a p: option to obtain the current coin prices. That didn't work though, because this command requires two arguments, which are the comma-separated list of coins and the reference currency. But, getopts only allows you to use one argument per option. To fix that, I moved the coin price command out of the gecko_api() function, and placed it at the end of the file, like this:

```
gecko_api $1
shift $((OPTIND-1))
[[ -n $1 ]] && [[ -n $2 ]] && curl -X 'GET' \
  "https://api.coingecko.com/api/v3/simple/price?ids=$1&vs_
currencies=$2&include_market_cap=true&include_24hr_vol=true&include_24hr_
change=true&include_last_updated_at=true&precision=true" \
  -H 'accept: application/json' | jq
```

The call to the gecko_api() function now only requires one positional parameter, which will be the selected -h, -l, or -c option, or the combined -hlc set of options. If you want to use each option separately, rather than combining them, you'll need to change gecko_api $1 to either gecko_api $1 $2 $3 or gecko_api $@.

So, adapting the original Coingecko scripts to use getopts was really quite easy. But, what's the advantage? Well, in this case, there's really only one. That is, by using getopts option switches, you can now perform more than one task by running this script just a single time. That's something that you can't do with the original scripts. Regardless, you can use this as a template for your own scripts in which using getopts might be more advantageous.

Now, let's check out a cool system monitoring script.

The Tecmint Monitor Script

I borrowed this handy Linux-only tecmint_monitor.sh script from the Tecmint website, and tweaked it a bit to make it work better on newer Linux systems. The author released it under the Apache 2.0 free software license, so I was able to upload the tweaked version to GitHub for your convenience. (I've also provided a link to the original Tecmint article in the *Further Reading* section.)

I'm not going to explain the whole script here, because the author has done a stellar job of explaining it by inserting comments everywhere. But, I will point out a few things about it.

The first thing to note is that the author has done things a bit differently with the `case` construct. Instead of placing all of the code that he wants to execute into the `case` options, he instead just uses the `case` options to set either the `iopt` or `vopt` variable, depending upon whether the `-i` or the `-v` option was chosen. Here's how it looks:

```
while getopts iv name
do
        case $name in
          i)iopt=1;;
          v)vopt=1;;
          *)echo "Invalid arg";;
        esac
done
```

The executable code is placed within a pair of `if. .then` constructs. Here's the first one:

```
if [[ ! -z $iopt ]]
then
{
wd=$(pwd)
basename "$(test -L "$0" && readlink "$0" || echo "$0")" > /tmp/scriptname
scriptname=$(echo -e -n $wd/ && cat /tmp/scriptname)
su -c "cp $scriptname /usr/bin/monitor" root && echo "Congratulations! Script
Installed, now run monitor Command" || echo "Installation failed"
}
fi
```

So, if the value of the `iopt` variable is not of zero length, meaning that the `-i` option was chosen, then this script installation routine will run. It's not a very complex command. All it does is prompt you to enter the root user's password, copy the `techmint-monitor.sh` script to the `/usr/bin/` directory, and change its name to `monitor`.

Now, there is a slight problem here that I haven't fixed. It's just since the author created this script in 2016, it's become more common for Linux users to not assign a password to the root user account. In fact, that's the default behavior for the Ubuntu distros, and it's optional for many other distros. (In fact, I've never assigned a root user password here on this Fedora workstation.) So, the `su -c` command here won't work; because it expects you to enter the root user password when it prompts you to. So, if you haven't assigned a password to the root account, you'll always get an authentication failure if you run the script without using `sudo`. But, the script works fine when I do run it with `sudo`, so I didn't bother to change this.

Next, we have the `if`. `.then` construct for the `vopt` variable, which looks like this:

```
if [[ ! -z $vopt ]]
then
{
#echo -e "tecmint_monitor version 0.1\nDesigned by Tecmint.com\nReleased Under
Apache 2.0 License"
echo -e "tecmint_monitor version 0.1\nDesigned by Tecmint.com\nTweaked by
Donnie for more modern systems\nReleased Under Apache 2.0 License"
}
fi
```

All this option does is show version information about the script. At the bottom, I added the `Tweaked by Donnie` line to show that I modified the original script. (You might say that I made a tweak here to show that I made some tweaks.)

Next, we see a long `if`. `.then` construct that does the real work. It begins with `if [[ $# -eq 0 ]]`, which means that if no options were chosen, the code in this `if`. `.then` construct will execute.

Within this big, long `if`. `.then` block are the commands that obtain various types of system information. I had to tweak the command for checking DNS server information because the author made it look for the IP address of the DNS server on a specific line of the `resolv.conf` file. I changed it so that it will look for any lines that begin with the text string `nameserver`, which looks like this:

```
# Check DNS
#nameservers=$(cat /etc/resolv.conf | sed '1 d' | awk '{print $2}')
nameservers=$(cat /etc/resolv.conf | grep -w ^nameserver | awk '{print $2}')
echo -e '\E[32m'"Name Servers :" $tecreset $nameservers
```

I also tweaked the Check Disk Usages command, in order to make it more portable. Here's how it looks:

```
# Check Disk Usages
#df -h| grep 'Filesystem\|/dev/sda*' > /tmp/diskusage
df -Ph| grep 'Filesystem\|/dev/sda*' > /tmp/diskusage
echo -e '\E[32m'"Disk Usages :" $tecreset
cat /tmp/diskusage
```

All I did here was to add the `-P` option to the `df` command, so that the `df` output will always be POSIX-compliant. Of course, you can also add more drives to this if you need to.

Finally, at the very end, we have the `shift $(($OPTIND -1))` command. The script will actually run just fine if you comment this line out, because we don't have to deal with any non-option arguments. Still though, a lot of people believe that it's good form to always add this line to the end of a script that uses getopts, just to ensure that all option information is cleared out when the script exits.

In all of these examples, you've seen me use `while` loops to implement `getopts`, because that's my own personal preference. However, if you prefer to use a `for` loop instead, that's also perfectly fine. The choice is yours.

All right, I think that just about does it for our discussion of getopts. Let's summarize and move on.

Summary

In this chapter, we've looked at `getopts`, which gives us a cool and easy way to create scripts that recognize Linux and Unix-style option switches that might have their own arguments. We began with a review of what command options and arguments are, and then cleared up a possible point of confusion about getopt and getopts. After a presentation about how to use getopts, we wrapped up with a review of a couple of real-world scripts that use it.

In the next chapter, we'll look at how shell scripting can be a big help to security professionals. I'll see you there.

Questions

1. Which of the following statements is true?

    a. You should always use getopt, because it's easier to use than getopts.

    b. getopt can handle arguments that contain blank spaces, but getopts can't.

    c. getopt requires you to use one or more shift commands with every option, but getopts doesn't.

    d. getopts can handle long options, but getopt can't.

2. In this `while getopts :a:b:c options;` do line, what does the first colon do?

    a. It suppresses error messages from the shell.

    b. It causes the -a option to require an argument.

    c. It doesn't do anything.

    d. The colons cause the options to be separated from each other.

3. You need to create a script that accepts options, options with arguments, and non-option arguments. Which of the following commands must you insert into the script to make non-option arguments work?

    a. `shift $(($OPTARG -1))`

    b. `shift $(($OPTIND +1))`

    c. `shift $(($OPTIND -1))`

    d. `shift $(($OPTARG +1))`

Further Reading

- Small getopts Tutorial: `http://web.archive.org/web/20190509023321/https://wiki.bash-hackers.org/howto/getopts_tutorial`
- How can I handle command-line options and arguments in my script easily?: `http://mywiki.wooledge.org/BashFAQ/035`
- How to Use OPTARG in Bash: `https://linuxsimply.com/bash-scripting-tutorial/functions/script-argument/bash-optarg/`
- A Shell Script to Monitor Network, Disk Usage, Uptime, Load Average and RAM Usage in Linux: `https://www.tecmint.com/linux-server-health-monitoring-script/`

 Note: The following links contain extra information about `OPTIND`.

- How to Use getopts to Parse Linux Shellscript Otions: `https://www.howtogeek.com/778410/how-to-use-getopts-to-parse-linux-shell-script-options/`
- How does the OPTIND variable work in the shell builtin getopts: `https://stackoverflow.com/questions/14249931/how-does-the-optind-variable-work-in-the-shell-builtin-getopts`
- How to Use "getopts" in Bash: `https://linuxsimply.com/bash-scripting-tutorial/functions/script-argument/bash-getopts/`

Answers

1. c
2. a.
3. c

Join our community on Discord!

Read this book alongside other users, Linux experts, and the author himself.

Ask questions, provide solutions to other readers, chat with the author via Ask Me Anything sessions, and much more. Scan the QR code or visit the link to join the community.

`https://packt.link/SecNet`

18

Shell Scripting for Security Professionals

In this chapter, we'll do things a bit differently. Instead of showing you new scripting concepts, I'll show you how to use the concepts that you've already learned to perform chores that a security professional might need to do.

Of course, you could do many of these chores with a more complex program, such as nmap. But, there may be times when these tools won't be available to you. In this chapter, I'll show you some simple scripts that can do some of these jobs.

Topics in this chapter include:

- Simple scripts for auditing
- Creating simple firewall scripts
- Searching for existing security-related scripts
- Okay, I know that you're anxious to get started. So, let's go.

Technical Requirements

For the Linux demos in this chapter, I'll use a Fedora Server virtual machine. That's because these demos will use features and utilities that are unique to Red Hat-type distros, such as Fedora. However, you can easily adapt them to other Linux distros, such as Ubuntu or Debian, if you desire.

I'll also be showing you some things on OpenIndiana and FreeBSD. On your FreeBSD virtual machine, I'm assuming that you've already installed bash, and set up a normal user account with full sudo privileges, as I've shown you in *Chapter 12, Automating Scripts with here Documents and expect*.

Also, as always, you can grab the scripts from Github by running:

```
git clone https://github.com/PacktPublishing/The-Ultimate-Linux-Shell-
Scripting-Guide.git
```

Simple Scripts for Auditing

If you're used to using nmap, you already know how awesome it is. You can use it for many types of auditing and network security chores, such as scanning ports or identifying operating systems on remote machines. But, if you ever find yourself in a situation where nmap isn't available to you, know that you can do some of your nmap chores with some simple shell scripts. Let's begin with something simple.

Identifying an Operating System

You can get a rough idea of what operating system is running on another machine by pinging it, and looking at the **Time-to-Live (TTL)** figure in the response. Here's how it works:

- 64: If the TTL of a ping response is 64, then the operating system of the target machine is Linux, some sort of BSD, or macOS.
- 128: A 128 TTL indicates that the target machine is running Windows.
- 255: This indicates that the target machine is running either Solaris or a Solaris clone, such as OpenIndiana.

Here's the output of a normal ping command. (Note that I'm using the -c1 option, which means that I'm only sending one ping packet.) This shows the TTL field:

```
donnie@fedora:~$ ping -c1 192.168.0.18
PING 192.168.0.18 (192.168.0.18) 56(84) bytes of data.
64 bytes from 192.168.0.18: icmp_seq=1 ttl=128 time=5.09 ms
--- 192.168.0.18 ping statistics ---
1 packets transmitted, 1 received, 0% packet loss, time 0ms
rtt min/avg/max/mdev = 5.086/5.086/5.086/0.000 ms
donnie@fedora:~$
```

In the second line of output, you see ttl=128, which indicates that I've just pinged a Windows machine. Now, here's the os-detect.sh script, which automatically interprets the TTL field:

```
#!/bin/bash
ttl=$(ping -c1 $1 | head -2 | tail -1 | cut -d= -f3 | cut -d" " -f1)
echo "The TTL value is $ttl."
if [[ $ttl == 64 ]]; then
        echo "A TTL of $ttl indicates either a Linux, BSD, or macOS operating
system."
elif [[ $ttl == 128 ]]; then
        echo "A TTL of $ttl indicates a Windows operating system."
elif [[ $ttl == 255 ]] ; then
        echo "A TTL of $ttl indicates a Solaris/OpenIndiana operating system."
else
        echo "There was no recognized TTL value."
fi
```

In the second line, I'm using the $1 positional parameter to represent the IP address of the target machine. I'm also piping the ping output into head and then tail in order to isolate the second line of output, which contains the TTL field. I then pipe this second line into cut, using the = as the field delimiter to isolate the third field, which in this example with Windows is 128 time. Finally, I pipe the value of this third field into cut, in order to isolate just the TTL number. This TTL number will be the value of the ttl variable.

Finally, we have the if. .elif. .else construct to identify the target machine's operating system. Now, here's the script in operation:

```
donnie@fedora:~$ ./os-detect.sh 192.168.0.18
The TTL value is 128.
A TTL of 128 indicates a Windows operating system.
donnie@fedora:~$ ./os-detect.sh 192.168.0.20
The TTL value is 64.
A TTL of 64 indicates either a Linux, BSD, or macOS operating system.
donnie@fedora:~$ ./os-detect.sh 192.168.0.19
The TTL value is 255.
A TTL of 255 indicates a Solaris/OpenIndiana operating system.
donnie@fedora:~$
```

For the record, the first machine is running Windows 10, the second one is running FreeBSD, and the third one is running OpenIndiana. So, that's easy, right? Hang on though, because I do need to point out a couple of caveats.

First, is the obvious fact that this script can't provide much detail about the operating systems on the target machines. In fact, it can't even differentiate between Linux, BSD, or macOS operating systems. The second caveat is that you can only use this script to scan machines that are on your local network, because sending ping packets across a network boundary changes the TTL value. Thirdly, you can run this script from either a Linux or a BSD machine, but you can't run it from a Solaris/OpenIndiana machine. That's because Solaris and OpenIndiana use a different implementation of the ping utility that doesn't show anything other than the fact that the target machine is up. And lastly, if the target machines have firewalls that are configured to block ping packets, then this script won't work at all.

So, even though this script could be a handy tool for a quick analysis of machines on your local network, you'll need to use nmap or some other equivalent tool to get more detailed information, to scan machines on another network, or to scan machines with firewalls that block ping packets. For example, using nmap with the -A option allows nmap to somewhat accurately detect the operating system of the target machine. Here's how it looks when I scan a FreeBSD 14 machine:

```
donnie@fedora:~$ sudo nmap -A 192.168.0.20
. . .
. . .
Device type: general purpose
Running: FreeBSD 12.X|13.X
```

```
OS CPE: cpe:/o:freebsd:freebsd:12 cpe:/o:freebsd:freebsd:13
OS details: FreeBSD 12.0-RELEASE - 13.0-CURRENT
Network Distance: 1 hop
Service Info: OS: FreeBSD; CPE: cpe:/o:freebsd:freebsd
Okay, that's cool. Let's now scan some ports.
. . .

. . .
donnie@fedora:~$
```

Okay, you see what I meant when I said that nmap's operating system detection is *somewhat* accurate. The scan results show that I'm scanning a FreeBSD 12 or FreeBSD 13 machine, even though it's really a FreeBSD 14 machine. But, FreeBSD 14 is still quite new, so it's probable that the fingerprint for it hasn't yet been added to the nmap database. On the positive side, at least this accurately tells us that it's some sort of FreeBSD machine, instead of just telling us that it could be FreeBSD, Linux, or macOS.

On the other hand, you might find times when our simple script works better. For example, look at what happens when I do an nmap -A scan on an OpenIndiana machine:

```
donnie@fedora:~$ sudo nmap -A 192.168.0.19
. . .

. . .
No exact OS matches for host (If you know what OS is running on it, see
https://nmap.org/submit/ ).
. . .

. . .
donnie@fedora:~$
```

As you saw earlier, our script correctly identified this machine as either a Solaris or OpenIndiana machine. But, nmap can't identify it at all.

A Simple Port-scanning Script

This is a cool little script that you can use to scan either local or remote machines for open network ports. If you're new to network scanning, a network port can be in any one of three states. Here are the relevant definitions of those states:

- open: An open port is one that has an associated network service running, and that is not blocked by a firewall. For example, you would expect to find Port 22 open on a server that has its Secure Shell service running, and Port 443 open on a webserver that's using an encrypted connection. By observing which ports on a remote machine are open, you can tell which network services are running on that machine.

- closed: A closed port is one that does not have an associated service running, and that is not blocked by a firewall.

- filtered: A filtered port has been blocked by a firewall.

This script works by using the network capability that's built into the GNU implementation of bash that comes on Linux and newer versions of macOS. It works by using either the /dev/tcp or the /dev/udp device on your Linux system. What's crazy though, is that you won't find either of these device files in the /dev/ directory. That's because they're hard-coded into the bash executable. You can use the strings utility to verify that, as you see here:

```
donnie@fedora:~$ strings /bin/bash | grep tcp
/dev/tcp/*/*
donnie@fedora:~$ strings /bin/bash | grep udp
/dev/udp/*/*
donnie@fedora:~$
```

> In case you're wondering, strings allows you to view text strings that are embedded into binary executable files. Also, be aware that this networking capability is only built into the GNU implementation of bash, which means that you can run these commands on either Linux or a newer version of macOS, but not on other Unix/Unix-like distros such as FreeBSD or OpenIndiana.

The simplest way to illustrate this is to manually query a port that will provide feedback. Here, I'm querying Port 13 on a remote network time server:

```
donnie@fedora:~$ cat < /dev/tcp/time.nist.gov/13
60372 24-03-03 21:04:44 58 0 0 544.5 UTC(NIST) *
donnie@fedora:~$
```

You'll also get feedback from Port 22, the SSH port, as you see here:

```
donnie@fedora:~$ cat < /dev/tcp/192.168.0.20/22
SSH-2.0-OpenSSH_9.3 FreeBSD-20230719
donnie@fedora:~$
```

This one takes a bit longer to complete, because it takes a while for the authentication timer on the target machine to time out.

> In both of these examples, note how I'm using the input redirector (<) to obtain input from the /dev/tcp device. Then, after the /dev/tcp/ part, I place the IP address of the target machine, and finally the port that I want to scan.

Most ports won't provide you with any kind of feedback. But, you can still tell if a port is open by how quickly the command executes. For example, if you query Port 53 on a DNS server, you should see that the command completes execution immediately, as you see here with the Google DNS server:

```
donnie@fedora:~$ cat < /dev/tcp/8.8.8.8/53
donnie@fedora:~$
```

So, I know that Port 53 is open. But, if I query a port that isn't open, such as Port 54 in this case, it will be a very long time before the command-prompt returns with an error message, as you see here:

```
donnie@fedora:~$ cat < /dev/tcp/8.8.8.8/54
bash: connect: Connection timed out
bash: /dev/tcp/8.8.8.8/54: Connection timed out
donnie@fedora:~$
```

Now, let's leverage this knowledge by creating the `bash-portscan1.sh` script, like this:

```bash
#!/bin/bash
host=$1
startport=$2
stopport=$3
ping=$(ping -c 1 $host | grep bytes | wc -l)
if [ "$ping" -gt 1 ]; then
  echo "$host is up";
else
  echo "$host is down. Quitting";
  exit
fi
for ((counter=$startport; counter<=$stopport; counter++)); do
        (echo >/dev/tcp/$host/$counter) > /dev/null 2>&1 && echo "Port
$counter open"
done
```

It's rather long, so I'll break it down into sections. Here's the top part:

```bash
#!/bin/bash
host=$1
startport=$2
stopport=$3
```

To run this script, you'll need to specify either the hostname or the IP address of the target machine, along with the range of ports that you want to scan. Easy enough so far, right? Next, we want to verify that the target machine is actually up, and create a variable assignment that we can use in the next step. Here's how that looks:

```bash
ping=$(ping -c 1 $host | grep bytes | wc -l)
```

The value of the `ping` variable will be greater than 1, most likely 2, if the target machine is up and accessible. If the target machine isn't accessible, the value will just be 1. To see how this works, run this from the command-line, leaving off the `wc -l` part, like so:

```
donnie@fedora:~$ ping -c1 192.168.0.20 | grep bytes
PING 192.168.0.20 (192.168.0.20) 56(84) bytes of data.
```

```
 64 bytes from 192.168.0.20: icmp_seq=1 ttl=64 time=0.506 ms
donnie@fedora:~$ ping -c1 192.168.0.200 | grep bytes
PING 192.168.0.200 (192.168.0.200) 56(84) bytes of data.
donnie@fedora:~$
```

I first pinged a machine that's up, and got two lines of output. I then pinged a fictitious machine, and only received one line of output. The wc -1 command will count those lines and assign the appropriate value to the ping variable.

Next, we have the if. .else block that causes the script to exit if the target machine isn't up. Here's how that looks:

```
if [ "$ping" -gt 1 ]; then
   echo "$host is up";
else
   echo "$host is down. Quitting";
   exit
fi
```

> Note how I had to surround $ping with a pair of double quotes. That's because the value of ping will contain blank spaces, non-alphanumeric characters, and might consist of more than one line. Without the double quotes, bash won't interpret the value of ping correctly.

Finally, we have the for loop that does the actual port scan. Here's how it looks:

```
for ((counter=$startport; counter<=$stopport; counter++)); do
          (echo >/dev/tcp/$host/$counter) > /dev/null 2>&1 && echo "Port
$counter open"
done
```

This starts by assigning the value of the startport variable to the counter variable. The loop will continue as long as the value of counter is less than or equal to the value of stopport.

Now, here's how it looks when I run the script:

```
donnie@fedora:~$ ./bash-portscan1.sh 192.168.0.20 20 22
192.168.0.20 is up
Port 22 open
donnie@fedora:~$ ./bash-portscan1.sh 8.8.8.8 53 53
8.8.8.8 is up
Port 53 open
donnie@fedora:~$
```

In the first instance, I scanned a range of ports, beginning with Port 20 and ending with Port 22. Then, I scanned only Port 53 on the Google DNS server.

So you see, this works fine with either local or remote targets.

So far, we've only scanned TCP ports. But, you can also scan UDP ports by making one simple modification, as I've done in the `bash-portscan2.sh` script. In the `for` loop, just change `tcp` to `udp`, so that it will look like this:

```
for ((counter=$startport; counter<=$stopport; counter++)); do
        (echo >/dev/udp/$host/$counter) > /dev/null 2>&1 && echo "Port
$counter open"
done
```

Of course, you can fancy things up a bit more if you like. For example, you could combine the TCP and the UDP scan functions together into one script, and have some sort of menu that allows you to choose the one you want to do. Heck, for that matter, you could even add a `yad`, `dialog`, or `xdialog` interface. (I've shown you the techniques for all this in *Chapter 16, Creating User Interfaces with yad, dialog, and xdialog*.)

Now, you can get more detailed information about your target by using `nmap` to perform the scan, which would look something like this:

```
donnie@fedora:~$ sudo nmap -sS 192.168.0.20
Starting Nmap 7.93 ( https://nmap.org ) at 2024-03-03 17:12 EST
Nmap scan report for 192.168.0.20
Host is up (0.00044s latency).
Not shown: 999 closed tcp ports (reset)
PORT    STATE SERVICE
22/tcp open   ssh
MAC Address: 08:00:27:45:A4:75 (Oracle VirtualBox virtual NIC)
Nmap done: 1 IP address (1 host up) scanned in 6.01 seconds
donnie@fedora:~$
```

This `-sS` type of scan, which is known as a SYN packet scan, requires `sudo` privileges. However, you can also do a `-sT` type of scan, which doesn't require `sudo` privileges. Scanning open ports with our homemade script runs almost instantaneously. But scanning closed or filtered ports can be, but not always, faster with `nmap`. Still though, there is one possible advantage for using our script. It's just that certain types of `nmap` scans can be blocked by adding a few rules to the target machine's firewall. So, if you try to run an `nmap` scan against a machine and get no results, you might try using the script, instead. On the other hand, scanning open ports with the script can be a bit less stealthy, because it will leave tell-tale messages in the target machine's system log files. For example, here's the set of messages that resulted from using the script to scan Port 22 on an AlmaLinux 9 machine:

```
Mar  6 13:25:20 localhost sshd[1601]: error: kex_exchange_identification:
client sent invalid protocol identifier ""
Mar  6 13:25:20 localhost sshd[1601]: error: send_error: write: Broken pipe
Mar  6 13:25:20 localhost sshd[1601]: banner exchange: Connection from
192.168.0.16 port 38680: invalid format
```

Using the script to scan other open ports will create similar messages, while scanning closed ports won't create any messages at all. If you use the script to scan an open webserver port, such as Port 80 or Port 443, you'll instead see messages like this one in the webserver's access_log file:

```
192.168.0.16 - - [06/Mar/2024:13:38:49 -0500] "\n" 400 226 "-" "-"
```

But, nmap won't create any messages like these unless the target machine's firewall is configured to log packets that come from nmap scans. So, there are advantages and disadvantages for both approaches.

> On Red Hat-type machines, such as AlmaLinux, Rocky Linux, and RHEL, these messages will show up in the /var/log/secure file. On other distros, these messages might show up in either the /var/log/messages file or the /var/log/syslog file. Some Linux distros, such as Debian, no longer create any of these files by default. For them, you'll need to either use the sudo journalctl command to view the messages, or install the rsyslog package from the normal distro repository so that you can have the normal text-mode log files..

Now, let's do something a bit more complex.

Auditing the root User Account

Since I'm a security geek, I always advocate setting up Linux and Unix systems with the root user account disabled. That's easy to do on many modern Linux systems, because you can configure things properly in the system installer. In fact, the Ubuntu installer won't even let you enable the root user account, and will just automatically add the account that you created for yourself to the sudo group. (You can enable the root user account after you've installed the operating system, even though that's not recommended practice.) For other Linux distros, such as Debian, Fedora, or members of the RHEL family, enabling the root user account during installation is optional. On most Unix-like systems such as FreeBSD and OpenIndiana, the installer will assign a password to the root user account. On FreeBSD, after installation has been completed, you'll have to manually install sudo, set up a normal user account to use it, and then disable the root user account. On OpenIndiana, the normal user you create when you install the operating system will already be configured to have full sudo privileges, and the root account will also be enabled.

So now, you want an easy way to audit your systems to see if the root user on them is enabled. Let's begin by setting up a script that works equally well on either Linux or OpenIndiana systems.

Creating the root Account Auditing Script for Linux and OpenIndiana

We'll begin with the rootlock_1.sh script, which you can download from the Github repository. This is another one of those scripts that's too long to show here in its entirety. That's okay though, because it's easier to explain if I break it down into sections.

The first thing I want to do is to initialize a couple of variables, like so:

```
#!/bin/bash
os=$(uname)
quantity=$(cut -f3 -d: /etc/passwd | grep -w 0 | wc -l)
```

OpenIndiana and most Linux systems come with bash installed by default, and both use the same shadow file system. So, the same exact script works for either one. Eventually though, I might want to modify it so that it will run on some of the BSD-type operating systems, which are set up differently. To prepare for that, I'll use the output of the uname command as the value for the os variable, so that I can ensure that the correct code will always run on each operating system. I also want to know how many user accounts there are that have an assigned UID value of 0, so I'll create the quantity variable to keep track of that. To obtain that value, I need to use the cut -f3 -d: command to look at the third field of each passwd file entry, and then pipe that into the grep -w 0 command to only find the lines that contain nothing but a 0 in that field. Finally, I use the wc -l command to count the number of lines that match this criterion.

Remember that the UID value of 0 is what gives user accounts full root user privileges. On most operating systems, you should never see more than one UID 0 user account. On some BSD-type systems, you'll see either two or three UID 0 accounts. One will be the root account, which might have either csh or sh assigned as the default shell. A second one will be the toor account, which will have sh assigned as the default shell. DragonflyBSD has a third UID 0 account which is called, installer. So, if you want to write one script that will cover all of these different operating systems, you'll need to write code that will account for each one having a different number of UID 0 accounts. (We'll look at all that later in this section.)

Next, I've created the linux_sunos function, which contains the bulk of the working code. Here's how it looks:

```
linux_sunos() {
        if [ $quantity -gt 1 ] ; then
                echo "CRITICAL.  There are $quantity accounts with UID 0."
        else
                echo "OKAY.  There is only one account with UID 0."
        fi
        echo
        echo
        rootlock=$(awk 'BEGIN {FS=":"}; /root/ {print $2}' /etc/shadow | cut
-c1)
        if [ "$rootlock" == $ ] ; then
                echo "CRITICAL!!  The root account is not locked out."
        else
                echo "The root account is locked out, as it should be."
        fi
}
```

The top part is easy. It's just an if. .then. .else construct that alerts you if there are more than one UID 0 accounts in the /etc/passwd file.

Next, I use an awk command, with its output piped into cut -c1, to find the root user account line in the /etc/shadow file, and to isolate the value of the first character of the second field of that line. That value will be assigned to the rootlock variable. So, what is so significant about that character? Well, here's the deal.

On Linux, Unix, and Unix-like systems, a list of user accounts is kept in the /etc/passwd file. This file must always be world-readable, so that users can access their user account information when they log in. Many years ago, when I was young and still had a full head of hair, user passwords were also kept in this passwd file. Eventually, someone figured out that keeping passwords in a world-readable file is a security problem, and invented the **shadow file system**. Now, the hashed values of all users' passwords are in the /etc/shadow file on Linux and Solaris/OpenIndiana systems, which requires root privileges to read. (It's a bit different on BSD-type systems, as I'll show you in just a bit.) For example, here's the entry for my own user account on my Fedora Server virtual machine:

```
donnie:$y$j9T$PfB847h88/LNURBaDxBbWdYI$bRXbrMUrTM7JwWifuDfjt6oFl0FFdYEzcwJHF5r/
kG5::0:99999:7:::
```

(Note that this is one long line that wraps around on the printed page. Also note that I changed a couple of characters, to prevent revealing the real hash value.)

What I want you to note is the prefix of this hashed value, which is y. The leading $ indicates that this account is enabled, and the whole y thing indicates that the password was hashed by the **ye-scrypt** hashing algorithm.

Since Fedora is a cutting-edge, somewhat experimental Linux distro, you can expect it to use new technologies that aren't yet widely used by the rest of the Linux ecosystem. Such is the case here with Fedora's use of yescrypt. On most modern Linux distros, you'll see a 6 prefix on the password hash, which indicates that they're using the SHA512 hashing algorithm. Although SHA512 hashes are very difficult to crack, yescrypt hashes are supposed to be even more difficult, which enhances password security.

For our present purposes, it doesn't matter which hashing algorithm is in use. All we care about is that leading $, because that's what tells us that the account is enabled. If anything other than a $ is in that first position, then the account is disabled. For best security, you want to see something like any of these three lines in the /etc/shadow file:

```
root:!::0:99999:7:::
root:*::0:99999:7:::
root:*LK*::0:99999:7:::
```

Now, here's the sort of thing that you don't want to see:

```
root:$y$j9T$TZqIDctm8w7ESbopARa5f1$RKjMWhZ9zS4KZ5dPvSODo2nAIH4s8GwZTA4TJNnoh3B:19
844:0:99999:7:::
```

On this virtual machine, the root account is enabled, as indicated by the leading $. And, this takes us back to the linux_sunos function in our script. Let's take another look at the line that creates the rootlock variable:

```
rootlock=$(awk 'BEGIN {FS=":"}; /root/ {print $2}' /etc/shadow | cut -c1)
```

As I pointed out before, this awk command isolates the second field of the root user's entry, which is the password field. Piping the awk output into the cut -c1 command isolates the first character of that field. The value of that character is then assigned as the value of the rootlock variable.

Next up is the code that determines whether or not the root user account is locked:

```
if [ "$rootlock" == '$' ] ; then
                echo "CRITICAL!!  The root account is not locked out."
        else
                echo "The root account is locked out, as it should be."
        fi
```

This says that if the first character of the second field of the root user's entry is a $, then the account is not locked. If that first character is anything other than a $, then the account is locked, and all is good.

Note that in this if. .then. .else construct I had to surround $rootlock with a pair of double quotes. That's because on some Linux distros, such as Ubuntu, you might see an * in the password field of the root user's shadow file entry. Without the double quotes, the shell will interpret the * as a wildcard, and will cause $rootlock to return the list of files in the current working directory. Using the double quotes allows the $ to do its job, while forcing the shell to interpret the * in a literal manner.

For good measure, I also surrounded the $ with a pair of single quotes, to ensure that that the shell would interpret it correctly. (It actually worked fine when I tested it without the single quotes, but it's better to be safe.)

Now, at the very end of the script, after the function, you see this:

```
if [ $os == Linux ] || [ $os == SunOS ] ; then
        linux_sunos
else
        echo "I don't know this operating system."
fi
```

The value of the os variable should be Linux on a Linux system, and SunOS on an OpenIndiana system. Either way, the linux_sunos function will run. If the value of os is anything else, the user will see an error message.

Finally, let's test this script to see what happens. Here's what it looks like on the Fedora workstation that I'm using to write this:

```
donnie@fedora:~$ sudo ./rootlock_1.sh
[sudo] password for donnie:
OKAY.  There is only one account with UID 0.
The root account is locked out, as it should be.
donnie@fedora:~$
```

Very cool, it all looks good.

To see how it looks when the root account is enabled, I pulled up my Fedora Server virtual machine, which has never had the root account enabled. I enabled the root account like this:

```
donnie@fedora-server:~$ sudo passwd root
Changing password for user root.
New password:
Retype new password:
passwd: all authentication tokens updated successfully.
donnie@fedora-server:~$
```

Easy, right? All I had to do was to assign a password to the root user account. Now, let's run the script:

```
donnie@fedora-server:~$ sudo ./rootlock_1.sh
OKAY.  There is only one account with UID 0.
CRITICAL!!  The root account is not locked out.
donnie@fedora-server:~$
```

Now, let's add the option to disable the root account, as you see in the rootlock_2.sh script. We'll do that by embedding another if. .then. .else construct within the one that's already there. Here's how it looks:

```
if [ $rootlock == $ ] ; then
                echo "CRITICAL!!  The root account is not locked out."
                echo "Do you want to disable the root account? (y/n)"
                read answer
                if [ $answer == y ] ; then
                        passwd -l root
                else
                        exit
                fi
        else
                echo "The root account is locked out, as it should be."
        fi
```

Here's how running the modified script looks:

```
donnie@fedora-server:~$ sudo ./rootlock_2.sh
OKAY.  There is only one account with UID 0.
```

```
CRITICAL!!  The root account is not locked out.
Do you want to disable the root account? (y/n)
y
Locking password for user root.
passwd: Success
donnie@fedora-server:~$
```

To disable an account, the passwd -l command places a pair of exclamation points in front of the password hash, like this:

```
root:!!$y$j9T$ckYOQzoMU0mr9gQkjqz/
K0$QDNV0unG1XAfBwViY.7a6JR8VaMpIGObGzXIN0vxGQA:19847:0:99999:7:::
```

The password hash is still there, but the operating system can no longer read it. This will allow you to unlock the account by running:

```
donnie@fedora-server:~$ sudo passwd -u root
[sudo] password for donnie:
Unlocking password for user root.
passwd: Success
donnie@fedora-server:~$
```

To both delete the password and disable the account, place a passwd -d root command on the line before the passwd -l root command, so that the construct will now look like this:

```
if [ $rootlock == $ ] ; then
                echo "CRITICAL!!  The root account is not locked out."
                echo "Do you want to disable the root account? (y/n)"
                read answer
                if [ $answer == y ] ; then
                        passwd -d root
                        passwd -l root
                else
                        exit
                fi
        else
                echo "The root account is locked out, as it should be."
        fi
```

Note that you can't use both the -l and -d options for passwd in a single command. To use both options, you'll need to run two separate commands. Also note that if you just use the -d option, you'll delete the password hash but the account is still considered as enabled. Running passwd -l after running passwd -d will both delete the password hash and disable the account.

And, although you probably already know this, I'll tell you anyway. Before you disable the root user account, be darned sure that you're logged in as a normal user with full sudo privileges, instead of as the root user. That way, there will be no chance of accidentally disabling the root account on a machine for which nobody else has any admin privileges.

The only way to re-enable root's account now is to create a new password, as you've already seen.

That covers it for Linux and OpenIndiana. Let's see if we can make this work on FreeBSD.

Modifying the root Account Auditing Script for Use on FreeBSD

On BSD-type operating systems, such as FreeBSD, the /etc/master.passwd file is used instead of the /etc/shadow file. In addition to the UID 0 root user account in the /etc/passwd file, there's the toor user account, which is also a UID 0 account. So, we'll need to add a freebsd function to work with these differences.

Up through FreeBSD 13, the root user account has csh assigned as its default shell, and the toor account has sh assigned as the default shell. Now, on FreeBSD 14, both of these UID 0 accounts have sh as the default shell.

The simplest way to do this is to add a new function, which I'll call freebsd. (Really, what else would I call it?) You'll find this new function in the rootlock_3.sh script that's in the Github repository. Let's break this new function into sections to see what we have. Here's the top part:

```
freebsd() {
        if [ $quantity -gt 2 ]
        then
                echo "CRITICAL.  There are $quantity accounts in the passwd
file with UID 0."
        else
                echo "OKAY.  There are only two accounts in the passwd file
with UID 0."
                echo
                echo
        fi
```

This is the same as the `linux_sunos` function that we just looked at, except that it now checks for more than two UID 0 accounts in the `passwd` file. Here's the next part:

```
rootlock=$(awk 'BEGIN {FS=":"}; $1 ~ /root/ {print $2}' /etc/master.passwd |
cut -c1)
        if [ "$rootlock" == '$' ] ; then
                echo "CRITICAL!!  The root account is not locked out."
                echo "Do you want to disable the root account? (y/n)"
                read answer
                if [ $answer == y ] ; then
                        pw mod user root -w no
                fi
        else
                echo "The root account is locked out, as it should be."
        fi
```

I had to modify the `awk` command so that it will only find "root" in the first field of a line, as you see here with the `$1 ~ /root/` part:

```
rootlock=$(awk 'BEGIN {FS=":"}; $1 ~ /root/ {print $2}' /etc/master.passwd |
cut -c1)
```

That's because, unlike the Linux and OpenIndiana shadow files, the FreeBSD `master.passwd` file lists users' default home directories. As you see here, the default home directories for the first three users are set to the `/root/` directory:

```
root:*:0:0::0:0:Charlie &:/root:/bin/csh
toor:*:0:0::0:0:Bourne-again Superuser:/root:
daemon:*:1:1::0:0:Owner of many system processes:/root:/usr/sbin/nologin
```

Having `/root/` instead of `$1 ~ /root/` in the `awk` command causes the script to read all three of these lines, instead of just the first one that's for the root user. This prevents the script from properly detecting if the root user account is enabled. That's because if the script sees a $ in field 2 of the root line, and then sees an * in field 2 of the toor and daemon lines, it will assign the * as the final value of `rootlock`. Because of that, the script will always show that the root account is locked, even when it isn't.

I also had to change the commands that lock the root and toor accounts, because the FreeBSD version of `passwd` doesn't have the proper option switches to do that. So, I replaced the two `passwd` commands with:

```
pw mod user root -w no
```

This handy command both removes the password and locks the account at the same time.

Since FreeBSD also has the toor account with UID 0, I've added another section to check for that:

```
toorlock=$(awk 'BEGIN {FS=":"}; /toor/ {print $2}' /etc/master.passwd | cut
-c1)
```

```
        if [ "$toorlock" == '$' ] ; then
                echo "CRITICAL!!  The toor account is not locked out."
                echo "Do you want to disable the toor account? (y/n)"
                read answer
                if [ $answer == y ] ; then
                        pw mod user toor -w no
                fi
        else
                echo "The toor account is locked out, as it should be."
        fi
}
```

Only one line in the master.passwd file contains the word "toor", so I didn't need to tell awk to look for the /toor/ pattern in only the first field. Other than that, it's the same as what I've just shown you for the root user. (Of course, since this is the end of the function, I've included the closing curly brace at the end.)

Finally, I've modified the final part of the script so that it will automatically choose which function to run:

```
if [ $os == Linux ] || [ $os == SunOS ] ; then
        linux_sunos
elif [ $os == FreeBSD ] ; then
        freebsd
else
        echo "I don't know this operating system."
fi
```

You've seen this sort of thing before in previous chapters, so you likely already know what's going on with this.

 Once again, I'm reading your mind. You're thinking about how cool this script is, and how much you'd like to use it on an entire fleet of mixed Linux, Unix, and Unix-like servers. The problem though, is that this script is written for bash and uses some of the bash advanced features that don't work on many of the legacy sh shells. That's great if you can install bash on all of your Unix and Unix-like servers, but that might not be an option. Also, if you're working with Internet of Things devices that run lightweight versions of Linux, you might not be able to install bash on them either. So, what do you do? Well, hang on, because I'll explain all of that in *Chapter 19, Shell Script Portability*.

I think that this about covers it for the rootlock scripts. Let's look at one more auditing script before wrapping up this section.

Creating a User Activity Monitoring Script

In this scenario, you want to see a record of when other users have logged into the system, and what they're doing with their sudo privileges. To do that, let's create the `user_activity_1.sh` script. Here's the top section:

```
#!/bin/bash
if [[ $1 == "" ]] ; then
        echo "You must specify a user name."
        echo "Usage: sudo ./user_activity_1.sh username "
        exit
fi
```

This tells you that you have to supply a user name when invoking this script. If you don't specify a user name, you'll see this message, and the script will exit. Here's the next part:

```
if [[ -f /var/log/secure ]] ; then
        logfile=/var/log/secure
elif [[ -f /var/log/auth.log ]] ; then
        logfile=/var/log/auth.log
elif [[ -n $(awk /suse/ /etc/os-release) ]] ; then
        logfile=/var/log/messages
else
        echo "I don't know this operating system."
        exit
fi
```

Most Linux and some Unix/Unix-like distros store user authentication messages in either the /var/log/secure file or the /var/log/auth.log file. SUSE and openSUSE are notable exceptions to this rule, because they store this information in the /var/log/messages file.

 I'm assuming here that you're working with a distro that has either rsyslog or syslog installed. This script won't work if all you have is journald.

Finally, here's the part that does the actual work.

```
username=$1
echo "=== User Account Activity ===" > user_activity_for_"$username"_$(date
+"%F_%H-%M").txt
# Check user activity in system logs
echo "=== Recent Logins ===" >> user_activity_for_"$username"_$(date +"%F_%H-
%M").txt
last | grep $username >> user_activity_for_"$username"_$(date +"%F_%I-%M").txt
```

```
# Check sudo command usage
echo "=== Sudo Command Usage ===" >> user_activity_for_"$username"_$(date
+"%F_%H-%M").txt
grep sudo "$logfile" | grep $username >> user_activity_for_"$username"_$(date
+"%F_%H-%M").txt
```

Okay, it's easy. It's just creating a report file with the user's name and a timestamp in the filename. The last command creates the record of the user's logins, and the grep command searches through the designated file for all lines that contain the *sudo* text string. Then, it pipes that output into grep to search for all lines that contain the designated user name.

Now, let's run the script to see what that Donnie character has been doing:

```
donnie@fedora-server:~$ sudo ./user_activity_1.sh donnie
[sudo] password for donnie:
donnie@fedora-server:~$ ls -l user_activity_*
-rwxr--r--. 1 donnie donnie     921 May 14 18:11 user_activity_1.sh
-rw-r--r--. 1 root    root   276170 May 14 18:11 user_activity_for_
donnie_2024-05-14_18-11.txt
donnie@fedora-server:~$
```

Very cool. You see that the script has created a report file with my username and the current date and time in the filename. Here's a snippet of what you'll see in that report file:

```
=== User Account Activity ===
=== Recent Logins ===
donnie   pts/1        192.168.0.16      Tue May 14 15:30 - 16:41  (01:11)
donnie   pts/0        192.168.0.16      Tue May 14 15:22    still logged in
donnie   tty1                           Mon May 13 17:33 - 17:44  (00:11)
donnie   pts/0        192.168.0.16      Mon May 13 14:43 - 17:44  (03:01)
=== Sudo Command Usage ===
Dec  8 14:17:32 localhost sudo[993]:  donnie : TTY=tty1 ; PWD=/home/donnie ;
USER=root ; COMMAND=/usr/bin/dnf install openscap-scanner scap-security-guide
Dec  8 14:17:32 localhost sudo[993]: pam_unix(sudo:session): session opened for
user root(uid=0) by donnie(uid=1000)
Jan 30 13:02:43 localhost sudo[955]:  donnie : TTY=tty1 ; PWD=/home/donnie ;
USER=root ; COMMAND=/usr/bin/dnf -y upgrade
```

 I've tested this script on Fedora Server, Ubuntu Server, openSUSE, FreeBSD, and OpenBSD. (Note that I installed bash on both of the BSD distros.)

Okay, I think that that's about it for the auditing scripts. Let's see what we can do with a firewall script.

Creating Simple Firewall Scripts

In this scenario, you need to create a text file with a list of IP addresses that you want to block. You then need to create a shell script that will read that list of IP addresses, and then create firewall rules that will block them. There are two ways that you can do this. First, there's the hard way. And then, there's the easy way.

The hard way consists of reading the list of addresses into a variable array, and then creating a for loop that will create a blocking rule for each IP address that's in the array. Okay, it's not that hard, but it is a bit harder than we would like. (I'll show you the easy way after I show you the hard way. That way, you'll be more appreciative of the easy way.)

Creating an IP Address Blocking Script for Red Hat Distros

Red Hat-type distros, such as Fedora, AlmaLinux, Rocky Linux, Oracle Linux, and of course Red Hat Enterprise Linux, use firewalld as their firewall management utility, and nftables as the actual firewall engine. To my knowledge, the only non-Red Hat Linux distros that come with this setup installed by default are SUSE and openSUSE.

The firewall-cmd utility is the main way to manage firewalld rules, policies and configuration. To see how this works, let's do a couple of hands-on labs.

Hands-on Lab: Create the Script with an Array and a for loop

In this lab, you'll create a script that builds a variable array by reading the list of IP addresses from the ip-address_blacklist.txt file. You'll then use a for loop to create a firewall rule for each IP address in the list.

1. On the Fedora Server virtual machine, create the ip-address_blacklist.txt file, with one IP address on each line. Make it look something like this:

```
donnie@fedora-server:~$ cat ip-address_blacklist.txt
192.168.0.14
192.168.0.84
192.168.0.7
192.168.0.12
192.168.0.39
donnie@fedora-server:~$
```

2. Now, create the firewall-blacklist_array.sh script, which uses a variable array and a for loop. Make it look like this:

```
#!/bin/bash
declare -a badips
badips=( $(cat ip-address_blacklist.txt) )
for ip in ${badips[*]}
do
```

```
         firewall-cmd --permanent --add-rich-rule="rule family="ipv4" source
address="$ip" drop"
done
firewall-cmd --reload
```

The first thing we're doing here is to declare and build the badips array, as I showed you in *Chapter 8, Basic Shell Script Construction*. This array obtains its values from the ip-address_blacklist.txt file that we've just created. Within the for loop, you see the firewall-cmd command that creates a firewall rule for each IP address that we loaded into the badips array. Whenever you use the --permanent option the firewall-cmd command will write the new rules to the proper configuration file. But, it won't load the new rules into the running firewall. The final firewall-cmd --reload command loads the new rules so that they will take effect.

3. Run this script on your Fedora virtual machine. You should receive one success message for each IP address, and a final success message after the reload command. Here's how it looks:

```
donnie@fedora-server:~$ sudo ./firewall-blacklist_array.sh
success
success
success
success
success
success
donnie@fedora-server:~$
```

4. To verify that the rules have taken effect, use the nft list ruleset command, and then scroll back to where you'll see the new rules. Here's how that looks:

```
donnie@fedora-server:~$ sudo nft list ruleset
. . .

. . .

chain filter_IN_FedoraServer_deny {
            ip saddr 192.168.0.14 drop
            ip saddr 192.168.0.84 drop
            ip saddr 192.168.0.7 drop
            ip saddr 192.168.0.12 drop
            ip saddr 192.168.0.39 drop

     }
. . .

. . .

donnie@fedora-server:~$
```

5. To see if the rules have been added permanently, look at the proper configuration file in the /etc/firewalld/zones/ directory, like this:

```
donnie@fedora-server:~$ sudo cat /etc/firewalld/zones/FedoraServer.xml
. . .
. . .
<rule family="ipv4">
    <source address="192.168.0.14"/>
    <drop/>
  </rule>
  <rule family="ipv4">
    <source address="192.168.0.84"/>
    <drop/>
  </rule>
  . . .
  . . .
donnie@fedora-server:~$
```

Note that the name of this configuration file will be different on other distros, such as AlmaLinux, Rocky Linux, Red Hat Enterprise Linux, or SUSE/openSUSE.

Also, be aware that different Linux distros come with different firewall management utilities. For example, Ubuntu comes with the **Uncomplicated Firewall** (ufw) firewall manager, and other distros might just have you use plain nftables without a management utility. Once you know the proper firewall management commands for your particular distro, it's a simple matter to modify this script to work with it. (If you need to learn more about Linux firewalls, you might like to check out one of my other books, *Mastering Linux Security and Hardening*, which is available from both Amazon and directly from Packt Publishing.)

End of lab.

Okay, that wasn't too difficult, was it? Hang on, though. Let's make this even easier with xargs.

Hands-on Lab: Creating the Script with xargs

Back in *Chapter 7, Text Stream Filters–Part 2*, I introduced you to the xargs utility. I showed you a few examples of how to use it in the context of text stream filters, and I also promised that I would show you more examples of how to use it later. You can vastly simplify this type of script by using xargs instead of variable arrays and for loops. As before, I'll show you how it's done with the Red Hat family.

1. Create the firewall-blacklist_xargs.sh script, like this:

```
#!/bin/bash
xargs -i firewall-cmd --permanent --add-rich-rule="rule family="ipv4" source
```

```
address={} drop" < ip-address_blacklist.txt
firewall-cmd --reload
```

(Note that the xargs line is a long line that wraps around on the printed page.)

As before, the first command is just a normal `firewall-cmd` command that creates the blocking rules. In this case, we're preceding the command with `xargs -i` so that it will read the list of IP addresses from the `ip-address_blacklist.txt` file, one at a time. In a normal `firewall-cmd` command, you would place either an IP address or a range of IP addresses after the `source address=` part. This time though, we've placed a pair of curly braces there. The xargs utility will cause the `firewall-cmd` command to run once for each IP address that it finds in the `ip-address_blacklist.txt` file. Each time that the command runs, the next IP address in the list will be placed within the pair of curly braces. The `--permanent` option in this `firewall-cmd` command is what saves the new rules to the proper rules file. Using this `--permanent` option requires you to run the `firewall-cmd --reload` command in order to make the new rules take effect.

2. Edit the `ip-address_blacklist.txt` file to add a few more IP addresses. Then, run the script. The output should now look something like this:

```
donnie@fedora-server:~$ sudo ./firewall-blacklist_xargs.sh
Warning: ALREADY_ENABLED: rule family=ipv4 source address=192.168.0.14 drop
success
Warning: ALREADY_ENABLED: rule family=ipv4 source address=192.168.0.84 drop
success
Warning: ALREADY_ENABLED: rule family=ipv4 source address=192.168.0.7 drop
success
Warning: ALREADY_ENABLED: rule family=ipv4 source address=192.168.0.12 drop
success
Warning: ALREADY_ENABLED: rule family=ipv4 source address=192.168.0.39 drop
success
success
success
success
donnie@fedora-server:~$
```

3. Verify that the new rules have taken effect:

```
donnie@fedora-server:~$ sudo nft list ruleset
. . .

. . .
chain filter_IN_FedoraServer_deny {
            ip saddr 192.168.0.14 drop
            ip saddr 192.168.0.84 drop
            ip saddr 192.168.0.7 drop
            ip saddr 192.168.0.12 drop
```

```
            ip saddr 192.168.0.39 drop
            ip saddr 212.12.3.12 drop
            ip saddr 172.10.0.0/16 drop
    }
. . .

. . .
donnie@fedora-server:~$
```

Note how with the last rule, I opted to block an entire IP address subnet. This capability could come in handy if you ever need to block an entire country from accessing your server, for example.

 If you ever do need to block an entire country, you can find lists of IP address ranges for various countries here:

https://lite.ip2location.com/ip-address-ranges-by-country

4. Open the /etc/firewalld/zones/FedoraServer.xml file in your text editor, and remove the rules that you've just created.

5. Finally, clear the rules out of the running firewall by doing:

```
donnie@fedora-server:~$ sudo firewall-cmd --reload
success
donnie@fedora-server:~$
```

End of lab.

Now, is that slick, or is that slick? I mean, by using xargs instead of variable arrays and for loops, you've vastly simplified this script. Also, using xargs makes your scripts more portable. That's because you can use xargs on pretty much any type of Linux, Unix, or Unix-like shell. On the other hand, you can use variable arrays with bash, but not with certain variations of sh. (I'll talk more about portability in *Chapter 19, Shell Script Portability*.) So really, having xargs in our toolbox is what I call a win-win!

Next, let's see if we can save ourselves a bit of work.

Searching for Existing Security-related Scripts

A basic tenet of computer programming is to reuse code as much as possible. Otherwise, every programmer in the world would waste huge amounts of time trying to always reinvent the proverbial wheel. So, if you find yourself in need of a script and don't know how to write it yourself, you can search for one either by using your favorite search engine or by searching on Github.

The only catch with using search engines is that you might have to try several different search terms to find what you need. For example, I tried the following search terms on DuckDuckGo:

- bash scripts for security audit
- bash scripting for pentesters

- bash scripts for security administrators
- bash scripting for cybersecurity

As a matter of full disclosure, I have to say that most of these search results were for courses and books for which you'll have to pay. If that's what you need or want, then great. But, mixed in with all that you might find some gems that will either help you with your immediate problem or that will give you some good ideas for your own scripts.

For more concise and useful search results, you might consider searching for scripts on Github. Here, for example, I searched for the term, *bash security scripts*:

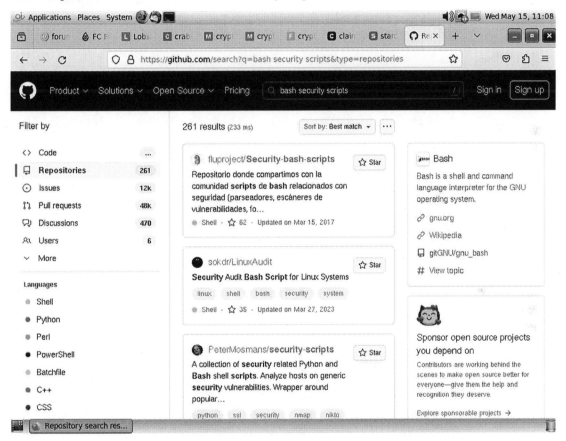

Figure 18.1: Searching for bash security scripts on Github

You'll find lots of repositories from many different authors like this. Most, if not all, of these scripts are released under a free-as-in-freedom software license, so you can download them and use them as you wish. Of course, you'll want to review and test the scripts before you put them into production use. Some of them will work on your systems without modification, and some won't. So, just because you're able to find scripts that someone else has already written doesn't mean that you can just skate by without any knowledge of shell scripting.

All right, I think that about covers it. Let's summarize and then move on to the next chapter.

Summary

In this chapter, I didn't introduce a lot of new scripting concepts as I normally do. Instead, I showed you how to use the concepts that you already know to create scripts that might be useful to a security-conscious administrator. You've seen how to create shell scripts that can do simple port scans or operating system identification. Then, you saw how to create auditing scripts that can show if the root user account is enabled, when a normal user is logging into the system, and what a normal user is doing with his or her sudo privileges. After that, I showed you a script that can read a list of IP addresses, and automatically create firewall rules to block those addresses. Finally, I showed you some tips about how to find and use scripts that other people have already created.

In the next chapter, we'll talk a bit about shell script portability. I'll see you there.

Questions

1. When you do a port scan of a remote machine and find ports that are in a closed state, what does that mean?

    a. That the ports are blocked by a firewall.

    b. That the ports are not blocked by a firewall, and that the associated services for those ports are not running.

    c. That the ports are not blocked by a firewall, and that the associated services for those ports are running.

    d. That the remote machine can't be reached by your port scanner.

2. You're looking for the /etc/shadow file on a FreeBSD system, but can't find it. What could be the problem?

    a. FreeBSD keeps its account passwords in the /etc/passwd file.

    b. FreeBSD keeps its account passwords in the /var/lib/ directory.

    c. FreeBSD uses the /etc/master.passwd file instead of the /etc/shadow file.

    d. FreeBSD doesn't require passwords.

3. Which of the following statements is true?

    a. There is no advantage to using xargs in your scripts.

    b. Using xargs can make your scripts easier to create, easier to read, and can enhance script portability.

    c. Using xargs makes your scripts more complex and harder to understand.

Further Reading

- Introduction to Bash for Cybersecurity: `https://medium.com/@aardvarkinfinity/introduction-to-bash-for-cybersecurity-56792984bcc0`
- Shell Scripting and Security: `https://www.linuxjournal.com/content/shell-scripting-and-security`
- HackSploit Blog-Bash Scripting: `https://hackersploit.org/bash-scripting/`
- Is Bash the Secret Weapon of Cybersecurity Experts?: `https://cyberinsight.co/is-bash-used-in-cyber-security/`
- Secure Scripting: A Step-by-Step Guide to Password Automation in Linux with Bash: `https://medium.com/@GeorgeBaidooJr/secure-scripting-a-step-by-step-guide-to-password-automation-in-linux-with-bash-12aa6b980acf`

Answers

1. b
2. c
3. b

Join our community on Discord!

Read this book alongside other users, Linux experts, and the author himself.

Ask questions, provide solutions to other readers, chat with the author via Ask Me Anything sessions, and much more. Scan the QR code or visit the link to join the community.

`https://packt.link/SecNet`

Leave a Review!

Thank you for purchasing this book from Packt Publishing—we hope you enjoy it! Your feedback is invaluable and helps us improve and grow. Once you've completed reading it, please take a moment to leave an Amazon review; it will only take a minute, but it makes a big difference for readers like you.

Scan the QR code below to receive a free ebook of your choice.

https://packt.link/NzOWQ

19

Shell Script Portability

As we'll see in a bit, many different shells are available for Linux, Unix, and Unix-like operating systems. Thus far though, we've mainly just been working with bash. The big advantage of bash is that it comes already installed on most Linux distros, macOS, and OpenIndiana. It normally isn't installed by default on the BSD-type distros, but you can install it yourself, if you need to.

The big advantage of bash is that it can use different scripting constructs that can make life easier for scripters. The big disadvantage of bash is that many of these bash constructs aren't always available in non-bash shells. That's not a big problem if you can install bash on all of your machines, but that's not always possible. (I'll explain why in just a bit.)

In this chapter, I'll show you some of the bash alternatives that you might encounter, and how to make your shell scripts run on a wide variety of these shells.

Topics in this chapter include:

- Running bash on non-Linux systems
- Understanding POSIX compliance
- Understanding the differences between shells
- Understanding bashisms
- Testing scripts for POSIX compliance

That about does it for the introduction. So now, let's dig in.

Technical Requirements

I'm using Fedora, Debian, and FreeBSD virtual machines for this chapter. If any of you are using a Mac, you can try the scripts on it as well, if you like. As always, you can get grab the scripts from GitHub by doing:

```
git clone https://github.com/PacktPublishing/The-Ultimate-Linux-Shell-
Scripting-Guide.git
```

Running bash on Non-Linux Systems

Before we talk about the alternatives to bash, let's talk about using bash on non-Linux operating systems. I mean, the easiest way to make your shell scripts portable is to have the same shell everywhere.

As I mentioned in the introduction, bash is already installed on most Linux-based operating systems, as well as on macOS and OpenIndiana. If you want to use bash on a BSD-type distro, such as FreeBSD or OpenBSD, you'll need to install it yourself. I've already shown you how to install bash on FreeBSD in *Chapter 8, Basic Shell Script Construction*. To refresh your memory, I'll show you again:

```
donnie@freebsd14:~ $ sudo pkg install bash
```

It's just as easy on any other BSD-type distro, except that they all use different package managers. Here's the table of commands for the various BSDs:

BSD Distro	Command to install bash
FreeBSD	`sudo pkg install bash`
OpenBSD	`sudo pkg_add bash`
DragonflyBSD	`sudo pkg install bash`
NetBSD	`sudo pkgin install bash`

Table 19.1: Commands to install bash on the BSD distros

Now, if you were to run a script with the #!/bin/bash shebang line on any of these BSD distros, you would get an error message that looks like this:

```
donnie@freebsd14:~ $ ./ip.sh
-sh: ./ip.sh: not found
donnie@freebsd14:~ $
```

This message is a bit misleading because it gives the impression that the shell can't find the script. In reality, the script can't find bash. That's because, unlike what you're used to seeing on Linux and OpenIndiana, bash isn't in the /bin/ directory on BSD distros. Instead, the BSD distros have bash in the /usr/local/bin/ directory. There are a couple of ways to fix this, which we'll look at next.

Using env to Set the bash Environment

The first way to ensure that your scripts can always find bash is to replace the #!/bin/bash line in your scripts with:

```
#!/usr/bin/env bash
```

This causes the script to look for the bash executable in the user's PATH environment, instead of in a specific, hard-coded location.

I've shown you in *Chapter 3, Understanding Variables and Pipelines* how to use the env command to view the environmental variables that are set in bash. In this case, I'm using env to specify the shell that I want to use to interpret this script.

This is the easiest method, but there are a few potential problems with it.

- If you specify an interpreter for which multiple versions are installed, you won't know which version will be invoked by the script. If for some crazy reason a machine has multiple versions of bash installed, you won't know which version that #!/usr/bin/env bash will invoke.

- Using #!/usr/bin/env bash could be a security problem. The normal bash executable is always installed in a directory for which only someone with root privileges can add, remove, or modify files. But, let's say that a malicious hacker were to gain access to your own normal user account. In that case, he or she wouldn't need to obtain root privileges in order to plant a malicious fake bash in your own home directory, and to alter your PATH environment so that the fake bash would be invoked instead of the real bash. Using the hard-coded #!/bin/bash line would prevent that problem.

- With #!/usr/bin/env bash, you won't be able to invoke any bash options on the shebang line. For example, let's say that you need to troubleshoot a troublesome script, and you want to run the script in debug mode. Using #!/bin/bash --debug will work, but using #!/usr/bin/env bash --debug won't work. That's because the env command can only recognize one option parameter, which in this case would be bash. (It will never see the --debug option.)

 For now, don't worry about what the --debug option is doing. I'll show you more about debugging shell scripts in *Chapter 21, Debugging Shell Scripts.*

Although using #!/usr/bin/env bash seems like the simplest solution, I prefer to avoid it whenever possible. So, let's look at another solution that's a bit more secure and reliable.

Creating a Symbolic Link to bash

My preferred solution for ensuring that your scripts can find bash works the same on all of the BSD distros. You just have to create a symbolic link to the bash executable in the /bin/ directory. Here's how it looks:

```
donnie@freebsd14:~ $ which bash
/usr/local/bin/bash
donnie@freebsd14:~ $ sudo ln -s /usr/local/bin/bash /bin/bash
Password:
donnie@freebsd14:~ $ which bash
/bin/bash
donnie@freebsd14:~ $
```

To use the `ln -s` command to create a link, you would first specify the path to the file to which you want to link. Then, specify the path and name for the link that you want to create. Note how after I created the link, the `which` command now finds `bash` in the `/bin/` directory, instead of in the `/usr/local/bin/` directory. That's because `/bin/` is listed before `/usr/local/bin/` in the default `PATH` setting, as you see here:

```
donnie@freebsd14:~ $ echo $PATH
/sbin:/bin:/usr/sbin:/usr/bin:/usr/local/sbin:/usr/local/bin:/home/donnie/bin
donnie@freebsd14:~ $
```

You can now use the `#!/bin/bash` shebang line on your BSD machine, the same as you would on a Linux machine.

Okay, this is all good if you can have `bash` installed on all of your systems. But, what if you can't? What if you need to write scripts that will run on `bash` as well as on alternate shells? To answer that, we'll first need to look at something called **POSIX**.

Understanding POSIX compliance

Way back in the Stone Age of Computing, there was no such thing as standardization. In order to keep things relevant, let's begin our history with the advent of Unix.

AT&T, who created Unix in the early 1970s, wasn't allowed to market it until 1983. This was due to an anti-trust legal case that the U.S. government had filed against AT&T back in 1956. (I don't know the details of the case, so please don't ask.) But, they were allowed to license the code to other vendors so that they could sell their own modified implementations. Because of this, several different implementations of Unix emerged, which weren't always completely compatible with each other. These different implementations included the **Berkeley Software Distribution (BSD)**, **Microsoft Xenix**, and **SunOS**. In 1983, AT&T was finally allowed to market its own **System V Unix**. Making things more interesting was the wide variety of shells that eventually became available for these various Unix systems. The Thompson shell came first, and was superseded by the Bourne shell a few years later. Other shells, such as the C shell and the Korn shell, soon followed. Finally, in the early 1990s, Linus Torvalds created the Linux kernel, which was a clean slate reimplementation of the Unix kernel. Nowadays, Linux-based operating systems have mostly supplanted Unix-based systems, and the Bourne Again Shell (`bash`) is the dominant shell for Linux-based systems.

In the 1980s, customers began demanding some semblance of standardization between the various Unix vendors. This culminated in the creation of the **POSIX** standard by the **IEEE Computer Society** in 1988.

IEEE stands for **Institute of Electrical and Electronics Engineers**. Curiously however, all you'll see on their website is IEEE, with no explanation of what it stands for.

POSIX stands for **Portable Operating System Interface**.

Finally, for those of you who are outside the U.S., AT&T stands for **American Telephone and Telegraph**.

And yes, it really is true that Microsoft used to be a Unix vendor.

The main purpose of POSIX is to ensure that shells and utilities work the same way across all implementations of Unix. For example, if you know how to use the ps utility on Solaris/OpenIndiana, then you also know how to use it on FreeBSD. The big problem is that while many Unix implementations and their default shells are POSIX-compliant, some are only partially compliant. On the other hand, most Linux-based operating systems are only partially POSIX-compliant. That's because many Linux utilities use different option switches that their Unix/Unix-like brethren don't use, and bash itself has programming features that aren't available in POSIX-compliant shells. For example, you can use an if [-f /bin/someprogram] type of construct to test for the presence of a file in a POSIX-compliant shell, but you can't use if [[-f /bin/someprogram]]. (I'll explain more about this in a few moments.)

 POSIX also defines which programming libraries must come with any given implementation of Unix. However, this is mainly of interest to actual programmers, rather than to shell scripters.

To be fair, I'll admit that POSIX compliance might never become an issue for you if you only work on Linux servers or workstations. But, let's say that you work with a large fleet of servers with a mix of Unix, BSD, and Linux systems. Now, let's say that some of those Unix and BSD servers are still running legacy systems for which bash isn't available. You might find it necessary to create POSIX-compliant shell scripts that will run on every server in the fleet without modification. Also, **Internet of Things (IoT)** devices are generally very low-resource devices that might not be able to run bash. Instead, they'll have something more lightweight, such as ash or dash. In general, these lightweight, non-bash shells will be POSIX-compliant, and won't be able to run scripts that use bash-specific features.

Now that you have a good understanding of what POSIX is all about, let's talk about the differences between the various shells.

Understanding the Differences Between Shells

In addition to defining a specific shell that you want to use, such as /bin/bash or /bin/zsh, you can also define the generic /bin/sh shell to make your scripts more portable, as you see here:

```
#!/bin/sh
```

This generic sh shell allows you to run your scripts on different systems that might or might not have bash installed. But, here's the problem. Years ago, sh used to always be the Bourne shell. Nowadays, sh is still the Bourne shell on some operating systems, but is something else entirely on other operating systems. Here's the breakdown of how it works:

- On most BSD-type systems, such as FreeBSD and OpenBSD, sh is the old-school Bourne shell. According to the sh man page, it only supports POSIX-compliant features, plus a few BSD extensions.

- On Red Hat-type systems, sh is a symbolic link that points to the bash executable.

- On Debian/Ubuntu-type systems, sh is a symbolic link that points to the dash executable. dash stands for **Debian Almquist Shell**, which is a faster, more lightweight implementation of the Bourne shell.

- On Alpine Linux, sh is a symbolic link that points to ash, which is a lightweight shell that's built into the busybox executable. (On Alpine Linux, bash is not installed by default.)

- On OpenIndiana, which is a **Free Open Source Software** fork of Oracle's Solaris operating system, sh is a symbolic link that points to the ksh93 shell. This shell, which is also known as the Korn shell, is somewhat compatible with bash. (It was created by a guy named David Korn, and has nothing to do with any vegetable.) However, the default login shell for OpenIndiana is bash.

- On macOS, sh points to the bash executable. Interestingly, zsh is now the default user login shell for macOS, but bash is still installed and available for use.

> Using #!/bin/sh will only work if you're careful about making your scripts portable. If sh on your machine points to something other than bash, it won't work for scripts that require advanced features that are specific to bash. So, if you use sh, be sure to test it on different systems to ensure that everything works as it should.

Before we get to the testing part though, let's look at the concept of bashisms, and how to avoid them.

Understanding Bashisms

A **bashism** is any feature that's specific to bash, and that won't work with other shells. Let's look at a few examples.

Using Portable Tests

For our first example, try running this command on your Fedora virtual machine:

```
donnie@fedora:~$ [[ -x /bin/ls ]] && echo "This file is installed.";
This file is installed.
donnie@fedora:~$
```

Here, I'm testing for the presence of the ls executable file in the /bin/ directory. The file is there, so the echo command is invoked. Now, let's run the same command on a FreeBSD virtual machine:

```
donnie@freebsd14:~ $ [[ -f /bin/ls ]] && echo "This file is installed."
-sh: [[: not found
donnie@freebsd14:~ $
```

This time I get an error, because the default user login shell on FreeBSD is sh, instead of bash. The problem here is that the [[. . .]] construct isn't supported on the FreeBSD implementation of sh. Let's see if we can fix that:

```
donnie@freebsd14:~ $ [ -f /bin/ls ] && echo "This file is installed."
This file is installed.
donnie@freebsd14:~ $
```

Very cool, this works. So now, you're wondering why anyone would use the non-POSIX [[. . .]] construct instead of the more portable [. . .]. Well, it's mainly because certain types of tests don't work with [. . .]. For example, let's look at the test-test-1.sh script:

```
#!/bin/bash
if [[ "$1" == z* ]]; then
    echo "Pattern matched: "$1" starts with 'z'."
else
    echo "Pattern not matched: "$1" doesn't start with 'z'."
fi
```

When I invoke this script, I'll supply a word as the $1 positional parameter. If the first letter of the word is "z", then the pattern will match.

> In this script, z* is a regular expression. We're using this regular expression to match all words that begin with the letter "z". Any time you do regular expression matching within a test, you have to place it within a double square bracket, or [[. . .]], construct.
>
> (I explained about regular expressions in *Chapter 9, Filtering Text with grep, sed, and Regular Expressions.*)

Here's how it works:

```
donnie@fedora:~$ ./test-test-1.sh zebra
Pattern matched: zebra starts with 'z'.
donnie@fedora:~$ ./test-test-1.sh donnie
Pattern not matched: donnie doesn't start with 'z'.
donnie@fedora:~$
```

Now, look at the test-test-2.sh script, which uses [. . .]:

```
#!/bin/bash
if [ "$1" == z* ]; then
    echo "Pattern matched: "$1" starts with 'z'."
else
    echo "Pattern not matched: "$1" doesn't start with 'z'."
fi
```

This is identical to the first script, except that it uses single square brackets for the test instead of double square brackets. Here's what happens when I run the script:

```
donnie@fedora:~$ ./test-test-2.sh zebra
Pattern not matched: zebra doesn't start with 'z'.
donnie@fedora:~$
```

You see that this test doesn't work with the single square brackets. That's because the single square bracket construct doesn't recognize the use of regular expressions. But, if using double square brackets doesn't work on certain implementations of sh, then how can I make this script portable? Well, here's one solution:

```sh
#!/bin/sh
if [ "$(echo $1 | cut -c1)" = z ]; then
    echo "Pattern matched: "$1" starts with 'z'."
else
    echo "Pattern not matched: "$1" doesn't start with 'z'."
fi
```

Instead of using the z* regular expression to match any word that begins with the letter "z", I'm just echoing the word into the cut -c1 command in order to isolate the first letter. I also changed the == in the test to =, because == is also considered a bashism.

 The == actually does work with the FreeBSD implementation of sh, but it might not work on other implementations. For example, it doesn't work on dash, which is invoked by #!/bin/sh on Debian/Ubuntu-type distros.

While I was at it, I changed the shebang line to #!/bin/sh, because I'll also want to test this on FreeBSD with the Bourne shell. So, will this work? Let's try it on Fedora, on which #!/bin/sh points to bash:

```
donnie@fedora:~$ ./test-test-3.sh zebra
Pattern matched: zebra starts with 'z'.
donnie@fedora:~$ ./test-test-3.sh donnie
Pattern not matched: donnie doesn't start with 'z'.
donnie@fedora:~$
```

Yeah, it works fine on Fedora. Now, let's see what happens on FreeBSD:

```
donnie@freebsd14:~ $ ./test-test-3.sh zealot
Pattern matched: zealot starts with 'z'.
donnie@freebsd14:~ $ ./test-test-3.sh donnie
Pattern not matched: donnie doesn't start with 'z'.
donnie@freebsd14:~ $
```

Yes indeed, it works like a champ. And, for the record, I also tested it on a Debian machine with dash, and it works fine on it, as well.

Now, let's look at our next portability problem.

Making Portable Arrays

Sometimes, you need to create and manipulate lists of items in your shell scripts. With bash, you can create variable arrays the same as you can with languages such a C, C++, or Java. For example, let's look at the ip-2.sh script:

```
#!/bin/sh
echo "IP Addresses of intruder attempts"
declare -a ip
ip=( 192.168.3.78 192.168.3.4 192.168.3.9 )
echo "ip[0] is ${ip[0]}, the first item in the list."
echo "ip[2] is ${ip[2]}, the third item in the list."
echo "*********************************"
echo "The most dangerous intruder is ${ip[1]}, which is in ip[1]."
echo "*********************************"
echo "Here is the entire list of IP addresses in the array."
echo ${ip[*]}
```

This is identical to the ip.sh script that I showed you in *Chapter 8, Basic Shell Script Construction*, except that I changed the shebang line to #!/bin/sh. To refresh your memory, I'm using the declare -a command to create the ip array, and the ip= line to populate the array. This should work fine on my Fedora machine, since the Fedora sh points to bash. Let's see if it does:

```
donnie@fedora:~$ ./ip-2.sh
IP Addresses of intruder attempts
ip[0] is 192.168.3.78, the first item in the list.
ip[2] is 192.168.3.9, the third item in the list.
*********************************
The most dangerous intruder is 192.168.3.4, which is in ip[1].
*********************************
Here is the entire list of IP addresses in the array.
192.168.3.78 192.168.3.4 192.168.3.9
donnie@fedora:~$
```

Yes, it does work.

Now, let's see how it looks on FreeBSD:

```
donnie@freebsd14:~ $ ./ip-2.sh
IP Addresses of intruder attempts
./ip-2.sh: declare: not found
./ip-2.sh: 4: Syntax error: word unexpected (expecting ")")
donnie@freebsd14:~ $
```

The problem this time is that the Bourne (sh) shell on FreeBSD can't use variable arrays. To make this script portable, we'll need to find a work-around. So, let's try this ip-3.sh script:

```sh
#!/bin/sh
set 192.168.3.78 192.168.3.4 192.168.3.9
echo "$1 is the first item in the list."
echo "$3 is the third item in the list."
echo "*********************************"
echo "The most dangerous intruder is $2, which is the second item of the list."
echo "*********************************"
echo "Here is the entire list of IP addresses in the array:"
echo "$@"
```

Instead of building an actual array this time, I'm using the set command to create a list of IP addresses that I can access with positional parameters. I know, you thought that positional parameters were only for passing arguments in from the command line when you invoke the script. But what you see here is just another way to use them. The big question though is, does this work? Let's see what it does on the FreeBSD machine:

```
donnie@freebsd14:~ $ ./ip-3.sh
192.168.3.78 is the first item in the list.
192.168.3.9 is the third item in the list.
*********************************
The most dangerous intruder is 192.168.3.4, which is the second item of the
list.
*********************************
Here is the entire list of IP addresses in the array:
192.168.3.78 192.168.3.4 192.168.3.9
donnie@freebsd14:~ $
```

Once again, we have achieved coolness.

  Note that when using set and positional parameters, we're not creating an actual array. Instead, we're just *simulating* an array. But hey, whatever works, right?

You can also build a simulated array from a text file, using the cat command. First, let's create the iplist.txt file, which looks like this:

```
donnie@fedora:~$ cat iplist.txt
192.168.0.12
192.168.0.16
192.168.0.222
```

```
192.168.0.3
donnie@fedora:~$
```

Now, create the ip-4.sh script, like this:

```
#!/bin/sh
set $(cat iplist.txt)
echo "$1 is the first item in the list."
echo "$3 is the third item in the list."
echo "*******************************"
echo "The most dangerous intruder is $2, which is the second item of the list."
echo "*******************************"
echo "Here is the entire list of IP addresses in the array:"
echo "$@"
```

And, here's what I get when I run this on FreeBSD:

```
donnie@freebsd14:~ $ ./ip-4.sh
192.168.0.12 is the first item in the list.
192.168.0.222 is the third item in the list.
*******************************
The most dangerous intruder is 192.168.0.16, which is the second item of the
list.
*******************************
Here is the entire list of IP addresses in the array:
192.168.0.12 192.168.0.16 192.168.0.222 192.168.0.3
donnie@freebsd14:~ $
```

So yeah, it's looking good.

Next, let's address something that hasn't been a problem for us yet, but could be in the future. That is, the use of echo.

Understanding Portability Problems with echo

So far, we haven't encountered any problems with using echo in our scripts. That's only because we haven't used any of echo's advanced formatting features. To demonstrate, run this command on your Fedora virtual machine:

```
donnie@fedora:~$ echo -e "I want to fly \vto the moon."
I want to fly
              to the moon.
donnie@fedora:~$
```

The \v that you see in the \vto the moon string inserts a vertical tab, which causes the output to be broken into two lines, with preceding tabs on the second line.

To use the \v tag, I had to use echo with the -e option. Now, try this again without the -e:

```
donnie@fedora:~$ echo "I want to fly \vto the moon."
I want to fly \vto the moon.
donnie@fedora:~$
```

You see that without the -e, the \v doesn't insert the vertical tab as it's supposed to do.

The big problem with echo is that there's no consistency in how the various non-bash shells handle its option switches. For example, let's open a dash session on our Debian machine to see what happens on it:

```
donnie@debian12:~$ dash
$ echo -e "I want to fly \vto the moon."
-e I want to fly
                        to the moon.
$ echo "I want to fly \vto the moon."
I want to fly
                        to the moon.
$
```

You see that on dash, echo -e inserts a -e at the beginning of the output string. But, if we omit the -e, the output displays correctly. That's because the POSIX standard doesn't define the -e option for echo. Instead, it just allows echo to recognize the backslash formatting options, such as \v, by default.

The best way to have consistent output from your scripts is to use printf instead of echo. Here's what that looks like on dash:

```
donnie@debian12:~$ dash
$ printf "%b\n" "I want to fly \vto the moon."
I want to fly
                        to the moon.
$
```

When using printf, you need to place the formatting options ahead of the string that you want to output. In this case, the %b enables the use of the backslash formatting options within the output string, and the \n means to append a newline to the end of the output. You see that I've combined these two options within the "%b\n" construct. The cool part is that you can run this command on any of your virtual machines, with any shell, and the output will always be consistent.

Finally, let's look at the ip-5.sh script, which uses printf instead of echo:

```
#!/bin/sh
set 192.168.3.78 192.168.3.4 192.168.3.9
printf '%s\n' "$1 is the first item in the list."
printf '%s\n' "$3 is the third item in the list."
printf '%s\n' "*********************************"
```

```
printf '%b\n' "The most dangerous intruder is \v$2,\v which is the second item
of the list."
printf '%s\n' "********************************"
printf '%s\n' "Here is the entire list of IP addresses in the array:"
printf '%s\n' "$@"
```

For all but one of the printf lines, I used the "%s\n" formatting option, which just means to print out the specified text string with a newline at the end. In the fourth printf line, I used the "%b\n" option, which means to allow the use of backslash formatting options in the text. You then see that I surrounded the $2 positional parameter with a pair of \v options in order to insert a pair of vertical tabs. Here's how it looks when I run the script:

```
donnie@fedora:~$ ./ip-5.sh
192.168.3.78 is the first item in the list.
192.168.3.9 is the third item in the list.
********************************
The most dangerous intruder is
                                          192.168.3.4,
                                                           which is
the second item of the list.
********************************
Here is the entire list of IP addresses in the array:
192.168.3.78
192.168.3.4
192.168.3.9
donnie@fedora:~$
```

The cool part is, as I said before, the printf output will be consistent on all shells.

Okay, now that you've seen some examples of bashisms, let's look at how to test our scripts for POSIX compliance.

Testing Scripts for POSIX Compliance

It's always important to test your shell scripts before putting them into production. This becomes even more important when you create scripts that need to run on a wide variety of operating systems and shells. In this section, we'll look at a few ways to perform that testing.

Creating Scripts on a POSIX-compliant Shell

When you first start creating your scripts, you might want to use an interpreter shell that's completely POSIX-compliant. Be aware though, that some POSIX-compliant shells still allow you to use certain bashisms. That's because POSIX defines a *minimum* standard that an operating system or shell must meet, and doesn't prohibit adding extensions. For example, sh on FreeBSD allows these two bashisms:

- Using echo -e for output.
- Using == for text string comparisons.

Now, I haven't extensively tested sh on FreeBSD to see exactly how many bashisms it allows. But, the fact that it allows at least these two means that we can't use it to determine if our scripts will work on our entire network.

The most fully POSIX-compliant shell that comes already installed on any operating system is dash. I've already mentioned that if you run a #!/bin/sh script on a Debian/Ubuntu-type system, it will use dash as the script interpreter. The benefit is that if you create a script that will run on dash, it will most likely also run correctly on every other shell.

Well, almost. Remember what I showed you just a while ago with echo -e. I showed you that on bash, you must use the -e option to include any backslash formatting options. Here's what I mean:

```
donnie@fedora:~$ echo -e "I want to fly \vto the moon."
I want to fly
                     to the moon.
donnie@fedora:~$ echo "I want to fly \vto the moon."
I want to fly \vto the moon.
donnie@fedora:~$
```

So on bash, the \v formatting option doesn't work unless you use echo with the -e switch. On dash, it's the opposite, as you see here:

```
donnie@debian12:~$ dash
$ echo -e "I want to fly \vto the moon."
-e I want to fly
                     to the moon.
$ echo "I want to fly \vto the moon."
I want to fly
                to the moon.
$
```

So, if you use echo commands in your scripts, they might work properly on dash, but not on bash. Your best bet, as I've mentioned before, is to use printf instead of echo. Aside from that though, if you do create scripts that will run on dash, you'll also want to test them on bash. I don't know how many POSIX-specific things there are that will run on dash but not on bash. But, we do know about this echo -e thing.

The **Policy-compliant Ordinary Shell** (posh) is a shell that's even more strictly POSIX-compliant than dash. The main problem with it is that the Debian/Ubuntu-type distros appear to be the only ones that have it in their repositories. On the other hand, you can easily install dash on pretty much any Linux distro, as well as on some of the Unix-like distros, such as FreeBSD.

At any rate, you can read more about posh here:

How to check your shell scripts for portability: https://people.redhat.com/~thuth/blog/general/2021/04/27/portable-shell.html

And, speaking of testing, let's look at ways to do that.

Using checkbashisms

This cool checkbashisms utility will look through your scripts for anything that might not work on non-bash shells. First though, you'll need to install it. Here's how to do it:

On Fedora:

```
donnie@fedora:~$ sudo dnf install devscripts-checkbashisms
```

On Debian/Ubuntu:

```
donnie@debian12:~$ sudo apt install devscripts
```

On FreeBSD:

```
donnie@freebsd14:~ $ sudo pkg install checkbashisms
```

On macOS:

Install the Homebrew system, and then install the checkbashisms package with:

```
macmini@MacMinis-Mac-mini ~ % brew install checkbashisms
```

 For directions on how to install the Homebrew system on your Mac, go to: https://brew.sh

Basic usage of checkbashisms is easy. If the script that you want to test has #!/bin/sh as its shebang line, then just enter:

```
donnie@fedora:~$ checkbashisms scriptname.sh
```

By default, checkbashims only checks scripts that have the #!/bin/sh shebang line. If your script uses something else as the shebang line, such as #!/bin/bash, then use the -f option to force it to check the script, like so:

```
donnie@fedora:~$ checkbashisms -f scriptbashname.sh
```

For the first example, let's take another look at the ip-2.sh script:

```
#!/bin/sh
echo "IP Addresses of intruder attempts"
declare -a ip
ip=( 192.168.3.78 192.168.3.4 192.168.3.9 )
echo "ip[0] is ${ip[0]}, the first item in the list."
echo "ip[2] is ${ip[2]}, the third item in the list."
echo "*********************************"
```

```
echo "The most dangerous intruder is ${ip[1]}, which is in ip[1]."
echo "**********************************"
echo "Here is the entire list of IP addresses in the array."
echo ${ip[*]}
```

Now, let's see what checkbashisms has to say about it:

```
donnie@fedora:~$ checkbashisms ip-2.sh
possible bashism in ip-2.sh line 3 (declare):
declare -a ip
possible bashism in ip-2.sh line 5 (bash arrays, ${name[0|*|@]}):
echo "ip[0] is ${ip[0]}, the first item in the list."
possible bashism in ip-2.sh line 6 (bash arrays, ${name[0|*|@]}):
echo "ip[2] is ${ip[2]}, the third item in the list."
possible bashism in ip-2.sh line 8 (bash arrays, ${name[0|*|@]}):
echo "The most dangerous intruder is ${ip[1]}, which is in ip[1]."
possible bashism in ip-2.sh line 11 (bash arrays, ${name[0|*|@]}):
echo ${ip[*]}
donnie@fedora:~$
```

Well, that's certainly no surprise, because we already established that some non-bash shells can't do arrays. And, I've already shown you how to deal with that.

Okay, here's a bashism that you haven't seen yet, in the math6.sh script:

```
#!/bin/sh
start=0
limit=10
while [ "$start" -le "$limit" ]; do
  echo "$start... "
  start=$["$start"+1]
done
```

This is a while loop that echoes the number 0 through 10, followed by a string of three dots, each on its own line. Here's how its output looks:

```
donnie@fedora:~$ ./math6.sh
0...
1...
2...
3...
4...
5...
6...
7...
```

```
8...
9...
10...
donnie@fedora:~$
```

It looks good here on Fedora with bash. But, will it work on Debian with dash? Let's see:

```
donnie@debian12:~$ ./math6.sh
0...
./math6.sh: 4: [: Illegal number: $[0+1]
donnie@debian12:~$
```

What's the problem? Perhaps checkbashisms can tell us:

```
donnie@debian12:~$ checkbashisms math6.sh
possible bashism in math6.sh line 6 ('$[' should be '$(('):
  start=$["$start"+1]
donnie@debian12:~$
```

The problem is in line 6. It's just that bash can use the [. . .] construct for performing integer math. But, other shells have to use the ((. . .)) construct. So, let's fix that in the math7.sh script:

```
#!/bin/sh
start=0
limit=10
while [ "$start" -le "$limit" ]; do
  echo "$start... "
  start=$(("$start"+1))
done
```

That should work much better, right? Well, let's see:

```
donnie@debian12:~$ ./math7.sh
0...
./math7.sh: 6: arithmetic expression: expecting primary: ""0"+1"
donnie@debian12:~$
```

No, it's still broken. So, let's give it another checkbashisms scan:

```
donnie@debian12:~$ checkbashisms math7.sh
donnie@debian12:~$
```

Whoa, now. What's going on here? The checkbashisms scan says that my code is good, yet the script is still clearly broken when running on dash. What's up with that? Well, after a bit of experimentation, I discovered that surrounding the variable name that's within the math expression with a pair of quotes is also a bashism. But, it's one that checkbashisms doesn't catch. Let's fix that in the math8.sh script:

```
#!/bin/sh
```

```
start=0
limit=10
while [ "$start" -le "$limit" ]; do
  echo "$start... "
  start=$(($start+1))
done
```

Okay, will this now finally work? Drum roll, please!

```
donnie@debian12:~$ ./math8.sh
0...
1...
2...
3...
4...
5...
6...
7...
8...
9...
10...
donnie@debian12:~$
```

Indeed, it now works like a champ.

So, you've seen that checkbashisms is a great utility that can really help you out. But, as with most things that mankind has invented, it isn't perfect. It can flag a lot of problematic, non-POSIX code, but it does allow some bash-specific things to slip through. (It would be nice if there were a list of things that checkbashisms misses, but there isn't.)

All right, let's move on to our next code-checking utility.

Using shellcheck

The shellcheck utility is another great code-checking tool that can also check for bashisms. It's available on most Linux and BSD distros. Here's how to install it:

On Fedora:

```
donnie@fedora:~$ sudo dnf install ShellCheck
```

On Debian/Ubuntu:

```
donnie@debian12:~$ sudo apt install shellcheck
```

On FreeBSD:

```
donnie@freebsd14:~ $ sudo pkg install hs-ShellCheck
```

On macOS with Homebrew installed:

```
macmini@MacMinis-Mac-mini ~ % brew install shellcheck
```

To demo this, let's go back to the Debian machine, and scan the same scripts that we scanned with checkbashisms. We'll begin with the ip-2.sh script. Here are the relevant parts of the output:

```
donnie@debian12:~$ shellcheck ip-2.sh
In ip-2.sh line 4:
ip=( 192.168.3.78 192.168.3.4 192.168.3.9 )
   ^-- SC3030 (warning): In POSIX sh, arrays are undefined.
In ip-2.sh line 5:
echo "ip[0] is ${ip[0]}, the first item in the list."
                 ^------^ SC3054 (warning): In POSIX sh, array references are
undefined.
. . .
In ip-2.sh line 11:
echo ${ip[*]}
     ^------^ SC2048 (warning): Use "${array[@]}" (with quotes) to prevent
whitespace problems.
     ^------^ SC3054 (warning): In POSIX sh, array references are undefined.
     ^------^ SC2086 (info): Double quote to prevent globbing and word
splitting.
. . .
donnie@debian12:~$
```

You see that shellcheck does warn us that we can't use arrays in POSIX-compliant scripts. It also warns us about issues involving good programming practices that aren't necessarily POSIX issues. In this case, it reminds us that we should surround variable expansion constructs, ${ip[0]} in this case, with a pair of double quotes in order to prevent whitespace problems. Of course, that's a moot point here, because the ${ip[0]} construct here is part of the array definition that we can't use anyway.

Now, let's try the math6.sh script:

```
donnie@debian12:~$ shellcheck math6.sh
In math6.sh line 6:
  start=$["$start"+1]
        ^-----------^ SC3007 (warning): In POSIX sh, $[..] in place of $((..))
is undefined.
        ^-----------^ SC2007 (style): Use $((..)) instead of deprecated $[..]
For more information:
  https://www.shellcheck.net/wiki/SC3007 -- In POSIX sh, $[..] in place of
$(...
  https://www.shellcheck.net/wiki/SC2007 -- Use $((..)) instead of
```

```
deprecated...
donnie@debian12:~$
```

As expected, shellcheck detects the non-POSIX way of doing math. So, that's good.

Scanning math7.sh gives us this:

```
donnie@debian12:~$ shellcheck math7.sh
donnie@debian12:~$
```

Here, we see the same problem that we saw with checkbashisms. That is, math7.sh has the variable name that's within the math construct surrounded by a pair of double quotes, as you see in the start=$(("$start"+1)) line. We've already established that this works on bash but not on dash, yet shellcheck doesn't flag this as a problem.

Finally, let's try this with math8.sh. As you'll recall, this is the script that we finally got to work on dash. Here's how that looks:

```
donnie@debian12:~$ shellcheck math8.sh
In math8.sh line 6:
  start=$(($start+1))
            ^----^ SC2004 (style): $/${} is unnecessary on arithmetic variables.
For more information:
  https://www.shellcheck.net/wiki/SC2004 -- $/${} is unnecessary on
arithmeti...
donnie@debian12:~$
```

In this case, the script works perfectly well on our Debian/dash machine. Here, shellcheck is pointing out a stylistic issue that doesn't affect whether the script will actually work. If you recall from *Chapter 11, Performing Mathematical Operations*, I showed you that when recalling the value of a variable that's within a math construct, it's not necessary to preface the variable name with a $. I mean, it doesn't hurt anything if you do, but it's not necessary.

Specifying a Shell with the -s Option

Another benefit of using shellcheck is that you can use the -s option to specify which shell that you want to use for testing your script. Even if the shebang line in your script is #!/bin/sh, and sh on your machine points to a non-bash shell, you can still test it against bash, like this:

```
donnie@debian12:~$ shellcheck -s bash ip-2.sh
In ip-2.sh line 11:
echo ${ip[*]}
     ^------^ SC2048 (warning): Use "${array[@]}" (with quotes) to prevent
whitespace problems.
     ^------^ SC2086 (info): Double quote to prevent globbing and word
splitting.
Did you mean:
```

```
echo "${ip[*]}"
For more information:
  https://www.shellcheck.net/wiki/SC2048 -- Use "${array[@]}" (with quotes)
t...
  https://www.shellcheck.net/wiki/SC2086 -- Double quote to prevent globbing
...
donnie@debian12:~$
```

By testing against bash, we no longer get the warning about how we can't use arrays. All we get this time is just a reminder that we should surround variable names with double quotes.

> With the -s option, you can specify sh, bash, dash, or ksh. (Curiously, it doesn't work with zsh.)

Hands-on Lab — Using -s to Scan Function Libraries

You can also use the -s option to scan function library files that don't have a shebang line. To see how that's done, let's scan the sysinfo.lib file that we last encountered back in *Chapter 14, Using awk-Part 1*.

> The scripts and library files in this section are too large to show here in their entirety. So, be sure to download them from the GitHub repository.

1. First, copy the sysinfo.lib file to sysinfo_posix.lib, like so:

    ```
    donnie@debian12:~$ cp sysinfo.lib sysinfo_posix.lib
    donnie@debian12:~$
    ```

2. Then, scan it for bash, since it was originally only meant to be used on bash. Here's the relevant output:

    ```
    donnie@debian12:~$ shellcheck -s bash sysinfo_posix.lib
    In sysinfo_posix.lib line 19:
                if [ $(uname) = SunOS ]; then
                     ^------^ SC2046 (warning): Quote this to prevent word
    splitting.
    . . .
    In sysinfo_posix.lib line 48:
                    cd /Users
                    ^-------^ SC2164 (warning): Use 'cd ... || exit' or 'cd
    ... || return' in case cd fails.
    Did you mean:
    ```

```
            cd /Users || exit
 . . .
donnie@debian12:~$
```

3. For bash, shellcheck didn't find any show-stopping problems. But, it does suggest some improvements that could prevent problems. First, it suggests that I surround the uname command
   substitutions with double quotes, in case uname returns a text string that contains either white
   space or special characters that the shell could misinterpret. In reality, though, this will never
   be a problem in this script, because we know that uname will never return anything except for
   a plain-text, purely alphabetic string. But, let's fix it anyway. In this case, the if [$(uname)
   = SunOS]; then line will become:

```
if [ "$(uname)" = SunOS ]; then
```

   We'll do the same thing for every occurrence of the uname command substitution.

4. The second suggestion we see is to insert a graceful exit mechanism in case the script can't cd
   into the /Users/ directory. Again, we know that this won't be a problem in this script, because
   we know that the specified directory will always be present. But again, let's fix it anyway. Let's
   take that cd /Users line and change it to:

```
cd /Users || return
```

   We'll do the same thing for all of the cd commands in the open_files_users() function. That
   way, if a cd command fails, the script will just continue running without this function.

5. Now, let's say that we want to make this script portable, so that we won't have to install bash
   on all of our systems. As I mentioned before, dash is the most POSIX-compliant shell that's
   widely available for most Linux and BSD-type distros. So, let's use -s dash to scan the file again:

```
donnie@debian12:~$ shellcheck -s dash sysinfo_posix.lib
 . . .

 . . .
In sysinfo_posix.lib line 55:
            if [[ $user != "lost+found" ]] && [[ $user != "Shared" ]];
then
                 ^-------------------------^ SC3010 (error): In dash, [[ ]]
is not supported.
                                            ^--------------------^
SC3010 (error): In dash, [[ ]] is not supported.
 . . .

 . . .
In sysinfo.lib line 71:
                echo "${os:12}"
                      ^------^ SC3057 (error): In dash, string
indexing is not supported.
```

```
. . .
. . .
donnie@debian12:~$
```

6. We've seen the first problem in previous scripts. It's just that the [[. . .]] construct isn't supported on some non-bash shells, such as dash. Fortunately, there's no reason that requires us to use the double square brackets in this case, so we can just replace them with single square brackets. So, we'll change the offending line to:

```
if [ $user != "lost+found" ] && [ $user != "Shared" ]; then
```

7. The second problem is one that we haven't seen yet. The "${os:12}" type of variable expansion is another bashism that won't work on either Bourne shell or dash. To refresh your memory, the os variable is defined in the system_info() function that's toward the end of the file. The variable definition, when done from the command-line, looks like this:

```
donnie@debian12:~$ os=$(grep "PRETTY_NAME" /etc/os-release)
donnie@debian12:~$ echo $os
PRETTY_NAME="Debian GNU/Linux 12 (bookworm)"
donnie@debian12:~$
```

But, we don't want the PRETTY_NAME= part to show up in the report. All we want is just the name of the operating system. This PRETTY_NAME= string consists of 12 characters. On bash, we can strip those 12 characters away by doing:

```
donnie@debian12:~$ echo "${os:12}"
"Debian GNU/Linux 12 (bookworm)"
donnie@debian12:~$
```

It looks good there, but watch what happens when I try this in a dash session:

```
donnie@debian12:~$ dash
$ os=$(grep "PRETTY_NAME" /etc/os-release)
$ echo "${os:12}"
dash: 2: Bad substitution
$
```

Oh dear, that doesn't work at all. Fortunately, this is an easy fix. We'll just use a POSIX-compliant form of variable expansion, which looks like this:

```
$ echo "${os#PRETTY_NAME=}"
"Debian GNU/Linux 12 (bookworm)"
$
```

Instead of specifying the number of characters to strip from the beginning of the text string, we just specify the actual portion of the text string to strip. And, I replaced the : with a #. Easy, right?

This is one of the great mysteries of life that I haven't yet figured out. Most bashisms were created as either a simpler way to do things, or to allow bash to do things that other shells can't do at all. In this case, the bash way of performing variable expansion isn't any easier than the POSIX way. So why did the bash developers even bother to give us this new, non-POSIX way? Your guess is as good as mine.

At any rate, you can read more about POSIX-compliant variable expansion here:

POSIX shell cheat sheet: `https://steinbaugh.com/posts/posix.html`

8. Next, we need to scan the script that uses this function library. Start by copying the system_info. sh to system_info_posix.sh:

```
donnie@debian12:~$ cp system_info.sh system_info_posix.sh
donnie@debian12:~$
```

9. Now, scan the system_info_posix.sh script for dash compatibility:

```
donnie@debian12:~$ shellcheck -s dash system_info.sh
. . .
. . .
In system_info_posix.sh line 5:
title="System Information for $HOSTNAME"
                              ^-------^ SC3028 (error): In dash, HOSTNAME
is not supported.
In system_info_posix.sh line 31:
if [[ -f /usr/local/bin/pandoc ]] || [[ -f /usr/bin/pandoc ]]; then
   ^--------------------------^ SC3010 (error): In dash, [[ ]] is not
supported.
                                     ^----------------------^ SC3010
(error): In dash, [[ ]] is not supported.
. . .
. . .
donnie@debian12:~$
```

The first thing we see is that "In dash, HOSTNAME is not supported." That seems strange, because all I'm doing here is calling the value of an environmental variable. But, it says that it doesn't work, so I'll change it to use command substitution with the hostname command, like so:

```
title="System Information for $(hostname)"
```

The next problem is the same old problem that we've seen before with the double square brackets. It's another case where double square brackets aren't necessary anyway, so I'll change it to single square brackets, like so:

```
if [ -f /usr/local/bin/pandoc ] || [ -f /usr/bin/pandoc ]; then
```

10. Next, let's copy the `sysinfo_posix.lib` file to its proper place in the `/usr/local/lib/` directory:

```
donnie@debian12:~$ sudo cp sysinfo_posix.lib /usr/local/lib/
donnie@debian12:~$
```

11. Now, edit the `system_info_posix.sh` script so that it will source the new function library, and use sh as the interpreter shell. Make the top part of the script look like this:

```
#!/bin/sh
# sysinfo_page - A script to produce an HTML file
. /usr/local/lib/sysinfo_posix.lib
```

12. Finally, copy the `system_info_posix.sh` script and the `sysinfo_posix.lib` file to other machines with other operating systems. You should find that this script and function library will work well on other Linux distros, as well as on FreeBSD, OpenIndiana, and macOS.

End of lab

So, we've covered `checkbashisms` and `shellcheck`. Shall we cover one more handy script-checking utility? Indeed we shall, and we shall do it now.

Using shall

The `checkbashisms` and `shellcheck` utilities act as **static code checkers**. This means that instead of actually running the scripts to see if they work, these two utilities just look through the code to detect problems. Sometimes though, it's helpful to have a **dynamic code checker** that will actually run the code to see what happens. That's where `shall` comes in.

`shall` is a bash script that you can download from the author's GitHub repository. The easiest way to install it is to clone the repository, like this:

```
donnie@debian12:~$ git clone https://github.com/mklement0/shall.git
```

Then, go into the `shall/bin/` directory, and copy the `shall` script to the `/usr/local/bin/` directory, like so:

```
donnie@debian12:~$ cd shall/bin
donnie@debian12:~/shall/bin$ ls -l
total 28
-rwxr-xr-x. 1 donnie donnie 27212 May 27 18:20 shall
donnie@debian12:~/shall/bin$ sudo cp shall /usr/local/bin
donnie@debian12:~/shall/bin$
```

Now, here's the cool part. With only a single command, `shall` can test your scripts against sh, bash, dash, zsh, and ksh. (It doesn't matter which interpreter shell you specify in the scripts' shebang line.) Most Linux and BSD distros have these various shells in their package repositories, so you can install ones that aren't installed already.

Of course, dash and bash are already installed on our Debian machine, so let's install zsh and ksh:

```
donnie@debian12:~$ sudo apt install zsh ksh
```

Let's begin by testing our ip-2.sh script. The output is too long to show in its entirety, so I'll just show some relevant sections. Here's the top part:

```
donnie@debian12:~$ shall ip-2.sh
X  sh@ (-> dash)                            [0.00s]
   IP Addresses of intruder attempts
   ip-2.sh: 4: Syntax error: "(" unexpected
```

The first check was for sh, which on Debian really means dash. You see here that the script couldn't run, because dash can't work with arrays. The next check is for bash, which looks like this:

```
√ bash                                      [0.00s]
   IP Addresses of intruder attempts
   ip[0] is 192.168.3.78, the first item in the list.
   ip[2] is 192.168.3.9, the third item in the list.
   *********************************
   The most dangerous intruder is 192.168.3.4, which is in ip[1].
   *********************************
   Here is the entire list of IP addresses in the array.
   192.168.3.78 192.168.3.4 192.168.3.9
```

The zsh and ksh checks that follow look the same. At the very bottom of the output, you'll see this:

```
FAILED - 1 shell (sh) reports failure, 3 (bash, zsh, ksh) report success.
donnie@debian12:~$
```

This means that our ip-2.sh script runs fine on bash, zsh, and ksh, but it won't run on dash.

But, as cool as shall is, it isn't quite perfect. To see what I mean, create the fly.sh script, like this:

```
#!/bin/sh
#
echo -e "I want to fly to the \v moon."
printf "%b\n" "I want to fly to the \v moon."
```

This is just a simple little script that demonstrates the problem with using echo -e in your scripts, as I showed you a few pages back. Here's what happens when I test fly.sh with shall:

```
donnie@debian12:~$ shall fly.sh
√ sh@ (-> dash)                             [0.00s]
   -e I want to fly to the
                                 moon.
   I want to fly to the
                          moon.
```

```
√ bash                                          [0.00s]
   I want to fly to the
                              moon.
   I want to fly to the
                              moon.
. . .
OK - All 4 shells (sh, bash, zsh, ksh) report success.
donnie@debian12:~$
```

So, shall says that the script ran correctly on all four shells. But, at the top of the output, you see that the -e shows up in the echo output with dash, which is the problem that I showed you before. The bottom line here is that when you use shall, don't just depend on what the status line at the bottom of the output says. Look at the output for all of the shells, and ensure that the output is what you really want to see.

The only other problem with shall isn't really with shall, but with sh. Remember that sh points to a different shell on different Linux, BSD, and Unix distros. You can install shall on any of these distros, as long as you can install bash on them. Then, just copy the shall script to the machine on which you want to test sh scripts.

A man page is embedded into the shall script. To see it, just do:

shall --man

Okay, I think that about does it for this chapter. Let's summarize and move on.

Summary

Script portability is important if you need to create scripts that will run on a wide variety of Linux, Unix, or Unix-like operating systems. I began by showing you how to install bash on various BSD-type distros, and how to ensure that your scripts will find bash on them. After that, I explained the POSIX standard, and why it's needed. Then, I showed you some bashisms, and some cool utilities that can test your scripts for them.

In the next chapter, we'll talk about shell script security. I'll see you there.

Questions

1. For shell scripters, what is the most important reason for following the POSIX standard?

   a. To ensure that scripts will only run on Linux operating systems.

   b. To ensure that scripts can run on a wide variety of Linux, Unix, and Unix-like operating systems.

   c. To ensure that all operating systems are running bash.

   d. To ensure that scripts can use the advanced features of bash.

2. Which of the following is a dynamic code checker?

    a. `checkbashisms`

    b. `shellcheck`

    c. `shall`

    d. `will`

3. Which of the following statements about `sh` is true?

    a. On every operating system, `sh` is always the Bourne shell.

    b. On every operating system, `sh` is a symbolic link that points to `bash`.

    c. `sh` represents a different shell on different operating systems.

4. You want to solve a math problem, and assign its value to a variable. Which of the following constructs would you use for best portability?

    a. `var=$(3*4)`

    b. `var=$[3*4]`

    c. `var=$[[3*4]]`

    d. `var=$((3*4))`

Further Reading

- UNIX Vs Linux: How Are They Different?: `https://www.maketecheasier.com/unix-vs-linux-how-are-they-different/`

- What is the difference between "#!/usr/bin/env bash" and "#!/usr/bin/bash"?: `https://stackoverflow.com/questions/16365130/what-is-the-difference-between-usr-bin-env-bash-and-usr-bin-bash`

- Writing Bash Scripts that aren't Only Bash: Checking for Bashisms and Using Dash: `https://www.bowmanjd.com/bash-not-bash-posix/`

- A Brief POSIX Advocacy: `https://www.usenix.org/system/files/login/articles/login_spring16_09_tomei.pdf`

- A Guide to POSIX: `https://www.baeldung.com/linux/posix`

- How can I test for POSIX compliance of shell scripts?: `https://unix.stackexchange.com/questions/48786/how-can-i-test-for-posix-compliance-of-shell-scripts`

- Making Unix Shell Scripts POSIX-compliant: `https://stackoverflow.com/questions/40916071/making-unix-shell-scripts-posix-compliant`

- Rich's sh (POSIX shell) Tricks: `http://www.etalabs.net/sh_tricks.html`

- Dash–ArchWiki: `https://wiki.archlinux.org/title/Dash`

- POSIX shell cheat sheet: `https://steinbaugh.com/posts/posix.html`

- Is there a minimally POSIX.2 compliant shell?: `https://stackoverflow.com/questions/11376975/is-there-a-minimally-posix-2-compliant-shell`

Answers

1. b
2. c
3. c
4. d

Join our community on Discord!

Read this book alongside other users, Linux experts, and the author himself.

Ask questions, provide solutions to other readers, chat with the author via Ask Me Anything sessions, and much more. Scan the QR code or visit the link to join the community.

https://packt.link/SecNet

20

Shell Script Security

Thus far, we haven't talked a whole lot about shell scripting security. Frankly, it's because it's one of those things that you might never have to worry about. I mean, a lot of times you'll just be writing scripts for your own use, that you'll just be running from your home directory on your own local machine. Even if you're an administrator who needs to create scripts that perform some sort of administrative task, you might only need to either run them on from your own home directory or share them with other *trusted* administrators who just run them from their own home directories. In these cases, shell scripting security isn't necessarily a huge deal.

However, you may at times need to share your script with other users or administrators that you don't fully trust. In these cases, shell scripting security is *extremely important*, and should be a major part of your scripting focus. For example, you might have some sort of administrative script that you need to place into a directory that administrators with only limited permissions can access. In those cases, you also need to ensure that nobody can modify it, and that only certain designated administrators can execute it. You'll also want to design the script in a way that will prevent bad actors from using it to perform command injection attacks.

Topics in this chapter include:

- Controlling Access to Your Scripts
- Understanding SUID and SGID Considerations
- Avoiding Sensitive Data Leakage
- Understanding Command Injection with eval
- Understanding Path Security

If you're ready, let's get going.

Technical Requirements

I'll mainly be working with Fedora Server and Ubuntu Server virtual machines. But, the techniques that I'll show you should work on just about any Linux distro. I'll also be showing you some things on a FreeBSD 14 virtual machine, and an OpenIndiana virtual machine.

As always, you can grab the scripts by doing:

```
git clone https://github.com/PacktPublishing/The-Ultimate-Linux-Shell-
Scripting-Guide.git
```

Controlling Access to Your Scripts

A lot of the scripts that you create might be just for yourself or your co-workers. Or, they might be for general distribution to the public. In all of these cases, you might not need to worry about having any kind of access control on your scripts.

But, there might also be times when you need to create scripts that only certain people can access. The methods that you can use for this include:

- Assigning sudo privileges
- Assigning an Access Control List
- Obfuscating plain-text scripts

We'll begin by looking using sudo.

Assigning sudo Privileges

sudo is a handy security feature that is installed by default on macOS, OpenIndiana and most Linux distros. It's also available for installation on most BSD-type distros and any Linux distros on which it isn't installed by default. The most common way to use sudo is to allow non-privileged users to run programs with root user privileges. (You can also use sudo to allow users to run programs with the privileges of other non-root users, such as a database user. I'm not going to go into all that now though, because I'm trying to keep things simple.)

Now, here's what makes sudo so cool. Let's say that you want a particular user to run one particular program with root user privileges. With sudo, you don't have to give that user the root user password. Instead, just configure the user's sudo privileges for the program, and then let the user enter his or her own password whenever he or she needs to run the program. Let's look at how that works.

Hands-on Lab – Configuring sudo

In this lab, you'll create a simple script, and configure sudo so that only designated users can run it.

1. Create the sudo_demo1.sh script, like this:

    ```
    #!/bin/bash
    echo "This is a demo of sudo privileges."
    ```

2. Copy the script to the /usr/local/sbin/ directory:

    ```
    donnie@ubuntu2404:~$ sudo cp sudo_demo1.sh /usr/local/sbin/

    donnie@ubuntu2404:~$ ls -l /usr/local/sbin/sudo_demo1.sh
    -rw-r--r-- 1 root root 55 Jul  6 19:24 /usr/local/sbin/sudo_demo1.sh
    ```

```
donnie@ubuntu2404:~$
```

As you see, copying this script to `/user/local/sbin/` caused the ownership of the file to automatically change to the root user.

3. Set permissions on the sudo_demo1.sh file so that only the root user can access it:

```
donnie@ubuntu2404:~$ cd /usr/local/sbin/
donnie@ubuntu2404:/usr/local/sbin$ sudo chmod 700 sudo_demo1.sh

donnie@ubuntu2404:/usr/local/sbin$ ls -l sudo_demo1.sh
-rwx------ 1 root root 55 Jul  6 19:24 sudo_demo1.sh
donnie@ubuntu2404:/usr/local/sbin$
```

Note how in the chmod 700 command, the 7 assigns read, write, and execute privileges to the root user. The two 0s remove all privileges from the *group* and from *others*. But, how do we obtain the value of 7 in the *user* position? Here's the breakdown on how it works:

The *read* permission has a value of 4.

The *write* permission has a value of 2.

The *execute* permission has a value of 1.

In this case, we want the user to have full read, write, and execute permissions. Adding the values of all three of those permissions gives us a value of 7.

(I know that this is a rather cursory explanation, but for now, please bear with me.)

4. Create a non-privileged user account for Horatio.

On Debian/Ubuntu, do:

```
sudo adduser horatio
```

On Fedora and other Red Hat-type distros:

```
sudo useradd horatio
sudo passwd horatio
```

5. Begin configuring sudo by entering:

```
sudo visudo
```

This command will open the `/etc/sudoers` file in either nano, vi, or vim, depending upon which operating system you're working with. Beyond that, the directions are the same.

6. Scroll down until you see this line:

```
root    ALL=(ALL:ALL) ALL
```

Directly below that line, place this line:

```
horatio ALL=(ALL:ALL) /usr/local/sbin/sudo_demo1.sh
```

Save the file as you would with a normal text editor.

I know that the ALL=(ALL:ALL) thing looks confusing, but it's really quite simple. Here's the TL;DR of what it means:

ON_HOSTS=(AS_USER:AS_GROUP_MEMBER) ALLOWED_COMMANDS

Now, here's the more specific breakdown:

The first ALL means that the specified user can run this command on all machines on the local network. Optionally, you can replace this ALL with the hostname of a particular machine or groups of machines on which you want this user to be able to run this command.

The second ALL means that the specified user can run this command as all users, including the root user.

The third ALL means that Horatio can run this command as a member of all groups, including the root user's group. (Note that this is optional. You can also just omit the group, and set this to ALL=(ALL).)

In the root line, the final ALL means that the root user can run all privileged commands. In the horatio line, the final ALL is replaced by the specific command that we want to allow Horatio to run.

7. Open another terminal window on your host machine, and log into the virtual machine with Horatio's account.

8. Have Horatio test this by first trying to run the script without sudo, and then with sudo, like this:

```
horatio@ubuntu2404:~$ sudo_demo1.sh
-bash: /usr/local/sbin/sudo_demo1.sh: Permission denied

horatio@ubuntu2404:~$ sudo sudo_demo1.sh
[sudo] password for horatio:
This is a demo of sudo privileges.
horatio@ubuntu2404:~$
```

You see that Horatio can run the script with his sudo privileges.

9. Have Horatio attempt to view the script's source code, like so:

```
horatio@ubuntu2404:~$ cd /usr/local/sbin
horatio@ubuntu2404:/usr/local/sbin$ less sudo_demo1.sh
sudo_demo1.sh: Permission denied
```

```
horatio@ubuntu2404:/usr/local/sbin$ sudo less sudo_demo1.sh
Sorry, user horatio is not allowed to execute '/usr/bin/less sudo_demo1.
sh' as root on ubuntu2404.
horatio@ubuntu2404:/usr/local/sbin$
```

Horatio can't view or edit the source code, because he doesn't have the proper sudo privileges for that. He has sudo privileges to do one thing, and one thing only, as the root user, which is just to execute the sudo_demo1.sh script.

That does it for our introduction to the mysteries of sudo. Let's move on to our next method of controlling access to scripts.

Using an Access Control List

If you've ever been a Windows administrator, you likely know that the NTFS filesystem on Windows allows you to grant really fine-grained permissions settings on files and directories. Sadly, the filesystems on Linux, Unix, and Unix-like systems don't have such fine-grained access control built into them. But, we can make up for that deficiency somewhat by using an **Access Control List**, or **ACL**. Let's look at how to do that in this hands-on lab.

Hands-on Lab — Setting an ACL for Horatio on Linux

In this lab, we'll create another script for which only Horatio will have permission to run. To keep things simple, just use the same virtual machine that you used for the previous lab, so that you won't have to create another user account.

1. You'll find everything you need for setting up ACLs already installed on your Fedora virtual machine. If you're using a Debian/Ubuntu type of machine, you might have to install the acl package by doing:

    ```
    sudo apt install acl
    ```

2. Log into your own normal user account, and create the acl_demo.sh script, like this:

    ```
    #!/bin/bash
    echo "This is a demo of ACLs."
    ```

3. Copy the script to the /usr/local/sbin/ directory, and note how the ownership automatically changes to the root user:

    ```
    donnie@ubuntu2404:~$ vim acl_demo.sh
    donnie@ubuntu2404:~$ sudo cp acl_demo.sh /usr/local/sbin/
    [sudo] password for donnie:
    donnie@ubuntu2404:~$ cd /usr/local/sbin/
    donnie@ubuntu2404:/usr/local/sbin$ ls -l acl_demo.sh
    -rw-r--r-- 1 root root 44 Jul 24 20:56 acl_demo.sh
    donnie@ubuntu2404:/usr/local/sbin$
    ```

4. In order for an ACL to work, you'll need to remove all permissions from group and others, like this:

```
donnie@ubuntu2404:/usr/local/sbin$ sudo chmod 700 acl_demo.sh
donnie@ubuntu2404:/usr/local/sbin$ ls -l acl_demo.sh
-rwx------ 1 root root 44 Jul 24 20:56 acl_demo.sh
donnie@ubuntu2404:/usr/local/sbin$
```

This is because the whole point of using an ACL is to prevent everyone who hasn't been set up with an ACL from accessing the file.

5. Use getfacl to verify that no ACL has been set:

```
donnie@ubuntu2404:/usr/local/sbin$ getfacl acl_demo.sh
# file: acl_demo.sh
# owner: root
# group: root
user::rwx
group::---
other::---

donnie@ubuntu2404:/usr/local/sbin$
```

6. In another terminal window, log into Horatio's account, and try to run the acl_demo.sh script, like so:

```
horatio@ubuntu2404:~$ acl_demo.sh
-bash: /usr/local/sbin/acl_demo.sh: Permission denied
horatio@ubuntu2404:~$
```

You see that Horatio has been denied.

7. Go back to your own terminal window. Create an ACL so that Horatio will have read and execute permissions on the acl_demo.sh script, like so:

```
donnie@ubuntu2404:/usr/local/sbin$ sudo setfacl -m u:horatio:rx acl_demo.
sh

donnie@ubuntu2404:/usr/local/sbin$ ls -l acl_demo.sh
-rwxr-x---+ 1 root root 44 Jul 24 20:56 acl_demo.sh
donnie@ubuntu2404:/usr/local/sbin$
```

Here's the breakdown of the command:

- -m: This means to modify the existing ACL. It will also create an ACL if one hasn't been created yet.
- u:horatio: This means that we're creating an ACL for user horatio.

- rx: This means that we're granting the read and execute permissions for this file to the specified user.
- Note the + at the end of the permissions settings for this file. This indicates that an ACL has been created.

8. Use getfacl to verify that the ACL was created properly:

```
donnie@ubuntu2404:/usr/local/sbin$ getfacl acl_demo.sh
# file: acl_demo.sh
# owner: root
# group: root
user::rwx
user:horatio:r-x
group::---
mask::r-x
other::---

donnie@ubuntu2404:/usr/local/sbin$
```

The user:horatio:r-x line indicates that the ACL has been created for Horatio.

9. Go back to Horatio's terminal window, and have him try to run the script:

```
horatio@ubuntu2404:~$ acl_demo.sh
This is a demo of ACLs.
horatio@ubuntu2404:~$
```

This time, Horatio has achieved coolness.

10. There is one downside to using an ACL instead of sudo. That is, sudo automatically assumes that a user needs to read a shell script in order to execute it. So, sudo allows a user to execute the script without explicitly setting the read permission for that user. This means that the user won't be able to use any utility such as cat or less to view the contents of the script file. When using an ACL, the read permission and the execute permission both have to be explicitly set on the script to allow someone to run it. So, when using an ACL, you won't be able to prevent the user from viewing the contents of the file. You can prove that by having Horatio view the file, like so:

```
horatio@ubuntu2404:~$ cat /usr/local/sbin/acl_demo.sh
#!/bin/bash

echo "This is a demo of ACLs."
horatio@ubuntu2404:~$
```

The bottom line here is that if you want to prevent users from viewing the contents of your scripts, set them up with the appropriate sudo privileges instead of using an ACL. On the other hand, if you don't mind that users can view the script's source code, then using an ACL is definitely an option.

Space doesn't allow for me to present more than just a cursory coverage of permissions settings, sudo, and ACLs in this chapter. If you need more information about them, I have entire chapters devoted to each of these topics in my *Mastering Linux Security and Hardening* book.

That's does it for sudo and ACLs on Linux. Let's now see how to do it on FreeBSD 14.

Hands-on Lab – Setting an ACL for Horatio on FreeBSD 14

You'll find everything you need for creating ACLs already installed on FreeBSD 14. Let's begin.

1. Create Horatio's user account by doing:

```
donnie@freebsd14:~ $ sudo adduser
```

The FreeBSD adduser command is interactive, similar to the adduser command on Debian and Ubuntu. After you invoke it, you'll just need to enter Horatio's information, as prompted. Here's what it looks like:

```
donnie@freebsd14:~ $ sudo adduser
Password:
Username: horatio
Full name: Horatio Black Cat
Uid (Leave empty for default):
Login group [horatio]:
Login group is horatio. Invite horatio into other groups? []:
Login class [default]:
Shell (sh csh tcsh bash rbash zsh rzsh ksh93 nologin) [sh]:
Home directory [/home/horatio]:
Home directory permissions (Leave empty for default):
Use password-based authentication? [yes]:
Use an empty password? (yes/no) [no]:
Use a random password? (yes/no) [no]:
Enter password:
Enter password again:
Lock out the account after creation? [no]:
Username   : horatio
Password   : *****
Full Name  : Horatio Black Cat
Uid        : 1002
Class      :
Groups     : horatio
Home       : /home/horatio
Home Mode  :
Shell      : /bin/sh
Locked     : no
OK? (yes/no) [yes]:
adduser: INFO: Successfully added (horatio) to the user database.
Add another user? (yes/no) [no]:
Goodbye!
donnie@freebsd14:~ $ ▊
```

Figure 20.1: Adding a user account to FreeBSD

In case you're wondering about the **Full Name** field, it's just that Horatio really is a black cat who's been visiting me lately.

2. Use the same `acl_demo.sh` script that you used for the Linux lab. Copy it to the `/usr/local/sbin/` directory, and verify that ownership has changed to the root user:

```
donnie@freebsd14:~ $ sudo cp acl_demo.sh /usr/local/sbin/
Password:
donnie@freebsd14:~ $ cd /usr/local/sbin/
donnie@freebsd14:/usr/local/sbin $ ls -l acl_demo.sh
-rw-r--r--  1 root wheel 44 Jul 29 15:42 acl_demo.sh
donnie@freebsd14:/usr/local/sbin $
```

3. Apply the 700 permissions setting to `acl_demo.sh`. This will mean that the root user will have read, write, and execute permissions, and that *group* and *others* have no permissions.

```
donnie@freebsd14:/usr/local/sbin $ sudo chmod 700 acl_demo.sh
donnie@freebsd14:/usr/local/sbin $ ls -l acl_demo.sh
-rwx------  1 root wheel 44 Jul 29 15:42 acl_demo.sh
donnie@freebsd14:/usr/local/sbin $
```

4. In another terminal window, log into Horatio's user account on the FreeBSD machine. Then, have him attempt to run the `acl_demo.sh` script.

```
horatio@freebsd14:~ $ acl_demo.sh
-sh: acl_demo.sh: Permission denied
horatio@freebsd14:~ $ sudo acl_demo.sh
Password:
horatio is not in the sudoers file.
This incident has been reported to the administrator.
horatio@freebsd14:~ $
```

5. Go back to your own terminal window, and set the ACL for Horatio, like so:

```
donnie@freebsd14:/usr/local/sbin $ sudo setfacl -m u:horatio:rx:allow
acl_demo.sh
Password:
donnie@freebsd14:/usr/local/sbin $
```

Note that the command is slightly different this time, because Linux uses the **Network Filesystem version 4 (NFSv4)** style of ACLs, and FreeBSD uses the POSIX style of ACLs. It's not a big difference, though. It's just that with FreeBSD, you have to add `allow` to the `setfacl` command.

6. Verify that the ACL has been properly set:

```
donnie@freebsd14:/usr/local/sbin $ getfacl acl_demo.sh
# file: acl_demo.sh
# owner: root
# group: wheel
      user:horatio:r-x-----------:-------:allow
            owner@:rwxp--aARWcCos:-------:allow
            group@:------a-R-c--s:-------:allow
         everyone@:------a-R-c--s:-------:allow
donnie@freebsd14:/usr/local/sbin $
```

You see that indeed, Horatio does have read and execute permissions for this script.

7. Go back to Horatio's terminal, and have him try to run the `acl_demo.sh` command:

```
horatio@freebsd14:~ $ acl_demo.sh
This is a demo of ACLs.
horatio@freebsd14:~ $
```

It works, which means that Horatio has now achieved coolness on FreeBSD.

Next, let's give this a try on OpenIndiana.

Hands-on Lab – Setting an ACL for Horatio on OpenIndiana

Doing this on OpenIndiana will be considerably different, because it doesn't use `setfacl` or `getfacl` to manage ACLs. Instead, it uses `chmod` for managing both normal permissions settings and ACLs. You'll once again use the same `acl_demo.sh` script that you used for the previous labs.

1. Create Horatio's user account, like this:

```
donnie@openindiana:~$ sudo useradd -m horatio
donnie@openindiana:~$ sudo passwd horatio
donnie@openindiana:~$
```

 The `-m` option tells `useradd` to create the new user's home directory. On the Open-Indiana version of `useradd`, this is normally the only option switch that you'll need.

2. There's no `/usr/local/` directory on OpenIndiana, so just copy the `acl_demo.sh` script to the `/usr/sbin/` directory, instead. Then, verify that the ownership has changed to the root user.

```
donnie@openindiana:~$ sudo cp acl_demo.sh /usr/sbin/
donnie@openindiana:~$ cd /usr/sbin/
donnie@openindiana:/usr/sbin$ ls -l acl_demo.sh
-rw-r--r--   1 root      root           44 Jul 29 16:14 acl_demo.sh
```

```
donnie@openindiana:/usr/sbin$
```

3. Change the permissions setting of the `acl_demo.sh` file to 700, as you did in the previous labs:

```
donnie@openindiana:/usr/sbin$ sudo chmod 700 acl_demo.sh
donnie@openindiana:/usr/sbin$ ls -l acl_demo.sh
-rwx------   1 root      root          44 Jul 29 16:14 acl_demo.sh
donnie@openindiana:/usr/sbin$
```

4. In another terminal window, log into Horatio's account. Have him try to run the `acl_demo.sh` script:

```
horatio@openindiana:~$ acl_demo.sh
-bash: /usr/sbin/acl_demo.sh: Permission denied
horatio@openindiana:~$ sudo acl_demo.sh
Password:
horatio is not in the sudoers file.
This incident has been reported to the administrator.
horatio@openindiana:~$
```

5. Now, apply an ACL for Horatio, granting him both read and execute privileges for the `acl_demo.sh` script:

```
donnie@openindiana:/usr/sbin$ sudo chmod A+user:horatio:rx:allow acl_
demo.sh

Password:
donnie@openindiana:/usr/sbin$
```

 Note how instead of using `setfacl -m u:horatio`, OpenIndiana uses `chmod A+user:horatio`. The A+ in this case just means that we're adding an ACL.

6. Go back to Horatio's terminal, and have him try to run the script:

```
horatio@openindiana:~$ acl_demo.sh
This is a demo of ACLs.
horatio@openindiana:~$
```

Yes, indeed. Even on OpenIndiana, Horatio has achieved coolness.

If you need to learn about OpenIndiana administration, you'll find that the official documentation at the OpenIndiana website is rather lacking. Fortunately, OpenIndiana is a fork of Oracle's Solaris operating system, which means that you can use the official Solaris documentation, instead. (I've placed a link to the relevant page in the *Further Reading* section.)

I think that that about covers it for ACLs. Let's move on to another way to control access to your scripts.

Obfuscating Plain-Text Scripts

You can also hide the contents of your shell scripts and prevent anyone from tampering with them by using the shc utility to convert your scripts into obfuscated executable binary files. And, you can do some things with shc that you can't do with either sudo or ACLs. Specifically, shc allows you to:

- Create an executable file that can run on only one machine.
- Set expiration dates for the executable files.
- Create executable files that can't be traced with debugging utilities such as strace or truss. (I'll explain those in just a bit.)

Let's begin by installing shc.

Installing shc

It's easy to install on Linux, FreeBSD, and macOS. Here's how it's done:

On Fedora:

```
sudo dnf install shc gcc
```

On Debian/Ubuntu:

```
sudo apt install shc gcc
```

Note that on Linux, you also need to install the gcc package so that you will have a C compiler that will work with shc. On FreeBSD, the C compiler gets installed as part of the operating system.

On FreeBSD:

```
sudo pkg install shc
```

On macOS with Homebrew installed:

```
brew install shc
```

Sadly, shc isn't available for OpenIndiana.

Hands-on Lab — Using shc

For this lab, you'll create the supersecret.sh script on your Fedora virtual machine. Also, go ahead and boot up your Debian/Ubuntu virtual machine, so that you can test your compiled scripts on it.

1. Using shc is simple. To demo, let's create the supersecret.sh script, like this:

```
#!/bin/bash

cat << secret
This document contains secrets that could impact the entire world!
Please don't let it fall into the wrong hands.

secret
```

This is just a simple *here document* that prints out a message, which looks like this:

```
donnie@fedora:~$ ./supersecret.sh
This document contains secrets that could impact the entire world!
Please don't let it fall into the wrong hands.

donnie@fedora:~$
```

2. The next step is to convert the shell script into an obfuscated binary file, like so:

```
donnie@fedora:~$ shc -f supersecret.sh -o supersecret
donnie@fedora:~$
```

As you see, I'm using the -f option to point to the shell script that I want to obfuscate, and the -o option to save the obfuscated binary file with the specified filename. This operation also creates a C language source file, as you see here:

```
donnie@fedora:~$ ls -l supersecret*
-rwxrwxr-x. 1 donnie donnie 15984 Jul  1 16:55 supersecret
-rwxr--r--. 1 donnie donnie   149 Jul  1 16:47 supersecret.sh
-rw-r--r--. 1 donnie donnie 18485 Jul  1 16:55 supersecret.sh.x.c
donnie@fedora:~$
```

shc works by first creating this C source code file, and then by calling a C compiler to compile the C source code into the binary file. You can prove that this works by trying to open the binary file with cat, like so:

```
donnie@fedora:~$ cat supersecret
@@@@@@◆@@@@◆
◆
@@a
    a
```

```
        @ @dd�-�=@�=@�>>@�88@8@@xx@x@DDS�td88@8@@P�
td`  ` @` @llQ�tdR�td�-�=@�/lib64/ld-linux-x86-64.so.20GNU
����GNUu[�C����@W�{�g���GNU0�@�ĉ���kĹ�@9�J<5Q
�.u n��`X��C{�!D�!D�Dg Dmallocgetpidstat__libc_start_
mainfprintfputenvmemsetstrlenstrdupgetenvmemcmpsprintfexecvpstderrmemcpyato
llstrerror__errno_locationexit__isoc99_sscanffwritecalloctime__
environlibc.so.6GLIBC_2.7GLIBC_2.14GLIBC_2.33GLIBC_2.34GLIB������
������u�iart__�ii��?
@�?@
· · ·
donnie@fedora:~$
```

If you can read that, then you're better than I am.

3. Try running this new `supersecret` binary, and you'll see that it works just like the script:

```
donnie@fedora:~$ ./supersecret
This document contains secrets that could impact the entire world!
Please don't let it fall into the wrong hands.

donnie@fedora:~$
```

Okay, let's be real. You're not going to obfuscate a simple script that does nothing but print out a message. I mean, anyone who can execute this binary file can still see the message. So, let's just say that your script contains a lot of additional code or data that you want to hide from everyone, including even the authorized users of the script. You also want to ensure that nobody can modify your scripts. In cases like that, `shc` is definitely a useful tool.

4. By default, `shc` creates binary files that will only run on the machine on which they were created. For example, let's see what happens when I transfer the `supersecret` binary that I created on this Fedora machine to an Ubuntu machine:

```
donnie@ubuntu2404:~$ ./supersecret
./supersecret: 3(�i��'(�qX5�@�й���ZBhas expired!
Please contact your provider jahidulhamid@yahoo.com
donnie@ubuntu2404:~$
```

That's definitely a handy security feature, because it allows you to control where your program can be run. So, if a malicious hacker were to somehow find your program and download it, he or she wouldn't be able to run it. The only catch is that we see the default `Please contact your provider. . .` message that's built into `shc`.

5. The default `Please contact your provider. . .` message doesn't mean anything to us, because it provides us with a bogus contact address. On the Fedora machine, fix that by adding the `-m` option and a custom message, like this:

```
donnie@@fedora:~$ shc -f supersecret.sh -m "You cannot run this program on
this machine." -o supersecret
donnie@fedora:~$
```

6. Transfer the new supersecret binary file to the Debian/Ubuntu machine, and try to run it. You should now see your custom message, like this:

```
donnie@ubuntu2404:~$ ./supersecret
./supersecret: ��]b+    �!����(��TR��0#50��fo_�7has expired!
You cannot run this program on this machine.
donnie@ubuntu2404:~$
```

Of course, you could also add your own contact address, if you really wanted to.

7. Sometimes though, you might want to create binary files that will run on any machine that's running the same operating system as the machine on which you created them. To do that, just relax the security a bit with the -r option, like so:

```
donnie@@fedora:~$ shc -rf supersecret.sh -o supersecret
donnie@fedora:~$
```

When I transfer this new binary file to my Ubuntu machine, it will run just fine, as you see here:

```
donnie@ubuntu2404:~$ ./supersecret
This document contains secrets that could impact the entire world!
Please don't let it fall into the wrong hands.

donnie@ubuntu2404:~$
```

8. Also, understand that shc creates binary files that can run on only one type of operating system. To see how that works, let's transfer the binary that I created on my Fedora machine to a FreeBSD machine. Here's what happens when I try to run it:

```
donnie@@freebsd14:~ $ ./supersecret
ELF binary type "0" not known.
-sh: ./supersecret: Exec format error
donnie@freebsd14:~ $
```

But, if you transfer the original script to the FreeBSD machine and then run shc on it, you'll get a binary that will run on FreeBSD.

 The good news here is that shc works exactly the same on FreeBSD as it does on Linux. So, you won't even have to modify your shc commands.

9. The next shc option I'll cover is the -e option, which allows you to set an expiration date on your program. Just specify the expiration date in the day-month-year (dd/mm/yyyy) format, like so:

```
donnie@fedora:~$ shc -e 02/07/2024 -rf supersecret.sh -m "This binary
file has expired. Contact me at donnie@any.net if you really need to run
it." -o supersecret
donnie@fedora:~$
```

I'm doing this on 1 July 2024, so I'll have to come back tomorrow to see if this actually works. So bye for now, I'll see you tomorrow.

10. Okay, it's now 2 July 2024, and I'm back. Let's see if this supersecret binary file still works:

```
donnie@fedora:~$ ./supersecret
./supersecret: has expired!
This binary file has expired. Contact me at donnie@any.net if you really
need to run it.
donnie@fedora:~$
```

Cool, the expiration date option works just fine.

> **Remember:** Even when you obfuscate your scripts with shc, you'll still need to use either sudo or an ACL to control who can execute them on a particular machine.

Now, let's see about making our executables untraceable.

Hands-on Lab – Creating Untraceable Executables

As you'll see in the next chapter, we have several tracing tools available to help programmers debug programs. These tools include strace for Linux systems, truss for FreeBSD, and either dtrace or dtruss for macOS. For Linux, there's also ltrace, which can trace calls to programming libraries.

> The strace, dtrace, truss, and dtruss utilities can trace the **system calls** that a program makes. The easiest way to explain system calls is that they're the mechanism that programs use to communicate with the operating system kernel.

The problem for us is that either a malicious actor or an unauthorized non-malicious actor could also use the information that these utilities provide to reverse engineer one of your compiled scripts. This could allow these unauthorized parties to see secrets that you don't want them to see.

What information would we not want unauthorized people to see? Here are two examples:

The names and locations of sensitive files that your program accesses: These files could reveal secrets to unauthorized actors.

Embedded passwords: Even if you encrypt passwords, using strace, truss, dtrace, or dtruss on your compiled binary file will reveal the plain-text passwords. (You'll soon see that in the *Avoiding Sensitive Data Leakage* section.)

Needless to say, either of these cases can represent a serious security problem. So to be sure, just get into the habit of making your shc binaries untraceable, as I'm about to show you in this section.

Here's how it works:

1. On the Fedora machine, install strace and ltrace, like this:

```
donnie@fedora:~$ sudo dnf install strace ltrace
```

2. On the Fedora machine, create a new supersecret binary without either the expiration date or the custom message.

```
donnie@fedora:~$ shc -f supersecret.sh -o supersecret
donnie@fedora:~$
```

3. Create a file that contains strace data about the supersecret binary, like this:

```
donnie@fedora:~$ strace ./supersecret 2> supersecret1_trace.txt
This document contains secrets that could impact the entire world!
Please don't let it fall into the wrong hands.

donnie@fedora:~$
```

Note that the strace output gets sent to stderr, which is why you have to use the 2> redirector.

4. Open the supersecret1_trace.txt file in less. What you'll see is a jumbled up mess that looks something like this:

```
execve("./supersecret", ["./supersecret"], 0x7ffd6152bd00 /* 58 vars */)
= 0
brk(NULL)                               = 0x14345000
arch_prctl(0x3001 /* ARCH_??? */, 0x7ffe27faa7c0) = -1 EINVAL (Invalid
argument)
```

```
access("/etc/ld.so.preload", R_OK)        = -1 ENOENT (No such file or
directory)
openat(AT_FDCWD, "/etc/ld.so.cache", O_RDONLY|O_CLOEXEC) = 3
. . .

. . .
```

For the most part, you would need to be a C language kernel programmer to understand what's going on with this. However, as we'll soon see, you might be able to glean some really important information if you know how to look for it.

5. Count how many lines are in the supersecret1_trace.txt file, like this:

```
donnie@fedora:~$ wc -l supersecret1_trace.txt
297 supersecret1_trace.txt
donnie@fedora:~$
```

So, there are 297 lines of output in the supersecret1_trace.txt file.

 Note that for all of these examples, you might get a different number of output lines on your own machines.

6. Perform an ltrace operation on the supersecret binary, saving the output to the supersecret1_ltrace.txt file. Then, count the number of lines in the supersecret1_ltrace.txt file, like so:

```
donnie@fedora:~$ ltrace ./supersecret 2> supersecret1_ltrace.txt
This document contains secrets that could impact the entire world!
Please don't let it fall into the wrong hands.

donnie@fedora:~$ wc -l supersecret1_ltrace.txt
7270 supersecret1_ltrace.txt
donnie@fedora:~$
```

You see that there are 7270 lines in the supersecret1_ltrace file.

7. Create a new supersecret binary. This time though, use the -U option to make this binary untraceable.

```
donnie@fedora:~$ shc -Uf supersecret.sh -o supersecret
donnie@fedora:~$
```

You won't have to delete the original binary before you do this, because this new command will overwrite the original binary.

8. Run strace on the supersecret binary again, saving the output to the supersecret2_tract. txt file.

```
donnie@fedora:~$ strace ./supersecret 2> supersecret2_trace.txt
Killed
donnie@fedora:~$
```

This time, strace was prevented from doing its job.

9. Even with the -U option, you'll still get some output sent to the output file. However, it will be much less than you got without the -U. Verify that by counting the lines in the supersecret2_ trace.txt file.

```
donnie@fedora:~$ wc -l supersecret2_trace.txt
34 supersecret2_trace.txt
donnie@fedora:~$
```

This time, there are only 34 lines of output, which is way less than the 297 lines that we had without the -U switch. So, this is further proof that the -U option prevents an strace operation from being successful.

10. Now, do an ltrace on the supersecret binary, and save the output to the supersecret2_ltrace. txt file:

```
donnie@fedora:~$ ltrace ./supersecret 2> supersecret2_ltrace.txt
donnie@fedora:~$
```

11. Count the lines in the supersecret2_ltrace.txt file:

```
donnie@fedora:~$ wc -l supersecret2_ltrace.txt
4 supersecret2_ltrace.txt
donnie@fedora:~$
```

Wow! There are only four lines in the output file this time. That's a far cry from the 7270 lines that we had without the -U option.

On FreeBSD, the shc commands to create the obfuscated binary files are identical to what you've seen on Linux. But, to perform system call tracing on FreeBSD binaries, use truss instead of strace, like so:

```
donnie@freebsd14:~ $ truss ./supersecret 2> supersecret1.truss.
txt
```

As far as I've been able to tell, there's no FreeBSD equivalent to the Linux ltrace command.

On macOS, you have the dtrace and dtruss commands. But to use them, you'll have to boot your machine into **Recovery** mode and disable the **System Integrity Protection** (**SIP**). I don't recommend doing that unless you absolutely, positively have to.

You'll also see that dtrace is available on OpenIndiana. But, since shc isn't available on OpenIndiana, I won't bother to cover it.

Next, let's see if we can decrypt this script.

Decrypting shc Binaries

Many years ago, when I showed shc to the students in my first shell scripting class, it was somewhat easy to crack the shc algorithm in order to convert a binary file back to the original shell script. So at that time, shc wasn't a very secure option. Now, due to shc developers taking advantage of improvements in modern operating system kernels, it's a lot harder to crack shc. But, there are a couple of utilities that are *supposed* to crack shc, or at least that's what their developers say.

This might be a bit of a spoiler, but I'll share it anyway.

As you'll soon see, the binaries that shc creates are currently safe from this type of cracking attack. But, there's always the possibility that someone could come up with better cracking tools in the future. So, think of this section as a framework for performing your own tests on any cracking tools that might come out in the future.

Let's take a quick look at these utilities, shall we?

Hands-on Lab: Testing UnSHc

This lab will familiarize you with the UnSHc utility. I'm using a Fedora Server virtual machine, but you can use either another Linux virtual machine or a FreeBSD virtual machine if you desire.

1. Download UnSHc from Github by doing:

    ```
    donnie@fedora-server:~$ git clone https://github.com/yanncam/UnSHc.git
    ```

2. Once it's downloaded, which only takes a few seconds, cd into the UnSHc/latest/ directory, and copy the unshc.sh script to the /usr/local/bin/ directory:

    ```
    donnie@fedora-server:~$ cd UnSHc/latest/
    ```

```
donnie@fedora-server:~/UnSHc/latest$ ls
unshc.sh
donnie@fedora-server:~/UnSHc/latest$ sudo cp unshc.sh /usr/local/bin/
donnie@fedora-server:~/UnSHc/latest$
```

3. In the `UnSHc/sample/` directory, you'll see an example shell script, along with the corresponding C source code file and compiled binary file.

 Note that this C source code file and binary file were both generated by a very old version of `shc`. (The reason why I mention this will become apparent in just a moment.)

Copy the binary file, which is `test.sh.x`, to your home directory:

```
donnie@fedora-server:~/UnSHc/sample$ ls
test.sh  test.sh.x  test.sh.x.c
donnie@fedora-server:~/UnSHc/sample$ cp test.sh.x ~
donnie@fedora-server:~/UnSHc/sample$ cd
donnie@fedora-server:~$
```

4. Attempt to decrypt the `test.sh.x` file, like so:

```
donnie@fedora-server:~$ unshc.sh test.sh.x
```

The output should look something like this:

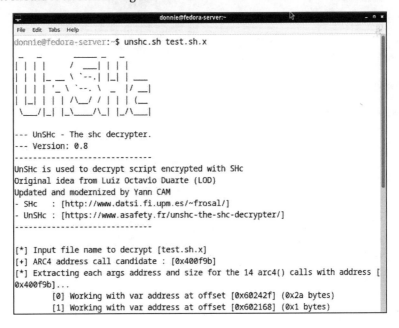

Figure 20.2: Using UnSHc

5. Verify that the test.sh.x binary file actually did get decrypted, like this:

```
donnie@fedora-server:~$ ls -l test*
-rw-r--r--. 1 donnie donnie   193 Jul  5 14:04 test.sh
-rw-r--r--. 1 donnie donnie 11440 Jul  5 14:01 test.sh.x

donnie@fedora-server:~$ cat test.sh
#!/bin/bash
# This script is very critical !
echo "I'm a super critical and private script !"
PASSWORDROOT="SuPeRrOoTpAsSwOrD"';
myService --user=root --password=$PASSWORDROOT > /dev/null 2>&1
donnie@fedora-server:~$
```

Okay, so that works just fine.

6. Next, try to decrypt a binary file that you created with the current version of shc. (You can use the binary file that you created in the *Using shc* lab, or you can create a new one.) Do it like this:

```
donnie@fedora-server:~$ unshc.sh supersecret
. . .

. . .
UnSHc is used to decrypt script encrypted with SHc
Original idea from Luiz Octavio Duarte (LOD)
Updated and modernized by Yann CAM
- SHc   : [http://www.datsi.fi.upm.es/~frosal/]
- UnSHc : [https://www.asafety.fr/unshc-the-shc-decrypter/]
----------------------------
[*] Input file name to decrypt [supersecret]
[-] Unable to define arc4() call address...
donnie@fedora-server:~$
```

As you see this time, the operation failed. So, the binary didn't get decrypted, and the original shell script was not reconstructed.

7. To see why the operation failed this time, go into the UnSHc/ directory and open the README. md file. Close to the top of the file, you'll see this paragraph:

Due to the many problems since shc 4.0.3, there seems to be a need for clarification. In shc 4.0.3 many structural changes have been incorporated, so that shc now makes use of various security mechanisms provided by the linux-kernel itself. Therefore, it is now almost impossible to extract the original shell script at all with current UnSHc version, if the new shc version was used. This requires a more in-depth approach, which means that a modified bash or a modified linux-kernel is needed to bypass the security measures.

So you see that the current version of shc is much more secure than the older versions.

I also tested UnSHc on a FreeBSD machine, and got the same results. That tells me that the security enhancements that prevent you from successfully using UnSHc are also in the current FreeBSD kernel.

Also, I tested another shc cracker that's called deshc-deb. If you'd like to play with it, you can download it by doing:

```
git clone https://github.com/Rem01Gaming/deshc-deb.git
```

(Spoiler alert: deshc-deb doesn't work either.)

Okay, I know, that was a lot of work to show you that something doesn't work. But, I figured that you might want to see for yourself, instead of just accepting my say-so for it. Seriously though, the bottom line is that shc is a good, secure way to obfuscate your scripts, in case you really need to do that. And, due to improvements in the Linux and FreeBSD kernels, the current decrypting utilities no longer work. However, you still need to take precautions to avoid sensitive data leakage, as you'll see a bit later in the *Avoiding Sensitive Data Leakage* section. Next though, let's look at a pair of permissions setting that could get you into trouble.

Understanding SUID and SGID Considerations

SUID and **SGID**, which stand for **Set User Identity** and **Set Group Identity**, are permissions settings that you can place on executable files. These two permissions settings are not only handy, but are also mandatory on certain executable files that deal with certain functions of Linux, Unix, and Unix-like operating systems. However, if you set SUID or SGID on programs that you create yourself, you could be opening your system up to all kinds of security problems. Before I explain why that is, I need to explain what SUID and SGID actually do and why they're needed.

First, let's go into the /bin/ directory, and look at the permissions settings for the rm executable, like so:

```
donnie@fedora:/bin$ ls -l rm
-rwxr-xr-x. 1 root root 61976 Jan 17 19:00 rm
donnie@fedora:/bin$
```

Here's the breakdown of what you're seeing:

- The root root portion of this output indicates that this file belongs to the root user, and is associated with the root user's group.

- The permissions settings are at the beginning of the line, and are divided into three sections. The rwx settings are for the *user* of the file, which in this case is the root user. (In the Linux/ Unix world, we refer to the *owner* of the file as the file's *user*.) The rwx here means that the root user has read, write, and executable permissions for this file.

- The next group of settings, which is r-x, is for the *group*, which in this case is for the root group. This means that members of this group, which in this case consists of only the root user, have read and executable permissions for this file.

- Finally, we have the third group of settings, which again is r-x. This group of settings is for *others*. This means that anyone who isn't the root user or a member of the root group can invoke the rm command, even though the rm executable belongs to the root user. The catch with this is that a normal, unprivileged user can only use rm to remove files and directories with permissions settings that allow the normal user to do so. (Normally, this would mean that the normal user can only remove his or her own files and directories.) Removing any other files and directories with rm requires root privileges.

Now, there are times when a normal user who doesn't have either root or sudo privileges needs to do something that requires root privileges. The most common task of this sort is when a normal user needs to change his or her own password. Changing a password requires modifying the /etc/shadow file on Linux and OpenIndiana systems, and the /etc/master.passwd file on FreeBSD and most other BSD-type systems. But, look at the permissions settings of the shadow file on my Fedora workstation:

```
donnie@fedora:/etc$ ls -l shadow
----------. 1 root root 1072 May 10 17:33 shadow
donnie@fedora:/etc$
```

Okay, this looks very strange, because there are no permissions of any kind on this file for anybody. In reality, the root user does have read and write permissions on this file. It's just that Red Hat-type operating systems, such as Fedora, use another mechanism to grant those permissions to the root user. (I don't want to go into what that mechanism is, because it's beyond the scope of our present topic.)

More typical is what you see on this Debian machine:

```
donnie@debian12:/etc$ ls -l shadow
-rw-r-----. 1 root shadow 1178 Mar 23 13:13 shadow
donnie@debian12:/etc$
```

Here, we see that only the root user has read and write permissions, and that the shadow group only has read permissions. Either way though, a normal user who needs to change his or her own password needs to modify this file, without invoking root or sudo privileges. How can that be accomplished? Well, with SUID, of course.

Adding the SUID permission to an executable file allows any normal user to execute that file with the same privileges as that file's user. For example, look at the permissions settings on the passwd executable:

```
donnie@fedora:/bin$ ls -l passwd
-rwsr-xr-x. 1 root root 32416 Jul 19  2023 passwd
donnie@fedora:/bin$
```

This time, we see rws as the permissions setting for the *user*, which again in this case is the root user. The lower-case s here means that the executable permission is set for the root user, and that the SUID permission is also set. In the third permissions group, you see r-x, which means that normal, unprivileged users can run this program. The SUID permission is what allows the normal user to change his or her own password, which requires modifying either the /etc/shadow file or the /etc/master. passwd file. So now, let's see if this works for Frank, who has no root or sudo privileges:

```
frank@debian12:~$ passwd
Changing password for frank.
Current password:
New password:
Retype new password:
passwd: password updated successfully
frank@debian12:~$
```

Indeed it does, thanks to the SUID setting on the passwd executable.

> I should point out that the SUID setting on the passwd executable only works if a user is setting his or her own password. To set anyone else's password, a user would still need to have the proper sudo privileges. (And no, I don't know how the operating system developers can make SUID work selectively like that.)

The SGID setting on executable files works the same way, except for groups. For example, look at the settings for the write executable:

```
donnie@fedora:/bin$ ls -l write
-rwxr-sr-x. 1 root tty 24288 Apr  7 20:00 write
donnie@fedora:/bin$
```

In this case, you see the s setting in the *group* permissions, which means that any user who executes this program has the same privileges as the associated group. In this case, we're talking about the tty group, which is a system group that allows its members to send output to the terminal. The SGID permission here allows a normal user to use write to send messages to another user who's logged into another terminal, like so:

```
donnie@fedora-server:~$ write frank
The server is shutting down in five minutes.
donnie@fedora-server:~$
```

After entering the write frank command, I hit **Enter**. I then entered the message and hit *Ctrl-d* to actually send the message. Thanks to the SGID setting on write, I was able to make that message show up on Frank's terminal, as you see here:

```
frank@fedora-server:~$
Message from donnie@fedora-server on pts/1 at 17:01 ...
```

```
The server is shutting down in five minutes.
EOF
```

So, what does all this have to do with shell scripting? Well, it's just that even though SUID and SGID are mandatory on certain executable files that are part of the operating system, they can be a security hazard if you set them on executable files that you create. By doing so, you can inadvertently allow normal users to do things that they shouldn't be allowed to do, and you can also allow intruders to invoke malicious code that could affect the entire system.

So, the general rule is to never, but *never*, set either SUID or SGID on programs of your own creation, unless you really know what you're doing and can avoid the security problems.

 By the way, here's how to set the SUID permission on files:

```
donnie@fedora-server:~$ ls -l newscript.sh
-rwxr--r--. 1 donnie donnie 0 Jun 25 17:13 newscript.shdonnie@fedora-server:~$
chmod u+s newscript.sh
donnie@fedora-server:~$ ls -l newscript.sh
-rwsr--r--. 1 donnie donnie 0 Jun 25 17:13 newscript.sh
donnie@fedora-server:~$
```

 Setting SGID looks like this:

```
donnie@fedora-server:~$ ls -l newscript2.sh
-rw-r--r--. 1 donnie donnie 0 Jun 25 17:15 newscript2.sh
donnie@fedora-server:~$ chmod g+s newscript2.sh
donnie@fedora-server:~$ ls -l newscript2.sh
-rw-r-Sr--. 1 donnie donnie 0 Jun 25 17:15 newscript2.sh
donnie@fedora-server:~$
```

But, for shell scripters, there's a bit of good news. That is, if you set either SUID or SGID on a shell script, it will have no effect at all. This is because the kernels of Linux, Unix, and Unix-like operating systems contain code that cause the operating system to ignore SUID and SGID settings on any executable script file that contains a shebang line. So, contrary to what you might see in other shell scripting tutorials, setting either of these dangerous permissions on your scripts isn't a problem, because they will have absolutely zero effect. However, they *might* have an effect on any binary files that you create with shc, so watch out for them.

Unfortunately, I haven't been able to extensively test the effects of SUID and SGID permissions on the binary files that you create with shc. So, just be aware that you don't want to see either of these permissions settings on those binary files.

I should also mention that it is possible to mount filesystem partitions with the nosuid option, which would cause the SUID and SGID permissions to be completely ignored on any files that are within that partition. In fact, many modern Linux and Unix distros already mount certain important partitions, such as the /tmp/ filesystem, with the nosuid option by default. Unfortunately, showing you how to set this option on your own partitions is beyond the scope of this book. In fact, I really can't, because the procedure differs for the various Linux and Unix distros, as well as for the various filesystem formats that they use. If you need to know how to set the nosuid option, your best bet is to consult the documentation for your particular distro.

Okay, let's talk about data leakage.

Avoiding Sensitive Data Leakage

As a systems administrator, there's a very good chance that you'll eventually have to deal with some sort of sensitive data, such as passwords, financial information, or customer information. You'll always want to ensure that your scripts don't inadvertently cause any sensitive data to leak out to any unauthorized people. Let's look at some ways that that could happen, and how to prevent it.

Securing Temporary Files

At some point, you might need to create scripts that store some sort of ephemeral data in a temporary file. Reasons that you might need to do this include:

- Processing a large amount of data without using excessive system memory.
- Storing the intermediate results of some sort of complex operation.
- Storing temporary data for logging debugging information.
- Allowing different processes or scripts to communicate with each other.

Since the /tmp/ directory is the most common place to store temporary files, let's begin this topic with and explanation of it.

Understanding the /tmp/ Directory

As I just said, the most common place to store temporary files is in the /tmp/ directory. The good part about this directory is that it is world-readable and world-writable, as you see here:

```
donnie@fedora-server:~$ ls -ld /tmp
drwxrwxrwt. 17 root root 340 Jun 27 14:27 /tmp
donnie@fedora-server:~$
```

This is good, because it provides a common, well-known place that different scripts and processes can access. Indeed, this directory isn't just used by your shell scripts. It's also used by various operating system processes. Here on the Fedora virtual machine, you see that it's storing temporary data from various systemd processes:

```
donnie@fedora-server:/tmp$ ls -l

total 0
drwx------. 3 root root 60 Jun 27 13:44 systemd-private-
d241f12536d0464393f30d8552359053-chronyd.service-RKt6x4
drwx------. 3 root root 60 Jun 27 13:44 systemd-private-
d241f12536d0464393f30d8552359053-dbus-broker.service-plcC5i
drwx------. 3 root root 60 Jun 27 13:45 systemd-private-
d241f12536d0464393f30d8552359053-httpd.service-SB6D6A
. . .

. . .
drwx------. 3 root root 60 Jun 27 13:44 systemd-private-
d241f12536d0464393f30d8552359053-systemd-resolved.service-uBl3YB
donnie@fedora-server:/tmp$
```

As you see here, every file or directory that gets created in /tmp/ is set with restrictive permissions, so that only the *user* of those files or directories can access them. Also, take another look at the permissions settings for the /tmp/ directory itself:

```
drwxrwxrwt. 17 root root 340 Jun 27 14:27 /tmp
```

At the end of the permissions string, you see a t in place of an x. This means that the executable permission is set for *others*, so in that sense it does the same job as the x. So, anybody can enter that directory. But, the t, which is known as the **sticky bit**, also makes it so that different users can't delete each other's files or directories, unless they have root privileges. (This would be true even if the files and directories were set with world-writable permissions.)

 I know that this is a rather cursory explanation of the sticky bit, but a fuller explanation is beyond the scope of this book. You'll find a lot more about it in my *Mastering Linux Security and Hardening* Book.

Okay, now that you understand the /tmp/ directory, let's look at how you can create scripts that will create temporary files. Understand though, that there are two ways to do it. First there's the wrong way, and then there's the right way.

The Wrong Way to Create Temporary Files

So now, let's say that you really need to write a script that creates temporary files. How would you do it, and how would it be a security concern? Well, before I show you the right way to create temporary files, let me show you the wrong way, in this tmp_file1.sh script:

```
#!/bin/bash
echo "This temporary file contains sensitive data." > /tmp/donnie_temp

cat /tmp/donnie_temp
```

Run this script, and you'll see this in the /tmp/ directory:

```
donnie@fedora-server:~$ ls -l /tmp/donnie_temp
-rw-r--r--. 1 donnie donnie 45 Jun 27 16:02 /tmp/donnie_temp
donnie@fedora-server:~$
```

You see that the read permission is set for the *user*, *group*, and *others*. The write permission is only set for the *user*. So, I'm the only person who can write to this file, but every unprivileged user who's logged into the server can read it. That's not what you want if you're really dealing with sensitive data. The other problem is that this script is using a predictable naming convention for the temporary file, which makes it easy for attackers to perform **sym link attacks**.

Trying to explain how **sym link attacks** work is way beyond the scope of this book. For now, let's just say that they can cause bad things to happen, such as:

Leakage of sensitive data.

Injection of false data.

Denial of service attacks.

If you want to learn more about sym link attacks, check out the references in the *Further Reading* section.

Also, bear in mind that security threats don't always come from unauthorized intruders. Authorized system users who can easily access the /tmp/ directory can also be threats.

Now that you've seen the wrong way to do business, let's look at the right way.

The Right Way to Create Temporary Files

The absolute best way to create temporary files is to use the mktemp utility. Here's how it works from the command-line:

```
donnie@fedora-server:~$ mktemp

/tmp/tmp.StfRN1YkBB

donnie@fedora-server:~$ ls -l /tmp/tmp.StfRN1YkBB

-rw-------. 1 donnie donnie 0 Jun 27 16:50 /tmp/tmp.StfRN1YkBB
donnie@fedora-server:~$
```

This is cool, because it solves both of the problems that we had in the previous demo. First, it automatically sets restrictive permissions on the files that it creates, so that nobody but the person who created them can access them. Secondly, it creates files with random filenames, which makes the files safe from sym link attacks. Let's see how this works in the `tmp_file2.sh` script:

```bash
#!/bin/bash

temp_file=$(mktemp)

echo "This file contains sensitive data." > "$temp_file"
```

In the `temp_file=$(mktemp)` line, I'm using command substitution to assign the output of the `mktemp` command to the `temp_file` variable. Since `mktemp` creates files with random filenames, the name of the temporary file will be different every time you run the script. The `echo` line is just sending some output into the temporary file. Anyway, let's see what we have when we run this script:

```
donnie@fedora-server:~$ ./tmp_file2.sh

donnie@fedora-server:~$ cat /tmp/tmp.sggCBdUd1M
This file contains sensitive data.
donnie@fedora-server:~$
```

As we've already noted above, the file is set with restrictive permissions, so that only I can access it:

```
donnie@fedora-server:~$ ls -l /tmp/tmp.sggCBdUd1M

-rw-------. 1 donnie donnie 35 Jun 27 17:00 /tmp/tmp.sggCBdUd1M
donnie@fedora-server:~$
```

Okay, this is all cool, and it looks good. But, we still don't have a way to automatically delete our temporary files when we no longer need them. I mean, even though they're all set with restrictive permissions, you still don't want them hanging around when they're no longer needed. Now, you might be tempted to just put an `rm` command at the end of the script, as you see here in the `tmp_file3.sh` script:

```bash
#!/bin/bash

temp_file=$(mktemp)

echo "This file contains sensitive data." > "$temp_file"

rm "$temp_file"
```

Sure, that works in a simple script like this one. But, if you're creating a complex script that could possibly exit without running to completion, the `rm` command might not get invoked. So, your best bet is to use a **trap** that will delete the temporary file, even if the script exits prematurely. Here's how that works, in the the `tmp_file4.sh` script:

```
#!/bin/bash

trap 'rm -f "$temp_file"' EXIT

temp_file=$(mktemp)

echo "This file contains sensitive data." > "$temp_file"

ls -l /tmp/tmp*

cat "$temp_file"
```

When you execute a script, it always opens in a new child shell. When the script has either run to completion or has exited prematurely, the child shell closes. The second line in this script, the `trap` line, specifies a command to run when that child shell closes. In this case, we want the `rm -f` command to run. (The `-f` switch forces the `rm` command to delete files without prompting the user.) After the echo line, which sends some text into the temporary file, I've added two lines that will prove that the temporary file really does get created. Anyway, here's what happens when I run the script:

```
donnie@fedora-server:~$ ./tmp_file4.sh

-rw-------. 1 donnie donnie 35 Jun 28 15:07 /tmp/tmp.6t5Qqx5WqZ

This file contains sensitive data.

donnie@fedora-server:~$ ls -l /tmp/tmp*

ls: cannot access '/tmp/tmp*': No such file or directory

donnie@fedora-server:~$
```

So, when I ran the script, it showed me the file and then showed me its contents, as I had hoped it would. But when I ran the `ls -l /tmp/tmp*` command afterwards, it showed that no `tmp` file exists. This proves that the `trap` command in the script really did delete the temporary file.

As good as all this looks, there's still one more modification that I'd like to show you in the `tmp_file5.sh` script, as you see here:

```
#!/bin/bash

trap 'rm -f "$temp_file"' EXIT

temp_file=$(mktemp) || exit 1
```

```
echo "This file contains sensitive data." > "$temp_file"

ls -l /tmp/tmp*

cat "$temp_file"
```

The only thing I did here was to add `|| exit 1` to the `temp_file` line. This makes it so that if for some weird reason the `mktemp` command can't create the temporary file, the script will exit gracefully with exit code 1. In reality, it might not be needed here, because it's almost a sure bet that `mktemp` will be able to create the temporary file. But, it's considered good programming practice to provide a graceful exit mechanism, and it certainly doesn't hurt anything to have it.

 Note that you can also create temporary directories in the `/tmp/` directory by using `mktemp` with the `-d` option switch.

Okay, you now know how to work with temporary files in a secure manner. Now, let's move on to something else that can be a bit of a bugaboo. That is, how to securely use passwords in scripts.

Using Passwords in Shell Scripts

The information in this section can help you out with two different scenarios:

- You need to create a script that a certain administrator or group of administrators will use, and place it where they can all access it. These administrators all have limited privileges, and what they need to do requires the password to some remote server. But, you don't want them to know that password, because you don't want to allow them to actually log into that server. All you want them to do is just one specific job, such as copying files to that server.

- You need to create a script for your own use that requires a password to a remote server. You want to set the script up to automatically run at a regularly scheduled time, as either a `cron` job or as a `systemd` timer job. If the script has to prompt you for a password, the job will be interrupted and won't run to completion.

In both cases, you'll need to embed a password into your script. But, there's a danger that your password might leak out to unauthorized parties. Naturally, you'll want to prevent that. So, let's see how.

Hands-on Lab — Encrypting Passwords

For this scenario, I'll show you a solution that I borrowed from the *How-to Geek* website. It's a good solution as far as it goes, but it's only a partial solution, as you'll soon see. First though, let's encrypt a password and create a script that uses it. Then, I'll show you the complete solution.

I've placed the link to the original *How-to Geek* article in the *Further Reading* section. Also, to avoid re-inventing the proverbial wheel, I won't repeat the extensive explanations that the author of this article has already provided.

1. To begin, you'll need a system with both the openssl and the sshpass packages installed. The openssl package is normally installed on pretty much every Linux, Unix, or Unix-like operating system, so you won't have to worry about that. You'll only need to worry about installing sshpass.

 You'll use openssl to encrypt your password, and sshpass to automatically pass your password to the ssh client.

The sshpass package is in the normal repositories for Fedora, Debian/Ubuntu, and FreeBSD. The package name is the same in all cases, so just use your normal package manager to install it.

Just for fun, I'll be using the FreeBSD virtual machine for this lab, but you can use either of your Linux virtual machines if you desire. (The procedure will be the same, regardless.)

2. Create the .secret_vault.txt file that contains the encrypted password for the remote server that you want to access, like this:

```
donnie@freebsd14:~ $ echo 'Chicken&&Lips' | openssl enc -aes-256-cbc -md
sha512
-a -pbkdf2 -iter 100000 -salt -pass pass:'Turkey&&Lips' > .secret_vault.
txt
donnie@freebsd14:~ $
```

In this command, Chicken&&Lips is the password for the remote server that you want to access, and Turkey&&Lips is the password that you'll need to decrypt the password. (Why you need this decryption password will become clear in a few moments.) Chicken&&Lips is the password that you'll encrypt.

3. Use the chmod 600 .secret_vault.txt command to set the read and write permissions for yourself, and to remove all permissions from everyone else:

```
donnie@freebsd14:~ $ ls -l .secret_vault.txt
-rw-r--r--  1 donnie donnie 45 Jul 31 16:31 .secret_vault.txt
donnie@freebsd14:~ $ chmod 600 .secret_vault.txt
donnie@freebsd14:~ $ ls -l .secret_vault.txt
-rw-------  1 donnie donnie 45 Jul 31 16:31 .secret_vault.txt
donnie@freebsd14:~ $
```

4. Look in the .secret_vault.txt file, and you'll see the sha512 hash value of your remote server password:

```
donnie@freebsd14:~ $ cat .secret_vault.txt
U2FsdGVkX18eeWfcaGbr0/4Fd70vTC3vIjVgymXwfCM=
donnie@freebsd14:~ $
```

5. Create the go-remote.sh script, using your own information for the Remote_User, Remote_Password, and Remote_Server:

```
#!/bin/bash
# name of the remote account
Remote_User=horatio

# password for the remote account
Remote_Password=$(openssl enc -aes-256-cbc -md sha512 -a -d -pbkdf2 -iter
100000 -salt -pass pass:'Turkey&&Lips' < .secret_vault.txt)

# remote computer
Remote_Server=192.168.0.20

# connect to the remote computer and put a timestamp in a file called
script.log

sshpass -p $Remote_Password ssh -T $Remote_User@$Remote_Server << _
remote_commands

echo $USER "-" $(date) >> /home/$Remote_User/script.log

_remote_commands
```

 As you'll see explained in the original *How-to Geek* article, the password for decrypting the Remote_Password has to be in the script, in plain-text. The author of the article doesn't consider this a problem, because the .secret_vault.txt file is a so-called hidden file that's in your own home directory, and because the permissions on it are set so that only the file owner can access it. However, that explanation only makes sense if the plain-text script is in a location that nobody else can access. (I'll explain more about that in just a bit.)

Instead of hard-coding the information for the remote user, remote server, and remote server password into the body of the script, I'm assigning the values for this information to the Remote_User, Remote_Password, and Remote_Server variables. To obtain the decrypted password that I need to assign to the Remote_Password variable, I'm using the stdin (<) redirector to read the password hash from the .secret_vault.txt file into the openssl command.

The sshpass -p command passes Horatio's password, from the Remote_Password variable, to the ssh client. Since we don't need for Horatio to open a remote terminal, we'll disable that with the -T option for ssh. The _remote_commands *here document* contains a single command that will be executed on the remote server. That is, it will create a script.log file that contains a timestamp in Horatio's home directory.

6. In order for this script to work, you'll need to have Horatio's public SSH key for the remote server in your .ssh/known_hosts file. So, before you try to run the script, have Horatio log into the remote server in the normal manner, and then have him log back out, like so:

```
donnie@freebsd14:~ ssh horatio@192.168.0.20
. . .
. . .
horatio@ubuntu2404:~$ exit
donnie@freebsd14:~
```

7. Execute the go-remote.sh script. You should see the login information from the remote server come up momentarily, and then be returned to the command prompt of your local machine.

8. Log into Horatio's account on the remote server. You should see the script.log file that contains a timestamp. It should look something like this:

```
horatio@ubuntu2404:~$ ls -l script.log
-rw-rw-r-- 1 horatio horatio 38 Jul 31 21:34 script.log
horatio@ubuntu2404:~$ cat script.log
donnie - Wed Jul 31 17:34:44 EDT 2024
horatio@ubuntu2404:~$
```

If you see the script.log file in Horatio's home directory, you have achieved coolness. But, is this really a complete solution? Well, no. Let's look at some potential problems that the author of this *How-to Geek* article doesn't address.

Understanding the Problems with this Solution

Again I ask, is the solution that I've just presented a good one? Well, that depends upon a few factors. I mean, if you have the script and the hashed password in your own home directory where only you can access it, it might be okay. But, here's an important consideration. Some operating systems, such as FreeBSD and older implementations of Linux, have users' home directories open to other users by default. Anyone who can get into your home directory can read the encryption password in your plain-text script, and see the name of the file that contains the encrypted password. In fact, let's take a look at that.

Home Directory Permissions on FreeBSD

Here's how it looks on FreeBSD:

```
donnie@freebsd14:~ $ cd ..
donnie@freebsd14:/home $ ls -l
```

```
total 17
drwxr-xr-x  9 donnie   donnie  68 Jul 31 17:52 donnie
drwxr-xr-x  2 horatio horatio 10 Jul 30 17:38 horatio
donnie@freebsd14:/home $ cd horatio/
donnie@freebsd14:/home/horatio $ ls
donnie@freebsd14:/home/horatio $ ls -a
.              .cshrc         .login_conf    .mailrc       .sh_history
..             .login         .mail_aliases  .profile      .shrc
donnie@freebsd14:/home/horatio $
```

As you see, by default, FreeBSD sets the read and execute permissions for *others* on users' home directories. In this case, it means that Horatio can see what's in my directory, and I can see what's in his directory, without having to use any kind of administrative privileges. Fortunately, I can easily fix that for myself, like this:

```
donnie@freebsd14:/home $ chmod 700 donnie/
donnie@freebsd14:/home $ ls -ld donnie/
drwx------  9 donnie donnie 68 Jul 31 18:01 donnie/
donnie@freebsd14:/home $
```

The chmod 700 command preserves the read, write, and execute permissions that I have for myself, and removes all permissions for everyone else. To ensure that any future users have this restrictive permissions settings on their FreeBSD home directories, create the /etc/adduser.conf file with that setting, like this:

```
donnie@freebsd14:~ $ sudo adduser -C
```

This is an interactive utility that prompts you for a lot of information. Accept the defaults for everything except for the Home directory permissions (Leave empty for default): line. For it, enter 700 as the value. Test your setup by creating another user account. You should see that the new user will have restrictive permissions set on his or her home directory, as you see here for the account that I just created for Vicky:

```
donnie@freebsd14:/home $ ls -ld vicky/
drwx------  2 vicky vicky 9 Jul 31 18:04 vicky/
donnie@freebsd14:/home $
```

 Also, keep in mind that when you install FreeBSD, the user account that the installer creates for you will have the more open permissions settings for your home directory. So, after you complete the installation, be sure to set your home directory permissions to the more restrictive value. Then, run the sudo adduser -C command to create the /etc/adduser.conf file, as I've just shown you.

Home Directories on Linux

Home directory permissions on Linux aren't as much of a problem, because many modern Linux distros create home directories with restrictive permissions by default. For example, here's how they look on any Red Hat-type system, such as Fedora, and on Debian 12:

```
donnie@fedora:/home$ ls -l
total 0
drwx------. 1 donnie donnie 25094 Jul 31 13:46 donnie
donnie@fedora:/home$
```

And, here's how they look on Ubuntu 22.04 and newer:

```
donnie@ubuntu2404:/home$ ls -l
total 12
drwxr-x--- 13 donnie  donnie  4096 Jul 31 22:22 donnie
drwxr-x---  3 horatio horatio 4096 Jul 31 21:34 horatio
drwxr-x---  2 vicky   vicky   4096 Jul  6 19:05 vicky
donnie@ubuntu2404:/home$
```

The only difference with Ubuntu is that it has read and execute permissions for the user's private group, where the Red Hat distros and Debian don't. That's okay because either way, nobody can access the home directories except for their respective owners.

Home Directories on Other Linux or Unix Distros

Other Linux or Unix distros might have other ways of doing business with their users' home directories. If you work with any of them, be sure to check the home directory permissions settings, and make any necessary changes.

Okay, that does it for home directory permissions. But, what if you need to place a script somewhere else where other administrators can access it? Let's see what we can do about that.

Hands-on Lab: Making an Untraceable Binary

If other administrators need to access a script that requires an embedded password, you might have to place both it and the encrypted password file into some other directory, such as /usr/local/bin/ or /usr/local/sbin/. In those cases, you'll want to ensure that nobody can read or modify the script, and that nobody can trace it. That's because anyone who can read your script, the go-remote.sh script in this case, can see the password that you need to decrypt the remote server password, as well as the name of the file that contains the remote server password. And of course, anyone who can edit this file can add extra commands to do possibly nasty things on the remote server.

Fortunately, you can easily solve this problem by using shc to turn your scripts into executable binary files, as I showed you a few pages back in the *Controlling Access to Your Scripts* section. But, when you do this, you absolutely *must* use shc with the -U option to make the binary untraceable.

If you don't make your binary files untraceable, anyone who can access the files can use debugging utilities such as strace, truss, dtrace, or dtruss to obtain the plain-text password, even if it has been encrypted with the strongest algorithm known to mankind.

1. To demonstrate, go back to the same virtual machine that you used to create the go-remote. sh script. Turn the script into an executable binary, using shc without the -U option:

```
donnie@freebsd14:~ $ shc -f go-remote.sh -o go-remote
donnie@freebsd14:~ $
```

2. Using truss on FreeBSD or strace on Linux, create the trace1.txt trace file of the go-remote executable.

On FreeBSD:

```
donnie@freebsd14:~ $ truss ./go-remote 2> trace1.txt
```

On Linux:

```
donnie@fedora-server:~$ strace ./go-remote 2> trace1.txt
```

3. Open the trace1.txt file, and scroll down until you see Horatio's password for the remote server. In my own file, it was on line 191, and it looks like this:

```
read(3,"Chicken&&Lips\n",4096)                    = 14 (0xe)
```

Yes indeed, Chicken&&Lips really is Horatio's password for the remote server.

4. Re-create the go-remote binary, using the -U option to make it untraceable:

```
donnie@freebsd14:~ $ shc -Uf go-remote.sh -o go-remote
donnie@freebsd14:~ $
```

5. Repeat *Step 2*, except this time save the output to the trace2.txt file:

6. Open the trace2.txt file and search for Horatio's password. (Spoiler alert: This time, you won't find it.)

 Now, after all this, I need to let you in on a little secret. That is, that neither Horatio's username nor the address of the remote server shows up in the truss or strace output. So, anyone who were to trace your binaries will have the password, but no username or server address. But, don't think that you're all good because of this. Remember, you need to think like a malicious hacker. Any malicious hacker worth his or her salt would already have used other means to map the servers on your network, and would have found a way to enumerate a list of possible usernames. So, even though this procedure only gives hackers one piece of the puzzle, it's still an important piece that can be combined with the other pieces.

All right, I think we're about through with this topic. Let's now take a quick look at secure coding practices.

Understanding Command Injection with eval

Another major problem with shell script security involves scripts that accept input from untrusted users or untrusted sources. If the script is coded incorrectly, an attacker could use it to inject malicious commands as the script's input. Before we look at examples of that, let's look the eval command, which facilitates passing data or commands into a script.

Using eval on the Command-line

The eval command is a shell builtin that's available on most shells. It's very handy when used properly, but dangerous when used improperly. Before we get into that, let's look at how eval works on the command-line.

Okay, eval is one of those commands that can be really complex to fully understand. So, to keep things simple, I'll be presenting some rather simplistic eval demos in this section. Even though they'll demonstrate things that you'll never do in real life, they'll serve the purpose of demonstrating the concepts.

For anyone who would like to see more in-depth coverage of eval, I'll drop some links into the *Further Reading* section.

The best way to think of eval is that you can use it to dynamically process commands that the shell would normally treat as meaningless text strings. For example, let's say that we want to find the date from three weeks ago. We would use date with the --date= option, like this:

```
donnie@fedora-server:~$ date
Wed Aug  7 02:48:23 PM EDT 2024
donnie@fedora-server:~$ date --date="3 weeks ago"
Wed Jul 17 02:48:25 PM EDT 2024
donnie@fedora-server:~$
```

As you see, I just used the "3 weeks ago" text string as the argument for the --date option, which works just fine. Now, let's assign this date command to the threeweeksago variable and echo back the results, like this:

```
donnie@fedora-server:~$ threeweeksago='date --date="3 weeks ago"'
donnie@fedora-server:~$ echo $threeweeksago
date --date="3 weeks ago"
donnie@fedora-server:~$
```

As you see, the echo command just returned the text string that I assigned to the variable. For some real magic, watch what happens when I replace echo with eval:

```
donnie@fedora-server:~$ eval $threeweeksago
Thu Jul 18 04:02:14 PM EDT 2024
donnie@fedora-server:~$
```

Now, let's wait a few minutes and run this again.

```
donnie@fedora-server:~$ eval $threeweeksago
Thu Jul 18 04:05:10 PM EDT 2024
donnie@fedora-server:~$
```

Look carefully, and you'll see that the second eval command has updated the time value. This sort of thing can be handy in scripting, because it allows you to assign a command to a variable, and then use that variable throughout the rest of the script. This allows you to execute the command in various parts of the script, without having to type out the entire command multiple times. But, as I've already mentioned, there's both a safe way and a dangerous way to use eval. Let's first look at the safe way.

Using eval Safely

Let's take a look at the eval-test1.sh script to see a simple example of safe eval usage:

```
#!/bin/bash

threeweeksago='date --date="3 weeks ago"'
eval $threeweeksago
```

Running the script looks like this:

```
donnie@fedora-server:~$ ./eval-test1.sh
Thu Jul 18 04:19:25 PM EDT 2024
donnie@fedora-server:~$
```

The reason this is safe is because we're feeding eval a text string that comes from within the script itself. As long as you have the permissions on this script locked down so that nobody can modify it, it's perfectly sane and safe. Using eval in this way makes it impossible for attackers to insert their own malicious commands.

Of course, this script is rather pointless, because it doesn't do anything at all useful. So, let's look at a more practical example in the eval-test2.sh script:

```
#!/bin/bash

desiredDate='date --date="1 month ago"'
datestamp=$(eval "$desiredDate")

echo "I'm creating a report with the $datestamp timestamp in the filename." >
```

```
somefile_"$datestamp".txt
```

Here, I'm using eval within a command substitution construct to create the value for the datestamp variable. I'll use then use this datestamp variable to insert a datestamp into both the text file, and the name of the text file. Here's how it looks when I run the script:

```
donnie@fedora-server:~$ ./eval-test2.sh
donnie@fedora-server:~$ ls -l somefile_Thu*
-rw-r--r--. 1 donnie donnie 90 Aug  8 16:42 'somefile_Thu Jul 18 04:42:31 PM
EDT 2024.txt'

donnie@fedora-server:~$ cat "somefile_Thu Jul 18 04:42:31 PM EDT 2024.txt"
I'm creating a report with the Thu Jul 18 04:42:31 PM EDT 2024 timestamp in the
filename.
donnie@fedora-server:~$
```

As you see, it works just fine. And, if I were to run this command a few moments later, I would see a new file with a new timestamp. And of course, if I were to decide to change the --date value to something else, such as "1 month ago", I would only have to make the change in the desiredDate= line, instead of having to change it multiple times throughout the script.

So, now that I've shown you the safe way to use eval, let's look at the dangerous way.

Using eval Dangerously

The eval-test3.sh script shows a very simple example of what you *never* want to do:

```
#!/bin/bash
eval $1
```

Yeah, I know what you're thinking. Nobody would ever create such a simplistic script that uses eval in this manner. That's okay though, because it serves the purpose of demonstrating the concept. Let's try it out to see what happens.

```
donnie@fedora-server:~$ ./eval-test3.sh 'date --date="1 day ago"'
Wed Aug  7 05:14:48 PM EDT 2024
donnie@fedora-server:~$
```

As you see, the date command gets passed into eval as positional parameter $1. This seems safe enough, but is it really? The key here is that anyone who runs this script can insert any command that he or she wants to run. For example, let's say that this script is in the /usr/local/bin/ directory. The permissions are set so that nobody can modify it, but also so that every non-privileged user can execute it. So, what could a malicious hacker accomplish with this? Let's see.

```
donnie@fedora-server:~$ eval-test3.sh 'cat /etc/passwd'
root:x:0:0:root:/root:/bin/bash
bin:x:1:1:bin:/bin:/sbin/nologin
. . .
```

```
. . .
charlie:x:1009:1009::/home/charlie:/usr/bin/zsh
horatio:x:1010:1010::/home/horatio:/bin/bash
donnie@fedora-server:~$
```

This particular example might not seem like a big deal, because the `passwd` file is world-readable anyway. But then, it could be a big deal under certain circumstances. For example, let's say that you're running a web server, and you have a shell script set up as a CGI script.

 CGI stands for **Common Gateway Interface**. You can create CGI scripts from various programming languages, including shell scripting. These CGI scripts can perform various functions on web servers, such as counting users, or even serving out content.

A full explanation of setting up web servers and how to hack them is way beyond the scope of this book. For now, let's just say that there are some clever hackers out there who can find and exploit poorly designed CGI scripts on web servers. That's especially true if the web server security isn't set up properly.

A malicious hacker who hasn't been able to log into the web server wouldn't be able to view the `passwd` file. But, if he or she were to find that this poorly-designed script is performing some sort of CGI function, he or she might be able to view the `passwd` file to enumerate the server's users. (But then, maybe not. Proper web server security measures might prevent this from happening, even if the script is insecure.)

For another example that might be more probable, let's say that you've placed the `eval-test3.sh` script in the `/usr/local/sbin/` directory, and have it set up so that only the root user has executable permissions, like this:

```
donnie@fedora-server:/usr/local/sbin$ ls -l eval-test3.sh
-rwx------. 1 root root 21 Aug  8 17:20 eval-test3.sh
donnie@fedora-server:/usr/local/sbin$
```

You then invoke the `sudo visudo` command to set up Charlie so that he has root privileges to run the `eval-test3.sh` script, but nothing else. Here's the line that does that:

```
charlie ALL=(ALL)          /usr/local/sbin/eval-test3.sh
```

Let's see how that works.

```
charlie@fedora-server:~$ eval-test3.sh 'cat /etc/passwd'
bash: /usr/local/sbin/eval-test3.sh: Permission denied
charlie@fedora-server:~$ sudo eval-test3.sh 'cat /etc/passwd'
[sudo] password for charlie:
root:x:0:0:root:/root:/bin/bash
. . .
. . .
```

```
charlie:x:1009:1009::/home/charlie:/usr/bin/zsh
horatio:x:1010:1010::/home/horatio:/bin/bash
charlie@fedora-server:~$
```

Charlie didn't do any harm this time, but what about next time? Let's see:

```
charlie@fedora-server:~$ sudo eval-test3.sh 'systemctl stop httpd'
charlie@fedora-server:~$
```

This time, Charlie did some real damage. He shut down the web server, causing a Denial-of-Service attack. Ordinarily, Charlie wouldn't have the power to do this. But, because he has sudo privileges to run the eval-test3.sh script, and that script contains the eval $1 line, Charlie can now run any command he wants to run, including system administrative commands.

As I said at the beginning of this section, I've tried to keep the explanation of eval simple. To see more complex and somewhat more realistic eval scenarios, I would like to draw your attention to two really good articles that I've found. The first one is on Medium.com, and is the absolute best write-up I've found that covers a real-world way to exploit poorly-written scripts with eval:

The perils of Bash eval:

https://medium.com/dot-debug/the-perils-of-bash-eval-cc5f9e309cae

The second one, at the Earthly.dev site, shows how to perform a **reverse shell attack** with an eval script. (If you don't know what a reverse shell attack is, you'll find the explanation in the article.) Anyway, you can find it here:

Bash eval: Understanding and (Safely) Using the Power of Dynamic Code Evaluation:
https://earthly.dev/blog/safely-using-bash-eval/

Also, there has been at least one instance of a real-life shell script vulnerability that involved an incorrect usage of eval. This involved the installation script for Gradle, which is an automated build tool for software development. You can read about it here:

CVE-2021-32751:

https://cve.mitre.org/cgi-bin/cvename.cgi?name=CVE-2021-32751

Now that you understand the dangers of eval, let's consider whether or not we even have to use it.

Using Alternatives to eval

Many times, you'll be able to use a safe alternative to eval. Let's look at a few examples.

Using Command Substitution

In the eval-test1.sh script that I showed you at the beginning of this section, you could have replaced eval with a command substitution construct.

Here's how it looks in the `eval-test1-alternative.sh` script:

```
#!/bin/bash

threeweeksago=$(date --date="3 weeks ago")
echo $threeweeksago
```

Run the script, and you'll see that it behaves exactly the same as the `eval` version:

```
donnie@fedora-server:~$ ./eval-test1-alternative.sh
Mon Jul 22 04:36:14 PM EDT 2024
donnie@fedora-server:~$ ./eval-test1-alternative.sh
Mon Jul 22 04:37:23 PM EDT 2024
donnie@fedora-server:~$
```

Granted, it doesn't really matter in this case, because the script doesn't accept external input. So, it's perfectly safe to use `eval` with it. But, if you create a script that does accept external input and you have the choice between using `eval` and using command substitution, your best bet is to go with command substitution.

 Remember: Always go with the safest option for your scripts.

Evaluating if eval is Necessary

In some cases, using `eval` doesn't even do anything that we can't do without it. For example, look at the `eval-test4.sh` script:

```
#!/bin/bash
a=$1
eval echo $(( a + 1 ))
```

When you run this script, you'll pass in a number as positional parameter $1. The arithmetic operator in the `eval` line will increment the number by 1, and display the result. Here's how that looks:

```
donnie@fedora-server:~$ ./eval-test4.sh 36
37
donnie@fedora-server:~$
```

Now, let's remove the `eval` command, so that the script looks like this:

```
#!/bin/bash
a=$1
echo $(( a + 1 ))
```

Running the script without eval gives us this:

```
donnie@fedora-server:~$ ./eval-test4.sh 36
37
donnie@fedora-server:~$
```

The output is identical to what it was when we used eval, which tells me that eval isn't even needed here. So, the only thing that eval does here is to add an attack vector that we definitely don't need.

 Remember: Don't use eval when it isn't necessary.

A similar scenario involves assigning a command to a variable, as we see here in the eval-test5.sh script:

```
#!/bin/bash
checkWebserver="systemctl status httpd"
eval $checkWebserver
```

Running this script will indeed show us the status of the web server service:

```
donnie@fedora-server:~$ ./eval-test5.sh
● httpd.service - The Apache HTTP Server
 . . .
 . . .
```

As before, we can accomplish the same thing without using eval at all, as you see here in the eval-test6.sh script:

```
#!/bin/bash
checkWebserver="systemctl status httpd"
$checkWebserver
```

Run this script, and the results will be identical to what they were when you used eval. So again, eval isn't needed.

Another example of this is the value5.sh script that I showed you in *Chapter 10—Understanding Functions*. To refresh your memory, here's what it looks like:

```
#!/bin/bash
valuepass() {
        local __internalvar=$1
        local myresult='Shell scripting is cool!'
        eval $__internalvar="'$myresult'"
}
```

```
valuepass result
echo $result
```

I've already explained this in *Chapter 10*, so for now I'll just say that I'm using eval here as a mechanism to help pass values in and out of the valuepass function. But, if you refer back to *Chapter 10*, you'll see that this is only one of several methods that I showed you for passing values in and out of a function. Using eval here is perfectly safe, since this script is only passing values internally. But, if you ever need to create a function that accepts external values from either the script's user or an external text file, you'll want to use one of the alternative methods.

I think that covers it for eval. Let's look at one last possible coding problem, and then move on to the next chapter.

Understanding Path Security

The possibility—however remote it may be—exists that someone could plant a trojaned version of some system utility on your system, and then manipulate a user's PATH setting so that the trojaned utility would be invoked, instead of the real one. The trojaned utility could do a variety of nasty things, such as exfiltrating sensitive data or performing a ransomware attack by encrypting important files. Before I show you a script, let's see how this looks on the command-line. Let's begin by showing you where the executable file for the normal ls command is located:

```
donnie@fedora-server:~$ which ls
alias ls='ls --color=auto'
    /usr/bin/ls
donnie@fedora-server:~$
```

We see that it's located in the /usr/bin/ directory, as it should be. Now, let's create a bogus ls, in the form of a script, and place it into the /tmp/ directory. Here's the ls script:

```
#!/bin/bash
echo "This is a trojaned ls file. This command does something nasty."
/usr/bin/ls
```

Of course, the echo command is harmless, but a real malicious hacker would replace that with something that isn't harmless. After running the malicious command, the script will then invoke the normal ls command.

Next, let's manipulate the user's PATH setting so that this script will get invoked instead of the real ls.

```
donnie@fedora-server:~$ PATH=/tmp:$PATH
donnie@fedora-server:~$
```

Finally, we'll invoke ls:

```
donnie@fedora-server:~$ ls
This is a trojaned ls file. This command does something nasty.
```

```
 04:26:53              Jul
 18                    link.txt
 . . .

 . . .

 ip_addresses.csv           variables.txt
 ipaddress_list_2024-06-03.txt
donnie@fedora-server:~$
```

This time, the bogus ls was invoked, because the /tmp/ directory is the first directory in the user's PATH setting.

By default, the shell scripts that you create will use your normal PATH settings to find the utilities and programs that the script invokes. For example, when you want to invoke the ls command in a script, just add a line that says ls instead of /usr/bin/ls. By doing that though, any attacker who can manipulate a user's PATH setting could cause the script to run a bogus, trojaned program. There are three things you can do to prevent that.

- **Method 1:** Make the script unreadable and untraceable, as I showed you in the first portion of this chapter. That way, attackers won't be able to see which utilities that the script is invoking, which means that they won't know which utilities to replace with a trojaned version.

- **Method 2:** Explicitly set a new PATH at the top of the script. Here's how that would look, in the path-test1.sh script:

```
#!/bin/bash
PATH=/bin:/sbin:/usr/local/bin:/usr/local/sbin
ls -l
```

- **Method 3:** Use the entire path to every command that you place in the script. So, for example, when you want to invoke awk, have the line say /bin/awk instead of just awk.

One problem with the third method is that it could make your scripts less portable. That's because some operating systems, such as FreeBSD, might have the executable files for certain utilities stored in directories that are different from what you're used to. For example, FreeBSD has the executable files for many of its utilities in the /usr/local/bin/ directory, instead of in the /usr/bin/ as we're used to seeing on Linux operating systems. So, if you want to ensure that your scripts will run on as many operating systems as possible, your best bet is to forget about Method 3. Using Method 2 will be much easier and just as effective.

And now, you're wondering how an attacker could possibly manipulate someone's PATH setting like this. Well, I can think of two possible scenarios.

Attack Scenario 1: Compromising the User's Account

One way that an attacker can manipulate a user's PATH setting is to first gain access to the user's account. If the attacker has already accomplished that, then it's game over anyway and path security would be the least of the user's problems. So, your best bet would be to ensure that users' accounts are configured securely, to prevent anyone from breaking in.

Attack Scenario 2: Social Engineering

An attacker could also possibly use social engineering to trick a user into running a program that would alter the user's shell configuration files.

 In the world of cybersecurity, **social engineering** can take many forms. For example, it can come by way of a scam email with a link to a malicious file, or it could come by way of a face-to-face encounter. In any case, the goal is to convince the victim to perform some sort of action that could cause a breach of security.

For this scenario, I'm using the Fedora Server virtual machine.

1. First, let's look at the `harmless-program.sh` script:

    ```
    #!/bin/bash

    echo "This program is harmless."
    echo "Trust me!"

    echo "PATH=/tmp:$PATH" >> /home/"$USER"/.bashrc
    echo "export PATH" >> /home/"$USER"/.bashrc
    ```

2. Run the script, and note that it places an extra PATH directive at the end of the `.bashrc` file. This extra directive overrides the PATH directive that's at the top of the file. This new setting won't take effect right away, but it will the next time that the user either logs into the system or opens another terminal window.

3. Log out and then log back in again. Prepare to be amazed at what happens when you try to do a directory listing:

    ```
    donnie@fedora-server:~$ ls
    You've just been pwned!
    You really should learn to protect yourself
    against social engineering attacks.
     acl_demo.sh              link.txt
    . . .

    . . .
    ipaddress_count.sh         user_activity_original.sh
     ip_addresses.csv          user_agent.tsv
     ipaddress_list_2024-06-03.txt     variables.txt
    donnie@fedora-server:~$
    ```

Of course, in real life the script would have done something a bit more nasty. Also, distributing this sort of malicious program as a script would be a bit obvious.

4. So, let's use shc to convert this to an untraceable executable binary. Also, use the -r option so that the binary will execute on other Linux machines.

```
donnie@fedora-server:~$ shc -rUf harmless-program.sh -o harmless-program
donnie@fedora-server:~$
```

5. Before you try to execute the binary, open the .bashrc file in your text editor, and delete the two lines that were added by the script.

6. Log out and then log back in.

7. Execute the new harmless-program binary.

8. Log out and then log back in. Then, execute the ls command. You should see the same results that you saw in Step 3.

9. Finally, open the .bashrc file in your text editor and delete the two lines that were added by the harmless-program program.

> If you do a web search for articles related to shell scripting security, you'll find several that talk about path security attacks. Curiously though, I've never seen a single one that explains how someone might execute such an attack.
>
> Also, this scenario provides a prime example of why all personnel who use a computer should learn to recognize and avoid social engineering attacks.

Okay, I think that this about covers things for this topic. So, let's wrap up and move on.

Summary

In this chapter, we covered topics that are important to a security-conscious Linux or Unix administrator. We began with a discussion of how to control access to your important scripts, and showed various methods of doing so. Next, we looked at considerations about the SUID and SGID permissions settings, and then we looked at a few different ways to prevent your scripts from leaking sensitive data. We then looked at how using the eval command in scripts can be quite dangerous, and wrapped up with a discussion of path security.

In the next chapter, we'll talk about debugging buggy scripts. I'll see you there.

Questions

1. Which of the following is true about the eval command?

    a. It's always safe to use eval in your scripts.

    b. It's always dangerous to use eval in your scripts.

    c. It's only safe to use eval in your scripts if it only takes input from and external source.

    d. It's only safe to use eval in your scripts if it only takes input from within your script.

2. Which two of the following statements are true about the /tmp/ directory? (Choose two.)

    a. It's completely secure, because only administrative users can enter it.

    b. Anybody can create files in it.

    c. Anybody can read files that mktemp creates in the /tmp/ directory.

    d. Any files that mktemp creates in the /tmp/ directory can only be read by the user who created them.

3. How would you prevent an attacker from obtaining information from a binary that you've created with shc?

    a. It's never possible to obtain information from an shc binary.

    b. Use shc with the -U option.

    c. Use shc with the -u option.

    d. There's nothing you can do to prevent this.

4. Before you set an Access Control List on a file, what must you do to that file?

    a. Remove all permissions from *group* and *others*.

    b. There's nothing that you need to do.

    c. Ensure that *user*, *group*, and *others* all have read, write, and execute permissions.

    d. Change ownership of the file to the root user.

5. What's the best way to ensure that any temporary files that your script creates in the /tmp/ directory always get deleted?

    a. After you run the script, go into the /tmp/ directory and delete the temporary files yourself.

    b. Automatically delete the files with an rm command at the end of the script.

    c. Automatically delete the files with a trap command at the beginning of the script.

    d. No action is needed, because your script will always automatically delete its temporary files.

Further Reading

- Setting and Displaying ACLs on ZFS File in Compact Format—Oracle Solaris ZFS Administration Guide: https://docs.oracle.com/cd/E23823_01/html/819-5461/gbchf.html#scrolltoc

- Shell Scripts and Security: https://stackoverflow.com/questions/8935162/shell-scripts-and-security

- Shell Script Security: https://developer.apple.com/library/archive/documentation/OpenSource/Conceptual/ShellScripting/ShellScriptSecurity/ShellScriptSecurity.html

- How to Securely Work with Temporary Files in Linux Shell Scripting: https://youtu.be/zxswimoojh4?si=ERfbJ04U2LJzQE60

- Why is SUID disabled for shell scripts but not for binaries?: https://security.stackexchange.com/questions/194166/why-is-suid-disabled-for-shell-scripts-but-not-for-binaries

- Dangers of SUID shell scripts: `https://www.drdobbs.com/dangers-of-suid-shell-scripts/199101190`
- Using the trap builtin to catch interrupts for graceful event handling in the shell: `https://www.shellscript.sh/trap.html`
- Reverse Engineering Tools in Linux—strings, nm, ltrace, strace, LD_PRELOAD: `https://www.thegeekstuff.com/2012/03/reverse-engineering-tools/`
- Reverse Engineering with strace: `https://function61.com/blog/2017/reverse-engineering-with-strace/`
- How to Use Encrypted Passwords in Bash Scripts: `https://www.howtogeek.com/734838/how-to-use-encrypted-passwords-in-bash-scripts/`
- Beginners Guide for eval Command on Linux: `https://linuxtldr.com/eval-command/`
- How to Use eval in Linux Bash Scripts: `https://www.howtogeek.com/818088/bash-eval/`
- Eval Command and Security Issues: `http://mywiki.wooledge.org/BashFAQ/048`
- Code Injection: `https://owasp.org/www-community/attacks/Code_Injection`
- Securing Shell Scripts: `https://www.admin-magazine.com/Archive/2021/64/Best-practices-for-secure-script-programming`

Answers

1. d
2. b and d
3. b
4. a
5. c

Join our community on Discord!

Read this book alongside other users, Linux experts, and the author himself.

Ask questions, provide solutions to other readers, chat with the author via Ask Me Anything sessions, and much more. Scan the QR code or visit the link to join the community.

`https://packt.link/SecNet`

21

Debugging Shell Scripts

If you've ever written a beautiful looking script, only to be disappointed when it doesn't work properly, don't feel alone. This happens to all of us, and even happened to me a few times when I was creating scripts for this book. (I know, shocking, right?)

The debugging process should begin the moment that you begin to design your code. Put careful thought into the design, test each portion as you write it, and—for goodness' sake—use a text editor with color-coded syntax highlighting. (That color highlighting will prevent you from making a multitude of typographical errors.)

Topics in the chapter include:

- Understanding common scripting errors
- Not Enough Quoting
- Creating a Wild Loop
- Using shell script debugging tools and techniques
- Using echo Statements
- Using xtrace for Debugging
- Checking for Undefined Variables
- Checking for Errors with the -e Option
- Using bash Debugger
- Debugging a script with bashdb
- Getting help with bashdb

If you're ready, let's get started.

Technical Requirements

For this chapter, I'm mainly just using the Fedora workstation that I'm using to create this Word file. But, you can use whichever Linux virtual machine that you like, as long as it has a desktop environment installed. (One of the demos requires a desktop.)

For the final topic, I'll show you how to install and use `bashdb` on Debian/Ubuntu, Fedora, FreeBSD, and macOS.

As always, you can grab the scripts by doing:

```
git clone https://github.com/PacktPublishing/The-Ultimate-Linux-Shell-
Scripting-Guide.git
```

Understanding Common Scripting Errors

The most important step in debugging is understanding the common errors that could cause your scripts to either outright fail, or to give you incorrect results. Let's look at a few examples.

Not Enough Quoting

You can have a few different problems if you don't surround variable names with quotes. Here are some examples.

Filenames with Blank Spaces

For this demo, I've moved into an empty directory in order to keep the files I'll be creating separate from the files in my main home directory. I want to create some files with a timestamp in the filename. To do that, I'll use the `date` command, without any option switches.

First, I'll create a file from the command-line using touch:

```
donnie@fedora:~/quoting_demo$ touch somefile_$(date).txt
donnie@fedora:~/quoting_demo$
```

Okay, let's look at the file:

```
donnie@fedora:~/quoting_demo$ ls -l
total 0
-rw-r--r--. 1 donnie donnie 0 Aug 20 15:08 03:08:51
-rw-r--r--. 1 donnie donnie 0 Aug 20 15:08 20
-rw-r--r--. 1 donnie donnie 0 Aug 20 15:08 2024.txt
-rw-r--r--. 1 donnie donnie 0 Aug 20 15:08 Aug
-rw-r--r--. 1 donnie donnie 0 Aug 20 15:08 EDT
-rw-r--r--. 1 donnie donnie 0 Aug 20 15:08 PM
-rw-r--r--. 1 donnie donnie 0 Aug 20 15:08 somefile_Tue
donnie@fedora:~/quoting_demo$
```

Whoa, now. What's going on here? Instead of having one file, I have seven. Each file has a portion of the current date in its filename. Well, the problem is that `date`, without any option switches, produces output with blank spaces in it, like this:

```
donnie@fedora:~/quoting_demo$ date
```

```
Tue Aug 20 03:13:23 PM EDT 2024
donnie@fedora:~/quoting_demo$
```

So when the shell saw those blank spaces, it thought that I wanted to create multiple files, instead of just one. Let's delete all of these files, and try this again with some quotes:

```
donnie@fedora:~/quoting_demo$ touch somefile_"$(date)".txt
donnie@fedora:~/quoting_demo$ ls -l
total 0
-rw-r--r--. 1 donnie donnie 0 Aug 20 15:15 'somefile_Tue Aug 20 03:15:37 PM EDT
2024.txt'
donnie@fedora:~/quoting_demo$
```

You see how I've surrounded the command substitution construct with a pair of double quotes, which causes the shell to ignore the blank spaces. So now, I have just one file with the correct filename.

Problems with Unset Variables

For our next scenario, let's look at the quote_problem1.sh script:

```
#!/bin/bash
number=1
if [ $number = 1 ]; then
        echo "Number equals 1"
else
        echo "Number does not equal 1"
fi
```

All it does is to tell us whether or not the value of number is 1. Running the script looks like this:

```
donnie@fedora:~$ ./quote_problem1.sh
Number equals 1
donnie@fedora:~$
```

Okay, it works fine. Now, I'll edit the file to change the value of number to 2, and run the script again. Here's how that looks:

```
donnie@fedora:~$ ./quote_problem1.sh
Number does not equal 1
donnie@fedora:~$
```

Now, let's try that with an unset variable, as you see in quote_problem2.sh:

```
#!/bin/bash
number=
if [ $number = 1 ]; then
        echo "Number equals 1"
else
```

```
        echo "Number does not equal 1"
fi
```

When we say that a variable is unset, it just means that we defined the variable, but haven't assigned a value to it. Let's see what happens with I try to run this script.

```
donnie@fedora:~$ ./quote_problem2.sh
./quote_problem2.sh: line 4: [: =: unary operator expected
Number does not equal 1
donnie@fedora:~$
```

The problem is that the if [$number = 1] test is looking for some sort of value for the number variable. But, number has no value, which breaks the test. Fortunately, it's an easy fix. All I'll have to do is to surround the $number that's in the test statement with a pair of double quotes, as you see in quote_problem3.sh:

```
#!/bin/bash
number=
if [ "$number" = 1 ]; then
        echo "Number equals 1"
else
        echo "Number does not equal 1"
fi
```

Running this script will show the correct results:

```
donnie@fedora:~$ ./quote_problem3.sh
Number does not equal 1
donnie@fedora:~$
```

This works because instead of having no value at all as we had before, number now effectively has the value of a blank space. A blank space isn't equal to 1, so the script works.

 It's normally better to always assign an initial value to your variables as you create them, in order to prevent these kinds of problems. However, it's sometimes desirable to use an unset variable. For example, you might want your script to do one thing if a variable is unset, or to do something else if the variable is set with a value. That's perfectly fine as long as you know how to use quotes to avoid these kinds of parsing problems.

To make this a bit more realistic, let's make quote_problem4.sh so that it will accept a user-defined value:

```
#!/bin/bash
number=$1
if [ $number = 1 ]; then
        echo "Number equals 1"
```

```
else
        echo "Number does not equal 1"
fi
```

Let's see how it works with different values:

```
donnie@fedora:~$ ./quote_problem4.sh 1
Number equals 1
donnie@fedora:~$ ./quote_problem4.sh 5
Number does not equal 1
donnie@fedora:~$ ./quote_problem4.sh
./quote_problem4.sh: line 4: [: =: unary operator expected
Number does not equal 1
donnie@fedora:~$
```

It works fine with either 1 or 5 as a value, but doesn't work when I don't supply a value. So, it appears that I forgot to quote the $number. Not to worry, I'll fix that in quote_problem5.sh:

```
#!/bin/bash
number=$1
if [ "$number" = 1 ]; then
        echo "Number equals 1"
else
        echo "Number does not equal 1"
fi
```

Let's see what we have now:

```
donnie@fedora:~$ ./quote_problem5.sh 1
Number equals 1
donnie@fedora:~$ ./quote_problem5.sh 5
Number does not equal 1
donnie@fedora:~$ ./quote_problem5.sh
Number does not equal 1
donnie@fedora:~$
```

It works like a champ, which means that once again, we've achieved coolness.

Since we've been working with tests, let's see what happens when we leave out a space, as I did in space_problem1.sh:

```
#!/bin/bash
number=$1
if ["$number" = 1 ]; then
        echo "Number equals 1"
else
```

```
          echo "Number does not equal 1"
fi
```

It's the same as the `quote_problem5.sh` script, except that I deleted the space between the [and the `"$number"`. Here's what happens when I run it:

```
donnie@fedora:~$ ./space_problem1.sh
./space_problem1.sh: line 4: [: =: unary operator expected
Number does not equal 1
donnie@fedora:~$
```

Amazingly enough, it gives me the exact same error message as when I forgot to quote my `$number` variable. So, this shows us two things. First, you need to be careful about placing spaces in your test conditions. Secondly, you can't always depend upon the shell's error message to tell you exactly what the problem is. In this case, the exact same message showed up for two completely different errors.

But wait! Here's one more way to troubleshoot this problem. We'll just use the -u shell option to check for uninitialized variables, as you see here in the `quote_problem6.sh` script:

```
#!/bin/bash -u
number=$1
if [ $number = 1 ]; then
        echo "Number equals 1"
else
        echo "Number does not equal 1"
fi
```

The only difference between this script and the previous one is that I added -u to the end of the she-bang line. Let's see what happens when I run it without supplying a value for `$1`:

```
donnie@fedora:~$ ./quote_problem6.sh
./quote_problem6.sh: line 3: $1: unbound variable
donnie@fedora:~$
```

This is cool, because it tells us exactly what the problem is, instead of just showing us a generic error message. If you need to see a more verbose message, just add the v option, like this:

```
#!/bin/bash -uv
```

Running the script now looks like this:

```
donnie@fedora:~$ ./quote_problem6.sh
#!/bin/bash -uv
number=$1
```

```
./quote_problem6.sh: line 3: $1: unbound variable
donnie@fedora:~$
```

 When you're finished debugging, be sure to delete the -u or -uv That's because it could cause problems in production scripts.

I'll show you more about using the -u option in just a few pages, in the *Using Shell Script Debugging Tools* section.

For the next problem, you'll need to buckle your seat belt. That's because things are going to get wild.

Creating a Wild Loop

When you create some sort of loop, it's real easy to accidentally create one that will run forever until you stop it. For example, let's look at the wild_loop1.sh script:

```bash
#!/bin/bash
# while loop running wild
count=30
limit=25
while [ "$count" -gt "$limit" ];
do
        echo $count
        (( count = (count + 1)))
done
```

This loop begins with a count value of 30, which will increment by 1 on each iteration of the loop. It's supposed to go until count reaches a value of 25. Okay, I know that the problem is blatantly obvious this time, but bear with me anyway. This could happen if a coder got in a hurry and just didn't notice it. Anyway, trying to run this will output a list of numbers that just keeps on going and going. No matter how fast you hit *Ctrl-c*, the output will scroll past the top of your terminal, so that you'll never get to see the top part of the output. So, I'll fix that by directing the output into a text file. First though, I'll open a second terminal window, and create a blank text file, like this:

```
donnie@fedora:~$ touch wild_loop.txt
donnie@fedora:~$
```

Next, while still in that window, I'll open the file with tail -f, in order to see the file as it gets updated:

```
donnie@fedora:~$ tail -f wild_loop.txt
```

I'll now go back to my first terminal window, and run the wild_loop1.sh script, like this:

```
donnie@fedora:~$ ./wild_loop1.sh > wild_loop.txt
```

I hit *Cntrl-c* after only a few seconds. But, as you see in the second window, the count really went wild:

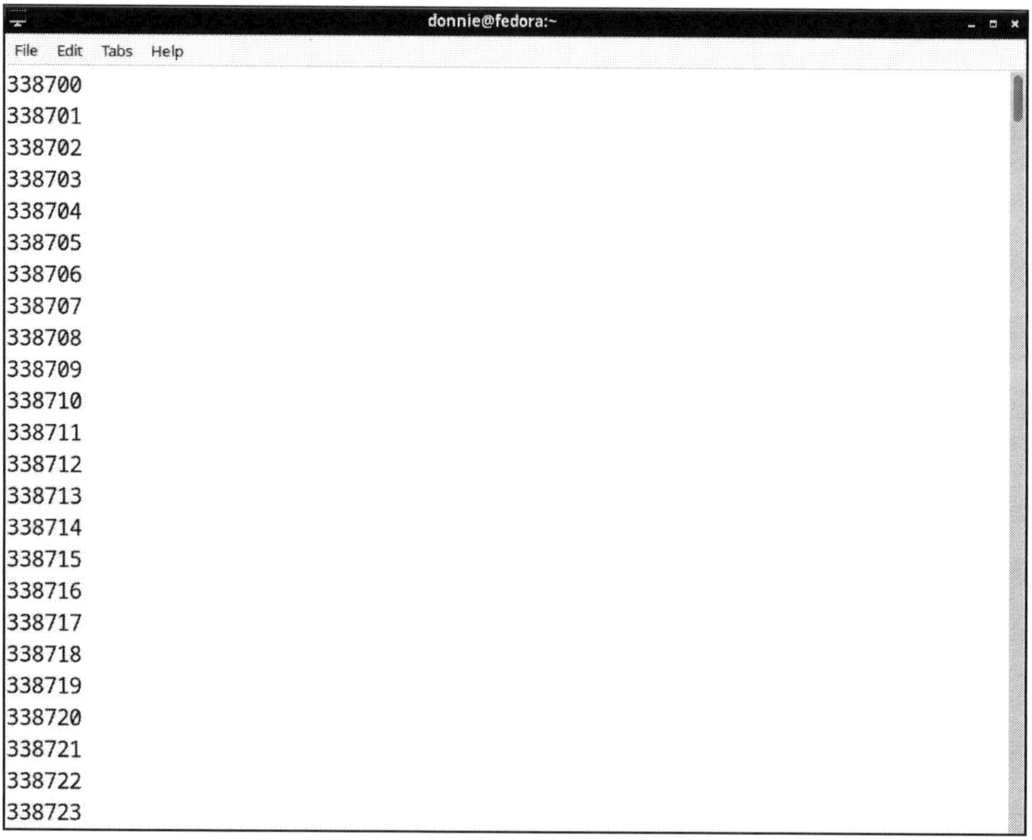

Figure 21.1: The wild loop is going wild!

Open the `wild_loop.txt` file in `less`, and you'll see that the script really does have the output begin at 30.

```
30
31
32
33
. . .
. . .
```

As I said before, the problem here is obvious. It's just that I accidentally reversed the values of count and limit. So, let's fix that in `wild_loop2.sh`:

```bash
#!/bin/bash
# while loop NOT running wild
count=25
limit=30
while [ "$limit" -gt "$count" ];
```

```
do
        echo $count
        (( count = (count + 1)))
done
```

This time, count is set to 25 and limit is set to 30. Running this script should work better. Let's see:

```
donnie@fedora:~$ ./wild_loop2.sh
25
26
27
28
29
donnie@fedora:~$
```

Oh yeah, that looks much better.

> There are a whole lot more shell scripting pitfalls that I could share with you. But, in the interest of not trying to reinvent the proverbial wheel, I'll end this here and instead share a few excellent resources that you might find useful.
>
> Filenames and Pathnames in Shell: How to do it Correctly:
>
> `https://dwheeler.com/essays/filenames-in-shell.html`
>
> Common Shell Script Mistakes:
>
> `https://www.pixelbeat.org/programming/shell_script_mistakes.html`
>
> BashPitfalls:
>
> `http://mywiki.wooledge.org/BashPitfalls`

All right, let's move on to the debugging tools.

Using Shell Script Debugging Tools and Techniques

There are a few different debugging tools that we can use, which include shellcheck, checkbashisms, and shall. We've already looked at them in *Chapter 19—Shell Script Portability*, so we won't look at them again here. Instead, I'll present some tools and techniques that we haven't covered yet.

Using echo Statements

Sometimes, if you have a problem with a shell script that you can't figure out, placing echo statements in strategic locations can help you find the problem.

You may see in other references that some people think of echo statements as the poor man's debugging tool. That's because echo is always available, and can be used if you can't use anything else.

Back in *Chapter 16, Creating User Interfaces with yad, dialog, and xdialog*, I showed you the xdialog-hello2.sh script, which can automatically detect two things.

- It can detect whether or not the Xdialog utility is present.
- It can also detect if your machine has a desktop environment installed.

If both a desktop environment and the Xdialog utility are detected, the script will run the graphical Xdialog utility. Otherwise, the script will run the ncurses-based dialog utility. Here's what the script looks like:

```bash
#!/bin/bash
command -v Xdialog
if [[ $? == 0 ]] && [[ -n $DISPLAY ]]; then
        diag=Xdialog
else
        diag=dialog
fi
$diag --title "Dialog message box" \
        --begin 2 2 \
        --msgbox "\nHowdy folks!" 15 50
clear
```

As a reminder, the DISPLAY environmental variable will have a non-zero length assigned value if a desktop environment is installed, and won't have an assigned value if no desktop environment is installed. The -n in the [[-n $DISPLAY]] statement tests for the presence of a non-zero length assigned value. (The -n actually stands for *non-zero*.) So, if the [[-n $DISPLAY]] test returns a value of 0, which means that the condition is *true*, then a desktop environment has been detected.

Originally though, the script looked like this, as you see in the xdialog-hello2-broken.sh script:

```bash
#!/bin/bash
command -v Xdialog
if [[ -n $DISPLAY ]] && [[ $? == 0 ]]; then
        diag=Xdialog
else
        diag=dialog
fi
$diag --title "Dialog message box" \
```

```
        --begin 2 2 \
        --msgbox "\nHowdy folks!" 15 50
clear
```

As you see, the only difference is that the test conditions in the two scripts are in a different order. The script that works has the [[$? == 0]] test first, and the broken script has the [[-n $DISPLAY]] condition first.

When I tried running the original script, which had [[-n $DISPLAY]] first, it just wouldn't work. I mean, it would work fine on desktop machines that had Xdialog installed or machines that were running in text mode. But, on desktop machines that didn't have Xdialog installed, it would always tell me that it is installed. And of course, running the script would always fail because it was trying to run Xdialog. I couldn't understand the reason for this, so I had to do some troubleshooting.

 I've never installed Xdialog on my Fedora workstation, so I can use it to show you my troubleshooting steps. When you try this demo, be sure to try it on a desktop-type virtual machine that also does not have Xdialog installed.

You can start troubleshooting by placing an echo $? command and a sleep 10 command just under the command -v Xdialog line. The script now looks like this:

```
#!/bin/bash
command -v Xdialog
echo $?
sleep 10
if [[ -n $DISPLAY ]] && [[ $? == 0 ]]; then
        diag=Xdialog
else
        diag=dialog
fi
$diag --title "Dialog message box" \
        --begin 2 2 \
        --msgbox "\nHowdy folks!" 15 50
clear
```

I wanted to see if the exit code would be 0 or 1, and the sleep 10 command would pause the script long enough so that I could see the echo $? output.

 I inserted the sleep 10 command to give myself ten seconds to see the output of the echo $? command. Otherwise, the clear command at the end would clear away the output before I could see it. If you prefer, you can omit the sleep 10 command, and instead just comment out the clear command. Either way works, so the choice is yours.

A 1 would mean that Xdialog is not installed, and a 0 would mean that it is installed. Placing the echo and sleep commands under the command -v Xdialog command would show me if the script was properly detecting if the package was installed. Running the script now looks like this:

```
donnie@fedora:~$ ./xdialog-hello2-broken.sh
1
```

The 1 exit code means that the script properly detects that Xdialog is not present. So, that portion of the script works. Next, you can comment out the whole if. . then. .else stanza, and place an [[-n $DISPLAY]] && echo $? statement and a sleep 10 statement just above it, like this:

```
#!/bin/bash
command -v Xdialog
[[ -n $DISPLAY ]] && echo $?
sleep 10
#if [[ -n $DISPLAY ]] && [[ $? == 0 ]]; then
 #        diag=Xdialog
#else
 #        diag=dialog
#fi
$diag --title "Dialog message box" \
        --begin 2 2 \
        --msgbox "\nHowdy folks!" 15 50
clear
```

Running the script with this modification looks like this:

```
donnie@fedora:~$ ./xdialog-hello2-broken.sh
0
```

The 0 exit code indicates a true condition, which means that a desktop environment is indeed installed. So, that part of the code also works properly.

At this point we need to start thinking logically. If the [[-n $DISPLAY]] returns a 0 exit code, how would that affect the [[$? == 0]] part? Well, it turns out that the $? in the second test condition was looking at the 0 exit code that was returned by the first test condition, instead of the exit code from the command -v Xdialog command. So on a desktop machine, the $? would always be looking at a 0 exit code, whether or not Xdialog was present. Fixing that was just a simple matter of swapping the order of the two test conditions, as you see above in the xdialog-hello2.sh script.

> In hindsight, the solution to this problem should have been obvious. But for some reason I was having a mental block that prevented me from seeing that. It just goes to show that even the best of us can sometimes be buffaloed by simple scripting errors.

All right, let's move on to the next debugging tool.

Using xtrace for Debugging

Using **xtrace** with your problematic scripts shows the actual execution of the commands in the scripts, along with their output. This can help you track down the source of your problems.

You can use xtrace mode in three different ways, which are:

- Append -x to the shebang line. This works for all shells that we've been working with. For example, if you're writing a bash script, then the shebang line will be #!/bin/bash -x. If you're creating a script where portability matters, you can use #!/bin/sh -x.
- Place a set -x command into the script where you want to turn on debugging mode.
- Run the set -x command from the command-line before you invoke a script.

To demo this, let's look at the xdialog-hello2-broken2.sh script, which has the same problem as the xdialog-hello2-broken.sh script that you saw in the previous section..

```bash
#!/bin/bash -x
command -v Xdialog
if [[ -n $DISPLAY ]] && [[ $? == 0 ]]; then
        diag=Xdialog
        sleep 10
else
        diag=dialog
        sleep 10
fi
$diag --title "Dialog message box" \
        --begin 2 2 \
        --msgbox "\nHowdy folks!" 15 50
clear
```

Here, I placed a -x at the end of the shebang line, and then placed a sleep 10 line after the diag=Xdialog line and the diag=dialog line. Now, let's run it.

```
donnie@fedora:~$ ./xdialog-hello2-broken2.sh
+ command -v Xdialog
+ [[ -n :0 ]]
+ [[ 0 == 0 ]]
+ diag=Xdialog
+ sleep 10
```

You can immediately see how this is even more useful than using echo commands. The [[-n :0]] line is the expansion of the [[-n $DISPLAY]] test. It shows that the DISPLAY variable does indeed have an assigned value (:0), which means that a desktop environment is installed. But, the real key here is the [[0 == 0]] line, which is the expansion of the [[$? == 0]] test. Invoking Xdialog from this script requires that $? equals 0, which would require that *both* of our test conditions return a 0.

This in turn requires that both Xdialog and a desktop environment are present. But, even though Xdialog is not installed on this machine, this script erroneously shows that it is, as you see in the diag=Xdialog line. So again, the only obvious answer is to swap the test conditions, as we did before, and test it again. After you do that, the [[$? == 0]] will expand to [[1 == 0]], which is what we want to see in this case.

> If you're using #!/usr/bin/env bash as your shebang line, than appending -x to the end of the shebang line won't work. That's because env only recognizes one option at a time, which in this case is bash. So instead, you'll need to either use set -x from the command-line before you run the script, or place a set -x command inside the script, like this:

```
#!/usr/bin/env bash
set -x
. . .
. . .
```

> If you use set -x on the command-line, you can turn debug mode back off by doing set +x.

If -x alone doesn't show you enough information, you can enable verbose mode by adding the v option, as you see in xdialog-hello2-broken4.sh:

```
#!/bin/bash -xv
command -v Xdialog
if [[ -n $DISPLAY ]] && [[ $? == 0 ]]; then
        diag=Xdialog
        sleep 10
else
        diag=dialog
        sleep 10
fi
$diag --title "Dialog message box" \
        --begin 2 2 \
        --msgbox "\nHowdy folks!" 15 50
clear
```

Here's the output:

```
donnie@fedora:~$ ./xdialog-hello2-broken4.sh
#!/bin/bash -xv
command -v Xdialog
```

```
+ command -v Xdialog
if [[ -n $DISPLAY ]] && [[ $? == 0 ]]; then
        diag=Xdialog
    sleep 10
else
        diag=dialog
    sleep 10
fi
+ [[ -n :0 ]]
+ [[ 0 == 0 ]]
+ diag=Xdialog
+ sleep 10
```

In addition to what we saw before, we now see the entire script echoed back at us. We also see that the value of the `diag` variable is `Xdialog`. Since `Xdialog` isn't installed on this machine, the `diag` value should be `dialog`.

If you need a permanent record of your debugging for further study, you can redirect the `-x` output into a text file. The `-x` output is considered as `stderr` output, so you'll redirect it like so:

```
donnie@fedora:~$ ./xdialog-hello2-broken4.sh 2> debug.txt
```

 When you're through debugging, be sure to remove the `-x` or set `-x` options from your script before you put it into production.

Okay, let's move on to our next trick.

Checking for Undefined Variables

As I said at the beginning of this chapter, in the *Understanding Common Scripting Errors* section, it's sometimes desirable to define a variable in a script without assigning an initial value to it. But, sometimes it isn't. You can track down uninitialized variables by appending a -u to the end of your shebang line. In bash for example, you can use `#!/bin/bash -u`, which will turn this feature on for the entire script. Or, you can place a `set -u` command any place in the script where you'd like to start checking. For example, let's look at the `unassigned_var1.sh` script, which has variable checking turned off:

```
#!/bin/bash
echo "The uninitialized myvar, without setting -u, looks like this : " $myvar
echo
myvar=Donnie
echo "I've just initialized myvar."
echo "The value of myvar is: " $myvar
```

Here's the output:

```
donnie@fedora:~$ ./unassigned_var1.sh
The uninitialized myvar, without setting -u, looks like this :
I've just initialized myvar.
The value of myvar is:  Donnie
donnie@fedora:~$
```

As you see, without the -u setting, the script runs to completion. It's just that trying to echo the value of the uninitialized myvar just shows us a blank space. Next, let's turn on variable checking by adding the -u option, as you see in the unassigned_var2.sh script:

```
#!/bin/bash -u
echo "The uninitialized myvar, without setting -u, looks like this : " $myvar
echo
myvar=Donnie
echo "I've just initialized myvar."
echo "The value of myvar is: " $myvar
```

Let's see what this does:

```
donnie@fedora:~$ ./unassigned_var2.sh
./unassigned_var2.sh: line 2: myvar: unbound variable
donnie@fedora:~$
```

This time the script failed as soon as it saw the uninitialized variable.

You can set the -u option anywhere in the script you like, by using set -u, as you see here in the unassigned_var3.sh script:

```
#!/bin/bash
echo "The uninitialized myvar, without setting -u, looks like this : " $myvar
echo
echo "I'm now setting -u."
set -u
myvar=Donnie
echo "I've just initialized myvar."
echo "The value of myvar is: " $myvar
echo
echo "Let's now try another uninitialized variable."
echo "Here's the uninitialized " $myvar2
```

So now, I have one uninitialized variable at the top, on line 2. (Let's just say that for whatever reason, I want this particular variable to be uninitialized.) I then turn on variable checking on line 5. Let's see how this runs:

```
donnie@fedora:~$ ./unassigned_var3.sh
```

```
The uninitialized myvar, without setting -u, looks like this :
I'm now setting -u.
I've just initialized myvar.
The value of myvar is:  Donnie
Let's now try another uninitialized variable.
./unassigned_var3.sh: line 11: myvar2: unbound variable
donnie@fedora:~$
```

Before I turn on variable checking, the uninitialized `myvar` just shows us a blank space. After I turn on variable checking, I initialized `myvar` with a value of `Donnie`, and it prints out normally. But, the uninitialized `myvar2` at the end crashes the script.

If you search the web for shell scripting security tutorials, you'll find several that tell you to make either `-u` or `set -u` a permanent part of your scripts. The authors of these tutorials say that it enhances the security of your scripts, without giving any convincing explanation of why or how. Using `-u` or `set -u` is great for debugging, but it should only be used for just that—debugging! So, when you're through debugging your scripts, be sure to remove the `-u` or the `set -u` before you place the script into production. Otherwise, your scripts could give you some rather unpredictable results.

Also, be aware that using `-u` can also help you detect typos in your scripts. For example, if you define a variable as `mynum=1`, but accidentally call back the value with `$mymum`, the `-u` will detect that `mymum` is an unset variable.

That about does it for the discussion of uninitialized variables. Let's move on to our next trick.

Checking for Errors with the -e Option

Our next trick is to use either the `-e` shell option or the `set -e` command to test our scripts for errors that cause commands within the script to fail. Let's look at the `bad_dir1.sh` script to see how that works.

```
#!/bin/bash
mkdir mydir
cd mydire
ls
```

With this, I want to create the `mydir` directory, `cd` into it, and then do a file listing. But, my typing isn't up to what it should be today, so in the `cd` line I accidentally typed `mydire`, instead of `mydir`. Let's see what happens when I run it.

```
donnie@fedora:~$ ./bad_dir1.sh
./bad_dir1.sh: line 4: cd: mydire: No such file or directory
 15827_zip.zip
 18.csv
 2023-08-01_15-23-31.mp4
 . . .
```

```
. . .
yad_timer.sh
yad-weather.sh
zoneinfo.zip
donnie@fedora:~$
```

Yeah, this problem is obvious, but that's okay. That's because the -e option does more than just identify the problem. It would cause the script to immediately exit if any command fails. Let's put this option into the bad_dir2.sh script to see how that works.

```
#!/bin/bash -e
mkdir mydir
cd mydire
ls
```

All I did here was to insert the -e option. Now, I'll delete the mydir directory that the first script created, and try running this one.

```
donnie@fedora:~$ rm -rf mydir
donnie@fedora:~$ ./bad_dir2.sh
./bad_dir2.sh: line 4: cd: mydire: No such file or directory
donnie@fedora:~$
```

Using -e also works when the failing command is part of a compound command structure, as you see in bad_dir3.sh.

```
#!/bin/bash -e
mkdir mydir && cd mydire
ls
```

As before, I'll delete the mydir directory that the previous script created, and then run bad_dir3.sh, which looks like this:

```
donnie@fedora:~$ ./bad_dir3.sh
./bad_dir3.sh: line 3: cd: mydire: No such file or directory
donnie@fedora:~$
```

So again, the -e stopped this script in its tracks when the cd command failed.

 I know what you're thinking, and I know that that's a bit creepy. You're thinking that the kinds of errors that -e would detect are fairly obvious. That's because with these types of errors, the shell will display an error message that pinpoints the problem. So then, why do we need -e? Well, think of -e and set -e as more of a safety mechanism than a debugging tool. For example, if the next command after trying to cd into a non-existent directory is to rm all files, then allowing the script to run after the cd command fails could be disastrous.

Okay, I've told you the good stuff about -e and set -e. Now, let me tell you some not-so-good stuff.

Understanding the Problems with set -e and -e

Although -e and set -e can be helpful, they can also cause you headaches. Sometimes, they can actually break a script that worked before. Here's what I mean.

The set -e and -e settings work by detecting if a command in the script returns an exit code of something other than 0.

 Remember that an exit code of 0 indicates a successful command execution, and a non-0 exit code indicates a failure.

Sometimes though, you'll need for some commands in your script to return a non-0 exit code in order for the script to work. This makes the operation of set -e and -e unpredictable, at best. For example, take a look at this set_e_fails1.sh script:

```
#!/bin/bash
set -e
i=0
let i++
echo "i is $i"
```

 Note that let i++ is a bashism that I haven't yet shown you. You can replace it with i=$((i + 1)) in order to make the script portable to non-bash shells.

This creates the i variable with a value of 0, increments that value by 1, and then prints out the final value of i. But, watch what happens with the -e setting:

```
donnie@fedora:~$ ./set_e_fails1.sh
donnie@fedora:~$
```

Well, it prints out nothing. Let's see what happens if I comment out the set -e command, like so:

```
#!/bin/bash
# set -e
i=0
let i++
echo "i is $i"
```

Let's run it again.

```
donnie@fedora:~$ ./set_e_fails1.sh
```

```
i is 1
donnie@fedora:~$
```

So, the script runs perfectly fine without the set -e, but inserting the set -e breaks it. I know, that's crazy, right? To help us figure out what's going on, let's create the set_e_fails2.sh script, like so:

```
#!/bin/bash
i=0
echo "Exit code after setting the value of i: " $?
let i++
echo "Exit code after incrementing i: " $?
echo "i is $i"
echo "Exit code after displaying new value of i: " $?
```

The only difference is that I omitted the set -e line, and inserted echo statements that display the exit code of each command. Now, to run it:

```
donnie@fedora:~$ ./set_e_fails2.sh
Exit code after setting the value of i:  0
Exit code after incrementing i:  1
i is 1
Exit code after displaying new value of i:  0
donnie@fedora:~$
```

The Exit code after incrementing i: 1 line shows us the problem. It's just that for some truly bizarre reason that I don't understand, the let i++ command produces an exit code of 1, even though the command is successful. So in this case, using -e created a problem, instead of solving one. (Curiously though, using the portable i=$((i + 1)) construct will return exit code 0, which will prevent this problem. I have no idea why that is.)

I mentioned in the *Checking for Undefined Variables* section that some articles you'll find on the web recommend making either -u or set -u a permanent part of your scripts, in order to enhance security. These authors actually recommend making both the -e/set -e and -u/set -u a permanent part of your scripts. But, as I've just demonstrated, -e/set -e can be rather unpredictable, and could cause you more problems than it solves. At any rate, if you do use this tool for troubleshooting, be sure to delete it from your scripts before you place them into production.

Although my personal belief is that -e and set -e can be useful when used with caution, that's actually a controversial opinion. In the following article, you'll see a lengthy write-up about why you should never, ever use -e or set -e:

BashFAQ105—Greg's Wiki:

`https://mywiki.wooledge.org/BashFAQ/105`

This author's belief is that you would be better served by creating your own error checks, rather than relying on -e/set -e.

If you like, give the page a visit, and work through the examples that the author provides. The author also provides a link to a page with the counter-argument to this, so be sure to check that out as well so that you can decide for yourself.

Okay, let's move on to our final debugging tool.

Using bash Debugger

The **bash Debugger**, which you'll normally see referred to as **bashdb**, allows you to step through a bash script, one command at a time. This allows you to see what each command in the script is doing before moving on to the next command. It's pretty simple to use, once you get installed.

You'll find a lot of bashdb tutorials on the web, but a lot of them are very old, and show you an obsolete method for installing bashdb. That's because years ago, bashdb was included in the repositories of pretty much every Linux distro. So, you could install it with your normal package manager as those tutorials showed.

Unfortunately, for some strange reason, bashdb has been removed from most, if not all, Linux repositories. So now, if you want to run bashdb on Linux, you'll need to compile it from source code as I'm about to show you.

On the other hand, bashdb is in the FreeBSD repository and in the Homebrew repository for macOS, so you're all good there.

Okay, let's look at installing bashdb.

Installing bashdb on Linux

As I mentioned above in the info box, you'll need to install bashdb from source code. Don't fret though, because it's easy.

1. You'll first need to install the autoconf and texinfo packages from your normal distro repository, using your distro's normal package manager.

2. Download the bashdb source code by doing:

```
git clone https://github.com/rocky/bashdb.git
```

3. cd into the bashdb/ directory that the git command created.

4. Run the following set of commands to compile and install bashdb:

```
./autogen.sh
./configure
make && make check
sudo make install
```

That's all there is to it.

Installing bashdb on FreeBSD

This is even easier. Just do:

```
sudo pkg install bashdb
```

Installing on macOS

On a Mac with Homebrew installed, just do:

```
brew install bashdb
```

Now that bashdb is installed, let's see if we can actually use it.

Debugging a Script with bashdb

Let's start with a clean, unmodified copy of the original broken xdialog script, which I'll call xdialog-hello2-broken5.sh, which looks like this:

```
#!/bin/bash
command -v Xdialog
if [[ -n $DISPLAY ]] && [[ $? == 0 ]]; then
        diag=Xdialog
else
        diag=dialog
fi
$diag --title "Dialog message box" \
        --begin 2 2 \
        --msgbox "\nHowdy folks!" 15 50
clear
```

As you've seen in the *Using xtrace for Debugging* section, the problem is that the script won't properly detect if both Xdialog and a desktop display are installed. Let's step through this with bashdb to see what it can tell us. Begin like so:

```
donnie@fedora:~$ bashdb ./xdialog-hello2-broken5.sh
bash debugger, bashdb, release 5.2-1.1.2
Copyright 2002-2004, 2006-2012, 2014, 2016-2019, 2021, 2023 Rocky Bernstein
This is free software, covered by the GNU General Public License, and you are
welcome to change it and/or distribute copies of it under certain conditions.
(/home/donnie/xdialog-hello2-broken5.sh:3):
3:    command -v Xdialog
bashdb<0>
```

This runs the first command in the script, and then dumps us out at the bashdb command prompt. To run the next command, just enter step, like so:

```
. . .
. . .
bashdb<0> step
(/home/donnie/xdialog-hello2-broken5.sh:4):
4:    if [[ -n $DISPLAY ]] && [[ $? == 0 ]]; then
bashdb<1>
```

Here, we see the DISPLAY variable that's inside the test construct. Let's examine that variable to see what its value is, by using the examine command:

```
. . .
. . .
```

```
bashdb<1> examine DISPLAY
declare -x DISPLAY=":0"
bashdb<2>
```

The declare -x part means that bashdb is marking the DISPLAY variable for export to subsequent commands. But, that's not the important part. What's important is that the DISPLAY variable has a value of :0, which means that the [[-n $DISPLAY]] test will return a value of 0 to indicate a true condition.

Instead of using the examine DISPLAY command, you can use the print $DISPLAY command, like so:

```
bashdb<1> print $DISPLAY
:0
bashdb<2>
```

This way, the only thing that shows up is just the actual DISPLAY value.

At this point, we need to put on our thinking caps and ponder what it means to have this DISPLAY test come before the $? test. Well, we've already come up with that answer when we used the echo statement and xtrace methods to troubleshoot this. It's just that if we do the DISPLAY detection first, the $? value in the second test will always be 0, even if no Xdialog executable is detected. But, for the sake of showing you a bit more, let's say that we haven't figured that out, and need to see more of what the script is doing. To do that, enter the series of commands that you see in the next snippet:

```
bashdb<2> step
(/home/donnie/xdialog-hello2-broken5.sh:4):
4:    if [[ -n $DISPLAY ]] && [[ $? == 0 ]]; then
[[ $? == 0 ]]
bashdb<3> step
(/home/donnie/xdialog-hello2-broken5.sh:5):
5:            diag=Xdialog
bashdb<4> print $diag
bashdb<5> step
(/home/donnie/xdialog-hello2-broken5.sh:10):
10: $diag --title "Dialog message box" \
bashdb<6> print $diag
Xdialog
bashdb<7>
```

I started this by issuing two step commands, which gets me down to where the diag variable is defined and what its assigned value is. I then issued the print $diag command, but nothing showed up. Then, I issued another step command, followed by another print $diag command. At that point, I finally see that the diag variable has the value of Xdialog, even though Xdialog isn't installed on this workstation.

> The clear advantage of using bashdb is that I didn't have to modify the script in order to debug it. As you see, I didn't have to add any echo statements to obtain the value of the DISPLAY and diag variables. I also didn't have to add a sleep command or comment out the ending clear command in order to prevent the screen from clearing before I could see the DISPLAY value. Obviously, this is a big win for bashdb.

Of course, you might at times need to find extra information about what you can do with bashdb. Let's look at that next.

Getting Help with bashdb

When you install bashdb, a man page will get installed with it. Frankly though, it doesn't tell you much. Fortunately, bashdb has a built-in help function that you can use any time that you're at the bashdb command-prompt. Just enter the help command, and you'll see this:

```
bashdb<0> help
Available commands:
-------------------
   action     complete   display  export  history  print    search  source   undisplay
   alias      condition  down     file    info     pwd      set     step     untrace
   backtrace  continue   edit     finish  kill     quit     shell   tbreak   up
   break      debug      enable   frame   list     return   show    trace    watch
   clear      delete     eval     handle  load     reverse  signal  tty      watche
   commands   disable    examine  help    next     run      skip    unalias

Readline command line editing (emacs/vi mode) is available.
Type "help" followed by command name for full documentation.
bashdb<1> █
```

Figure 21.2: The bashdb help display

This shows the list of available `bashdb` commands. To see how to use a particular command, just enter `help` followed by the command name, like so:

```
bashdb<1> help break
**break** [*loc-spec*]

Set a breakpoint at *loc-spec*.

If no location specification is given, the current line will be used.

Multiple breakpoints at one place are permitted, and useful if conditional.

For *loc-spec* paths with space characters please use octal escape, e.g.:
break /some/path\040with\040spaces/script.sh:3

See also:
---------

"tbreak" and "continue"

Aliases for break: b
bashdb<2> █
```

Figure 21.3: Getting help for the break command

That about wraps things up for this chapter. Let's summarize and move on.

Summary

In this chapter, we covered some cool tips and tricks that can help you troubleshoot your code. We began by looking at some common shell scripting errors, and showed how to find them in a broken script. We then looked at some common debugging tools and techniques. For the `-u` and `-e` shell options, I showed you both the pros and the cons of using them. Finally, I showed you how to install and use `bashdb`.

In the next chapter, we'll take a brief look at scripting with `zsh`. I'll see you there.

Questions

This time, instead of presenting you with questions to answer, I'll present you with some buggy shell scripts. Try running them to observe the errors, and then try to debug them. Can you debug them? Sure you can. I have faith in you.

1. We'll start with the `bug1.sh` script:

```
#!/bin/bash
echo "Fix this script...I've got bugs"
a=45
if [$a -gt 27 ]
then
```

```
echo $a
fi
exit
```

2. Here's the bug2.sh script:

```
#!/bin/bash
echo "Fix this script...I've got bugs"
for i in 1 2 3 4 5 6 7 8 9
do
echo $i
exit
```

3. Now, for bug3.sh:

```
#!/bin/bash
echo "Fix this script...I've got bugs"
scripts=$(ls | grep [a-z]*.sh)
echo $scripts
exit
```

4. Here's the fourth and final, bug4.sh:

```
#! /bin/bash
echo '1 2 3' > sample.data
cut -d' ' -f1,3 sample.data | read x z
echo $((x+z))
```

Further Reading

- Writing Shell Scripts—Lesson 9: Stay Out of Trouble: http://linuxcommand.org/lc3_wss0090.php
- How to Debug Bash Scripts: https://linuxconfig.org/how-to-debug-bash-scripts
- 15 Essential Bash Debugging Techniques and Tools: https://www.fosslinux.com/104144/essential-bash-debugging-techniques-and-tools.htm
- Debugging a Bash Script: https://www.baeldung.com/linux/debug-bash-script
- 5 Simple Steps On How to Debug a Bash Shell Script: https://www.shell-tips.com/bash/debug-script/#gsc.tab=0
- Filenames and Pathnames in Shell: How to do it Correctly:
- https://dwheeler.com/essays/filenames-in-shell.html
- Common Shell Script Mistakes:
- https://www.pixelbeat.org/programming/shell_script_mistakes.html
- BashPitfalls:
- http://mywiki.wooledge.org/BashPitfalls

- Debugging your shell scripts with bashdb: `https://www.linux.com/news/debug-your-shell-scripts-bashdb/`
- Debugging bash scripts with the bashdb debugger: `https://dafoster.net/articles/2023/02/22/debugging-bash-scripts-with-the-bashdb-debugger/`
- Using BashDB to Debug Your Shell Scripts—YouTube: `https://www.youtube.com/watch?v=jbOQJDSTksA`
- BASH Debugger documentation: `https://bashdb.sourceforge.net/bashdb.html`
- The Bash Trap Trap: `https://medium.com/@dirk.avery/the-bash-trap-trap-ce6083f36700`

Answers

1. In the `if` statement, you need to insert a blank space between the [and the $a.

2. You need to place a done statement after the `echo $i` statement.

3. There are a couple of problems with this script. First, the regular expression is set up wrong, which causes you to get either no or incorrect output from this script. Instead of

   `[a-z]*.sh`, it should be `[a-z].sh`. (The * actually isn't needed for this.)

 You can review the concept of regular expressions in *Chapter 9—Filtering Text with grep, sed, and Regular Expressions.*

There's also the fact this regular expression isn't doing much for us. Unless you have scripts with filenames that consist of nothing but either digits or upper-case characters, this grep command is going to show you all of the scripts in your directory. So, you could probably just omit the grep command altogether, and go with a simple `ls *.sh` command.

Finally, in the echo statement, you need to surround the variable with a pair of double quotes, like this:

```
echo "$scripts"
```

This will prevent problems with filenames that have blank spaces in them.

4. This script is supposed to take values from the first and third field of the `sample.data` file that the script created, and add them together. The values of the first and third fields are 1 and 3, so the sum of the two should be 4. However, here's how it looks when you run it:

```
donnie@fedora:~$ ./bug4.sh
0
donnie@fedora:~$
```

The problem is that the cut command on line 3 is piping its output into the read command. The problem with that is that the read command is built into the shell, instead of having its own executable file.

That's significant, because you can only pipe output of one command into a command that has its own executable. So, you can't pipe output into a command that's a shell builtin.

Instead of using a pipe, you can instead send the first and third field values to the `tmp.data` file, and then use the input redirector to obtain the input from the `tmp.data` file, as you see here in the bug5.sh script:

```
#! /bin/bash
echo '1 2 3' > sample.data
cut -d' ' -f1,3 sample.data > tmp.data
read x z < tmp.data
echo $((x+z))
```

Another option would be to use a *here* document, as you see in the bug6.sh script:

```
#! /bin/bash
echo '1 2 3' > sample.data
read -r x z <<<$(cut -d' ' -f1,3 sample.data)
echo $((x+z))
```

Either way, you'll now see the correct results:

```
donnie@fedora:~$ ./bug5.sh
4
_____:~$ ./bug6.sh
4
donnie@fedora:~$
```

Join our community on Discord!

Read this book alongside other users, Linux experts, and the author himself.

Ask questions, provide solutions to other readers, chat with the author via Ask Me Anything sessions, and much more. Scan the QR code or visit the link to join the community.

```
https://packt.link/SecNet
```

22

Introduction to Z Shell Scripting

Thus far, we've mainly talked about bash, since it's the preeminent login shell and scripting environment for Linux. In recent years, a fairly new kid on the block, **Z Shell** (zsh) has been gaining a bit of popularity as a default login shell. But, even on the operating systems that come with zsh as the login shell, bash is still there, and bash is what most people still use for scripting purposes. Be aware though, that scripting in zsh does have certain advantages, such as better math capabilities, enhanced variable expansion, and the ability to use native zsh commands instead of utilities such as find, grep, or sed. These features can help you create scripts that are a bit simpler and lighter than equivalent bash scripts.

Most articles and YouTube videos that you see about zsh focus on the user interface enhancements, and very few focus on zsh scripting. Unfortunately, the few books and tutorials that do focus on zsh scripting aren't very well-written, and you won't get much out of them. Hopefully, I can provide some clarification.

Rather than present a detailed tutorial, I'd like to just present a high-level overview of zsh scripting, so that you can decide for yourself if it's for you.

Topics in this chapter include:

- Introducing zsh
- Installing zsh
- Understanding the Unique Features of zsh Scripting
- Using zsh Modules

If you're ready, let's dig in.

Technical Requirements

You can use any of your Linux virtual machines for this chapter. As always, you can grab the demo scripts by doing:

```
git clone https://github.com/PacktPublishing/The-Ultimate-Linux-Shell-
Scripting-Guide.git
```

Introducing zsh

Z Shell was created in 1990 by Paul Falstad. It's an extension of the Bourne Shell, but also includes features from bash, Korn Shell (ksh), and C Shell (tcsh).

> The **C Shell,** which used to be somewhat popular with Unix and Unix-like distros, is vastly different from anything you've seen. Writing a C Shell script is more akin to writing a C language program than it is to what you're used to. So if you're a C language programmer, you might like it. If you're not, then you might not like it so much.

Z Shell comes as the default login shell for both macOS and Kali Linux. For pretty much everything else, you'll need to install it yourself. As far as zsh scripting goes, most of what you've learned about scripting in bash also applies to scripting in zsh. So, in this chapter I'll just present the unique features of zsh, and show you some simple scripting examples.

Installing zsh

The zsh package is available in all Linux and BSD-type distros that I've tried, as well as on OpenIndiana. The package name is zsh in all cases, so you can just install it with your normal package manager.

On the BSD distros, you'll have the same path problem that you had with bash. That is, on BSD distros, the zsh executable is in the /usr/local/bin/ directory, instead of the /bin/ directory. That's okay, though. Just create a symbolic link in the /bin/ directory, as you did for bash. On my FreeBSD machine, the command looks like this:

```
donnie@freebsd-zfs:~ $ which zsh
/usr/local/bin/zsh
donnie@freebsd-zfs:~ $ sudo ln -s /usr/local/bin/zsh /bin/zsh
donnie@freebsd-zfs:~ $ which zsh
/bin/zsh
donnie@freebsd-zfs:~ $
```

Now, if you need to run your zsh scripts on Linux, OpenIndiana, and BSD machines, you can use the same shebang line, which looks like this:

```
#!/bin/zsh
```

If you want to use zsh as your temporary login shell, you can just enter zsh at your normal shell's command prompt. If you want to set zsh as your permanent login shell, use the chsh command on Linux and the BSD distros, and the passwd command on OpenIndiana. Here's how that looks on Linux and the BSD distros:

```
donnie@ubuntu2404:~$ chsh -s /bin/zsh
Password:
donnie@ubuntu2404:~$
```

Here's how it looks on OpenIndiana:

```
donnie@openindiana:~$ passwd -e
Enter existing login password:
Old shell: /bin/bash
New shell: /bin/zsh
passwd: password information changed for donnie
donnie@openindiana:~$
```

 Note that when you change the shell for your own user account, you'll be prompted to enter your own user password. However, this has nothing to do with sudo, because even non-privileged users can use chsh on Linux/BSD distros and passwd -e on OpenIndiana to change their own default shells.

The first time you log in with zsh, you'll be presented with a setup menu that looks like this:

```
This is the Z Shell configuration function for new users,
zsh-newuser-install.
You are seeing this message because you have no zsh startup files
(the files .zshenv, .zprofile, .zshrc, .zlogin in the directory
~).  This function can help you with a few settings that should
make your use of the shell easier.

You can:

(q)  Quit and do nothing.  The function will be run again next time.

(0)  Exit, creating the file ~/.zshrc containing just a comment.
     That will prevent this function being run again.

(1)  Continue to the main menu.

--- Type one of the keys in parentheses ---
```

Hit the **1** key to go to the main menu, and choose your preferred setup options. The configuration will be saved to the .zshrc file in your home directory.

Next, let's look at some of the unique features of zsh scripting.

Understanding the Unique Features of zsh Scripting

When you script in zsh, you can take advantage of certain enhancements that aren't in bash. Here's a quick review of some of those enhancements.

Differences in Variable Expansion

In *Chapter 8—Basic Shell Script Construction*, I explained the concept of **variable expansion**, which is also sometimes called **parameter expansion**. This allows you to write cool scripts that do cool things, such as changing the filename extensions on a whole batch of files at a time. Most of the same variable expansion constructs that are in bash are also in zsh, but zsh has additional ones that provide additional capabilities. Let's look at a few examples.

Substituting Values

Substituting values in zsh works the same as it does in bash, with one exception. That is, if you substitute a value in a text string that includes an exclamation point, you'll have to escape it in a zsh script. For example, here's how it works in bash:

```
donnie@fedora:~$ unset name
donnie@fedora:~$ echo "Hello, ${name:-Guest}!"
Hello, Guest!
donnie@fedora:~$ name=Horatio
donnie@fedora:~$ echo "Hello, ${name:-Guest}!"
Hello, Horatio!
donnie@fedora:~$
```

As I explained in *Chapter 8*, the `variable_name:-default_value` construct supplies a default value for any variable that doesn't yet have a value assigned to it. This same construct is supposed to work in zsh, but watch what happens when I try it:

```
ubuntu2404% unset name
ubuntu2404% echo "Hello, ${name:-Guest}!"
dquote> "
Hello, Guest

ubuntu2404%
```

When I hit the **Enter** key after typing the echo command, zsh takes me to the dquote> prompt. If I hit the " key a second time, I get the output that I want. To get it right the first time, I'll just place a \ before the !, like this:

```
ubuntu2404% unset name
ubuntu2404% echo "Hello, ${name:-Guest}\!"
Hello, Guest!
ubuntu2404% name=Horatio
ubuntu2404% echo "Hello, ${name:-Guest}\!"
Hello, Horatio!
Ubuntu2404%
```

So, with the \ in front of the exclamation point, it works just fine. I don't know why the ! needs to be escaped in zsh, but whatever works, right?

Substituting Substrings

Substring substitution partly works in bash, but not completely. Here's what I mean.

I'll first create the name variable with the value of lionel. Then, on both bash and zsh, I'll attempt to replace the first lower-case *l* with an upper-case *l*. First, on bash, like so:

```
donnie@fedora:~$ echo $SHELL
/bin/bash
donnie@fedora:~$ name="lionel"
donnie@fedora:~$ echo "${name/l/L}"
Lionel
donnie@fedora:~$
```

Now, on zsh:

```
ubuntu2404% echo $SHELL
/bin/zsh
ubuntu2404% name="lionel"
ubuntu2404% echo "${name/l/L}"
Lionel
ubuntu2404%
```

In the ${name/l/L} construct, you see that I first listed the variable name with a forward slash and the letter that I want to replace, followed by another forward slash and the letter that I want to substitute. As you can see, this works on both bash and zsh. I can also replace both both occurrences of the lower-case *l* by using two forward slashes after the name variable, like so:

On bash:

```
donnie@fedora:~$ echo "${name//l/L}"
LioneL
donnie@fedora:~$
```

On zsh:

```
ubuntu2404% echo "${name//l/L}"
LioneL
ubuntu2404%
```

Again, this works on both bash and zsh. So, if this works on both shells, why am I showing this to you? Well, it's just that on bash, this only works if the text string doesn't contain any blank spaces.

Here's an example of what I mean:

On bash:

```
donnie@fedora:~$ names="Donnie and Vicky and Cleopatra"
donnie@fedora:~$ echo "${names//and/&}"
Donnie and Vicky and Cleopatra
donnie@fedora:~$
```

This time, I wanted to replace all occurrences of *and* with an ampersand. But, this doesn't work on bash because the text string contains blank spaces. So, let's try this on zsh.

On zsh:

```
ubuntu2404% names="Donnie and Vicky and Cleopatra"
ubuntu2404% echo "${names//and/&}"
Donnie & Vicky & Cleopatra
ubuntu2404%
```

On zsh, having a text string with blank spaces doesn't matter.

Translating Between Upper and Lower Case

Here's an example of the exact opposite situation. This time, I'll show you something that works on bash, but not on zsh. Then, I'll show you the alternative method for zsh.

First, let's say that we want to capitalize the first letter of the value that's assigned to the name variable. Here's how to do it on bash:

```
donnie@fedora:~$ name=horatio
donnie@fedora:~$ echo "${name^}"
Horatio
donnie@fedora:~$
```

All I did here was to place a ^ after the name variable in the echo statement. Now, let's say that I want to capitalize all letters. I'll do that by using two ^ characters, like this:

```
donnie@fedora:~$ echo "${name^^}"
HORATIO
donnie@fedora:~$
```

If you have a text string with all upper-case characters, use either one or two commas to convert either the first letter or all letters to lower-case, like this:

```
donnie@fedora:~$ name=HORATIO
donnie@fedora:~$ echo "${name,}"
hORATIO
donnie@fedora:~$ echo "${name,,}"
horatio
```

```
donnie@fedora:~$
```

On zsh, none of this works at all, as you see here:

```
ubuntu2404% name=horatio
ubuntu2404% echo "${name^}"
zsh: bad substitution
ubuntu2404% echo "${name^^}"
zsh: bad substitution
ubuntu2404% name=HORATIO
ubuntu2404% echo "${name,}"
zsh: bad substitution
ubuntu2404% echo "${name,,}"
zsh: bad substitution
ubuntu2404%
```

 I'm showing you this because some zsh scripting books say this will work on zsh. But, as you see, it definitely doesn't.

So, what's the alternative on zsh? Well, you just use a builtin zsh function. Let's first use the U function to convert an entire text string to upper-case:

```
ubuntu2404% name=horatio
ubuntu2404% echo "${(U)name}"
HORATIO
ubuntu2404%
```

Instead of placing a pair of ^ characters after the name variable, I just placed a (U) before the name variable.

As far as I've been able to find, there's no function that converts just the first letter. So, let's convert the first letter like this, instead:

```
ubuntu2404% name=horatio
ubuntu2404% capitalized_name=${name/h/H}
ubuntu2404% echo $capitalized_name
Horatio
ubuntu2404%
```

This is the same method that I've just shown you in the previous section.

Next, let's do some globbing.

Extended File Globbing

"What's **file globbing**", you say? Well, you've actually been working with it throughout this book. It's just that I've never told you what it's called. All it means is that you can use wildcard characters, such as the * and the ?, to work with multiple files at the same time. For example, you can do this:

```
donnie@fedora:~$ ls -l *.zip
-rw-r--r--. 1 root    root        32864546 Jul 27  2023 15827_zip.zip
-rw-r--r--. 1 root    root        49115374 Jul 27  2023 21261.zip
-rw-r--r--. 1 root    root        36996449 Jul 27  2023 46523.zip
. . .

. . .
-rw-r--r--. 1 root    root        21798397 Jul 27  2023 tmvx.zip
-rw-r--r--. 1 root    root           60822 Jul 27  2023 U_CAN_Ubuntu_20-04_LTS_
V1R4_STIG_SCAP_1-2_Benchmark.zip
-rw-r--r--. 1 root    root          425884 Jul 27  2023 zoneinfo.zip
donnie@fedora:~$
```

All I'm doing here is using the * wildcard to view all of the .zip files in my directory.

You can do all this and more in zsh. The only catch is that you need to have the extendedglob feature turned on. To verify that it is, look in the .zshrc file in your home directory. You should see a line that looks something like this:

```
setopt autocd beep extendedglob nomatch notify
```

If the extendedglob option is there, then you're good. If it isn't, just add it in. So now, let's look at a few examples of extended globbing.

> Why is extended file globbing on zsh useful? Well, it's just that in many cases, you'll be able to use the extended globbing features of zsh instead of using the find utility. You might find this easier than using find. Or, you might prefer using find, if that's what you're used to using. I'll let you make the decision.
>
> Also, for demo purposes, I'm mainly showing you this with the ls utility. But, you can also use globbing with other utilities, such as cp, mv, rm, chmod, or chown.

Filtering ls Output

With this cool feature enabled, you can do cool things like excluding files that you don't want to see. For example, let's say that you want to see all files in your directory except for the .sh files. Just do this:

```
ubuntu2404% ls -d ^*.sh
bashlib-0.4              My_Files
demo_files               supersecret
deshc-deb                supersecret_trace.txt
Documents                sysinfo.html
```

```
encrypted_password        sysinfo_posix.lib
encrypted_password.sh.x.c  test.sh.x
expand_1.txt                       user_activity_for_donnie_2024-05-12_09-30.txt
expand_2.txt                       user_activity_for_donnie_2024-07-22_10-40.txt
expand.txt                 user_activity_for_horatio_2024-07-06_07-12.txt
FallOfSudo                 while_demo
file2.txt                          while_demo.sh.x.c
file3.jpg
ubuntu2404%
```

The ^ that precedes the *.sh is a negation symbol. This is what prevents the ls command from showing you the .sh files.

Note that I had to include the -d option for ls. Otherwise, you'll also see files in any subdirectories that you might have. For some reason, the ^ filters out the unwanted files in
my top level directory, but it doesn't filter out the unwanted files in the subdirectories. So,
without the -d, you'll also see all files that are in the subdirectories, including the ones
that you want to filter out.

You can use the *~ operator to accomplish the same thing. Here's how that looks:

```
ubuntu2404% ls -d *~*.sh
bashlib-0.4            My_Files
demo_files            supersecret
deshc-deb                      supersecret_trace.txt
Documents                   sysinfo.html
encrypted_password     sysinfo_posix.lib
encrypted_password.sh.x.c  test.sh.x
expand_1.txt                       user_activity_for_donnie_2024-05-12_09-30.txt
expand_2.txt                       user_activity_for_donnie_2024-07-22_10-40.txt
expand.txt                 user_activity_for_horatio_2024-07-06_07-12.txt
FallOfSudo                 while_demo
file2.txt                          while_demo.sh.x.c
file3.jpg
ubuntu2404%
```

As you see, the output is identical to that of the ls -d ^.sh output. To exclude multiple types of files,
just use the *or* operator (|), like this:

```
ubuntu2404% ls -d *~(*.sh|*.jpg|*.txt|*.c)
bashlib-0.4  Documents                My_Files            sysinfo_posix.lib
demo_files   encrypted_password  supersecret    test.sh.x
deshc-deb    FallOfSudo               sysinfo.html  while_demo
ubuntu2404%
```

So in this case, I filtered out the `.sh`, `.jpg`, `.txt`, and `.c` files. Now, let's look at our next trick.

Grouping ls Searches

Something else that you can't do in bash is to group your ls searches, like this:

```
ubuntu2404% ls -ld (ex|test)*
-rw-r--r-- 1 donnie donnie    52 Apr 29 20:02 expand_1.txt
-rw-r--r-- 1 donnie donnie   111 Apr 29 20:02 expand_2.txt
-rw-r--r-- 1 donnie donnie    51 Apr 29 20:02 expand.txt
-rwxrw-r-- 1 donnie donnie    48 Jun 30 20:26 test.sh
-rw-rw-r-- 1 donnie donnie     0 Jul  5 19:31 test.sh.dec.sh
-rwxr-xr-x 1 donnie donnie 11440 Jul  5 19:12 test.sh.x
ubuntu2404%
```

Here, I'm using the | symbol as an *or* operator, to view all files with either ex or test as the first portion of their filenames.

Using Globbing Flags

As you know, Linux and Unix operating systems are normally case-sensitive. So, if you were to use the ls `*.jpg` command to view all JPEG-type graphics files, you would completely miss any files that might have the `*.JPG` extension. With zsh, you can use **globbing flags** to make your commands case-insensitive. Here's an example:

```
ubuntu2404% touch graphic1.jpg graphic2.JPG graphic3.jpg file3.jpg
ubuntu2404% ls *.jpg
file3.jpg  graphic1.jpg  graphic3.jpg
ubuntu2404% ls (#i)*.jpg
file3.jpg  graphic1.jpg  graphic2.JPG  graphic3.jpg
ubuntu2404%
```

The `(#i)` in the second ls command is the globbing flag. The # indicates that it's a flag, and it will precede the pattern that you want to match.

The `(#l)` flag will match either a lower-case or upper-case pattern if you specify a lower-case pattern for your search. If you specify an upper-case pattern, then it will only match the upper-case pattern. Here's how that looks:

```
ubuntu2404% ls (#l)*.jpg
file3.jpg  graphic1.jpg  graphic2.JPG  graphic3.jpg
ubuntu2404% ls (#l)*.JPG
graphic2.JPG
ubuntu2404%
```

You see here that when I specified `*.jpg` as the pattern, it also found the `.JPG` file. But, when I specified `.JPG` as the pattern, it only found the `.JPG` file.

Now, let's expand some directories.

Expanding Directories

You can use **globbing qualifiers** to view different types of directories or files. We'll start with the qualifiers for directories, which are:

- *(F): This expands non-empty directories.
- *(^F): This expands both plain files and empty directories.
- *(/^F): This only expands empty directories.

First, let's look at the non-empty directories that are in my home directory.

```
ubuntu2404% ls *(F)
bashlib-0.4:
bashlib       config.cache   config.status   COPYING   Makefile       README
bashlib.in   config.log       configure       INSTALL   Makefile.in


. . .

. . .
My_Files:
afile.txt                    somefile.txt     yetanotherfile.txtx
anotherfile.txt                 somepicture.jpg   yetanotheryetanotherfile.txt
haveicreatedenoughfilesyet.txt    somescript.sh
ubuntu2404%
```

You see here that this command shows the non-empty directories and their contents. But, it doesn't show any files that are in my top-level home directory. So, it's all good.

Now, I want to see all of the files that are in my top-level home directory, along with any empty directories that might also be there. I'll do that like this:

```
ubuntu2404% ls *(^F)
acl_demo.sh              rsync_password.sh
diskspace.sh                shutdown-update.sh
. . .

. . .
rootlock_2.sh                while_demo.sh.x.c


Documents:


empty_directory:
ubuntu2404%
```

The two empty directories show up at the bottom of the output.

Finally, I only want to see the empty directories, like so:

```
ubuntu2404% ls *(/^F)
Documents:

empty_directory:
ubuntu2404%
```

Pretty cool, eh?

Next, let's look at file expansion.

Expanding Files

There are several ways to expand files. First, we'll expand by either the file or directory file types.

Expanding Files and Directories

If you want to see the files in your directory, but don't want to see any directories, do this:

```
ubuntu2404% ls *(.)
acl_demo.sh              rsync_password.sh
diskspace.sh                  shutdown-update.sh
encrypted_password     sudo_demo1.sh
. . .
. . .
rootlock_1.sh                  while_demo.sh
rootlock_2.sh                  while_demo.sh.x.c
ubuntu2404%
```

If you only want to see your directories, both empty and non-empty, do this:

```
ubuntu2404% ls *(/)
bashlib-0.4:
bashlib      config.cache  config.status  COPYING  Makefile      README
bashlib.in  config.log       configure      INSTALL  Makefile.in
. . .
. . .

Documents:

empty_directory:

FallOfSudo:
fallofsudo.py  LICENSE      main.png  README.md

My_Files:
```

```
afile.txt                          somefile.txt    yetanotherfile.txtx
anotherfile.txt                           somepicture.jpg  yetanotheryetanotherfile.txt
haveicreatedenoughfilesyet.txt     somescript.sh
ubuntu2404%
```

Okay, I think you see what's going on with this. Let's move on to look at file permissions.

Expanding by File Permissions

In *Chapter 20, Shell Script Security*, I explained about how file and directory permissions work. Let's do a quick review.

The permissions settings are divided between the *user*—which is what we call the owner of the file or directory—the *group*, and *others*. Each of these can have any combination of read, write, and executable permissions set for any given file or directory. If you need to search for files or directories with certain permissions settings, you can use the find utility. On zsh, you can use **globbing qualifiers** instead of find. Here's the list of the qualifiers that you'll work with:

For the user:

- r: The user has the read permission.
- w: This denotes files for which the user has the write permission.
- x: The user has the executable permission.
- U: This looks for files or directories that belong to the current user.
- s: This looks for files with the SUID permission set.

For the group:

- A: The group has the read permission.
- I: The group has the write permission.
- E: The group has the executable permission.
- G: This looks for files or directories that belong to the current user's group.
- S: This looks for files or directories that have the SGID permission set.

For others:

- R: Others have the read permission.
- W: Others have the write permission.
- X: Others have the executable permission.
- t: This looks for directories that have the sticky bit set.

So, how does all this work? Well, let's say that you're in the /bin/ directory, and you want to see all of the files that have the SUID permission set. Just do something like this:

```
ubuntu2404% cd /bin
ubuntu2404% ls -ld *(s)
-rwsr-xr-x 1 root root  72792 Apr  9 07:01 chfn
```

```
-rwsr-xr-x 1 root root    44760 Apr  9 07:01 chsh
-rwsr-xr-x 1 root root    39296 Apr  8 15:57 fusermount3
-rwsr-xr-x 1 root root    76248 Apr  9 07:01 gpasswd
-rwsr-xr-x 1 root root    51584 Apr  9 14:02 mount
-rwsr-xr-x 1 root root    40664 Apr  9 07:01 newgrp
-rwsr-xr-x 1 root root    64152 Apr  9 07:01 passwd
-rwsr-xr-x 1 root root    55680 Apr  9 14:02 su
-rwsr-xr-x 1 root root   277936 Apr  8 14:50 sudo
-rwsr-xr-x 1 root root    39296 Apr  9 14:02 umount
ubuntu2404%
```

If you're in your own home directory and want to see all of the SUID files that are on the entire filesystem, just make your search recursive, like this:

```
ubuntu2404% ls -ld /**/*(s)
-rwsr-xr-x 1 root root          85064 Feb  6  2024 /snap/core20/2264/usr/bin/chfn
-rwsr-xr-x 1 root root          53040 Feb  6  2024 /snap/core20/2264/usr/bin/chsh
. . .

. . .
-rwsr-xr-x 1 root root         154824 Jul 26 02:32 /usr/lib/snapd/snap-confine
ubuntu2404%
```

Unlike find, ls isn't inherently recursive. So, if want to search through all of the lower-level subdirectories of the directory you're already in, just do this:

```
ubuntu2404% pwd
/home/donnie
ubuntu2404% ls -l **/*(s)
zsh: no matches found: **/*(s)
ubuntu2404%
```

The only difference between this and the full filesystem search is that I used **/*(s) instead of /**/*(s). (Of course, there are no SUID files in my home directory, which is to be expected.)

If you need to actually do something with this ls output, you can create a zsh script, like this find_suid.sh script:

```
#!/bin/zsh

ls -ld /**/*(s) > suid_files.txt
```

It's just a simple little script that creates a text file with a list of the SUID files on your system. But hey, who says we can't fancy it up a bit? Let's see what we can do in the find_suid2.sh script:

```zsh
#!/bin/zsh

suid_results_file=$1

if [[ -f "$suid_results_file" ]]; then
        echo "This file already exists."
        exit
fi
ls -ld /**/*(s) > "$suid_results_file"
```

With this script, you'll specify the name of the file where you want the results to be saved. If there's already a file with that filename, the script will give you a warning message and then exit.

You can use any of the other globbing qualifiers in the same manner. For example, let's say that you need to search through the entire filesystem for files that belong to you. Let's see how that works:

```
ubuntu2404% ls -ld /**/*(U) | less
```

This will make for a very long list, so I have to pipe this into less to prevent the output from scrolling off the top of the screen. Here's some of what you'll see:

```
crw--w----  1 donnie tty    136, 0 Sep  3 20:04 /dev/pts/0
crw-------  1 donnie tty      4, 1 Sep  3 19:24 /dev/tty1
drwxr-x--- 13 donnie donnie  4096 Sep  3 20:02 /home/donnie
-rw-rw-r--  1 donnie donnie    44 Jul 24 20:53 /home/donnie/acl_demo.sh
drwxr-xr-x  2 donnie donnie  4096 Jun 29 21:10 /home/donnie/bashlib-0.4
. . .

. . .
-rw-r--r--  1 donnie donnie     0 Sep  3 19:24 /sys/fs/cgroup/user.slice/user-
1000.slice/user@1000.service/memory.reclaim
-rwxrwxrwx  1 donnie donnie  2155 Jul  5 19:31 /usr/bin/deshc
```

As you see, a typical Linux system has files that belong to you all over the place.

This is one clear advantage that zsh has over every other shell, including bash. The extended file globbing capabilities of zsh can replace much of the functionality of find, but with much simpler syntax. (Of course, you can also use this trick with other utilities besides ls, such as cp, mv, rm, chmod, or chown.)

> You can also use `zsh` file globbing to replace utilities such as `grep`, `awk` and `tr`. Honestly though, the syntax for globbing commands that replace those utilities is so convoluted that you're better off using the utilities. On the other hand, using `zsh` file globbing instead could make your scripts somewhat lighter and faster. And, you can use file globbing in those rare cases where you might find that the utilities aren't installed.
>
> At any rate, if you want to read about the additional file globbing capabilities of `zsh`, here's the link:
>
> Zsh Native Scripting Handbook:
>
> `https://github.zshell.dev/docs/zsh/Zsh-Native-Scripting-Handbook.html`
>
> You can also find out more about both file globbing and variable expansion by reading the `zshexpn` man page.

All right, let's talk briefly about arrays.

Understanding zsh Arrays

This will be quick, because there are only three things that I want to point out about `zsh` arrays. The first thing is that instead of having array index numbers begin with 0, as is the case with `bash` arrays, the index numbers for `zsh` arrays begin with 1. Here's how it looks on `bash`:

```
donnie@fedora:~$ mybasharray=(vicky cleopatra horatio)
donnie@fedora:~$ echo ${mybasharray[0]}
vicky
donnie@fedora:~$ echo ${mybasharray[1]}
cleopatra
donnie@fedora:~$
```

You see how using an index number of 0 brings up the first name in the list, and an index number of 1 brings up the second name. Now, here's how it looks on `zsh`:

```
ubuntu2404% myzsharray=(vicky cleopatra horatio)
ubuntu2404% echo ${myzsharray[0]}

ubuntu2404% echo ${myzsharray[1]}
vicky
ubuntu2404% echo ${myzsharray[2]}
cleopatra
ubuntu2404%
```

This time, the index number of 0 brings up nothing, because index 0 doesn't exist.

The second big difference is in how you can view the entire contents of an array. With bash, you need to do something like this:

```
donnie@fedora:~$ echo ${mybasharray[@]}
vicky cleopatra horatio
donnie@fedora:~$
```

You can still do this on zsh if you like, but you don't have to. Instead, you can just view the contents of the array the same as you'd view the value of a normal variable, like this:

```
ubuntu2404% echo $myzsharray
vicky cleopatra horatio
ubuntu2404%
```

Finally, I want to show you how to eliminate duplicate entries that might be in a array. To demonstrate, let's create an array with a list of fruits, like this:

```
ubuntu2404% fruits=(orange apple orange banana kiwi banana apple orange)

ubuntu2404% echo $fruits
orange apple orange banana kiwi banana apple orange
ubuntu2404%
```

As you see, there are several duplicates in the list. To get rid of the duplicates, just do this:

```
ubuntu2404% echo ${(u)fruits}
orange apple banana kiwi
ubuntu2404%
```

Replacing the (u) with (U) prints out the entire list in upper-case letters.

```
ubuntu2404% echo ${(U)fruits}
ORANGE APPLE ORANGE BANANA KIWI BANANA APPLE ORANGE
ubuntu2404%
```

Combine the u with the U, and you'll eliminate duplicates and print out the list in upper-case letters.

```
ubuntu2404% echo ${(uU)fruits}
ORANGE APPLE BANANA KIWI
ubuntu2404%
```

To show this in practice, let's look at the fruit_array.sh script:

```
#!/bin/zsh

fruits=(apple orange banana apple orange kiwi)
echo "Let's look at the entire list of fruits."
for fruit in $fruits; do
```

```
        echo $fruit
done
echo "****************"
echo "****************"
echo "Now, let's eliminate the duplicate fruits."
printf "%s\n" ${(u)fruits}
```

In the first stanza, I'm using a `for` loop to print out each individual fruit that's in the `fruits` array. In the second stanza, I wanted to print out each individual fruit, without the duplicates. Using `echo` would have printed all of the fruits out on a single line, as I showed you in the command-line example above. So instead of `echo`, I used `printf`. Here, the `%s` parameter tells `printf` to print the designated text strings, which in this case is each member of the array. The `\n` option inserts a newline after each fruit. Running the script looks like this:

```
ubuntu2404% ./fruit_array.sh
Let's look at the entire list of fruits.
apple
orange
banana
apple
orange
kiwi
****************
****************
Now, let's eliminate the duplicate fruits.
apple
orange
banana
kiwi
ubuntu2404%
```

 There are actually a lot more things that you can do with arrays than I can show you here. To read about them, take a look at the `zshexpn` man page.

That does it for arrays. So now, let's talk about math.

Enhanced Math Capabilities

In *Chapter 11—Performing Mathematical Operations*, I explained that `bash` has only limited builtin math capabilities, and that it can only work with integers. For anything beyond that, you'll need to use an external program, such as `bc`, in your `bash` scripts. On the other hand, `zsh` has expanded math capabilities built right in.

For our first example, let's try to divide 5 by 2 from the zsh command-line:

```
ubuntu2404% echo $((5/2))
2
ubuntu2404%
```

Well, that wasn't what I wanted. I should see a final answer of 2.5, instead of 2. What's going on? The answer is that to perform floating point math, you have to explicitly express one of the numbers as a floating point number. So, let's fix that.

```
ubuntu2404% echo $((5.0/2))
2.5
ubuntu2404%
```

Much better. By expressing the first number as 5.0 instead of 5, the floating point math works. Unfortunately though, the zsh math isn't quite perfect. I mean, it worked fine for this division example, but watch what happens when I try any other operation:

```
ubuntu2404% echo $((2.1+2.1))
4.2000000000000002
ubuntu2404% echo $((2.1*2))
4.2000000000000002
ubuntu2404% echo $((2.1-2))
0.10000000000000009
ubuntu2404% echo $((2.1%2))
0.10000000000000009
ubuntu2404%
```

For some reason that I don't understand, zsh adds extra trailing digits after the decimal point. It wouldn't matter much if they were all zeros, but you also have the spurious 2 and 9 at the end, which throws off our calculations. Fortunately, we can easily correct that by just assigning the results to a variable, like so:

```
ubuntu2404% ((sum=2.1+2.1))
ubuntu2404% echo $sum
4.2000000000
ubuntu2404%
```

The trailing zeros are still there, but at least the spurious 2 and 9 digits aren't.

 Even after some rather extensive research, I was never able to find any command or option switch that I can use to specify the number of digits to show past the decimal point.

Grouping math operations, in order to specify their precedence, looks like this:

```
ubuntu2404% ((product=(2.1+2.1)*8))
ubuntu2404% echo $product
33.6000000000
ubuntu2404%
```

If just simple math isn't enough for you, you can load the mathfunc module, which I'll show you in the next section.

Using zsh Modules

A lot of zsh functionality is contained in loadable zsh modules. I can't cover all of the zsh modules in this chapter, so let's just look at some of the more useful ones.

First, let's see which modules get loaded into a zsh session by default:

```
ubuntu2404% zmodload
zsh/complete
zsh/computil
zsh/main
zsh/parameter
zsh/stat
zsh/terminfo
zsh/zle
zsh/zutil
ubuntu2404%
```

There are a lot more optional modules that you can load yourself by using the zmodload command, as we'll see next.

 To read about all of the available zsh modules, see the zshmodules man page.

Now, let's get a bit more specific by looking at the mathfunc module.

Using the mathfunc Module

If you want to create some really fancy math scripts without having to use an external utility such as bc, just load the mathfunc module, like this:

```
ubuntu2404% zmodload zsh/mathfunc
ubuntu2404%
```

This module provides functions for trigonometry, logarithms, exponentiation, as well as some other math functions. You can see all the functions that the modules provide, like this:

```
ubuntu2404% zmodload -lF zsh/mathfunc
+f:abs
+f:acos
+f:acosh
+f:asin
+f:asinh
. . .

. . .
+f:y0
+f:y1
+f:yn
ubuntu2404%
```

So now, let's say that you want to see the square root of 9. Do it like this:

```
ubuntu2404% ((squareroot=sqrt(9)))
ubuntu2404% echo $squareroot
3.0000000000
ubuntu2404%
```

Now, let's put this into the `squareroot.sh` script:

```
#!/bin/zsh
zmodload zsh/mathfunc
your_number=$1
((squareroot=sqrt(your_number)))
echo $squareroot
```

 Note here that I've had to place a `zmodload zsh/mathfunc` command at the beginning of this script. That's because every time you close your terminal or log out of your machine, any modules that you've loaded from the command-line will automatically unload. So, you'll have to add this `zmodload` command to your scripts.

Here, I'm using the your_number variable to contain the value of the number that the user specifies for the $1 parameter. Let's see if it works.

```
ubuntu2404% ./squareroot.sh 9
3.0000000000
ubuntu2404% ./squareroot.sh 25
5.0000000000
ubuntu2404% ./squareroot.sh 2
```

```
1.4142135624
ubuntu2404%
```

Oh yeah, it works just fine, and all without messing with any external programs, such as bc.

 All of the other mathfunc functions work in a similar manner. Use your own imagination and the scripting concepts that I've shown you for bash to come up with your own zsh math scripts.

That does it for your introduction of the mathfunc module. Next, let's briefly look at the datetime module.

The datetime Module

The datetime module does pretty much the same job as the date utility. You can use either one to do cool things, like creating files with timestamps in their filenames. It's not loaded by default, so let's do that now:

```
ubuntu2404% zmodload zsh/datetime
ubuntu2404%
```

Now, let's see what it provides:

```
ubuntu2404% zmodload -lF zsh/datetime
+b:strftime
+p:EPOCHSECONDS
+p:EPOCHREALTIME
+p:epochtime
ubuntu2404%
```

Here's the breakdown of what you're looking at:

- strftime: This is the only function that this module contains. You can use it the same as you'd use the date utility.
- EPOCHSECONDS: This environmental variable is an integer value that represents the number of seconds that have elapsed since the beginning of the Unix epoch. This variable is also available in bash.
- EPOCHREALTIME: This environmental variable is a floating point value that represents the number of seconds that have elapsed since the beginning of the Unix epoch. Depending upon the particular system, this value can be to either nanosecond or microsecond accuracy. This variable is also available in bash.
- epochtime: This variable contains two components. It's like the EPOCHREALTIME variable, except that the decimal point is replaced by a blank space. This variable is not available in bash.

The Unix epoch began on 1 January, 1970. In the early days of Unix, Unix developers decided that the easiest way to set the time on a Unix computer would be to express it as the number of seconds that have elapsed since that date.

You can see the current values of the three variables like this:

```
ubuntu2404% echo $EPOCHSECONDS
1725470539
ubuntu2404% echo $EPOCHREALTIME
1725470545.8938724995
ubuntu2404% echo $epochtime
1725470552 124436538
ubuntu2404%
```

Now, let's create the `zsh_time.sh` script that uses the `strftime` function:

```
#!/bin/zsh
zmodload zsh/datetime

timestamp=$(strftime '%A-%F_%T')
echo "I want to create a file at $timestamp." > "timefile_$timestamp.txt"
```

The `strftime` function uses the same date and time formatting options as the `date` utility uses. In this case we have:

- %A: This is the day of the week.
- %F: This is the date in YYYY-MM-DD format.
- %T: This is the time in HH:MM:SS format.

The only real difference between using `date` and `strftime` is that with `date`, you have to precede the string of formatting options with a +, like this:

```
date +'%A-%F-%T'
```

 The `strftime` function has its own man page, which you can view by doing `man strftime`.

After I run the script, I should have my file:

```
ubuntu2404% ./zsh_time.sh
ubuntu2404% ls -l timefile_*
-rw-rw-r-- 1 donnie donnie 58 Sep  4 18:16 timefile_
Wednesday-2024-09-04_18:16:37.txt
```

```
ubuntu2404% cat timefile_Wednesday-2024-09-04_18:16:37.txt
I want to create a file at Wednesday-2024-09-04_18:16:37.
ubuntu2404%
```

 I've covered what I believe are the most useful modules. If you want to read about the rest of the zsh modules, take a look at the zshmodules man page.

I think that this will just about do it for our introduction to zsh scripting. Let's wrap up and move on.

Summary

In this chapter, I introduced you to the concept of scripting in zsh instead of in bash. I began by showing you how to install zsh, if it isn't installed already. I showed you some of the differences between bash and zsh features that could impact how you'd write a zsh script. These include differences in file globbing, variable expansion, array indexing, and math operations. Along the way, I showed you how these zsh features can help you build scripts that are simpler, yet more functional, than bash scripts.

The main problem with zsh scripting, other than the fact that bash is much more prevalent, is the lack of documentation. There are plenty of tutorials and articles about setting up a zsh user environment, but very little about zsh scripting. Hopefully, you'll be able to use the knowledge that I've provided here to write some cool zsh scripts.

In the next and final chapter, I'll introduce you to the idea of using PowerShell on Linux. (Yes, you read that correctly.) I'll see you there.

Questions

1. Which command would you use to view all of the zsh modules that have been loaded into your zsh session?

    a. zmodls

    b. zmod -l

    c. zmodload -l

    d. zmodload

2. You want to load the math function module. Which of these commands would you use?

    a. zmod mathfunc

    b. zmod zsh/mathfunc

    c. zmodload -l mathfunc

    d. zmodload -l zsh/mathfunc

    e. zmodload zsh/mathfunc

3. What is a major difference between the way that bash and zsh handle arrays?

    a.   There is no difference.

    b.   bash array indexing begins at 1, zsh array indexing begins at 0.

    c.   bash array indexing begins at 0, zsh array indexing begins at 1.

    d.   bash can work with arrays, but zsh can't.

4. Which zsh command would you use to view all of the `.png` files and all of the `.PNG` files that are in your directory?

    a.   `ls *.png`

    b.   `ls (#i).png`

    c.   `ls (#l).PNG`

    d.   `ls *.PNG`

5. You only want to view the empty directories that are in your current working directory. Which of these zsh commands would you use?

    a.   `ls -l *(/^F)`

    b.   `ls -l *(^F)`

    c.   `ls -l *(F)`

    d.   `ls -ld`

Further Reading

- The Z Shell Manual: `https://zsh-manual.netlify.app/`
- What is ZSH, and Why Should You Use It Instead of Bash?: `https://www.howtogeek.com/362409/what-is-zsh-and-why-should-you-use-it-instead-of-bash/`
- ZSH for Starters: Exploring Linux's Elegant Shell: `https://www.fosslinux.com/133167/zsh-for-beginners-exploring-linuxs-elegant-shell.htm`
- How to Write Script for ZSH: `https://www.linuxtoday.com/blog/writing-scripts-for-zsh/`

Answers

1. d
2. e
3. c
4. b
5. a

Join our community on Discord!

Read this book alongside other users, Linux experts, and the author himself.

Ask questions, provide solutions to other readers, chat with the author via Ask Me Anything sessions, and much more. Scan the QR code or visit the link to join the community.

https://packt.link/SecNet

23

Using PowerShell on Linux

PowerShell started its life as a closed-source, proprietary product that could only be installed on Windows operating systems. Now though, it's Free Open Source Software, and is freely available for use on Linux-based and macOS-based machines.

I can't give you a complete course on PowerShell in this chapter, because it's something that would require an entire book. Instead, I'll just give you a high-level overview of the PowerShell philosophy, show you how to install it, and provide some useful examples. I'll also provide some rationale on why you, as a Linux or Mac administrator, might like to learn PowerShell. And of course, you'll find plenty of PowerShell reference material links both throughout the chapter and in the *Further Reading* section.

Topics in this chapter include:

- Installing PowerShell on Linux and macOS
- Reasons for Linux and Mac Admins to Learn PowerShell
- Differences Between PowerShell Scripting and Traditional Linux/Unix Scripting
- Viewing the Available PowerShell Commands
- Getting Help with PowerShell Commands
- Real-World Cross-Platform PowerShell Scripts

If you're ready, let's get started.

Technical Requirements

You can use a Fedora, Ubuntu, or Debian virtual machine for this. You won't be using your FreeBSD or OpenIndiana virtual machines, because PowerShell isn't available for them.

As always, you can grab the scripts by doing:

```
git clone https://github.com/PacktPublishing/The-Ultimate-Linux-Shell-
Scripting-Guide.git
```

Installing PowerShell on Linux and macOS

We'll first look at the methods for installing PowerShell on Linux, and then look at how to install it on macOS.

Installing PowerShell on Linux via a snap Package

The snapd system is a universal software packaging system that was invented by the developers of Ubuntu. It comes installed by default on Ubuntu operating systems, and can be installed on most other Linux distros.

If you're setting up a new Ubuntu Server, you can choose to install a selection of snap packages, including PowerShell, from the Ubuntu installer. Here's what that looks like:

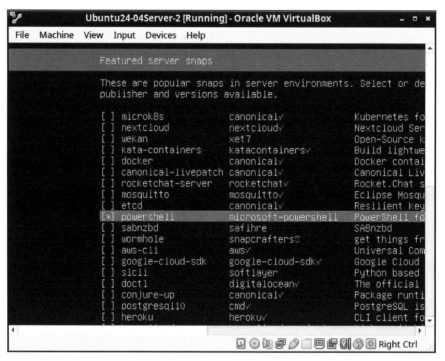

Figure 23.1: Selecting the PowerShell snap package during Ubuntu installation

You can install snapd on non-Ubuntu distros, but the installation instructions vary for different distros. You can find the installation instructions here:

https://snapcraft.io/docs/installing-snapd

Once you've installed snapd, you can install PowerShell by doing:

```
sudo snap install powershell --classic
```

Installing PowerShell on Fedora

On a Fedora system, you can use any of several methods for installing PowerShell. For example, you can install it either via a `.rpm` package, or via a Docker container. You'll find detailed instructions for each of these methods, along with a few more, here:

`https://fedoramagazine.org/install-powershell-on-fedora-linux/`

Installing PowerShell on macOS

You can install PowerShell on a Mac via the Homebrew system. You'll find detailed instructions for that here:

`https://learn.microsoft.com/en-us/powershell/scripting/install/installing-powershell-on-macos?view=powershell-7.4`

Invoking PowerShell

Once PowerShell is installed, invoke it by entering the `pwsh` command. Your command-prompt will then look something like this:

```
PS /home/donnie>
```

Now, before I show you any demos, let's address the burning question of the day. Why should a Linux or Mac person such as yourself learn a scripting language that was invented at Microsoft?

Reasons for Linux and Mac Admins to Learn PowerShell

Scripting in PowerShell is a somewhat different experience from scripting in the traditional Linux and Unix shells. But, it's not hard, and you might even like it once you get used to it. At any rate, there are some valid reasons why a Linux administrator might like to learn PowerShell. Let's take a look at some of those reasons.

Working with Mixed Operating System Environments

The first reason is simply one of both convenience and flexibility. A lot of enterprises and organizations run a mixed bag of Linux and Windows servers, and usually run Windows on their workstations. It might be helpful if you could run one common scripting language across your Windows and Linux platforms. And, if you're a Windows administrator who now needs to learn Linux administration, you might find it easier to do it with PowerShell, which you'll likely already know. In fact, let me tell you a story about my own reason for learning PowerShell.

Throughout the years 2010 and 2011, I worked with a client who had taken on the Nagios company as one of his clients. The Nagios company produces the Nagios network monitoring system, which can monitor pretty much every type of network device. (This includes servers that run either Linux or Windows, as well as various types of networking equipment.) My client's job was threefold. He was to produce training documentation, conduct Nagios training classes, and fly around the country to set up Nagios monitoring systems for clients of the Nagios company.

Anyway, every time my client needed to do anything with Windows servers, he would turn to me, because I knew Windows Server and he didn't.

 Okay, I've been guarding a dark secret, and I hope you won't think badly of me. It's just that back in 2006, before I got involved with Linux, I obtained my Microsoft Certified Systems Engineer (MCSE) certification for Windows Server 2003. When I first got into Linux, I thought that I would never use my MSCE training. Boy, was I wrong.

Unfortunately, my MCSE training didn't include anything about PowerShell, because it hadn't yet been invented. So, in order to come up with Windows Server monitoring solutions for my client, I had to give myself a crash course on PowerShell scripting.

The bottom line here is that if you're involved with setting up any kind of network monitoring solution, even if you're a Linux admin, learning PowerShell could be useful.

PowerShell Commands Can Be Simpler

The second reason is that in some cases, PowerShell is just easier to deal with. You've seen how in the traditional Linux/Unix shell languages, commands to perform a certain task can become quite long and convoluted. For example, let's say that you want to view all of the system processes that are using 200 Megabytes or more of the machine's Random Access Memory (RAM), and you want to see only certain fields of the output. The traditional Linux/Unix way of doing this would involve using the ps command with the proper option switches, and then piping the ps output into awk, like this:

```
donnie@fedora:~$ ps -eO rss | awk -F' ' '{ if($2 >= (1024*200)) {printf("%s\
t%s\t%s\n",$1,$2,$6);}}'

PID        RSS      COMMAND
3215 338896    /usr/lib64/chromium-browser/chromium-browser
3339 247596    /usr/lib64/chromium-browser/chromium-browser

. . .

. . .

21502       614792   /usr/lib64/firefox/firefox
23451       369392   /usr/lib64/firefox/firefox
donnie@fedora:~$
```

So, what's the problem with this? Well first, you need to be familiar with the ps option switches, as well as with the various ps output fields. In this case, the ps -e command shows us something like this:

```
donnie@fedora:~$ ps -e
     PID       TTY        TIME        CMD
       1        ?      00:00:04     systemd
       2        ?      00:00:00     kthreadd
       3        ?      00:00:00     pool_workqueue_release
. . .
```

```
. . .
   28122  ?              00:00:00      Web Content
   28229  ?              00:00:00      kworker/7:0
   28267  pts/1          00:00:00      ps
donnie@fedora:~$
```

But, that doesn't show the RSS field, which contains the memory use data that we want to see. So, I'll add the O rss option, so that the final ps command will be ps -eO rss. It should now show something that looks like this:

```
PID     RSS   S TTY      TIME      COMMAND
 1     29628  S ?        00:00:04  /usr/lib/systemd/systemd --switched-root
--sys
 2       0    S ?        00:00:00  [kthreadd]
 3       0    S ?        00:00:00  [pool_workqueue_release]
. . .

. . .
27199    0    I ?        00:00:00  [kworker/8:2]
27262   62216 S ?        00:00:00  /usr/lib64/firefox/firefox -contentproc
-child
27300   5060  R pts/1    00:00:00  ps -eO rss
donnie@fedora:~$
```

The problem now is that that's more than we want to see. Piping this output into awk will filter out all of the unwanted stuff. But, to use awk, you'll need to know what's in every field of the ps output, so that you'll know what fields to list in the awk command. In this case, we want to see the PID, RSS, and COMMAND fields, which are fields 1, 2, and 6. We want to see all processes for which field 2 has a number that's greater than 200 Megabytes, which we're expressing here as (1024*200).

 Remember that the true definition of a Megabytes is 1024 Kilobytes. Since awk doesn't understand measurements in Bytes, Kilobytes, Megabytes, and so forth, you'll have to express your memory measurements as either a math formula or a normal integer. (The integer product of 1024*200 is 204800.)

Finally, the printf command will print out just the fields that we want to see, with the proper formatting options.

Okay, that's doable. But, can we simplify that with PowerShell? Let's see.

```
PS /home/donnie> Get-Process | Where-Object WorkingSet -ge 200MB


NPM(K)    PM(M)     WS(M)     CPU(s)     Id  SI ProcessName
------    -----     -----     ------     --  -- -----------
     0     0.00    331.27      40.27   3215 …10 chromium-browser --enable-n…
     0     0.00    227.35      11.00   3674 …10 chromium-browser --type=ren…
```

```
       0      0.00     221.48      15.93     3369 …10 chromium-browser  --type=ren…
       0      0.00     228.37      19.19     3588 …10 chromium-browser  --type=ren…
 . . .

 . . .
       0      0.00     402.61     271.87     8737 …10 soffice.bin
       0      0.00     971.86   1,004.20     5869 …12 VirtualBoxVM

PS /home/donnie>
```

Yeah, I'm thinking that that's a lot easier. It's a lot shorter, which will make it less prone to error. The only field name you need to know is the WorkingSet (WS) field, which is equivalent to the RSS field in ps. Also, you see that we can pipe the output of one command (Get-Process) into another command (Where-Object), similarly to how we pipe the output of a Linux/Unix utility into another one. The best part is that this command is so intuitive, that I think you can figure out what it's doing without me even explaining it.

All right, let's move on to the next reason for learning PowerShell.

Enhanced Builtin Math Capabilities

If you need to create scripts that are heavy on math, PowerShell might be just what you need. You can do floating point math without loading any external program, and a function library is available for advanced math functions. Let's look at some examples.

First, let's do a simple division operation, like so:

```
PS /home/donnie> 5 / 2
2.5
PS /home/donnie>
```

As you see, PowerShell does floating point math by default, without having to invoke any special tricks. Now, let's put some different math problems into the math1.ps1 script, which looks like this:

```
param([Float]$number1 = "" , [Float]$number2 = "")


$sum = $number1 + $number2
Write-Host "The sum of these numbers is: " $sum
Write-Host "***********"
$divideresult= $number1 / $number2
Write-Host "Division of these two numbers results in: "$divideresult
Write-Host "***********"
$multiplyresult = $number1 * $number2
Write-Host "Multiplying these two numbers results in: " $multiplyresult
Write-Host "***********"
$modulo = $number1 % $number2
Write-Host "The remainder from dividing these two numbers is: " $modulo
```

The first thing to note here is the param line at the top. This is the directive that creates the positional parameters that I'll use to pass arguments into the script. Instead of using $1 and $2 as positional parameters, I'm using param to create the $number1 and $number2 positional parameters. Note how I need to create both positional parameters with just one param directive. If I use two separate param lines, the script will error out, because it won't recognize the second param line. Also, I've specified that the number1 and number2 variables that I'm using for the positional parameters will be of the floating point number type.

The rest of the script is a straightforward demonstration of how to do addition, division, multiplication, and modulo operations. Instead of using echo or printf statements, I'm using PowerShell's native Write-Host command. Also, note how variable names will always be preceded by a $, whether you're defining them or calling back their values. Now, let's run the script with 5 and 2 as our arguments:

```
PS /home/donnie> ./math1.ps1 5 2
The sum of these numbers is:  7
**********
Division of these two numbers results in:  2.5
**********
Multiplying these two numbers results in:  10
**********
The remainder from dividing these two numbers is:  1
PS /home/donnie>
```

Easy enough, right? Well, doing more advanced math in PowerShell is just as easy. To demonstrate, let's create the math2.ps1 script, like so:

```
param([Float]$number1 = "")


$tangent = [math]::Tan($number1/180*[math]::PI)
Write-Host "The tangent of $number1 degrees is:  $tangent."
Write-Host "**********"
$cosine = [math]::Cos($number1/180*[math]::PI)
Write-Host "The cosine of $number1 degrees is: "$cosine
Write-Host "**********"
$squareroot = [math]::Sqrt($number1)
Write-Host "The square root of $number1 is: " $squareroot
Write-Host "**********"
$logarithm = [math]::Log10($number1)
Write-Host "The base 10 logarithm of $number1 is: " $logarithm
```

Here, you see how I'm using the [math]:: construct to call in the functions that calculate the tangent, cosine, square root, and logarithm of my specified number. The only slight catch is that the tangent and cosine functions work with radians by default. To make it work with degrees, I had to divide the number of degrees that I input by 180, and then multiply that by the value of pi (π).

Now, let's run this with 45 as my argument:

```
PS /home/donnie> ./math2.ps1 45
The tangent of  45  degrees is:  1.
***********
The cosine of 45 degrees is:  0.7071067811865476
***********
The square root of 45 is:  6.708203932499369
***********
The base 10 logarithm of 45 is:  1.6532125137753437
PS /home/donnie> vim
```

Oh yeah, looking good.

> You can read more about PowerShell math, including a more complete list of its math
> functions, here:
>
> https://ss64.com/ps/syntax-math.html

Next, let's look at some fundamental differences between PowerShell and the more traditional shells.

Differences Between PowerShell Scripting and Traditional Linux/Unix Scripting

PowerShell still uses many of the same programming constructs as other scripting languages use, such as functions, loops, if constructs, and so forth. But, as you've already seen there are also some differences in the basic design of PowerShell that set it apart from traditional Linux/Unix shell scripting. Let's look at a few examples.

Using Filename Extensions and the Executable Permission

Throughout this book, you've seen me create normal Linux/Unix scripts with the .sh extensions on their filenames. In reality, you don't have to use any filename extension on normal Linux/Unix scripts. This means that the somescript.sh script would work just as well if the its filename were just somescript. With PowerShell, the .ps1 filename extension is mandatory for all PowerShell scripts. Without it, your PowerShell script just won't run.

On the other hand, it's not necessary to set the executable permission on PowerShell scripts, as it is for traditional Linux/Unix scripts. As long as the script file has .ps1 at the end of its filename, and as long as you're in the PowerShell environment, the script will run.

PowerShell is Object-oriented

The traditional Linux and Unix shell scripting languages are strictly **procedural languages**. This means that the commands in the program or script that you create will work on data from some external source.

That source could be the keyboard, a file, a database, or even a *here* document that's embedded within the script or program. Understand that the data and the commands that work on them are completely separate entities.

With **object-oriented programming**, which you'll sometimes see referred to as **OOP**, the data and the procedures that operate on the data are packaged together in an **object**. This allows you to do cool things, like telling a numerical object to double itself. It also allows you to create other objects that inherit characteristics from their parent objects.

 I know that this is a simplified explanation of object-oriented programming. But, a detailed explanation is way beyond the scope of this book. Of course, if you've ever programmed in languages like C++ or Java, you'll know what I'm talking about.

PowerShell Uses Cmdlets

Most PowerShell commands are actually referred to as **Cmdlets**, which you'll pronounce as *command-lets*, while others are either aliases or functions. Each Cmdlet takes the form of a verb and a noun separated by a hyphen, such as Get-Content, which gets (reads) from a file, or Set-Content, which writes to a file. The way this works on Windows machines is that every Windows subsystem has its own set of Cmdlets. For example, a Windows machine that acts as a **Domain Name System (DNS)** server would have a set of Cmdlets to work with DNS, and a **Microsoft Exchange** server would have Cmdlets for working with Exchange.

The Linux and Mac versions of PowerShell have far fewer sets of Cmdlets, because all of the Windows-specific stuff has been stripped out. You'll find what you need to work with Linux or macOS, but nothing else.

As you see, these Cmdlets are a lot different from the commands that Linux/Unix admins are used to using. For that reason, you might consider using aliases to help ease the transition to PowerShell. Let's check that out next.

Using Aliases on PowerShell

On Windows machines, PowerShell has aliases already set up that allow you to use Linux/Unix commands in place of PowerShell commands. (Microsoft did this on purpose to make it easier for Linux/Unix admins to learn PowerShell.) For example, here's how to list files in your current directory on PowerShell for Linux:

```
PS /home/donnie> Get-ChildItem


    Directory: /home/donnie


UnixMode          User Group   LastWriteTime      Size Name
--------          ---- -----   -------------      ---- ----
drwxr-xr-x        donnie donnie  6/29/2024 21:10   4096 bashlib-0.4
```

```
drwx------        donnie donnie    7/4/2024 23:59        4096 demo_files
. . .

. . .
-rw-rw-r--        donnie donnie    9/3/2024 22:26          67 zsh_fruits.txt
-rwxrw-r--        donnie donnie    9/4/2024 18:17         141 zsh_time.sh

PS /home/donnie>
```

You see that the Get-ChildItem command does pretty much the same job as an ls -l command. On a Windows machine, there will already be a PowerShell alias that allows you to use the ls command to run the Get-ChildItem command. Here's how that looks on one of my Windows machines:

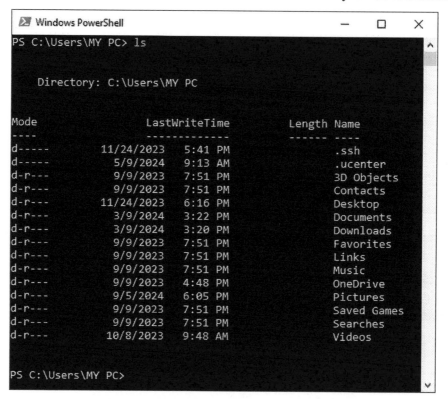

Figure 23.2: Using the ls PowerShell alias on Windows

So yeah, this looks just like the Get-ChildItem command. But, if you open a PowerShell session on Linux or Mac and run the ls command, you won't invoke the alias, because no aliases are set up by default. Instead, you'll invoke the actual ls command from your Linux or Mac operating system. Here's how that looks:

```
PS /home/donnie> ls
acl_demo.sh            rootlock_1.sh
bashlib-0.4            rootlock_2.sh
date_time.sh              rsync_password.sh
```

```
. . .
. . .
hello.sh                zsh_fruits.txt
My_Files                zsh_time.sh
rootlock_1a.sh
PS /home/donnie>
```

You see that this looks nothing like Get-ChildItem. In fact, it's just the normal output from your normal ls command.

Fortunately though, you can create your own aliases on PowerShell, which can make typing PowerShell commands much easier. You can create aliases with either the Set-Alias or the New-Alias Cmdlets. Let's first create the alias that will make ls run the Get-ChildItem command, using Set-Alias:

```
PS /home/donnie> Set-Alias -Name ls -Value Get-ChildItem
PS /home/donnie> ls


    Directory: /home/donnie


UnixMode          User Group          LastWriteTime          Size Name
--------          ---- -----          -------------          ---- ----
drwxr-xr-x        donnie donnie        6/29/2024 21:10        4096 bashlib-0.4
drwx------        donnie donnie        7/4/2024 23:59         4096 demo_files
. . .
. . .
-rw-rw-r--        donnie donnie        9/3/2024 22:26           67 zsh_fruits.txt
-rwxrw-r--        donnie donnie        9/4/2024 18:17          141 zsh_time.sh


PS /home/donnie>
```

The other way is to use New-Alias, like so:

```
PS /home/donnie> New-Alias ls Get-ChildItem
PS /home/donnie>
```

Either way works equally well, but it's only a temporary fix. Once you close your PowerShell session, you'll lose the alias. To make your aliases permanent, you'll need to edit your PowerShell profile file. You can find where it's supposed to be by doing:

```
PS /home/donnie> echo $profile
/home/donnie/.config/powershell/Microsoft.PowerShell_profile.ps1
PS /home/donnie>
```

The only problem is that the .config/ directory is there, but neither the powershell/ subdirectory nor the Microsoft.PowerShell_profile.ps1 file is. So, you'll need to create them.

You can just use your normal Linux/Mac command to create the `powershell/` subdirectory, like this:

```
PS /home/donnie> mkdir .config/powershell
PS /home/donnie>
```

Then, use your favorite text editor to create the `Microsoft.PowerShell_profile.ps1` file within that new `powershell/` subdirectory. Add this line to create the `ls` to `Get-ChildItem` alias:

```
New-Alias ls Get-ChildItem
```

You can add as many aliases to this file as you like. Just remember to log out of your PowerShell session, and then log back in to ensure that the new profile takes effect.

 Important: If you intend to create PowerShell scripts that will run on multiple machines, be aware that the aliases that you've created might not be available on some of them. Your best bet in that case will be to forget about using your own aliases, and just use the native PowerShell commands.

Next, let's see how to view the available PowerShell Commands.

Viewing the Available PowerShell Commands

To see what commands are available to you, just do:

```
PS /home/donnie> Get-Command

CommandType     Name                 Version     S
                                                 o
                                                 u
                                                 r
                                                 c
                                                 e
-----------     ----                 -------     -
Alias           Get-PSResource       1.0.4.1     M
Function        cd..
Function        cd\
Function        cd~
Function        Clear-Host
Function        Compress-Archive     1.2.5       M
. . .
```

```
. . .
Cmdlet              Write-Verbose       7.0.0.0     M
Cmdlet              Write-Warning       7.0.0.0     M


PS /home/donnie>
```

Under `CommandType`, you see that we have aliases, functions, and Cmdlets. Under the `Source` column, you see the letter `M`, which means that these commands are all stored in some PowerShell module.

Of course, there aren't nearly as many PowerShell commands for Linux as there are for Windows. To see how many there are, just do this:

```
PS /home/donnie> Get-Command | Measure-Object | Select-Object -Property Count


Count
-----
  293


PS /home/donnie>
```

Here, we begin by piping the output of the `Get-Command` Cmdlet into the `Measure-Object` Cmdlet. The official explanation of `Measure-Object`, according to the help file, is that it calculates the property values of certain types of objects. In this case, we only want to see one of those calculations, which shows us how many commands there are. We'll do that by piping the `Measure-Object` output into `Select-Object -Property Count`, which works the same as the Linux/Unix `wc -l` command. After all that, we see that there are 293 PowerShell commands available on this Linux machine.

As I've mentioned a few pages back in the *PowerShell Uses Cmdlets* section, all Cmdlets are in the *Verb-Noun* format. You can use `Get-Command` with either the `-Verb` or `-Noun` options to see all of the commands for a particular verb or noun. For example, let's see all of the available commands for the Date noun:

```
PS /home/donnie> Get-Command -Noun 'Date'


CommandType     Name          Version     S
                                          o
                                          u
                                          r
                                          c
                                          e

-----------     ----          ----        -
Cmdlet          Get-Date      7.0.0.0     M
Cmdlet          Set-Date      7.0.0.0     M


PS /home/donnie>
```

We see that there are only two Cmdlets for Date. Let's see how many there are for the Set verb:

```
PS /home/donnie> Get-Command -Verb 'Set'

CommandType        Name                    Version    S
                                                      o
                                                      u
                                                      r
                                                      c
                                                      e

-----------        ----                    -------    -
Function           Set-HostnameMapping     1.0.1      H
Function           Set-PSRepository        2.2.5      P
Cmdlet             Set-Alias               7.0.0.0    M
Cmdlet             Set-Clipboard           7.0.0.0    M
. . .
. . .
Cmdlet             Set-StrictMode          7.4.5.500  M
Cmdlet             Set-TraceSource         7.0.0.0    M
Cmdlet             Set-Variable            7.0.0.0    M

PS /home/donnie>
```

Now, you're wondering how to find out what all of these PowerShell commands do. Well, let's look at that next.

Getting Help with PowerShell Commands

This one is easy. Just use the Get-Help Cmdlet, followed by the name of the command for which you need information. For example, you can see information about the Get-Module Cmdlet like this:

```
PS /home/donnie> Get-Help Get-Module
```

What you'll see will resemble a normal Linux/Unix man page.

At the bottom of every Get-Help screen, you'll see commands that will show you how to see even more information. For example, if you need to see examples of how to use the Get-Module Cmdlet, do this:

```
PS /home/donnie> Get-Help Get-Module -Examples
```

Sometimes, the help page for the command that you need to learn about isn't available. In those cases, either run the `Update-Help` Cmdlet, or append the `-Online` option to the end of your `Get-Help` command.

Another great resource is the PowerShell Commands page, which you can find here: `https://ss64.com/ps/`

(Of course, a lot of the listed commands are Windows-specific, but you'll also find quite a few that are cross-platform.)

Okay, I think that this does it for the PowerShell theory. Let's look at a couple of real-world examples of PowerShell scripts.

Real-World Cross-Platform PowerShell Scripts

To come up with some real-world examples of cross-platform PowerShell scripts, I did a DuckDuckGo search for the *PowerShell script examples Linux* text string. The coolest thing I found is the *Mega Collection of PowerShell Scripts* on Github. You can use `git` to download it by doing:

```
git clone https://github.com/fleschutz/PowerShell.git
```

Once it's downloaded, `cd` into the `PowerShell/scripts/` directory, and take a look at what's there. For our first example, let's look at something simple that will run on all platforms.

The write-marquee.ps1 Script

The `write-marquee.ps1` script is truly cross-platform, because it doesn't use any commands that are specific to any particular operating system. All it does is create a marquee message that flows across on your screen. I can't show the entire script here, but you can look at your own local copy. So, let's just look at the individual parts of it to see how it's set up.

At the top, you see the comment section, which is surrounded by `<#` and `#>`. Actually, these are more than just comments. If you do `Get-Help ./write-marquee.ps1`, you'll see that everything that's within the `<#` and the `#>` will come up as a help screen, like this:

```
PS /home/donnie/PowerShell/scripts> Get-Help ./write-marquee.ps1
NAME
    /home/donnie/PowerShell/scripts/write-marquee.ps1
SYNOPSIS
    Writes text as marquee
. . .
. . .
REMARKS
    To see the examples, type: "Get-Help /home/donnie/PowerShell/scripts/write-
marquee.ps1 -Examples"
```

```
    For more information, type: "Get-Help /home/donnie/PowerShell/scripts/
write-marquee.ps1 -Detailed"
    For technical information, type: "Get-Help /home/donnie/PowerShell/scripts/
write-marquee.ps1 -Full"
    For online help, type: "Get-Help /home/donnie/PowerShell/scripts/write-
marquee.ps1 -Online"
PS /home/donnie/PowerShell/scripts>
```

Next, the `param([string]$Text =` line creates the string-type variable that contains the marquee message. It looks like this:

```
param([string]$Text = "PowerShell is powerful - fully control your computer!
PowerShell is cross-platform - available for Linux, Mac OS and Windows!
PowerShell is open-source and free - see the GitHub repository at github.
com/PowerShell/PowerShell! PowerShell is easy to learn - see the tutorial
for beginners at guru99.com/powershell-tutorial.html! Powershell is fully
documented - see the official PowerShell documentation at docs.microsoft.com/
en-us/powershell", [int]$Speed = 60) # 60 ms pause
```

The `[int]$Speed = 60) # 60 ms` pause part at the end of the variable definition determines the speed at which the marquee message will flow across the screen.

Next up is the `StartMarquee` function, which looks like this:

```
function StartMarquee { param([string]$Line)

  $LinePos = $HOST.UI.RawUI.CursorPosition
  $LinePos.X = 2
  $LinePos.Y -= 2
  foreach($Pos in 1 .. $($Line.Length - 80)) {
          $HOST.UI.RawUI.CursorPosition = $LinePos
          Write-Host -noNewLine "$($Line.Substring($Pos,80))"
          Start-Sleep -milliseconds $Speed
  }

}
```

Figure 23.3: The StartMarquee function

After drawing the marquee box and using `$LinePos` lines to ensure that everything gets properly positioned, you see the `foreach` loop that prints the message out to the screen, one letter at a time.

Finally, after the function definition, you see the function call:

```
StartMarquee "
+++ $Text +++ $Text +++ $Text +++ $Text +++ $Text +++ $Text +++ $Text +++ $Text
+++ $Text +++ $Text +++ $Text +++ $Text +++
```

```
"
exit 0 # success
```

The function call passes the `$Text` variable, which contains the marquee message, into the `StartMarquee` function. In between each iteration of the `$Text` message, there will be three plus signs (+++). The script will keep running until it's gone through all iterations of the `$Text` message. Anyway, here's how it looks when I run it on my Ubuntu Server virtual machine:

```
PS /home/donnie/PowerShell/scripts> ./write-marquee.ps1

our computer! PowerShell is cross-platform - available for Linux, Mac OS and Win
```

Figure 23.4: Running the write-marquee.ps1 script

Pretty cool, eh? Now, let's look at something that's even more cool.

The check-cpu.ps1 Script

The `check-cpu.ps1` script attempts to retrieve the model number and name of your machine's CPU, along with the CPU temperature.

 If you want to see the CPU temperature, you'll need to run this directly on a host Linux machine, instead of in a virtual machine. Running this in a virtual machine won't allow the script to access the host machine's temperature sensors.

I say *attempt*, because when I run this script on my Fedora workstation, I get this:

```
PS /home/donnie/PowerShell/scripts> ./check-cpu.ps1
✓ 64-bit CPU (16 cores, ) - 48°C OK
PS /home/donnie/PowerShell/scripts>
```

So, all it shows me is that I'm running some sort of 64-bit CPU with 16 cores. The actual truth is that this machine is running an Intel(R) Xeon(R) CPU E5-2670, with eight cores and hyperthreading enabled. But, if I run this same script on a Windows 10 machine, I'll get this:

```
PS C:\Users\donni\Documents\PowerShell\scripts> .\check-cpu.ps1
⊞ Intel(R) Core(TM)2 Quad CPU    Q9550  @ 2.83GHz (AMD64, 4 cores, CPU0, 2833MHz, CPU socket) - no temp
PS C:\Users\donni\Documents\PowerShell\scripts>
```

Figure 23.5: The check-cpu.ps1 script on a Windows machine

On this ancient (circa 2008) Dell that's running Windows 10 Pro, the script properly reports that the CPU is an old-school Core 2 Quad, model number Q9550. On the other hand, the script properly reported the CPU temperature on the Linux machine, but not on the Windows machine. That part is easy to explain. It's just that some computer motherboards, especially older ones, have temperature sensors that aren't compatible with modern operating systems.

As far as getting the CPU model right, it seems that the PowerShell command for Linux can't do that, but the command for Windows can. Let's take a look at the script to see what's going on with that.

Toward the top of the `check-cpu.ps1` script, you see the `GetCPUArchitecture` function, which looks like this:

```
function GetCPUArchitecture {
        if ("$env:PROCESSOR_ARCHITECTURE" -ne "") { return "$env:PROCESSOR_
ARCHITECTURE" }

        if ($IsLinux) {
                $Name = $PSVersionTable.OS
                if ($Name -like "*-generic *") {
                        if ([System.Environment]::Is64BitOperatingSystem) {
return "x64" } else { return "x86" }
                } elseif ($Name -like "*-raspi *") {
                        if ([System.Environment]::Is64BitOperatingSystem) {
return "ARM64" } else { return "ARM32" }
                } elseif ([System.Environment]::Is64BitOperatingSystem) {
return "64-bit" } else { return "32-bit" }
        }
}
```

As you see, there's a bit of difference in the syntax from what you're used to in normal Linux/Unix scripting. One difference is that instead of surrounding a test condition with square brackets, Power-Shell uses parentheses. Like this, for example:

```
if ("$env:PROCESSOR_ARCHITECTURE" -ne "") { return "$env:PROCESSOR_
ARCHITECTURE" }
```

All this line does is to return the value of the PROCESSOR_ARCHITECTURE environmental variable, if one exists. The rest of this function is specifically for Linux, as evidenced by the `if (IsLinux)` stanza. You see here that it detects whether the CPU is x86, x86_64, or ARM. For ARM, it detects whether it's a 32-bit or 64-bit version.

The only part of this function that Windows uses is the first line, which is the `if ("$env:PROCESSOR_ARCHITECTURE" -ne "") { return "$env:PROCESSOR_ARCHITECTURE" }` line. And, the only thing that this does on my Windows 10 machine is to insert the "AMD64" string into the information that you see in the above graphic. On Windows, all other CPU information is obtained from the **Windows Management Instrumentation** (**WMI**) interface. The code for that is in the `else` clause of the `try` stanza, which begins on line 44. (The `else` clause begins on line 54.) Here's how it looks:

```
try {
        Write-Progress "Querying CPU status..."
        $status = "✅"
        $arch = GetCPUArchitecture
```

```
if ($IsLinux) {
        $cpuName = "$arch CPU"
        $arch = ""
        $deviceID = ""
        $speed = ""
        $socket = ""
} else {
        $details = Get-WmiObject -Class Win32_Processor
        $cpuName = $details.Name.trim()
        $arch = "$arch, "
        $deviceID = "$($details.DeviceID), "
        $speed = "$($details.MaxClockSpeed)MHz, "
        $socket = "$($details.SocketDesignation) socket"
}
```

You see in the if..else construct that if the machine is running Linux, it will call the GetCPUArchitecture function, and retrieve the CPU information from it. In the else section, you see the code for Windows. Although the script does obtain one piece of information for Windows from the PROCESSOR_ARCHITECTURE environmental variable, it obtains most of the CPU information from the **Windows Management Instrumentation** (**WMI**) subsystem. As it happens, the PROCESSOR_ARCHITECTURE variable doesn't contain any information for this particular Fedora workstation. So, all I get on this machine is just the generic message about whether I'm running a 32-bit or 64-bit machine, and whether it's an x86 or an ARM machine. That's okay though, because I can modify the script to fix that.

Open the check-cpu.ps1 script in your editor, and scroll down until you see this line in the try stanza, which should be line 47:

```
$arch = GetCPUArchitecture
```

We're going to leave that line alone, because Windows also uses the GetCPUArchitecture function. Instead, we're going to add the following line after the if ($IsLinux) { line, which is line 48:

```
$arch = Get-Content /proc/cpuinfo | Select-String "model name" | Select-Object
-Unique
```

Instead of obtaining its value from the GetCPUArchitecture function, the arch variable now gets its value from a command substitution construct.

We see here a couple of other ways in which PowerShell scripting is different.

First, anytime you work with a PowerShell variable, you need to precede the variable name with a $. This means that whether you're defining a variable or calling back its value, you need that $. Secondly, you see that in PowerShell, you don't surround the command substitution construct with $( ). Instead, just write the command as you normally would.

Okay, let's break this line down.

- Get-Content: This does the same job as the Linux/Unix cat command.
- Select-String: This does the same job as the Linux/Unix grep command.
- Select-Object -Unique: This does the same job as the Linux/Unix uniq command. We need it here because my machine has 16 virtual cores, and I only want to see the information for one of them.

Running the modified script on my Fedora workstation looks like this:

```
PS /home/donnie> ./check-cpu.ps1
⚠   model name      : Intel(R) Xeon(R) CPU E5-2670 0 @ 2.60GHz CPU (16 cores, )
- 57°C HOT
PS /home/donnie>
```

That's much better, but it's not quite perfect. I really want to get rid of the "model name" text string at the start of the output. So, let's make one more slight edit to the script, like so:

```
$longarch = Get-Content /proc/cpuinfo | Select-String "model name" | Select-Object -Unique

$arch = $longarch -replace "model name\t: ", ""
```

All I did here was to change the $arch to $longarch in the original $arch line. I'll use that as my intermediate variable. Then, I added a new $arch line that uses the -replace "model name\t: ", "" command to delete the "model name" string, along with the following tab character, colon, and blank space. In this case, the -replace command is doing the same job as the Linux/Unix sed command. To put this into context, here's how the relevant portion of the modified try stanza now looks:

```
try {
        Write-Progress "Querying CPU status..."
        $status = "✓"
        $arch = GetCPUArchitecture
        if ($IsLinux) {
                $longarch = Get-Content /proc/cpuinfo | Select-String "model
name" | Select-Object -Unique
                $arch = $longarch -replace "model name\t: ", ""
                $cpuName = "$arch CPU"
                $arch = ""
                $deviceID = ""
                $speed = ""
                $socket = ""
        }
```

Here's what running the new script looks like:

```
PS /home/donnie> ./check-cpu.ps1
⚠ Intel(R) Xeon(R) CPU E5-2670 0 @ 2.60GHz CPU (16 cores, ) - 62°C HOT
PS /home/donnie>
```

Perfect. This is exactly what I want to see, other than the fact that my workstation is running a bit hot for some reason. (Tomorrow, I'll open it up to see if I need to blow out any dust bunnies.) The best part is that this is still a cross-platform script, because I didn't do anything that would affect how it runs on Windows.

Okay, I think that does it for our introduction to the mysteries of PowerShell. Let's summarize and then wrap things up.

Summary

In this final chapter, I've shown you a bit about scripting in PowerShell on a Linux machine. I started by showing you a bit of history, and then showed you the philosophy of scripting on PowerShell and how it differs from scripting in traditional Linux/Unix shells. You also saw the basics about how to use PowerShell commands, and how to obtain help for the commands. Finally, I showed you some real world examples of actual PowerShell scripts that work on either Windows or Linux. But, as I've said before, all I can do in just one chapter is to present a high-level overview of PowerShell scripting. If you need to learn more about it, there are plenty of resources both on-line and in books.

Oh, I almost forgot the most important thing. I also showed you some reasons about why you, as a Linux or Mac administrator, might want to consider scripting in PowerShell. Yeah, it's different and takes a bit of getting used to. But, there are some definite benefits, especially if you need to work in a mixed environment of Linux, macOS, and Windows computers.

This wraps up not only *Chapter 23*, but also the book. Along the way, you went from a command-line beginner to a shell-scripting guru. Of course, you might not be able to remember everything off the top of your head, and that's okay. Just use this book, and any other resources you can find, as ready-references if you ever need help in creating an awesome script.

Anyway, it's been a long journey, but I've enjoyed it, and hope that you have as well. Take care, and maybe we'll meet up again some time.

Further Reading

- PowerShell Core for Linux Administrators Cookbook: https://www.packtpub.com/en-us/product/powershell-core-for-linux-administrators-cookbook-9781789137231
- I switched from bash to PowerShell, and it's going great!: https://www.starkandwayne.com/blog/i-switched-from-bash-to-powershell-and-its-going-great/index.html
- Install PowerShell on Fedora Linux: https://fedoramagazine.org/install-powershell-on-fedora-linux/
- PowerShell equivalents for common Linux/Bash commands: https://mathieubuisson.github.io/powershell-linux-bash/

- Bash vs. PowerShell: Comparing Scripting Shells: `https://smartscripter.com/bash-vs-powershell-choosing-the-right-scripting-shell/`

- PowerShell differences on non-Windows platforms: `https://learn.microsoft.com/en-us/powershell/scripting/whats-new/unix-support?view=powershell-7.4`

- PowerShell's Equvalent to Linux's ls -al: An In-depth Guide: `https://thelinuxcode.com/equivalent-of-linux-ls-al-in-powershell/`

- Bash vs PowerShell Cheat Sheet: `https://blog.ironmansoftware.com/daily-powershell/bash-powershell-cheatsheet/`

Leave a Review!

Thank you for purchasing this book from Packt Publishing—we hope you enjoyed it! Your feedback is invaluable and helps us improve and grow. Please take a moment to leave an Amazon review; it will only take a minute, but it makes a big difference for readers like you.

`https://packt.link/r/1835463576`

Scan the QR code below to receive a free ebook of your choice.

`https://packt.link/NzOWQ`

packt.com

Subscribe to our online digital library for full access to over 7,000 books and videos, as well as industry leading tools to help you plan your personal development and advance your career. For more information, please visit our website.

Why subscribe?

- Spend less time learning and more time coding with practical eBooks and Videos from over 4,000 industry professionals
- Improve your learning with Skill Plans built especially for you
- Get a free eBook or video every month
- Fully searchable for easy access to vital information
- Copy and paste, print, and bookmark content

At www.packt.com, you can also read a collection of free technical articles, sign up for a range of free newsletters, and receive exclusive discounts and offers on Packt books and eBooks.

Other Books You May Enjoy

If you enjoyed this book, you may be interested in these other books by Packt:

Linux Kernel Programming

Kaiwan N. Billimoria

ISBN: 9781803232225

- Configure and build the 6.1 LTS kernel from source
- Write high-quality modular kernel code (LKM framework) for 6.x kernels
- Explore modern Linux kernel architecture
- Get to grips with key internals details regarding memory management within the kernel
- Understand and work with various dynamic kernel memory alloc/dealloc APIs

- Discover key internals aspects regarding CPU scheduling within the kernel, including cgroups v2
- Gain a deeper understanding of kernel concurrency issues
- Learn how to work with key kernel synchronization primitives

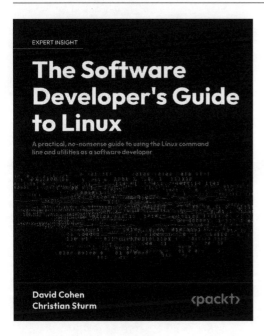

The Software Developer's Guide to Linux

David Cohen, Christian Sturm

ISBN: 9781804616925

- Learn useful command-line tricks and tools that make software development, testing, and troubleshooting easy

- Understand how Linux and command line environments actually work

- Create powerful, customized tools and save thousands of lines of code with developer-centric Linux utilities

- Gain hands-on experience with Docker, SSH, and Shell scripting tasks that make you a more effective developer

- Get comfortable searching logs and troubleshooting problems on Linux servers

- Handle common command-line situations that stump other developers

Packt is searching for authors like you

If you're interested in becoming an author for Packt, please visit authors.packtpub.com and apply today. We have worked with thousands of developers and tech professionals, just like you, to help them share their insight with the global tech community. You can make a general application, apply for a specific hot topic that we are recruiting an author for, or submit your own idea.

Join our community on Discord!

Read this book alongside other users, Linux experts, and the author himself.

Ask questions, provide solutions to other readers, chat with the author via Ask Me Anything sessions, and much more. Scan the QR code or visit the link to join the community.

https://packt.link/SecNet

Index

Symbols

/tmp/ Directory 543, 544

A

Access Control List (ACL) 521
  setting, for Horatio on FreeBSD 14 524-526
  setting, for Horatio on Linux 521-524
  setting, for Horatio on OpenIndiana 526-528
  using 521

action 371, 372

aliases 81-86, 633-636

American Telephone and Telegraph (AT&T) 490

apache access log
  parsing 226-228

Apache webserver logs
  searching, for cross-site
    scripting 281-283

Application Programming Interface (API) 303

arrays
  using 191-194, 407, 408

array variables 190, 191

associative array 379

awk command 369, 370
  busybox 370
  gawk 370
  mawk 370
  nawk 370

awk programming variables
  using 401

awk script construction 397, 398

B

bash 1
  env command, using 488, 489
  running, on Non-Linux Systems 488
  Symbolic Link, creating 489, 490

bashdb
  help, obtaining 593, 594
  installing, on FreeBSD 590
  installing, on Linux 590
  installing, on macOS 590
  script, debugging 591-593
  using 589, 590

bashism 492
  Portable Arrays making 495-497
  Portable Tests, using 492-494

bc program files
  floating point math, performing with 315, 316
  using 320-323
  using, in interactive mode 316-320
  using, in shell scripts 323-328
  using, modes 315

Berkeley Software Distribution
  (BSD) 178, 237, 490

break command 210, 211

built-in variables 386

C

case construct 213-215

cat utility
using 91-96

character sets 234, 235

check-cpu.ps1 script 641-644

Cmdlets 633

CoinGecko 303

CoinGecko API
coingeck.sh script, creating 303-306
using 303

command arguments
using 18, 19

command chaining 21
with semicolon 21

command history 35-39

command-line
printing from 172-174
shell options, setting from 78-81

command options
hands-on practice 16-18
using 16

command sequences
command chaining, with semicolon 21
conditional command execution, with double
ampersands 22
using 21

command structure 15
command arguments, using 18, 19
command options, using 16

command substitution 180, 201-204

Comma Separated Value (.csv) files 104
empty fields, filling 284-286

Common Gateway Interface (CGI) 558

Common Unix Printing Software (CUPS) 172

compiled programming
versus interpreted programming 11, 12

conditional command execution
with double ampersands 22
with double pipes 22

conditional statements
using 399, 400

configuration files 72
bash global configuration files, in Fedora 72-74
bash global configuration files, on Debian 76
users' configuration files, in Fedora 74, 75
users' configuration files, on Debian 76, 77

continue command
using 211, 212

CPU generation
finding 403-407

cross-platform PowerShell scripts 639
check-cpu.ps1 script 641-644
write-marquee.ps1 script 639-641

cross-site scripting attacks (XSS) 281

C shell 600

cut
using 98, 99

D

datetime module 620
using 620, 621

Debian
bash global configuration files 76
default editor, setting 77
users' configuration files 76, 77

Debian Almquist Shell 491

directories
expanding 609

Domain Name System (DNS) server 633

double ampersands
used, for conditional command execution 22

double pipes
used, for conditional command execution 22

do. .while construct 206, 207

dynamic code checkers 511

dynamic data
here documents, creating with 339-341

E

echo 223, 224
Portability Problems 497-499

echo statements
using 577-580

embedded passwords 533

environmental variables 45-48
reviewing 69, 70

errors
checking, with -e option 585, 586

escaping 39

eval command 555
command substitution, using 559
eval-test1.sh script, using 556, 557
eval-test3.sh script, using 557, 558
if eval, evaluating 560-562
using, on command-line 555, 556

executable permission 632

existing security-related scripts
searching for 482, 483

exit codes 219
standard shell exit codes 219
user-defined exit codes 219-223

expand
using 122, 123

expect
using, for security implications 349, 350
using, with responses 346-349

expr command
using 310-312

expressions
integer math, performing with 309

extended file globbing 606
directories, expanding 609
files and directories, expanding 610, 611
files, expanding 610
files, expanding by permissions 611-614
globbing flags, using 608
ls Output, filtering 606-608
ls Searches, grouping 608

F

favorite search engine
using 7

Fedora
bash global configuration files 72-74
PowerShell, installing on 627
users' configuration files 74, 75

field separators 374

file descriptor 56

file globbing 606

file mode string 27

filename extensions 632

file types
block device 27
character device 27
directories 27
named pipes 27
regular files 27
sockets 27
symbolic links 27

find 64, 65
used, for performing multiple actions 30, 31
using 23-30
using, to perform other commands 31-33

floating-point math
performing, with bc program files 315
using 409, 410

for construct 209, 210

for..in construct 208, 209

for loop 20
  using 407, 408
format (fmt)
  using 149-151
Fred's ImageMagick Scripts
  using 365
FreeBSD
  bashdb, installing on 590
  gsed, installing on 237
FreeBSD problem solution 551
  Home Directories on Linux 553
  Home Directories, on other Unix Distros 553
  Home Directory Permissions 551, 552
Free Open Source Software 492
function 289-291
  calling 293, 294
  creating 293, 294
  defining 291-293
  positional parameters, passing 294-296
  using, in here documents 341-346
  using, in shell scripts 293
  values, passing 296-299
function libraries
  creating 299-301

G

getopts
  purpose 447
  using 449-452
  versus getopt 448
getopts, real-world examples
  modified coingecko script 453, 454
  tecmint_monitor script 454-456
global variable 296
globbing flags 608
globbing qualifiers 609, 611
GNU bash Debugger (gbd) 190
GNU Project 7

grep 267
  basic search 267-269
  basic search, with extend syntax 275
  consecutive duplicate words, searching 276
  extended regular expressions, using 275
  fixed-strings regular expressions, using 279
  words beginning with certain letter,
      searching 277
  words with digits, searching 278
grep, advanced searches 269
  ^ Metacharacter, using 275
  carriage return, handling 271-273
  case-insensitive searches, making 270, 271
  social security numbers, searching 274
  source code files, auditing 273
  whole words, searching 269, 270
gsed
  installing, on FreeBSD 237
  installing, on macOS 237
  installing, on OpenIndiana 238
GUI, creating with yad 420
  data entry form, creating 420-424
  drop-down list, creating 424, 425
  file checksum utility, creating 426, 427
  form buttons, programming 431, 432
  GUI front-end, creating for
      ImageMagick 428-430
  yad basics 420
  yad file manager, using 425
GUI text editors 10, 11

H

hard drive
  beta-testing 228, 229
head
  using 133-135, 137, 138
here documents (heredoc)
  creating, with dynamic data 339-341
  creating, with static data 333-338

functions, using in 341-346
  using 331, 332
here script 331
Homebrew
  reference link 237
Homebrew system installation
  reference link 501
Horatio on FreeBSD 14
  used, for setting Access Control
    List (ACL) 524-526
Horatio on Linux
  used, for setting Access Control
    List (ACL) 521-524
Horatio on OpenIndiana
  used, for setting Access Control
    List (ACL) 526-528
HTTP status code 384
human user accounts 373-375
Hypertext Markup Language 340

I

if. .then construct 204, 206
  using 224, 225
image files
  batch-processing 364
ImageMagick
  image files, batch-processing 364
  image properties, viewing 358, 359
  images, customizing 359-364
  images, displaying 356, 358
  images, resizing 359-364
  installing 355
info pages 7
input from commands
  obtaining 388-394
input from text files
  human user accounts 373-375
  obtaining 372

regular expressions, using 386-388
  webserver access logs, parsing 375-386
input/output redirection 55, 56
Institute of Electrical and Electronics Engineers
  (IEEE) 490
integer math
  performing, with expressions 309
  performing, with integer variables 314, 315
integer math, with expressions
  echo, using with math expressions 312-314
  expr Command, using 310-312
integer variables
  integer math, performing with 314, 315
internationalization and localization
  capabilities 370
Internet of Things (IoT) 491
interpreted programming
  versus compiled programming 11, 12
IP address blocking script
  creating, for Red Hat distros 478
  creating, with array 478-480
  creating, with for loop 478-480
  creating, with xargs 480-482

J

Javascript injection attack 281
join
  using 102-105

K

Korn shell 179
KWrite text editor 10

L

limit string 332
Linux
  used, for installing bashdb 590
  used, for installing PowerShell 626

Linux Documentation Project 7

literals 234

local variable 296

loops 204

  break command, using 210, 211

  case construct 213-215

  continue command 211, 212

  do. .while construct 206-208

  for construct 209, 210

  for. .in construct 208, 209

  if. .then construct 204-206

  positional parameters, using 216-218

  until construct 212, 213

M

macOS

  used, for installing bashdb 590

  used, for installing gsed 237

  used, for installing PowerShell 627

manual pages 4-6

math expressions

  echo, using with 312-314

mathfunc module 618

  using 618, 619

metacharacters 39, 234

  character sets 234, 235

  escaping 39, 40

  modifiers 234-236

  positional anchors 234, 235

Microsoft Exchange server 633

Microsoft Xenix 490

mixed operating system environments

  working with 627, 628

modifiers 234-236

multi-line records

  working with 413, 414

multiple actions

  performing, with find utility 30, 31

multiple commands

  command sequences, using 21

  executing 20

  find utility, using 22-30

  multiple actions, performing with find 30, 31

  running 20, 21

multiple files

  modifying 281

N

Nagios 222

natural sort 377

network connectivity

  checking 301, 302

Network Filesystem version 4 (NFSv4) 525

Non-Linux Systems

  used, for running bash 488

non-standard filename extensions

  converting 354, 355

normal characters 39

Number of Record (NR) 386

numbering lines (nl)

  using 125-133

numbers in line

  summing 401, 402

O

object-oriented programming (OOP) 633

octal dump (od) utility

  using 138-143

OpenIndiana 179, 600

  used, for installing gsed 238

option switches

  single-letter options 16

  whole-word options 16

P

parameter expansion 194, 602

passwords
  encrypting 548-551
  using, in shell scripts 548

paste
  using 100-102

Path Security 562, 563
  social engineering 564, 565
  users account 563

pattern 371, 372

PDF engine 340

pdflatex engine 340

pipelines 49-51

pipes 64, 65

plain-text scripts
  obfuscating 528
  shc Binaries, decrypting 536
  shc, installing 528
  shc, using 529-532
  Untraceable Executables, creating 532-536

Policy-Compliant Ordinary Shell (posh) 500

Portability Problems
  with echo 497-499

Portable Operating System
    Interface (POSIX) 490

positional anchors 234, 235

positional parameter 72
  using 216-218

POSIX Compliance 490, 491
  checkbashisms, using 501-504
  shellcheck, using 504-506
  used, for testing shell scripts 499

POSIX-compliant shell
  used, for creating shell scripts 499, 500

POSIX-compliant variable expansion
  reference link 510, 511

PowerShell 2
  aliases 633-636
  Cmdlets 633
  commands 636-638
  enhanced builtin math capabilities 630-632
  help, obtaining with commands 638, 639
  installing, on Fedora 627
  installing, on Linux via snap package 626
  installing, on macOS 627
  invoking 627
  object-oriented 632, 633
  reference link 627
  simpler commands 628-630

PowerShell math
  reference link 632

printer driver 172

printf command 410
  using 410-413

procedural languages 632

Process ID (PID) 389

programming variables 48, 49

pr
  using 166-172

Q

quoting 39-42

R

records 371

recursive commands
  running 33
  using 33-35

Red Hat distros
  IP address blocking script, creating 478

redirectors 64, 65

Regex101 281
  reference link 281

RegexBuddy 280
  reference link 280

RegexMagic 280
  reference link 280

regular expressions (regexp) 234
  using 386-388

repeat character 276

Resident Set Size (RSS) 390

responses
  automating, with expect 346-349

result variable 298

return command 296

reverse shell attack 559

root privileges 12

root user account
  auditing 467
  script, creating for Linux 467-473
  script, creating for OpenIndiana 467-473
  script, modifying for FreeBSD 473-475

S

scripting errors 570
  filenames, with blank spaces 570, 571
  issues, with unset variables 571-574

scripting variables 188
  and shell levels 188, 189
  case sensitivity 189
  creating 188
  deleting 188
  read-only variables 190

scripts
  access control 518
  Access Control List (ACL), using 521
  Plain-Text Scripts, obfuscating 528
  sudo privileges, assigning 518

search path 23

sed program files
  compound scripts 263-265

  lines, appending in text file 260, 261
  lines, copying from one file to another 263
  lines, modifying in text file 261, 262
  text, substituting 262
  using 260

sed script 236

sed substitution script 239

semicolon
  used, for command chaining 21, 22

Sensitive Data Leakage
  avoiding 543
  passwords, using in shell scripts 548
  temporary file, securing 543

set -e and -e settings
  using 587, 588

Set Group Identity (SGID) 539-543

Set User Identity (SUID) 539-543

shadow file system 469

shall
  using 511-513

shc
  installing 528
  using 529-532

shc binaries
  decrypting 536
  UnSHc utility, testing 536-539

shebang line 178

shell 1-3, 491, 492

shell builtin 220

shellcheck
  -s option, using to scan function
      libraries 507-510
  specifying, with -s option 506
  using 504-506

shell commands
  Favorite Search Engine, using 7
  info pages 7
  Linux Documentation Project 7

manual pages 4-6
  using, for issue solving 4

shell options
  setting, from command-line 78-81

shell script construction 178, 179
  logged-in users, counting 180-182

shell scripts
  creating, on POSIX-compliant Shell 499, 500
  function, using 293
  passwords, using 548
  testing, for POSIX Compliance 499
  Text Editor, used for creating 8

shell sessions 71, 72
  interactive shells 71
  login shells 71
  non-interactive shells 71
  non-login shells 71
  reviewing 71

simple firewall scripts
  creating 478
  IP address blocking script, creating for Red Hat
    distros 478

simple port-scanning script 462-467

simple scripts, for auditing 460
  operating system, identifying 460-462
  root user account, auditing 467
  simple port-scanning script 462-467
  user activity monitoring
    script, creating 476, 477

single-letter options 16

snapd, installing on non-Ubuntu distros
  reference link 626

snap package
  PowerShell, installing on Linux 626

social engineering 564

sort utility
  using 105-117

split
  using 151-154

standard error (stderr) 56-63

standard input (stdin) 55-60

standard output (stdout) 56, 57
  file descriptor, using 58
  file overwrites, preventing 57, 58

standard shell exit codes 219-222

static code checkers 511

static data
  here documents, creating with 333-338

sticky bit 544

Stream Editor 236
  blank lines, deleting 252
  Edsel, modifying to Studebaker 256, 257
  entire lines of text, modifying 257
  items, deleting from list 249-252
  lines of text, appending 253-255
  lines of text, inserting 256
  list of cars, modifying 244-247
  list of Hollywood actors, modifying 242, 243
  multiple operations, performing 255
  office memo, modifying 239-242
  portability issues 236, 237
  q command, using 258
  r command, using 259
  using, in shell scripts 265, 266
  w command, using 258
  whole-word substitution, performing 247-249

subshell 186

sudo privileges 12
  assigning 518
  configuring 518-521

SunOS 490

sym link attacks 545

System Integrity Protection (SIP) 536

System V Unix 490

T

Tab Separated Value (.tsv) files 378

tac
  using 96-98

tail
  using 136-138

tee command 63, 64

temporary file
  creating 544-548
  securing 543
  /tmp/ Directory 543, 544

terminal emulator 3

ternary operator 410

test performance 182
  conditions 186, 187
  if. .then construct, using 184
  test condition, enclosing within square
      brackets 183, 184
  test keyword, using 182, 183
  tests types, using 184, 186

text editor
  used, for creating shell scripts 8

text files
  used, for obtaining input 372

text-mode text editors 8-10

text-stream filter 55, 90
  cat 91-96
  cut 98, 99
  join 102-105
  paste 100-102
  sort 105-117
  tac 96-98

third-party repository installations
  automating 283, 284

token 332

tr
  using 154-162

U

UI, creating with dialog and xdialog 433
  dialog basics 433-435
  dialog or xdialog, selecting
      automatically 437-439
  SSH login interface, creating 442-445
  widgets, adding 439-441
  xdialog basics 435-437

undefined variables
  checking for 583-585

unexpand
  using 124, 125

uniq
  using 143-147

UnSHc
  testing 536-539

until construct 212, 213

untraceable binary
  making 553-555

untraceable executables
  creating 532-536

user activity monitoring script
  creating 476, 477

User Agent string 379

user-defined exit codes 219-223

User ID Numbers (UIDs) 373

V

variable expansion 194, 602
  error message, displaying 197, 198
  extended file globbing 606
  matching patterns 200, 201
  substrings, substituting 603, 604
  upper and lower case, translating
      between 604, 605
  values, substituting 602
  value, substituting for set variable 195

value, substituting for unset variable 194

variable offset, using 198-200

variable value, assigning 196

variable offset 198

Virtual Set Size (VSZ) 390

W

wc

using 147-149

webserver access logs

parsing 375-386

while loop

using 401

whole-word options 16

wild loop

creating 575, 576

Windows Management Instrumentation (WMI) 642, 643

write-marquee.ps1 script 639-641

X

xargs

using 162-165

Xdialog 578-580

xtrace

using, for debugging 581-583

Y

yad 420, 432

basics 420

file manager 420

yescrypt hashing algorithm 469

Z

Z shell (zsh) 1, 599, 600

arrays 614-616

enhanced math capabilities 616-618

features 601

installing 600, 601

variable expansion 602

zsh modules 618

datetime module, using 620, 621

mathfunc module, using 618, 619

using 618

Download a free PDF copy of this book

Thanks for purchasing this book!

Do you like to read on the go but are unable to carry your print books everywhere?

Is your eBook purchase not compatible with the device of your choice?

Don't worry, now with every Packt book you get a DRM-free PDF version of that book at no cost.

Read anywhere, any place, on any device. Search, copy, and paste code from your favorite technical books directly into your application.

The perks don't stop there, you can get exclusive access to discounts, newsletters, and great free content in your inbox daily.

Follow these simple steps to get the benefits:

1. Scan the QR code or visit the link below:

https://packt.link/free-ebook/9781835463574

2. Submit your proof of purchase.
3. That's it! We'll send your free PDF and other benefits to your email directly.

Made in the USA
Las Vegas, NV
23 April 2025

21270312R00383